HOKKAIDO

45°

· Sapporo

· Muroran

· Aomori

Akita · Morioka

Yamagata · Kamaishi

Niigata · Sendai

Utsunomiya · Fukushima

· Maebashi · Mito

Saitama · Chiba

Tokyo · Kimitsu

OCEAN

· Naha

OKINAWA

日英対訳 [第11版]

JAPAN

NIPPON
THE LAND AND ITS PEOPLE

日鉄総研

ISBN978-4-930825-31-5
Copyright © 2019 by
Nippon Steel Research Institute Corporation

第 11 版の発行にあたって

「日本―その姿と心―」の第 10 版を発行（2014 年 9 月）してから 5 年が経過しました。

この間、日本では、2011 年 3 月 11 日に発生した東日本大震災（地震と津波）の発生から 8 年を経て、後遺症は未だ残るものの、経済的な被害・損害はほぼ回復しつつあります。また、2019 年 4 月末に今上天皇が生前退位し上皇となられ、同時に皇太子が天皇に即位し年号が「平成」から「令和（れいわ）」に変わりました。

一方目を日本の外に転じますと、イギリス政府は EU 当局との EU からの離脱（Brexit）条件の交渉に臨んでいますが、交渉は難航しその行く末は混とんとしています。また、「アメリカ・ファースト」を標榜するトランプ大統領は、アメリカの貿易収支が大幅な赤字となったことを理由に、中国、EU、日本等に対し多額の関税をかけ、さらに中国がアメリカの知的財産権を侵害しているとの理由で、多くの輸入製品に対して制裁関税を課す事態となっています。北朝鮮・イランの核兵器廃絶をめぐるアメリカとの駆け引きの行方は未だ不透明です。

30 年間に及ぶ平成の時代（1989〜2019 年）は、世界規模での戦争のない平和な時代でしたが、他方でベルリンの壁の崩壊（冷戦の終止符）等から始まり変動の激しい時代でした。

よかれあしかれ予想しにくいことが世界各地で起きる可能性は十分あります。しかし我々はどのようなことが起ころうとも、しっかりと未来を見据え、人類の繁栄と幸福を追求し続けることこそが世界の進むべき道であるとの信念を堅持しなければなりません。そのためには、世界の人々がお互いに自国の事だけでなく他国の事もよく理解し、常日頃からお互いを理解するためのコミュニケーションを持続することが肝要です。

この本は、日本の気候・風土の特徴を、地理、歴史、政治、経済、社会、科学技術および文化という切り口から紹介しています。日本の事を日本人にだけでなく、外国の人々にもよく理解し

ていただくために、日本語と英語で要領よく紹介することに努めました。執筆陣は事実（Fact）が最も重要なことであると認識し、最新の重要な出来事も漏らさないようにするとともに、客観的な統計をできるだけ広範囲に引用しました。

日本を訪れた海外からの人々は、2018年の実績で3千万人を超えました。2019年9月に日本でラグビー・ワールドカップが開催され、2020年7月から東京オリンピック・パラリンピックが開催されることになっています。訪日外国人がますます増えることが予想されます。

改訂にあたりましては、話題性のある事柄を取り上げながら紹介することに心がけました。具体的には、次のような事項です。

1．日本に特有な天皇制度について

2019年5月1日から天皇とともに元号が「令和」に変わりました。「令和」の典拠は日本の最古の歌集『万葉集』であり、「令和」には「人々が美しく心を寄せあうなか文化が生まれ育つという意味が込められている」（安倍総理大臣談話：4月1日）のです。外国の方々は日本の象徴天皇とはどのような立場にあり、歴史的にどのような役割を果たされてきたのかに関心を持たれるでしょう。「2 歴史」の項では、日本の天皇制・国家体制の成立とその変遷をうかがうことのできる事柄について加筆しました。

2．日本のエネルギー問題と戦争の放棄を唱える憲法の定め、および憲法改正問題

日本は、生活と経済活動に欠かせないエネルギーの60％以上を中東の石油・天然ガスに依存せざるを得ないという状況に置かれているなかで、その輸送を受け持つタンカー等の安全保障について、日本はもっと積極的に関与すべきとの世論があります。戦争の放棄を定めた憲法の規定との関係についての論点を紹介し、憲法改正に関して最近話題となる他の改正テーマについても触れました（「3 政治（2）政治 a）日本国憲法」）。日本経済に及ぼすエネルギー問題については、「4 経済（3）日本経済が直面する4つの重要課題 a)

エネルギー確保」の項に詳しく記述しました。
3. 天然資源に恵まれない日本での技術開発の現状

　天然資源の乏しい日本が経済先進国の一員としてたえず国際社会で一定の役割を果たすには、優れた先端技術の開発を怠らないことが非常に重要です。日本の企業や研究開発機関は具体的にどのような技術を開発し実用化しているか、「6 科学技術（1）先端科学技術」の項で紹介しました。

4. 少子高齢化と働き方改革

　多くの経済先進諸国は少子高齢化社会の到来を迎えており、日本はその先頭グループにあります。終戦直後の 1947 年の国内総出生数は約 250 万人でしたが、2018 年においては 95 万人と急減しています。他方、日本人の平均寿命は 1947 年の男性 50 歳、女性 54 歳から、2017 年には男性 81 歳、女性 87 歳へと急伸し高齢者層の人口が急増しています。このことが社会に深刻な問題をもたらしています。一つは高齢者層の年金・医療・介護等の社会保障関係費用の増大です。政府と地方公共団体のかかえる借金は 1,100 兆円を超えていますが、借金の大きな要因の一つはこの費用の急激な増加への対応のためです。もう一つは深刻な労働力不足問題です。労働生産性の向上が喫緊の課題であり、政府はその対応として裁量労働制の採用に取り組んでいます。2019 年 4 月より外国人労働者の受け入れのための道が少し広げられました。さらに女性の労働力を掘り起こすことも図られていますが、子育て期の女性に対しては、きめの細かい子育て支援に十分留意しなければなりません。総じて、少子高齢化問題への対応は将来の日本社会のありように大きな影響を与えることになります。「4 経済（6）企業経営と雇用 c）雇用関係 7）働き方改革」の項で最近の動きを紹介しました。

　また、「5 社会（2）少子高齢社会」の項で日本社会の現状を紹介していますので合わせてご覧ください。

5. 温暖な気候と四季に恵まれた日本の特有な文化・風土

　「7 文化」の項は、この本が狙いとする「日本を知ってもらう」ために有意義な事柄を紹介するものです。今回の改訂

にあたり、日本の主な年中行事(「7 文化(10)風俗・習慣・娯楽 b)主な年中行事」)の内容を充実し、加えて日本の代表的ペットを紹介しました(「e)日本の代表的ペット」)。また、2015年以降に日本で新たに選定された4つの世界遺産を紹介しました。

東京オリンピック・パラリンピックを観戦するために来日される方々のために、「(8)オリンピック」という項目を設け、2020年夏季オリンピック・パラリンピック競技東京大会の概要と会場の全体像を紹介しました。あらかじめお読みいただければより興味深くオリンピック・パラリンピックを楽しんでいただけるでしょう。

今回の改訂においても、急速に変化していく世界の状況をできるだけ直近に至るまで取り込むことに努めました。しかしなお多くの重要な事項を見落とし、あるいは内容に不十分な点があると思います。読者の皆様のご批評をお願いいたします。

改訂にあたっては、当社の川人敦夫、吉橋宏および阿部一正が執筆・編集を担当し、澤田奈々恵が編集補助を担当しました。英文翻訳は、John Bowen さんと Daniel Heller さんにお願いいたしました。

この本が少しでも読者の皆様のお役に立つことを祈念します。今後も内容の充実にいっそう努力してまいりますので、引き続き皆様のご支援とご鞭撻をお願い申し上げます。

2019年5月
　　第11版執筆陣を代表して　　　　日鉄総研㈱
　　　　　　　　　　　　　　　　　元社長　阿 部 一 正

執筆・編集に際して留意した点

1) 各項目の解説は事典的なものではなく、話題の一例を示したものである。具体的な例や客観的なデータをできるだけ引用して、外国との対比・関連性について述べるなど、外国人の理解を得やすいように心がけた。
2) 和文と英文を対比して収録した。
3) 解説に関する補足を巻末に付記した。
4) 他の文献からの引用については、その文献名・著者名（および訳者名）を引用個所に表示したほか、主な参考文献・資料などは一括して巻末に列記した。
5) 文中の単位などは次の通りとした。
   年　号：西暦
   時　代：西暦の世紀または日本史で使用されている時代名
   　　　　もしくは元号
   度量衡：メートル法（ヤード・ポンド法を付記）
   金　額：円または米ドル
   温　度：摂氏（華氏を付記）
6) 英文の綴りは米国式とした（固有名詞の場合を除く）。
7) 英文中（見出しを除く）、日本語音をローマ字綴りで表示した普通名詞については、それが英語化しているか否かを問わず、項目ごとに初出するもののみ斜体（イタリック）で表示した（例：*kimono, judo, shogun*）。
8) 英文中の固有名詞は、新聞、書物、映画、等々の出版物名、作品名に限り斜体（イタリック）で表示した（例：*Kojiki, Rashomon*）。
9) 英文中、日本人名（号を含む）の表記順については、古今を問わず日本語の読み順通りとした（例：Ashikaga Yoshimitsu, Katsushika Hokusai, Natsume Soseki, Yukawa Hideki）。
10) 本の大きさ、装丁は、携帯して手軽に活用し得るように配慮した。

Foreword to the Eleventh Edition

Five years have passed since the publication of the tenth edition of Nippon: the Land and its People (September 2014).

Eight years have passed since the Great East Japan Earthquake occurred on March 11, 2011, and although the aftermath remains, the country is recovering from the economic damage it suffered. At the end of April 2019 the Emperor abdicated, becoming the Emperor Emeritus, and the Crown Prince assumed the imperial throne, completing the transition from the Heisei era to the Reiwa era.

Abroad, the UK government is negotiating with the EU authorities over the terms of Britain's exit (Brexit) from the European Union. However, the negotiations are difficult and the way ahead is unclear. In the U.S., President Trump, who advocates "America First" policy, has imposed heavy tariffs on imports from China, the EU, Japan, and other countries, citing as the reason the large deficit the U.S. is running in its balance of trade, and is imposing punitive customs duties on many imports from China in retaliation for China's violations of U.S. intellectual property rights. The future of the political bargain between the U.S. and North Korea and Iran over the abolition of nuclear weapons is also still unclear.

Although the 30 years of the Heisei era (1989–2019) was a time of peace, with no global wars, it was also a time of major change, starting with the fall of the Berlin Wall that marked the end of the Cold War.

There is a good chance that things that are difficult to predict will happen around the world. But no matter what happens, the path the world has to follow is to firmly believe in the future and continue to pursue prosperity and happiness for all mankind. To that end, it is essential that people throughout the world have a good understanding of other countries as well as their own, and continue to communicate with each other on a daily basis.

This book provides an introduction to the characteristics of Japan's climate and natural features from the perspectives of its geography, history, politics, economy, society, science and technology, and culture. The information is provided in English and Japanese in order to give both Japanese and foreigners a better understanding of the country. The authors recognize that facts are of first importance, and therefore have endeavored to ensure that the latest important events are included, and cited wide range of objective statistics as much as possible.

Japan had more than 30 million foreign visitors in 2018. With Japan hosting the Rugby World Cup in September 2019 and the Tokyo Olympics and Paralympics in July to September 2020, the number of foreign visitors to Japan is expected to greatly increase.

In preparing the eleventh edition, the focus was on including the following topical matters and concerns.

1. Japan's Imperial System

The era name changed to Reiwa on May 1, 2019, the day on which the new emperor ascended the throne. Reiwa was derived from the *Manyoshu*, the oldest anthology of Japanese poetry. In a statement made on April 1, Prime Minister Abe said that "The name Reiwa includes the meaning of culture coming into being and flourishing when people bring their hearts and minds together in a beautiful manner." Foreigners are interested in knowing about the position of the Emperor as the symbol of Japan and the role that emperors have played historically. Section 2, History, includes a description of the Japanese imperial system and the establishment of, and transition to, the system of state.

2. Japan's Energy Problem, its Constitution that Renounces War, and the Constitutional Amendment Issue

With Japan having to rely on oil and natural gas from the Middle East for more than 60% of the energy essential to its existence and economic activities, public opinion is that Japan should have a more active involvement in securing the safety of the tankers used for the transportation of the oil and gas it uses. We describe the issue in the context of the constitutional renunciation of war, and touch on the subject of amending the constitution and other recent topics related to amendments (section 3, Government, part (2) Government, a) The Japanese Constitution). The energy issues affecting the Japanese economy are described in detail in section 4, Economy, part (3) Four Important Issues Facing the Japanese Economy, a) Securing Energy.

3. Technology Development in a Japan with Few Natural Resources

For Japan, with its paucity of natural resources, to play its role as a member of the international community of economically advanced countries, it has to keep developing outstanding, advanced technologies. Some specific examples of technologies that Japanese companies and R&D institutions have developed and put to practical use are described in part (1) Advanced Science and Technology of section 6, Science and Technology.

4. Declining Birthrate, Aging Society and Workplace Reforms

Japan is in the forefront of the many advanced economies that are facing the arrival of a declining birthrate and an aging society. The total number of births in 1947 right after the end of the war was about 2.5 million, but by 2018 it had fallen sharply, to 950,000. At the same time, the average life expectancy of the Japanese people have risen from 50 years for males and 54 years for females in 1947, to 81 years for males and 87 years for females in 2017. This rapid aging of the population has given rise to a number of serious problems in society. One is the increase in social security related expenses, such as pensions and medical and nursing care for the elderly. The debts of the national and local governments now exceed 1,100 trillion yen, with one of the major causes being the response to the rapid increase in costs. Another problem is that there is a serious labor shortage. Improving labor productivity is an urgent issue, and the government is responding by adopting a discretionary labor system. Also, from April 2019, it was made easier to bring in foreign workers. There is also a focus on expanding the participation of women in the labor force, which requires giving full consideration to supporting the child-care needs of women who are raising children. In general, the response to the problems of declining birthrate and the aging of the population will have a profound effect on the future of Japanese society. Recent developments are covered in section 4, Economy, part (6) Business Management and Employment, c) Employment, 7) Workplace Reforms.

See also to the current situation of Japanese society in the section 5, Society, part (2) Aging Society with Declining Birth Rate.

5. Unique Aspects of Japanese Culture, and Mild Climate with Four Distinct Seasons

Section 7, Culture, is an introduction to things that are useful for knowing about Japan, which is the aim of this book. In preparing the eleventh edition, part (10), Customs, Manners and Pastimes, b) Main Annual Festivals, of the Culture section was expanded, and a section e) on Japanese pets was added. We also introduce four Japanese properties that have been added to the list of World Heritage Sites since 2015.

For those coming to Japan to watch the Tokyo 2020 Olympics and Paralympics, overviews of the Summer Olympics and Paralympic Games and the venues are included (in the Culture section, part (8) The Olympics). It is our hope that reading this information in advance will enhance your enjoyment of the events.

In this edition, we also endeavored to provide an up-to-date picture of the rapidly changing world situation. However, we think we may have omitted many important issues and inadequately explained others. We would appreciate readers bringing any such shortcomings to our attention.

The work of writing and editing the new and updated text was done by our company employees, Mr. Kawahito Atsuo, Mr. Yoshihashi Hiroshi and Mr. Abe Kazumasa, with edit assistant Ms. Sawada Nanae. The English translation was done by Mr. John Bowen, with editing and input by Dr. Daniel Heller.

The editors hope that readers find this book useful in some small way. We are committed to making continual improvements in content and accuracy. Your ongoing support and encouragement in our endeavors will be greatly appreciated.

May 2019

On behalf of the authors of the Eleventh Edition,
Former President,　Abe Kazumasa
Nippon Steel Research Institute Corporation

Editors' Note

1) No attempt has been made to produce an encyclopedia.
   Instead, we have tried to limit ourselves to a single aspect of each topic and to make the accompanying commentary easy for those not familiar with Japan to understand by including concrete examples, data and comparisons with other countries.
2) Corresponding Japanese and English commentaries appear on opposing pages.
3) Supplementary information relating to our commentary has been included at the back of the book.
4) Quotations are accompanied by the title of the reference, the name of the author (and translator if any). A list of references appears at the back of the book.
5) Dates are according to the Western calendar. Eras are in some cases referred to by century of the Western calendar and in others by era names commonly used in Japanese history.
   Weights and measures are metric with English system equivalents given in parentheses.
   Monetary values are given in yen and/or U.S. dollars.
   Temperatures are in degrees Celsius with conversions into degrees Fahrenheit given in parentheses.
6) American spelling has been used (except for some proper nouns).
7) Japanese common nouns used in the book (except those in the headings) are italicized the first time they appear in each topic (*e.g.*, *kimono*, *judo*, *shogun*), irrespective of whether or not they have been Anglicized.
8) Proper nouns are italicized only in the case of the names and tiles of newspapers, books, films and other such publications and works (*e.g.*, *Kojiki*, *Rashomon*).
9) The names (including pseudonyms) of Japanese individuals through all ages, whether contemporary or historical, are written in the usual Japanese order, with the family name preceding the given name (e.g., Ashikaga Yoshimitsu, Katsushika Hokusai, Natsume Soseki, Yukawa Hideki).
10) A pocket-size format has been used so the book can be easily carried as a handy reference.

目 次

1 地 理
- a) 位置・国の広さ ……………………………………………… 32
- b) 気候 ……………………………………………………………… 34
- c) 地形 ……………………………………………………………… 36
- d) 地震・津波 …………………………………………………… 38
- e) 人口 ……………………………………………………………… 40
- f) 山・川・湖 …………………………………………………… 40
- g) 植物 ……………………………………………………………… 42
- h) 動物 ……………………………………………………………… 44

2 歴 史
- a) 日本人の祖先・日本国の起源 …………………………… 46
- b) 古代（4～12世紀）………………………………………… 48
- c) 中世・近世（12～19世紀前半）………………………… 50
- d) 近代（19世紀後半～1945年）…………………………… 56
- e) 現代（その1）（1945～1980年代前半）……………… 62
- f) 現代（その2）（1980年代後半以降）………………… 66

3 政 治
(1) 天 皇
- a) 天皇の憲法上の地位 ……………………………………… 78
- b) 皇室の歴史 …………………………………………………… 78
- c) 天皇・皇后 …………………………………………………… 80
- d) 天皇の退位 …………………………………………………… 80
- e) 女性天皇・女系天皇 ……………………………………… 82

(2) 政 治
- a) 日本国憲法 …………………………………………………… 84
- b) 統治機構 ……………………………………………………… 88
- c) 選挙 ……………………………………………………………… 90
- d) 治安・警察庁・海上保安庁 …………………………… 96
- e) 自衛隊 ………………………………………………………… 100

(3) 外 交
- a) 日本外交の基本方針 ……………………………………… 102
- b) 地域別の外交 ………………………………………………… 104
- c) 分野別外交 …………………………………………………… 118

(4) 国旗など
- a) 国旗 ……………………………………………………………… 126
- b) 国歌 ……………………………………………………………… 126

- c) 国花 ……………………………………………………… 126
- d) 元号 ……………………………………………………… 128

4 経 済
(1) 日本経済の概況
- a) 経済規模 ………………………………………………… 130
- b) 産業構造 ………………………………………………… 130
- c) 産業基盤 ………………………………………………… 132
- d) 対外経済 ………………………………………………… 132

(2) 戦後経済の歩み
- a) 戦争による疲弊からの復興（1945～1950年代前半）
  ……………………………………………………………… 134
- b) 高度成長期（1950年代後半～1960年代）…………… 134
- c) 安定成長期（1970年代～1980年代前半）…………… 136
- d) バブルの生成（1980年代後半～1990年代初）……… 136
- e) バブルの崩壊と長期景気低迷（1990年代初～2000年）
  ……………………………………………………………… 138
- f) 好況感なき回復から世界同時不況へ（2001～2011年）
  ……………………………………………………………… 138
- g) 東日本大震災以降（2011年～）……………………… 140

(3) 日本経済が直面する4つの重要課題
- a) エネルギー確保 ………………………………………… 142
- b) 財政再建 ………………………………………………… 146
- c) 第4次産業革命（IoT・ビッグデータ・AI）への対応
  ……………………………………………………………… 148
- d) 少子・高齢化社会・人口減少への対応 ……………… 150

(4) 対外経済
- a) 貿易 ……………………………………………………… 150
- b) 国際収支 ………………………………………………… 154
- c) 対外経済協力 …………………………………………… 156

(5) 主要産業の動向 …………………………………………… 158
- a) 第1次産業 ……………………………………………… 160
- b) 第2次産業 ……………………………………………… 166
- c) 第3次産業 ……………………………………………… 188

(6) 企業経営と雇用
- a) 概況 ……………………………………………………… 210
- b) 企業経営の変革 ………………………………………… 212
- c) 雇用関係 ………………………………………………… 222

5 社 会
(1) 人口動態
- a) 総人口 …………………………………………………… 232

		b) 平均寿命・死亡原因	232
		c) 世帯数・家族構成	234
		d) 結婚・離婚	236

(2) **少子高齢社会**
  a) 少子化の現状と将来 ……………………………………………… 238
  b) 高齢化の現状と将来 ……………………………………………… 240
  c) 少子高齢社会の問題 ……………………………………………… 242
  d) 少子化社会の対策 ………………………………………………… 242
  e) 高齢化社会の対策 ………………………………………………… 246
  f) 女性の社会進出 …………………………………………………… 246
  g) 単身赴任 …………………………………………………………… 250

(3) **社会保障**
  a) 概要 ………………………………………………………………… 250
  b) 社会保障制度を取り巻く状況の変化と問題点 ………………… 252
  c) 社会保障制度の内容 ……………………………………………… 254
  d) 社会保険 …………………………………………………………… 256

(4) **教　育**
  a) 学校教育制度 ……………………………………………………… 262
  b) 教育制度の発展 …………………………………………………… 266
  c) 教育普及率 ………………………………………………………… 268
  d) 教育への経済的支援 ……………………………………………… 270
  e) 大学 ………………………………………………………………… 270
  f) 大学院 ……………………………………………………………… 274

(5) **情報通信社会（ICT）**
  a) 日本の ICT の現状 ………………………………………………… 274
  b) ICT による日本成長戦略 ………………………………………… 276
  c) スマートフォン社会の到来 ……………………………………… 278
  d) インターネット …………………………………………………… 282
  e) ビッグデータ利活用の開始 ……………………………………… 284
  f) ネットワーク利用に伴う問題点 ………………………………… 288

(6) **環境保全**
  a) 戦後日本の環境問題 ……………………………………………… 290
  b) 環境保全に対するグローバルな視点 …………………………… 292
  c) 分野別の環境課題 ………………………………………………… 292
  d) 国民の取り組み …………………………………………………… 310
  e) 最近の重要なキーワード ………………………………………… 310

6　科学技術
(1) **先端科学技術**
  a) ライフサイエンス分野 …………………………………………… 314
  b) 超電導技術 ………………………………………………………… 320
  c) 発光ダイオード（LED） ………………………………………… 322

d）	宇宙開発	324
e）	ナノテクノロジー	328
f）	化学分野	328
g）	ロボット	330
h）	エネルギー	332
i）	スーパーコンピュータ	334
j）	先端医療	336

(2) 日本の製造業技術・ものづくりの技の強み

a）	高効率大型火力発電所	342
b）	鉄道関連技術	344
c）	石油・シェールガス生産用のパイプ	346
d）	ミシン	346
e）	その他のユニークな技術	346

(3) 諸技術の組み合わせによる業務運営効率化のためのシステムの追求 … 348

(4) 日本の科学技術の現状

a）	科学技術基本計画	350
b）	研究開発費および予算	354
c）	ノーベル賞受賞者	354
d）	自然科学系学位（博士号）新規取得者	354
e）	自然科学系論文数	354
f）	特許出願件数	356
g）	技術貿易	356

(5) 日本の科学技術の課題と対策

a）	イノベーションの産学連携	358
b）	科学技術開発の国際化	358
c）	博士号取得者の活用	360
d）	若手・女性・外国人研究者の登用	360
e）	科学技術経営者の育成	362
f）	次の時代を担う人材の育成	362

7　文　化

(1) 日本文化の特質

a）	序	366
b）	稲作に根ざす日本文化	366
c）	自然に対する感性・繊細な芸術描写	368
d）	外国文化の吸収と融合	370

(2) 文字・言語・文学

a）	日本語	372
b）	文字	374
c）	外国人の日本語学習	378
d）	日本語のなかの外来語	380

e)	日本の文学	382
f)	短歌・俳句	388

(3) 日本美術の歴史
- a) 縄文時代（紀元前1万年頃～紀元前4～3世紀頃） …… 392
- b) 弥生時代（紀元前10世紀頃～紀元後3世紀中頃）…… 392
- c) 古墳時代（3世紀中頃～7世紀末頃） …… 394
- d) 飛鳥白鳳時代（592～710年） …… 394
- e) 奈良時代（710～794年） …… 394
- f) 平安時代（794～1185年） …… 396
- g) 鎌倉時代・南北朝時代（1185～1392年） …… 396
- h) 室町時代（1338～1573年） …… 398
- i) 安土桃山時代（1573～1603年） …… 398
- j) 江戸時代（1603～1868年） …… 400
- k) 近代・現代（明治時代・大正時代・昭和時代・平成時代）（1868年～） …… 402
- l) 国宝・重要文化財 …… 404
- m) クローン文化財 …… 404

(4) 演劇・芸能
- a) 伝統的な演劇・芸能 …… 406
- b) 能・狂言 …… 406
- c) 歌舞伎 …… 408
- d) 組踊（くみおどり） …… 410
- e) 文楽（人形浄瑠璃） …… 410
- f) 邦楽 …… 412
- g) 日本舞踊 …… 414
- h) 大衆芸能 …… 414

(5) 伝統芸術・工芸
- a) いけばな …… 418
- b) 茶道 …… 418
- c) 書道 …… 420
- d) 日本画 …… 420
- e) 陶磁器 …… 422
- f) 漆器 …… 424
- g) 日本刀 …… 426
- h) 人形 …… 428
- i) 扇子（せんす） …… 430
- j) 羽子板 …… 430
- k) 庭園 …… 432
- l) 盆栽 …… 432

(6) 建築・住居
- a) 家屋 …… 434

	b） 建築物	436

(7) スポーツ
	a） 概要	438
	b） 相撲	438
	c） 柔道	440
	d） 剣道・弓道・薙刀（なぎなた）・空手道	442
	e） 野球	444
	f） サッカー	446
	g） マラソン・駅伝マラソン	446

(8) オリンピック
	a） 概説	448
	b） 2020年夏季オリンピック・パラリンピック競技東京大会（概要）	448
	c） 2020年夏季オリンピック・パラリンピック競技東京大会（全体像と課題）	450

(9) 宗　教
	a） 概説	452
	b） 神道	454
	c） 仏教	456
	d） 禅	458
	e） キリスト教	458

(10) 風俗・習慣・娯楽
	a） 着物（和服）	460
	b） 主な年中行事	462
	c） 国民の祝日	466
	d） 郷土色豊かな祭りや伝統的行事	470
	e） 日本の代表的ペット	476
	f） 外国と異なる日本の習慣	480
	g） 名刺	480
	h） 判子（はんこ：印鑑ともいう）	482
	i） 風呂敷	482
	j） そろばん	482
	k） 賭け事	484
	l） パチンコ・パチスロ	484
	m） カルタ	486
	n） 碁（囲碁）・将棋・麻雀	488
	o） 日本の流行歌とクラシック音楽	490
	p） 日本映画（邦画とも呼ぶ）	496
	q） 日本のマンガ	500
	r） メディアコンテンツ	502

(11) 食物・飲み物
	a） 食生活	506

b）	和食（日本料理）	510
c）	酒	514
d）	飲み物	516
e）	タバコ	518
f）	自動販売機の普及	520

⑿ **日本人について**
- a） 国民性 …… 520
- b） 日本人の集団帰属意識 …… 522
- c） 武士道 …… 522
- d） 切腹 …… 524
- e） 日本人の微笑 …… 526
- f） 日本人の自己紹介のしかた …… 526

⒀ **日本の文化力**
- a） 文化力の再認識 …… 528
- b） 文化芸術立国にむけた政府の方針 …… 528

⒁ **観　光**
- a） 日本の自然景観を楽しむ …… 532
- b） 日本の歴史や文化財をたずねる …… 532
- c） 日本にある世界遺産 …… 536
- d） 日本での宿泊 …… 548

⒂ **日本のノーベル賞受賞者** …… 550

［付録］
〔統計資料〕
- (1) 主要各国の面積と人口 …… 558
- (2) 日本の主要都市人口 …… 559
- (3) 日本の統治機構 …… 560
- (4) 各国の国内総生産（GDP）と1人あたりGDP …… 562
- (5) 日本の産業別国内総生産 …… 563
- (6) 主要国のエネルギー自給率 …… 564
- (7) 主な国の農産物自給率 …… 564
- (8) 産業別就業人口割合 …… 565
- (9) 日本の学校体系図 …… 566

〔参考文献〕 …… 567
〔年　表〕 …… 569
〔索　引〕 …… 579

Contents

1 **Geography**
 a) Location and Size of Japan 33
 b) Climate of Japan 35
 c) Geographical Features of Japan 37
 d) Earthquakes and Tsunamis 39
 e) Population of Japan 41
 f) Mountains, Rivers and Lakes of Japan 41
 g) Plants of Japan 43
 h) Japanese Wildlife 45

2 **History**
 a) Origin of the Japanese People and the Japanese Nation 47
 b) Ancient Times (4th century to 12th century) 49
 c) Middle Ages and Early Modern Ages (12th century to early 19th century) 51
 d) Modern Times (Mid-19th century to 1945) 57
 e) Recent Times I (1945 to mid-1980s) 63
 f) Recent Times II (Mid-1980s on) 67

3 **Government**
 (1) The Emperor
  a) Constitutional Status of the Emperor 79
  b) History of the Imperial House 79
  c) The Imperial Family 81
  d) The Emperor's Abdication 81
  e) Female Emperor and Matrilinear Emperor 83
 (2) Government
  a) The Japanese Constitution 85
  b) Japanese System of Government 89
  c) Elections 91
  d) Public Safety, National Police Agency, and Japan Coast Guard 97
  e) Self-Defense Forces 101
 (3) Diplomacy
  a) Basic Principles of Japanese Diplomacy 103
  b) Country-Specific Diplomacy 105
  c) Field-Specific Diplomacy 119

(4) The National Flag etc.
- a) The National Flag ... 127
- b) The National Anthem ... 127
- c) National Flower ... 127
- d) Use of Eras in Reckoning Years ... 129

4 Economy
(1) Overview of the Japanese Economy
- a) Scale of the Economy ... 131
- b) Industrial Structure ... 131
- c) Industrial Foundation ... 133
- d) External Economic Relations ... 133

(2) Postwar Economic Progress
- a) Recovery from the Ruins of War (1945 to mid-1950s) ... 135
- b) Rapid Economic Growth (Mid-1950s through 1960s) ... 135
- c) Stable Growth (1970s to mid-1980s) ... 137
- d) Bubble Economy (Mid-1980s to early 1990s) ... 137
- e) Collapse of the Bubble and Protracted Recession (Early 1990s to 2000) ... 139
- f) From the Muted Economic Recovery to the Global Recession (2001 to 2011) ... 139
- g) After the Great East Japan Earthquake (from 2011) ... 141

(3) Four Important Issues Facing the Japanese Economy
- a) Securing Energy ... 143
- b) Fiscal Reconstruction ... 147
- c) Response to the Fourth Industrial Revolution (IoT, Big Data, AI) ... 149
- d) Response to Aging Society, Declining Birthrate, and Shrinking Population ... 151

(4) External Economic Relations
- a) Trade ... 151
- b) International Balance of Payments ... 155
- c) External Economic Cooperation ... 157

(5) Industrial Trends ... 159
- a) Primary Industries ... 161
- b) Secondary Industries ... 167
- c) Tertiary Industries ... 189

(6) Business Management and Employment
- a) Overview ... 211
- b) Transformation of Business Management ... 213
- c) Employment ... 223

5 Society

(1) Population Dynamics
- a) Total Population ··· 233
- b) Average Life Span and Causes of Death ············· 233
- c) Number of Households and Family Composition ········· 235
- d) Marriage and Divorce ································· 237

(2) Aging Society with Declining Birth Rate
- a) Low Birth Rate ··· 239
- b) Aging Population ······································· 241
- c) Low Birth Rate Issues ································· 243
- d) Efforts to Avoid a Low-Birth-Rate Society ············ 243
- e) Aging-Society Measures ······························· 247
- f) Social Advancement of Women ························ 247
- g) Taking a Post Away from One's Family ··············· 251

(3) Social Security
- a) Overview ·· 251
- b) Problems and Changes in Circumstances Related to the Social Security System ······························· 253
- c) Elements of the Social Security System ·············· 255
- d) Social Insurance ·· 257

(4) Education
- a) Japanese Educational System ························· 263
- b) Development of the Educational System ············· 267
- c) Education Rate ··· 269
- d) Financial Support for Education ······················ 271
- e) Colleges and Universities ····························· 271
- f) Graduate Schools ······································· 275

(5) Information and Communication Society
- a) Information and Communication Technology (ICT) in Japan ·· 275
- b) Japan's ICT-Based Growth Strategy by ICT ········· 277
- c) The Advent of the Smartphone Society ··············· 279
- d) Internet ··· 283
- e) The Start of Big Data Utilization ···················· 285
- f) Network Usage Issues ································· 289

(6) Preservation of the Environment
- a) Environmental Problems in Post-War Japan ········· 291
- b) Preservation of the Environment from a Global Perspective ··· 293
- c) Environmental Issues in Different Fields ············ 293
- d) Community Efforts ···································· 311
- e) Recent Important Keywords ·························· 311

6 Science and Technology

(1) Advanced Science and Technology
- a) Life Sciences ⋯ 315
- b) Superconducting Technology ⋯ 321
- c) Light-Emitting Diode (LED) ⋯ 323
- d) Space Exploration ⋯ 325
- e) Nanotechnology ⋯ 329
- f) Chemical Sector ⋯ 329
- g) Robotic Process Automation ⋯ 331
- h) Energy ⋯ 333
- i) Supercomputers ⋯ 335
- j) Advanced Medical Treatment ⋯ 337

(2) Strength of Japanese Manufacturing Technology
- a) High-Efficiency Large-Scale Thermal Power Plants ⋯ 343
- b) Railway-Related Technology ⋯ 345
- c) Pipes for Petroleum and Shale Gas Production ⋯ 347
- d) Sewing Machines ⋯ 347
- e) Other Unique Technologies ⋯ 347

(3) Combining Technologies to Optimize Operational Efficiency
⋯ 349

(4) Science and Technology in Japan
- a) Science and Technology Basic Plan ⋯ 351
- b) R&D Expenditures and Budget ⋯ 355
- c) Nobel Prize Winners ⋯ 355
- d) Doctorates in the Natural Sciences ⋯ 355
- e) Natural Science Research Papers ⋯ 355
- f) Number of Patent Applications ⋯ 357
- g) Technology Trade ⋯ 357

(5) Japanese Science and Technology—Issues and Countermeasures
- a) Industry-University Collaborative Innovation ⋯ 359
- b) Internationalizing Science and Technology Research ⋯ 359
- c) Utilizing Graduates with Doctor's Degrees ⋯ 361
- d) Creating Opportunities for Junior, Female, and Foreign Researchers ⋯ 361
- e) Training Science and Technology-Minded Business Leaders ⋯ 363
- f) Developing Human Resources for Future Generations ⋯ 363

7 Culture

(1) Unique Aspects of Japanese Culture
- a) Introduction ⋯ 367
- b) Japanese Culture, Rooted in Rice Cultivation ⋯ 367

- c) Sensitivity to Nature and Subtleties of Depictions in Art ... 369
- d) Absorbing and Assimilating Foreign Cultures ... 371

(2) Writing System, Language and Literature
- a) The Japanese Language ... 373
- b) Writing System ... 375
- c) Learning Japanese by Foreigners ... 379
- d) Loanwords ... 381
- e) Japanese Literature ... 383
- f) Tanka and Haiku ... 389

(3) History of Japanese Art
- a) Jomon Period (10,000 B.C. to 400 or 300 B.C.) ... 393
- b) Yayoi Period (10th century B.C. to mid-3rd century A.D.) ... 393
- c) Tumulus Period (Mid-3rd century to late 7th century) ... 395
- d) Asuka Hakuho Period (592 to 710) ... 395
- e) Nara Period (710 to 794) ... 395
- f) Heian Period (794 to 1185) ... 397
- g) Kamakura Period and the Period of North and South Dynasties (1185 to 1392) ... 397
- h) Muromachi Period (1338 to 1573) ... 399
- i) Azuchi-Momoyama Period (1573 to 1603) ... 399
- j) Edo Period (1603 to 1868) ... 401
- k) Modern Period and Today (Meiji era, Taisho era, Showa era, and Heisei era) (from 1868) ... 403
- l) National Treasures and Important Cultural Assets ... 405
- m) Cloned Cultural Properties ... 405

(4) Dramas and Entertainments
- a) Traditional Theater and Entertainments ... 407
- b) Noh and Kyogen ... 407
- c) Kabuki ... 409
- d) Kumi-odori ... 411
- e) Bunraku (Joruri Puppet Theater) ... 411
- f) Japanese Music ... 413
- g) Japanese Dancing ... 415
- h) Popular Entertainment ... 415

(5) Traditional Arts and Crafts
- a) Ikebana ... 419
- b) Tea Cult ... 419
- c) Calligraphy ... 421
- d) Japanese Painting ... 421
- e) Ceramic Ware ... 423

f)	Lacquer Ware	425
g)	Japanese Swords	427
h)	Dolls	429
i)	Folding Fans	431
j)	Hagoita	431
k)	Gardens	433
l)	Bonsai	433

(6) Buildings
- a) Houses ……………………………………………………… 435
- b) Large Buildings ……………………………………………… 437

(7) Sports
- a) Overview ……………………………………………………… 439
- b) Sumo …………………………………………………………… 439
- c) Judo …………………………………………………………… 441
- d) Kendo, Kyudo, Naginata, and Karatedo ………………… 443
- e) Baseball ……………………………………………………… 445
- f) Soccer ………………………………………………………… 447
- g) Marathons and Road Relay Races ………………………… 447

(8) The Olympics
- a) Outline ………………………………………………………… 449
- b) Overview of the Tokyo 2020 Summer Olympics and Paralympics …………………………………………………… 449
- c) Overall Theme and the Issues Facing the Tokyo 2020 Summer Games ……………………………………………… 451

(9) Religion
- a) Overview ……………………………………………………… 453
- b) Shinto ………………………………………………………… 455
- c) Buddhism ……………………………………………………… 457
- d) Zen Buddhism ………………………………………………… 459
- e) Christianity …………………………………………………… 459

(10) Customs, Manners and Pastimes
- a) Kimono (Japanese Dress) …………………………………… 461
- b) Main Annual Festivals ……………………………………… 463
- c) National Holidays …………………………………………… 467
- d) Local Festivals and Traditional Events …………………… 471
- e) Japanese Pets ………………………………………………… 477
- f) Customs and Beliefs Peculiar to Japan …………………… 481
- g) Name Cards …………………………………………………… 481
- h) Seal Stamps (Seal Impressions) …………………………… 483
- i) Furoshiki ……………………………………………………… 483
- j) Abacus ………………………………………………………… 483
- k) Betting ………………………………………………………… 485

l)	Pachinko and Pachisuro	485
m)	Japanese Card Games	487
n)	Go (Igo), Shogi, Mah-jong	489
o)	Japanese Popular Songs and Classical Music	491
p)	Japanese Films	497
q)	Japanese Comics (manga)	501
r)	Media Content	503

(11) Food and Drink

a)	The Japanese Diet	507
b)	Japanese Cuisine	511
c)	Sake and Other Alcoholic Drinks	515
d)	Beverages	517
e)	Tobacco	519
f)	Proliferation of Automatic Vending Machines	521

(12) About the Japanese

a)	The Japanese Character	521
b)	Japanese Group Consciousness	523
c)	Bushido	523
d)	Seppuku	525
e)	The Japanese Smile	527
f)	How Japanese Introduce Themselves in Business Situations	527

(13) Japanese Cultural Power

a)	Renewed Awareness of Cultural Power	529
b)	Government Policies Directed at Creating a Culturally and Artistically Vibrant Nation	529

(14) Sightseeing

a)	Japan's Natural Scenery	533
b)	Historical and Cultural Treasures in Japan	533
c)	Japanese Properties on the World Heritage List	537
d)	Lodgings in Japan	549

(15) Nobel Prize Winners ……… 551

Appendix

(1)	Area of Selected Countries	558
(2)	Population of Selected Cities in Japan	559
(3)	Government of Japan	560
(4)	GDP and Per Capita Income	562
(5)	GDP by Industry in Japan	563
(6)	Self-Sufficiency in Energy	564
(7)	Self-Sufficiency in Food Crops	564
(8)	Breakdown of Industrial Sector of Employed Persons	

	15 Years Old and Over	565
(9)	Japanese School System	566

日　本
—その姿と心—

JAPAN

**NIPPON
THE LAND
AND
ITS PEOPLE**

1 地理

a) 位置・国の広さ

日本は、アジア大陸の東側に東西、南北それぞれ約 3,000 km（1,860 マイル）にわたって位置する弧状の島国で、本州・四国・九州・北海道の 4 つの主な島と、散在する 7,000 弱の島からなっている。これらをすべて含めて日本列島と総称されている。

首都東京は、東経 140 度（ニューギニア島・オーストラリア中央部とほぼ同経度）、北緯 36 度（中国の青島・イランのテヘラン・地中海のマルタ島・ジブラルタル海峡・アメリカのグランドキャニオンなどとほぼ同緯度）にある。

東京から各地への距離は次のとおりである。

ニューヨーク	10,850 km	(6,740	マイル)
ロサンゼルス	8,740 〃	(5,430	〃)
リオデジャネイロ	18,560 〃	(11,530	〃)
ロンドン	9,560 〃	(5,940	〃)
パリ	9,740 〃	(6,050	〃)
ベルリン	8,910 〃	(5,540	〃)
ローマ	9,880 〃	(6,140	〃)
モスクワ	7,500 〃	(4,660	〃)
テヘラン	7,680 〃	(4,770	〃)
ナイロビ	11,200 〃	(7,000	〃)
デリー	5,860 〃	(3,640	〃)
シンガポール	5,320 〃	(3,310	〃)
北京	2,100 〃	(1,300	〃)
ソウル	1,160 〃	(720	〃)
シドニー	7,830 〃	(4,870	〃)

国土面積は約 37 万 8,000 km²（14 万 6,000 平方マイル）で、マレーシアよりわずかに大きく、中国やアメリカの 25 分の 1・ブラジルの 23 分の 1・インドネシアの 5 分の 1 にあたる。しかし国連海洋法条約で定められた領海を含む排他的経済水域（EEZ：Exclusive Economic Zone）で比較すると、日本は 447 万 km² でカナダに次いで世界第 6 位である。EEZ では日本は中国やブラジルよりも大きい。

1 Geography

a) Location and Size of Japan

Japan is an island nation lying off the east coast of Asia. It has the general shape of a crescent and extends north-south and east-west, each about 3,000 km (1,860 miles) from tip to tip. The country is made up of four main islands (Honshu, Shikoku, Kyushu and Hokkaido) which together with smaller islands of a little fewer than 7,000 are collectively referred to as the Japanese Archipelago.

The nation's capital, Tokyo, lies at 140° east longitude (on a line with New Guinea and central Australia) and 36° north latitude (about the same as Tsingtao, Tehran, Malta, the Strait of Gibraltar, and the Grand Canyon).

Below are the distances between Tokyo and some of the other major cities of the world:

New York	10,850 km	(6,740 miles)
Los Angeles	8,740 km	(5,430 miles)
Rio de Janeiro	18,560 km	(11,530 miles)
London	9,560 km	(5,940 miles)
Paris	9,740 km	(6,050 miles)
Berlin	8,910 km	(5,540 miles)
Rome	9,880 km	(6,140 miles)
Moscow	7,500 km	(4,660 miles)
Tehran	7,680 km	(4,770 miles)
Nairobi	11,200 km	(7,000 miles)
Delhi	5,860 km	(3,640 miles)
Singapore	5,320 km	(3,310 miles)
Beijing	2,100 km	(1,300 miles)
Seoul	1,160 km	(720 miles)
Sydney	7,830 km	(4,870 miles)

Japan's land area of about 378,000 km^2 (146,000 square miles) is slightly larger than that of Malaysia, one twenty-fifth that of China, one twenty-fifth that of the United States (U.S.), one twenty-third that of Brazil, and one fifth that of Indonesia. However, the area of Japan's Exclusive Economic Zone (EEZ) as prescribed by the United Nations Convention of the Law of the Sea amounts to 4.47 million km^2 (1.73 million square miles), which is the world's sixth largest following

EEZ の内側では、魚類などの海産資源、石油・天然ガス・メタンハイドレートなどのエネルギー資源、マンガンその他の希少金属（レアメタル）を含む鉱物資源の排他的経済開発が認められる。近年、東アジアの海域で、いくつかの小島の領有権をめぐって周辺国家が争っているのは、その背景に国家主権の問題と並んで、EEZ のもつ経済的安全保障の問題があるからである。

　なお、国土の面積・領海について、2013 年からの噴火活動で小笠原諸島の無人島、西之島（東京都）の面積が約 9 倍に広がった。それにより領海が 70 km² 広くなった。

b) 気候

　日本列島は南北に長く、南は亜熱帯から北は亜寒帯まで広範囲にわたっているが、大部分の地域は温帯に属しており、海洋性の温暖な気候で、四季の区別がはっきりしている。ただし、複雑な地形や海流の影響により、気候の地域差が顕著である。

　起伏に富んだ山脈が日本列島を縦断し、その標高も高い部分は 3,000 m（9,840 フィート）におよんでいるため、太平洋側と日本海側の気候の差が大きい。太平洋側では、夏は南東の季節風が吹いてむし暑く、冬は乾燥した晴天が多い。日本海側では、冬は大陸方面からの北西の季節風による降雪が多い。この地方は世界有数の豪雪地帯で、新潟県などでは、積雪が 4 〜 5 m（13〜16 フィート）にも達するところがある。

　北海道を除く地域では、6 月上旬から 7 月中旬にかけて梅雨と呼ばれる高温多湿の雨期がある。台風シーズンとなる 8 月から 10 月にかけて、日本列島は南西部を中心に暴風雨圏内に入ることも珍しくなく、台風の進路には多大な関心が払われる。本州・北海道の内陸部（とくに盆地）では降雨量が少なく、気温の上下差が大きいところがある。また、瀬戸内海の沿岸部は、前述の梅雨期以外は概して雨が少なく、気候は温暖である。

Canada. Japan's EEZ is larger than those of China and Brazil.

The resources Japan has the exclusive right to develop economically within its EEZ include fishery and other marine resources, energy resources such as petroleum, natural gas and methane hydrate, and manganese, rare earth metals and other mineral resources. The disputes over territorial rights that have emerged among countries bordering the East Asian Seas in recent years are rooted as much in the economic security aspect of EEZs as in national sovereignty concerns.

Nishinoshima, an uninhabited island of the Ogasawara Island group that is part of the administrative district of Tokyo, underwent a nine-fold increase in area due to volcanic eruption activity that started in 2013, This increased the area of Japan's territorial waters to 70 square kilometers.

b) Climate of Japan

Although Japan's considerable north-south length extends from the subfrigid zone to the subtropical zone, most of the country lies in the temperate zone and enjoys a moderate, oceanic type of climate with four distinct seasons. Still, the climate differs markedly from region to region owing to the effects of the complex topography and varying ocean currents.

Ranges of rugged mountains that run nearly the full length of the country and rise to as high as 3,000 meters (9,840 feet) give the Pacific and Sea of Japan sides of Japan vastly different climatic patterns. On the Pacific side, the summers are hot and humid with prevailing seasonal winds from the southeast. The winters are dry and marked by many clear days. On the Sea of Japan side, northwesterly winter winds off the Asian continent bring regular, heavy snows that makes this area one of the snowiest regions on earth. In Niigata Prefecture, for example, annual snowfalls of 4 to 5 meters (13 to 16 feet) are not unusual.

From early June to mid-July, all areas except the northernmost island of Hokkaido have a hot and very humid rainy season called the "*tsuyu* (or *baiu*)." And during the typhoon season, which runs from August to October, typhoon-force wind and rain may strike any part of Japan, with the southwestern areas being the most vulnerable. Once a typhoon appears on the weather map, people throughout the country keep an anxious eye on its path. The inland regions of Honshu and Hokkaido, particularly the basins in these areas, receive little rain and are subject to large temperature variations. On the other hand, the coastal regions of the Inland Sea lying between the islands of Honshu and Shikoku, though also quite dry except during the rainy season, have a moderate

日本の大部分の地域で、もっともよい季節は春と秋で、とくに新緑の萌（も）える4～5月ごろと、さわやかで木の葉の色づく9月下旬から11月中旬ごろまでの山野の風景が美しい。
　梅雨・台風・豪雪はいずれも愉快なものではない。なかでも、風水害の大部分は台風がもたらす。台風のころはちょうど稲の開花から結実期にあたるので、農家の心配も大きい。しかしながら、これらが与える自然の恵みも大きい。梅雨期の降雨は稲作になくてはならないものであり、台風時の大雨や冬の積雪は水資源を豊かにする。

　なお、近年の地球温暖化現象に伴って、以下のような観測報告がある。「日本の平均気温も年による変動が大きいものの長期的に上昇傾向で、100年あたり1.15℃の割合で上昇しており、世界平均（0.68℃／100年）を上回っている。また、日最高気温が35℃以上の猛暑日や最低気温が25℃以上の熱帯夜の日数もそれぞれ増加傾向を示している。降水にも変化が表れており、日降水量1mm以上の降水日数は減少傾向にある一方、日降水量が100mm以上の大雨の日は増加傾向にある。」

c）地形

　日本列島は太平洋や日本海などの海に囲まれ、大陸とは浅い大陸棚で接している。太平洋側には非常に深い日本海溝や伊豆小笠原海溝がある。

　日本の地形は変化に富んでいる。川は短く急流で、山あいでは深い峡谷をつくり、海岸線は複雑に入りくんでいる。風光明媚なところが多く、温泉地も点在している。

　日本の国土の約4分の3は山地および丘陵地で、国土の3分の2は森林に覆われており、森林率は67％と世界の国々の中でも高い。農業用地は12％、宅地は3％で、工

climate.

In almost all parts of Japan the best seasons are spring and autumn. The countryside is especially beautiful during April and May when all is freshly green, and between late September and mid-November when the air is stimulating and the leaves have changed color.

There is no pretending that the rainy season, the typhoons, and the heavy snows are pleasant aspects of the Japanese climate. The typhoons, for example, are responsible for the major share of the wind and flood damage suffered by Japan and they are particularly worrisome for rice-farmers, as it is in the typhoon season that the rice plant blooms and ripens. Still each of the aspects of the climate is in its own way a natural blessing: the rains which fall during the baiu are indispensable to a good rice crop, and the precipitation that comes in the form of typhoon rains and heavy snows makes an invaluable contribution to Japan's water resources.

The global warming phenomenon of recent years has given rise to the following kind of observation reports. "Although Japan's average temperature fluctuates from year to year, it has risen over the long term at the rate of 1.15°C per 100 years, exceeding the world average of 0.68°C per 100 years. Hot days with temperatures of 35°C or above and tropical nights with a low temperature of 25°C or above are also on the increase. Precipitation is also changing, with the number of days on which precipitation is 1 mm or more showing a decline, while at the same time days of heavy rain with a daily precipitation of 100 mm (3.9 inches) or more are on the rise."

c) Geographical Features of Japan

The islands of Japan are bounded by the Pacific Ocean on the east and the Japan Sea on the west. They are connected with the Asian mainland by the relatively shallow-lying continental shelf. On the Pacific side of the islands are two regions of extreme depth known as the Japan Deep and the Izu-Ogasawara Deep.

Japan has a great deal of variety in its topographical features. Its rivers are short and fast-flowing and form deep gorges in the mountainous areas. All of the major islands have highly irregular coast lines. Wherever the traveler goes in Japan, he will be impressed by the many places of scenic beauty. The countryside is dotted with hot springs, many of which have become popular resorts.

About three-quarters of Japan's land area is mountainous or hilly and two-thirds is covered with forest. The country's forest coverage rate of 67% is one of the highest in the world. Agricultural land accounts for

業用地はわずか0.4％にすぎない。

d）地震・津波

日本列島は環太平洋地震帯の上にあり、火山活動も活発で、世界でも有数の地震多発地帯となっている。

2011年3月11日午後2時46分、仙台市の東70kmの海底を震源とする超巨大地震が発生した。地震の規模はマグニチュード9.0で、これは日本周辺での観測史上最大の地震（東日本大震災）であり、世界中の人々を震撼させたものである。死者・行方不明者は18,537人で、死者の93％は津波が原因とされている（2013年9月時点）。このほかに避難後の震災関連死が2,688人出たとされる。避難者は地震直後に40万人以上、建物の全壊・半壊合わせて約40万戸、停電840万戸余り、断水40万戸におよんだ。また、火災も345件発生し、千葉県から岩手県にかけて石油コンビナート、石油・ガス備蓄基地、製鉄所ガスホルダーなどが火災により損傷し、多くの一般住宅も焼失した。

この地震の特質は、巨大地震とこれに伴う巨大津波により重大な人的・物的被害をもたらしたことと、これに加えて原子力発電所の崩壊という重大事故が発生したことである。崩壊した原子炉から大量の放射性物質が広範囲に拡散する、という経験したことのない重大かつ深刻な災害となり、日本の産業、経済、社会にとって長期・甚大な被害をあたえた。また、この震災は日本の原子力・エネルギー政策に大きな影響をあたえている。

日本における地震について、文字による最初の記録は、416年8月と言われている（日本書紀）が、特に地震とこれに起因する津波による被害が大きかったものとして、869年7月に東日本北部（岩手県沖から福島県沖）に発生した貞観地震（推定マグニチュード8.3〜8.6）が伝えられている（日本三代実録）。

20世紀以降では、東京を中心とした首都圏に壊滅的な被害を与えた1923年の関東大震災（マグニチュード7.9）をはじめとして、1933年の昭和三陸地震（マグニチュード8.4）、最近では1995年の阪神・淡路大震災（マグニ

12% and residential land for 3%. A mere 0.4% is devoted to industrial purposes.

d) Earthquakes and Tsunamis

Lying on the circum-Pacific earthquake zone, the Japanese Archipelago is the site of considerable volcanic activity and is one of the world's most seismologically active areas.

At 2:46 p.m. on March 11, 2011, a massive earthquake took place having its epicenter under the seabed 70 km to the east of Sendai city. Known as the Great East Japan Earthquake, it had a magnitude of 9.0, making it the biggest earthquake in Japan's recorded history, and its effects were felt around the world. As of September 2013, the number of dead and missing stood at 18,537, with about 93% of the deaths being due to the accompanying tsunami. An additional 2,688 earthquake-related deaths happened after evacuation. Immediately after the earthquake, the number of evacuees rose to over 400,000, approximately 400,000 buildings were totally or partially destroyed, 8.4 million houses suffered electric power outages, and some 400,000 houses were without water. A total of 345 fires broke out and from Iwate to Chiba, petrochemical complexes, oil and gas storage facilities and steelworks' gas holders suffered fire damage, and many ordinary houses were also destroyed by fires.

In addition to the major damage to life and property, the huge tsunami brought on by the earthquake caused extensive damage to a nuclear power station, triggering a major nuclear accident. Large amounts of radioactive material from the damaged nuclear reactors were spread over a wide area, creating an unprecedentedly major, serious disaster that inflicted enormous damage on Japan's industry, economy and society. The earthquake also had a major impact on Japan's nuclear energy policy.

The oldest recorded earthquake in Japanese history occurred in August 416, according to the *Nihonshoki* (Chronicles of Japan). However, the Jogan Earthquake of July, 869, was particularly notable for the major extent of the damage due to the quake and the associated tsunami, as described by the *Nihon Sandai Jitsuroku* (The True History of Three Reigns of Japan). The Jogan Earthquake struck the offshore part of northeastern Japan, from Iwate Prefecture to Fukushima Prefecture.

A number of severe earthquakes have hit Japan since the beginning of the twentieth century. The most disastrous of these was the Great Kanto Earthquake of 1923 (magnitude of 7.9), which caused catastrophic damage in and around Tokyo. Recent ones include the Great Hanshin and

チュード 7.2)、2004 年の新潟県中越地震（マグニチュード 6.8）が発生し、2011 年には前述の東日本大震災が発生した。その後も震度 4 ～ 5 クラスの地震は全国各地でたびたび発生しているが、2016 年 4 月には、熊本県益城町で震度 7（マグニチュード 7.3）の地震が発生し死者 204 人の犠牲者が出ている。

また、2018 年 9 月に北海道胆振地方中東部を震源とする震度 7（マグニチュード 6.7）の地震が発生し、死者 41 人の犠牲者が出た。なお、この地震の影響で道内の半分の電気を供給していた苫東厚真火力発電所が被災して発電不能となり、このため北海道全域が数日間ブラックアウト（停電）し、各方面に多大な損害を与えた。

e）人口

日本の総人口は 2018 年 4 月（人口推計確定値） 1 億 2,650 万人であり、これは同年、中国（14 億 1,505 万人）、インド（13 億 5,406 万人）、アメリカ（3 億 2,677 万人）、インドネシア（2 億 6,680 万人）、ブラジル（2 億 1,087 万人）、パキスタン（2 億 0,081 万人）、ナイジェリア（1 億 9,588 万人）、バングラデシュ（1 億 6,637 万人）、ロシア（1 億 4,397 万人）、メキシコ（1 億 3,076 万人）に次いで世界第 11 位である。

日本の人口密度は 1 km² 当たり 341 人（2018 年）であり世界 25 位である。

人口の分布は、温暖で交通・産業の発達した太平洋側の海岸沿いの平野に多く、本州の南関東から北九州にかけて人口の 70％が集まっている。また、工業の発展にともなって、人口が都市に集中し農村では著しく減少した。

人口 100 万人以上の都市は、東京 23 区（930 万人、2017 年）を筆頭に横浜市、大阪市、名古屋市など 12 ある。

f）山・川・湖

日本の約 70％は山地で本州の中央部には飛騨・木曽・赤石の 3 つの山脈があって、3,000 m 級（1 万フィート級）の山々がそびえている。これらはそれぞれ北・中央・南アルプスとも呼ばれ、また、総称して日本アルプスといわ

Awaji Earthquake of 1995 (7.2), the Mid-Niigata Prefecture Earthquake of 2004 (6.8), and the aforementioned Great East Japan Earthquake of 2011. These have been followed by the frequent occurrence of earthquakes with a seismic intensity of 4 to 5 throughout the country, but in April 2016 an earthquake with an intensity of 7 (magnitude 7.3) occurred in the town of Mashiki, Kumamoto Prefecture, which resulted in 204 deaths.

In September 2018, there was also a major earthquake in the central-eastern area of the Iburi district of Hokkaido. The earthquake, which had an intensity of 7 (magnitude 6.7), resulted in 41 fatalities. The Tomato-Atsuma thermal power station, which supplies power used by half of Hokkaido, was damaged in the quake, causing blackouts throughout the prefecture for several days and considerable damage.

e) Population of Japan

Japan has a population of 126.50 million, putting it in eleventh place after China (1,415.05 million), India (1,354.06 million), the U.S. (326.77 million), Indonesia (266.80 million), Brazil (210.87 million), Pakistan (200.81 million), Nigeria (195.88 million), Bangladesh (166.37 million), Russia (143.97 million), and Mexico (130.76 million), as of April 2018 (Estimated population values).

Japan has a population density of 341 people per square kilometer (2018) 25th in the world.

The population is greatest along the Pacific seaboard where the weather is mild and the transportation and industrial facilities are most highly developed. In fact, approximately 70% of the nation's people live on the strip of coastal plain between Tokyo and the northern part of Kyushu. Advancing industrialization has been accompanied by a population shift toward the large cities and a marked population decline in the agricultural areas.

Of the twelve cities in Japan with populations of over one million, the largest are the 23 wards of Metropolitan Tokyo (9.30 million, 2017), Yokohama, Osaka and Nagoya.

f) Mountains, Rivers and Lakes of Japan

About 70% of Japan's land area is mountainous. The most prominent mountains are found in the Hida, Kiso, and Akaishi ranges of central Honshu where the highest peaks are in the 3,000-meter class (10,000-foot class). These three ranges are, in the order named, often referred to

れ、これは1896年に、イギリス人ウェストンによって名付けられた。

富士山は、標高3,776 m（12,388フィート）の日本でもっとも高い山である。典型的な円錐形活火山で、美しい広い裾野をもち、冬には中腹まで雪に覆われ一層美しさを増す。1707年に大噴火があったが、それ以後約300年の間噴火していない。富士山は2013年、世界文化遺産に登録された。日本第2の標高の山は南アルプスの北岳で3,193 m（10,468フィート）である。2017年時点で、日本には浅間山・阿蘇山・桜島・雲仙岳・三原山など111の活火山がある。

川は短くて急流が多く、もっとも長い信濃川でも367 km（228マイル）である。落差の大きい急流は水力発電に適し、美しい峡谷をつくっているが、交通にはほとんど利用できず、洪水を起こす危険もある。日本第2の長流は利根川で322 km（200マイル）である。

湖の多くは山間部にあり、水が澄んでいて眺めのよいものが多い。もっとも大きい琵琶湖の面積は674 km^2（260平方マイル）で、西ヨーロッパ最大のレマン湖（ジュネーブ湖）の約1.2倍である（なお、北米五大湖最小のオンタリオ湖の30分の1）。また、もっとも深い湖は田沢湖で、水深423 m（1,388フィート）である。日本第2の湖は面積168 km^2（65平方マイル）の霞ヶ浦であり、土砂などによって外海と分離してできた。

g）植物

日本は気候の地域差が顕著であるため、植物の生態は複雑で種類も豊富である。日本にある約4,500種の植物のうち、約1,000種は日本固有種である。

北海道をふくむ日本北部には、針葉樹でもトドマツやハイマツなどシベリア地域と似かよった植物がみられる。本州中央部から九州の平地には、クリなどの温帯落葉樹が多い。東北地方から中部山岳地帯には、ブナ・カエデなどが広がる。山々は5月から6月に美しい新緑におおわれ、秋には色とりどりの紅葉に彩られる。

as the North, Central, and South Alps. Collectively, they are called the Japanese or Nihon Alps. These designations were introduced into the Japanese vocabulary by Walter Weston, an Englishman, in 1896.

Mt. Fuji is Japan's highest peak with an altitude of 3,776 meters (12,388 feet). An almost perfectly conical volcano with beautiful wide-flowing skirts, the mountain's beauty is most stunning in winter when its upper half is covered with snow. Mt. Fuji's most recent eruption was a major one in 1707, about three hundred years ago. Mt. Fuji was designated as a World Heritage Site in 2013. Japan's second-highest peak, at 3,193 meters (10,468 feet), is Mount Kita, in the South Alps. Japan has 111 active volcanoes (2017), the most famous of which are Mt. Asama, Mt. Aso, Mt. Sakurajima, Mt. Unzen, and Mt. Mihara.

Most Japanese rivers are short and fast flowing. Even the longest, the Shinano River, is a mere 367 km (228 miles) from source to mouth. Though fast streams which drop from great heights have certain advantages when applied to hydroelectric power generation and are apt to provide picturesque canyons, they are all but impossible to use as waterways and are susceptible to flooding. Japan's second-longest river, at 322 km (200 miles), is the Tone River.

Most of Japan's lakes are in the mountains and many offer fine views thanks to their clear water and scenic surroundings. The largest is Lake Biwa, whose area of 674 km^2 (260 square miles) is about 1.2 times that of Lake Léman (Lake Geneva), the largest lake in Western Europe, about one-thirtieth that of Lake Ontario, the smallest of the Great Lakes in North America. Japan's deepest lake is Lake Tazawa which reaches a depth of 423 meters (1,388 feet). Lake Kasumigaura is the second largest lake in Japan with an area of 168 km^2 (65 square miles). It is a body of water cut off from the ocean mostly by river sedimentation.

g) Plants of Japan

Japan's considerable regional differences in climate give the country a complex ecological landscape and an abundant variety of plants. Of Japan's 4,500 or so kinds of plants, around 1,000 are indigenous.

Many of the trees of Hokkaido and other northern regions are similar to those of Siberia, including the Sakhalin fir, Siberian dwarf fir, and other conifers. The trees at lower altitudes between central Honshu and Kyushu are mainly temperate zone deciduous types such as the Japanese chestnut. Beech and maple are common through the mountain areas between the Tohoku District and the Chubu Mountain Range. The hillsides are covered with beautiful fresh green foliage in May and June and set ablaze with red and yellow tints in the autumn.

サクラは日本人にはことのほか愛され、日本全土で植林されている。サクラにはソメイヨシノ（染井吉野）、八重桜、枝垂（しだれ）桜、早咲きの河津桜で知られる寒桜など、代表的な4つの種類があるが、もっとも親しまれているのはソメイヨシノである。毎春、サクラの開花は沖縄から始まり、日本列島を北上する。花は1週間で散ってしまうが、「桜前線」を追って旅行すれば、約3カ月間サクラの花を楽しむことができる。

春は、さまざまな食べられる野草や山菜が摘める季節である。秋は、山林にキノコ狩りに出かけるシーズンになる。キノコのなかでは、マツタケはその香りから高価で珍重されている。

h）動物

日本は植物相が複雑なので、動物相も寒帯性動物から熱帯性動物まで、多様である。

北海道には、ヒグマなどシベリアの動物と同種のものがいる。本州には中国大陸・朝鮮半島と共通した動物がたくさんいる。典型的なものはキツネ・タヌキである。また、本州にはシカ・キジなどの固有種がいる。このほかに、高山地帯の鳥で四季に応じて羽根の色を変えるライチョウがいる。かつて本州に生息していたニホンオオカミは絶滅している。

日本には北海道を除くどの地方にも、固有種のニホンザルが生息している。サルは本来熱帯性の動物であるが、ニホンザルは青森県下北半島（北緯42度）にも生息しており、サルの生息分布の北限になっている。ヨーロッパや北アメリカにはサルはいない。雪の中ではねまわったり、温泉に入るサルが見られるのは日本だけである。

沖縄や南西諸島には、特別天然記念物に指定され大切に保護されているイリオモテヤマネコ・アマミノクロウサギ・カンムリワシなどの貴重種のほか毒蛇のハブなどの熱帯性動物も多い。

The Japanese are particularly fond of the cherry tree and have planted it throughout the country. There are four representative varieties of *sakura* (Japanese flowering cherry tree) include Somei Yoshino, Yaezakura, Shidarezakura, and Kanzakura such as the early-flowering Kawazuzakura, but by far the most familiar variety is the Somei Yoshino. Each spring, the cherry blossom season begins in Okinawa and moves gradually northward through the other islands. Although at each place the petals fall after about a week, a person traveling north with the "cherry blossom front" would be able to enjoy the blossoms for nearly three months.

Spring is the time for picking a variety of edible wild herbs and plants, and autumn the time for a trip into the woods to gather mushrooms. While many kinds of mushrooms are picked, the high-priced *matsutake* mushroom (Armillaria matsutake) is particularly prized, for its splendid aroma.

h) Japanese Wildlife

Japan's highly diverse flora has led to the development of a multifarious fauna including arctic animals, tropical animals, and everything in between.

The island of Hokkaido has many of the same animals found in Siberia: the brown bear and others. The island of Honshu has many animal species in common with mainland China and the Korean Peninsula. Typical of these are the fox and raccoon dog. Honshu also has a number of animals and birds not found elsewhere, such as the Japanese deer and Japanese pheasant. Another is the snow grouse, a high mountain bird whose feathers change color with the seasons. The Japanese wolf, a former denizen of Honshu, is extinct.

A single species of monkey (the *Nihon-zaru* or Japanese macaque) inhabits all parts of Japan other than Hokkaido. Although monkeys are basically tropical animals, the Nihon-zaru is an exception. It lives as far north as the Shimokita Peninsula in Aomori Prefecture (about 42 degrees north latitude), the most northern region monkeys are known to inhabit. Monkeys do not live in the wild in Europe or North America. Only in Japan can one see monkeys frolicking in deep snow and in hot springs.

Many of the animals in Okinawa and the other Nansei Islands are valuable, protected tropical species that are designated as special natural monuments, such as the Iriomote wildcat, the Amami rabbit and the Crested serpent eagle, and there are also poisonous snakes such as the *habu*.

2 歴史

a) 日本人の祖先・日本国の起源

　日本列島には旧石器時代から人間が住み始め、これまで最古のもので3万年以上前の石器や人骨が出土している。この人々が日本人の祖先であるとする見方が有力である。その後も中国大陸や朝鮮半島、東南アジアなどからさまざまな人達が渡来して文化を伝え、しだいに混血し現在の日本人が形成されていったと考えられている。日本民族はモンゴロイド（ニグロイド、コーカソイドと並ぶ三大人種の一つ）に属しており、日本人の乳児の多くは、モンゴロイドに顕著な小児斑という青い斑紋が臀部に現れる。

　紀元前1万年から紀元前4～3世紀ごろまでの縄文時代の人々は、おもに狩猟・漁労・採集などによって生活し、独特の文様をもつ世界最古の土器といわれる縄文土器を作っていた。3世紀ごろまでの弥生時代には、稲作が広く行われ、金属器も使われるようになり、その後の日本人の生活の原型が形作られた。よく知られている三内丸山遺跡（青森県）は縄文時代の、また吉野ヶ里遺跡（佐賀県）は弥生時代の集落跡である。

　弥生時代末期の3世紀前半、中国の歴史書によると、日本では邪馬台国の女王・卑弥呼が統治する倭国という連合王国が栄えた。当時の日本は多くの小国家に分かれ抗争も多かったが、卑弥呼の出現により国内は安定したと伝えられる。なお、邪馬台国の所在地については、北九州説と近畿説とがあり、まだ結論が出ていない。
　4世紀には、近畿地方に比較的大きな勢力をもつ豪族が出現したが、最後にこれを統一したのが後の天皇家につながると言われるヤマト王権（大和朝廷ともいう）である。ヤマト王権は、5世紀ごろまでに、九州から東北地方南部までを支配した。
　このように長い期間をかけて徐々に国が統一されていったので、何年何月をもって日本の国が生まれたと決めるこ

2 History

a) Origin of the Japanese People and the Japanese Nation

Humans began living on the islands of Japan from the Old Stone Age (Paleolithic Period). The oldest stone implements and human bones discovered date back more than thirty-thousand years. The prevailing view is that these early inhabitants are the primary ancestors of the Japanese people. Later, when people of various origins began migrating to Japan from China, Korea and Southeast Asia, they and their cultures were gradually absorbed by the earlier settlers. Today's Japanese are thought to be the result of this blending. The Japanese people belong to the Mongoloid race (one of the world's three major racial classifications along with the Negroid and Caucasoid races), and most Japanese newborns have a distinctive blue mark known as the Mongolian spot at the base of the spine.

During the Jomon period that extended from ten thousand years ago up to the fourth to third century B.C., people depended mainly on hunting, fishing and gathering for their livelihood. The Jomon people are credited with creating pottery vessels generally accepted to be the oldest pottery in the world, which they decorated with characteristic rope-impressed (*jomon*) patterns. In the ensuing Yayoi period, which lasted to around the third century A.D., the Japanese mastered the art of rice cultivation, began to use metal implements, and set the fundamental patterns of Japanese life. Well-known remains of these periods include the Jomon ruins at Sannaimaruyama in Aomori Prefecture and the Yayoi ruins at Yoshinogari in Saga Prefecture.

According to Chinese historical records, a united kingdom called Yamatai said to be ruled by Queen Himiko flourished in Japan in the first half of the third century near the end of the Yayoi period. The records report that Japan was divided into numerous small warring countries until Himiko brought stability. Yamatai's location is uncertain, with opinion divided between northern Kyushu and Kinki.

In the fourth century, relatively powerful clans emerged in the Kinki region. These were consolidated into what finally became known as the Yamato court, which later evolved into the Imperial Family. Until around the fifth century, the Yamato court ruled an area extending from Kyushu to the southern part of the Tohoku District.

Thus the foundation of Japan was a gradual process that continued over many years and it is therefore impossible to set any date as that on

とはできない。8世紀に編さんされた史書『古事記』（712年）および『日本書紀』（720年）には、紀元前660年に初代の神武天皇が建国し即位したと書かれている。その即位の日が現在の暦では2月11日にあたるため、この日を「建国記念の日」として国民の祝日としている。

b）古代（4〜12世紀）

　4〜5世紀にかけてヤマト王権により統一された日本は、大陸から文字・国家制度・仏教・儒教・工芸技術などの文物を導入して国の基礎をかためた。このころ大王（天皇）は、有力な豪族の協力によって政治を行っていた。国民は主として稲作中心の農業に従事していた。

　3世紀後半から7世紀前半は古墳時代と呼ばれ、天皇家や豪族の大規模な墳墓が多数築造された。はじめは近畿地方など西日本が中心であったが、関東地方や東北地方にも広がっていった。これまで全国で16万基以上の古墳跡が確認されている。

　7世紀に中国（隋・唐）の制度にならい、日本も法治国家体制（律令制度に基づく政治体制）をつくった。土地や人民は、豪族の支配から離れて国のものとなり、一般農民は1人2,300 m^2（0.57エーカー：米の収穫量を基準）の土地を国から与えられて一定の税金（租庸調）を納め、国防にも従事することになった。

　それまでの日本の政治は、有力豪族（蘇我氏等）の協力を必須とする政治であったが、これを天皇中心の政治へ移行する一連の国政改革が推進されていた。聖徳太子は推古天皇のもと、遣隋使（618年に隋が滅び唐が建ったのでそれ以降は遣唐使）を派遣し中国の文化・制度を学び、十七条の憲法や人材登用のための冠位十二階（604年）を定めるなど中央集権国家体制の基盤づくりをめざしていた。その基盤の上に、646年から中大兄皇子（のちの天智天皇）らが進めた政治改革（大化の改新）の中で律令制度が積極的に取り入れられていった。

which the nation came into existence. In the *Kojiki* (Records of Ancient Matters: 712) and the *Nihonshoki* (Chronicles of Japan: 720), two ancient chronicles compiled in the eighth century, it is recorded that the Emperor Jinmu began his reign in the year 660 B.C. and the date given for his ascension, February 11, is now set aside as a Japanese holiday called National Foundation Day.

b) Ancient Times (4th century to 12th century)

After consolidation of Japan into a single nation by the Yamato court in the fourth and fifth centuries, the foundations of the country were strengthened by introducing various aspects of continental learning and culture. These included the Chinese writing system, various social systems, religion (Buddhism), ideology (Confucianism), and arts and crafts. The emperors of this period ruled in cooperation with a number of powerful families. The common people were for the most part engaged in agriculture centered on the production of rice.

From late in the third century to early in the seventh century, the Imperial and other powerful families took to building many huge tumuli (ancient burial mounds). At the beginning of this period, called the Kofun (Tumulus) Period, the custom was limited to the Kinki and other western regions of the country but it later spread to the Kanto and Tohoku districts. More than 160 thousand burial mound remains have been discovered so far.

In the seventh century, a constitutional form of government modeled after that of China (Sui and T'ang) was introduced (a political structure based on legal and administrative codes). The land and the people were no longer under the control of powerful families but were put under the direct rule of the state. Each farmer was granted 2,300 m^2 (0.57 acres, the standard measure of rice crop yield) of land and was required to pay a prescribed (in kind; So-Yo-Cho) tax and contribute a certain amount of his time to defending the nation.

Until that time, Japanese politics required the cooperation of powerful families (such as the Soga clan), but a series of national reforms were being promoted to shift this to emperor-centric politics. Under the Empress Suiko, Prince Shotoku dispatched envoys to China to study Chinese culture and systems, firstly under the Sui Dynasty, and subsequently, after the fall of the Sui Dynasty in 618, under the Tang Dynasty, to establish the foundation of a centralized national state, such as by formulating in 604 the Seventeen Article Constitution and the merit-based Twelve Level Cap and Rank System of selection and promotion. Building on that foundation, the code of law known as

（注）冠位十二階：官僚制度の中に取り込む人材の位階制度。個人に与えられる位（12の異なる色の冠を授ける）で世襲の対象にならない。蘇我氏等の貴族層の秩序（氏姓制度）ではない。しかし中国の「科挙」のような厳格な試験による人材採用制度ではなく、次第に世襲化していった。このため律令国家としては中国のような堅固な官僚機構は育たなかった。

　なお、律令の一つに墳墓に関する法律（薄葬令）があった。身分に応じて墳墓の規模などを制限し、天皇陵の造営に費やす時間を7日以内に制限するなど人民の負担を軽減することが進められている。これにより結果的に古墳時代は終わりを告げることとなる。

　この律令制度は8世紀から崩れ始めた。貴族が徐々に土地を私有化して荘園にしていったからである。貴族は土地と人民を支配して富をたくわえ、藤原氏等の一部名門貴族が天皇に代わって事実上政治を支配する権限（摂政・関白制度）を掌握することになる。これにより平安朝文化に代表される独自の貴族文化を形成する礎を確立することとなる。

　奈良に都（平城京）が置かれたとき（710年）から、都が京都（平安京）に移されるまで（794年）の時期を奈良時代と呼び、平安京に移されて、貴族から武士の政権（鎌倉幕府）ができるまで（1185年）を平安時代と呼ぶのが一般的である。

c) 中世・近世（12〜19世紀前半）

　貴族に使われていた武士は、各地方で農民を直接支配することにより力をつけ、12世紀の終わりに貴族から政権を奪取し（武士の棟梁であった源頼朝による鎌倉幕府の創立）、以後19世紀後半（1868年、明治政府成立）まで約700年間武士が政権を持ち続けた。

the *ritsuryo* system was implemented from 646 in the Taika Reforms, promoted by Prince Naka-no-Oe (later to become Emperor Tenji) and others.

Note: The Twelve Level Cap and Rank System was incorporated in the bureaucratic system. Twelve differently colored caps were used to confer rank on individuals. The ranks were not hereditary, in contrast to the system of clans and hereditary court titles. However, since the conferring of ranks did not involve the kind of rigorous examination system that was used in China for recruiting civil service personnel, the Japanese system gradually became increasingly hereditary, and as a result, did not produce the kind of robust bureaucracy of a ritsuryo state such as China's.

The ritsuryo code included a law related to burials. This prescribed that the size of a grave or tomb was to be in accordance with the status of the deceased, and to lighten the burden on the people stipulated that no more than seven days was to be spent on the construction of an imperial tomb, bringing the kofun (tumulus) period to an end.

This ritsuryo system started to crumble in the eighth century as the nobility began taking private possession of the land and establishing manors. With both the land and the people under their control, the aristocrats of the period were able to amass great fortunes and establish the foundation of their own independent culture, as typified by the culture of the Heian period. Members of the powerful Fujiwara clan, for example, effectively took over the reins of government by acting as regents to the emperor.

From 710 when the capital was located in Nara (Heijo-kyo) until 794 when the capital was transferred to Kyoto (Heian-kyo) is referred to as the Nara period, and from the transfer to Heian-kyo until the shift in political power from the nobility to the warrior class took place, and the Kamakura shogunate was established in 1185, is referred to as the Heian period.

c) Middle Ages and Early Modern Ages (12th century to early 19th century)

Warriors employed by the nobility to keep the peasants under control took advantage of their position of direct control over the farmers to greatly expand their power, until late in the twelfth century they were able to seize power from the nobility and Minamoto no Yoritomo established the Kamakura shogunate. The rule of the warrior class lasted nearly seven hundred years, finally coming to an end in the latter half of the nineteenth century with the formation of the Meiji government in

武士の棟梁は天皇から征夷大将軍に任命されて幕府（将軍の中央政府）を設け、各地域の封建領主（大名という）を支配した。これらの封建領主は、土地と人民を支配することについて将軍から承認をうけ、将軍に対して忠誠を誓った。

　1274年と1281年の2度にわたる元軍の日本遠征（蒙古襲来）に対し、鎌倉幕府は大名を指揮してよく防御したが、外敵との戦いであったため功績のあった大名たちに恩賞によって十分に報いることができず、徐々に大名たちの信用を得られなくなってきた。
　1333年、後醍醐天皇は、大名の足利尊氏らの支援を受けて、幕府を討伐し、鎌倉幕府は滅亡した。後醍醐天皇は政治を貴族、武士階級に任せることなく、天皇自身の親政による革新的で急進的な新政権を打ち立てた（建武の新政）。しかしこの政治は貴族、武士双方から受け入れられず、わずか3年後、足利尊氏の離反により新政権は崩壊した。後醍醐天皇は京都から吉野に逃れて朝廷（南朝）を開いたため、朝廷が京都の北朝と吉野の南朝に並立することになった。1336年、足利尊氏は北朝の天皇から征夷大将軍の位をもらい受け、室町幕府を開いた。しかし、南朝は独自に天皇親政の政治を行い、世の中は安定しなかった。その後、室町幕府の画策により1392年に北朝と南朝は合一する。この間の56年を南北朝時代という。

　南北朝が一本化すると、室町幕府は権力基盤が安定するが、将軍の世代交代が進むにつれ、一方で幕府を支える管領（かんれい：将軍を補佐する有力大名）と呼ばれる一部の大名の力が強まるとともに、他方で守護、地頭と呼ばれる地方の大名の力も増大し、いざこざが絶えなかったがとりわけ1467年から1477年にかけて内乱状態が継続した（応仁の乱）。このため幕府は徐々に衰退し、15世紀末から16世紀末にかけては大名間の戦乱が頻発した。全国各地に戦国大名とよばれる勢力が出現し相互に離合集散しながら戦闘を繰り返した。この戦乱の期間を戦国時代と呼ぶ。戦国時代の末期、戦国大名の織田信長・豊臣秀吉が事実上政権を掌握していた時代（1568年の信長の入京から

1868.

Formally, the leading warrior would be appointed by the emperor as his "*shogun* in charge of conquering barbarian territories" and with this designation would set up the central government under the shogun (shogunate or *bakufu*) and take leadership over the feudal lords (*daimyo*) in the various parts of the country. In return for the shogun's recognition of their right to rule over their territory and people, the lords would pledge their loyalty to the shogun.

Under the direction of the Kamakura shogunate, the former army put up a good defence against the Mongol attacks of 1274 and 1281. However, as those were battles against a foreign enemy, the shogunate was unable to reward the feudal lords sufficiently for their achievements, and therefore gradually lost their trust.

In 1333 Emperor Godaigo, with the support of Ashikaga Takauji and other lords, defeated the shogun, bringing down the Kamakura shogunate. Emperor Godaigo set up an innovative and radical new administration (the Kenmu restoration) which was based on his own direct rule without the delegation of politics to the nobility or warrior class. However, this was rejected by both nobility and warriors, and without the support of Ashikaga Takauji, the administration collapsed after just three years. Godaigo escaped to Yoshino, where he established what became known as the South court, in contrast to the North court which continued to function in Kyoto. In 1336, Ashikaga Takauji was appointed "shogun in charge of conquering barbarian territories" by the emperor of the North court and proceeded to set up the Muromachi shogunate. However, with Emperor Godaigo implementing his own direct rule in the South court, it was an unstable time. In 1392, the Muromachi shogunate orchestrated the unification of the two courts. The 56 years it took to achieve this is called the South and North Courts period.

The unification stabilized the power base of the Muromachi shogunate, but each change of shogun saw a growth in the power of the feudal lords acting as the shogun's deputies, a fundamental part of the shogunate, while at the same time the lords acting as governors and estate stewards also grew more powerful, and the constant quarrelling by the sides eventually led to the Onin War, a civil strife that lasted from 1467 to 1477. This weakened the shogunate and led to a period from late in the 15th century to the end of the 16th century that was marked by almost constant fighting and realignments among feudal warlords that emerged across the nation. This time became known as the Age of Warring States. From the end of this period until the seizing of power by the warlords Oda Nobunaga and Toyotomi Hideyoshi (from Nobunaga's

1600年の関ヶ原の戦いまで）を安土桃山時代と呼ぶ。

この間1543年、ポルトガル人を乗せた船が九州の南端からほど近い種子島に漂着し、鉄砲（火縄銃）の技術が日本に伝わったのが、日本とヨーロッパの初めての出会いであった。以後イエズス会宣教師が鹿児島に上陸しキリスト教が伝来した。また西国大名とポルトガルやスペインとの間で貿易（南蛮貿易）も盛んに行われた。

1603年、戦国時代を制した（関ヶ原の戦いで勝利した）大名の徳川家康は江戸（今の東京）に徳川幕府（江戸幕府ともいう）を開き、以後260年余り日本を統治した。徳川幕府は、国の統治機構としての幕藩体制を確立して全国の大名を支配し、国内戦争を防止する体制を確立した。また、社会階級を固定化し、その相互移動を禁じる「士農工商」の身分制度を敷き、これにより国の経済基盤（米の生産）を支える農民を完全に支配した。さらに、幕府は1639年には外国との外交関係を断ち、外国との往来を禁止する「鎖国」政策をとった。政治的幕藩体制と「土地・米本位制」の経済体制のもとで、幕府は圧倒的な財力を基盤に、政治的・軍事的に諸大名を支配し、国内は長い平和が続いた。その間に工業や商業が発達し、文化の発展、教育の普及もめざましく、次の近代国家発展期の基礎をつくった。

また各地に設けられた「寺子屋」では、「読み・書き・そろばん」が教えられ、識字率をはじめとする民衆の教育レベルの向上に役立った。

しかし、19世紀後半になって幕府の支配体制に経済的・政治的な陰りが見え始めた。その原因の第一は貨幣経済の発達である。持続する平和な期間に工業や商業が発達し、米を通貨とする経済が貨幣経済に転換した。そのため、米のみを支配する幕府および武士階級は商品・貨幣を握る商人階級の経済力に依存するようになった。その結果、幕府の支配統制力は弱まった。第二は強力な幕府対抗勢力の台頭である。もともと外様大名として不満を持っていた西日本地方の薩摩、長州など有力な諸藩（西南雄藩）は、幕府

entry into Kyoto in 1568 to the battle of Sekigahara in 1600) is referred to as the Azuchi-Momoyama period.

It was during this period that Japan first made contact with Europe thanks to the landing of a storm-blown Portuguese ship on the island of Tanegashima, near the southern tip of Kyushu, in 1543, an event that gave the Japanese a chance to learn about firearms (matchlock guns). Not long after, Jesuit missionaries began arriving in Kagoshima to spread the Christian faith. And trade between merchants under the feudal lords in the region and Portugal, Spain, soon began to flourish.

In 1603, the Tokugawa shogunate was established in Edo (now Tokyo) by the warlord Tokugawa Ieyasu (the victor at the battle of Sekigahara), and remained in power for more than 260 years. The Tokugawa shogunate succeeded in putting a stop to regional conflicts by establishing the shogunate and *han* (regional domain) system in which the country was divided into many domains each of which a shogun-appointed lord governed. It also implemented a caste system that ranked warriors at the top, followed by farmers, artisans and tradesmen, and strictly prohibited migration between classes. This gave it total control over the farmers at the core of the country's rice-dominated economy. In 1639, the shogunate broke off all relations with foreign countries, prohibited foreign travel and entered an era of isolation. The shogunate-dominant political system, along with a land-rice dominated economic system, gave the Tokugawa shogunate overwhelming financial power that it used to keep the feudal lords under tight political and military control and maintain a long peaceful period throughout the country. With peace came industrial and commercial development, cultural development and a dramatic spread of education, thus laying the foundation for the ensuing period of development into a modern nation.

The numerous village classrooms (*terakoya*) that sprouted up throughout the country to teach reading, writing, and how to use an abacus (arithmetic) played a particularly important role in increasing literacy and the general level of education of the common people.

Toward the middle of the 19th century, the economic and political strength of the Tokugawa shogunate began to show signs of decline. The first cause was the emergence of a monetary economy. As industry and commerce developed in the sustained peaceful environment, the economy using rice as currency gave way to a monetary economy. This made the shogunate and warrior class, who had control of only rice, dependent on the economic power of the merchant class, whose wealth was in merchandise and money. The power of the shogunate to control and govern diminished as a result. Another reason for the

の鎖国政策に反して独自の貿易や産業により財力を蓄え、農民をも取り込んだ新鋭兵器を装備した強力な近代的軍事力を組織して、幕府に対抗した。第三は、200年以上続いた幕府の鎖国政策の破たんである。ヨーロッパ諸勢力は18世紀前半からしきりに幕府に対して開国を迫るような状況になっていた。

d）近代（19世紀後半～1945年）

［立憲君主国家の確立とその終焉］

　1853年、圧倒的な武力を誇示するアメリカの提督ペリーが率いる艦隊の来日を契機とし、幕府はやむなく鎖国を解き、通商貿易を容認する条約を締結した。これが極めて不平等な条約であったため、反幕府勢力は、幕府の開国・不平等条約締結の弱腰を責めたて、かねて復権をうかがっていた天皇・宮廷勢力と結託し、いよいよ幕府を攻めた。そこで、幕府は一大名としての徳川家存続を目指して、1867年に大政奉還（政権を幕府から天皇へ返還）を行った。翌1868年に西南雄藩が主導して、明治天皇を頂点にいただく新政府（明治政府）が成立した。これを明治維新という。

　この間の幕府と反幕府間のせめぎあいは明らかな内戦であったが、この際の両勢力の賢明な指導者の措置により、地方においてはいくつかの戦闘が起きたものの、首都である江戸における大規模な武力衝突は避けられた。

　1869年には、明治政府は確固たる中央集権国家の早期実現を目指し、それまで封建領主たる各藩が治めていた領土や領民を天皇に返還させ、各藩の藩主は「知藩事」に任命された（これを版籍奉還という）。しかし、これでは従来の藩主が知藩事と名前が変わっただけであまり大きな効果はなく、1871年、全国の藩を廃止して、中央政府が管理する県と府に置き換える「廃藩置県」が実行された。こ

shogunate's loss of power was the emergence of strong anti-shogunate forces. The feudal lords of Satsuma, Choshu and other leading feudal domains in western Japan, who came under the Tokugawa shogunate's rule after it had consolidated power and were known as *tozama daimyo* (outsider lords), had long been discontent. These domains built financial strength by engaging in trade and industrial activities in violation of the shogunate's isolation policy and confronted the shogunate by organizing strong, up-to-date military forces that were equipped with advanced weapons and were also supported by the farmers. Still another reason was the collapse of the shogunate's isolation of trade that had been in effect for more than 200 years. European powers had been pressing the shogunate to open up Japan from the first half of the 18th century.

d) Modern Times (Mid-19th century to 1945)
Establishment of Constitutional Monarchy and Its Demise

By an intimidating show of force, the squadron led by Commodore Perry arriving from the United States (U.S.) in 1853 forced the Tokugawa Shogunate to agree to abandon isolation and conclude a treaty that accepted overseas trade and commerce. As the treaty was seen as extremely unfair, the anti-shogunate forces exploited the discontent with the shogunate's weak-kneed stance on the opening of the country and the one-sided treaty to join hands in conspiracy with the emperor and the imperial court, which had been waiting for a chance to resume power, and attacked the shogunate. At this juncture, the shogunate, seeking to preserve the daimyo status of the House of Tokugawa, moved to restore political authority to the Emperor in 1867. In the following year, the powerful domains of the southwest took the lead in forming a new government (Meiji government) under Emperor Meiji. This is known as the "Meiji Restoration of 1868."

Although what took place was clearly a civil war and there were a number of local conflicts, there was no major military conflict in the city of Edo where the feudal government was located (today's Tokyo). This good fortune can be attributed to the wisdom of the leaders on both sides.

With the aim of achieving the early realization of a strong, centralized state, in 1869 the Meiji government ordained that the domains and people who had been governed until then by each feudal lord be returned to the emperor. However, this did not have much effect as it was just a matter of changing the name of the former *han* lord, so in 1871 the han were abolished and replaced by prefectures administered by the central government. This established a consistent tax collection

れによって中央政府による一貫した徴税権が確立し、財政も安定化し、近代国家としての軍備や教育の普及に弾みがついた。

　幕府倒壊後から20年の間に、日本は欧州諸国に範をとる諸施策を実行して、近代国家に発展していった。士農工商の身分制度の廃止とともに武士階級の経済的・社会的特権もなくなった。統治制度の面では、内閣制度の設置、憲法の制定（議会の開設、司法権の独立、国民の権利義務等を定め、ドイツ国憲法にならい天皇を頂点とするいわゆる立憲君主制度である大日本帝国憲法の制定）、ドイツ式陸軍とイギリス式海軍の設立、地方制度の改革などが行われた。経済の面では、土地制度の改革と官営事業による殖産興業、貨幣制度の統一が行われた。社会文化の面では、近代的学校制度が確立された。このようにして、日本社会は欧米の文化・制度を積極的に取り込んでいった。

　これらの近代化により国力は充実したが、他方で日本はアジア各地で権益拡大を図るアメリカ・イギリス・フランス・オランダ・ロシアなど列強諸国との間で利害が衝突することとなった。

　日本と清国との間で、朝鮮の支配権を争って、1894年から1895年にかけて戦争が起きる（日清戦争）。当時大国であった清国に近代化途上の日本が予想に反して勝利したため、列強諸国はおおいに日本をけん制することとなった。

　日清戦争に勝利した日本は、下関条約により清国から遼東半島（旅順や大連がある重要戦略地域）を割譲される。しかし、これはロシアの南下政策に反するものであり、ロシアはドイツ、フランスを誘ってこれに干渉してきたため、日本はこれを返還した（三国干渉）。このような状況の中で1904年に日露戦争が勃発した。この戦争は日本の国運を賭けた戦争であった。そのため、日本は、1902年にイギリスとの間で日英同盟を結び、もしロシア以外の国が日本に宣戦布告したときは、イギリスは日本のために参戦するという約束を取り付け、さらにアメリカに対して

right by the central government, which stabilized public finances and gave momentum to military preparedness and the spread of education of a modern state.

The twenty-year period immediately following this transition saw the new Meiji Government implement a wide range of measures modeled on European examples and designed to set Japan on its way to becoming a modern nation. The warrior-farmer-artisan-tradesman caste system was abolished and the warrior class was deprived of its social and economic privileges. Administrative innovations included the introduction of the cabinet system; the promulgation of a constitution which provided for independent legislative and judiciary branches of government and set forth the rights and obligations of the citizens; the establishment of the Constitution of the Empire of Japan modeled on the German constitution as a constitutional monarchy with the emperor at its head; the establishment of an army modeled after that of Germany and a navy modeled after that of Britain; and various reforms in the systems of local government. On the economic side, the system of land ownership was revised, modern industries were promoted under direct government management, and a uniform monetary system was instituted. Social and cultural reforms included the establishment of a modern system of education. Thus, vigorous measures were taken to assimilate Western culture into the Japanese social structure.

Although these efforts at modernization greatly enhanced Japan's power internationally, this in turn led to conflicts with the major powers that were attempting to expand their interests in Asia, most notably the U.S., Great Britain, France, Holland, and Russia.

The Sino-Japanese War of 1894–1895 between Japan and Qing Dynasty China was fought for dominance in Korea. China was a major power at the time, and when it was unexpectedly defeated by Japan, which was still modernizing, it resulted in Japan having constraints placed on it by the great powers.

Following Japan's victory, the Shimonoseki Peace Treaty was signed, under which China ceded Liaodong Peninsula (an important strategic area with Port Arthur and Dalian). However, this ran up against Russia's southern policy aimed at securing a warm-water port, so Russia persuaded Germany and France to intervene (Tripartite Intervention), forcing Japan to recede the territory. These were the circumstances that led to the outbreak of the Russo-Japanese War in 1904. It was a war on which Japan staked the fate of the nation. Thus, in 1902 Japan and Great Britain signed the Anglo-Japanese Alliance, under which Britain would come to the aid of Japan if any country other than Russia declared war

は、当時のセオドア・ルーズベルトに対し、アメリカの世論が日本の不利にならないように画策してくれる約束を取り付けていた。結果として日本は強国ロシアを陸海において破り、1905年にアメリカの仲介でポーツマス条約により戦争は終結した。その後1910年8月、日本は朝鮮の同意を得て同国を併合した。

国内では、19世紀の終りごろから産業革命が進み、資本主義が発達し、第一次世界大戦においては、連合国側について勝利し、敗戦国ドイツのアジアにおける権益を一部受け継ぐ等国力はますます増し、政治面においても政党政治が一般化するようになり、近代化はますます進んだ。

しかし、1929年の世界大恐慌の影響で経済が行きづまるなか、軍部が台頭して、しだいに日本の政治や外交を支配するようになる。1931年の満州事変（中国の遼東半島に駐留していた日本軍の出先機関が主導となり、満州（現在の瀋陽あたり）の権益を狙って事実上の日本の傀儡（かいらい）国家である満州国を建国した）、1932年の五・一五事件（5月15日に、武装した海軍の青年将校たちが総理大臣官邸に乱入し、内閣総理大臣犬養毅を殺害した）、1933年の国際連盟脱退、1936年の二・二六事件（2月26日から29日にかけて、陸軍青年将校が1,483名の下士官兵を率いて起こしたクーデター事件）を経て、1937年には北京市南西部にある盧溝橋で日本軍と中国国民革命軍との衝突事件を端緒として日中戦争（日華事変ともいう）が勃発し、事実上戦争状態に突入した。アジアにおける、日本と列強諸国との間の権益の争いは一層激化し、列強諸国は日本の海外資産凍結、石油等の重要資源の対日輸出禁止などの対抗措置をとるようになった。

1941年12月8日、ついに日本はアメリカ・イギリス・オランダに対し宣戦を布告した。日中戦争から1941年の宣戦布告までの戦争状態を大東亜戦争と呼ぶ。1939年ドイツがヨーロッパで口火を切った戦争は、1940年に三国同盟を結んだ日本・ドイツ・イタリアとアメリカ・イギリスなどの連合国との間の第二次世界大戦へと拡大していっ

on Japan. With respect to America, Theodore Roosevelt provided a commitment to a plan that worked to ensure American public opinion would not be to Japan's detriment. Following Japan's defeat of the mighty Russian forces on both land and sea, the war was brought to a close in 1905 with the Treaty of Portsmouth mediated by the U.S. In August 1910, Japan annexed Korea with Korea's agreement.

Domestic developments continued to maintain a rapid pace. By the end of the nineteenth century, Japan's industrial revolution was well under way and the groundwork of capitalism had been laid. In World War I and the following years, there were victories on the side of the Allies and Japan was strengthened by the seizure of some German possessions in Asia, political parties became an accepted part of the governmental system and the process of modernization continued apace.

However, the military then took advantage of the stalling of the Japanese economy under the pressure of the Great Depression of 1929 to rise to political prominence and gain increasing control over both domestic and international policy. The military's increased influence was soon seen in the Manchurian Incident (Mukuden Incident) of 1931 (led by a garrison stationed on the Liaodong Peninsula in China, the Japanese military established what was a de facto puppet state of Japan, Manchukuo, around what is now Shenyang, with the aim of securing rights and interests on Manchuria), the May 15 Incident of 1932 (armed naval officers forced their way into Prime Minister Inukai Tsuyoshi's official residence and assassinated him), Japan's withdrawal from the League of Nations in 1933, and the February 26 Incident of 1936 (a coup d'état attempt on February 26–29 by 1,483 noncommissioned soldiers led by young army officers). In 1937 there was a clash between the Japanese army and the Chinese National Revolutionary Army at the Marco Polo Bridge in the southwestern part of Beijing, an incident that ended up touching off the outbreak of war between Japan and China. As the race between Japan and the major powers to establish stronger influence in Asia intensified, the major powers imposed various countermeasures against Japan, including the freezing of its overseas assets and prohibition of petroleum and other vital raw material exports to Japan.

On December 8, 1941, Japan declared war on the U.S., Great Britain, and the Netherlands. The state of war from the Sino-Japanese War to the Declaration of War in 1941 is called the Greater East Asia War. The war touched off by Germany in Europe in 1939 had thus grown into a worldwide conflict between the Rome-Berlin-Tokyo Axis of the Tripartite Pact signed in 1940 and the U.S., Great Britain and other

た。
　当初、三国同盟側が優勢であったが、やがて形勢は逆転した。日本は、はじめの半年間に東南アジアと西南太平洋の広大な地域を占領下に収めたが、その後、連合国軍は反撃に転じた。1945年3月末アメリカ軍は沖縄に上陸し、同年8月6日に広島、9日長崎に世界史上初の原子爆弾を投下し、さらにソ連が日ソ中立条約を犯して対日参戦した。こうした打撃によって、日本はポツダム宣言を受け入れて1945年8月15日降伏し、戦争は終わった。すでにイタリアとドイツは降伏していたので、これによって第二次世界大戦は終結した。

e）現代（その1）（1945〜1980年代前半）
［占領政策下の日本］

　アメリカ軍を主力とする連合国軍の占領と間接統治のもとで、日本は民主主義的平和国家への道を歩むこととなった。民主化への基盤として、新憲法の制定（日本国憲法：アメリカの主導のもとに起草、1947年発行）、婦人参政権を認めた選挙法の施行、労働者の権利を守る労働関係法の制定、財閥の解体、過度経済集中の排除、農地解放などの施策が断行された。

　1951年、サンフランシスコ平和条約の調印により、日本は独立を回復した。しかし、米・ソの対立（冷戦）のために、この時点で条約に調印したのはアメリカおよび西側自由主義諸国だけであった。同じ日、日本とアメリカは日米安全保障条約を締結し、アメリカは日本を防衛し、日本はアメリカに基地を提供することに合意した。その後1960年の条約更新時に、自由民主党の岸信介首相の政権はアメリカの日本防衛義務を明記させ、不平等問題を決着した。こうして日本は西側陣営の一員となった。戦後の民主化施策の断行と独立の回復は、ほぼ吉田茂首相の政権下で行われた。

　日本は、その後も東側社会主義諸国との友好関係を回復する努力を続けた。1956年には日ソ共同宣言がまとまり（鳩山一郎首相政権）、同年日本の国際連合加盟が承認され

Allies.

Although the Axis Powers had the upper hand in the beginning, the situation later reversed. The control that Japan had gained over a vast region in the southwestern Pacific during the first six months of action was thereafter pushed back by an Allied counteroffensive. The landing of American troops on Okinawa at the end of March, 1945 was followed by the dropping of atomic bombs on Hiroshima (August 6) and Nagasaki (August 9), the first use of nuclear weapons ever, and the Soviet Union's entry into the war against Japan, in contravention of the neutrality pact between Japan and the Soviet Union. These blows led Japan to accept the Potsdam Declaration and surrender on August 15, 1945, bringing the war to an end. As Italy and Germany had already surrendered, the Second World War came to an end.

e) Recent Times I (1945 to mid-1980s)
Japan under the Occupation Policy

Under the postwar occupation and indirect rule of the Allied Forces, primarily the U.S. military, Japan began to rebuild itself into a peaceful, democratic nation. The foundation for a democratic society was laid through the enactment of a new constitution (the Japanese constitution, drafted under American leadership and enacted in 1947), an election law recognizing women's suffrage, and a labor relations law for protecting workers' rights, along with decentralization of monopolistic enterprises (*zaibatsu*), implementation of agrarian reform, and other measures.

Japan's independence was restored with the signing of a peace treaty in San Francisco in 1951. However, owing to the antagonism (the Cold War) between the U.S. and the Soviet Union, the treaty was signed only by the U.S. and other free world countries. On the same day, Japan and the U.S. also concluded the Japan-U.S. Treaty of Mutual Cooperation and Security, under which the U.S. agreed to defend Japan and Japan to provide the U.S. with military bases. At the time the treaty was renewed in 1960, the administration of Prime Minister Kishi Nobusuke, who belong to the LDP (Liberal Democratic Party) clarified that the U.S. was committed to defend Japan, settling the issue of the claimed inequality of the treaty. Thus it was that Japan became a member of the Western Bloc. The implementation of democratization measures after the war and the recovery of independence were carried out almost entirely under the administration of Prime Minister Yoshida Shigeru.

Japan also made efforts to restore friendly relations with the socialist countries of the Eastern Bloc. A joint declaration agreed on with the Soviet Union in 1956 (by Prime Minister Hatoyama Ichiro's administra-

た。

　1969年に行われた、アメリカのニクソン大統領と佐藤栄作首相との首脳会談で沖縄返還が約束された。サンフランシスコ平和条約の下で沖縄はアメリカの施政権下に置かれていたが、ニクソンはベトナム戦争の近年中の終結を考慮し、日米安全保障条約の延長（1960年の改正からほぼ10年経過し、1970年の更新時期が迫っていた）を条件に返還を約束したものである。約束どおり、安全保障条約は延長され1972年5月15日に沖縄は本土に復帰した。

　1972年には、田中角栄首相が訪中し、中国側は周恩来首相との間で共同声明を発表して中華人民共和国との国交は回復し、さらに1978年には日中平和友好条約が正式に調印された。なお、この田中首相の訪中は、前年1971年7月15日の、世界を揺るがしたアメリカのキッシンジャー国務長官の突然の訪中（いわゆるニクソンショック）に触発されたものである。これにより日本は台湾を中国の一部と認める結果になった。

［石油危機と高度経済成長］
　1973年に、第4次中東戦争（エジプト・シリア軍がイスラエルに対しシナイ半島等の領土を奪還するために起こした）が勃発し、これが原因でいわゆる第1次石油危機が起きる。中東諸国の原油生産縮小により石油価格が高騰するとともにインフレーションが加速、消費財価格の便乗値上げ行為が多数発生し、さらにはトイレットペーパーがスーパーの店頭から消えてしまうというような騒動が起きた。これらの問題が契機となって、1977年に独占禁止法にカルテル行為（談合行為）に対する課徴金納付命令等の制裁規定が導入され、規制が強化された。
　さらに、1979年には前年に起きたイラン革命によりイランでの石油生産が中断し、原油の需給がひっ迫し、原油価格が高騰し、いわゆる第2次石油危機が起きた。
　この間に日本は高度経済成長をはたし、1975年にはアメリカ・イギリス・フランス・西ドイツ・イタリアとともに第1回主要先進国首脳会議（サミット）にも参加した（なお、1977年のロンドンサミットに参加した福田赳夫首相が、1929年の世界大恐慌の唯一の体験者として、保護

tion) led to approval of Japan's membership in the United Nations in the same year.

In the summit between President Nixon of America and Prime Minister Sato Eisaku held in 1969, the return of Okinawa was promised. In accordance with the Treaty of San Francisco, Okinawa came under the administrative authority of the U.S. However, Nixon had been thinking about the ending of the Vietnam War. It had been almost ten years since the Japan-U.S. Treaty of Mutual Cooperation and Security had been revised in 1960, and it would soon be up for renewal, in 1970. With consideration given to his view that the Vietnam War would soon be concluded, Nixon promised to return Okinawa provided the treaty was extended. The Security Treaty was extended and on 15 May 1972 Okinawa reverted to Japan.

During a visit Prime Minister Tanaka Kakuei made to China in 1972, the restoration of diplomatic relations between Japan and the People's Republic of China was announced in a joint statement with Prime Minister Zhou Enlai. The Treaty of Peace and Friendship between Japan and the People's Republic of China was signed in 1978. Tanaka had been inspired to make his trip by the sudden visit of U.S. Secretary of State Henry Kissinger to the People's Republic of China on July 15, 1971, which shook the world (the so-called Nixon shock). This resulted in Japan recognizing Taiwan as part of China.

Oil Crisis and High Economic Growth

In 1973, the Fourth Middle East War broke out when Egypt, Syria and other Arab countries launched an attack against Israel to recapture territory in the Sinai Peninsula. This led to the first oil crisis, as oil production by Middle Eastern countries decreased, causing oil prices to soar and increasing inflation. There were widespread price hikes on consumer goods and toilet paper disappeared from supermarket shelves. Taking these problems as an opportunity, in 1977 Antimonopoly Act regulations were strengthened by the introduction of sanction provisions such as surcharge payment orders for cartel action (bid rigging).

In 1979, when oil production in Iran was interrupted due to the Iranian revolution of the previous year, the price of crude oil soared, bringing about the second oil crisis.

Japan achieved rapid economic growth during this period. In 1975, it joined the U.S., Great Britain, France, West Germany, and Italy at the first summit conference of leading industrially advanced nations. (Prime Minister Fukuda Takeo, who took part in the 1977 London Summit, famously warned the participants of the rise of protectionism, saying he

貿易主義の台頭を参加者に戒めた逸話は有名である)。

1980年代には、日本経済はいっそう国際競争力を強め、1985年9月、先進五ヵ国(日・米・英・西独・仏)蔵相・中央銀行総裁会議での合意(プラザ合意:日本円の対外為替レートの急激な上昇を容認)による重圧にも耐え抜くことができた。巨額の貿易黒字、低い失業率、消費者物価の安定など日本の経済指標の上昇は、めざましいものがあった。ドル換算による1人あたりの国民所得も、世界のトップクラスに上昇した。

このような戦後の経済的発展は、日本人のライフスタイルにも大きな変化をもたらした。とりわけ、1964年以降の変化は顕著で、東海道新幹線が開通し、東京オリンピックがアジアではじめて開催された。「3種の神器」といわれたテレビ・電気洗濯機・電気冷蔵庫などの家電製品や乗用車の普及、高速道路網・内外航空路の整備、電話・ファクシミリなどの通信網の発達によって、国民の生活は便利で快適なものになった。強い日本円のおかげで、年間1,000万人もの日本人が、海外旅行に出かけるようになった。

f) 現代(その2)(1980年代後半以降)
[石油の確保と自衛隊の派遣・憲法問題]

石油の87%を中東に依存する日本は、中東に紛争が発生するたびにエネルギー問題と石油の輸送にかかわる海外出兵問題(戦力および交戦権の否認:憲法第9条)に直面せざるを得なくなる。ペルシャ湾岸の石油資源をめぐって1980年から1988年まで9年間にわたって続いたイラン・イラク戦争においては、世界各国の石油タンカーの安全を保障するためにアメリカは各国に対し機雷を除去する目的で掃海艇の派遣を要請した。日本では、憲法上の問題から自衛隊を派遣する考えは毛頭なく、海上保安庁の巡視船をペルシャ湾に派遣するか否かが深刻に議論された。また、1990年8月に、石油価格の上昇を狙って石油の減産を主張するイラクと石油輸出国機構(OPEC)との折り合いがつかず、イラクが突如クウェートに侵攻した事件が引き金となり、1991年1月に国際連合が多国籍軍の派遣を決定しイラクを空爆していわゆる湾岸戦争が始まった。この際

was the only person there who had first-hand experience of the Great Depression of 1929.)

The international competitiveness of the Japanese economy continued to strengthen also in the 1980s, enabling it to withstand the pressure that was triggered by the Plaza Accord (which accepted the rapid appreciation in the Japanese yen's foreign exchange rate) and continued through the latter half of the decade. The period was marked by rapidly ascending economic indicators: a huge trade surplus, low unemployment, and stable commodity prices. Per capita income, as stated in U.S. dollars, rose to the level of the highest anywhere in the world.

This economic development of the postwar years profoundly altered the Japanese lifestyle. The changes became particularly noticeable from 1964, the year when the Tokaido Shinkansen (bullet train) line went into operation and the first Olympiad to take place in Asia was held in Tokyo. The spread of TVs, washing machines, and refrigerators (then called the "three status symbols") and other home electrical appliances, the emergence of private automobiles, the building of an expressway network and domestic and overseas airway networks, and the development and improvement of telephone, facsimile and other communications systems combined to make life easier and more enjoyable. Encouraged by the strong yen, people also took to overseas travel, at the rate of 10 million annually.

f) Recent Times II (Mid-1980s on)
Securing Oil and Dispatching Self-Defense Forces, Constitutional Issues

Every time there is a conflict in the Middle East, Japan, which depends on the Middle East for 87% of its oil, has to face the problem of energy concerns and the overseas involvement of military personnel in the transportation of oil, a problem rooted in the renouncement of war and the right of belligerency set out in Article 9 of its Constitution. During the Iran-Iraq War which lasted from 1980 to 1988, the U.S. asked countries to send minesweepers in order to secure the safety of oil tankers from around the world traversing the waters of the Persian Gulf. In Japan, the idea of dispatching Self-Defense Forces was not considered, due to constitutional issues, and there was a serious discussion about whether to send a patrol boat of the Japan Coast Guard. In addition, in August 1990, Iraq, which had been advocating reducing oil production to drive up the price but could not reach a compromise with the Organization of the Petroleum Exporting Countries (OPEC), suddenly invaded Kuwait, an event that in January 1991 led to the United

には、自衛隊の海外派遣は憲法違反かどうかで侃々諤々（かんかんがくがく）の議論があった。結局、資金援助として約130億ドル（約1兆7,000億円）の拠出と掃海艇の派遣を実施したが、国際的には「日本はカネだけ出して済ませようとしている」という厳しい評価にさらされることになった。

このような批判を受けて、日本においても「国際社会の一員として『カネ』だけでなく『汗』も流すべき」という世論が形成され、宮沢喜一首相の政権下で、1992年6月に国際平和協力法（PKO法：Peace Keeping Operation）が成立し、文民警察官とともに、厳しい行動制限の下にではあるが、陸上自衛隊が国連カンボジア暫定統治機構（UNTAC）に参加するに至った。

その後、2003年3月にはいわゆるイラク戦争（第2次湾岸戦争）がおきる。これは、第1次湾岸戦争の終結にあたって、国際連合との間でイラクは大量破壊兵器の不保持を義務付けられたが、これに違反しているという推測で、アメリカ、イギリス、オーストラリア、ポーランド等の有志連合（フランス、ドイツ、ロシア等は反対）が国連の決議なしで一方的にイラクへ侵攻したものである。当時の小泉純一郎首相はアメリカの支持を表明し、非戦闘地域に限り自衛隊を派遣する「イラク特別措置法」を成立させ、人道支援のため自衛隊をイラクに派遣した（合計800人）。なお、イラクでは大量破壊兵器は発見されず、その後2006年12月にはそれまで捕捉されていたサダム・フセイン大統領が処刑され、さらにテロが頻発しゲリラ戦が長引き、ようやく2011年12月14日に至って、アメリカ軍の完全撤収によってブッシュ大統領から代わったバラク・オバマ大統領がイラク戦争の終結を正式に宣言した。

[財政の立て直しと公共企業体の民営化]
1980年代半ば、日本電信電話公社や日本専売公社など、大きな公共企業体の民営化が行われ、1985年にそれぞれ日本電信電話株式会社（NTT）と日本たばこ産業株式会社（JT）になった。1987年には日本国有鉄道（国鉄）が7つの鉄道会社（JR）に分割・民営化された（中曽根康弘首相政権）。1989年には、日本では初めて税率3％の消費税（付加価値税）が導入された。この税は1997年に5％に引上げられ、2014年4月には8％へ引き上げられた。

Nations deciding to dispatch a multinational force and bomb Iraq, marking the start of the Gulf War. In that case, there was a fierce debate as to whether dispatching a Self-Defense Force was constitutional. In the end, Japan provided financial assistance amounting to about 13 billion dollars (about 1.7 trillion yen) and sent a minesweeping boat, but internationally it was criticized for just being willing to give away money.

In response to such criticism, public opinion got behind the idea that as a member of the international community, Japan should be willing to give effort as well as money. Accordingly, in June 1992 the administration of Prime Minister Miyazawa Kiichi enacted the Act on Cooperation with United Nations Peacekeeping Operations and Other Operations, and along with civilian police officers, the Ground Self Defense Force joined the United Nations Transitional Authority in Cambodia (UNTAC), albeit acting under severe restrictions.

The so-called Iraq War (the Second Gulf War) began in March 2003, when a "coalition of the willing" that included the U.S., Britain, Australia, and Poland invaded Iraq unilaterally without a resolution of the United Nations. This step was taken because at the conclusion of the first Gulf War Iraq had been forbidden to possess weapons of mass destruction, but was conjectured to be in violation of this obligation. A number of countries including France, Germany, and Russia were opposed to the move and did not take part in the invasion. Prime Minister Koizumi Junichiro announced his support for the U.S. and passed the "Iraq Special Measures Law" to dispatch Self-Defense Force personnel to non-combat regions to provide humanitarian assistance. In all, 800 personnel were sent to Iraq. No weapons of mass destruction were found in Iraq. Saddam Hussein was captured and held until his execution in December 2006. There were frequent terrorist acts as guerrilla warfare continued until, on December 14, 2011, following the complete withdrawal of the U.S. military, the Iraq War was officially declared over by President Barack Obama.

Reconstruction of Finance and Privatization of Government Corporations

In the mid-1980s, several large government corporations were privatized. Nippon Telegraph and Telephone Public Corporation and Japan Tobacco & Salt Public Corporation became Nippon Telegram and Telephone Corporation (NTT) and Japan Tobacco Incorporated (JT) in 1985. Japanese National Railways was split into seven railway companies and privatized as the JR Group in 1987 (by the administration of Prime Minister Nakasone Yasuhiro). Another big change was the introduction of a 3% consumption tax (a form of value-added tax) in

[東西冷戦の終了と歴史認識]
　1989年、ベルリンの壁開放に象徴される、東ヨーロッパ社会主義諸国で、議会制民主主義への転換、市場経済の導入などの諸民主化の改革が連続して起こった。これによって東欧社会主義国は消滅し、同年末に米ソ首脳（ブッシュ（父）大統領・ゴルバチョフ書記長）がマルタ会談で冷戦の終結を宣言した。1991年には、ソビエト社会主義共和国連邦が解体され消滅した。

　1990年代初頭の歴代政権は、戦前の日本の朝鮮半島に対する植民地支配や中国大陸などへの侵略行為について謝罪と反省をすべきであるという考え（歴史認識）を口頭では表明していた。1994年6月に自由民主党、社会党、さきがけの3党による連立政権が成立し、社会党出身の村山富市が首相になると、村山は戦後50年目の節目の年に当たる1995年5月に歴史認識を国会の決議に付すことを考えた。しかし3党の合意は得られなかったので、同年8月15日に次のような村山談話（一部抜粋）を閣議決定した。「・・・我が国は、遠くない過去の一時期、国策を誤り、戦争への道を歩んで国民を存亡の危機に陥れ、植民地支配と侵略によって、多くの国々、とりわけアジア諸国の人々に対して多大の損害と苦痛を与えました。私は、未来に過ち無からしめんとするが故に、疑うべくもないこの歴史の事実を謙虚に受け止め、ここに改めて痛切な反省の意を表し、心からのお詫びの気持ちを表明いたします。・・・」。この談話はその後の歴代の内閣に受け継がれている。

[バブル経済の崩壊と構造改革]
　バブル経済は、1980年代中盤の「円高不況」対策および諸外国からの「内需拡大」要求対策として実施された大幅かつ長期間に渡る金融緩和政策によってもたらされたものであった。日銀は、1985年から1987年にかけて公定歩合を5％から2.5％まで低下させ、これにより生み出された余剰資金は株式と不動産に向かった。株価は3年間で3倍に上昇し、地価も急速に上昇し「狂乱地価」とも言われた。これを抑えるため、日銀は公定歩合を1989年5月か

1989. The tax was raised to 5% in 1997 and to 8% in April 2014.

End of the Cold War and Historical Awareness

In 1989, in the socialist countries of Eastern Europe, a series of transitions to parliamentary democracy and democratization reforms such as the introduction of a market democracy took place, symbolized by the opening up of the Berlin Wall. The result was the disappearance of the Eastern European socialist countries and, at the end of the year, at the Malta Summit between the U.S. President George H. W. Bush and Soviet General Secretary Mikhail Gorbachev, the two leaders declared an end to the Cold War. The dissolution of the Union of Soviet Socialist Republics took place in 1991.

Successive regimes in the early 1990s expressed an idea (historical awareness) that there should be verbal apologies for, and reflections on, colonial rule on the Korean Peninsula before the war and invasions into the Chinese continent. When the coalition government with the Liberal Democratic Party, the Social Democratic Party, and the New Party Sakigake was formed in June 1994, Murayama Tomiichi from the Social Democratic Party became the prime minister. Murayama had historical awareness, and had the idea of presenting a resolution to the National Assembly in May 1995, which was the 50th year after the war ended. However, since the agreement of the three parties could not be obtained for that date, the Cabinet decided on August 15 for the Murayama discourse. The following is an excerpt. "…During a certain period in the not too distant past, Japan, following a mistaken national policy, advanced along the road to war, only to ensnare the Japanese people in a fateful crisis, and, through its colonial rule and aggression, caused tremendous damage and suffering to the people of many countries, particularly to those of Asian nations. In the hope that no such mistake be made in the future, I regard, in a spirit of humility, these irrefutable facts of history, and express here once again my feelings of deep remorse and state my heartfelt apology…". The discourse has been handed down from cabinet to cabinet.

Collapse of Bubble Economy and Structural Reforms

The bubble economy was brought about by the large and long-term monetary easing policy implemented as a measure against the high yen recession in the mid-1980s, and demands from other countries that Japan expand domestic demand. Between 1985 and 1987 the Bank of Japan reduced the official discount rate from 5% to 2.5%, and the surplus money generated thereby went into stocks and real estate. Stock prices tripled in three years and land prices rose rapidly to what were called "crazy prices." To curb this, between May 1989 and August 1990

ら1990年8月にかけて6％まで上昇させた。これにより株価、地価が半値以下に暴落し、「バブル経済」の崩壊が始まった。この結果金融機関の抱える不良債権は100兆円に及び、この不良債権処理を政府主導の金融再編および公的資金の投入ならびに民間企業の財務圧縮により行うことになった。そのため日本経済はおよそ10年の間低迷を続けた。

2001年から小泉純一郎首相政権による一連の日本の「構造改革」が実施された。具体的には、政府・行政組織の再編成（1府（総理府）21省から1府（内閣府）12省へ：実質的な再編成は橋本龍太郎首相前政権によって行われた）、道路公団および郵政事業の民営化、石油公団の廃止や、金融、雇用ほか各分野での規制緩和などである。また、2002年には「知的財産立国」が宣言され、産業基盤としての知的財産の創造が大いに奨励され、関連法制度が幅広く改正・整備された。

政府・民間による一体となった不良債権の処理と中国など新興国向けの輸出増加により、景気はゆるやかに回復に向かった。

しかし、2008年にアメリカのサブプライムローン問題をきっかけとして世界同時不況（リーマンショック）が起こった。日本も景気が急速に悪化し、製造業の大幅な減産、失業者の急増など、深刻な経済・社会問題に直面した。ドルやユーロの価値の急激な下落の余波を受けて円は記録的な高水準が続き、日本経済はデフレ不況に陥った。

2006年に小泉政権から引き継いだ安倍、福田、麻生の自由民主党（自民党）政権はそれぞれ短命に終わり、2009年に行われた総選挙の結果自民党から民主党に政権が変わった。しかし政権を握った民主党政府や日銀の対応の遅れから円高の是正、景気の回復は進まなかった。民主党政権では3年余りの間に首相が鳩山、菅、野田と変わり、発足時に掲げた10数項目の公約も大半が実施されず、逆に消費税引き上げ、TPPへの参加表明など公約に反する政策決定が行われて、国民の支持は急落した。

the Bank of Japan raised the official discount rate to 6%. As a result, stocks and land prices plunged to half or less the peak level, starting the collapse of the bubble economy. Non-performing loans held by financial institutions reached 100 trillion yen and had to be disposed of by government-led financial restructuring, the injection of public funds, and financial retrenchment by private enterprises. This caused the Japanese economy to stagnate for some 10 years.

During this period, the Koizumi Junichiro Administration carried out a series of structural reforms starting from 2001. This process included a reorganization of the national administrative structure (from one office: the Prime Minister's Office, and twenty-one ministries and agencies to one office: the Cabinet Office, and twelve ministries, a substantial reorganization that had been carried out by the previous administration under Prime Minister Hashimoto Ryutaro), privatization of the postal services and Japan Highway Public Corporation, abolition of Japan National Oil Corporation, and deregulation of the financial, employment, and other sectors. The "Intellectual property nation" declaration was made in 2002, promoting the creation of intellectual property as an industrial base, for which the related legal system was amended and expanded.

Once the combined efforts of the government and the private sector got the bad debt problem substantially under control and exports to China and other emerging countries started to rise, the economy began to recover gradually.

But in 2008 the global economy was plunged into recession by the U.S. subprime mortgage crisis (the Lehman shock). Japan's economy went into a freefall. The country soon faced sharp declines in industrial output, rapid increases in unemployment, and other severe economic and social issues. Plummeting dollar and euro values pushed the yen to record high levels, and the economy fell into a deflationary slump.

The Koizumi Liberal Democratic Party (LDP) Administration, which stepped down in 2006, was followed by three short-lived LDP Administrations, of Abe, Fukuda, and Aso. Although the general election of 2009 shifted power from the LDP to the Democratic Party of Japan (DPJ), the new administration made no progress in weakening the strong yen or invigorating the economy, because both it and the Bank of Japan responded too slowly. The DPJ installed three prime ministers in just over three years (Hatoyama, Kan, and Noda), and not only failed to make good on most of its dozen or so campaign promises but even took policy actions contrary to its commitments, such as deciding to raise the consumer tax rate and oppose participation in the Trans-Pacific

また対外的にも、沖縄の基地問題に対し、既に日本の橋本龍太郎首相政権とアメリカの両政府で合意されていた「普天間飛行場を名護市辺野古崎へ移転しその跡地を日本に返還する」等という方針を、2006年5月に鳩山由紀夫首相はこれを一方的に見直すと主張した。このような日本政府の基本方針のゆらぎからアメリカの対日信頼感が損なわれ、加えて東シナ海や日本海の島々の領有をめぐって中国、韓国との関係も急速に冷え込むなど日本外交の主体性が問われることとなった。1990年代はじめからの10年、それに引き続く2000年代はじめの10年間、政治、経済および社会の低迷状態は「失われた10年」あるいは「失われた20年」とも言われた。

[デフレ脱却から景気回復へ]
　この間2011年3月に発生した東日本大震災と相まった国民の先行き不安の払しょくと、局面打開の期待を背景に、2012年の末に行われた総選挙で自民党は圧勝し、自民党・公明党連合は衆議院議席の3分の2を獲得して政権に復帰した。これを受けて成立した第2次安倍晋三首相政権は、デフレ脱却・景気回復を目指して、思い切った金融緩和政策をはじめとしたアベノミクスと呼ばれる経済政策を打ち出した。経済は政権成立前から素早く反応し、短期間に円安、株高方向に進み、輸出産業を中心とする企業の収益などにプラス効果が現れ、内閣支持率も高水準を維持した。

　2013年7月の参議院選挙も自民党・公明党連合は圧勝し、総数の過半数を大幅に上回る議席を獲得して、「衆参のねじれ」（衆議院では多数だが参議院では少数）が解消し、政局はより安定した。

　その後、野党は離合集散を繰り返し混とんとしている。すなわち、2016年3月、民主党に維新の会の一部が合流し民進党が結成されたが、2016年7月参議院議員通常選挙の結果、自民党・公明党連合は135議席から146議席へ増加、野党の民進党は64議席から49議席へ減少。さら

Partnership. It quickly lost the support of the Japanese people.

Diplomatic difficulties also arose. Most notably, U.S. trust in Japan was undermined by the government's vacillating stance on the Okinawan military base issue; although the administration of Prime Minister Hashimoto Ryutaro and the U.S. administration had agreed that Futenma Air Station would be moved to Henokozaki, Nago City, and the site returned to Japan, in May 2006 Prime Minister Hatoyama Yukio unilaterally insisted on reviewing that plan. And, relations with China and South Korea rapidly deteriorated as territorial disputes over small islands in the East China Sea and the Japan Sea intensified. These and other problems cast doubt on Japan's foreign policy principles. The prolonged period of political, economic and social stagnation that continued from the 1990s into the early 2000s has been called Japan's "lost decade" or "two lost decades."

From Deflation to Recovery of Economy

The general election held late in 2012, the first following the catastrophic earthquakes and tsunamis of March 2011, came at a time when people wanted to get rid of their anxiety about the future and were eager for change. Against this backdrop, the LDP won a landslide victory that returned the LDP-Komeito coalition to power with a two-thirds majority in the House of Representatives. The coalition chose Abe Shinzo for his second term as prime minister, and the new Abe administration promptly launched an ambitious economic easing stimulus program, called "Abenomics," centered on a drastic financial initiative aimed at ending deflation and restoring economic growth. The Abenomics strategy fueled a recovery that had started from before Abe took over, so the economy reacted quickly. Almost immediately, the yen began to weaken and stock prices began to rise. Before long, a positive effect on revenues was seen among businesses in the export-centered industries. Support for the Abe Cabinet stayed high.

The LDP-Komeito coalition also won the House of Councilors election of July 2013 by a wide margin. By taking enough of the contested seats to realize an overwhelming majority, the two parties put an end to the "divided Diet" (where the ruling administration had a majority of seats in the House of Representatives but a minority of seats in the House of Councilors).

Since then, the opposition parties have been in constant motion, repeatedly realigning themselves. In March 2016, part of the Japan Innovation Party merged with the Democratic Party of Japan to form the Democratic Party, and the result of the House of Councilors election held in July 2016 was that the coalition between the LDP and Komeito

に、2017年9月、希望の党が結党（都民ファーストの会が主たる母体）され、希望の党は一部が民進党に合流したが、2017年10月、民進党の多くの議員が脱退し立憲民主党を結党した。

　2017年10月衆議院議員総選挙（定数465）の結果、自民党・公明党連合は313議席に対し、立憲民主党が55議席、希望の党が50議席、共産党が12議席、日本維新の会が11議席となった。なお、2018年5月に希望の党と民主党は新しい党（国民民主党）を立ち上げ合流した。

ended with 146 seats, up from 135 seats, while the seats held by the opposition Democratic Party declined to 49 from 64 seats. In September 2017, the Party of Hope formed a party (with Tomin First no Kai as the parent body), and part of the Party of Hope merged with the Democratic Party, but in October 2017 most of the members of the Democratic Party left to form the Constitutional Democratic Party of Japan.

As a result of the general election of the House of Representatives held in October 2017 (465 seats), the LDP-Komeito coalition had 313 seats, the Constitutional Democratic Party of Japan 55, the Party of Hope 50, the Communist Party 12 seats, and the Japan Innovation Party 11. With that being the status, in May 2018, the Party of Hope and the Democratic Party launched a new party called the Democratic Party for the People.

3　政治

(1) 天皇

a) 天皇の憲法上の地位

　　天皇は、現行憲法では日本国の象徴であり、日本国民統合の象徴であって、この地位は、主権を持っている日本国民の総意に基く、と定められている。天皇は、憲法の定める国事に関する行為のみを行い、国政に関する権能をもたない。国事に関する行為には、内閣の助言と承認を必要とし、内閣がその責任を負う。

　　国事に関する行為とは、国会の指名に基づく内閣総理大臣の任命、内閣の指名に基づく最高裁判所長官の任命、また内閣の助言と承認に基づく憲法改正、法律・政令および条約の公布、国会の召集、衆議院の解散、総選挙施行の公示、栄典の授与、批准書およびその他の外交文書の認証、外国の大・公使の接受などである。

　　このように、天皇は政治上の権限をもたないが、外交儀礼上は元首として扱われる。

b) 皇室の歴史

　　日本の現存する最古の史書によると、紀元前660年に初代の天皇が即位したことになっている。しかし、天皇（古代には大王と呼んだ）の存在を史実に即して説明できるのは、4～5世紀以降の時代である。7世紀に中国の法律制度を導入して、天皇はみずから政治をすることになったが、実際に政治を行った期間は短かった。9世紀以後、約1,000年にわたって政治は貴族や武士によって行われた。しかし、各時代の実権者は、天皇を倒してみずから天皇になるということはなく、政治の大権を天皇から授かるという形を取った。

3 Government

(1) The Emperor

a) Constitutional Status of the Emperor

The present constitution of Japan declares that the Emperor shall be the symbol of the State and of the unity of the people, deriving his position from the will of the people with whom resides sovereign power. The Emperor performs only such acts in matters of state as are provided for in the Constitution without having any powers related to government. The advice and approval of the Cabinet is required for all acts of the Emperor in matters of state and the Cabinet is responsible for these acts.

Acts in matters of state performed by the Emperor include appointment of the Prime Minister as designated by the Diet (Japan's national legislative body); appointment of the Chief Judge of the Supreme Court as designated by the Cabinet; promulgation of amendments of the constitution, laws, cabinet orders and treaties; convocation of the Diet; dissolution of the House of Representatives; proclamation of general election of members of the Diet; awarding of honors; attestation of instruments of ratification and other diplomatic documents; and receiving of foreign ambassadors and ministers as approved and advised by the Cabinet.

Thus the Emperor has no governmental powers but is treated as the head of state in diplomatic and ceremonial functions.

b) History of the Imperial House

According to the oldest Japanese history book still in existence, the first Emperor (in ancient times called the Great King) assumed the Imperial Throne in the year 660 B.C. On the basis of more objective historical facts, however, the earliest date for which the existence of an emperor can be confirmed is somewhere in the fourth to fifth century A.D. After the introduction of a Chinese type legal system in the seventh century, the Emperor did for a time actually govern in his own right but this period of true imperial rule was short-lived. For a period of about one thousand years beginning in the ninth century, the country was under the control of the nobility and their successors, the warrior class. However, at no point in history did the actual power holder overthrow the Emperor and assume the Imperial Throne. Rather,

19世紀、大政奉還（1867年）によって、天皇は再び国の統治権を行使することになったが、実際は立法・行政・司法の三権分立の形をとった立憲君主制であった。第二次世界大戦後、現行憲法による天皇および皇室の形になった。

以上のように、日本の天皇は古代以来みずから国政の実権を掌握するということはほとんどなく、そのため政争に直接まきこまれることが少なかった。天皇が日本国民統合の中心であるとする観念を国民の間に強く根づかせたのは、古代以来の伝統と権威に加えて、天皇が時の政治の動きに対して超然とした存在であったという史実があるからであろう。

現行の皇室典範では、皇位継承者は天皇の男系男子のみと定められている。

c）天皇・皇后

126代目の天皇（今上天皇）のお名前は徳仁（なるひと）である。1960年2月23日に生誕、学習院大学と英国オックスフォード大学に学ばれ、2019年5月1日に皇位を継承された。

日本では通常、天皇の存命中はお名前を呼ぶことはしない。崩御後はおくり名をつける。たとえば、124代天皇のお名前は裕仁（ひろひと）であったが、在位の元号が昭和であったので、いまは昭和天皇と呼んでいる。

皇后のお名前は雅子で、民間（小和田家）の出身で、ハーバード大学と東京大学に学ばれた。

天皇夫妻の間に愛子内親王がおられる。なお、天皇の弟である秋篠宮文仁（ふみひと）親王が皇嗣（こうし）になられた。文仁親王には2006年生まれのご子息、悠仁（ひさひと）親王がおられる。

d）天皇の退位

天皇の退位は天皇が崩じた（死亡した）ときに生ずる（皇室典範第4条）とされている。しかし、2017年（平成29年）6月16日に公布された法律（天皇の退位等に関す

the rulers of the time based their governments on the sovereign right conferred upon them by the Emperor.

The Meiji Restoration (1867) placed the reins of government back in the hands of the Emperor, not as an absolute ruler but as the head of a constitutional monarchy comprising independent legislative, executive, and judiciary branches. The status of the Emperor and the Imperial House in Japan was redefined into its present form by the new constitution adopted following the Second World War.

Only very rarely throughout Japan's long history has the Emperor held actual power over the affairs of state and, as a consequence, he has seldom become directly involved in political struggles. The concept of the Emperor as the center about which the Japanese people are unified is very deeply rooted in the Japanese mind. This view of the Emperor arises not only from the long imperial tradition and respect for imperial authority, but also to a large extent from the fact that the Emperor has remained above day-to-day political matters.

The Imperial Household Act currently specifies that the person ascending to the Imperial Throne must be a male who is a descendant from the Emperor through a line of males.

c) The Imperial Family

The name of the present Emperor of Japan, the one hundred and twenty-sixth to occupy the Imperial Throne, is Naruhito. He was born on February 23, 1960 and became Emperor on May 1, 2019. He studied at Gakushuin University and in England at Oxford University.

The Japanese do not ordinarily refer to living emperors by name, and deceased emperors are referred to by names given posthumously. For example, the one hundred twenty-fourth Emperor's name was Hirohito, but he is now called the Emperor Showa because he ascended to the throne in the first year of the Showa era.

The Empress's name is Masako. Born a commoner, Owada Masako, she studied in the U.S. at Harvard University and at Tokyo University.

The Emperor and Empress have a daughter, Imperial Princess Aiko. The Emperor has a brother, Fumihito, Prince Akishino, who became the Imperial heir; Prince Akishino has a son, Prince Hisahito, who was born in 2006.

d) The Emperor's Abdication

An emperor's abdication is taken to occur upon his demise (Article 4 of The Imperial Household Act). However, in accordance with the Special Measures Law on the Imperial Household Act Concerning the

る皇室典範特例法：以下この項において特例法という）により、今上天皇（当時）に限り、特例法の施行日に退位することになった（特例法第 2 条）。その後政府は、特例法の施行日（天皇の退位日）を 2019 年（平成 31 年）4 月 30 日と定め、皇太子さま（当時）が退位日の翌日、2019 年 5 月 1 日に新天皇に即位した。また、退位後の天皇は上皇となられた。

　平成上皇に限りこのようになった経緯は、2016 年 8 月 8 日の平成上皇自らによる「お気持ち」を国民に直接表明したこと（地上波テレビ全局による放送）が端緒となった。その表明の内容については特例法第 1 条に詳述されている。すなわち、「天皇陛下が、28 年にわたり象徴としての活動に精励してこられ 83 歳と高齢になり、陛下御自身が今後活動を続けることが困難となると深く案じておられる。国民もこの陛下のお気持ちを理解し共感している。皇太子も 57 歳となり、陛下の代理として国事行為に精勤されている。これらを鑑みて退位と皇嗣の即位を実現する」というものである。次の天皇についても特例法の例によるかどうかは次世代の人々が決めることとし、現行の皇室典範はそのまま据え置き、あえて一代限りの特例という形をとった。

e）女性天皇・女系天皇
　皇室典範第 1 条には「皇位（天皇の地位）は皇統に属する男系の男子が、これを承継する」と規定され、同法第 2 条では天皇は皇族の中から選ぶこととされ、その順序が決められている。

　2019 年 5 月の時点で皇族は 18 人であり、今上天皇を除く皇位継承資格者（男性）は 3 人であるが、その一人である常陸宮殿下は 83 歳であられる。そこで皇統の安定承継が話題となることが多い。このような背景の下で、女性天皇や女系天皇の是非について大きな関心を呼んでいる。女性が天皇になることの是非が女性天皇問題である。女性天皇は歴史上過去に複数の例があるが、過去の例は、女性天

Abdication of His Majesty the Emperor and Other Matters (hereinafter referred to as the "Special Measures Law") promulgated on June 16, 2017, the present Emperor (the then) shall abdicate on the date the Special Measures Law comes into force (Article 2 of the Special Measures Law). The government decided that the date on which the Special Measures Law comes into force (the day of the Emperor's abdication) shall be April 30, 2019. The Crown Prince (the then) acceded to the position of Emperor on May 1, 2019. The retired Emperor became the Emperor Emeritus.

The way the matter applied only to the former Emperor (the Emperor Emeritus Heisei) went back to a broadcast the former Emperor made on August 8, 2016 (carried by all terrestrial TV channels) in which he expressed his "thoughts" to the nation. The gist of the address is included in Article 1 of the Special Measures Law, in which it is stated that "…His Majesty the Emperor has been assiduous in his activities as the symbol of the State for 28 years, and having reached the advanced age of 83, and after deep consideration, feels that in the future it will become difficult for him to continue carrying out those activities. The people understand and sympathize with His Majesty's feelings. His Highness the Crown Prince is now 57 and has been dedicating himself to representing His Majesty in the conduct of matters of State. In view of this, the abdication of His Majesty the Emperor and the accession of His Highness the Crown Prince to the Imperial Throne will be effectuated." Whether the exception of the Special Measures Law also applies to the following Emperor will be for the people of the next generation to decide. The current Imperial Household Act will remain as it is, with the exception being for the one generation.

e) Female Emperor and Matrilinear Emperor

Article 1 of the Imperial Household Act stipulates that "The Imperial Throne shall be succeeded to by a male offspring in the male line belonging to the Imperial Lineage," and Article 2 states the members of the Imperial Family to which the Imperial Throne can be passed, and the order in which the person is selected.

As of May 2019, the Imperial Family had eighteen members, of which, excluding the present Emperor, three were qualified to succeed to the throne (being male). One of them, His Imperial Highness Prince Hitachi, is 83 years of age. Thus, a stable imperial succession is a topic that frequently arises. Against this backdrop, there is considerable interest in the pluses and minuses of a female emperor or a matrilinear emperor. The pros and cons of a woman becoming an emperor is the

皇が皇后であったか、女性天皇が皇族の女性であり独身を貫いたケースで、いわばつなぎのような形で、その跡継ぎ（皇嗣）は皇族の中から選ばれ、皇統が絶えることはなかった。

これに対して、女系天皇とは、皇族の女性が天皇になった場合に、跡継ぎは、当該女性天皇の直系家族がなるという考えである。女性天皇が皇族の男性と結婚する場合は、問題ないが、皇族以外の男性と結婚する場合は、その配偶者はいわば天皇家の婿養子になると考えられる。ところが日本の天皇家では、皇族以外の女性が天皇家に嫁入りすることはあっても、皇族以外の男性が天皇家に婿養子になるというのは認められないと思われる。もし女性天皇が皇族以外の男性と結婚すると、当該女性天皇は配偶者である男性の家に入らなければならない。

それは、現在の皇統から外れた天皇が新しい王朝を設立することになる。そうすると少なくとも記録に残る限り1,500年続いている日本の天皇家の「万世一系の天皇」という体系が崩れてしまうのではないか。日本国憲法には「万世一系の天皇」という文言はない（大日本帝国憲法には明記されていた）が、女系天皇制度を認めるコンセンサスを得るのは難しいのではないだろうか。

（2）政治

a）日本国憲法

現在の日本国憲法は、太平洋戦争終結の翌年の1946年11月3日に公布され、1947年5月3日から施行された。

この憲法は、明治時代に制定された「大日本帝国憲法」の内容を、当時日本の占領政策を担っていたアメリカの指導の下で一新したものである。前憲法との違いをいくつかあげれば、象徴天皇、主権在民、平和主義、人権尊重、国際紛争を解決する手段としての戦争の放棄などである。

現行憲法が制定されて70年以上が経過した現在、政界また国民の間にも憲法改正の議論への関心が急速に高まっ

issue of a female emperor. Historically, there have been a number of female emperors, but in the past they were empress consorts, or the female emperor was a member of the imperial family who remained single, a stopgap, so to speak, and her successor (an imperial heir) was selected from the imperial family, so there was no break in the imperial line.

In contrast, in the case of a matrilinear emperor, when a female member of the imperial family has become Emperor, her successor will be a direct lineal descendant. If the female emperor marries a male member of the imperial family, there is no problem. However, if she marries a man who is not a member of the Imperial Family, he is considered to be a man adopted to be the husband of the Emperor. In the case of the Japanese Imperial Family, while a woman who is not an imperial family member may marry into the Imperial Family, it is unlikely that a man who is not an imperial family member would be permitted to be adopted into the imperial family. If the female emperor marries a man from outside the imperial family, she must enter the spouse's house.

That would mean that an emperor outside the present Imperial lineage would establish a new dynasty, which would mean the collapse of the "unbroken line of Emperors" that stretches back 1,500 years according to records. The Constitution of Japan does not mention an "unbroken line of Emperors" (although it was clearly stated in the Constitution of the Empire of Japan), but it is difficult to obtain a consensus on recognizing a matrilinear emperor system.

(2) Government

a) The Japanese Constitution

Japan's present Constitution was promulgated on November 3, 1946, the year following the end of the Pacific War, and went into effect on May 3, 1947.

Under the guidance of the United States (U.S.), which was responsible for the occupation policy of Japan at that time, the Constitution of the Empire of Japan enacted in the Meiji era was completely revised. A few of the points that distinguish it from the earlier constitution are that it defines the Emperor as the symbol of the state, affirms that sovereignty rests with the people, advocates peace, commits to respect for human rights, and renounces war as a means of settling international disputes.

Over 70 years have now passed since the present Constitution went into effect and moves to revise the constitution have intensified in

ている。

　憲法改正の論点については、いろいろな立場からいろいろな論点があげられている。一番かまびすしく議論されているのは自衛隊の合憲性の明確化の是非、すなわち安全保障の問題であろう。この背景としては、近年の中国、韓国、ロシアとの領土・領海に関する争い、中国の軍備拡充、北朝鮮のミサイル・核開発など国際関係の緊張増加、アメリカの世界的軍備再編に伴う在日米軍の縮小などの状況がある。日本の安全保障の観点から、自衛隊の性格と役割、海外派遣時の活動の実態などに照らして憲法第9条（戦争の放棄）の規定、特にその第2項（戦力の不保持、交戦権の否定）との整合性を求める主張が強くなっている。

　次に議論されている論点としては、憲法26条第2項後文の「義務教育は、これを無償とする」という問題であろうか。現在、小・中学校では授業料は無料である。小・中学校へ通うのは義務だと法律で定めているからである。では幼児教育、高等学校や大学についてはどう考えればよいのか。特に、幼児教育については、待機児童問題が大きく取り上げられているが、幼児教育が義務化されれば、待機児童問題は大幅に解決されるのではないか。この問題は、憲法にまで言及しなくとも、法律のレベルで解決できるかもしれないが、どこまでの教育を義務とするか、国民的な議論を踏まえて解決すべき問題である。

　緊急事態条項についての議論も盛んである。国際的なテロや大規模災害、他国からの武力行使の場合に、政府に権限を集中できるようにしておかなくてよいか。他方で、政府（行政）に立法と司法の権限を無制限に集中させると、三権分立構造が崩れ、国民の基本的人権が危うくなることにならないかという論点である。

　最近において緊急で現実的な問題としては参議院議員選挙における合区の解消問題がある。2016年の参議院議員通常選挙では、鳥取県と島根県、徳島県と高知県がそれぞれ合区して一つの選挙区とされた。これは、選挙権の一票の格差を解消させるためにとられた便法であった。しかし、この方法によるといずれかの県は代表者を国政の場へ送れない結果となる可能性があり、各都道府県の意見を等しく国政に反映させるという憲法の理念が実現されなくな

political circles and among the people of Japan. There are various discussions from different standpoints on revisions to the Constitution.

What is most frequently discussed are the pros and cons of clarifying the constitutionality of the Self-Defense Forces, that is, the issue of security. The main causes behind this are the deterioration of Japan's relationships with China, South Korea and Russia owing to territory and territorial water disagreements, military expansion by China, and nuclear bomb and ballistic missile tests conducted by North Korea. Another factor has been the tendency of the U.S. to reduce its military presence in Japan during a time of realignment of the U.S. military's presence around the world. In addition, questions have arisen about how well Article 9 of the Constitution fits with matters like strengthening defense, Japan's role in international affairs, and the functions and overseas deployment of the Self-Defense Forces.

The second most frequently discussed issue is about Article 26, paragraph 2 of the Constitution that states "…compulsory education be free." Currently, tuition is free at elementary and junior high school. That is because it is a legal obligation to attend elementary and junior high school. So what about preschool education, high school and university? A major problem in regard to preschool education is that of waiting lists, but wouldn't mandating preschool education go a long way to solving that problem? Maybe it could be solved at the legal level without referring to the Constitution, but how much education should be obligatory is something that should be resolved by a national debate.

There are also many discussions on emergency provisions. Should it be possible to allow control to be concentrated in the government in the case of international terrorism, large-scale disasters, or the use of force by other countries? On the other hand, if such centralized control of legislative and judicial powers by the government (administration) continues indefinitely, there is an argument that it could lead to the collapse of the system of separation of powers and endanger the people's basic human rights.

One actual, pressing problem that needs to be resolved is that of the combined districts in the ordinary election of the House of Councilors. Tottori Prefecture and Shimane Prefecture, and Tokushima Prefecture and Kochi Prefecture were each combined as a single constituency in the election of the House of Councilors in 2016. This was done as an expedient way to eliminate the disparity in the relative weight of a vote. However, this method could result in one of the prefectures not being able to send a representative to the Diet, thereby preventing the

るのではないか。この問題は、議論の行方によっては、現在の都道府県の区割りの是非、道州制、衆議院のほかに参議院は本当に必要なのかというさらに大きな論点を浮かび上がらせるかもしれない。

このほか、従前から首相公選制、環境権などの新しい概念の導入などの論点がある。制定から70年以上も全く修正されない憲法は世界でも稀有なものである。国民一人一人が、いろいろな意見に関心を持って、主体的に真剣に考えることが求められる。いずれも基本的人権の根幹にかかわる問題だからだ。

憲法改正は、衆参両院の総議員数の3分の2以上の賛成により発議され、国民投票の有効投票数の過半数の賛成によって決定される（憲法第96条および2010年施行の国民投票法（憲法改正手続き法ともいう））。

b) **統治機構**

日本の統治機構は立法・行政・司法の各機関が独立した三権分立制である。

国の唯一の立法機関である国会は、国権の最高機関で、衆議院と参議院の二院から成っている。両議院とも国民の選挙によって選出された議員で組織されている。国会の権限として、内閣総理大臣の指名、内閣不信任の決議、法律案の議決、予算の議決、条約の承認、裁判官に対する弾劾裁判、憲法改正の発議などがある。

行政権は内閣に属し、内閣は内閣総理大臣とその他の国務大臣で組織され、行政権の行使について国会に対し連帯して責任を負う。内閣は一般行政事務のほか、法律を執行し、外交関係を処理し、条約を締結し、予算を作成し、政令を制定する。これらの業務を分担するため、国務大臣を長とする1府12省庁がおかれている（2001年1月、内閣の重要政策に関して、各省より一段高い立場から企画立案・総合調整を行うために、内閣官房長官を補佐する内閣

realization of the constitutional philosophy of reflecting the opinion of each prefecture equally in the national government. Depending on the direction of the discussion, this problem may lead to the emergence of even greater issues such as the appropriateness of current prefectural districting, the system of reorganizing Japan into several regional blocs (*Doshusei*), and whether the House of Councilors is really necessary.

Other issues in dispute include the introduction of a prime ministerial public election system and the introduction of new concepts such as environmental rights. A Constitution that has not been modified at all for the more than 70 years since its enactment is a rarity in today's world. Every citizen needs to think independently and seriously on subjects on which there are various opinions. These are issues that are fundamental to basic human rights.

A two-thirds majority in both the House of Representatives and the House of Councilors is required to approve a constitutional amendment. Then, the amendment must receive more than half of the valid votes in a general referendum of the populace (Article 96 of the Constitution and the National Referendum Law of 2010 (also called the Constitutional Amendment Procedure Act)).

b) Japanese System of Government

The government of Japan is composed of a legislative branch, an administrative branch and a judiciary branch, each of which is independent of the others.

Legislative powers are vested in the Diet, which is the highest organ of state power and its sole law-making body. The Diet is made up of the House of Representatives and the House of Councilors, both of which consist of members elected by the people. Among the powers of the Diet are the power to designate the Prime Minister; the power to approve non-confidence resolutions in the Cabinet; the power to pass laws; the power to approve the budget; the power to approve treaties; the power to conduct trials of impeachment against judges; and the power to suggest the amendment of the Constitution.

The administrative power is vested in the Cabinet which consists of the Prime Minister and other ministers of state. In the exercise of its administrative power, the Cabinet is collectively responsible to the Diet. In addition to its general administrative functions, the Cabinet administers the law; manages foreign affairs; concludes treaties; prepares the budget; and enacts Cabinet orders. The work of carrying out these functions is divided among one office and twelve ministries and agencies, each of which is headed by one of the ministers of state.

府（総理府を改変）が設置されるとともに各省庁の再編（21省から12省へ）が行われた）。内閣の統一を保つために、内閣総理大臣は国務大臣の任免権をもつ。

　司法機関として裁判所がある。最高裁判所と下級裁判所（高等裁判所・地方裁判所・家庭裁判所・簡易裁判所）とからなる。すべての裁判官は、その良心にしたがい独立してその職権を行い、憲法および法律にのみ拘束される。最高裁判所の長官は内閣の指名に基づき天皇が任命し、そのほかの裁判官はすべて内閣が任命する。最高裁判所は、一切の法律・命令・規則または処分が憲法に適合するかしないかを決定する権限（違憲立法審査権）をもつ終審裁判所である。

　2009年5月から、裁判員制度が開始された。これは国民の司法への直接的参加を認め、事件ごとに国民のなかから選ばれた裁判員が裁判官とともに審理に参加する裁判制度をいう。国民が刑事裁判に参加することにより、裁判が身近で分かりやすいものになり、司法に対する国民の信頼の向上につながることが期待されている。裁判員裁判は原則として民間から選ばれる裁判員6人および裁判官3人で行われる。この制度は死刑または無期懲役・禁固に相当する重大な刑事事件を対象とする。

　日本国憲法において、行政権は国の統治機構のほかに、地方自治体にも認められており、地域住民の意思に基づく施政を行うとされている。

　全国に1都（東京都）、1道（北海道）、2府（大阪府、京都府）、43県（青森県から沖縄県まで）の包括的地方公共団体がある。都道府県のもとには、基礎的地方公共団体として1,718（2017年）の市区町村がある。

c）選挙

　国会議員、都道府県・市町村（東京の区を含む）の各首長、および各議会議員は、直接選挙で選ばれる。選挙権は、従来満20歳以上の男女全員に認められてきたが、2016年6月19日施行の改正公職選挙法により、満18歳以上の男女全員に認められることになり、約240万人が新たに有権者となった。最初に適用された選挙は2016年

(In January 2001, in order to plan and comprehensively coordinate the major policies of the Cabinet from a position higher than that of each ministry, a Cabinet Office (reformed Prime Minister's Office) was established to assist the Chief Cabinet Secretary and ministries were reorganized, reducing the number of ministries from 21 to 12.) The Prime Minister has the power to dismiss ministers of state in order to maintain the solidarity of the Cabinet.

The judiciary branch of government is made up of the Supreme Court and such inferior courts as the high courts, the district courts, the family courts, and the summary courts. All judges are independent in the exercise of their conscience and are bound only by the Constitution and the laws. The Chief Judge of the Supreme Court is designated by the Cabinet and appointed by the Emperor, and all other judges are appointed by the Cabinet. The Supreme Court is the court of last resort with the power to determine the constitutionality of any law, order, regulation, or official act (the power of judicial review).

In May 2009, the *saiban-in* (lay judge) system was launched to give ordinary citizens a direct role in the criminal judicial process. Lay judges selected separately for each trial hear the case together with professional judges. Having citizens participate in criminal trials is expected to make trials more familiar and easier to understand, leading to increased public confidence in the judicial system. In a saiban-in trial, as a rule, six lay judges selected from among adult citizens sit with three professional judges. The system applies to trials for serious crimes that carry a penalty of death or life imprisonment.

The Japanese Constitution confers administrative authority not only on the national government but also on local self-governments to enable administration based on the will of local people.

The country is divided into forty-seven prefectures as sub-national jurisdictions: namely Tokyo-to, Hokkaido, Osaka-fu, Kyoto-fu and 43 *ken* (from Aomori-ken in the north to Okinawa-ken in the south). These forty-seven prefectures encompass 1,718 (in 2017) municipalities (cities, special wards, towns, and villages).

c) Elections

Members of the Diet, prefectural governors, city, town, and village mayors and assembly members (including those of Tokyo's wards) are chosen by direct election. Formerly all men and women aged 20 years or older had the right to vote, but in accordance with the revised election law that went into force on June 19, 2016, the minimum voting age was lowered to 18, adding approximately 2.4 million new voters

7月10日投票の参議院議員通常選挙であった。被選挙権は、参議院議員と都道府県知事は30歳以上、それ以外は25歳以上の者にある。女性は1945年にはじめて選挙権と被選挙権を得た。

現在、国会議員と都道府県の知事および地方議会議員の大部分は、政党の党員であるかまたは政党の推薦を受けた者である。選挙運動は、ポスター・テレビ・立会演説会・街頭演説・インターネットなどにより行われる。選挙は無記名自由投票で行い、選びたい人の氏名を、選挙によっては政党名を自分で書く。

1994年に公職選挙法が改正され、衆議院議員総選挙は中選挙区制から小選挙区比例代表並立制に切り換えられた（2016年5月27日施行の改正公職選挙法により、議員定数は465議席であり、定員1の小選挙区289議席と全国11ブロックの比例代表176議席に分かれる）。

2009年8月に行われた衆議院議員総選挙では、民主党が圧勝し（308議席獲得。自由民主党は119議席に減少）、政権交代を果した。民主党のマニフェスト（政権公約）の主要施策は、税金の無駄使いの根絶と官僚の天下りの廃止、子供手当の支給、高速道路の無料化、高校授業料の無償化、農業の戸別所得補償、年金制度の一元化などであった。

しかしながら、約3年半の政権担当時に、公約はほとんど実行できず、2012年12月に行われた衆議院議員総選挙では、251議席減の57議席と惨敗した。代わりに自由民主党が294議席を獲得し、公明党との連立政権を発足させた。野党側はその後も勢力は回復できず、2014年12月の総選挙では、連立政権は合計で326議席に対し、民主党73議席、維新の会41議席であった。さらに2017年10月の衆議院議員総選挙では、連立政権は313議席（定数改正後の定数465の3分の2超）を獲得している。

to the electorate. The first election held under the revised law was an ordinary election of members of the House of Councilors held on July 10, 2016. The minimum age for members of the House of Councilors and prefectural governors is thirty and that for all other elected officials twenty-five. Women were first given the right to vote and the right to stand for office in 1945.

Most present members of the Diet, prefectural governors, and members of prefectural assemblies belong to a political party or were elected with the support of a political party. The election campaigns are conducted through various media including posters, television, speech meetings, street-corner oratory, and the Internet. Voting is done through free casting of secret ballots, with each voter writing in the name of a candidate, or the name of a political party.

The Election Law was revised in 1994. The old system of electing members of the House of Representatives from medium-sized districts was replaced by a system combining small, single-seat districts with large proportional representation districts (under the revised Election Law that went into effect on May 27, 2016, the number of seats is 465, divided between 289 members elected from single-seat districts under the single member plurality system and 176 elected from eleven separate electoral blocs under the proportional representation system).

In the General Election held in August 2009, the Democratic Party of Japan (DPJ) won a large majority of seats in the House of Representatives (308 seats, while the number of seats held by the Liberal Democratic Party (LDP) decreased to 119) and achieved a change of government. Among the DPJ's key election pledges were to eradicate wasteful spending of tax money and *amakudari* (golden parachuting; practice by retiring bureaucrats taking high-level positions in companies or organizations they once regulated), pay a child allowance, do away with some expressway tolls, make public high schools tuition-free, provide individual income support allowance for farmers, and create a unified pension system.

However, the DPJ made good on almost none of these promises during its approximately three and a half years in power, and the party was badly defeated in the General Election of December 2012. It lost 251 of 308 seats in the House of Representatives, while the Liberal Democratic Party captured 294 seats and formed a coalition government with the Komeito party. The opposition side were unable to recover their strength. In the general election held in December 2014 the coalition government captured a total of 327 seats, while the DPJ captured just 73 seats and the Japan Innovation Party 41. Also, in the general election

参議院も衆議院と同様に全国民を代表する選挙された議員で組織される。参議院議員通常選挙は全国規模の国政選挙であるが、総議員を一斉に選出するわけではなく半数改選であるから「総選挙」とは呼ばず、3年ごと（任期6年）の参議院議員選挙を「通常選挙」と呼んでいる。議員定数は242人であり、選挙区146議席と比例代表96議席に分かれる。選挙区は各都道府県に1つ（47）置かれ、人口に応じて各区から2～10人程度が割り当てられ、比例代表は全国統一で行う、とされてきた。しかし、2016年6月19日施行の改正公職選挙法により、同年7月の参議院議員通常選挙においては、鳥取県と島根県、徳島県と高知県がそれぞれ合区とされ（選挙区が2つ減って45となり、割り当て人数は、2～12人となった）、各都道府県に1つという原則に例外が生じる可能性ができた。なお、この参議院議員通常選挙では、自由民主党と公明党の連立政権は135議席から146議席へと増員させた。

　衆参両議員とも国民の代表であるので、選挙においては国民の意思が平等に反映されることが必要である（法の下の平等・憲法第14条）。2012年12月の衆議院議員選挙について、最高裁判所は次のような判決を下した。すなわち「衆議院は1票の格差が2倍以上、参議院は5倍以上であれば憲法違反状態である。本件はこの基準を満たしていないので憲法違反とはいえないが、違憲状態であり、さらに選挙制度の根本的改革を求める」という判決を出した。

　前述の、参議院議員の選挙において、法改正で合区を設定したのは、この判例等を受けて取られた救済措置であった。しかし、このことが各都道府県の民意を等しく国政に反映させるという憲法上の理念に反するのではないかという別の憲法問題を惹起した。そこで、さらにこの問題の発生も防ぐため、2018年7月18日、参議院議員の定数を6つ増やす法案が、与党の賛成多数で可決、成立した。埼玉

of the House of Representatives held in October 2017, the coalition government won 313 seats (more than two-thirds of the 465 set by the revised Election Law).

Like the House of Representatives, the House of Councilors also consists of members elected by and representative of the people. Although House of Councilors elections are national elections held throughout the country, they are referred to as "ordinary elections," not "general elections," because they are not held for all members at one time but for half of the members once every three years (for a six-year term of office). The number of House of Councilors members is fixed at 242, with 146 being elected from local constituencies and 96 by proportional representation. One constituency is assigned to each of the 47 prefectures, and the election by proportional representation is from a single nationwide electoral district. However, according to the Revised Public Offices Election Law that came into force on June 19, 2016, Tottori Prefecture and Shimane Prefecture, and Tokushima Prefecture and Kochi Prefecture, were regarded as combined districts in the House of Councilors ordinary election held in July of the same year (a decrease of two districts, to 45, and an allocation of 2 to 12 representatives per district), so that in principle, it was possible for an exception to occur to the principle that there be representation from each prefecture. In this ordinary election of the House of Councilors, the coalition government of the LDP and New Komeito increased the number of seats it held by 11, giving it 146 seats.

As the members of both Houses are representatives of the people, a fair electoral system that accurately represents the interests of the all voters is essential (equality under the law; Article 14 of the Japanese Constitution). On this point, regarding the election of House of Representatives in December 2012, the Supreme Court has ruled it to be unconstitutional for the electoral weight per vote to differ by a factor of twice or more in the case of the House of Representatives and of five times or more in the case of the House of Councilors. The fact that the House of Representatives is currently not in compliance with this standard is a major fairness issue.

In the above election of the House of Councilors, the setting up of the combined districts by the revision of the law was a remedial action in response to the court decisions. However, it raised another constitutional issue as to whether it was contrary to the constitutional philosophy of having the will of the people of each prefecture equally represented in the national administration. On July 18, 2018, a bill to increase the number of seats in the House of Councilors by six was approved by a

選挙区の定数を6から8に増やし（これで格差は3倍未満になる見通し）、比例代表定数を96から100に増加するというものである。比例代表に特定枠を設け、合区の対象県から出馬できなかった候補者をその特定枠から選出して救済しようというもの。1票の格差是正と関係ない比例代表の枠を広げ、人口減少社会の中で、定数を増加することに合理性はなく、与党からも反対が出た。

d）治安・警察庁・海上保安庁
1）警察庁

警察の組織は、内閣府の外局である国家公安委員会の下に警察庁があり、警察庁の指揮監督の下に各都道府県の警察本部（警察官総数259,800人：2018年）がある。

そのうち、東京都の本部だけは警視庁と呼ばれ別格の大きな組織である（総数43,500人）。これは東京には、皇居、各国大使館、国会、総理大臣官邸、最高裁判所、各中央官庁などの国の重要機関があること、また主要民間企業の本社、NHKや主要新聞・放送局・通信社の本部が集中しているからである。各都道府県警察本部の下に各地方の警察署がある。

警察は英語・フランス語でPoliceというが、この語源はラテン語で、国家を意味する。警察は、社会の安全や治安を維持し、秩序を守るための国の行政機関である。警察には〈1〉犯罪の予防、〈2〉発生した犯罪の捜査、〈3〉テロ対策、などの治安維持の主要な3つの役割がある。

日本では、水と安全はタダであるという観念が長年続いていた。強盗事件の対人口被害者率で日本はOECD加盟国平均の5分の1で、「日本の治安の良さは世界一」という定評がある。2017年の日本の犯罪件数（警察が把握した件数）は前年比8.1％減の91.5万件で、その74％が窃盗、4％が詐欺・横領・偽造・収賄などの知能犯、6％が暴行・傷害・脅迫などの粗

majority of the ruling party in order to prevent this problem occurring. The number of the Saitama electoral district's seats was increased by two, to eight (which is expected to reduce the vote-value disparity to under three), and the 96 proportional representation seats were increased to 100. For the proportional representation system, a special quota has been set up to help candidates get elected who were unable to run after their prefectural districts were combined. This drew opposition even from within the ruling party, since it does not make sense to make moves to broaden proportional representation within a shrinking population that are not related to correcting disparities in the value of a vote.

d) Public Safety, National Police Agency, and Japan Coast Guard
1) National Police Agency

Organizationally, the National Police Agency comes under the National Public Safety Commission, an extra-ministerial bureau of the Cabinet Office, and is responsible for directing and supervising the prefectural police departments (total number of police officers: 259,800 in 2018).

The department in Tokyo, called the Metropolitan Police Department, is much larger than the others, having 43,500 officers. This is because many important national and other institutions are located in Tokyo, including the Imperial Palace, foreign embassies, National Diet, Official Residence of the Prime Minister, the Supreme Court and the central government agencies, as well as the headquarters of major private enterprises, NHK, and the headquarters of major newspapers, broadcasting and communications companies. Each Prefectural Police Headquarters has numerous local police stations under it.

Keisatsu, known in English and French as the "police" (from the Latin word for "government"), is a national administrative body for maintaining public safety and keeping social order. The three main safety preservation duties of the police are <1> crime prevention, <2> criminal investigation, and <3> protection against terrorism.

The Japanese have long counted public safety, along with water, among the free of charge things in life. The fact that the ratio of robbery victims versus population in Japan is one-fifth the average among OECD members lends support to its reputation as the world's safest country. According to figures compiled by the police, the number of crimes in Japan in 2017 was about 915,000, a decrease of 8.1% compared to the preceding year. Larceny offences accounted for 74%,

暴犯、殺人・強盗など凶悪犯は0.5％、その他刑法犯15.5％であった。

　日本の警察の特徴は、警察署の下に置かれる「交番」と呼ばれる市民に身近な警官派出所があることである。交番は全国におよそ6,600箇所（東京都内に1,200箇所）ある。交番（KOBAN）は国際語として世界に通用している。日本の交番は地域のパトロール、交通整理などのほかに、幼児・生徒・両親の交通安全指導、地域の防犯・防災ネットワークの援助、落し物管理、迷子やはぐれたペットの保護、さらには住宅・事業所の戸別訪問など、防犯対策の助言や異常有無の確認を行うなど非常にきめの細かい住民サービスを行っている。

　交番のシステムは最近ではタイ、シンガポール、ハワイ、ブラジル、ホンジュラスなどでも採用され、KOBANで通用している。

2）海上保安庁

　海上保安庁は、1948年5月に発足し、国民が安心して海を利用し様々な恩恵を享受できるよう、関係国との連携・協力関係の強化を図りつつ、海上における犯罪の取締り、領海警備、海難救助、環境保全、災害対応、海洋調査、船舶の航行安全などの活動を行っており海上の警察、消防機能を担っている。

　日本の領土面積は約38万km^{2}と世界62位であるが、領海を含めた排他的経済水域（EEZ）の面積は領土面積の12倍、約447万km^{2}と広大である。

　2018年度の海上保安庁の人員は約1万4,000人、予算は約2,400億円、巡視船・巡視艇など455隻、航空機26機、ヘリコプター48機（2018年3月）を保有している。

　同時に、尖閣諸島周辺海域における中国公船及び中国漁船の活動状況の活発化に伴い、大幅に組織・装備・機能を充実させている。

fraud, embezzlement, forgery, bribery, and other white-collar offences for 4%, felonious and violent offences, including assault, inflicting bodily injury, intimidation for 6%, murder, robbery for 0.5%, and other criminal offenses for 15.5%.

A unique aspect of the Japanese police system is the ubiquitous citizen-friendly police department substation known as the *koban*. There are around 6,600 kobans nationwide, about 1,200 of them in Tokyo. The term koban (usually written KOBAN) has gained international recognition. Typical koban functions include neighborhood patrols and traffic direction. However, aside from these activities, the koban also provides local citizens with a long list of other of services. For example, a koban operates as a center that offers traffic safety instruction to preschool and school children and their parents, helps local citizens to organize and operate community crime and disaster prevention networks, serves as a lost-and-found office, takes custody of lost children and pets, and visits local homes and businesses door to door to offer security advice and survey community concerns.

Police boxes modeled after those in Japan, and going by the name of "KOBAN," have recently appeared in Thailand, Singapore, Hawaii, Brazil, Honduras and other regions.

2) Japan Coast Guard

The Japan Coast Guard (JCG; formerly the Maritime Safety Agency) was established in May 1948. It endeavors to strengthen liaison and cooperation with neighboring countries so that the Japanese people can feel secure as they enjoy the many blessings of the sea. Its activities encompass maritime and firefighting functions, including as they do maritime crime control, protection of territorial waters, sea rescue, environmental preservation, disaster management, oceanographic observation, and navigation safety assurance.

Although Japan ranks sixty-second in the world in terms of the area of its territorial land (about 380 thousand square kilometers), the area of its exclusive economic zone (EEZ), including the territorial area, is 12 times larger, at about 4.47 million square kilometers.

The JCG has around 14,000 personnel, a budget of 240 billion yen, 455 patrol vessels, patrol craft and other watercraft, 26 fixed-wing aircraft, and 48 helicopters (as of March 2018).

With the increasing activities of Chinese public ships and fishing vessels in the waters surrounding the Senkaku Islands, the JCG is greatly enhancing its organization, equipment and functions.

e）自衛隊

日本は、第二次世界大戦終了時に戦勝国によって全陸海軍が解体された。その後、朝鮮戦争を機に1954年、自衛隊が設立された。

自衛隊は、「わが国の平和と独立を守り、国の安全を保つため、直接侵略および間接侵略に対し、わが国を防衛することを主たる任務とし、必要に応じ公共の秩序の維持に当る」（自衛隊法第3条）ものとして設置されている。

自衛隊の最高指揮官は内閣総理大臣であり、通常の業務は防衛大臣があたり、文民統制を厳格に維持している。

我が国防衛政策の基本は、日米同盟を基軸に東アジア地域の平和と安定に貢献する、憲法の精神を守り専守防衛の姿勢を堅持することを根幹にしている。北朝鮮が2017年に水素爆弾や大陸間弾道弾の開発に成功し、このことが我が国をはじめ近隣諸国に対し脅威をもたらしている。さらに中国が急速に軍事力を強化させ、東・南シナ海へ積極的な進出を行っていることは、近隣諸国に対し第二次世界大戦後、最も深刻な安全保障、防衛上の危機感を与えている。国際協調・外交交渉による解決が望まれるところであるが、このような状況の中で、日米同盟関係、自衛隊の実力の真価が問われている。

自衛隊は、防衛大臣の指揮下にあり、陸上自衛隊・海上自衛隊・航空自衛隊で構成されている。自衛隊員はすべて志願制度によっている。2018年3月末の実員は、陸上自衛隊・統合幕僚本部約14.2万人、海上自衛隊約4.2万人、航空自衛隊約4.3万人の合計約22.7万人であり、2018年の防衛省の予算は、5兆1,900億円である。主要装備は、2018年3月末で、陸上自衛隊：戦車・装甲車等約1,630両、大型火砲500両、ヘリコプター等約389機、地対艦ミサイル5個連隊、地対空ミサイル5群、海上自衛隊：艦艇134隻・48万トン、対潜哨戒機等170機、航空自衛隊：作戦用航空機479機、地対空誘導弾6群等である。そのほかに核弾道ミサイルの脅威への対応としてイージス艦6隻を保有している。新規の主要事業として、陸上配備型イージス・システム（イージス・アショア）2基の整備に着手した。

e) Self-Defense Forces

At the end of the Second World War all of Japan's military forces were demobilized by the victorious countries. Today's Self-Defense Forces were established in 1954 following the end of the Korean War.

The reason for establishing the Self-Defense Forces is stated in Article 3 of the Self-Defense Forces Law as follows: "The main mission of the Self-Defense Forces shall be to protect the peace and independence and preserve the safety of Japan by defending it against direct and indirect attack and, when necessary, to help preserve public order."

The Self-Defense Forces are kept strictly under civilian control by giving the Prime Minister the highest right of command of the Self-Defense Forces and placing the actual day-to-day affairs of the Forces under the control of the Minister of Defense.

Fundamental Japan's national defense policy regards Japan-U.S. Security Alliance at its base maintaining peace and stability of Far East, and to be consistent with the spirit of the Constitution by maintaining exclusively defense oriented policy. In 2017 North Korea succeeded in developing a hydrogen bomb and continental ballistic missiles, posing a threat to Japan and neighboring countries. Furthermore, China is rapidly strengthening its military capabilities and actively entering the East and South China Sea, giving neighboring countries their most serious sense of security and defense crisis since the Second World War. While it is desirable to achieve a solution through international cooperation and diplomatic negotiation, the situation is calling into question the Japan-U.S. Security Alliance and the true value of the Self-Defense Forces' capabilities.

The Self-Defense Forces are divided into three branches: the Ground Self-Defense Force, the Maritime Self-Defense Force, and the Air Self-Defense Force, under the command of the Minister of Defense. All members are volunteers. As of the end of March 2018, the number of members actually in service totaled 227,000, with 142,000 in the Ground Self-Defense Force and Joint Staff Headquarters, 42,000 in the Maritime Self-Defense Force, and 43,000 in the Air Self-Defense Force. The Ministry of Defense budget for 2018 was 5.19 trillion yen. As principal weaponry, as of the end of March 2018, the Ground Self-Defense Force has about 1,630 tanks and armored cars, 500 pieces of heavy artillery, 389 helicopters and other aircraft, five anti-ship missile regiments and five anti-aircraft groups, the Maritime Self-Defense Force has 134 battleships (480,000 tonnes) and 170 antisubmarine patrol planes and other aircraft, and the Air Self-Defense Force has 479 combat and other aircraft. Japan also has six Aegis cruisers for defense

(3) 外交

a) 日本外交の基本方針

　　日本は1945年の第二次大戦終結後、連合軍による占領を経て、1951年世界主要国との講和条約を結び、1956年国際連合に加盟して国際社会復帰を果たした。以来日本は平和憲法の理念（日本国憲法第9条は戦争の永久放棄をうたっている）の下に専守防衛の基本姿勢に徹し、外交三原則を守るとともに、唯一の原爆被爆国として非核三原則を堅持している。

　　（外交三原則）
　　この原則は次のように定められている（外務省「外交青書」第1号 1957年）。
　　〈1〉国際連合の目的に沿って、国際社会の平和と安全に寄与する。
　　〈2〉自由、民主主義、基本的人権、不平等の是正、市場経済、多角的自由貿易体制などの普遍的価値を共有する自由主義諸国とともに行動し、自らの安全と繁栄を求める。
　　〈3〉アジア・太平洋地域の一国として、同地域の平和と安全に貢献する。
　　（非核三原則）
　　核兵器を〈1〉持たず、〈2〉作らず、〈3〉持ち込ませずという核に対する三原則を打ち出している。この原則は、1950年代から1980年代に日本の歴代内閣で標榜されてきた国是であるが、1972年10月9日に、当時の佐藤栄作内閣が閣議決定した。なお、これにより1974年に佐藤栄作首相はノーベル平和賞を受賞した。
　　戦後70年以上経過し、冷戦終結からも25年以上経過したが、今日の国際社会は、依然さまざまな問題に直面している。例えば、日本政府は、核廃絶に真剣に取り組み、2017年10月29日に日本が提出した核廃絶決議が144カ国の賛成を得て国連で決議されたが、他方で、アメリカの

against the threat of ballistic missile attacks. As part of a major new project, work has started on the installation of two ground-based Aegis (Aegis Ashore) ballistic missile defense stations.

(3) Diplomacy

a) Basic Principles of Japanese Diplomacy

Following the end of the Second World War in 1945, Japan went through a period of occupation by the Allied Forces. Its reemergence as a member of the international community started with the conclusion of a peace treaty with the world's leading countries in 1951 and was consummated when Japan became a member of the United Nations in 1956. Under the postwar "Peace Constitution" (Article 9 of the Constitution of Japan says that the Japanese people forever renounce war), Japan has consistently adhered to a basic stance of maintaining armed forces exclusively for defense and to three basic principles in its foreign relations. And as the only country ever to suffer an atomic attack, Japan is committed to the three nonnuclear principles.

(Three foreign policy principles)

These principles are stated as follows (Ministry of Foreign Affairs Diplomatic Bluebook No. 1, 1957).

<1> Contribute to the peace and security of the international community in accordance with the purpose of the United Nations.
<2> Work in concert with free nations that share such universal values as freedom, democracy, basic human rights, rectification of inequalities, market economy, and multilateral free trade, and pursue the security and prosperity of Japan itself.
<3> Contribute to Asian-Pacific peace and security as a member of the region.

(The three nonnuclear principles)

Three nuclear principles have been adopted: <1> not possessing or <2> not making nuclear weapons, and <3> not allowing their entry into Japan. This principle is a national policy that was advocated by successive Japanese cabinets from the 1950s to the 1980s, and on October 9, 1972, decided on by the Cabinet of Sato Eisaku. This led to Sato receiving the Nobel Peace Prize in 1974.

More than seventy years have passed since the end of the Second World War and more than twenty-five since the end of the Cold War, but the world still continues to encounter various problems. For its part, the Japanese government seriously addressed the abolition of nuclear weapons, and a resolution to ban nuclear weapons submitted by

核の傘下にある日本は依然として「核兵器禁止条約」には参加していない。

b）地域別の外交
1）北アメリカ

アメリカは日本と自由、人権、市場経済などの基本的価値および戦略的利益を共有する唯一の重要な同盟国である。日米安全保障体制を基軸とする日米同盟は、戦後70年にわたり日本の外交・安全保障の基盤となっている。

戦後、日本はアメリカとの安全保障体制のもと経済復興に専念し、廃墟の中から立ち上って世界の先進国の一員に列するまでになった。2つの国が互いに国を挙げて激闘した後に、1951年、一転して日米安全保障条約を締結し、さらに1960年には緊密な友好同盟関係（日本国とアメリカ合衆国との間の相互協力及び安全保障条約）を結び、その関係が70年近くにおよぶという事実は歴史的にきわめて稀な事例である。

同時にこの同盟が、日本と極東の平和と繁栄を通じて広くはアジア、世界の安定と繁栄にも大きな役割を果たしたことは歴史的事実である。日米両国は安全保障のほか、政治・経済・文化などの幅広い分野において協調している。

ところが、2017年1月からオバマ前大統領から引き継いだトランプ大統領は、アメリカの国益を優先する対外政策を内外に標榜している（アメリカ・ファースト）。2018年3月、アメリカの2017年の貿易収支が大幅な赤字となったことを理由に、トランプ大統領は、中国、日本等、赤字をもたらしている主要相手国に対し、当該国からの製品の輸入がアメリカにとって「脅威」であると認定し（通商拡大法232条）、自国の安全保障を理由に鉄鋼製品に対して25％、アルミ製品に対して10％の関税をかける措置をとった。これに対し中国は直ちに、アメリカ産のワイン、ナッツ類、豚肉等128品目に追加関税を課した。さらにアメリカは、翌4月に、中国がアメリカの知的財産を侵

Japan on October 29, 2017 was approved in the United Nations by 144 countries. On the other hand, Japan, which remains under the nuclear umbrella of the U.S., has not joined the Treaty on the Prohibition of Nuclear Weapons.

b) Country-Specific Diplomacy
1) North America

The U.S. is a unique ally especially important to Japan for being a country with which Japan shares not only such basic values as freedom, respect for human rights, and market economy but also common strategic interests. The Japan-U.S. Security Alliance, centered on security arrangements between Japan and the U.S., has been the foundation of Japanese diplomacy and security in over 70 years since the end of the Second World War.

Under the protection of the security arrangement with the U.S., postwar Japan concentrated on rebuilding its economy and rose from the ashes of the war to become one of the world's most economically and industrially advanced countries. With the signing of the Treaty of Mutual Cooperation and Security between Japan and the U.S. in 1951 (and again in 1960), Japan and the U.S. changed from bitter enemies to close friends who continue to maintain their friendship nearly seventy years on, which is a historically rare achievement.

By helping to bring peace and prosperity to Japan and the Far East, the Alliance has also played a major, historically significant role in promoting stability and prosperity broadly throughout Asia and worldwide. Collaboration between Japan and the U.S. is by no means limited to security arrangements but extends to a wide range of fields including politics, business and culture.

However, President Trump, who took over from President Obama in January 2017, is advocating a domestic and foreign policy of giving priority to the national interests of the U.S. ("America First"). In March 2018, citing the fact that the U.S. posted a major deficit in its international trade balance in 2017, President Trump announced that U.S. would impose 25% tariff on steel products and 10% tariff on aluminum products for security reasons and recognized importing products from major trading countries such as China and Japan are "threats" to the U.S. (under Article 232 of the Trade Expansion Act). China, for its part, immediately imposed additional tariffs on 128 items, including American wine, nuts, and pork. In addition, the U.S. cited Article 301 of the Trade Act in announcing that from April 2019 it would impose sanction duties on 1,300 items such as industrial robots, aircraft, and passenger cars,

害しているとの理由で、産業用ロボット、航空機、乗用車等1,300品目にも及ぶ製品に対し制裁関税を課す（通商法301条）との発表を行った。これに対して中国は、アメリカ産の大豆、牛肉、自動車、航空機等に対して追加の関税を課すと発表した。今後のアメリカと日本との経済上の協調関係がどうなるか懸念が生じている。

2）アジア・大洋州地域

21世紀に入り、世界は大きな変動の流れの中にある。その中でとくにアジア・大洋州地域はますます存在感を増し、世界の成長の主要なけん引役として注目されている。アメリカも引き続きアジア・大洋州地域を重視する政策を推し進めている。

ASEAN（東南アジア諸国連合）、中国、インドのGDP（名目国内総生産）の合計は、過去10年間に4倍に増えている（世界平均は2倍）。この地域では、APEC、RCEP、FTAAP、による複数国間での経済協力交渉が進んでいる。

特に中国は、1978年から経済の改革開放政策を進め、安くて豊富な労働力をもとに積極的に外国の企業・工場を誘致し資本や技術を取り込み始めた。さらに2001年には悲願のWTO（世界貿易機構）加入を認められ、それ以降の経済分野での躍進は目を見張るものがある。国内の石炭・鉄鉱石などの鉱物資源採掘を増加させるだけではなく、海外からも大量の原材料を調達し、鉄鋼・機械・化学・繊維などの分野で工業製品の生産量を伸ばし（例えば、世界鉄鋼協会の統計によると、2017年の世界鉄鋼生産量は約16億トンであるが、これは2000年当時の生産量約8億トンの倍に当たる。その増加した分のほとんどは、中国の生産によるものである）、21世紀における「世界の工場」と呼ばれるようになった。しかし、近年では鉄鋼製品をはじめとして過剰生産された工業製品が海外市場に溢れ深刻な貿易摩擦問題を引き起こしている。国内においては労働力が逼迫し、労働者の賃金は上昇を続けているため工場の統廃合による生産調整の段階になっている。当初は安くて豊富な労働力を求めた外国の企業には、中国は魅力のないものとなり、より安い労働力の調達先はベトナム・ミャンマー・バングラデシュなどへ移りつつある。

そのような状況の中で、習近平国家主席は、2013

citing as the reason China's infringement of U.S. intellectual property. In response, China announced that it would impose additional tariffs on soybeans, beef, automobiles, and aircraft from the U.S. Concerns have arisen as to future economic cooperation between the U.S. and Japan.

2) Asia and Oceania

The world has been marked by momentous changes since entering the twenty-first century. Amidst this, the rising presence of Asia and Oceania, and their emergence as key drivers of world economic growth, have been particularly striking. The U.S., for example, has been pushing forward with strategies focused on the Asian-Oceanian region.

The total of the GDPs (gross domestic product) of the ASEAN (Association of South-East Asian Nations) members, China and India has quadrupled over the past 10 years (twice the world average growth rate). APEC, RCEP and their moves toward realization of FTAAP are advancing economic cooperation negotiations in this region.

Since 1978 China has promoted an economic policy of reform and opening, actively attracting foreign companies and factories based on its cheap and abundant labor force and bringing in capital and technology. In 2001, China was able to join the World Trade Organization (WTO), something China had long wished for, and its economic growth became truly remarkable. As well as increasing its mining of domestic resources such as coal and iron ore, China imported large amounts of raw materials and increased the production of industrial products in such areas as steel, machinery, chemistry, and textiles. According to the statistics of the World Steel Association, world steel production in 2017 was about 1.6 billion tons, double the production volume of about 800 million tons from 2000, and most of that increase has been due to China's production. China became to be called "the factory of the world" in the 21st century. In recent years, however, overproduction has led to overseas markets being flooded by steel and other industrial products, causing serious trade friction problems. Due to the tight domestic labor market, the wages of workers are continuing to rise, in response to which production adjustments are being made by the consolidation and closing of factories. For foreign companies that initially sought cheap, abundant labor, China is becoming unattractive and the search for cheaper labor is moving to Vietnam, Myanmar, Bangladesh and other countries.

In September 2013, President Xi Jinping announced the Belt and

年9月「一帯一路」構想（ユーラシア各国と協力しシルクロード経済ベルトを建設する構想）を発表した。中央アジア・西アジア諸国に加えて東南アジア・南アジア諸国をも含む各国との経済協力構想を明らかにするとともに、アメリカと日本が主導するアジア開発銀行（ADB）に対抗して「アジアインフラ投資銀行（AIIB）」を設立し、豊富な資金力を背景に、中国の周辺諸国においてインフラ整備を支援して中国企業の進出の足がかりとし、政治的、軍事的にも存在感を高めようとしている。

他方、中国国内では2017年7月、国家政権転覆を先導した罪で服役中であったノーベル平和賞受賞者の劉暁波（リュウギョウハ）氏が死亡した。すると中国当局による劉氏および遺族に対する処遇をめぐり、各国政府やメディア等各界から憂慮の声が相次いだ。当局による活動家や少数民族等に対する締め付けは引き続き強化されていて、国際社会からは中国の人権状況を憂慮する声が上がっている。

今では世界第2位の経済大国となり、人口は14億人超を抱え、また強大な軍事力を有することとなった中国は、近年、軍事拠点・資源確保の両面から南シナ海での強引な海洋進出が目立ち、海洋周辺諸国をはじめとして世界各国から警戒と脅威の目で見られている。

- ASEAN（Association of South-East Asian Nations 東南アジア諸国連合）：東南アジア10カ国（インドネシア、シンガポール、タイ、フィリピン、マレーシア、ブルネイ、ベトナム、ミャンマー、ラオス、カンボジア）の経済、社会、政治、安全保障、文化の協力機構。人口6億、本部はジャカルタ。
- APEC（Asia-Pacific Economic Corporation アジア太平洋経済協力）：環太平洋地域の多国間経済協力のための非公式フォーラム。日本、アメリカ、カナダ、オーストラリアなど12カ国で発足、のちに中国、メキシコ、ロシアなどが参加して21カ国、環太平洋地域の持続的発展を目ざす。
- RCEP（Regional Comprehensive Economic Partnership 東アジア地区包括経済連携）：ASEANを基盤とする枠組み。ASEANが日本、中国、インド、オーストラリアと個別に組んで

Road Initiative, a proposal involving cooperation with Eurasian countries to build an economic belt along the Silk Road. As well as describing an economic cooperation concept that encompasses Central Asia and West Asian countries and Southeast Asia and South Asian countries, the proposal included the establishment of the Asia Infrastructure Investment Bank (AIIB), to counter the Asian Development Bank (ADB) led by the U.S. and Japan. Abundant financial resources would be used to support infrastructure development in China's neighboring countries, giving Chinese enterprises a foothold in those areas as part of China's endeavors to raise its political and military presence in the region.

In July 2017, Liu Xiaobo, a Nobel Peace Prize laureate, died in prison in China. He had been imprisoned on charges of inciting subversion of the state. His death led to anxiety from other governments and the media of the Chinese authorities for the way they had treated Liu and his bereaved family members. As the authorities strengthened their clampdown on activists and ethnic minorities, the international community announced its concerns at the state of human rights in China.

China currently has second largest economic power in the world, a population of more than 1.4 billion, and has a powerful military power. In recent years, as China has made prominent moves into the South China Sea in a blatant push to establish military bases and secure mineral resources, it is seen as a threat and countries around the world are keeping an eye on China.

- ASEAN (Association of South-East Asian Nations) is a regional association for economic, social, political, security, and cultural cooperation among ten South-East Asian countries (Indonesia, Singapore, Thailand, Philippines, Malaysia, Brunei, Vietnam, Myanmar, Laos, and Cambodia). The combined population of the member countries are 600 million. ASEAN's headquarter is in Jakarta.

- APEC (Asia-Pacific Economic Cooperation) is an informal forum for multinational economic cooperation in the Pacific Rim region. It was launched by twelve countries including Japan, the U.S., Canada, and Australia, and later joined by China, Mexico, Russia and a number of other countries. APEC currently has 21 participants striving to realize sustainable development around the Pacific.

- RCEP (Regional Comprehensive Economic Partnership) is a framework based on ASEAN. Through the framework, ASEAN aims a high-level cooperation by unifying FTAs (free trade agreements) individually organized with Japan, China, India, and Australia. In

いた FTA を一本化して高レベルの連携を目ざす協定。2011 年 11 月、日本と中国は、共同で ASEAN に対し、ASEAN + 3 （日本、中国、韓国）にオーストラリア、ニュージーランド、インドを加えた ASEAN + 6 の計 16 カ国で、経済連携協定の締結を提案し、翌年 11 月 ASEAN 側は交渉を開始することを宣言。2018 年 2 月、第 21 回の交渉会合が開かれた。
- FTAAP（Free Trade Area of Asia-Pacific　アジア太平洋自由貿易圏）：ASEAN + 3、TPP 諸国などの地域活動をさらに発展させたより包括的自由貿易協定。参加国 21。投資、サービス、電子取引、サプライチェーンの緊密化などにより貿易の円滑化を目ざす。しかし、RCEP の交渉が始まったことや、2013 年に日本が TTP 交渉に参加したこと、2017 年 1 月にアメリカが TPP からの離脱を表明したこともあり、各国の思惑も一致しておらず、さらにアメリカは 2 国間の自由貿易協定（FTA）を目論んでおり、関係が錯綜してまとまるかは不透明である。

3）アフリカ・中東地域

　北アフリカ・中東地域はヨーロッパ、サハラ以南のアフリカ、中央アジア、インドなどの南アジアを結び付けている地政学上の重要地点である。この地域は、石油、天然ガスなどのエネルギー資源を世界に供給する重要地域で、同時に国際通商上の主要な海上ルートでもある。輸入原油の 87％ を中東に依存する日本にとっては、ペルシャ湾・インド洋・マラッカ海峡・南シナ海にわたる「シーレーン」の安全確保は不可欠の条件である。

　2011 年から北アフリカ・中東を席巻したいわゆる「アラブの春」の変革によりいくつかの独裁政権が倒れ、新体制が構築されつつあるが、国内の宗教対立などで依然エジプトなど一部では混乱が続いている。特にシリアの内戦は深刻で、すでに死者 10 万人超を出しながら事態終息の見通しは立っていない。このような状況の中で、2014 年から 2015 年にかけてイラクとシリア両国の国境付近を中心に、イスラム過激派組織 IS（イスラミック・ステート）が出現し、武力行使、残虐なテロ行為等の猛威を振るい、挙句の果てに国家樹立を宣言した。その後この組織はアメリカ、ロシア

November 2011, Japan and China jointly proposed that ASEAN conclude an economic partnership agreement with 16 countries that include ASEAN Plus 3 (Japan, China, Korea) plus three additional countries (Australia, New Zealand, India) to form ASEAN Plus 6. In November 2012, ASEAN announced the launch of negotiations. The 21st round of negotiations was held in February 2018.

- FTAAP (Free Trade Area of Asia-Pacific) refers to a still more comprehensive free trade agreement for invigorating the regional activities of ASEAN Plus 3 and the TPP (Trans-Pacific Partnership) countries. There are 21 participating nations. The goal of FTAAP is to facilitate trade by, for example, cultivating closer ties in areas like investment, services, electronic trading, and supply chains. However, due partly to the fact that the RCEP negotiations have begun, Japan participated in the TTP negotiations in 2013, and in January 2017 the U.S. announced it was withdrawing from TPP, the expectations of each country are not in agreement. Furthermore, the U.S. is pursuing bilateral free trade agreements. Thus, the relationships are complicated and it is unclear whether they can be settled.

3) Africa and the Middle East

North Africa and the Middle East are located in a geopolitically important region that links Europe, Sub-Saharan Africa, Central Asia, and South Asian areas such as India. The region is an important supplier of energy resources, including oil and natural gas, to the world and is situated on a major maritime route for international commerce. The safety of the "sea lane" extending from the Persian Gulf, across the Indian Ocean, and through the Strait of Malacca to the South China Sea is indispensable for Japan, which imports 87% of its crude oil from the Middle East.

The transformation, called the Arab Spring, that swept through North Africa and the Middle East from 2011 brought down despotic governments and marked the start of political reform in a number of countries. Still, some countries remain in a state of unrest, owing to internal religious conflicts, as in Egypt, and other causes. The civil war in Syria has been especially fierce, with the death toll already over 100 thousand and no end in sight. The Islamic extremist organization IS (Islamic State) emerged from 2014 to 2015, mainly around the border between Iraq and Syria, and by using force and violence and cruel terrorist acts, declared the establishment of their nation. By October 2017, IS had been almost wiped out by counter-attacks launched by an international

の支援を含む国際包囲網の反撃を受けて、2017年10月にはほぼ一掃されている。また、アメリカはシリアのアサド政権が反体制派との戦闘で「化学兵器」を使用したと断定し、2017年4月には単独で、2018年4月にはイギリス・フランスとともに、巡航ミサイルマホークをシリアの軍事関連施設に発射した。

　これらの紛争と混乱により2018年7月現在、シリア難民は約490万人発生し、その多くはヨーロッパに逃れ、各国で深刻な政治問題を引き起こしている。

　アフリカ全体の発展に関しては、日本は1993年から5年ごとに「アフリカ開発会議」を日本で開催している。日本は第1回から一貫して、アフリカが援助対象にとどまらず、自助努力により持続的に成長し、やがては「世界の成長の原動力となる」という目標をこれら諸国と共有している。2017年8月に、モザンビークの首都マプトで、アフリカ諸国51カ国が参加し、河野外務大臣が出席してアフリカ開発会議閣僚会合が行われた。

4）欧州・EU（欧州連合）およびイギリスのEUからの離脱交渉

　EU28カ国を含む欧州は、日本にとって自由と民主主義、人権、法の支配、市場経済などの基本的価値を共有し、また経済、安全保障、科学、学術、文化、芸術などにおいても国際社会で主導的役割を果たす重要なパートナーである。

　近年EUは、ギリシャはじめ複数の加盟国の財政危機救済のための巨額な財政支出で全体の活力が弱まり、ドイツ、フランスなどへの負荷が増してきた。現在、EUは域内の経済・金融の統合により活力の再生に懸命に取り組んでいる。

　日本とEUの経済規模は大変大きく、合わせると全世界のGDPの4分の1を占めるとともに、貿易では世界の5分の1以上に達する。日本とEUが画期的な自由貿易協定を締結すれば、EUの対日輸出が32.7％拡大し、日本からEUへの輸出も23.5％増加するという試算がある。このような両者の基本認識に基づき、2013年3月25日に、当時の欧州委員会委員長、欧州理事会常任議長と安倍総理大臣との間で協定の交渉が開始され、2017年7月6日、日本とEUとは経済連携協定（EPA）と戦略的パートナーシップ（SPA）の政治的大枠合意に達した。EPAについては2017年12

encirclement force that included the support of the U.S. and Russia. The U.S. asserted that Syria's Assad regime used "chemical weapons" in combat against anti-government fighters, and in April 2017, acting alone, and in April 2018, acting with the United Kingdom (UK) and France, launched Tomahawk cruise missiles at facilities in Syria having a connection with military operations.

These conflicts and chaotic conditions have resulted in some 4.9 million Syrian refugees as of July 2018. Many of these refugees have fled to Europe, causing serious political problems there.

Japan has sought to promote development throughout Africa by hosting the Tokyo International Conference on African Development once every five years since 1993. From the very first conference, Japan's approach has been to go beyond simply assisting the African countries to sharing a vision aimed at achieving sustainable growth through self-help and Africa becoming an "engine of global growth." In August 2017, 51 African countries participated in the conference held in Maputo, the capital of Mozambique. Japan's Minister for Foreign Affairs, Kono Taro, attended the ministerial meeting of the conference.

4) Europe and the EU (European Union), and Britain's Exit Negotiation from the EU

Japan and Europe (including but not limited to the 28 countries of the EU) share fundamental values such as freedom, democracy, respect for human rights, rule of law, and market economy. Moreover, Europe is a partner playing a leading role in the international community in areas such as economy, security, science, academic field, culture, and art.

In recent years, the EU's overall vitality has been sapped by huge government expenditures for rescuing Greece and other member countries from their debt crises, with much of the burden falling on Germany and France. The EU is making an all-out effort to rebuild its strength through economic and financial integration within the Eurozone.

The economic scale of Japan and the EU is very large; together they account for a quarter of the world's GDP, and more than one-fifth of global trade. It has been calculated that if Japan and the EU were to conclude what would be an epochal free trade agreement, EU exports to Japan would increase by 32.7%, and exports from Japan to the EU could increase by 23.5%. Based on the fundamental recognition about this fact by both sides, on March 25, 2013, negotiations began on an agreement between the chairman of the European Commission, the President of the European Council, and Prime Minister Abe. On July 6, 2017, Japan and the EU reached an accord on a major political framework with an Economic Partnership Agreement (EPA) and a Strategic Partnership

月8日に交渉が妥結し2019年3月末に発効した。

　ところで、2016年6月23日にイギリスで、EUから脱退するか否かを問う国民投票が実施され、大方の予想に反して、僅差で脱退（Brexitという）が決まった。その結果、イギリスは2019年10月末をもってEUから離脱することになった。イギリスのEUからの離脱はEU域内だけでなく、日本にも政治・経済・社会の領域に大きな影響を及ぼすことになる。世界は、本当に脱退するのかを含め離脱条件交渉の行方を重大な関心をもって見守っている。

5）中南米
　中南米諸国の発展は目覚しいものがあるとともに、民主主義が育ちつつあり、経済、地球環境などの国際会議の舞台にもなり、国連での発言力が高まっている。

　またこの地域は、鉄鉱石、レアメタルなどの鉱物資源、食料などの重要な供給元であると同時に巨大市場としても期待される。日本は、資金・技術協力、インフラ整備やEPA（経済連携協定）・投資協定などによる進出日本企業の活動支援などにより、持続的な経済発展に協力するとともに、日本への資源・食糧供給に努めている。

　なお、地上デジタルテレビ放送の日本方式（移動体向けや災害時の緊急警報放送機能が可能）が中南米14カ国で採用されることが決定した（2017年1月現在）。

6）ロシア、中央アジア・コーカサス諸国
　ⅰ）ロシア
　　　日本政府はアジア・太平洋の重要性の増大と戦略環境の変化の中で、日本の国益のためにロシアとの協力関係が重要であるとの認識に立って首相・外相はじめ様々なレベルでの交流を行っている。ロシアもエネルギー輸出戦略の観点から、経済、外交の重点をアジア・太平洋地域に移しつつある。現下の日本のロシアとの重要懸案事項は、

Agreement (SPA). It was reported that a compromise agreement on the EPA was reached on December 8, 2017, which was effected at the end of March 2019.

On June 23, 2016, a referendum was held in the UK on whether to withdraw from the EU. Contrary to expectations, withdrawal ("Brexit") was decided by a slim majority. As a result, the UK is set to leave the EU at the end of October 2019. The withdrawal of the UK from the EU will have a major impact not only within the EU region but also to Japan's politics, economy, and society. The world is watching with the utmost interest concerning the direction of the negotiated withdrawal conditions, and whether the withdrawal actually takes place.

5) Central and South America

Central and South America is a rapidly developing region making noticeable strides toward stable democracy. Today, it is a frequent venue for international conferences on economic and environmental issues and other topics of global interest. This has helped to give the region a stronger voice in the United Nations.

Central and South America has drawn increasing attention as a supplier of iron ore, rare metals and other vital mineral resources, as well as food, and is also viewed as a huge and promising market. Japan is pushing forward with financial and technical cooperation, infrastructure initiatives, EPAs (Economic Partnership Agreements), investment agreements and other measures aimed at creating a better business environment for Japanese businesses active in the region. These efforts are aimed at enabling the region to achieve sustainable economic development, while also securing a source of resources and food supplies for Japan.

Up to January 2017, fourteen countries in Central and South America had decided to adopt the Japanese format for digital terrestrial TV broadcasting (with mobile user and emergency warning broadcast capability).

6) Russia, Central Asia, and the Caucasus

i) Russia

Against the backdrop of the increasing significance and strategic environment of the Asia-Pacific region, the Japanese Government considers cooperation with Russia as important to Japan's national interest. In this light, exchanges with Russia are being conducted at various levels, including summit meetings and foreign ministers' meetings. As one aspect of its energy export strategy, Russia is steadily shifting its economic and diplomatic focus to the Asia-Pacific region. The main

北方領土問題の解決と平和条約の締結、エネルギーの安全保障問題である。

　2016年12月、ロシアのプーチン大統領が訪日し、日ロ首脳会談が行われた。その結果、北方4島における共同経済活動を行うための協議を開始すること、また、元島民による墓参などのための手続きを改善することで一致した。

　ロシアと欧米諸国との間では、ウクライナ情勢（2014年3月のロシア軍によるクリミア併合）、ロシアによるアメリカ、ドイツ、フランス等の国政選挙への介入疑惑（2016～2017年）、シリアのアサド政権が反体制派との戦闘で「化学兵器」使用したと称して、これに対しミサイル攻撃等を行ったアメリカ、イギリス、フランスに対して、アサド政権を擁護するロシアが反発（2018年）、などの対立関係が続き、ロシアは孤立化する方向に進んでいるように見える。

　他方、中国とは、ユーラシア経済同盟と「一帯一路」構想の接合を進めるとともに、2度の合同軍事演習を実施するなど、緊密な関係を維持している。

ⅱ）中央アジア・コーカサス諸国

　日本は2012年、この地域の諸国との外交関係樹立20周年に当たり、「中央アジア＋日本」外相会議はじめ様々な要人交流を通じてさらなる関係強化を進めている。

　特にこの地域は、アジア、欧州、中東、ロシアを結ぶ地政学上のかなめの地点で、アフガニスタンの安定化、テロ・麻薬・武器の拡散防止など、国際社会の重要課題に取り組むための拠点として注目されている。

　中国は、この地域の諸国を「一帯一路」構想に組み込み、豊富な資金力を背景に、中国主導の国際秩序を構築する野心的な試みを推進している。中国からの投融資を受けて貨物の集積基地、港湾設備等に莫大な投資をした国もある。例えばインド洋に面するスリランカでは中国からの投融資を受けて、南部のハンバントタ港を大々的に整備し港湾施設を設置した。しかし、目論見通りに稼働率が上がらないため、中国からの投融資に対する

pending issues between Japan and Russia are resolution of the Northern Territories problem, conclusion of a peace treaty, and energy security concerns.

In December 2016, Russian President Vladimir Putin visited Japan for a Japan-Russia summit meeting, at which it was agreed to start negotiations on conducting joint economic activities in the four islands of the Northern Territories, and to improve procedures for allowing former residents of the islands to return to visit family graves.

Russia is perceived as conflicting with the U.S. and EU countries, moving towards a direction that is isolating it from the West due to confrontations over a number of issues, including the Ukraine situation (the annexation of Crimea by the Russian military in March 2014), suspicions of Russian interference in national elections in the U.S., Germany, France and other countries (2016–2017), and in Syria, Russia's defense of the Assad regime over accusations that the regime had used chemical weapons against anti-government forces, leading to missile strikes against the regime by the U.S., the UK, and France (2018).

At the same time, with China promoting the joining of a Eurasian economic alliance as part of its Belt and Road Initiative, Russia is maintaining its close relationship with China such as by carrying out two joint military exercises.

ii) Central Asia and the Caucasus

As 2012 marked the 20th anniversary of diplomatic relations with the countries of these regions, Japan used the occasion to establish further stronger ties with them through a "Central Asia plus Japan" foreign ministers' conference and various VIP exchanges.

This is a region of pivotal geopolitical significance bridging Asia, Europe, the Middle East and Russia. Its location makes it critical to efforts to stabilize Afghanistan, preventing the spread of terrorism, drugs, and weapons, and find solutions to other challenging issues facing the international community.

China is incorporating the countries in this region into its Belt and Road Initiative and, with its wealth of financial resources, is promoting ambitious attempts to build a Chinese-led international order. Some countries have used investments and loans from China to make huge investments in cargo collecting bases, and port facilities. Sri Lanka, for example, in the Indian Ocean, used investment and loans from China to build the major port of Hambantota in the south and set up extensive port facilities. However, the capacity utilization of the facility did not increase in line with expectations, making it impossible to reach the

返済のめどが立たず、当該港湾施設を運営する権利を 99 年の期限で中国国有企業に譲り渡した（債務のワナとも呼ばれる）。「一帯一路」構想は歓迎一辺倒から多くの国で懸念材料に変わりつつある。

  （注）・中央アジア諸国：カザフスタン、キルギス、タジキスタン、トルクメニスタン、ウズベキスタンの5カ国
    ・コーカサス諸国：アルメニア、アゼルバイジャン、グルジアの3カ国

c）分野別外交
 1) 国家安全保障
  ⅰ) 日本の外交基本政策

   日本は、外交基本三原則実現ための方策として、次の3つの安全保障政策を推進している。
    〈1〉日米安全保障体制（日本国とアメリカ合衆国との間の相互協力及び安全保障条約。本項において「日米防衛協定」という）堅持
    〈2〉適切な自国防衛力整備
    〈3〉国際平和と安全確保のための外交努力
  ⅱ) 米軍再編への対応

   冷戦終結後の世界は、地域紛争、国際テロ、大量破壊兵器・弾道ミサイルの拡散、海賊問題、サイバー攻撃など一国では処理できない地球規模の問題が起こっている。特に日本の周辺では北朝鮮の核実験・弾道ミサイルの開発、中国の軍備の拡大などによる緊張感が急速に高まっている。

   アメリカは、この事態に対処するため、軍事技術を最大限に活用し、機動性と効率性の高い防衛体制をめざして世界的軍事体制の再編成を計画し、日本を含む同盟・友好国に協力を求めてきた。日本は、軍事情報の共有・保護強化、米軍の再配備、横須賀基地への原子力空母ロナルド・レーガンの配備などの諸問題に協力している（日米防衛協定のためのガイドライン：2015年4月27日改定）。

   日本政府においても、かかる国際的緊張状況に米軍とともに対応するため、2014年7月1日、日本自体だけではなく、日本と密接な関係にある

loan repayment target. As a solution, the rights to operate the port facilities for 99 years were transferred to a Chinese state-owned enterprise in an arrangement referred to as "dept-trap diplomacy." As a result, instead of a warm welcome, many countries are regarding the Belt and Road Initiative with concern.

Note:
- Central Asian countries: Kazakhstan, Kyrgyz, Tajikistan, Turkmenistan, Uzbekistan.
- Caucasus countries: Armenia, Azerbaijan and Georgia.

c) Field-Specific Diplomacy

1) National Security

i) Japan's Basic Diplomatic Policy Stance

Japan pursues the following three basic diplomatic policies as measures for implementing its three fundamental diplomatic principles. <1> Firmly maintaining Japan-U.S. security arrangements (The Treaty of Mutual Cooperation and Security between Japan and the U.S., referred to in this section as "Japan-U.S. Defense Agreement"), <2> keeping up appropriate defense capabilities, and <3> engaging in diplomatic efforts for ensuring world peace and security.

ii) Response to U.S. Military Realignment

Regional wars, international terrorism, proliferation of weapons of mass destruction and ballistic missiles, maritime piracy, and cyber-attacks are some of the global issues of the post-Cold-War world that are beyond the power of a single country to deal with alone. Nuclear tests and ballistic missile development by North Korea and military growth in China have rapidly heightened tensions in the vicinity around Japan.

To meet this challenge, the U.S. plans to carry out a worldwide military realignment aimed at optimizing the use of military technology and realizing a highly mobile defense system. For this, it has called on the cooperation of its friends and allies, including Japan. Japan is collaborating a broad range of issues extending from the sharing of military information with enhanced security to the relocation of U.S. military facilities, and the deployment of the nuclear-powered aircraft carrier USS Ronald Reagan at Yokosuka Naval Base (Guidelines for Japan-US Defense Agreement, revised on April 27, 2015).

In order to be able to respond to international tensions with the U.S. military, in accordance with a Cabinet decision of July 1, 2014, in the event of an attack to Japan or on a close ally of Japan, such as the U.S.,

同盟国（アメリカ）等が攻撃されたときにも、集団的自衛権（日米防衛協定第5条：日本の領域に対して侵害が行われた場合の日本とアメリカの共通の危険への対処）を行使できるとの閣議決定を行っている。

iii）ミサイル防御システム（BMD）

　政府は、専守防衛の立場を堅持する日本を弾道ミサイルから守る唯一の手段が弾道ミサイル防御システムであるとの判断から、その整備を決断し、日米共同開発に合意した。その後日米の協力による共同研究・開発・生産が進められ（2017年、米軍のBMD対応型イージス艦2隻が日本に配備された）、日本のイージス艦も迎撃実験に参加した。

iv）テロ・海賊・麻薬対策

　日本は国内においては国際テロの直接的被害の経験がないが、アルカイダの対日テロ計画、中東海域やマラッカ海峡での海賊の横行、北アフリカ・アルジェリアでの邦人殺害事件など海外のテロからの防衛・安全確保も重要課題である。

　麻薬については、日本で不正使用される麻薬のほぼ全量が外国からの輸入である。この事情から、麻薬対策は、外からの供給の遮断、国内の乱用者による需要の削減に大別される。供給の遮断には、密輸阻止のための水際対策の徹底が肝心で、そのために政府は関係国家、国際機関、一般企業・市民からの情報収集及び港湾、空港での現物取り締まりを強化している。また需要の削減については、不法所持者、不法使用者の発見・指導に努めている。日本は麻薬規制が最も厳しく、少量の所持、栽培でも懲役刑が適用されるのはG7諸国の中で日本だけである。2018年4月時点において台湾からの麻薬の密輸が目立って多い。

v）自由で開かれたインド太平洋戦略

　政府は、2017年秋以来、成長著しいアジアと潜在力の高いアフリカを重要地域と位置づけ、「自由で開かれたインド太平洋戦略」、すなわちインド洋と太平洋でつないだ地域全体の安全と経済成長をめざしている。このため、アメリカ・インド・オーストラリアと法の支配に基づく海洋の自

Japan shall be able to exercise its right to collective self-defense (Article 5 of the Japan-US Defense Agreement: Dealing with a common danger to Japan and the U.S. in the case of an invasion into the territory of Japan).

iii) Ballistic Missile Defense (BMD) System

The Japanese Government considers ballistic missile defense to be the only system compatible with Japan's exclusively defense-oriented policy that is capable of offering protection against missile attack. It therefore decided to implement a BMD system, and the governments of Japan and the U.S. agreed to develop one jointly. Subsequent joint research, development and production efforts enabled a Japanese Aegis cruiser to participate in missile interception tests (in 2017 two U.S. BMD Aegis destroyers were deployed to Japan).

iv) Terrorism, Piracy, and Drug Countermeasures

Although Japan has never experienced direct damage from international terrorism inside the country, it urgently needs to defend and protect itself from overseas terrorism, including the threat of Al Qaeda's anti-Japan terrorism, the rampages of pirates in Middle Eastern waters and the Strait of Malacca, and incidents like the killing of Japanese in Algeria.

Almost all narcotics illegally used in Japan are brought in from overseas. In view of this situation, the war against drugs is being fought mainly on two fronts: preventing drugs from getting in and reducing demand by drug abusers inside the country. Strictly enforced border control is essential to stop illegal drug trafficking and cut off supplies. The government is therefore gathering information from relevant countries, international organizations, private companies, and individuals, while also tracking down drug smugglers at sea and airports. The effort to reduce abuser demand is focused on identifying and counseling illegal drug possessors and users. Japan regulates narcotic drugs very strictly. It is the only G7 country to give prison sentences for possessing or growing even minute amounts of drugs. As of April 2018, conspicuous amounts of narcotics are being smuggled in from Taiwan.

v) Free and Open Indo-Pacific Strategy

Since the autumn of 2017, the government has positioned Asia, with its rapid growth, and Africa, with its high potential, as important areas, that is "Free and Open Indo-Pacific Strategy", aiming for safety and economic growth throughout the whole region connected by the Indian Ocean and the Pacific Ocean. For this reason, Japan is strengthening collaboration with the U.S., India, and Australia to achieve freedom of

由の達成に向けて連携を強化している。
2）経済の安全保障
　ⅰ）WTO を補完する各種通商協定

　　日本は、WTO（世界貿易機関）の定める統一的なグローバル・ルールに従い、多角的自由貿易の発展に貢献し、またその恩恵も受けてきた。

　　しかし、日本のさらなる成長のためには、急速に成長・変化を遂げつつあるアジア・太平洋地域の需要を取り込むことが重要である。そのためには近年、迅速性が問われる WTO を補完する手段として、2 国間または少数国家間の FTA、EPA、RCEP さらに ACTA が重要な役割を担うようになってきた。

　　日本は、TPP への加盟について、既存加盟 11 カ国の承認を得て 2013 年 7 月から交渉に参加した。交渉では、原則　すべての貿易の関税を削減しゼロにすること、ヒト・モノ・サービス・カネの移動をほぼ完全に自由にすることがめざされているが、条約の規定が非常に複雑である事や参加各国ともそれぞれがメリット・デメリットを持つため、妥結が懸念されていたが、2018 年 12 月末に発効した。

- FTA（Free Trade Agreement　自由貿易協定）：特定の国・地域の物とサービスの貿易自由化を目的とする協定。
- EPA（Economic Partnership Agreement　経済連携協定）：FTA を基礎として、さらに投資、人（看護師・介護師など）の移動、政府調達、知的財産（特許・著作権など）のルールづくりなど、より広い分野での経済関係強化を目的とする協定。日本はこれまでに 18 カ国・1 地域との間で締結した。
- TPP（Trans-Pacific Partnership　環太平洋パートナーシップ協定）：加盟国間の工業製品、農林水産物、知的財産権、人の移動、金融、医療・保健サービスなど 20 分野を例外なしに対象とし、関税の全面撤廃をめざし、参加表明国 12（オーストラリア、ブルネイ、カナダ、チリ、日本、マレーシア、メキシコ、ニュージーランド、ペルー、シンガポール、アメリカ、ベトナム）であった。ところが、

the oceans based on the rule of law.
2) Economic Security
i) Trade Agreements that Complement WTO

Japan has contributed to and benefited from the development of multilateral free trade under the uniform global rules of the World Trade Organization (WTO).

To ensure future economic growth, however, Japan must involve itself in the demand of the rapidly expanding and transforming Asia-Pacific markets. In recent years, therefore, FTA, EPA, RCEP and ACTA arrangements between two or a small number of countries have come to play an important complementary role to the slower-moving WTO.

Japan had expressed an interest in joining the TPP, and upon receiving the approval of the 11 existing members, entered the talks in July 2013. Although the negotiations are aimed to reduce all trade tariffs to zero and eliminating substantially all restraints on the movement of people, goods, services and money, it has become increasingly clear that the provisions of the agreement are very complex and disparate merits and demerits among the participating countries raised concerns about whether an agreement could be reached, but the agreement finally came into force at the end of December 2018.

- FTA (Free Trade Agreement): An agreement to abolish customs duties and liberalize trade in goods and services between specified countries or regions.
- EPA (Economic Partnership Agreement): An agreement based on an FTA that aims to strengthen economic relations in a broader range of areas by, for example, defining rules on investment, movement of people (e.g., nurses and caregivers), government procurement, and intellectual property (patents, copyrights etc.). Japan has so far concluded FTAs with 18 countries and one region.

- TPP (Trans-Pacific Partnership): An agreement that envisions abolition of all tariffs between member countries without exception in 20 categories including industrial products, agricultural, forestry and fishery products, intellectual property rights, human mobility, and financial, medical, and health services. Twelve countries have pledged to participate: Australia, Brunei, Canada, Chile, Japan, Malaysia, Mexico, New Zealand, Peru, Singapore, the U.S., and Vietnam. In January 2017 the U.S. announced it was pulling out of the TPP. The U.S. accounts for a particularly high volume of trade,

2017年1月に貿易量が格別多いアメリカが突然離脱を表明し、発効のめどが立たなくなった（成立間もないトランプ政権は、多国間貿易交渉よりも2国間交渉の方が自国に有利だと主張）。しかし、2017年11月、アメリカを除く11カ国の間で内容の見直しが行われ、2018年3月チリで署名式を行い、同年12月末に発効したものである。

- ACTA（Anti-Counterfeiting Trade Agreement 偽造品の取引の防止に関する協定）：日本は偽造品や知的財産保護のために最初の締約国になった。

ⅱ）エネルギーの安全保障

日本のエネルギー自給率はわずか9.5％であり、この脆弱なエネルギー構造と、伸び続ける需要や昼夜間における需要格差の拡大といった多くの課題の対応に迫られている。

（詳細については 4 経済（3）日本経済が直面する4つの重要課題 a）エネルギー確保の項参照）

ⅲ）ODA（Official Development Assistance）：政府開発援助

1954年に始まった日本のODAは1976年の戦後賠償終了とともに急速に拡大し、1991年から2000年までの10年間は世界最大の供与国であった。しかし、2012年にはアメリカに次ぎ世界第2位となり、2017年は50億ドルで、OECDの経済協力委員会加盟国23カ国の供与額総額の7.3％で、23カ国中4位である（支出総額ベース）。なお、中国に対するODAは2018年度をもって終了した。

2008年、日本政府の2大援助機関が統合された。すなわち独立行政法人国際協力機構（新JICA）のもとに、国際協力銀行（JBIC）の海外経済協力部門が統合され、技術協力、有償資金協力、無償資金協力の3つを一元的に実施する統合援助機関として援助の一層の効率化が図られることとなった。日本のODAは、⟨1⟩地球環境、⟨2⟩途上国の経済発展、⟨3⟩民主化・市場経済化支援、⟨4⟩国際平和、⟨5⟩極度の貧困と飢餓の克服などを含んでいる。

so with its sudden withdrawal, it became impossible to say when the agreement could go into effect. Shortly after the Trump administration took over it argued that bilateral negotiations were better for the U.S. than multilateral negotiations. In November 2017, the agreement was reviewed by the 11 remaining countries, which signed a new TPP (TPP 11) at a ceremony held in Chile on March 8, 2018. Finally, it went into effect at the end of December 2018.

- ACTA (Anti-Counterfeiting Trade Agreement): A multinational agreement for preventing product counterfeiting and protecting intellectual property, which Japan was one of the first to sign.

ii) Energy Security

With an energy self-sufficiency of only 9.5%, Japan has a pressing need to deal with its fragile energy structure, and numerous other issues such as steadily rising energy demand and increasing disparity between day and night demand.

(For details, see Chapter 4 Economy, Section (3) Four Important Issues Facing the Japanese Economy, a) Securing Energy)

iii) ODA (Official Development Assistance)

Although Japan launched an ODA program in 1954, it was not until the completion of war reparations to Asian countries in 1976 that its ODA began expanding very rapidly. During the decade between 1991 and 2000, Japan was the world's top-ranking provider of ODA. In 2012 it moved to second place after the U.S. (ranking by total disbursements). In 2017 Japan was in fourth place, providing 5 billion dollars in ODA, which accounted for 7.3% of the total amount of ODA from the 23 member countries of the OECD's Economic Cooperation Committee. ODA to China ended in fiscal 2018.

In 2008, the Japanese Government's two largest aid organizations were merged. Specifically, part of the Japan Bank for International Cooperation (JBIC) was merged into the Japan International Cooperation Agency (as the new JICA). The merger was aimed at boosting aid efficiency by creating an integrated aid organization for unified orchestration of cooperation in the three areas of technical assistance, loan aid, and grant aid. Japanese ODA includes: <1> ensuring environmental sustainability, <2> promoting the economic development of emerging nations, <3> supporting the development of democracies and free-market economies, <4> achieving world peace, and <5> eradicating extreme poverty and hunger.

(4) 国旗など

a） 国旗

日本の国旗は日の丸または日章旗といわれている。両方とも昇る太陽の旗という意味である。白地の中心の赤い円は太陽を表す。昔から神社の旗やのぼりに用いられ、16世紀ごろから日本を表す旗として船に揚げられた。

「太陽の出る所」という意味の国号（日本）とも合致するので、1870年に商船に揚げる国旗として制定された。1999年には日章旗が国旗として法制化された。

国旗としての正式な寸法は、縦横比が2対3、日章の直径は縦の長さの5分の3、日章は旗面の中央となっている。

b） 国歌

日本の国歌として歌われている『君が代』の歌詞は、10世紀に完成した『古今和歌集』に収録されている和歌であるが、作者は不明である。曲は明治時代になって宮内省の林広守により作曲され、慣習的に「国歌斉唱」の際に用いられるようになった。

『君が代は　千代に八千代に　さざれ石の　巌となりて苔のむすまで』
歌詞の意味は、「天皇の御世（みよ）は小さな小石が岩になって、その岩に苔が生えるほど先まで永遠に続くように」である。『君が代』は1999年に国歌として法制化された。

c） 国花

日本では桜が国を代表する花と考えられているが、国花としての法制度はない。桜は日本の神話にも現れており、桜の花の散り方の潔（いさぎ）よさが、武士の人生観に結びつけられた。

日本各地に桜の名所があり、満開の桜の木の下で酒宴を開くのが日本人の楽しみになっている。日本の桜の70％から80％はソメイヨシノという品種である。

(4) The National Flag etc.

a) The National Flag

The national flag of Japan is called the *Hi-no-Maru* or the *Nisshoki*. Both words mean "the flag of the rising sun." The sun is represented by a red circle at the center of a white field. The design had been used on shrine flags and banners for many years before being adapted as a flag for indicating the nationality of Japanese ships in the sixteenth century.

So well did the flag match the name of the country (meaning place from where the sun rises) that it was formally designated as the national flag for use on merchant ships in 1870. It became Japan's national flag by law in 1999.

In its official size, the flag has a hoist of two against a fly of three and the sun is a circle whose center is at the center of the flag and whose diameter is three fifths the hoist.

b) The National Anthem

The words of *Kimigayo*, which is sung as Japan's national anthem, were taken from a *waka* poem found in *Kokinwakashu*, a collection of waka poems dating back to the tenth century. The poet's name is unknown. The anthem's melody was written by Hayashi Hiromori, an imperial court musician in the Meiji era. Over the years, this became the song the Japanese traditionally sang together as their national anthem.

The words of the anthem mean: "May the reign of the Emperor continue for all generations and for all eternity—the time it takes for small pebbles to grow into a great rock and become covered with moss." Kimigayo became Japan's national anthem by law in 1999.

c) National Flower

The Japanese have long thought of the *sakura* (cherry blossom) as the flower which symbolizes the nation, but it has not been designated as the national flower by law. The sakura is mentioned in ancient myths, and the way its petals fall while still at the height of their beauty was interpreted by the old warrior class as symbolic of resignation and grace in death, qualities which the warriors rated high.

There are numerous cherry blossom viewing spots throughout the country and one of the pleasures of life among the Japanese is the chance to hold a sake drinking party beneath a grove of cherry trees in full bloom. Among the various kinds of cherry trees, the Somei Yoshino

また、皇室の紋章が菊であるため、菊も日本を代表する花とされている。

d）元号

東洋の国には時代ごとに呼び名をつけるところがある。古代中国には、皇帝が時をも支配するという思想があった。日本では、7世紀に「大化」と号したのが最初である。日本の制度では、天皇が元号の終わりと次の元号の始まりを定めてきた。

しかし、19世紀後半の「明治」以降は、おのおのの天皇は一代に一つの元号を用いるという原則（一世一元制）が定められた。すなわち、天皇が前天皇の位をついだ年を元年とし、天皇が亡くなるまで、同一元号を使用する。「明治」以降は、「大正」、「昭和」、「平成」と続き、現在の元号は「令和」である。

なお、2017年6月16日に公布された「天皇の退位等に関する皇室典範特例法」により、前の天皇は、2019年4月30日に退位し、翌日の5月1日から、元号は「令和」となった。

is the most popular and accounts for 70 to 80% of the total number.

The chrysanthemum is another flower which, because of its use in the Imperial Crest, is considered to be symbolic of Japan.

d) Use of Eras in Reckoning Years

Some oriental countries name (number) years by eras. In ancient China, even time was thought to come under the emperor's rule. Japan began reckoning years by era in the seventh century, starting with the Taika era. Under the Japanese system, it was the emperor who decided when one era would end and the next begin.

In the latter half of the nineteenth century, however, it was decided that from the Meiji Era on, each emperor's reign would constitute one era (the practice of assigning one era name to the reign of each emperor). That is to say, the year in which an emperor ascended to the throne would be the first year of a new era which would continue to his death. The Meiji era was followed by the Taisho era, Showa era, Heisei era, and the Reiwa era.

In accordance with the "Special Measures Law on the Imperial Household Act Concerning the Abdication of His Majesty the Emperor and Other Matters" promulgated on June 16, 2017, the former Emperor abdicated on April 30, 2019, and the Reiwa era started on May 1.

4 経済

(1) 日本経済の概況

a) 経済規模

　日本経済は、国内・外の経済不振と行き過ぎた円高の影響で低迷を続け、2008年のリーマンショックに引き続き、2011年の東日本大震災の影響も受け、経済規模を示す国民総生産（GDP）が2007年度の530兆円から2011・2012年度は490兆円と7.4％縮小した。2012年12月に再び政権復帰した安倍晋三政権は大胆な金融政策、機動的な財政政策、民間投資を喚起する成長戦略のいわゆるアベノミクス政策を実施し、さらに米国、EU、中国および新興国の好調な経済の状況も受け、日本経済は引き続き回復しつつあり、2017年度末には国民総生産が547兆円と5年間で7.9％経済成長した。

　2017年時点では、日本のGDP総額は世界第3位である。アメリカの4分の1、中国の5分の2、ドイツの1.3倍、イギリス・フランス・インドの1.9倍、ロシア・韓国の3.2倍である。
　国民1人当たりのGDPは日本はドル換算で3万8,450ドルで、アメリカの5万9,790ドルに対し、64.3％であり、フランス・イギリスと同じレベルで、韓国の1.3倍、ロシアの3.5倍、中国の4.4倍、インドの19倍である（2017年 IMF 調査）。

b) 産業構造

　第二次世界大戦後の日本経済は、まず第2次産業を中心に発展し、続いて第3次産業が急速に拡大した。第3次産業は1970年代に GDP の50％を超え、2016年には72.0％に達した。その結果、1995年には33.8％と GDP の3分の1を占めていた第2次産業の比率は、2016年には26.8％と相対的に低下したが、依然として日本経済の重要な柱であり、高度の技術と製品によって世界経済に寄与している。第1次産業の比率は縮小を続けて1.2％となった。これは工業国に共通な傾向とはいえ、日本の場合食料や木材の輸入依存度が特に高いため、食の安全などの観点から、

4 Economy

(1) Overview of the Japanese Economy

a) Scale of the Economy

Due to domestic and international stagnation, the effect of an excessive appreciation of the yen, the Lehman shock in 2008, followed by the impact of the Great East Japan Earthquake in 2011, caused the gross domestic product (GDP), which shows the scale of an economy, to decline by 7.4% from 530 trillion yen in fiscal 2007 to 490 trillion yen in fiscal 2011 (April 2011 to March 2012). The administration of Abe Shinzo, who returned to power again in December 2012, implemented so-called Abenomics, "bold monetary policy," "flexible fiscal policy," and a "growth strategy to encourage private investment." With the strong economic conditions of the United States (U.S.), the EU, China and newly emerging economies, the Japanese economy continued to recover, and at the end of fiscal 2017 the GDP stood at 547 trillion yen, a growth of 7.9% over a five-year period.

At the end of 2017, Japan's GDP was the world's third largest. It was one-fourth that of the U.S.'s, two-fifths that of China's, 1.3 times that of Germany's, 1.9 times that of the UK's, France's and India's, and 3.2 times that of Russia's and South Korea's.

The Japanese per capita income is equivalent to about 38,450 dollars, which is approximately 64.3% of the U.S. per capita income of $59,790, about the same as the per capita income of France and the UK, 1.3 times that of South Korea, 3.5 times that of Russia, 4.4 times that of China, and 19 times that of India (IMF survey 2017).

b) Industrial Structure

Following the end of the Second World War, the Japanese economy developed rapidly, starting with the secondary industries. This was followed by the rapid growth of the tertiary industries, which in the 1970s accounted for more than 50% of the gross national product (GDP), a figure that in 2016 reached 72.0%. The result of this was a relative decrease in the percentage of GDP accounted for by the secondary industries, from 33.8% in 1995 to 26.8% in 2016. Manufacturing continues to be an important pillar of the Japanese economy, contributing to the world's economy through advanced technology and products. The ratio of the primary industries has continued to contract, and is now

農林水産業の維持が大きな課題になっている。

c）産業基盤

　日本は石灰石など限られたものを除いて見るべき鉱物資源を持たない。したがって、エネルギー・資源の確保は特に重要な課題である。農業用地や工業用地も限られており、比較的恵まれていた水産資源についても、国際的な取り決めなどのため利用可能量は減少している。

　このため日本は海に囲まれた地形を利用して、大規模な海面埋め立てによって対処している。工業については、専用港を持つ臨海工業地帯が発達した。また、東京湾・大阪湾を中心に次世代産業の基盤整備も行われている。

　人的資源については、豊富で優秀な人材が経済発展を支えてきたが、最近では、少子・高齢化の影響を受け15歳以上65歳未満の生産年齢人口が徐々に減少してきており、2018年では深刻な人手不足状況となっており、今後は官民あげて、働き方改革・生産性向上対策・外国人労働者の導入などの対応策が必要となっている。

d）対外経済

　日本は、資源の多くを海外に依存する一方、レベルの高い工業力によって製品を生み出すため、経済における輸出入の役割が大きい。

　貿易の相手地域は全世界にわたるが、近年では中国を中心にアジア諸国の比率が高くなっている。

　国際収支は1980年代以降、貿易収支、経常収支とも黒字基調で推移してきた。しかし、2011年の貿易収支は、東日本大震災と原子力発電所休止の影響による化石燃料輸入の増加を主因として、31年ぶりの赤字となった。2016年および2017年は、貿易収支、経常収支ともに世界経済の好調、化石燃料価格の下落、企業の国際競争力強化、円安の効果により輸出が増加し、大幅な黒字となった。

1.2%. While this trend is one that is common to industrialized countries, Japan has a particularly high dependence on imports for its food and timber, so from the standpoint of food safety, food security and other such perspectives, maintaining the agriculture, forestry and fisheries industries are major issues in Japan.

c) Industrial Foundation

Apart from a few exceptions, such as limestone, Japan possesses very few mineral resources, so securing energy resources and other natural resources is of particular importance. Agricultural land and industrial land are limited, and while Japan is relatively blessed when it comes to fishery resources, the usable amount is decreasing due to international agreements and other factors.

Japan is surrounded by water, and offsets its limited land by using large-scale sea landfill, and is developing infrastructure for next-generation industries mainly in Tokyo Bay and Osaka Bay.

Japan's abundant, excellent human resources supported its economic development, but with the gradual decrease in the working-age population aged 15 to 65 due to the low birthrate and the aging of the population, there were already serious labor shortages, generating a need for future response strategies by public and private sectors, such as work reforms, and measures such as productivity improvements and the introduction of foreign workers in 2018.

d) External Economic Relations

While Japan relies on other countries for most of its resources, the products produced by its high-level industrial capabilities means that both imports and exports play a major role in its economy.

Japan's trading partners span the world, but in recent years Asian countries, led by China, account for an increasing proportion of its trade.

From the 1980s Japan maintained a surplus in its international trade and current accounts. In 2011, however, for the first time in 31 years, Japan posted a trade account deficit, mainly due to the Great East Japan Earthquake and the impact of an increase in imports of fossil fuels resulting from the shutting down of nuclear power stations. In 2016 and 2017, the strong global economy, combined with declines in the prices of fossil fuels, stronger international competitiveness of companies and the depreciation of the yen, boosted exports, leading to significant trade and current account surpluses.

（2）戦後経済の歩み

a）戦争による疲弊からの復興（1945～1950年代前半）

　　第二次世界大戦終了時（1945年）の日本経済は、総力戦による疲弊、空襲による破壊などによってほぼ壊滅状態にあり、鉱工業生産は、開戦時（1941年）の7分の1に落ち込んでいた。しかし、その後の日本経済は、「奇跡」とさえ言われる復興ぶりを示した。

　　それには、国民の復興への意欲と努力に加えて、アメリカを中心とする連合軍の占領政策と政府の産業政策が大きく寄与した。連合軍は、それまでの日本の経済力が財閥、大地主などに集中していたことが日本の軍事力を支え、民主的な経済運営を妨げていたとして、財閥解体・独占禁止、農地改革、労働権の確立の3つの基本政策を実施した。同時に日本政府は、経済資源を産業の基礎である石炭、電力、鉄鋼に集中させる政策で産業の再興を促した。

　　さらに、1950年に勃発した朝鮮戦争は、参戦した米軍からの4億ドルに及ぶ資材・サービスの需要をもたらし、復興への歩みを確実なものとした。
　　こうして1955年にはGNPが戦前の水準を回復し、政府の経済白書は「もはや戦後ではない」と宣言した。

b）高度成長期（1950年代後半～1960年代）

　　1950年代後半から、日本経済は平均年10％の高成長を続けた。需要面では、自由貿易の利益と円安に維持された為替レートに支えられた輸出拡大、テレビ・冷蔵庫・洗濯機などの家庭電化製品をはじめとする内需の拡大があり、供給面では、国民の高い貯蓄性向に支えられた銀行の積極的融資による投資資金の確保と、必要な資源と最新の設備・技術の輸入とによって、生産規模拡大、効率・品質の向上が実現された。

　　国際競争に対処するため、合併等による企業規模拡大も進み、財閥解体で非効率な規模に分割されていた企業の再

(2) Postwar Economic Progress

a) Recovery from the Ruins of War (1945 to mid-1950s)

At the end of the Second World War, in 1945, exhausted from the total warfare and the destruction caused by air raids, the Japanese economy lay more or less devastated. Mining and manufacturing production had fallen to one-seventh of the level at the start of the war in 1941. However, this was followed by what was called a "miracle" recovery.

In addition to the nation's desire and efforts to recover, a major contribution was made by the occupation policies of the Allied Forces, led by the U.S., and the government's industrial policies. The Allied Forces held that Japan's economic power had been concentrated in the hands of the zaibatsu and major landowners had supported Japan's military might and prevented the economy from being managed democratically. Therefore three fundamental policies were introduced: dissolution of the zaibatsu and prohibition of monopolies; agrarian land reform; and the establishment of labor rights. At the same time, the Japanese government adopted policies that promoted the revival of industry by channeling economic resources into coal, electric power, and steel, which were fundamental to industry.

The road to recovery was solidified in 1950 with the outbreak of the Korean War, and the intervention of the U.S., which generated 400 million dollars in demand for supplies and services for U.S. forces.

By 1955 the gross national product (GNP) had recovered to the prewar level, prompting an Economic White Paper to state that the Japanese economy could "no longer be termed postwar."

b) Rapid Economic Growth (Mid-1950s through 1960s)

From the second half of the 1950s, Japan's economy grew at a high average annual rate of 10%. On the demand side, export growth was helped by the benefits of free trade and an exchange rate that kept the yen low. Moreover, there was also an expansion of internal demand for televisions, refrigerators, washing machines, and other household appliances. On the supply side, the securing of investment funds due to aggressive financing efforts by banks, supported by the nation's high savings rate, and imports of the necessary resources and the latest equipment and technology, led to increased production and improvements in efficiency and quality.

To respond to international competition, enterprises expanded their scale of operations through mergers, and companies that had been

統合も認められた。

ただ、このころから、高度成長の陰の部分として、公害問題が新たな社会問題となった。

c）安定成長期（1970年代～1980年代前半）

1970年代に入ると、経済成長は鈍化し始めた。家庭電化製品等の需要が一巡したことがその基調にあったが、国外からの撹乱要素も相次いでいた。

1971年のニクソン米国大統領によるドルの金兌換停止の影響で、円の為替相場は23年間続いた1ドル360円から、1973年までに1ドル260円台に急騰し、好調だった繊維・鉄鋼をはじめとする工業製品の輸出の停滞を招いた。1973、1979年の2度の石油危機も、エネルギー資源を輸入に頼る日本産業を痛撃した。

しかし、産業界は、省エネルギー技術の開発、コンピュータの活用による効率化と品質向上、繊維産業・重化学工業から自動車・エレクトロニクスなどの高付加価値産業への移行等でこの危機を克服した。これにより、年3％前後の安定成長が維持された。輸出競争力も回復し、貿易黒字が拡大した。

d）バブルの生成（1980年代後半～1990年代初）

日本の貿易黒字が拡大する一方で、アメリカの対外経済の不均衡が問題となったことから、1985年に先進5カ国がドル安誘導の協調介入（プラザ合意）を実施した。その結果、1ドル235円だった円は1年で160円台となり、さらに高騰を続けて1988年には120円台となった。

この急激な円高に対処するため、日本の輸出産業は、東南アジア・中国の低コスト国や需要地である欧米諸国への生産拠点の移転を積極的に進めた。しかし、これは後に国内産業の空洞化を招く一因にもなった。

他方、政府は内需拡大を国際公約とし、公共事業の拡大、減税等の政策を実施した。一時引き締め策を取った日本銀行も低金利政策に転じた。これらにより生じた潤沢な国内資金は、土地や株式への投機的な投資に向かい、地価、株価の高騰を招いて、いわゆる「バブル経済」が出現した。

divided up into inefficiently small units by the dissolution of the monopolistic enterprises (*zaibatsu*) were allowed to re-integrate.

However, a dark side of the high rate of economic growth was that pollution became a new societal issue.

c) Stable Growth (1970s to mid-1980s)

Entering the 1970s, economic growth started to slow. Demand for home appliances and other products had run its course, and there were a number of external disruptive factors.

In 1971, the U.S. president, Richard Nixon, took the dollar off the gold standard, the effect of which was that after 23 years of having an exchange rate of 360 yen to the dollar, the rate soared to 260 yen to the dollar by 1973, causing exports of industrial products such as textiles and steel, which had been brisk, to stagnate. There were also two oil crises, in 1973 and 1979, which impacted Japanese industry, with its reliance on imported energy resources.

However, industry was able to weather these crises by developing energy-saving technology, using computers to increase efficiency and quality, and moving from the textiles and heavy chemical industries to high-value-added industries such as cars and electronics. This made it possible to maintain stable annual growth of around 3%. Export competitiveness recovered, and the trade surplus grew.

d) Bubble Economy (Mid-1980s to early 1990s)

The growth of Japan's trade surplus meant a corresponding imbalance in the U.S.' external account, which in 1985 led to the implementation of the Plaza Accord by the five developed countries that intervened in concert to devalue the dollar. As a result, in one year the yen went from 235 yen to the dollar to 160 yen, and continued its rapid rise, reaching 120 yen by 1988.

In response to this rapid appreciation of the yen, Japan's export industries moved production bases to the low-cost nations of Southeast Asia and China and the demand areas of Europe and the U.S. This was one factor that later caused the hollowing-out of industries in Japan.

The government also made international public commitments to expand internal demand, causing it to expand public works projects and decrease taxes. The Bank of Japan, which at one point had resorted to tight-money measures, switched to a low-interest policy. The high fluidity of internal funds produced by this policy was channeled into investments in property and securities, causing property and share prices to skyrocket, forming a "Bubble Economy."

e）バブルの崩壊と長期景気低迷 （1990年代初〜2000年）

　　1990年代初めになると、実態を離れて膨らんだ経済は破綻し、バブルが崩壊した。地価や株価の下落で景気は急減速した。その影響で、大手銀行や証券会社の経営破綻が相次ぎ、金融システムへの信頼喪失で、投資の過度な減退や多数の企業倒産等が生じた。

　　政府は70兆円に及ぶ公的資金の投入で金融秩序の回復に努めるとともに、国債発行や地方債の発行容認などで財政面から内需増加の景気刺激を図った。しかし、十分な成果が得られないまま、国および地方自治体の財政は大きな負債を背負うことになった。

　　企業は雇用削減を含む事業の再編成を余儀なくされ、倒産・失業の増加、所得の減少が深刻化した。この状態は約10年間続き、「失われた10年」と呼ばれた。

f）好況感なき回復から世界同時不況へ （2001〜2011年）

　　2001年ごろから、政府は金融機関への大規模な公的資金投入に踏み切り、日本銀行もゼロ金利と呼ばれる極度の金融緩和政策を実施した。1996年に始まった金融制度改革も機能し始めた。銀行・証券の兼業容認、海外金融機関の活動への規制緩和等を含む、いわゆる「日本式ビッグバン」である。これらにより、潤沢な資金の供給が促された。

　　この間に、製造業は設備・人員・負債の過剰の解消に努め、金融機関の抱える不良債権の処理も進んだ。これらの効果で、株価の持ち直し、企業収益の改善、設備投資の回復などが軌道に乗り始めた。中国市場の拡大やアメリカの不動産バブルのもたらす輸出需要も回復を助けた。

　　しかし、コスト削減を主体とする企業業績の改善は賃金上昇や雇用増には結びつかず、「好況感なき景気回復」と呼ばれる状況が続いた。また、規制緩和の一つとして進められた労働力の流動化により、派遣労働などの不安定な就

e) Collapse of the Bubble and Protracted Recession (Early 1990s to 2000)

In the early 1990s, the economic bubble, which had become far removed from the actual economic situation, collapsed. Land and stock prices plummeted, drastically slowing growth. This led to a series of failures of major banks and securities companies, undermining confidence in the financial system, resulting in excessive cutbacks in investment and many corporate bankruptcies.

In response, the government implemented an economic stimulus package that used 70 trillion yen in public funds in an effort to restore financial order and called for the issuing of national and local government bonds to stimulate internal demand. But the results were not enough, and the efforts left the national and local governments heavily in debt.

Businesses were forced to implement restructuring programs, which included laying off employees. Because of this and the rising number of business failures and unemployment, the decline in personal income became increasingly serious. This extended period of social and economic stagnation became known as Japan's "Lost Decade."

f) From the Muted Economic Recovery to the Global Recession (2001 to 2011)

From around 2001 the government embarked on a large-scale investment of public funds in financial institutions, and the Bank of Japan implemented an ultra-easy monetary policy that lowered interest rates to nearly zero. Financial system reforms that were initiated in 1996 started to have an effect. This was the so-called Japanese "Big Bang," which allowed institutions to run both banking and security operations and eased restrictions on the activities of overseas financial institutions. These measures smoothed the way for the supply of ample funds.

In the meantime, the manufacturing industry made efforts to eliminate excess facilities, personnel and debt, and progress was made in the cleanup of bad debts by the financial sector. As stock prices rose, corporate profits improved and capital investment recovered, the economy started to get back on track. The recovery was also helped by China's market growth and export demand generated by a property bubble in the U.S.

However, as it was a muted recovery, with the improvements in corporate results having been achieved mainly by cutting costs, it did not lead to higher wages and employment. Also, one aspect of deregulation that increased labor mobility was an expansion of temporary and other

労形態が拡大し、正規社員と派遣労働者・パート社員との賃金格差という新たな問題が現れてきた。

さらに、2008年に、アメリカで発生したサブプライムローン問題によって大手投資銀行リーマンブラザーズが破綻し（リーマンショック）、これが大規模な金融危機を招き、その影響は全世界に及んだ。日本経済も深刻な危機に陥り、政府の景気対策にもかかわらず回復の兆しを見せず、2年連続してマイナス経済成長となった。2009年には、自由民主党（自民党）から民主党への政権交代があったが、民主党政権も効果的な政策を実施できず、景気低迷は続いて、「失われた10年」はついに「失われた20年」になった。

g）東日本大震災以降（2011年～）

2011年3月11日、東日本を激烈な地震と、それに伴う巨大津波が襲い、東北から北関東に及ぶ広大な地域の沿岸部に壊滅的な損害を与えた。

さらに、それに起因する東京電力福島第一原子力発電所の原子炉の水蒸気爆発は、放射能による広範囲にわたる周辺地域の汚染をもたらし、福島県を中心とした市民生活および産業に長期にわたる影響を残した。

しかも、震災と原子力発電所の事故の影響は、被災地だけでなく、全国の原子力発電所の休止による電力不足、サプライチェーンの混乱などによって全国、世界各国の自動車産業に及んだ。

福島第一原子力発電所の事故は、日本の原子力発電所（原発）全体の安全性への危惧を強め、原子力利用のあり方、ひいてはエネルギー政策全般の再検討が必要になった。すでに長期的な低迷を続けていた日本経済は、この震災を境に、景気回復に加えて復興とエネルギー問題の深刻化という困難な課題を抱えることになった。

2012年12月、総選挙によって自由民主党が大差で勝利し、公明党との連立で政権に復帰した。

安倍政権は、景気回復を最優先の政策目標とし、その実現手段として、「大胆な金融政策」、「機動的な財政政策」、「民間投資を喚起する成長戦略」の「三本の矢」を挙げた。いわゆる「アベノミクス」である。

insecure forms of employment that gave rise to the fresh problem of a growing wage gap between regular employees and temporary or part-time workers.

Furthermore, in 2008 came the so-called Lehman Shock, named after the collapse of Lehman Brothers, a major investment bank, brought down by its involvement in the subprime loan problem in the U.S. This set off a major financial crisis. The impact was felt worldwide. The Japanese economy fell into a serious crisis, with no signs of recovery even after government stimulus measures, and underwent two consecutive years of negative growth. In 2009, the reins of power passed from the Liberal Democratic Party (LDP) to the Democratic Party of Japan (DPJ), but with the new administration also unable to implement effective measures, the economy continued to stagnate. Soon, the "Lost Decade" became the "Lost Two Decades."

g) After the Great East Japan Earthquake (from 2011)

On March 11, 2011, a violent earthquake and giant tsunami hit the east side of Japan, inflicting devastating damage along large area of the eastern seaboard, from Tohoku down to the Northern Kanto plain.

This also caused steam explosions in Tokyo Electric Power Company's Fukushima Daiichi Nuclear Power Station, contaminating the surrounding area with radioactive material that will have a long-term impact on people's lives and on industry, centering in Fukushima prefecture.

Moreover, in addition to the impact the earthquake and nuclear power station accident had on the local region, there were power outages caused by the shutdown of all of Japan's nuclear power plants and supply-chain disruption that extended to car industries around the world.

The Fukushima Daiichi accident also increased fears about the safety of all of Japan's nuclear power plants, requiring a review of the use of nuclear power and, by extension, of the nation's overall energy policy. With the Japanese economy already in a prolonged downturn, the Great East Japan Earthquake (Tohoku earthquake) brought with it the difficult issues of reconstruction and the worsening of the energy problem.

In the general election held in December 2012, the LDP scored a major victory, returning to power in a coalition with the Komeito.

Economic recovery being the most important goal, Prime Minister Abe Shinzo set out his "Three Arrows" to achieve that policy goal as being "bold monetary policy," "flexible fiscal policy," and a "growth strategy to encourage private investment." Collectively, this was dubbed "Abenomics."

具体的には、国債発行を含む豊富な資金の供給によって公共事業、企業投資などを活発化させるとともに、2％の物価上昇を目標として掲げる「脱デフレ」政策で消費増や賃金引き上げを促そうとしている。さらに、この政策が行き過ぎた円高の是正につながり、輸出拡大に寄与することも期待された。

　金融政策をになう日本銀行も、安倍政権の任命によって2013年3月に就任した黒田東彦総裁の下で大胆な金融緩和を実施している。これらにより、株式価格の上昇、円高の是正が進み、GDP・雇用総数も2013年から2018年まで6年間連続で増加している。

（3）日本経済が直面する4つの重要課題

a）エネルギー確保

　日本の一次エネルギー供給量の内訳を原発事故後の2017年度で見ると、石油39.1％、石炭25.1％、天然ガス23.4％、原子力1.5％、水力4.1％、再生エネルギー・地熱等7.7％（カロリーベース）であり、原子力が2010年度に比べて9.8％減少した。資源的には水力、再生エネルギー・地熱以外ほとんど持たず、エネルギー資源の自給率は2014年度の6.4％を底にやや回復して2017年度は9.5％（国際エネルギー機関推計）になっている。日本にとってエネルギー資源の確保とエネルギーの節約は引き続き極めて重要な問題である。

　このうちエネルギーの節約については、官民ともに高い意識を持って取り組んでおり、GDP単位当たりのエネルギー消費量はアメリカの60％程度、中国、インドの20％程度と、世界トップクラスの低い水準を実現している。

　資源確保では、資源国との開発協力、調達先の多様化を進めている。特に、石油、天然ガス輸入の70％を中東地域に頼っていることにはエネルギー安全保障面での懸念もあり、2017年には、アメリカにおけるシェールオイル・ガスやロシアのサハリン天然ガスの使用量も増加した。また、石油、天然ガスの備蓄体制の整備も進めており、石油については、2017年1月時点で全国の消費量の約半年分の備蓄がある。再生可能エネルギーの開発・普及にも努めてきたが、エネルギー供給に占める比率はまだ低く、コスト削減も含めてさらに強化が必要である。

Specifically, it involved energizing public enterprises and corporate investment by supplying ample funds, by issuing national bonds, and using de-deflationary policies in the form of a price inflation target of 2% to encourage an increase in consumption and higher wages. It was also anticipated that the policy would help achieve export growth brought about by a correction to the excessively high yen.

Under the Governor, Kuroda Haruhiko, who was appointed in March 2013 by the Abe administration, the Bank of Japan, which is responsible for monetary policy, also implemented bold monetary easing measures. As a result of these moves, share prices rose, the exchange rate of the yen underwent a correction, and GDP and total employment increased for the six straight years from 2013 to 2018.

(3) Four Important Issues Facing the Japanese Economy

a) Securing Energy

In fiscal 2017, that is, after the nuclear power accident, 39.1% of Japan's primary energy came from oil, 25.1% from coal, 23.4% from natural gas, 1.5% from nuclear power, 4.1% from hydropower, and 7.7% from renewable energies and geothermal energy and the like (calorie basis), so nuclear power had decreased by 9.8% compared to 2010, the year prior to the accident. However, except in the case of hydropower and renewable and geothermal energy, Japan has almost no energy resources and the nation's energy self-sufficiency bottomed out at 6.4% in 2014, then rose to 9.5% in fiscal 2017 (International Energy Agency estimate). So for Japan, securing energy resources and conserving energy continue to be important issues.

Both the public and private sectors have been tackling energy conservation with a high awareness. At 60% that of the U.S.'s and around 20% that of China's and India's, Japan's level of energy consumption per unit of gross national product (GDP) ranks among the lowest in the world.

To secure resources, Japan is carrying out collaborative development projects with countries that possess such resources, and is diversifying its procurement sources. With the reliance on the Middle East for 70% of its oil and natural gas imports being of particular concern from the perspective of energy security, in 2017 more shale oil and gas from the U.S. and more natural gas from Sakhalin, Russia, were used. Progress is also being made with setting up facilities for storing oil and natural gas; as of January 2017, Japan had about a six-month store of oil. Although there has been a focus on developing and diffusing the use of renewable energy, it still only accounts for a small part of the energy supply. More

今、世界では、温室効果ガスの人為的な排出量と植物などの吸収源による除去量とのバランスを達成する「脱炭素社会」を今世紀後半に実現するべく、化石燃料利用への依存度を引き下げることなどによって炭素排出を低減していく「脱炭素化」の動きが活発になっている。

　2018年7月、政府は新たなエネルギー基本計画案を閣議決定した。2030年に向けて再生可能エネルギー比率を電源の22〜24％と主力電源化するために取組みを強化する。焦点の原子力発電（原発）比率は昼夜を問わず安定的に発電できる「重要なベースロード電源」との位置づけを踏襲し20〜22％としている。原発は停止している設備の再稼働を安全に配慮しながら着実に進め、廃炉処理も確実に進める。2018年7月時点で再稼働済みの原発は9基にとどまる。原発は安全の確保や廃炉の費用など多くの論点があるものの、電源の中核のひとつに据えることを変えていない。また温暖化ガスの排出量が多いと国内外から批判を受ける石炭火力発電は2030年も電源の26％を見込む。このため高効率化を前提に「環境負荷の低減を見据えつつ活用していく」としている。

　2050年に向けては世界の気候温暖化の阻止・脱炭素化の流れを踏まえ、再生可能エネルギーについて「最重要主力電源」を目指す方針を提示した。太陽光や風力発電システムのコスト低減をはかるほか、課題である送電線網の改革も進める。

　なお電力については、これまで地域別の9つの電力会社が担当地域内の発電と送電を併せて行ってきたが、東日本大震災の経験などから、2020年4月から発電と送電を分離することにより、地域を超えた弾力的な電力供給を図り、併せて、2013年から新たな発電事業者の電力販売を容易にするという方針が決定された。さらに2017年からガスの小売全面自由化が開始され、競争活性化が図られている。

　また2018年9月、北海道地震で北海道地域の半分以上の電力を供給していた火力発電所が被災し、北海道全域がほぼ2日間停電に追い込まれた（ブラックアウト）。地震・台風など自然災害にたびたび襲われる日本は、広範囲

efforts are needed, including to reduce costs.

Decarbonization movements are under way aimed at reducing carbon emissions by reducing dependence on fossil fuels, with the goal of realizing a decarbonized society by the second half of the century in which there is a balance between anthropogenic greenhouse gas emissions and their removal by sinks such as plants.

In July 2018, the Cabinet approved the draft of a new strategic energy basic plan. A strong effort will be made to bring the ratio of renewable energy ratio to 22–24% as a main power source in 2030. This will be followed by a nuclear power generation ratio of 20–22%, positioned as an important base-load power source that can generate power stably day and night. Nuclear power plants in shutdown will gradually be restarted while giving full regard to safety. Work on decommissioning of reactors will be carried out with safety and reliability. As of July 2018, only nine nuclear reactors have been restarted. Although nuclear power plants face many issues such as ensuring safety and the high cost of decommissioning reactors, there is no change in their positioning as a core power supply. Similarly, coal-fired thermal power plants, which are criticized both domestically and abroad due to their emitting large amounts of greenhouse gases, are expected to form 26% of the power supply, even in 2030. For this reason, the government is promoting their conversion to high efficiency coal power generation while focusing on reducing their environmental burden.

Looking towards 2050, based on current global climate change prevention and decarbonization trends, the policy focus is on making renewable energy the most important major power source. In addition to reducing the cost of solar and wind power generation systems, reform of transmission networks will also be promoted to resolve existing issues.

Up until now Japan's nine regional electric power companies have been responsible for both the generation and delivery of electricity in their respective regions, but following the experience of disasters such as the Great East Japan Earthquake, a policy has been decided on that seeks to achieve a more flexible inter-regional power supply system by separating the generation and delivery, starting from April 2020. In 2013, a policy direction was set to make it easier for new power producers to sell their electricity. Natural gas retailing was fully liberalized in 2017, which has stimulated competition.

In September 2018, thermal power plants that supplied more than half the electricity used in Hokkaido were damaged by a Hokkaido earthquake, causing almost total blackouts throughout Hokkaido for almost two days. Japan, which is frequently hit by natural disasters such as

地域の停電を避けなければならない。国民の生命、生活を守る観点から地域を超えた電力融通が極めて重要な課題となっている。

b) 財政再建

　政府は、1970年代初めからほぼ毎年国債を発行してきた。その結果、日本の財政は1990年代初めから大幅な赤字を続けており、特に2008年のリーマンショック以降はさらに赤字幅が拡大した。政府と地方自治体の長期債務残高は、2010年度末に862兆円を超え、2017年度末には1,093兆円に達した。このうち865兆円が国の長期債務残高で、GDPの1.56倍を超えている。この累積債務を埋め合わせるため、2017年度には34.4兆円の国債が発行された。

　日本の財政の大幅な赤字の原因は、海外主要国との法人税減税競争、急速な高齢化に伴う毎年約1兆円の社会保障支出の自然増、公共投資、発行済み国債の返済にかかる支出などが増加しているためである。近年は国債の償還と利払いだけで年23兆円以上が必要になっており、2018年度予算の国債費は23.3兆円で、一般会計予算の歳出97.7兆円の23.8％を占めている。

　このような問題先送り、後世代にツケを回す、さらには世界トップクラスの過大な国債依存状態をこのまま続ければ、国債の金利が上がり、金利の支払いさえ困る状況に陥るとの批判がある。政府は、長引くデフレから抜け出し、景気を上向かせることが先決であり、それによって税収を増加させることが財政再建にもつながるはずだとしている。しかし、過去の債務に関わる元利払い以外の支出と、公債発行などを除いた収入との収支均衡であるプライマリー・バランスへの着地点は、2026年に先延ばしとなっている。

　歴代内閣は財政再建を重要な課題にしており、すでに省庁再編、国営事業の民営化、国立大学・研究施設の独立採算化等で行政の効率化を進めてきた。また2007年には郵政民営化も実現した。これらの歳出削減努力に勝る徹底した歳出削減と急速な高齢化に対応した増税策を講じなければならない。

earthquakes and typhoons, has to be able to avoid wide-area blackouts. Ensuring electric power interchanges among regions is an extremely important task in the context of protecting the lives and livelihoods of citizens.

b) Fiscal Reconstruction

From the beginning of the 1970s the government has issued bonds nearly every year. As a result, Japan has run a large fiscal deficit from the early 1990s, a deficit that became particularly large following the "Lehman Shock" in 2008. At the end of fiscal 2010, the outstanding long-term debt of the central and regional government exceeded 862 trillion yen, and by the end of fiscal 2017 had reached 1,093 trillion yen. The national debt accounted for 865 trillion of this amount, or more than 1.56 times the gross domestic product (GDP). In order to make up for this accumulated debt, in fiscal 2017, 34.4 trillion yen in government bonds were issued.

Japan's major fiscal deficits are due to competition in corporate tax cuts with major countries, a natural increase in social security expenditures of about 1 trillion yen annually due to the rapid aging of the population, public investment, and interest payments on outstanding government bonds. In recent years 23 trillion yen or more a year is required for interest payments and redemption of government bonds; in fiscal 2018, the cost of servicing the debt will be 23.3 trillion yen, accounting for 23.8% of the general account budget of 97.7 trillion yen.

There is a criticism that if the problem is thus postponed, passing the bill to future generations, and Japan's globally top-level dependence on excessive government bonds continues, interest rates on the bonds will rise, making it a difficult problem to even pay the interest. However, the government stance is that the decision to escape from the prolonged deflation and get the economy back on track is the first priority, and that the increasing tax revenues from a stronger economy will also lead to fiscal reconstruction. However, arrival at a primary balance, which is the balance of expenses other than principal interest payments related to past obligations and income excluding bond issuance, etc., has been postponed to 2026.

With fiscal reconstruction being an important issue for successive Cabinets, there has been a focus on increasing government efficiency by moving ahead with the restructuring of government ministries, the privatization of state-owned businesses, and the implementing of independent accounting for national universities and research institutions. In 2007 the postal service was privatized. Even greater

政府は 2014 年 4 月から消費税を 8 ％へ引き上げ、2019 年 10 月からさらに 10％に引き上げることを決定している。ただし、これが実施されても、食料品などへの軽減税率（8 ％の維持）の適用、幼児教育・保育、一部高等教育・私立高校の無償化を併せておこなうため、約 2.5 兆円の収支改善しか見込めず、財源不足の解消には全く至らないと試算されている。

c）第 4 次産業革命（IoT・ビッグデータ・AI）への対応

　第 1 次産業革命の発端は、18 世紀後半にイギリスで始まり、水力や蒸気機関を動力とした機械を導入し、作業能率を大幅に上昇させることに成功した。
　第 2 次産業革命は、19 世紀後半にアメリカとドイツを中心に起こり、世界に普及し、電力や石油を使った内燃機関を用い大量生産が可能になったほか、重化学工業技術が飛躍的に進歩した。

　第 3 次産業革命は 20 世紀後半に始まり、コンピュータ・通信やロボットにより産業の各方面で自動化が可能となり、生産性を大幅に高めた。

　第 4 次産業革命は、工場の機械装置をはじめとし、あらゆるものをインターネットにつなぐ IoT によって社会全体と産業構造の変革をもたらす。人工知能（AI）やロボットなどによる自動化技術を駆使し、新事業やサービスを生み出す計画は実践段階に入っている。
　サイバースペース（コンピュータやネットワークの中に広がるデータ領域）と現実が融合し、また、財・サービスを提供する側と消費者との垣根も取り払われるなど新たなビジネスモデルが生み出されている（e コマース、仮想通貨等）。多くの社会的な課題が徐々に解決されるとともに、生活の質も向上していく。このような第 4 次産業革命の波は世界を席巻しており、産業構造が大きな変化を遂げようとしている。情報化・デジタル化の波は、新興国・発展途上国での普及がより早く、シェアリングエコノミーやキャッシュレス決済への対応は、法的規制や生活習慣の違いも起因して日本はアメリカのみならず中国・インドにも

expenditure reduction efforts are needed and taxes have to be raised to cope with spending cuts and the rapid population aging that are beyond these expenditure reduction efforts.

In April 2014 the government raised the consumption tax rate to 8%, and decided to further raise the rate to 10% in October 2019. However, because a reduced tax rate (kept at 8%) will be applied to groceries, at the same time childhood education, and child care as well as higher education and private high school for some will become free of charge, it will only improve the balance by about 2.5 trillion yen, which is estimated not even come close to eliminating the revenue shortfall.

c) Response to the Fourth Industrial Revolution (IoT, Big Data, AI)

The first industrial revolution began in Britain in the late eighteenth century. It introduced machinery driven by hydraulic power and steam engines and succeeded in greatly increasing working efficiency.

The second industrial revolution took place mainly in America and Germany in the latter half of the 19th century and spread throughout the world. It made mass production possible by using electricity and internal combustion engines fueled by petroleum, and led to dramatic advances in heavy chemical industrial technology.

The third industrial revolution began in the second half of the 20th century. Using computers, communication and robots, it enabled the application of automation in various industrial fields, greatly improving productivity.

The fourth industrial revolution brings innovation to the whole society and industrial structures through IoT, which connects everything to the Internet, including plant machinery and equipment. Plans that use artificial intelligence (AI), and robots to drive automation technology that creates new businesses and services are becoming practical.

New business models have been created in which cyberspace (data areas in computers and networks) and the real world are integrated, and barriers between providers of goods and services and consumers disappear (e-commerce and virtual, or crypto, currencies, etc.). Such models are gradually resolving many social problems and improving the quality of life. The waves of the fourth industrial revolution are sweeping across the world, bringing major changes to industrial structures. Computerization and digitization are spreading more quickly in emerging economies and developing countries, and due to differences in legal regulations and lifestyle, in these areas, Japan's responses to sharing economies and cashless settlements trails China and India as

リードされている。

d）少子・高齢化社会・人口減少への対応

2017年の日本の出生数は94.6万人と2年連続して100万人を切り、一方、2017年の死亡数は139.4万人と少子化・人口減少は深刻な状況となっている。また2017年の日本の平均寿命は男性81.09歳、女性は87.26歳と伸び続けている。少子・高齢化・人口減少問題はどんどん進んでいる。国立社会保障・人口問題研究所が発表した報告書によれば、2010年時の人口1億2,806万人から減少の一途をたどり、約50年後には1億人を割り、人口構成は逆ピラミッド型となり深刻な問題である。

例えば、日本の社会保障制度の基本である年金制度は賦課方式で、現役の働き手世代が年金受取世代の負担を負っているため、高齢者が激増し、働く世代が大幅に縮小すれば、年金財政がいずれ破綻してしまう危険性が極めて高い。また日本の政府・自治体の借金が1,100兆円を超えており、働き手が少ない世代では膨大な借金を返済することが困難となる。日本社会全体に共通する重大な課題であり、このため生産性の向上、働き方改革、働き手確保なども喫緊の課題となる。

（4）対外経済

a）貿易
1）貿易構造

日本の貿易は、基本的には資源・原材料を輸入して工業製品を輸出するという加工貿易型の構造だと言えるが、最近では、輸入においても工業製品の比率が高まっている。これは、工業分野でも国際的な相互依存関係が進展していることを示すとともに、日本企業の海外展開の結果でもある。主要部品等を輸出し、新興国等に置かれた海外拠点でそれを製品に加工して日本に逆輸入する例が増えており、食品でも、海外に農場や養殖施設を持ち、その生産物を加工食品などの形で

d) Response to Aging Society, Declining Birthrate, and Shrinking Population

The number of births in Japan in 2017 was 946 thousand, under one million for the second year in a row, and the number of deaths in 2017 was 1.394 million. The declining birthrate and shrinking population have become a serious matter. The average life expectancy in Japan in 2017 continued to increase, standing at 81.09 years for males and 87.26 years for females. There is the growing problem of a declining birthrate and shrinking population. According to a report released by the National Institute of Population and Social Security Research, the population has been in a steady decline from the 2010 figure of 128.06 million, and will fall below 100 million in about 50 years, when the shape of the population pyramid will be a reverse pyramid. It is indeed a serious problem.

For example, the pension system, which is the basis of Japan's social security system, is a pay-as-you-go system, in which the active working generation funds the pensioners. Therefore, there is a very high risk that a major increase in the number of aged persons and a major decrease in the number of active workers will cause the pension finance system to collapse. Moreover, while the debts of the Japanese government and municipalities exceed 1,100 trillion yen, it is difficult to repay huge debts in a generation that has few workers. This is a serious problem that permeates the entire Japanese society, and therefore there is an urgent need to improve productivity, reform work methods, and secure workers.

(4) External Economic Relations

a) Trade

1) Trade Structure

While Japan's trade basically has a "processing trade" type structure comprising imports of resources and raw materials and exports of industrial products, recently industrial products account for an increasing share of imports. This shows the increasing international interdependence of the industrial sector and the growing overseas expansion of Japanese companies. Reverse imports are on the increase, in which main components are exported from Japan to bases located in emerging economies to be processed into final products and imported back to Japan. There are also many instances now in which companies

輸入する例が多くなっている。

2）輸出

2017年、日本の輸出額は、前年比12％増の78.3兆円となった。国別では、第1位はアメリカで全輸出の19.3％を占め、第2位は中国19.0％、第3位は韓国7.6％となった。

商品別では、半導体等製造装置（韓国、中国、アメリカ）、自動車（アメリカ、オーストラリア、カナダ）、鉄鋼（中国、タイ、台湾）などが増加した。また、アメリカ向けは15.1兆円（7％増）となり、中国向けの14.9兆円（21％増）を上回った。アメリカは、5年連続でわが国最大の輸出相手国となった。

輸出品は大部分が工業製品であり、2017年では、一般機械類が輸出額の19.9％、自動車15.1％、電気機器15.1％（半導体など電子部品5.1％を含む）、化学製品12.8％、自動車部品5.0％を占めている。その他の主なものは、鉄鋼4.2％、精密機械3.2％、船舶1.7％などである。

電子部品では、部品輸出に中国、韓国の電機企業や日本企業の海外拠点に供給されるものが多く、プラスチック類でも同じような形がみられる。

2017年、向け先では、アジアが54.8％で最も多い。中国、韓国以外は台湾5.8％、香港5.1％、タイ4.2％、シンガポール3.2％、ベトナム2.2％、インドネシア1.9％、マレーシア1.8％などASEAN（東南アジア諸国連合）の比率は15.2％と高い水準である。

その他地域では、EU向けが11.1％で、うちドイツが2.7％、イギリス2.0％、オランダ1.8％などである。また中南米4.0％、中東3.0％、大洋州2.9％、アフリカ1.1％となっている。その他主要国としてオーストラリア2.3％、メキシコ1.6％、インド1.3％、ロシア0.9％である。

3）輸入

2017年の日本の輸入は、前年比14.0％増の75.3兆円で、アメリカ、中国、ドイツに次ぐ世界第4位の輸入国である。増加の要因は原油価格が5年ぶりに前年比31％上昇の影響を受け、原油（サウジアラビア、UAE、クウェート）、石炭（オーストラリア、ロシア、インドネシア）、LNG（オーストラリア、マレー

have overseas farms and aquaculture facilities, the products of which are imported into Japan in the form of processed foods.

2) Exports

Japan's exports amounted to 78.3 trillion yen in 2017, an increase of 12% compared to the preceding year. In the first place, accounting for 19.3% of all export destinations, was the U.S., followed in second place by China, with 19.0%, with South Korea third, with 7.6%.

By product, sales of semiconductor manufacturing equipment (Korea, China, the U.S.), automobiles (the U.S., Australia, Canada), and iron and steel (China, Thailand, Taiwan) rose. The value of the exports to the U.S. was 15.1 trillion yen (7% increase), and to China was 14.9 trillion yen (21% increase). The U.S. was Japan's largest trading partner, with the export amount increasing for the fifth consecutive year.

Industrial items accounted for most of the exports in terms of value. In 2017, general machinery accounted for 19.9% of exports, automobiles for 15.1%, electrical equipment for 15.1% (include electronic components such as semiconductors for 5.1%), chemical products for 12.8%, and automotive parts for 5.0%. Other major items were steel, 4.2%, precision machinery, 3.2%, and ships, 1.7%.

In electrical equipment, exports of most component exports are supplied to Chinese and South Korean electrical machinery enterprises and overseas bases of Japanese companies, and this also applies to plastic parts.

In terms of export destination in 2017, Asia accounted for the largest share at 54.8%. In addition to China and South Korea, there was Taiwan at 5.8%, Hong Kong at 5.1%, and the Association of South East Asian Nations (ASEAN) at 15.2%, led by Thailand at 4.2%, Singapore at 3.2%, Vietnam at 2.2%, Indonesia at 1.9% and Malaysia at 1.8%.

By other regions, the EU accounted for 11.1%, with Germany being the top destination at 2.7%, followed by the UK at 2.0% and the Netherlands at 1.8%. Central and South America accounted for 4.0%, the Middle East for 3.0%, Oceania for 2.9%, and Africa for 1.1%. Other major countries included Australia at 2.3%, Mexico at 1.6%, India at 1.3% and Russia at 0.9%.

3) Imports

Japan's imports in 2017 rose 14.0% compared to the previous year, to 75.3 trillion yen making Japan the world's fourth largest importer after the U.S., China, and Germany. Factors behind the increase included a rise of 31% in oil prices (Saudi Arabia, UAE, Kuwait), the first such rise in five years, and increases in imports of coal (Australia, Russia, Indonesia), and LNG (Australia, Malaysia, the U.S.). At 9.5%, the

シア、アメリカ）など鉱物性燃料が増加した。原油の主な供給元である中東地域は 9.5％を占め、その内訳はサウジアラビア 4.1％、UAE 3.1％、カタール 1.6％などである。

また、最大の輸入相手国である中国からはコンピュータ機器（レノボ等）、スマートフォン（アップル・ファーウェイ等）、衣料の増加により、18.4 兆円（前年比 8％増）となり 2 年ぶりに増加した。

輸入額全体に占める鉱物性燃料のシェアは 20.9％（前年比 2.7％増）で、食料品 7.6％、原料品（木材、鉱石など）3.3％を合わせた原材料および半製品は 31.8％であり、製品輸入比率は 68.2％（前年比 2.6％減）となった。

主要な製品輸入品は、電気機器 14.6％、化学製品 11.7％、一般機械 9.7％、金属製品 4.0％、自動車等 2.9％、精密機械 2.7％などである。

この中には、日本企業の海外拠点による製品の逆輸入が含まれている。個別の品目で比較的多いのは、化学製品のうちの医薬品 3.5％、電機機器のうちの半導体等の電子部品 3.7％などである。身近な製品では、衣類が中国を中心に 4.1％を占めている。

相手地域ではアジアが 50.6％を占めた。その内訳は中国が 24.5％で、以下は韓国 4.2％、台湾 3.8％、タイ 3.4％、インドネシア 3.0％、マレーシア 2.9％、ベトナム 2.8％などである。

中国に次ぐのはアメリカの 10.7％で、航空機、医薬品、科学光学機器など工業製品のほか、肉類、穀物、大豆等の農産物でも主な輸入先である。

その他では、EU が 15.5％で、その内訳はドイツが 3.5％である。オーストラリアが石炭、鉄鉱石、LNG などで 5.8％、ロシア 2.1％、カナダ 1.6％である。地域別にみると、大洋州 6.6％、中南米 4.2％、アフリカ 1.2％などである。

b）国際収支

海外とのモノやサービス、利子・配当などの取引をまとめた経常収支は、2017 年 21 兆 8,742 億円の黒字で前年比 7.5％の増加であった。経常黒字は、東日本大震災の影響で 2014 年まで減少が続いていたが、2015 年から原燃料など資源安の影響で貿易収支が大幅に回復したことで黒字幅

Middle East was the main source of oil, with 4.1% coming from Saudi Arabia, 3.1% from the United Arab Emirates, and 1.6% from Qatar.

At 18.4 trillion yen, an increase of 8% from the previous year (the first increase in two years) China was the main source of imports, with computer equipment (Lenovo, etc.), smartphones (Apple, Huawei, etc.) and apparel all posting increases.

The share of the total import value of mineral fuels is 20.9% (an increase of 2.7% year-on-year), semi-finished goods, including food at 7.6% and raw materials at 3.3% (wood, ores, and so on), accounted for 31.8% of total imports, and the ratio of product imports was 68.2% (a decrease of 2.6% year-on-year).

Major imports are electrical equipment for 14.6%, chemical products for 11.7%, general machinery for 9.7%, metal products for 4.0%, automobiles for 2.9% and precision machinery for 2.7%.

A breakdown of industrial products, with some of these being reverse imports from overseas facilities of Japanese companies. Relatively high individual items were pharmaceuticals at 3.5% and electrical components, such as semiconductors used in electrical equipment, 3.7%. Among everyday items, clothing, mainly from China, accounted for 4.1%.

By region, Asia accounted for 50.6%, by country, China at 24.5%, South Korea at 4.2%, Taiwan at 3.8%, Thailand at 3.4%, Indonesia at 3.0%, Malaysia at 2.9%, Vietnam at 2.8%.

By country, at 10.7%, the U.S. was second to China, supplying aircraft, pharmaceuticals, and scientific optical instruments, and agricultural products such as meat, grain and soybeans.

The EU accounted for 15.5% of imports, of which Germany accounted for 3.5%. Australia (coal, iron ore, and LNG) accounted for 5.8%, Russia for 2.1%, Canada for 1.6.%. Oceania accounted for 6.6%, Central and South America for 4.2%, and Africa for 1.2%.

b) International Balance of Payments

The current account balance is a summary of transactions in goods, services, and interest and dividends with other countries. In 2017 Japan had a current account surplus of 21.8742 trillion yen, an increase of 7.5% from the previous year. The current account surplus had continued to decrease until 2014 due to the impact of the Great East

が増えた。

　経常収支の各項目をみると、貿易収支が4兆9,308億円と黒字を維持している。サービス収支は7,061億円の赤字であったが、旅行収支が1兆7,626億円の黒字、知的財産権などの使用料が2兆3,660億円の黒字となり、赤字額は大きく減少している。海外企業から受け取る配当金や債券の利子などを示す第一次所得収支は、前年比9.1％増の19兆7,397億円の黒字であった。この増加は、海外投資の成果と前年比3.1％の円安（2016年平均値108.79円／ドル、2017年平均値112.16円／ドル）の影響もある。

　足元の世界経済の状況は好調に推移しているが、国内の原子力発電所の低稼働状況などから、鉱物性燃料に依存する割合が高く、輸出競争環境の厳しさが継続しているため、政府は新興国・発展途上国向けインフラ輸出の拡大と訪日観光客誘致などを、重点施策の柱としている。

　外貨準備高とは、輸入代金の決済、対外債務の返済、自国通貨の為替レートの急激な変動を抑制するために行う為替市場介入などを目的として、財務省と日本銀行が保有する対外資産のことである。日本は2018年6月で1兆2,587億ドルを保有しており、中国に次ぐ世界第2位の水準である。

c）対外経済協力
　日本は、国際経済協力に力を入れており、2000年まで10年間は世界最大のODA（政府開発援助）供与国であった。その後、供与は減額した。現状は過去8年間5,500億円／年のODA予算を維持しており、2017年は5,527億円で、OECDの経済協力委員会（DAC）加盟23カ国の供与額の7.3％を占め、23カ国中4位である。

　その他、民間企業ベースでも、この5年間で毎年400億ドルから500億ドルの直接投資や国際機関への融資などの

Japan Earthquake, but since 2015 the surplus has improved as the trade balance underwent a dramatic recovery due to falls in the prices of raw fuels and other resources.

Looking at each item of the current account, Japan maintains a surplus in its trade account, which currently stands at 4.9308 trillion yen. Although there was a trade balance of services deficit of 706.1 billion yen, that has been significantly decreased by a travel balance surplus of 1.7626 trillion yen and a surplus of 2.366 trillion yen in charges for the use of intellectual property rights. The primary income balance, which shows dividends and interest on bonds received from overseas companies, showed a surplus of 19.7397 trillion yen, an increase of 9.1% compared to the previous year. This increase also reflects overseas investment results and a depreciation in the yen of 3.1% compared to the previous year (average of 108,79 yen/dollar in 2016; average of 112.16 yen/dollar in 2017).

The global economic conditions have been good, but with Japan's internal energy situation in which few nuclear power plants are in operation, there continues to be a high level of dependence on mineral fuels, creating a bleak environment for export competition. This being the case, the focal point of government policy has been to revitalize exports such as by expanding infrastructure exports to emerging economies, and to place emphasis on attracting tourists to Japan.

Foreign exchange reserves are defined as the amount of foreign assets held by the Ministry of Finance and the Bank of Japan for the settling of import payments, repayment of external debt, and intervening in foreign exchange markets to curb sudden fluctuations in the exchange rate of the local currency. Japan had $1.2587 trillion as of June 2018, making it the world's second largest holder of foreign currency reserves, first place being China.

c) External Economic Cooperation

Japan has focused on international economic cooperation, and in the ten years leading to 2000 was the world's leading provider of Official Development Assistance (ODA). Subsequently, its efforts in this area have decreased. Over the past eight years Japan has maintained an annual ODA budget of 550 billion yen. In 2017, the 552.7 billion yen it provided accounted for 7.3% of the assistance provided by the OECD's 23 Development Assistance Committee (DAC) member states, ranking it fourth among the other member states.

Also, in the past five years private sector enterprises have been involved in providing from 40 billion to 50 billion dollars a year in

資金提供実施や自然環境保護をはじめとする具体的活動などが活発に行われている。また、非営利団体の活動も積極的に行われており、農業、教育、医療などの多様な分野で現地に溶けこんで活動し、相手国の国民の福利の向上や経済発展の基礎づくりに寄与している。

(5) 主要産業の動向

2017年末時点の現況は、2012年12月から61カ月の景気回復期間となり、戦後2位のいざなぎ景気を超える長さとなっている。しかし、実質GDPの伸び率は1.5%と過去の景気回復に比べると低い。この5年間で就業者数は185万人増加。保育の受け皿拡大等により女性の就業者が152万人増加したことに加え、若者への支援等により若者の失業率は5.1%と1993年以来の低水準となった。4年連続で2%程度の賃上げが実現し、最低賃金も5年連続で増加した。働く人全体の所得は24兆円増加、企業収益や税収も増加し、デフレを克服しつつある状況である。2010年から2012年の行き過ぎた円高も修正され、第2次産業の国際競争力も改善された。第3次産業もサービス、通信、医療福祉、外食、輸送などが景気をけん引している。今後、自由貿易主義を標榜する日本としては、EUとの日欧経済連携（EPA）・TPPとの連携の成果、および日米・日中・日印・対ASEANとの貿易交渉の推進結果が、日本の産業の行く末に大きな影響を与える。

他方、アメリカトランプ政権は2017年の対中国貿易赤字額が2,758億ドルと過去最高に達したことを受け、2018年3月以降、中国製太陽光パネルなどにセーフガード措置を発動したほか、安全保障を根拠に鉄鋼、アルミ製品に対する追加関税を実施した。また、知的財産権の侵害や不正技術移転に対処するため、貿易慣行を理由とする通商法301条を根拠に、中国に対して追加関税、WTOへの提訴、投資制限などの方針を示している。25%の追加関税は2018年7月に340億ドル、8月に160億ドル、9月に2,000億ドルを第3弾として実施している。中国もこの動

direct investment and funding to international bodies, and in activities aimed at preserving the natural environment. In addition, nonprofit organizations are working locally on the ground in many areas including agriculture, education, and health care, to improve public welfare in partner countries and help build the foundation for economic development.

(5) Industrial Trends

The end of 2017 marked the 61st month of an economic recovery period that started in December 2012, longer than what is called the Izanagi boom that had marked the second longest period of postwar economic expansion. However, the real GDP growth rate is 1.5%, which is lower than past recoveries. The number of employed people increased by 1.85 million over the past five years. In addition to the fact that the number of female employees increased by 1.52 million due to the expansion of childcare facilities, the youth unemployment rate was 5.1%, the lowest it has been since 1993, thanks to youth support measures. Wages rose by about 2% for four years in a row and the minimum wage also increased five years in a row. The income of all workers increased by a total of 24 trillion yen, and the increases in corporate earnings and tax revenues are also overcoming deflation. The over-appreciation of the yen from 2010 to 2012 underwent a correction and the international competitiveness of the secondary industries improved. In the tertiary industries, the economy is being driven by services, communications, medical welfare, food services, transportation, and so forth. With Japan advocating free trade principles going forward, the outcome of the Japan-EU Economic Partnership Agreement (EPA) and collaboration with the Trans-Pacific Partnership (TPP), and the results of promoting trade negotiations with the U.S., China, India, and ASEAN will have a big influence on the future of Japanese industry.

After the U.S. recorded its biggest ever trading deficit of 275.8 billion dollars with China in 2017, the Trump administration implemented safeguard measures in March 2018 against solar panel products made in China. The U.S. later imposed additional tariffs on steel and aluminum products, on the grounds of national security. In addition, in order to cope with infringement of intellectual property rights and illegal technology transfers, the U.S. has cited Section 301 of its Trade Act relating to unfair trade practices and expressed its intentions to impose additional tariffs on Chinese products, institute a case with the WTO, restrict investment, and so forth. Additional tariffs of 25% are to be

きに対抗して米国製品に同額・同率の報復関税をかけているため、米中政府の対立が激化しており、世界第1位と第2位の経済大国同士の長期対立は世界経済に大きな悪影響を及ぼすことが危惧されるとともに、自由貿易のあり方について深刻な問題提起がなされている。

a）第1次産業

1）概要

日本の第1次産業の産業全体における相対的な比率は、2017年で就業人口の約3.4％、GDPの1.2％と、数字の上では小さく、食料の自給率はカロリーベースで38％、食料生産額ベースでは68％にとどまり、農林水産物の供給における海外依存度が高い。2018年にTPPが発効し、農産物の関税を引き下げられれば、構造的改善が必須となり国際競争力強化が迫られることとなる。課題としては、〈1〉若い農業従事者を増やす、〈2〉農業への参入障壁をなくす、〈3〉全農業用地の1割が農業放棄地になっているが、これを有効に活用する、〈4〉マーケティング、品種改良によるブランドの確立、食の安全管理、知的財産管理を徹底する、〈5〉ITの活用、空き工場の植物工場への転用、LEDなどの最新技術を導入して飛躍的に生産性の向上を図る、などであり従来の政府補助金に頼った守りの農業から大規模輸出もできる攻めの農業への転換である。

2）農業

日本の農業（畜産を含む）の就業者は、2017年に204万人で、GDPの1.0％を生み出した。しかし、就業者の高齢化が進んで65歳以上が66％に達しており、後継者確保が大きな課題である。また、農用地面積が国土の12.0％にすぎず、農家の80％の経営規模が2ha（5エーカー）に満たないことも経営効率化を妨げている。そのため、これまで基本的に自営農家にゆだねられていた農業へ、企業の参入や、農家間の経営受委託などによる規模拡大も試みられている。また、収益性の向上のため、耕作・加工・販売の一体化

implemented in three stages: 34 billion dollars in July 2018, 16 billion dollars in August and 200 billion dollars in September. Since China will also respond to that by applying retaliatory tariffs of the same amount and same rate to U.S. products, the standoff between the U.S. and China is set to intensify, amid concerns that a long-term confrontation between the world's No. 1 and No. 2 economic powers will have a huge negative impact on the world economy and raise serious issues about how free trade will proceed.

a) Primary Industries
1) Overview

Japan's primary industries employed 3.4% of the nation's workforce and accounted for 1.2% of the gross domestic product (GDP) in 2017, so in terms of numbers are small, with the country having a high dependence on foreign supplies of agricultural and marine products, and a food self-sufficiency of 38% on a calorie basis and 68% in terms of food production monetary value. If the TPP goes into effect in 2018 and reduces tariffs on agricultural products, it will be necessary to make structural improvements and strengthen international competitiveness. Issues to be tackled are: <1> increase the numbers of young farmers; <2> eliminate barriers to entering agriculture; <3> make effective use of abandoned farmland, which accounts for 10% of all agricultural land; <4> marketing, by establishing brands through the improvement of plant varieties, food safety management, and the careful management of intellectual property; <5> utilization of information technology, conversion of empty factories to use for plants, introduction of LEDs and other new technologies to achieve major improvements in productivity, and other moves to shift from conventional "passive" agriculture that relies on government subsidies to "aggressive" agriculture which produces products that can also be exported on a large scale.

2) Agriculture

In 2017, agriculture (including livestock farming) had a workforce of 2.04 million and accounted for 1.0% of GDP. Due to the aging of the workforce, 66% of the workers are 65 or older, so securing successors is a major issue. Also, only 12.0% of the nation's total land area is used for agriculture, and with 80% of farmers working less than 2 hectares (5 acres), it is difficult to increase efficiency. Up until now, therefore, the entry of companies into agriculture, which has basically been left to self-employed farmers, or to management trusts among farmers as a way of increasing the scale of farming operations. Integrating cultivation, processing and sales is also being promoted as way to improve

なども推進されている（農業の6次産業化）。

　農業の6次産業化：農業や水産業などの第1次産業が食品加工（第2次産業）・流通販売（第3次産業）にも業務展開している経営形態を表す（1次×2次×3次で6次産業化と呼ぶ）。

　最も重要な作物は日本人の主食であるコメであり、農家の60％が稲作を経営の柱としている。そのため関税等により保護されており、主食用は100％の自給率を維持している。飼料用として2017年、77万トン輸入している。ただ、国外からの輸入自由化への要求は強い。

　輸入品との競争は、その他の農産物ではすでに顕在化しており、生鮮野菜や伝統的な産物であるそば、こんにゃく、緑茶なども輸入されている。現状はおおむね生鮮野菜の70％は国産でまかなっている。野菜・果物の競争力強化をめざして品種や生産方法の改良に大きな努力が注がれており、世界各地で生産されているリンゴなどでも、高級品として高値で輸出されている。近年、ぶどう、ももの輸出額の伸びが続いており、ぶどうはシンガポール、桃はマレーシアで大きく販売を増やしている。2016年は野菜・果物ともに前年比6％の産出額増加となっている。

　畜産は、2016年に農業産出額の35％を占めたが、経営規模は養鶏を除いて極めて小さい。一部関税による保護はあるものの、輸入品との競争は厳しく、飼料の75％（栄養分換算）を輸入に依存する脆弱性もある。狭い国土での経営のため糞尿処理で高度な対策が必要なことなども不利であり、経営の集約化、施設の共同化などによる競争力強化が進められている。2016年は集約化効果・高級化もあり肉用牛の産出額は前年を7％上回り、過去5年間で産出額が47％増加している。

3）林業

　日本の国土面積の3分の2、約2,500万haは森林である。国産材の供給量は2002年を底に増加傾向にある。木材自給率も2002年の18.8％を底に上昇傾向で推移した。2017年は2,953万m^3を供給し、自給率36.1％となり30年前の水準に回復した。

profitability (the sixth industrialization of agriculture).

Sixth industrialization of agriculture: This represents a form of management in which primary industries such as agriculture and fisheries also develop business in food processing (secondary industry) and distribution (tertiary industry). (The name is derived from Primary industry × Secondary industry × Tertiary industry equals Sixth industrialization.)

The most important crop is rice, which is the staple food of the Japanese and the principal crop for 60% of farmers. Tariff protection is therefore used to maintain a self-sufficiency ratio of about 100% for staple food rice. In 2017 Japan imported 770,000 tons of rice for animal feed. However, there are strong demands from other countries for import liberalization.

There is also competition from imports of fresh vegetables and traditional Japanese foods such as buckwheat noodles, *konnyaku*, and green tea. Currently, 70% of fresh vegetables are domestically grown. Great efforts have been focused on strengthening competitiveness in fruit and vegetables by improving varieties and production methods, and even on exporting as high-priced luxury goods such as apple varieties from many parts of the world. In recent years, exports of grapes and peaches continue to grow, with sales of grapes to Singapore and peaches to Malaysia increasing. In 2016 output of both vegetables and fruits increased by 6% in terms of sales value compared to the previous year.

Livestock accounted for 35% of agricultural output value in 2016, but with the exception of poultry farming, all livestock farming is conducted on a very small scale. There is some tariff protection, but competition from import items is intense and the industry is vulnerable, relying on imports for 75% (in terms of nutrients) of the feed used. The need for advanced measures for treating manure in what is a limited land area is a further disadvantage. Moves are being made to strengthen competitiveness by centralizing management and sharing facilities. In 2016, consolidation and upgrading increased beef cattle production by 7% compared to the previous year, and the increase over the past 5 years has been 47% (sales value).

3) Forestry Industry

Two-thirds, or approximately 25 million hectares (6.2 million acres), of the land area of Japan is covered by forests. The domestic timber supply volume has been on the rise since bottoming out in 2002. The timber self-sufficiency ratio is rising after also bottoming out at 18.8% in 2002. In 2017, the supply volume was 29.53 million cubic meters, a

木材需要量のうち、2017年は製材用が32％、合板用が13％、パルプ・チップ用が40％であった。合板では、国産材に対応した技術開発や施設整備等を進めた結果、2017年の国内生産における国産材利用の割合は82％に上昇した。

地球環境保護の観点から、日本は、世界的な森林保全に配慮し、木材供給国での植林活動などを実施・支援している。国内でも、環境保全や水源涵養のため、新規就業者への支援、間伐材の用途拡大、ボランティアによる山林手入れなど、林業の維持・振興に官民による種々の努力が行われている。そのための財源にあてるため、2024年から森林環境税として国民1人あたり1,000円を徴収する方向で検討が進められている。

4）水産業

魚介類は日本人の重要な蛋白源であり、国民1人当たり消費量は、2016年で1日125gであった（水産白書2018）。

漁業の主体は海面漁業で、2016年の就業者は20万人、漁獲量は、430万トンであった。うち33万トンが遠洋漁業によるもので、アフリカの近くや北大西洋まで出かけて操業している。ほかに内水面漁業が6万トンある。養殖も盛んであり、高度な技術を応用して、カキ、ホタテ、ブリ類、マダイ、マグロなどを107万トン生産した。海面、内水面、養殖を合わせた全生産量は436万トンとなる。

世界的な食慣習の変化で海産物の消費が増えているため、資源保護の観点から漁獲量や漁業水域の規制が強化されていること、各国の漁獲競争が激化していることなどから、日本が利用できる漁業資源の確保が難しくなり、この25年間で日本の漁獲量は3分の1に減少している。そのため、魚介類でも自給が不可能となり、自給率は2016年で56％になっている。

日本やアイスランド、ノルエウェーなどの海洋国家は古来、鯨を食用とする食文化がある。一方、反捕鯨国は「商業捕鯨につながる調査捕鯨などの提案は認めない」という主張を崩さず、2018年9月の国際捕鯨

self-sufficiency ratio of 36.1%, representing a recovery to the level of 30 years ago.

In 2017, 32% of timber demand was for sawn lumber, 13% for plywood, and 40% for pulp and chips. As a result of advances in the development of technology and facilities for domestic timber, the proportion of domestic lumber used for domestic plywood production rose to 82% in 2017.

To protect the global environment and in consideration of worldwide forest conservation moves, Japan is implementing and supporting tree planting activities in countries that supply wood. Even in Japan, to protect the environment and conserve water resources, various efforts are being made by the public and private sectors to maintain and promote forestry, such as by helping to employ new workers, expand thinned-wood applications and using volunteer-based forest care activities. To devote further financial resources for that purpose, collecting 1,000 yen per citizen as a forest environmental tax from 2024 is under consideration.

4) Fisheries Industry

Seafood is an important source of protein for the Japanese people. Daily per capita fish consumption was 125 grams in 2016 (2018 Fisheries White Paper).

In 2016, Japan's fisheries industry had a workforce of 200,000 and a catch of 4.30 million tons, of which 330,000 tons was from deep-sea fishing operations as far as close to Africa and in the North Atlantic. Some 60,000 tons came from inland fresh-water fisheries. Aquaculture is also thriving, and from the application of advanced technology yielded 1.07 million tons of oysters, scallops, yellowtail, red sea bream, and tuna. Total production from sea, inland-water and aquaculture operations combined came to 4.36 million tons.

Because the consumption of seafood has increased with worldwide changes in dietary practices, regulation of fish catches and fishing areas has been strengthened to protect marine resources, and there is increased fishing competition between countries, which has made it more difficult for Japan to secure fishery resources it can utilize. In the past 25 years, Japan's catch has decreased to one-third what it used to be. This has made self-sufficiency in seafood impossible, and Japan's self-sufficiency ratio is now 56%.

In maritime nations such as Japan, Iceland and Norway, the eating of whale has been part of their food culture since ancient times. On the other hand, anti-whaling nations continued to reject Japan's proposal on scientific whaling that is related to commercial whaling, and in

委員会 (IWC : International Whaling Commission) において「捕鯨の解除は一切認められない」と決議された。これを受けて日本政府は 2018 年 12 月に IWC を脱退した。

b) 第2次産業
1) 建設業

建設業は、2017 年に全就業者の 7.6% の 501 万人を雇用し、GDP の 5.5% を生産した。現況は東日本大震災からの復興関連に続き、リニア中央新幹線建設、老朽化した社会インフラの補修・更新、東京オリンピック・パラリンピック施設建設に取りかかっている。巨大工事が重なり各現場は熟練技能工が慢性的に不足しており、体系的な育成が必要である。さらに 2025 年に大阪万国博覧会開催が決定し、大規模建設工事は長期にわたり継続されると予想される。

建設業にはおよそ 46.5 万の企業がある。ゼネコンと呼ばれる総合建設事業者には売上高が 1 兆円を超える企業も 5 社あるが、大半は中・小規模であり、単独で小規模な工事を行うほか、大手企業の下請けとして活動している。伝統的な社寺建築や海洋土木など特殊な技術で活躍する企業もある。

海外でも、長大橋、高層ビルなどで多くの実績を持ち、2017 年度の海外受注額は、現地法人によるものを含めて 1.85 兆円に達した。ただ、海外では中国・韓国との競争が厳しくなっている。

2) 製造業
i) 概要

製造業には、2017 年に 1,081 万人の就業者がおり、GDP の 21.0% を生み出した。経済全体における製造業の相対的比率は低下しているが、国内需要に加え、資源輸入をまかなう外貨を得るために必要な輸出品の大半を供給する分野としても、日本経済における重要性は依然として極めて高い。

ただし、製造業の中心は、かつての重化学工業から、エレクトロニクスなどへと移行している。さらに、半導体、パソコン、スマートフォン、液

September 2018, the International Whaling Commission (IWC) decided against lifting the ban on whaling. In response to this decision, the Japanese government withdrew from the IWC in December 2018.

b) Secondary Industries

1) Construction Industry

In 2017, the construction industry employed 5.01 million workers, or 7.6% of the workforce, and accounted for 5.5% of the gross domestic product (GDP). Following on from Great East Japan Earthquake-damage reconstruction-related projects, work is underway on the construction of the Linear Chuo Shinkansen (bullet train) line, the repair and renewal of aging infrastructure in society, and the construction of facilities for the Tokyo Olympic and Paralympic Games. On each of these overlapping giant construction project sites there is a chronic shortage of skilled workers, and a need for systematic training. Furthermore, it has been decided to hold the Osaka World Exposition in 2025, thus large-scale construction projects are expected to continue for a long time.

The industry comprises some 465,000 companies. While five of these are general construction firms with annual sales of over 1 trillion yen, the majority are small private contractors that work on their own or as subcontractors of large companies. Some are also companies with special skills, such as in the traditional architecture of temples and shrines and marine civil engineering.

Abroad, the industry has built many long bridges and high-rise buildings. In fiscal 2017, overseas orders, including those by local subsidiaries, came to 1.85 trillion yen. However, there is fierce competition from China and South Korea.

2) Manufacturing
i) Overview

In 2017 the manufacturing sector had a workforce of 10.81 million and accounted for 21.0% of the gross domestic product (GDP). Manufacturing accounts for relatively less of the overall economy than before, but in addition to domestic demand, it supplies most of the export demand to obtain the foreign currency to cover the import of resources, so its importance within the Japanese economy continues to be very high.

While it used to be centered on heavy chemical industries, it has now shifted to other sectors such as electronics. However, even in relatively advanced products such as semiconductors, personal computers,

晶テレビなど、比較的先端的な製品でも、技術・コストの両面で競争力を強めてきた中国、韓国、台湾などに圧倒されている。

日本の工業には、多くの国際的に知られた企業とともに、高度な技術と経験を持つ中小の専門企業が多数あり、高品質な精密金型、機械部品などを供給して工業全体の質的水準を高めている。ただ、これらの企業では、個人の技術に依存する部分が大きく、技能の継承、後継者の確保が重要な課題になっている。

ii) 金属工業

金属工業は、鉄鋼、非鉄金属、金属製品の3分野からなり、2015年には従業者97.0万人で42.2兆円の製品を出荷した。

鉄鋼業：日本は、2017年に粗鋼を1億466万トン生産した。これは世界の生産量の6.2％に当たり、中国に次ぐ世界第2位に位置する。

粗鋼の生産には、鉱石から製錬する高炉法と鉄くずから作る電炉法がある。高炉・電炉の双方を持つ一貫メーカーは4社で、粗鋼生産の4分の3を占め、広範な製品を生産している。

国際競争の激化の中で、世界の鉄鋼業で国境を越える大規模な再編が進み、日本企業の相対的地位と競争力が低下した。そのため、日本の一貫メーカーでも、2000年代になって上位企業間の合併が進み、2012年までに6社から4社に集約された。うち2社が粗鋼生産量で世界3位など10位以内に入っている。また、中国の生産過剰に伴う輸出量の増大が鉄鋼製品の価格破壊を惹起し、市場のバランスを崩して世界的な問題となっている。

日本の鉄鋼製品は、自動車用高強度薄鋼板（ハイテン材）、モーター・トランスに不可欠な電磁鋼板、極寒にも耐える高強度鋼管など、高い信頼度を要求される製品で国際的に高く評価されており、2017年には鋼材3,813万トンを輸出した。

海外では、日本の自動車メーカーの海外拠点などに高品質の材料を供給するため、海外鉄鋼メーカーとの合弁事業などの形で製造販売を行い、あ

smartphones, and Liquid Crystal Display (LCD) televisions, it is being overwhelmed by China, South Korea, Taiwan and increasingly competitive in terms of both technology and cost.

Japanese industry is comprised of many internationally known companies and numerous, specialized small and medium-sized enterprises that possess a high level of technology and experience and supply high-quality precision molds and machine parts that raise the overall quality standards of the industry. In large part, however, those companies depend on the technological skills of individuals, so securing successors that can carry on the skills has become an important task.

ii) Metals Industry

The metals industry comprises the three areas of steel, nonferrous metals, and metal products. In 2015 the metals industry had a workforce of 970,000 and shipped products worth some 42.2 trillion yen.

Steel Industry: Japan produced 104.66 million tons of crude steel in 2017, which accounted for 6.2% of world production. Japan is the world's second largest steel producer behind China.

Crude steel is produced by the blast furnace method of smelting from ore, and from scrap iron by the electric arc furnace method. There are four integrated manufacturers that have both blast furnaces and electric furnaces, and they are responsible for the production of three-fourths of the crude steel and produce a wide range of products.

While the international competition has been intensifying, the global steel industry is undergoing major cross-border restructuring, reducing the relative competitive position of the Japanese industry. Therefore in the 2000s even the top integrated manufacturers in Japan pursued mergers, which by 2012 had consolidated six companies into four. Two of the companies are in the top ten in the world in crude steel production, one of which ranks third in the world. An increase in exports due to excess production in China has caused the prices of steel products to collapse, leading to global problems of the supply-demand imbalance.

Japan's steel products include high-tensile sheet for automotive applications, electrical steel sheet that is essential for motors and transformers, high-strength steel tube able to withstand extreme cold and other internationally acclaimed products in which high reliability is a requirement. In 2017 Japan exported 38.13 million tons of steel materials.

To supply high-quality materials to overseas plants of Japanese auto manufacturers, Japanese companies are entering into joint-ventures with overseas steel producers to manufacture and sell their steel, and

るいは海外鉄鋼メーカーに技術を供与している。今後、自動車の海外現地生産化・軽量化・電気自動車（EV）化の流れに対応しなければならない。コストやリサイクル面で鉄の優位性はあるが、素材競争が激化している。

電炉メーカーは多数あり、事業内容も多様で、汎用品主体から特殊な高級品まで、それぞれ特徴を持って活動しているが、コストに占める比率の高い電気料金の上昇で厳しい経営状況にある。

非鉄金属工業：銅は、2016年に銅くずのリサイクルによるもの17万トンを含む155万トンの電気銅を生産した。主原料の鉱石はほぼ全量輸入に依存している。これに若干の輸入地金を加えて内需をまかなうほか、86万トンの地金、銅製品の輸出も行った。

アルミは、精錬に多量の電力を要するため、国内企業は大部分が精錬事業から撤退している。そのため、国内のアルミ需要は、輸入される新地金とリサイクルによる地金の加工という形でまかなわれている。日本のアルミ・リサイクル活動は極めて活発であり、2016年の地金供給の内訳は、輸入地金252万トン、国内再生地金119万トンであった。

リチウム、インジウム、コバルトなど、工業生産に不可欠なレアメタルは、全量輸入に依存しており、使用済みデジタル機器などからの回収・リサイクルに努めている。

ⅲ）一般機械・精密機械工業

一般機械：生産用機械器具などの一般機械を代表するのは金属工作機械である。生産台数では急拡大する中国が首位に立っているが、品質においては、日本はドイツとともに世界最高水準にある。しかし、金属工作機械は生産量が1990年から25年で約3分の1、生産金額は25％減となっている。2017年の国内生産額は1兆1,300億円であった。その中で台数、金額ともに、約90％がNC工作機械で、国際競争力もあり、生産量、生産金額を維持している。なお、金属工作機械の2017年の輸出額は7,862億円であった。

日本は産業用ロボットでは質・量とも世界を

providing technology to the producers. In the future, the industry must respond to the trend towards overseas local production of cars, weight reduction, and the move to electric vehicles (EVs). Steel has advantages in terms of cost and recycling, but competition is intensifying.

There are many manufacturers of electric furnaces which exhibit much variety, supplying a range of products, from general-purpose items to specialized, premium products and focusing on the features of each, but a rise in the price of electricity, which makes up a high percentage of the cost, is creating a difficult business environment.

Nonferrous Metal Industry: In 2016 electrolytic copper production came to 1.55 million tons, which included 170,000 tons recycled from copper scrap. Virtually all the raw ore has to be imported. Domestic demand was covered by the addition of a small amount of imported bullion, and 860,000 tons of bullion and copper products were exported.

Since it takes a lot of electric power to refine aluminum, for the most part domestic companies have withdrawn from the aluminum refining business. Therefore, domestic demand for aluminum is covered by importing new bullion and processing recycled aluminum. Aluminum recycling in Japan is extremely active: in 2016, supplies of aluminum consisted of 2.52 million tons of imported metal and 1.19 million tons of domestically recycled metal.

Lithium, indium, cobalt and other rare metals essential to industrial production are all imported, and efforts are made to recover and recycle such metals from used digital equipment.

iii) General Machinery & Precision Machinery Industries

General Machinery: Metal machine tools are representative of general machinery such as production machinery and equipment. China's rapid growth makes it the leader in terms of production volume, but Japan, along with Germany, ranks as the world's best in terms of quality. Production of metal machine tools decreased by one-third in the 25 years since 1990, and in value the decrease was 25%. Domestic production in terms of value amounted to 1.13 trillion yen in 2017. Of this total, some 90% in terms of both quantity and value were numerical control (NC) type machine tools that are internationally competitive, so production levels have been maintained in both quantity and value. Exports of metal machine tools in 2017 amounted to 786.2 billion yen.

Japan's industrial robots lead the world in terms of quality and

リードしており、2017年には前年比34.0％増の23.5万台を生産し、18.4万台を輸出した。国内の稼働数は28.7万台で、出荷金額は8,777億円であった。産業用ロボットは日欧中などにおける労働力人口減少、賃金上昇、品質向上のニーズ拡大を背景に、自動車・電子デバイス業界を中心に普及が進んできたが、今後は他業界や医療・福祉分野にも広がるであろう。

コマツに代表される建設用機械、エンジン、ベアリング、半導体製造装置などにも高度な技術を持ち、輸出でも重要な役割を果たしている。

精密機械工業：日本は、光学機器、時計、検査用機器など幅広い分野で高い技術を持っている。デジタルカメラ、レンズ交換式カメラは、日系企業3社が2017年全世界生産台数3,300万台の75％を占めている。ただし、国内生産比率は15％となっている。

日本製時計は、2017年に3億825万個を生産した。ただし、うち完成品は608万個で、大部分はムーブメントという半製品の形で輸出されている。

従来の精密機械は、光学と合体し、事業領域を半導体製造用部材やHDD用ガラスディスク、メガネレンズ、コンタクトレンズ、医療用内視鏡、カテーテル、人工臓器などの医療分野へと広がっている。

iv) 重電機器

大規模な電気設備である重電機器は、発電（火力発電所、原子力発電所、発電機など）、送電（変圧器、高圧遮断器など）、配電設備（電気開閉制御装置、ガス絶縁開閉装置など）に分類される。重電機器の2017年国内生産金額は過去10年で最高の3兆8,551億円であった。

v) 家庭用電気機器

家庭用電気機器の2017年国内生産金額は過去ピーク時1990年の2兆7,246億円に対し、30％減の1兆9,125億円であった。

空調機、冷蔵庫、洗濯機やテレビ、オーディオなどの家庭用電気機器の生産増加は、日本経済発

quantity, with production in 2017 amounting to 235,000 units, an increase of 34.0% compared to the previous year, of which 184,000 units were exported. The number of robots in operation in Japan amount to 287,000 units, with a shipment value of 877.7 billion yen. The use of industrial robots are spreading mainly in the automobile and electronic device industries in Japan, Europe, and China due to the decrease in the size of labor forces, rising wages, and increasing need for improved quality. In the future, their use will spread to other industries, as well as to the medical and welfare fields.

Japan's advanced technology in the areas of construction machinery, as typified by Komatsu's products, engines, bearings, and semiconductor fabrication equipment plays an important role in exports.

Precision Machinery: Japan has advanced technology in a wide range of product areas such as optical equipment, watches, and inspection equipment in digital cameras and interchangeable lens cameras, three Japanese companies account for 75% of the total production in the world, volume of 33 million units in 2017. However, the domestic production ratio is 15%.

Production of Japanese watches amounted to 308.25 million units in 2017. However, finished products accounted for 6.08 million units of that number, with most of the total being exported in the semi-finished form of movements.

Conventional precision machinery combined with optics has expanded its business domain to semiconductor manufacturing components, glass disks for hard disk drive applications, eyeglass lenses, contact lenses, and medical endoscopes, catheters, artificial organs, and other medical fields.

iv) Heavy Electrical Equipment

Heavy electrical equipment which is a large-scale electrical equipment can be categorised to power generation (thermal power plants, nuclear power plants, generators), power transmission (transformers, high-voltage circuit breakers), and power distribution equipment (electrical switching control equipment, gas insulated switchgear). Domestic production of heavy electric equipment in 2017 came to 3.8551 trillion yen, the largest amount in the past 10 years.

v) Home Appliances

Domestic production of home appliances in 2017 came to 1.9125 trillion yen, down 30% from the 1990 peak of 2.7246 trillion yen.

Japan's economic development was powered by increases in the production of home appliances such as air conditioners, refrigerators,

展の原動力であった。しかし近年は、高級機種を除く多くの製品で海外生産への移行が進み、さらには、急速に発展している中国企業などに市場を譲って撤退する事例も増えている。そのため、2017年の空調機、冷蔵庫、洗濯機の国内生産はそれぞれ514万台、182万台、97万台にとどまり、1990年のピーク時に比べて35〜80％減少している。さらに液晶テレビに至っては、2010年のピーク時に比べて30分の1に減少している。一方、新たに温水洗浄便座が283万台生産されている。日本企業は、4K・8K高解像度テレビ、家庭用燃料電池、電気自動車用電池・車載カメラ・安全運転サポート機器など、より高度な技術の開発と、新しいニーズの開拓に努めている。

vi) コンピュータ・エレクトロニクス機器工業

日本の半導体は、1980年代には世界シェアの50％以上を占めていた。日本のメーカーは、もともと大企業であり総合電機メーカーである。そのため、専業メーカーと比べて経営に小回りが利かない。その製品は品質・機能の高さと比較優位な低価格が評価されていた。その後、世の中は高機能高価格製品から汎用低価格製品へと需要が変化する。ところが日本の大企業は既存の顧客のニーズに対応するために、従来製品の改良を求めるための「持続的イノベーション」の追求にのみ注力し、従来製品の価値を破壊して全く新しい価値を生み出す「破壊的イノベーション」を追求するという視点を見失っていた。したがって、変化した需要に対応する価値を生み出すための素早い設備投資を行う決断ができにくく、結局世界のマーケットを韓国勢に奪われることになった。いわゆる「イノベーションのジレンマ」（Innovator's Dilemmma）に陥った、と言われている。

例えば「破壊的イノベーション」の典型的な成果としてスマートフォン、タブレット端末、クラウドコンピューティング、データ通信機器の出現が挙げられるが、これらを構成するマイクロプロセッサー（MPU）・メモリー（DRAMやNAND型フラッシュメモリ）・発光ダイオード（LED）・パワー半導体・イメージセンサーなど半導体の2017年度の世界におけるシェアは、アメ

washing machines, TVs, and audio devices. But in recent years, there has been a shift to overseas production in many products, with the exception of high-end models, and Japanese companies are withdrawing and increasingly relinquishing the market to rapidly developing countries such as China. Thus, domestic production in 2017 of air conditioners, refrigerators and washing machines amounted to 5.14 million, 1.82 million and 970,000 units, respectively, down 35 to 80% from the 1990 peak, and LCD TVs are down to one-thirtieth their 2010 peak. Meanwhile, 2.83 million units of warm water toilet seats are being produced. In an effort to spur new market needs, companies are focusing on developing even higher technologies such as 4K and 8K high-resolution TVs, home-use fuel cells, electric vehicle batteries, vehicle mounted cameras, safe driving support equipment, and so forth.

vi) Computer and Electronic Industries

In the 1980s Japan's share of the global semiconductor market was more than 50%. The Japanese manufacturers were large enterprises, general electrical equipment manufacturers, and lacked the management nimbleness of specialized manufacturers. These products had high reputation for superior quality and function, and the comparative advantage of their lower price. Subsequently demand underwent a change from high functionality, high-priced products to general purpose low-priced products. However, in order to meet the needs of existing customers, the large Japanese enterprises focused only on "sustaining innovation" for improving conventional products, losing sight of the "destructive innovation" viewpoint of tearing down the value of conventional products to create totally new value. It therefore became difficult to make quick capital investment decisions to create value corresponding to the changed demand, and eventually they ceded world market share to South Korea. They had fallen into the so-called "Innovator's Dilemma."

Typical results of destructive innovation include the emergence of smartphones, tablets, cloud computing, and data communication devices, which are composed of microprocessors (MPUs), memory (DRAM and NAND type flash memory), light-emitting diodes (LEDs), power semiconductors, image sensors, and other such semiconductor products. In fiscal 2017 American companies had the biggest share of the global semiconductor market with 28.9%, followed by South Korean companies with 20.7%, and Japan with just 7.0%, exposed

リカ系企業が第1位で28.9％、次いで韓国系企業が20.7％を占め、日本は7.0％に留まっており、急伸する中国半導体大手との激しい競争にさらされている。

日本では、2017年に412万台のパソコン・タブレット端末が生産された。これは世界シェアの1％である。また携帯電話・スマートフォンの2017年、日本国内生産の世界シェアは0.2％、日系企業のシェアも2.1％とサムスン、アップルおよびファーウェイに完敗している。情報化社会のキーツールであるパソコン・スマートフォンの失敗は痛手である。ただし、スマートフォンの部品の大多数は日本企業の製品である。例えば反射防止フィルム、カバーガラス、カメラレンズ用樹脂、光学フィルム、充電コネクター端子、バッテリー、多層基板用ソルダーレジストは日本の技術が支えている。

vii) 自動車工業

日本の自動車は、経済性と信頼性で海外市場に広く受け入れられている。2017年には国内だけで969万台を生産し、半数近い471万台を輸出したほか、海外生産が1,974万台あり、日系メーカーのグローバルな生産台数は2,943万台に達している。

自動車の海外生産は、原則として欧米諸国、中国、インドなどを含む消費地で行われているのが特徴である。低コスト化を主目的とすることが多い他の産業の例との相違であり、新興国に立地する場合も、相手国の市場に合わせた車を提供することを主な目的とするメーカーが多い。さらに、国外有力メーカーと広範囲な提携を行う例も多い。

日本の自動車は、排気ガスなどの厳しい環境基準をクリアしている。低燃費のハイブリッド車でも、世界をリードしている。ハイブリッド車の生産台数は世界最大であり、国内乗用車販売に占める比率は2016年34.8％に達している。

世界最大の自動車市場である中国は、自国に優位な電気自動車（EV）優先の政策を打ち出し、英仏政府も2040年までに、ガソリンおよびディーゼル車の販売を禁止する方針を決めたため、一挙

to fierce competition from the rapidly-growing major semiconductor companies of China.

In 2017 Japan produced 4.12 million personal computers and tablets. That corresponds to a 1% share of the world market. Also in 2017, mobile phones and smartphones produced domestically in Japan accounted for 0.2% of the world market, and Japanese companies' share is 2.1%, which is completely eclipsed by Samsung, Apple, and Huawei. To be defeated in personal computers and smartphones, key tools in an information society, is a hard blow. However, the majority of the parts used in smartphones are products of Japanese companies. Antireflection films, cover glass, resin for camera lenses, optical films, charging connector terminals, batteries, and solder resists for multilayer boards are all examples of products underpinned by Japanese technology.

vii) Automobile Industry

Japanese cars are widely popular in overseas markets due to their good fuel economy and reliability. In 2017 domestic production totaled 9.69 million units, of which 4.71 million, or nearly half, were exported. In addition, a further 19.74 million units were produced overseas, so global production volume by Japanese manufacturers reached 29.43 million units.

The feature of the overseas production of cars is that, in principle, it is done where the consumption takes place, including in the case of Europe, the U.S., China, and India. This is different from other industries in which production is carried out mainly to reduce costs, and even if the production is located in a developing country, it is generally done by manufacturers primarily to provide cars that match the market of the country concerned. Moreover, in many cases local production is done as a part of wide-ranging cooperation with leading foreign manufacturers.

Motor vehicles in Japan clear strict exhaust emissions standards. Furthermore, Japan leads the world in hybrid cars, with their low fuel consumption. Japan also leads the world in the number of hybrid vehicles produced, which in 2016 accounted for 34.8% of domestic passenger car sales.

China, the world's largest automobile market, has initiated a policy that gives priority to electric vehicles (EVs), which are favorable for that country, and with the decisions by UK and French governments to ban the selling of gasoline and diesel vehicles by 2040, competition in

に世界的な電気自動車開発の競争が激化してきている。

今後、自動運転、自動車のコネクテッド化、さらにシェアリング化や高齢化社会に適応する各種サービスの提供に向かって展開していくものと予想されている。内外の有力経営者は「これからは自動車メーカーでなく、移動手段の提供者という考え方に変わる必要がある。」と発言している。

排気量 660 CC 以下の「軽自動車」は日本の特徴的な車種であり、経済的な輸送手段として国民に広く利用されており、2017 年には 184 万台生産されている。

二輪車は 2017 年に 65 万台を生産し、46 万台を輸出した。ここでも海外生産が広く行われている。

viii) 造船・その他輸送機械工業

造船：2017 年の鋼船竣工量は、493 隻、1,307 万総トンであった。日本の造船業は、かつては世界の造船量の半分近くを占めたが、政府の資金援助を受けている中国、韓国の急激な追い上げにより、2017 年の竣工量は世界の 19.9％で、世界第 3 位となっている。しかし、LNG 船、環境規制対応船（排気ガスのクリーン化）などの技術力は国際的に高く評価されている。

その他輸送機械：日本は鉄道関連でも優れた技術を持ち、車両単体のほか、車両と運用システムをセットにした新幹線型高速鉄道の輸出なども行っている。また、電車・地下鉄車両の技術も優れており、欧米・アジア各国への輸出および現地生産も行われている。

航空・宇宙では、大型旅客機はすべて輸入しているが、それらの生産への参加や、小型機、観測用ロケットの生産などを行っており、観測用ロケットのイプシロンは、40 億円以下の低コストを目標に高い性能を実現しつつあり、国際的に注目されている。また、第二次大戦後に製造した唯一の国産旅客機ですでに引退している YS11 に次ぐ小型旅客機 MRJ も、2020 年納入開始をめざして米国で試験飛行中である。

global EV development is intensifying.

Future development of the industry is likely to be towards automated driving, connected cars, car sharing, and the provision of various services adapted to an aging society. Leading managers in Japan and abroad say that from now on, the companies need to think of themselves not as car manufacturers, but as providers of transportation means.

Kei vehicles having a maximum engine displacement of 660 cc are also characteristics of Japanese cars, and are widely used by people as an economical means of transport. Production amounted to 1.84 million units in 2017.

Production of motorcycles amounted to 650,000 units in 2017, of which 460,000 were exported. There is also widespread overseas production of motorcycles by Japanese manufacturers.

viii) Shipbuilding and Other Transportation Equipment Industries

Shipbuilding: There were 493 new steel ship completions in Japan in 2017, amounting to 13.07 million gross tons. Japan's shipbuilding industry used to account for half the world's shipbuilding, but China and South Korea, whose shipbuilders receive government subsidies, have caught up rapidly and in 2017, Japan's ship completions accounted for 19.9% of the world total, ranking the industry third in the world. The industry's technical capabilities in vessels such as LNG carriers, and environmentally compliant ships (cleaner exhaust gas systems), is internationally acclaimed.

Other Transportation Equipment: Japan has outstanding railway-related technology, and as well as individual rail cars, exports *Shinkansen* high-speed railways as sets of railcars and operational systems. It also has excellent train and subway car technology and exports to Europe, the U.S., and Asian countries, and is engaged in local production.

With respect to aerospace, Japan imports all its large passenger aircraft, but participates in their production, and produces small aircraft and rockets for scientific observation. The Epsilon rocket has attracted international attention for the low cost of under 4 billion yen for which it is aiming and in the process of achieving, and its high performance. A small passenger plane, the MRJ, now undergoing test flights, is scheduled to start shipping in 2020. The MRJ is undergoing test flights in the U.S. and will be the first airliner produced in post-WWII Japan since the NAMC YS-11, which is no longer being manufactured.

ix）化学工業

　化学工業は、「その最大の消費者は化学工業自身」と言われる重層的な構造を持ち、石油精製・アンモニア合成等の基礎材料からプラスチック等の中間材料、肥料から化粧品に至る広範な最終製品までの多様な製品を生産している。2016年の製品出荷額は、狭義の化学工業と石油・石炭製品工業を合わせて43.3兆円で、製造業全体の14.3％を占める重要分野である。

　しかし、石油を主原料とする日本の化学工業は、調達コストの低い天然ガスを利用している中東・欧米諸国に比べて不利であり、用地等の制約から設備規模の点でも十分な効率を得にくい状況にある。そのため各企業は、事業再編の推進、エチレンプラントの削減・共有化を行い、稼働率が2012年の78％から2017年98.5％に向上し、収益が改善した。硫酸、汎用プラスチック等からエンジニアリングプラスチックなどの高機能素材や高機能製品への転換で優位性を確保しようとしている。

　なお、深刻な問題となっているプラスチック汚染対策として、外食チェーンが相次いでストローなどを廃止する「脱プラスチック」の動きが趨勢となっている。プラスチック製品を手掛けてきた素材メーカーでは、微生物によって自然に分解される生分解性プラスチック製品の開発を急いでいる。

　医薬品の生産額は漸増傾向にあり、2015年には6兆8,200億円となった。しかし、大規模な開発体制を擁して長期間にわたり国際的に展開する欧米の巨大な製薬会社との新薬開発競争にさらされており、先発医薬品企業はアルツハイマー病予防薬、がん治療薬、循環器官用薬などの新薬開発に努めている。政府は社会保障費抑制も視野に安価なジェネリック薬の普及を80％まで高めるよう指導強化している。

　その他の製品では、合成ゴムが年産167万トン、販売額約5,700億円、化粧品がインバウンド需要も伸び2017年は販売額が前年比9.7％増の

ix) Chemical Industry

The chemical industry is described as being its own largest consumer. It has a multilayered structure that produces a broad and diverse range of end products, from the basic materials of petroleum refining and ammonia synthesis to intermediate materials such as plastics, and from fertilizer to cosmetics. In 2016, the combined production of the chemical industry, in the narrow sense, and the petroleum and coal products industry amounted to 43.3 trillion yen, making it a major sector accounting for 14.3% of the overall manufacturing industry.

However, Japan's chemical industry, which uses petroleum as its main raw material, is at a disadvantage compared to the Middle East and countries of the West that use natural gas having a low cost of procurement, and has difficulty obtaining sufficient efficiency from the standpoint of the scale of facilities, due to site and other constraints. Therefore the companies involved in the industry are promoting business restructuring and scaling back and sharing ethylene plants. Thus, the capacity utilization improved from 78% in 2012 to 98.5% in 2017, and revenues improved. Each company is trying to achieve a competitive advantage in the conversion of sulfuric acid and general-purpose plastics to high-performance materials and products such as engineering plastics.

Plastic pollution is a serious matter, and there are many moves to tackle the problem. Many restaurant chains, for example, have stopped using plastic straws, and materials manufacturers that work with plastics are urging the development of biodegradable plastic products that are naturally degraded by microorganisms.

The production value of pharmaceuticals has been gradually increasing, and in 2015 amounted to 6.82 trillion yen. However, in developing new drugs, Japan's pharmaceutical companies must compete with their giant counterparts in the West, which have large-scale development systems and can expand internationally over extended periods. The Japanese industry is looking to develop new drugs to prevent, for example, Alzheimer's and for treating cancer and circulatory organs. To control social welfare costs, the government is strengthening its focus on promoting the expanded use of low-priced generic drugs to 80% of drugs dispensed.

In other products, annual production of synthetic rubber continues to be strong, at present amounting to 1.67 million tons with sales of around 570 billion yen. Cosmetics continue to have comparatively robust 2017

1兆 6,370 億円となるなど、好調な状況である。

x) 繊維工業

繊維工業は、日本の工業化の初期には内需を満たすだけでなく輸出でも重要な役割を果たす基幹産業であった。しかし、近年は縮小傾向が続き、2015 年の製品出荷額は、1980 年に比べて 65% 減の 4 兆 690 億円に減少し、製造業全体の 0.8% となった。

この傾向は、需要の減退のためではなく、主として新興国への市場移譲によるものであり、素材である繊維、布類から縫製品まですべての分野で生じているが、特に顕著なのは衣類である。ユニクロなど日本企業が海外現地生産者を指導し、素材の提供、縫製工場の運営をおこない、消費者のニーズに合ったデザイン・品質を満たした製品を輸入している。アパレルメーカーは、より低賃金国を目指して中国からベトナム、インドネシアさらにバングラデシュ、カンボジア、ミャンマーなどに工場を移転するケースも多くなっている。

他方、国内生産では、高機能素材やブランド力のある衣類など、高付加価値製品の開発・生産で優位性を確保しようとしている。例えば、ゴルフクラブから、航空機、自動車など広い用途を持つ高機能素材として注目されている炭素繊維は、日本で開発された技術が世界の主流となっており、品質・生産量（2017 年、2.1 万トン）とも日本が世界の首位にいる。

伝統的な「着物」は、日常的に使われることは減っているが、絹に近い感触の化学繊維の開発・利用などで使いやすさを追求し、新しい需要の開拓を図っている。また、「着物」を作っていた伝統技術が日本の丁寧で繊細なモノづくりの基礎につながっているとみる識者が多い。

xi) 窯業・製紙・ゴム製品工業

窯業：セメント、ガラス、陶磁器などが含まれ、これと土石製品を合わせた 2015 年の製品出荷額は 7.6 兆円で、製造業出荷額の 2.4% を占めた。

金額で窯業の中心であるセメントは、原料を自

sales of around 1.637 trillion yen, an increase of 9.7% over the previous year, helped by growth in inbound demand.

x) Textile Industry

Textiles were a key industry that was important for exports as well as meeting domestic demand in the early days of Japan's industrialization. In recent years, however, the industry has been shrinking, until in 2015 the value of goods shipped amounted to 4.069 trillion yen, about 65% of what it was in 1980, accounting for 0.8% of overall manufacturing output.

This trend is not due to a decline in demand but rather to a transfer of the market to primarily emerging economies, and while this is happening in all areas of operations from textiles and cloths to sewn goods, it is particularly pronounced with respect to apparel. Japanese companies such as Uniqlo provide local producers overseas with guidance and materials, operate sewing factories, and import products that satisfy the design and quality needs of consumers. Many apparel manufacturers are moving their factories from China to countries where wages are lower, such as Vietnam, Indonesia, Bangladesh, Cambodia, and Myanmar.

On the other hand, domestic producers such as of clothing with brand power and high-performance textile material are trying to achieve a competitive advantage in the development and production of high-value-added products. For example, in carbon fiber, which is attracting attention as a high-performance material with a wide range of applications from golf clubs to aircraft and automobiles, technology developed in Japan has become the global mainstream, and has put Japan in first place in terms of both quality and production volume (21,000 tons in 2017).

Traditional *kimono* are no longer used so much for everyday wear, but attempts are being made to create new demand by the development and use of chemical fibers that provide a silk-like feel and ease of use. There are many knowledgeable people who consider that the traditional technology which goes into the making of kimonos led to the foundation of Japan's meticulous, fine manufacturing.

xi) Ceramics, Paper, and Rubber Industries

Ceramics: Shipments by the ceramics industry, which encompasses cement, glass, china and porcelain and the like, and stone and clay products, amounted to 7.6 trillion yen in 2015, accounting for 2.4% of manufacturing industry shipments.

In terms of money amount, cement is the center of the ceramics

給できる優位性を持つが、景気による需要の変化を受けやすく、近年の生産はやや低調で、2017年の生産量は5,487万トン、販売額は約3兆円であった。

2015年のガラス製品販売額は1兆6,170億円で、うち45％が安全ガラス、35％がガラス繊維製品、30％が板ガラスなどである。ガラス繊維をはじめとする機能性ガラスは、エレクトロニクス、住宅、自動車などで新しい用途が広がっており、国際競争力も強いため、企業は一層の技術開発、市場開拓に力を入れている。

高機能材料として重要性を増しているファインセラミックスでは、日本は質・量ともに世界をリードしており、2017年の販売額は4,870億円であった。

陶磁器のうち食器・花器類では、世界に知られた有名メーカーから多くの個性的な地方窯元まで、多様な製品を供給している。ただし、量的に陶磁器生産の大半を占めるのはタイル、衛生用品、碍子である。中でも、洗浄便座は家庭用電気機器が減少している中で唯一成長しており、優れた着想で世界的に注目されている。

製紙：2017年の日本の紙生産量は2,650万トンで、中国、アメリカに次ぐ世界第3位であった。主原料であるパルプの元になるチップと原木の多くは海外に依存しており、2016年の使用量の68％が輸入された。そのため日本企業は、輸出国において植林を行うなど、木材資源と環境の保護に努めている。

また、日本は古紙回収に力を入れており、2016年には回収率81.3％で、製紙原料の64.3％が古紙でまかなわれた。

ゴム製品：日本は中国、アメリカに次ぐ世界第3位のゴム消費国で、2016年に新ゴム換算で154万トンを消費した。うち128万トンが販売額3兆5,100億円のゴム製品となり、残りは他の産業で電線などの製品に使われた。ゴム製品のうち、1兆4,500億円が自動車用タイヤである。その他ゴムベルトなど各種の工業用製品も重要であり、2015年の販売額は1兆7,550億円であった。

なお、2016年に消費された原料ゴムは、44％

industry, having the advantage of self-sufficiency in raw materials. Being subject to changes in demand depending on the economy, in recent years production has been somewhat sluggish. Production in 2017 was 54.87 million tons and sales amounted to about 3 trillion yen.

Sales of glass products in 2015 amounted to 1.617 trillion yen, of which 45% was safety glass, 35% glass fiber products, and 30% flat glass. With the increase in applications for glass fiber and other functional glass in electronics, housing, automobiles, and other fields, and in view of their strong international competitiveness, companies are focusing more effort into technology and market development.

Fine ceramics are an increasingly important high-performance material in which Japan is a leader in terms of both quality and quantity. In 2017, sales of fine ceramics came to 487 billion yen.

Tableware and vase products encompass diverse products that come from sources ranging from world-famous companies to distinctive regional potteries. In terms of production volume, however, most ceramics products are tiles, sanitary goods or insulators. Amid the sinking sales of electric home appliances, the only item that shows growth is the washing toilet seat, an excellent idea that has caught on and attracted worldwide attention.

Paper: In 2017, Japanese production of paper amounted to 26.5 million tons, which was third in the world after China and the U.S. The industry relies on overseas sources for the majority of the raw wood chips used to form pulp, the main raw material, importing 68% of the amount used in 2016. Japanese companies are therefore working to protect timber resources and the environment such as by reforestation efforts in the exporting countries.

Japan also focuses on waste paper recovery, and had a recovery rate of 81.3% in 2011 in which waste paper accounted for 64.3% of paper stock.

Rubber: Japan is the third largest consumer of rubber, behind China and the U.S. In 2016 Japan used 1.54 million tons (in terms of new rubber), of which 1.28 million tons was in the form of rubber products which the industry sold for 3.51 trillion yen. The remainder was used by other industries for electric wire and other such products. Motor vehicle tires accounted for 1.45 trillion yen, but various other industrial rubber products such as rubber belts are also important and accounted for sales of 1.755 trillion yen in 2015.

Of the raw rubber used in 2016, 44% was natural rubber and 56%

が天然ゴム、56％が合成ゴムで、前者はすべて輸入された。

xii) 食料品工業

2015年の食料品の出荷額は38兆5,100億円で、製造業全体の11.9％を占めた。食料品産業は、規模的には成熟段階に入っているが、消費者の多様な要求に応じるため、内容は多様化しており、レトルト食品、冷凍食品などの加工度の高い製品や低カロリー食品の需要が拡大している。日本発のインスタントラーメンも依然堅調で、2016年には57億食が生産された。

2016年の清涼飲料の生産量は2,163万キロリットルで、内容も多岐にわたり、従来の炭酸飲料やコーヒー類に加え、緑茶、ミネラルウォーターが急増して上位に入ってきた。

酒類はやや減少して789万キロリットルで、主体はビールと、ビールに似ているが酒税率の差で価格が低い日本固有の製品「発泡酒」、「第三のビール」である。ただし、ビールの生産量は減少している。日本酒の生産量も減少しているが、ワインの一種として海外に進出するなど、新しい需要の開拓が進められている。政府は酒税収入が大幅に減少してきているため、10年かけて、ビール全般にかかる酒税率を均一化しようとしているが、企業の努力による新製品開発を阻害するのではないかとの指摘もある。

なお、肥満者や自動車運転者のため、味・香りなどは酒類に似るがアルコール、プリン体を含まない飲料も生産されている。

タバコは、政府の管理を受ける日本たばこ産業株式会社（JT）が独占的に製造しており、2017年には929億本を販売した。輸入は自由化されており、これを含む販売量は1,514億本で、JTのシェアは61.3％であった。近年、健康意識の高まりなどから、公共の場や路上での禁煙、タバコ税大幅引き上げなど喫煙を抑制する措置が進んでいる。ピークだった2000年に比べて55.2％減となっている。最近では煙の出ない電子タバコの普及が進んでいる。

synthetic, with all the natural rubber being imported.

xii) Food Industry

Shipments by the food industry in 2015 came to 38.51 trillion yen which accounted for 11.9% of the total for all industries. Although the industry is entering maturity in terms of its size, the content is diversifying to meet diverse and growing consumer demand for retort, frozen and other highly processed foods and low-calorie foods. Japan's instant ramen remained strong, with 5.7 billion units produced in 2016.

Soft drink production in 2016 amounted to 21.63 million kiloliters, and here too, the content was diverse, including in addition to the traditional carbonated beverages and coffees, rapid growth brought green tea and mineral water into the higher ranks.

Production of alcoholic beverages declined slightly, to 7.89 million kiloliters; this consisted mainly of beer, happoshu, and other Japanese sparkling beverages referred to as the "third-type of beer" that resembles beer but is cheaper due to differences between the liquor tax rates. However, beer production decreased. Production of sake is also decreasing, but development of new demand is helping it make some inroads abroad as a kind of wine. Although the government is attempting to uniformly apply the liquor tax rate on all beer and beer-like products over the course of ten years due to sharp decreases in liquor tax revenues, it has been pointed out that it might hinder corporate efforts to develop new products.

For people who are overweight or driving, there are beverages that contain no alcohol or purines but taste and smell like they do.

The government-managed Japan Tobacco (JT), which has a monopoly on the production of tobacco products, sold 92.9 billion cigarettes in 2017. Including imports, 151.4 billion cigarettes were sold, with the JT share accounting for 61.3%. In recent years, growing health awareness has led to increasing restrictions on smoking, including the banning of smoking in public spaces and streets, and steep hikes in the tobacco tax. Sales of tobacco products have declined 55.2% from the 2000 peak. Recently smokeless electronic tobacco products are becoming popular.

c）第3次産業
1）卸売・小売業

日本には 2017 年に 135.5 万の民営の卸売・小売事業所があり、約 1,053 万人の就業者を擁し、2016 年には、GDP の 13.7％を生み出した。

この分野には、年間販売額 10 兆円を超える巨大企業もあるが、事業所の大部分は小規模で、55％は従業員 4 人未満、10 人未満まで入れると 81％を占めている。このうち、地域に密着した個人商店などは、ネット通信販売、量販店、郊外型ショッピングモール、アウトレットモール、コンビニエンスストアなどの急速な発達に追われて急減している。国民の利便性、生活様式の変化に応じ、種々の新しい発想による店舗が現れている。

中心市街地の核であった百貨店や大型スーパーも、郊外型量販店、ネット通信販売などとの競争や消費者行動の変化で販売額を減少させ、撤退が相次いでいる。そのため、合併で経営力を高めるとともに、海外有名ブランドの出店、ショッピングモール化、美術展などのイベント開催で新しい魅力を作りだそうとしている。

コンビニエンスストア：米国生まれのコンビニエンスストアは、日本で独自の発展を遂げ「コンビニ」と略称されて国民に広く利用されている。

店舗の大部分は大手企業のフランチャイズである。大手 3 社の寡占化が進んでいる。店舗は、2017 年現在 55,500 店あり、飽和状況となっている。各店のレジは本部と回線で直結されていて、販売状況に応じて迅速な在庫補充が可能である。通常 24 時間営業であり、売れ筋商品を中心に、日用雑貨や食品の販売のほか、預貯金の出し入れや送金、通信販売代金・公共料金の振り込み、納税、郵便・宅配便の受付、航空機・高速バス・劇場・スポーツイベントのチケット取次など日常生活に必要な多様なサービスを提供して地域住民に必要な拠点となっている。消費者が欲している新たな商品、サービスの開発に努力しており、さらに災害時の地域支援機能も保持しつつある。

総合商社：「sogoshosha」として海外でも知られる大規模な商業企業であり、日本との対外貿易、三国間

c) Tertiary Industries
1) Wholesale and Retail

In 2017 the wholesale-retail sector comprised 1.355 million shops and businesses that employed some 10.53 million workers, and in 2016 accounted for 13.7% of GDP.

Although the sector includes large corporations with more than 10 trillion yen in annual sales, most of the businesses are small, with 55% having fewer than four employees, and 81% fewer than 10. The number of privately owned local shops has declined sharply, driven off by the rapid expansion of online and mail order sales, mass retailers, suburban shopping malls, outlet malls, and convenience stores. But various new stores with new ideas have appeared in response to changes in people's convenience and lifestyles.

Department stores and large supermarkets that used to be at the heart of urban areas now find themselves competing with suburban type mass retailers and online and mail order sales and changes in consumer behavior, and with sales falling, are leaving. They have also been improving their management capabilities through mergers, opening famous foreign brand shops, using the shopping mall format, and putting on fine art exhibitions and other events, all in an effort to create new attractions.

Convenience Stores: The convenience store (abbreviated to "*konbini*") is an American invention that has developed in an original way in Japan, where it is utilized very extensively.

Most of the stores are franchises of leading companies. An oligopoly of three major companies is developing. In 2017 there was a state of saturation, with some 55,500 stores. The cash registers of each store are connected directly to the head office, which enables stocks to be swiftly replenished as required. The stores usually operate 24 hours a day, and in addition to focusing on popular items, selling daily necessities and a broad range of food, provide a wide range of services that are needed in daily life, such as access to savings accounts, money transfers, mail order payments, the handling of payments to utilities and tax payments, acceptance of packages for home delivery, ticket agency services for air travel, high-speed bus services, theater, and sporting events, and more, making the stores a necessary base for local residents. They endeavor to develop new products and services that consumers want, and they hold regional support functions when disasters occur.

General Trading Companies (*sogoshosha*): Japan's giant trading companies are known throughout the world for the broad range of their

貿易、国内間取引と幅広い活動を行い、日本の経済活動の中で中核的な機能を果たしてきた。しかし、近年、商社各社は、それぞれの得意分野に経営資源を集中し、物流・保管機能、商社金融機能、海外での資源開発・エネルギー資源や食料の確保の強化および新興国での都市開発、工場用地・人材確保、販売網の構築、マーケティング・商品企画などを自ら推進し、ベンチャー起業の支援をしたり、大手コンビニエンスストアや小売業を傘下に治め、川下作戦を展開している商社もある。

　ネット通信販売（無店舗販売）：総務省統計局の家計消費動向調査によれば、2002年に比べると2017年のネット通信販売購入額は約10倍の1万円／月に増加している。特に、インターネット、テレビショッピングと迅速・確実な配送に加えて商品代金の回収まで行う宅配便とを組み合わせた消費者向け電子商取引の拡大は急速で、2017年には前年比9.3％増の16.5兆円となっており、小売業全体販売額約142.5兆円の11.6％を占める程成長している。対象も書籍や食品から家具、家電製品、自動車などの大型商品まで広範にわたっている。消費者向けより先行していた企業間電子取引は2016年で204.1兆円、すでに全取引の19.8％に達している。

　自動販売機：自動販売機は都市部では至るところにあり、2017年末の設置台数は、乗車券などを除く商品販売機だけで427.1万台、販売額は4.7兆円を超える。高額紙幣にはおつりが出るのはもちろん、売るものも、飲み物のほか、各種食品、雑誌、靴下、乾電池など多様である。飲み物では冷たいもの、熱いものが選べ、コーヒーの甘さも調整できる。カップ麺もすぐ食べられる形で出て来るなど、きめ細かい処理ができる。

2）金融・保険業

　金融・保険業は2017年に168万人を雇用し、2016年にはGDPの4.2％を生み出している。

　金融の本質は、資金を余剰している先から集め、不足している先に融通するところにある。この事業の性

activities in Japan's bilateral and trilateral foreign trade operations, and domestic business, and have been fulfilling a core function in Japan's economic activities. In recent years, however, they are concentrating management resources on their respective areas of strength and shifting to promoting areas such as their logistics and storage functions, trading company financial functions, overseas resource development, strengthening of their securing of energy resources and food, urban development in emerging countries, securing of factory sites and personnel, building sales networks, marketing, and product planning. There are trading companies that support start-ups and entrepreneurship, oversee major convenience store and retail business operations, and are developing downstream strategies.

Online and Mail Order (Nonstore) Retailing: According to a household consumption trends survey conducted by the Statistics Bureau of the Ministry of Internal Affairs and Communications, in 2017 the household monthly outlay on online purchases was 10,000 yen, a ten-fold increase compared with 2002. Consumer oriented e-commerce and TV shopping that in addition to speedy, secure shipping, combine the Internet and home delivery, and even the collection of product payments, is growing particularly rapidly, totaling 16.5 trillion yen in 2017 which represented a year-on-year increase of 9.3%, and has grown to where it accounts for 11.6% of the retail sales total of about 142.5 trillion yen. It encompasses a broad range of products, from books and foods to large items such as furniture, home appliances, and cars. Business-to-business e-commerce, which preceded the consumer oriented version, amounted to 204.1 trillion yen in 2016, or 19.8% of total transactions.

Automatic Vending Machines: Automatic vending machines are everywhere in urban areas. As of the end of 2017, excluding machines that sell tickets, there were 4.271 million machines selling over 4.7 trillion yen's worth of merchandise. They give change for high-denomination bank notes and sell drinks, various kinds of food, magazines, socks, batteries, and so forth. Customers can choose cold drinks or hot, or how sweet they want their coffee. Cup noodles pop out, ready to eat.

2) Finance and Insurance Industries

In 2017 the finance and insurance industries employed 1.68 million people, and in 2016 generated 4.2% of the gross national product (GDP).

The essence of finance is to gather surplus funds from one party to accommodate another party that has a shortage. The business inherently

質上、公共性が極めて高いことから、この事業を行うものに対しては、資金調達ならびに営業に対して、免許制ないし認可制・登録制などの規制が行われている。

2017年末の国内銀行の預金残高は、ゆるやかな景気回復に伴い前年比4.1％増の760兆円である。また家計の金融資産残高（現預金・株式・公社債・保険・個人年金など）は前年比3.9％増の188兆円となっている。

現在の日銀の金融政策は、デフレ脱却と持続的な経済成長の実現に向けた金融緩和が中心となっている。ゼロ金利の継続や資金量を大幅に増やすことによって景気を下支えしている。2014年10月から資金供給量は年間80兆円に拡大し、日銀が購入する資産も長期国債に加え上場投資信託、不動産投資信託も加え、「異次元の金融緩和」を実施しており、株式市場を下支えしている。

金融機関は日銀の低金利政策により、収益が悪化している。そのため効率化と国際競争力の強化をめざして大規模な再編が進められ、2017年末現在、ゆうちょ、三菱UFJ、みずほ、三井住友、農林中央金庫の5機関が総資産規模で世界の銀行上位50行に入っている。また地方銀行も経営が圧迫され、再編・合理化を進めている。

生命保険は2016年度末で保有契約額135兆円と7年間で2.2％と漸増状況となっている。資産運用収益は2016年度9兆780億円、資産運用利回り1.96％と安定している。損害保険は2016年度前年比1.4％減の8兆2,440億円の保険料収入となった。火災・自動車保険が人口減少もあり、伸び悩み状況となっているが、地震保険は東日本大震災以降、39％伸びている。

日本の郵便事業は、国営当時から本業のほかに貯蓄銀行機能を持っており、民営化後、その部分が分離されて証券業務、保険事業なども開始した。

クレジットカードは、買物などの売買決済手段として日本でも浸透している。発行枚数は2016年度に2億7,200万枚で、成人人口1人当り保有枚数は2.6枚、年間利用額は54兆円となっている。

has a very high public nature, so regulations such as licensing, approval, and registration systems are applied to those involved in the fund procurement and management.

Domestic bank deposits outstanding at the end of 2017 amounted to 760 trillion yen, 4.1% more than the previous year due to the gradual economic recovery. Household financial assets (cash deposits, stocks, public and corporate bonds, insurance, individual pensions, etc.) increased by 3.9%, to 188 trillion yen.

The current policy of the Bank of Japan is focused on monetary easing to end deflation and achieve sustained economic growth. The economy is being supported by continuing zero interest rates and significantly increasing the amount of funds. Since October 2014, funds have been expanded to 80 trillion yen annually, and assets purchased by the Bank of Japan are added to long-term government bonds, along with listed investment trusts and real estate investment trusts, implementing monetary easing that is done at a scale referred to as being of "another dimension" to support the stock market.

Bank revenues are worsening due to the Bank of Japan's low-interest policy. As a result, large-scale restructuring is being carried out to improve efficiency and strengthen international competitiveness. As of the end of 2017, the Japan Post Bank, Mitsubishi UFJ, Sumitomo Mitsui, Mizuho, and Norinchukin Bank were ranked among the world's top 50 banks in terms of total assets. The management of regional banks is also under pressure, and they are promoting reorganization and streamlining.

As of the end of fiscal 2016, life insurance contracts held amounted to 135 trillion yen, a gradual increase of 2.2% over seven years. Asset management revenue in fiscal 2016 was steady at 9.078 trillion yen with a 1.96% yield on asset investments. General insurance premium income decreased by 1.4% from the previous year to 8.244 trillion yen. Although fire and automobile insurance is sluggish due partly to the shrinking population, earthquake insurance has increased by 39% since the Great East Japan Earthquake.

In addition to its core business, the postal service in Japan also has a savings bank function from when it was state-owned. After it was privatized that part was split off and also started a securities business and insurance operations.

Credit cards are widely used in Japan to pay for store and other purchases. In fiscal 2016 the number of issued cards was 272 million, or an average of 2.6 cards per adult, which are used to pay 54 trillion yen per year.

一方、金融機関が発行するキャッシュカードは、ATM（現金自動預入支払機）で本人確認を行い、現金の引き出し、預け入れなどを行うためのものである。

　クレジットカードおよびキャッシュカードのいずれも、最近は磁気カードから偽造困難なカードへの切り替えが進んでいる。またキャッシュカードの場合、安全性がさらに高いとされる生体認証カードの導入も普及している。

　電子マネーとは、現金の代わりに、予めチャージまたは自動チャージしたプリペイドカード、もしくはクレジットカードでの後払いを設定したカードやスマートフォンなどで支払いをすることができる電子のお金である。日本では買い物や交通機関利用時に良く使用されているが、近年の海外観光客の増加もあり、現金支払いからスマートフォン決済が急速に増加すると予想されており、その環境整備が急がれている。

　「フィンテック（Fintech）」とは、金融を意味する「ファイナンス（Finance）」と、技術を意味する「テクノロジー（Technology）」を組み合わせた造語である。近年では概ね「ICT（Information and Communication Technology）を駆使した革新的、あるいは破壊的な金融商品・サービスの潮流」といった意味で利用されている。これまで金融機関が独占的に提供し、変化に乏しかった金融商品・サービスを、ICT を活用することによって、利用者の目線から「安く、早く、便利」に変えていこうとする動きが活発化している。

3）運輸・観光業
　ⅰ）概況
　　　日本の運輸業は、郵便事業を含めて 2017 年に 337 万人の従業者を擁し、GDP の 5.0％を生みだした。

　　　輸送手段別構成を見ると、2017 年度、貨物ではトンキロ（数量×距離）で自動車 51.1％、鉄道 5.1％、内航船 43.5％、航空 0.3％、人員では人キロで自動車 62.9％、鉄道 30.5％、客船 0.2％、航空 6.4％であった。

　　　日本はさまざまな自然と文化を活かして観光立国をめざしており、2018 年には訪日観光客 3,192 万人を達成した。

Cash cards issued by financial institutions are for operating an ATM (automatic teller machine). After the ATM has confirmed the user's identity the cardholder can withdraw or deposit cash, for example.

Credit cards and cash cards that store data magnetically are increasingly being replaced with ones less vulnerable to fraud. Also, cash cards are becoming available that utilize biometric authentication for still stronger security.

Electronic money can be used to make payments in place of cash using a prepaid card that is charged beforehand or automatically, or a card or smartphone set for post-payment by credit card. In Japan such cards are widely used for shopping and travelling on public transportation. With the recent increase in overseas tourists, payment by smartphone instead of cash is expected to increase rapidly, and preparation of the facilities for this is being urgently implemented.

"Fintech" is word coined by combining "finance" and "technology." In recent years it is used to broadly signify trends in innovative or destructively innovative financial products and services driven by information and communication technology (ICT). Up to now financial institutions have been exclusive providers of products and services that could not be modified by consumers. That is increasingly giving way to moves to use ICT to modify products and services to make them cheaper, faster, and more convenient from the user's point of view.

3) Transportation and Tourist Industries
i) Overview
When postal operations are included, Japan's transportation industry employed 3.37 million workers in 2017 and generated 5.0% of the gross national product (GDP).

A breakdown of transport by mode, in the case of freight, by ton-kilometers, was 51.1% by motor vehicle, 5.1% by railway, 43.5% by coastal ship, and 0.3% by airplane. Passenger transportation, by passenger-kilometers, was 62.9% by motor vehicle, 30.5% by railway, 0.2% by passenger ship, and 6.4% by airplane (fiscal 2017).

Japan is focusing on using its natural scenery and cultural attractions to become a tourism nation. In 2018, Japan was visited by 31.92 million tourists.

ii) 自動車輸送

2017年現在の道路延長は128万キロで、その82%が舗装されている。高速自動車国道9,319キロはじめ、高速道路網も発達している。

少子高齢化社会のもとで、配送を担うトラック運転手は大幅に不足している。トラック運転手の労働環境は厳しく、かつ長時間労働のわりに低賃金で、運転手の確保は難しい。特にインターネット通販の拡大により、宅配便の貨物量が急増している。荷物の即日配達や夜間の時間指定配達また再配達などである。こうした状況に対し、物流各社は、配達料金の大幅値上げにより運転手の待遇改善、倉庫や仕分けなど物流施設の自動化を図っている。また利用者も宅配ボックスの設置、コンビニや駅での宅配物の受け取りなど工夫を図っている。

2001年に運用が開始されたETC（有料道路料金無線自動決済システム）の利用は急速に普及し、2018年有料道路利用率は、91％に達している。

近年問題となっているのは、戦後の復興期から高度成長期にかけて急速に整備された高速道路、トンネル、橋、鉄道等交通インフラの老朽化であり、財政状況が苦しい中、補修・改修には膨大な費用と難しい工事が必要と予想され、計画的な対応が求められている。

iii) 鉄道輸送

2018年4月現在の鉄道延長（旅客営業線）は27,822 kmで、その73％がJR各社（Japan Railways）のものである。新幹線や都市部の地下鉄ではさらに建設が続いているが、地方などでは、人口減少と相まって採算性が悪く廃止されたり、減便される路線もある。

かつて貨物輸送の主役だった鉄道の比率は、自動車にその座を譲って3.8％にまで減少していたが、エネルギー効率に優れ、CO_2排出量も少ないことなどが改めて評価され、コンテナ利用、トラック、フェリー、内航海運と組み合わせた複合一貫輸送システム（モーダルシフト）の活用などにより、新しい需要の開拓を進め比率を5.1％ま

ii) Motor Vehicle Transportation

As of 2017 the length of all the roads in Japan was 1.28 million kilometers, 82% of which was paved. There is a well-developed high-speed road network, starting with 9,319 kilometers of national expressways.

With the birthrate declining and the society aging, truck drivers responsible for making deliveries are in short supply. Truck drivers have a tough working environment and are difficult to recruit, due to wages that are low considering the long working hours. In particular, the expansion of online mail order has increased the volume of the parcels that are being delivered. Then there are same day deliveries, time-designated evening deliveries and redeliveries, and so on. In response, distribution companies are trying to significantly raise delivery charges to improve drivers' treatment and automate distribution facilities such as warehouses and sorting systems. For their part, users are trying to help by setting up delivery boxes, and by receiving orders at convenience stores and rail stations.

Toll roads in Japan are equipped with a wireless system (called ETC), for collecting tolls automatically. Since it was launched in 2001 it has become very popular, and by 2018, it is used by 91% of toll road users.

An issue in recent years has been the aging of the highways, tunnels, and bridges built quickly from the postwar reconstruction period to the high-growth period. Even in the midst of the difficult fiscal conditions, these infrastructures need to be repaired and renovated, a difficult task that will be enormously costly and require a systematic approach.

iii) Railway Transportation

As of April 2018, the total length of Japan's railways (passenger lines) were 27.822 thousand kilometers. About 73% of the total is accounted for by the JR (Japan Railways) companies. While Shinkansen (bullet train) lines and urban subways continue to be built in sparsely populated areas that also face a declining population and where profitability is low, there have been cases in which routes have been abolished or reduced.

The railway used to be the main player in freight transportation, but its ratio declined to as low as 3.8% as motor vehicles assumed the role. But now the railway, with its excellent energy efficiency and low carbon dioxide emissions, is being re-evaluated. New demand for freight transportation by railways is being developed by using container freight trains, and a multimodal transportation system combining freight trains, trucks, ferries, and coastal shipping, which has brought the rate back up

で回復させている。

また、旅客輸送は 2017 年度に 4,318 億人キロで、全国平均で輸送量全体の 30.5% を占め、復調傾向にある。特に大都市圏では主要な交通機関になっており、東京の都心では、ピーク時に 2 分間隔で運行している。主要都市には地下鉄もあり、特に東京、大阪、名古屋には高密度の地下鉄網が整備されている。

高速鉄道で世界をリードする新幹線は、2011 年までに九州南端から北海道の函館までつながった。さらに、2015 年には北陸新幹線が金沢まで延長され、また函館から札幌への延伸工事も始まっている。現在、日本の最大の建設工事でもあるリニア中央新幹線は、最高設計速度 505 km／h の高速走行が可能な超電導磁気浮上式リニアモーターカーにより建設される。東京・名古屋間の 2027 年の開業を目指しており、2014 年 12 月に起工式が行われた。完成後は最速で 40 分で結ぶ予定。東京・大阪間の全線開業は 2037 年を目標とし、最速 67 分で結ぶ計画になっている。

在来型の路線も海底トンネルと長大橋で日本の主要 4 島を結んでいる。本州と北海道を結ぶ青函トンネルは 53.9 km で海底トンネルでは世界最長であり、本州と四国を結ぶ瀬戸大橋は、陸上部を含めて全長 13.1 km で、道路・鉄道併用橋では世界最長である。

日本の鉄道は、正確な定時運行で世界に知られている。異常発生時の自動停止など、安全措置も発達しており、運行システムを含む新幹線、在来型鉄道の総合技術は世界各地に輸出されている。

iv）海上輸送

2017 年度の船舶による国内輸送量は、旅客では全輸送量の 0.2% だったが、貨物では、工業原材料、鉄鋼など 1,809 億トンキロで、全輸送量の 43.7% を占めた。

外航船による貨物輸送は、輸出 1 億 6,770 万トン、輸入 7 億 6,760 万トン、三国間輸送 4 億

to 5.1%.

At 431.8 billion passenger-kilometers, passenger transportation in fiscal 2017 accounted for 30.5% of the transportation total on a nationwide average, and it is on the way to a recovery. Especially in metropolitan areas, public transit has become a major mode of transportation, with trains coming at two-minute intervals during peak times in the center of Tokyo. There are also subways in major cities, such as the high-density metro systems in Tokyo, Osaka, and Nagoya.

The Shinkansen, the world's leading high-speed train, had by 2011 linked the southern tip of Kyushu with the Hakodate in Hokkaido, where work has started to further extend the line to Sapporo. In addition, the Hokuriku Shinkansen was extended to Kanazawa in 2015. The Linear Chuo Shinkansen, which is currently the largest construction project in Japan, is currently being built with superconducting magnetically levitated linear motor cars capable of running at a maximum design speed of 505 km/h. A groundbreaking ceremony was held in December 2014, with the aim being to start operations between Tokyo and Nagoya in 2027. After completion, at top speed the journey between the two cities will take 40 minutes. When the entire line between Tokyo and Osaka is completed by the target year of 2037, the trip is scheduled to take 67 minutes at top speed.

The four main Japanese islands are linked by conventional lines via undersea tunnels and long bridges. The 53.9 kilometer Seikan Tunnel linking Honshu and Hokkaido is the longest undersea tunnel in the world, and the Great Seto Bridge that connects Honshu with Shikoku, at 13.1 kilometers long (including the land portion), is the world's longest road/railway bridge.

Japan's railways are known throughout the world for the precise punctuality of their operations, and they are fully equipped with safety systems, such as the one that stops the train automatically if something goes wrong. Comprehensive Shinkansen and conventional railway technology and operational systems are being exported to countries around the world.

iv) Marine Transportation

Japan's domestic transportation volume by ship in fiscal 2017 was 0.2% of the total transportation volume in the case of passengers, but in the case of freight, involving industrial raw materials and steel and the like, it was, at 180.9 billion ton-kilometers, 43.7% of the total transportation volume.

Cargo transportation by international trading vessels was 167.7 million tons exports, 767.60 million tons imports, and 439.4 million

3,940万トンで、輸入の場合、重量で36.6％がタンカー・LNG船による原油と液化天然ガスなどであった。

海運でも国際競争が激化しており、日本の業界は、タンカー、コンテナ船、鉄鋼専用船などの大型化で輸送コストの低減を追求している。2016年10月、深刻な海運不況に直面して、日本の大手海運会社3社の定期コンテナ船事業を統合した。

外航船による旅客輸送は、2017年、前年比27.2％増の253.3万人を達成した。2020年には訪日クルーズ客500万人を目指して国際旅客拠点港湾整備を急いでいる。また日本船による世界一周旅行なども定着しつつあり、日本人のクルーズ観光客の増加も期待されている。

v）航空輸送

航空会社の経営は、国外企業を含むLCC（ローコストキャリア）が相次いで参入して競争が激化している。これに対し既存の国内航空会社は、LCCへの参入・提携と高水準のサービスの提供による差別化との使い分けなど、経営の在り方を整理し、国際競争力を回復した。

2017年度に旅客で国内線1億212万人、国際線2,239万人、郵便物を含む貨物で国内線91万トン、国際線176万トンを輸送し、この5年で国際線利用客48％増、国内線利用客も11％増加している。

国際空港では、主力である成田空港の他、羽田空港を拡張して24時間化した。日本には97の空港があるが、主要都市に近い28空港以外では小規模なものが多い。しかし、LCCの乗り入れ連携と訪日観光客の急増にも恵まれ、利用客数は大幅に増加している。

vi）観光

政府は、急速な成長を遂げるアジアをはじめとする世界の観光需要を取り込もうとしている。人口減少・少子高齢化が進展する中、交流人口の拡大によって地域の活力を維持し、社会を発展させるとともに、諸外国のとの交流により、国際相互理解を深める大きな効果がある。訪日観光客は

tons cross-transport. In the case of imports, 36.6% by weight was oil and LNG by tanker and LNG carrier.

Even in shipping, international competition is intense. The Japanese industry is trying to reduce transportation costs through the use of larger vessels, including tankers, container ships and specialized steel carriers. In October 2016, in the face of a serious maritime recession, three of Japan's major shipping companies merged their regular container ship operations.

In 2017, 2.533 million passengers entered and left Japan by ship, a year-on-year increase of 27.2%. Japan is hurrying to improve international passenger port facilities to handle the 5 million cruise ship passengers expected to visit Japan in 2020. And with around-the-world trips on Japanese ships becoming established, the number of Japanese cruise ship tourists is expected to increase.

v) Air Transportation

The entry of low-cost carriers (LCCs), including foreign LCCs, is increasing competition. In response, existing domestic airlines have been forced to rethink how they manage themselves. They have made alliances with existing LCCs and launched their own LCCs, while differentiating their full-service flights by providing high-level service. In these ways, they have restored their international competitiveness.

In fiscal 2017 the airline industry transported about 102.12 million passengers on domestic routes and 22.39 million passengers on international routes. The amount of cargo transported, including mail, was 910 thousand tons on domestic routes and 1.76 million tons on international routes. Over the past five years, international passengers increased by 48% and domestic passengers by 11%.

In addition to the main international airport, Narita, Tokyo's other international airport, Haneda, recently has expanded and moved to around the clock operation. Japan has 97 airports, but except for the 28 located near major cities, most of them are small. However, due to the cooperation of the LCCs and the rapid increase of visitors to Japan, the number of passengers has increased substantially.

vi) Tourism

The government is trying to win over tourism demand from around the world, including from the rapidly growing region of Asia. With the shrinking population, the declining birth rate, and the aging of the population, the number of people who come to interact with Japan is expanding which maintains the vitality of local regions, develops society, and has great effect of deepening international mutual under-

2018年に3,192万人を超え、2020年の東京オリンピック・パラリンピック開催時は4,000万人を超えることを目標としている。

4）マスコミ

　i ）新聞業

日本には、2018年10月現在117種の日刊紙があり、総発行部数は前年比5.3％減の3,990万部（朝・夕刊セットのものは1部として）である。総数ではこれを上回る国もあるが、1,000世帯当たりの発行部数700部は世界で最も多い。2017年度の新聞社売上高は前年比3.1％減の1兆7,122億円となっている。

日本の新聞の特徴は、全国を対象として150万部以上を発行する「全国紙」と呼ばれる新聞が5紙あり、中には発行部数840万部に近いものもある。スポーツ紙や夕刊専門紙は主に鉄道駅などで販売されるが、全国紙、地方紙の大部分は契約者に各戸配達され、約30万人がこれに従事している。

新聞の発行部数は、テレビ、インターネットなど、速報性の高い情報源の発達の影響を受けてこの5年間で12.1％減と急速に減少しつつある。そのため、各新聞社は、合理化・効率化を図りニュースの背景の追求など、掘り下げた報道に力を入れるとともに、全国紙はじめ一部の新聞は、WEB上で読め、検索機能などを持つデジタル版を併せて発行している。

　ii ）出版業

日本は世界有数の出版国であり、2016年には、78,110点の新刊書籍と3,589種類の雑誌が発行された。2017年の国内出版総市場（出版売上額＋電子書籍売上額）は前年比4.3％減の1兆5,901億円となっている。既存の出版市場は13年連続のマイナス成長となっており、近年、特にコミック販売額の減少幅が大きく、コミックを含む雑誌市場は1990年代と比べて大きく減少している。一方、2017年の国内電子書籍市場は前年比15.8％増の2,200億円となっている。出版総市場に占める電子書籍のシェアは13.8％と増大している。

国内の出版総市場はマイナス成長となってお

standing. More than 31.92 million tourists visited Japan in 2018, and the target is to exceed 40 million by the opening of the Tokyo Olympic and Paralympic Games in 2020.

4) Mass Communication
i) Newspapers

As of October 2018, Japan had 117 daily newspapers with a total circulation of 39.9 million copies (counting morning and evening editions as one set), a year-on-year decrease of 5.3%. There are countries that have higher total circulations, but the circulation of 700 per 1,000 households is the world's highest. The sales of newspaper companies in fiscal 2017 declined 3.1% from the previous year, to 1.7122 trillion yen.

Five of Japan's newspapers are nationally distributed newspapers with circulations of at least 1.5 million copies. One of these papers has a circulation of close to 8.4 million. While sports and special evening editions are sold at railway stations and the like, the majority of national and regional newspapers are sold by monthly subscription and delivered to the subscribers' homes by some 300 thousand delivery personnel.

The effect of the latest news always being available through the various news sources on TV and the Internet, etc., effected the newspaper circulations to decline rapidly to 12.1% over the past five years. Newspaper publishers are responding by streamlining and efficiency endeavors, and pursuing extra background news and focusing on in-depth reports. Some national newspapers have also started publishing digital editions that can be read and searched on the Internet.

ii) Publishing

Japan is one of the world's leading publishing nations. In 2016, 78,119 new books and 3,589 magazines were published. The total domestic publication market (publisher revenue plus e-book sales) in 2017 was 1.5901 trillion yen, 4.3% less than the previous year. The publishing market has been experiencing negative growth for 13 years in a row, and in recent years, the decrease in comic sales is large, and the magazine market including comics has decreased greatly compared to the 1990s. The domestic e-book market in 2017 increased 15.8% year-on-year, to 220 billion yen. The share of e-books in the total publishing market rose to 13.8%.

The total publishing market in Japan is experiencing negative

り、出版社と書店数が大幅に減少している。印刷メディアを用いた出版物から電子書籍へのシフトはコミックを中心に進んでいるものの、少子・高齢化や文字離れ等の構造的な減少要因がそれを上回っていると考えられる。

ⅲ）放送業

　日本の放送は、ラジオ、テレビとも、公共放送であるNHK（日本放送協会）とその他多くの民間放送局によって行われる。NHKは、法律に基づいて受信機を持つ世帯から徴収する受信料で運営され、経営面などでは政府の監督を受ける。

　テレビ、ラジオは公共の電波を占有するため、放送法で以下の3点が規定されている。〈1〉放送を公共の福祉に適合するように規制し、その健全な発達を図る。〈2〉番組編集について、何人からも干渉・規制されない。公安・善良な風俗を害しない、政治的公平を保ち、報道は事実をまげない。意見が対立している問題はできるだけ多くの角度から論点を明らかにする。〈3〉放送番組の種別（教養番組、教育番組、報道番組、娯楽番組等）及び放送の対象とする者に応じて編集の基準を定め、それに従い放送番組の編集をする。

　民間放送は主に広告収入で運営される。ほかに多くのCATV局があり、多様な内容に地域情報などを含めて提供している。

　テレビには地上波放送と衛星放送があり、前者は2012年までにすべてデジタル化された。これにより、画質の向上のほか、双方向利用なども可能になった。移動体などに向けたワンセグ放送も行われている。2018年12月からは、衛星放送で本格的に家庭向け4K・8K放送が開始された。現行の高精細度テレビジョン放送（ハイビジョン、2K）に比べ、映像・動画の解像度（画素数）が高い4K・8Kの「スーパーハイビジョン」で行われる。

　なお、地上デジタルテレビ放送の日本方式ISDB-Tは、ワンセグ放送を併せて行えるなどの長所を持ち、2018年までに、南米を中心とする

growth, and the number of publishers and bookstores has drastically decreased. While a shift from publications that use printed media to e-books is advancing, mainly in comics, that is considered to be exceeded by structural decline factors such as the falling birthrate, the aging of society and people no longer reads as much as they used to.

iii) Broadcasting

Japan's television and radio broadcasters include one public company, Japan Broadcasting Corporation (NHK), and numerous private broadcasting stations. NHK is supported by a TV receiving fee that all households that have a TV receiver are required by law to pay. NHK management is subject to government oversight.

Because television and radio use the public airwaves, the following three points are prescribed by the Broadcasting Act. <1> Broadcasting shall be regulated so as to conform to the public welfare and to achieve the sound development thereof. <2> With respect to editing, broadcast programs must not be interfered with or regulated by any person. Political fairness must be maintained, not harming the public security and good morals, and reporting must not distort the facts. Points at issue must be clarified from as many angles as possible where there are conflicting opinions concerning an issue. <3> Standards must be stipulated for editing the broadcast programs in accordance with the target audience of the broadcasts and the classification of the broadcast program, meaning categories such as cultural programs, educational programs, news programs, entertainment programs, etc., and the broadcast programs must be edited in compliance with those standards.

Private broadcasters are run mainly on income from advertising fees. There are also many CATV stations that provide a variety of content and local information.

There is satellite TV broadcasting and terrestrial TV broadcasting. All terrestrial TV broadcasting had become digital by 2012, which improved image quality and also made two-way usage possible. There is also a system called 1seg for broadcasting to mobile terminals. In December 2018, satellite broadcasting started transmitting 4K and 8K broadcasts for home. Compared to current high-definition television broadcasting (Hi-Vision, 2K), this is done using 4K and 8K "Super Hi-Vision" with high-resolution video and animation (pixel count).

ISDB-T is a Japanese ground-based digital TV broadcasting system that can be used together with 1seg. The system has a number of advantages which has led to the technology being exported to 18 countries (as

18 カ国に技術輸出されている。
5) 情報・通信業

　産業分類による情報・通信産業には、電気通信、コンピュータソフトウェア制作、情報処理・提供サービス、インターネット付随サービス、前項で述べた各種マスコミ、映画や CD の制作など、広範な産業が含まれる。

　この定義による情報・通信産業は 2017 年に 226 万人を雇用し、GDP の 5.0％を生み出した。

　ここでは、上記の諸産業のうち、いくつかの産業の状況を示すが、現代社会が「情報化社会」と呼ばれるように、情報・通信の役割は、このような産業区分を超えて広がっている。

　ソフトウェア：ソフトウェア業は、2017 年に 70 万人の従業者を擁し、売上高は 14.1 兆円であった。ソフトウェアの内容は多岐にわたるが、近年注目されているのは電子ゲーム用ソフトウェアで、海外でも広く知られている。

　インターネット：インターネット利用者は、2017 年末に 1 億 84 万人で、利用率は 83.5％に達した。インターネットの利活用が進化し、普及が進んでいる。

　近年、インターネットの重要性が、益々増加しており、今後の世界経済成長およびイノベーションの主要な推進力となっていることは世界の共通認識である。2017 年の G7 イタリアのタオルミーナサミットにおいても、イノベーションと次世代生産革命によって引き起こされる「大きな変化」の機会をとらえ、各国がデジタル経済から十分な恩恵を受けられるよう図る。そのためには、クラウドコンピューティング、ソーシャルネットワーキングといった、各国の社会においてイノベーションを推進して新たな機会をとらえる必要があるとしている。このような認識のもとに、人々や企業によるデジタル世界へのアクセスを促進するとともに、人工知能を活用する。また情報の自由な流通を促進し、知的財産保護とサイバーセキュリティに関する政策を推進することで合意した。

　人口減少時代を迎えている日本にとっても、人・モノ・組織・地域などあらゆるものを「つなげる」ことで新たな価値創造を実現する ICT（Information and Communication Technology）を利活用して、需要喚起、生産性向上に資する。その結果、女性や高齢者などの

of 2018), mainly in South America.

5) Information and Telecommunication Industry

The information and telecommunication classification includes a wide range of industries such as telecommunications, computer software development, information processing and provision services, Internet associated services, and the production of the various kinds of mass communication listed above, and of movies and CDs.

In 2017 the information and telecommunication industry thus defined employed 2.26 million and generated 5.0% of GDP.

Here, the state of some of the industries mentioned above is described, showing how the role of the information and telecommunication industry extends beyond the classification, in much the same way that modern society is referred to as the "information society."

Software: In 2017 the software industry had a workforce of 700 thousand and sales of 14.1 trillion yen. The contents of software are many, but what has recently been attracting attention is electronic game software, which is also well-known abroad.

Internet: As of the end of 2017, 83.5% of Japanese, or 100.84 million people, are using the Internet, a utilization rate of 83.5%. The Internet continues to spread as its use and application evolve.

A common understanding throughout the world is that the Internet is becoming increasingly important and has become the main driving force of global growth and innovation. At the G7 Summit in Taormina, Italy, in 2017, it was recognized that in order for each country to fully benefit from the digital economy, it was necessary to seize the new opportunities provided by the big changes brought about by innovation and the next-generation revolution in production methods by utilizing cloud computing and social networking to drive social innovation in each country. Based on this recognition, access to the digital world for people and companies will be promoted and artificial intelligence utilized. There was also agreement to further the free circulation of information and promote policies on intellectual property protection and cyber security.

For Japan, which is entering an era of declining population, ICT (Information and Communication Technology) will be utilized to realize new value creation by "connecting" everything, including people, goods, organizations, regions, and so forth, contributing to improvements in productivity. This will bring sustainable growth by enabling

在宅勤務を可能とし、社会・労働参加を促進することで持続的成長が図られる。

6) 医療・福祉産業

我が国の医療制度は、主に医療施設と医療従事者によって構成され、国民皆保険の下、基本的にどの医療機関でも受診可能であり、世界最長の平均寿命を達成するなど、世界トップクラスの保健医療水準を実現している。

2016年10月現在、病院8,442施設、一般診療所約10.2万施設、歯科診療所6.9万施設、病床総数166.5万床、医師31.9万人、歯科医師10.5万人、薬剤師30万人、看護師147.3万人、医療・福祉産業総従事者799万人の医療体制である。病院数の70％、病床数の57％が民間で民間中心の医療提供体制となっている。2017年度の日本の総医療費は38.9兆円であり、急速な高齢化で2020年度では46.9兆円になると推測されている。

社会福祉とは、生活する上で支援や介助を必要とする人々に社会的サービスを提供し、自立や生活の安定を手助けする制度である。近年は家族構成や地域社会の変容にともない、必要とされる福祉が多様化している。

高齢化が進行し、介護の問題は家族だけでは負担しきれなくなった。そこで、介護を社会全体で支える仕組みを構築するため、2000年4月より介護保険制度が始まった。介護保険は、40歳以上のすべての人を加入者とし、保険料を納め、介護が必要と認定された場合は費用の一部を支払い、介護サービスを受けることができる。特に特別養護老人ホームは不足しており、2017年3月時点で30万人が待機状況となっている。

また大都市部を中心に認可保育所に入れない「待機児童」は2013～2016年までの4年間に保育所の定員数を43万人分増やしたが、働く主婦が増加しているため、待機児童の数は2009年以降、毎年2万人を超えて推移している。また保育士も不足している。

7) その他の第3次産業

その他の第3次産業には、電気・ガス・水道、不動産、宿泊・飲食、生活サービス、娯楽、研究、教育、NPO活動などの多様な分野および行政等の公務

women, elderly people, and others to e-commute from home, promoting greater participation in society and the labor force.

6) Medical and Welfare Industry

Japan's medical system consists mainly of medical facilities and medical staff. Under the national health insurance program, basically people are free to choose any medical institution they want. With its world-class health and medical standards, the Japanese people have the the world's longest average life expectancy.

As of October 2016, there are 8,442 hospitals, approximately 102,000 general clinics, 69,000 dental clinics, 1.665 million beds, 319 thousand doctors, 105 thousand dentists, 300 thousand pharmacists, and 1.473 million nurses. In all, the medical and welfare system employs 7.99 million people. It is primarily a private-sector healthcare delivery system in which 70% of the hospitals and 57% of the hospital beds are private. Total medical expenses in Japan in fiscal 2017 amounted to 38.9 trillion yen, and it is estimated it will be 46.9 trillion yen in 2020 due to the rapid aging of the population.

Social welfare is a system that provides social services to people who need assistance or nursing care, and helps them lead an independent, stable life. In recent years, the required welfare has diversified as the composition of families and local communities undergo changes.

As the population continues to age, the burden of nursing care became too heavy to be borne by the family alone. In April 2000, this led to the initiation of a long-term care insurance system as a mechanism to support nursing care throughout the entire society. People start paying nursing-care insurance premiums at the age of 40, and when care services are required, they pay part of the expenses involved. Special nursing homes for the elderly are in short supply, and as of March 2017 some 300 thousand people are on waiting lists.

Children who can't enter an authorized nursery schools due to lack of capacity, mainly in the center of big cities, are put on waiting lists. In the 4-year period 2013–2016, the number of capacity at nursery schools were increased by 430,000, but as more housewives are working, every year since 2009 more than 20,000 children are put on waiting lists. There is also a shortage of nursery school teachers.

7) Other Tertiary Industries

Other tertiary industries include electricity, gas, water, real estate, lodging, eating and drinking, life services, entertainment, research, education, and various other activities, such as those of NPOs and public

が含まれる。うち民間部門では、2016年に全産業の61.1% 3,531万人が従事しており、2016年にはGDPの50.4%を占めた。
　内容をみると、民間部門では宿泊・飲食サービス業417万人、その他サービス業455万人、生活・娯楽サービス業232万人、専門・技術・業務サービス業230万人、教育・学習支援業183万人、不動産・物品賃貸業148万人、電気・ガス19.4万人が続いている。

　現代社会では、生活の多様化などに応じて、絶えず従来の産業分類に当てはまらない多様な職種が生まれており、この分野は今後も拡大していくと予想される。

(6) 企業経営と雇用

a) 概況

　日本の伝統的な企業経営の特徴については、終身雇用、年功序列、企業内福祉の重視など指摘されてきた。また上場企業のような大企業における意思決定については「稟議（りんぎ）」方式と呼ばれる、組織の下部の発意に基づく集団的決定方式が多くの企業で採用されてきた。トップの強い指導力で運営される企業も少なくなかったが、大企業で広く用いられたこのシステムは、従業員と企業との一体感を生み出し、各人の発意を活かすことに役立ったことで、日本経済の発展に大きく貢献したと考えられ、その理念は今なお多くの企業の経営哲学の中に残されている。

　この伝統的な経営方式は、企業間の株式持ち合い、とりわけ企業とメインバンク、大口需要家などの取引先とが株式を持ち合う「安定株主」を形成し、株主総会での議決権の安定多数を確保するという慣行の上に成立してきたものである。
　現在の日本の株式会社制度は、1899年にドイツの制度に倣って制定されたものである。その後何度かの改正を経ているが、基本は今日においても、会社の重要な意思決定は株主で構成される株主総会が決め、日常の業務執行とその業務執行の監督は、株主総会で選任される取締役で構成される取締役会に委任され、同じく株主総会で選任され

service administration. Of these, in 2016, 35.31 million people were engaged in the private sector, corresponding to 61.1% of all industries and accounting for 50.4% of GDP in 2016.

Looking at the details, in the private sector, there are 4.17 million people in the lodging and food service industry, 4.55 million in the other services industry, 2.32 million in the life and entertainment service industry, 2.3 million in the professional, technical, and business service industry, 1.83 million in the education and learning support industry, 1.48 million in the real estate, goods rental, and leasing industry, and 194 thousand in the electricity and gas industry.

In modern society, in response to the diversification of life styles, various occupations that do not fit into traditional industrial classifications are constantly being born. This category is expected to expand in future.

(6) Business Management and Employment

a) Overview

The features of traditional Japanese corporate management are extolled as lifetime employment, seniority-based promotion, and emphasis on internal welfare. The *ringi* system of collective decision-making that builds on initiatives begun in the lower part of the organization is common in many listed large companies. Quite a few of the companies were managed by top management having strong leadership skills, but it is considered that this ringi system, which has been widely used by large corporations, made a major contribution to Japan's economic development because of its usefulness in creating a feeling of unity between the employees and the company and tapping the initiative of each person. That thinking still remains in the management philosophy of many companies.

In this traditional management style, companies are connected through cross-shareholdings, a main bank, and stable shareholding by major customers or suppliers, to ensure enough voting rights at shareholders meetings to maintain stability.

The current Japanese corporate system based on the German system was established in 1899. Although it has undergone several revisions since then, fundamentally, important decision-making is conducted at the general meeting of shareholders, and the daily execution of business and its supervision are delegated to a board of directors elected at the meeting of shareholders, at which auditors are also appointed who do

る監査役は、業務執行は行わず、取締役の業務執行について、法令定款に違反していないかをチェックするという制度になっている。

しかし、1990年代初頭のバブル経済の崩壊とそれに続く経済のグローバル化、新興国の経済発展、通信手段の発展による経済・社会システムの急激な変化などにより、経営システムは大きく変化している。

b）企業経営の変革

1）株式持ち合いの解消

企業間の株式の持ち合いの慣行が行われてきた背景には、企業の株式の価格が右肩上がりに上昇してきた実態がある。1960年末の日経平均株価は1,300円程度であったが、その後1990年初頭までの30年間、毎年10％以上の株価上昇が続き、3万8,000円まで達した。しかし、その後バブル経済がはじけ、株価は下がり続け、2001年には1万円を割り込む状況となる。こうなると企業が他社の株式を保有し続ける経済合理性はなくなる。

また、1989年から4年間にわたって行われた日米構造問題協議の中で、米国側から日本企業の系列関係が問題とされたが、これは株式の持ち合い構造が市場の公正競争を妨げているという指摘であった。これを契機に、株式保有制限、会社内容の開示、株主の権利の拡充（例えば、株主代表訴訟の容易化）、社外重役制度等、後述の3）項で取り上げるコーポレートガバナンスの観点からの法規制が行われることになる。このような背景のもとで、現在では持ち合い構造はほぼ解消してきた。

2）企業内部の意思決定システム

従来のシステムでは、例えば、大企業の取締役会では取締役の数が多く実質的な審議がなされにくいので、別に少数の役付取締役（常務、専務、副社長等）だけで構成される常務会等を設けて実質的な審議・決定をする、というように、企業の決定システムが重層化し、意思決定に時間がかかることや、責任の所在があいまいになりやすいという問題があった。しかし、企業活動がグローバル化すると、迅速かつ的確な決定が求められるようになった。その対応として、CEO

not have a business role but are there to check whether the directors' execution of their duties violates laws and regulations or the company's Articles of Incorporation.

However, with the collapse of the bubble economy in the early 1990s, rapid changes in economic and social systems caused by the subsequent economic globalization, the economic development of the emerging economies, and the rapid development of communication means, management systems have been undergoing huge changes.

b) Transformation of Business Management
1) Elimination of Cross-Shareholdings

Behind the practice of cross-shareholding between companies was the reality of the soaring prices of corporate shares. The Nikkei Stock Average at the end of 1960 stood at 1,300 yen, and in the subsequent 30 years up to the early 1990s stock prices continued to rise at 10% or more a year, reaching 38,000 yen. But then the bubble economy burst, and the Nikkei went down and kept going down, falling below 10,000 yen in 2001. In such a situation, the economic rationale for holding on to another company's shares disappeared.

Also, during the Japan-U.S. consultations on structural problems that took place over the four years starting 1989, the U.S. side brought up the keiretsu relationships as a problem, arguing that the cross-shareholding structure was preventing fair competition in the market. Taking this opportunity, laws and regulations from the perspective of corporate governance, as discussed below in section 3), have been introduced, along with limits on cross shareholding, requirements for greater company disclosures, expansion of shareholder rights (for example, simplification of shareholder representative litigation cases), external director systems, etc. Against this background, cross-shareholding structures were virtually eliminated.

2) Internal Decision-Making System

In the conventional system, for example, at the board of directors' meeting at a large company, it was hard to have substantive deliberations because of the large number of directors. So a separate executive board was set up comprised of a small number of titled directors (managing director, executive director and executive vice president) to carry out substantive deliberations and make decisions. So the problem then was the decision system became stratified, making a decision took time, and pinpointing where responsibilities lay became unclear. With the globalization of corporate activities, it became necessary to make

制度・執行役員制度の導入、大幅な権限移譲、企業内階層の簡素化など、意思決定過程を透明にする欧米型の経営手法を取り入れたシステムの導入が進んだ。

また、法制面においても、国際社会における競争力確保の観点から、会社経営の自由度を広げるための改正が行われるようになった。例えば、持株会社設立の禁止の解除、自己株式の取得・保有制限の撤廃などである。

- 持株会社（Holding Company）：他の会社の株式の保有のみを目的とする会社。例えば、既存会社の事業部門等をすべて子会社にして、親会社は子会社の株式を保有し、子会社管理に徹する（独占禁止法第9条の改正等、1997年）。
- 自己株式（Treasury Stock）：発行会社が保有している自社の株式。他社の株式との交換、役員・従業員への報酬の支払い（予め決めた価格で株式を購入できる権利：ストックオプション）等の為に保有する場合が多い（旧商法第211条ノ3の設定等、2003年）。

3）コーポレートガバナンス

従来、大企業の経営者の関心は内部管理に偏りがちであった。企業は、必要な資金を自ら株式や社債の発行によって市場から直接調達（直接金融）するよりも、メインバンクを中心とする金融機関を通して間接的に市場から借り入れる方法（間接金融）で賄ってきた。株式についてもその多くがメインバンクや大口取引先等の友好的な法人株主に保有され、さらにそれら法人同士が相互に持ち合っていた。欧米の経営者の大きな関心事である不特定多数の株主への対応などあまり必要なかったのである。取締役の多くが従業員から内部昇格で選ばれていたことも、内部重視傾向の一因であった。その結果、経営者の違法行為が隠ぺいされるという不適切な事例まで発生した。

しかし、先の2）項で述べたように、バブルがはじけて持ち合い構造が解消されるとともに、グローバル化の進展で海外投資家が日本企業の株式の多くの割合を保有することになり、海外取引先、海外競争業者など外部の利害関係者（ステークホルダー）が増加すると、それらの外部関係者との利害の調整と、国内では

quick, accurate decisions. This situation led to the introduction of the CEO and executive officer system, significant transfer of authority, and a simplified internal hierarchy. That is, the incorporation of Western type management methods with a transparent decision-making process.

In terms of the legal system, to ensure competitiveness in the international community, amendments were made to broaden the degree of freedom of company management. These included dropping the ban against establishing a holding company and removing restrictions on a company acquiring and holding treasury stock.

- Holding Company: A company formed only to hold shares of other companies. For example, all the business divisions of a company are made into subsidiaries, and the parent company holds the shares of the subsidiaries and focuses solely on administering them (revision of Article 9 of the Antimonopoly Act and other revisions, 1997).
- Treasury Stock: A company's shares owned by the issuing company. Often it is held to exchange with stocks of other companies, to pay remuneration to directors and employees (right to purchase stock at a predetermined price: stock options), etc. (Old Commercial Code Article 211-3, 2003).

3) Corporate Governance

Traditionally, Japanese managers of large companies' interest were biased toward internal control. Rather than raise the necessary funds directly from the market by issuing shares and bonds (direct financing), they preferred to borrow indirectly from the market by going through a main bank (indirect financing). With respect to shares, too, they preferred to have their shares held by friendly corporate shareholders such as the main bank or a large customer, and for these corporations to also hold each other's shares. This also meant there was not much need to respond to the demands of a large number of unspecified shareholders, which is a major source of concern for Western managers. The fact that most directors have been promoted internally up through the ranks also contributed to the tendency of Japanese companies to have an internal focus, which could lead to inappropriate actions such as hiding illegal activities by managers.

However, as described in the previous section 2), the bursting of the bubble economy largely eliminated the cross-holding structures, and in the process of globalization foreign investors were left holding a large percentage of the shares of Japanese companies. There was also an increasing number of overseas competitors and suppliers and other such external stakeholders, whose interests had to be balanced. It also

あまり例のなかった敵対的買収への対処など、国際基準に合致した企業統治体制づくりが避けられない状況となった。

このような背景のもとに、コーポレートガバナンス（企業統治）の議論が盛んになってきたのである。この議論は、大企業のあり方について、「誰のために」、「どのような方法で」運営されるべきかを論ずるものである。

この議論を受けて、2002年、新たな株式会社形態として「委員会等設置会社」を認める商法改正が行われた。この形態においては、監査役は廃止され、会社の取締役会は、経営の基本方針の決定、業務執行者の選任・解任のみを行い、取締役の大部分は業務執行には関与しない。社外取締役が過半数を占める3つの委員会がそれぞれ分担して、取締役の候補者の決定（指名委員会）、取締役の報酬の決定（報酬委員会）、会社業務執行の監査（監査委員会）を行い、日常の業務執行は、取締役会が選任する執行役に委任される。会社の業務執行と、監督・監査を明確に分ける（モニタリング・モデルと呼ばれる）ものである。

2006年には、それまで商法（会社編）、商法特例法、有限会社法等に分かれて規定されていた会社関係法律を統合・再編した新しい会社法が制定・施行された。同法は、まず従来カタカナ文語体で記載されていた規定をひらがな口語体に改めて一般人にも読みやすくしたことに画期的な点がある。また同法はコーポレートガバナンスを大いに意識し、企業の効率性の向上と並んで、企業の健全性と法令・企業倫理への適合（コンプライアンス）、取締役・従業員による法令違反を防止するための内部統制システムの整備などが定められた。

内部統制は、当該企業だけでなく、親会社・子会社を含めた企業集団全体を対象にしていることが重要である。企業の不祥事などが子会社を隠れ蓑にしてなされることが多いからである。1978年に義務付けられ2000年には単独決算よりも重視されるようになった連結決算制度の確立も、企業集団全体の内部統制を実現するために大いに効果があったと考えられる。

meant having to deal with hostile takeovers that had seldom been seen before in Japan, creating a situation in which developing a corporate governance system consistent with international standards became unavoidable.

Against this backdrop, discussions on corporate governance have flourished. For whom is a large company to be operated, and by what methods? Those were the types of questions that have been asked.

Amid this, in 2002 the Commercial Code was revised to allow for a "Ccompany with Committees etc." as a new corporate form. In this structure, the corporate auditors were abolished, the company's board of directors only decides basic management policy and the appointment and dismissal of executives, and most of the directors are not involved in the running of the business. There are three statutory committees, on which the majority of directors are outside directors, each with its own responsibilities. The nominating committee nominates directors, the remuneration committee decides directors' remuneration, and the audit committee audits corporate operations. The execution of daily business is delegated to executive officers appointed by the Board of Directors. Termed a monitoring model, it clearly separates supervision and auditing from the execution of the business.

In 2006, a new Companies Act was enforced. This consolidated and reorganized legal provisions and regulations that had been spread across a number of laws, including the Corporate Relations Act (a part of the Commercial Code), the Commercial Code Special Law, and the Limited Liability Company Law. The new Act also broke new ground by being written in colloquial hiragana style instead of the former katakana literary style, making it easier for the general public to read. The law showed great awareness of corporate governance, making it mandatory to establish an internal control system for preventing illegal acts by directors and employees, and is directed at improving efficiency and competitiveness and maintaining corporate soundness and compliance with the law and corporate ethics.

The focus of the internal control system is not just the company itself, but also the corporate group, including parent companies and subsidiaries, which is important because many cases of misconduct are disguised in subsidiaries. It became mandatory in 1978 for companies to have a consolidated accounting system, as it came to be commonly understood that it is a more effective means to achieve internal control by using a corporate group's overall consolidated accounting system, which in

さらに、2014年の会社法の改正により上場会社には社外取締役の設置が事実上強制された。同時に、前述の委員会等設置会社に加えて、新しく「監査等委員会設置会社」（従来の会社の監査役を廃止して、過半数が社外取締役で構成される監査等委員会を設置する会社）という、従来の会社に監査役を置かない会社形態を認めた。この監査等委員会設置会社に移行する上場企業の数は法改正直後から年々増加している。その理由は、2002年に認められた委員会等設置会社はモニタリング・モデルの実現により会社の透明性を図るという理念からは評価できるが、実際の多くの上場企業においては社長の事実上の経営者人事権は残したいので、委員会等設置会社の採用に踏み切れないという実態があるからである。また監査等委員会の取締役会に対するけん制力がより強化されたこと、従前の社外監査役のほかに、さらに社外取締役を設けるために、社外からの人材を確保することが容易でないという現実も考慮されたのである。なお従来の「委員会等設置会社」の名称は「指名委員会等設置会社」に変更された。
　ところで、日産自動車のカルロス・ゴーン取締役会長が役員報酬の開示義務（金融商品取引法）に違反した事件との関連で、日産自動車が設置した企業統治改革専門委員会は、2019年3月27日、経営体制の見直しへ提言をまとめた。その中で、日産自動車は現在「監査役会設置会社」を採用しているがこれを「指名委員会等設置会社」に改めることを提言している。指名委員会等設置会社の方が国際的にわかりやすく、一定程度の権限の集中を防げる（経営の監督と執行を明確に分離する）という理由である。社外の目を取り入れ（社外取締役が中心となって経営を監督する）、一連の不正の温床となった人事・報酬を巡るプロセスを透明化するためである。

　最近では法律による強制だけでなく、民間の有識者から提唱された上場企業のあるべき行動基準を定めた「コーポレートガバナンス・コード」や、さらには責任ある機関投資家に対する諸原則を定めた「スチュ

2000 was made to be more important than the non-consolidated system.

The amendment of the Companies Act in 2014 in effect mandates the appointment of outside directors by listed companies. At the same time, in addition to the above-mentioned "company with committees, etc." a new structure was permitted, a "company with an audit and supervisory committee" (a company that has abolished the former corporate auditor role and set up a statutory audit committee on which the majority of members are outside directors). The number of listed companies shifting to the "company with an audit and supervisory committee" structure following the amendment of the law is increasing year by year. The reason for this is that while the "companies with committees, etc." structure approved in 2002 can be evaluated highly as endeavoring to be transparent by realizing a monitoring model, in fact many of the listed companies are in effect managed by the president, who wants to retain the right to make personnel decisions, and so doesn't want to take the step of becoming a "company with committees, etc." Furthermore, the audit committee's ability to control the board of directors has been further strengthened, it is not easy to secure human resources from outside the company to establish outside directors in addition to the outside corporate auditor. The former title of a "company with committees, etc." has been changed to a "company with three statutory committees."

Following the matter of Carlos Ghosn, then chairman of Nissan Motors, being accused of being in violation of the legal obligation (under Japan's Financial Instruments and Exchange Act) to disclose his executive compensation, Nissan established a "Special Committee for Improving Governance," which on March 27, 2019, presented recommendations for making improvements to the company's corporate governance. One of the proposed improvements was for Nissan to implement a transition from being a company with statutory auditors to a company with three statutory committees. The reasons for doing that were that a company thus organized was easier to understand from an international perspective, and that, to a certain extent, it prevents the concentration of power (there being a clear separation between supervisory and executive functions). Outside directors are used to provide most of the management oversight, bringing transparency to the processes that surround personnel and compensation and form a hotbed of misconduct.

In recent years, In addition to legal enforcement, corporate governance codes that set out standards of behavior of listed companies proposed by private sector experts, and stewardship codes, which define various principles for responsible institutional investors, have been

ワードシップ・コード」などが制定され、証券取引所側からの後押しもあって多くの企業と機関投資家から順守されてきている。

4）ファイナンスにおける市場機能の重視

　従来、企業はメインバンクと密接な連携を保つことを重視して間接金融に多くを頼り、市場金利が安定的であったこともあって資金調達コストについてはあまり重視してこなかった。しかし金融のグローバル化が進む中で、金融の効率化を目指し、直接金融にも積極的に取り組み、より弾力的で低コストの資金調達を追求するようになっている。他方金融機関側も一層自由な資金運用を求めているため、企業と銀行の関係でも、必ずしも相互依存的ではない、市場機能を重視する金融施策が採用されるようになってきている。

5）企業再編の弾力化

　経済のグローバル化で企業活動が国境を超えて拡大すると、日本企業も従来の規模では国際競争への対処が難しくなり、国内企業間の合併、海外企業との提携などが活発化した。そのため、合併等の企業結合の可否を判断するための独占禁止法上の審査基準（市場の画定、商品シェア、代替性、輸入圧力等）もゆるやかになり、運用も弾力的になされる（例えば、2012年10月の新日本製鉄と住友金属工業の合併）など世界規模の競争力の必要性が考慮され、企業再編ルールに国際基準が取り入れられた。

6）地域への貢献と企業メセナ

　かつては企業による公害や不祥事の隠ぺいなどが社会的な大問題となったことがあったが、現在では、環境保護と周辺社会との良好な共生関係が企業の大きな関心事になっている。

　株式の持ち合いが盛んなころは、企業経営者にはとりわけ誠実性が求められた。持合い構造が消滅すると、企業の効率性・健全性の実現が経営者の課題となり、グローバル化が進展した現在は、様々なステークホルダーとの利害調整が重要となる。経営者には社会の一員としての企業の存在自体の是非が問われ、企業の社会的責任や公益性、共生が求められるようになっている。

proposed by private-sector experts and enacted, and are being backed up by stock exchanges, and complied with by corporations and institutional investors.

4) Emphasis on the Role of Market Mechanisms in Financing

Formerly, in a regime of relatively stable interest rates, companies placed emphasis on maintaining close, cooperative ties with a main bank, relied heavily on indirect funding, and did not place particular emphasis on the cost of procuring funding. However, amid the globalization of funding, there is an active focus on funding efficiency and efforts aimed at direct funding, as part of an endeavor to procure funds flexibly and at a low cost. On the other hand, financial institutions are given increasingly more freedom to manage their funds. As a result, the relationship between a company and its bank is not necessarily one of interdependency. Funding policies are now emphasizing on market mechanisms.

5) Flexible Business Reorganization

In the course of economic globalization of a company's cross-border activety expands, it is hard for a Japanese company of a conventional size to deal with international competition. In such cases, Japanese companies have tended to pursue a domestic merger or an overseas alliance. To determine the propriety or advisability of entering into the merger or alliance, carrying screening and appraisal based on the criteria involved, with reference to antitrust laws (definition of the market, the companies' share of the market, substitutability, import pressure, and so forth) has been done more loosely than in the past (for example, the October 2012 merger between Nippon Steel and Sumitomo Metal Industries). Taking into account the need to be competitive on the global stage international standards have been incorporated into the corporate restructuring rules.

6) Contribution to Local Regions and Corporate Philanthropy

Formerly companies have caused serious societal problems by generating pollution and concealing misconduct. Nowadays, a major corporate concern is protecting the environment and having a good, symbiotic relationship with the surrounding community.

When cross-shareholding was a thriving arrangement, managers were required above all to have integrity. When the cross-holding structure is eliminated, achieving corporate efficiency and soundness becomes the issue for the manager. Today, with the advance of globalization, coordinating the interests of a company's various stakeholders is important. When the rights and wrongs of the very existence of the company itself are called into question, corporate social responsibility and concern for the public interest and coexistence are required of management.

このような観点から、スポーツ活動や芸術活動の実施・少子高齢化社会に対する支援で社会全般の生活・文化に貢献する企業も増加しており、社内に保育所を設けたり、財団を設立して日本を代表するコンサートホールや美術館を運営する例も多い。

c）雇用関係
1）雇用関係の変化

日本の企業では、長い間、学校・大学卒業時の定期採用、所定の年齢までの終身雇用、勤続年数による昇進という雇用慣行と企業別労働組合とが雇用制度の主流であった。

しかし近年は、厳しさを増す経済環境や就業者の意識の変化によって、さらには少子高齢化社会の到来によって外国人労働者も含めた雇用の流動化が顕著になりつつあり、終身雇用を基礎とする雇用関係にも大きな影響を与えている。

2）雇用の流動化

高度成長時代が終わり、景気変動の影響が厳しさを増していること、産業構造の急激な変化によって労働力需給の質的ミスマッチが大きくなっていることなどから、企業の側から、終身雇用制によらない弾力的な要員管理への要請が出てくる。他方、就業者あるいは求職者の中には、自己の能力の十分な発揮のため、終身雇用という拘束を望まない若者や、経済不振による企業倒産などで職を失い、仮に不安定であっても仕事が欲しいという人々が増えてくる。

これらの要請に対応して、終身雇用契約による正社員以外に、パートタイマー、人材派遣会社からの期間職員、業務委託契約による在宅勤務者等非正規雇用就業者が増加している。異なるパートタイムの仕事を渡り歩いて暮らすフリーターと呼ばれる若者も少なくない。1995年には全就業者の19％だったこれら非正規雇用労働者の比率は、2017年には37.4％に達している（総務省）。

終身雇用制度を基本とする場合でも、経営状況悪化などへの対応として、特典を与えて早期退職を促す例はしばしば見られる。

Based on that perspective, there are a growing number of companies that contribute to the life and culture of society, encourage sporting and artistic activities, and offer support for facing the low-birthrate, aging society. There are many examples of corporations equipping company premises with day care facilities and which have established foundations and are running concert halls and museums that are so well known as to be considered representative of Japan itself.

c) Employment
1) Changes in the Employment Relationship

For a long time, yearly recruitment after graduating from school or university, lifetime employment to a fixed age, promotions based on years of service, and enterprise labor unions were the mainstream Japanese employment practices.

But in the increasingly severe economic climate and with employee's value changing, employment mobility including foreign workers are becoming noticeable and have big impact on the fundamental employment relationship that is rooted in lifetime employment and, due to the declining birthrate and the aging of the society.

2) Employment Mobility

When the period of high economic growth ended, the impact of the economic change became increasingly challenging, mainly due to the qualitative mismatch of labor supply and demand increasing owing to rapid changes in the industrial structure, and there were calls for a more elastic personnel management system that did not depend on lifetime employment. On the other hand, among young employees and job seekers there were some who wanted to give freer rein to their abilities who felt lifetime employment as restricting, and there were also a growing number of unfortunates who had lost their jobs to bankruptcies and wanted work, even if it wasn't stable employment.

In response to these requests, and in contrast to "full-time" employees who had entered into a lifetime employment contract, there was a growing number of non full-time employees which included part-timers, temporary workers from staffing agencies, and contract workers who worked from home. Another common type of young part-time worker was the "freeter," who hopped from job to job. In 1995, non full-time workers accounted for 19% of all employees; by 2017 the percentage had grown to 37.4% (Ministry of Internal Affairs and Communications).

Even if it is based on the lifetime employment system, when business conditions are bad, workers are often given incentives to take early retirement.

最近の雇用状況は次のとおりである。日本の就業者数は総務省統計局の 2018 年 3 月の速報値では、雇用者数は 5,872 万人前年比 144 万人の増加、63 か月連続の増加。正規の職員・従業員数は 3,417 万人、非正規の職員・従業員数は 2,111 万人、完全失業者数は男 103 万人、女 69 万人、合計 173 万人。完全失業率は 2.5％と世界他主要国と比較しても極めて好調である。

3 ）労働組合

　　欧米の労働組合がおおむね産業別あるいは職種別に組織されているのに対し、日本の組合は個々の企業を単位として組織されるのが一般的である。

　　ただし、近年増加しつつあるベンチャー企業などの新興企業では労働組合が組織されない例が多いことなどから、労働組合加入者は減少傾向にあり、2016 年には 994 万人で、全労働者の 17.3％であった。

　　他方で、パートタイマーの組合員は年々増加し、2016 年には 113 万人に達した。パートタイマーの数自体が増加していることと、企業内組合がこれらの人々の加入を進めていることによるとみられる。

　　日本の労働組合は、個々の企業を単位として組織されている労働組合が主で、企業別または企業内労働組合と呼ばれている。これは産業別あるいは職種別に組織されている欧米の産業別労働組合、職種別労働組合と対比されるもので、日本の労働組合の特徴として現在も引き継がれている。

　　企業別労働組合は同一産業内でまとまり、産業別労働組合を組織している。さらにこの民間の産業別労働組合および諸官庁・自治体労働組合の大部分が合流して日本労働組合総連合会（連合）という中央組織を構成している。連合は労働組合最大のナショナルセンターで約 686 万人（2017 年）の組合員を擁している。

4 ）労使関係

　　日本の労使は、相互の理解と信頼の基盤に立って良好な協力関係を維持してきた。組合の多くが企業内組合であり、日常的に経営者と情報を共有し易いこともそれを助けた。

　　賃金・給与等の基礎的労働条件の改善については、上位組織で要求内容を統一し、毎年春に経営者団体と

The recent employment situation is that according to the preliminary figures of the Statistics Bureau of the Ministry of Internal Affairs and Communications, the number of employed persons in March 2018 was 58.72 million, an increase of 1.44 million from the previous year, marking the 63rd consecutive monthly increase. The number of full-time employees was 34.17 million, the number of temporary staff and employees was 21.11 million, and the total number of unemployed was 1.03 million males and 690,000 females, for a total of 1.73 million. The unemployment rate was 2.5%, which is very low compared with other major countries around the world.

3) Labor Unions

In contrast to European and American unions that are generally organized by occupation or industry, most Japanese labor unions are organized by company.

However, start-up firms and other newly emerging companies that are growing in numbers often do not have an organized labor union, which is eroding union membership: in 2016 union members numbered 9.94 million, which was 17.3% of all workers.

On the other hand, the number of part-time workers who become union members are growing year by year, and by 2016 had reached 1.13 million. This is probably because the number of part-timers is growing and the company unions are encouraging them to join.

Most Japanese labor unions are organized separately by enterprises and are therefore called enterprise or in-house unions. This continues to be a feature of Japanese labor unions that distinguishes them from European and American unions organized by industry or occupation.

The enterprise unions are federated by industrial sector. Moreover, most of these private-sector federations and the national and local government worker unions (public-sector unions) are merged into a central organization called the Japanese Trade Union Confederation (*Rengo*). With 6.86 million members in 2017, Rengo is Japan's largest national center of labor unions.

4) Labor-Management Relations

Japanese management and labor have maintained an excellent cooperative relationship founded on mutual understanding and trust. This is helped by the fact that as most of the unions are enterprise unions, and it is easy to share information with management on a daily basis.

Every spring Japanese labor unions engage in a campaign, called "Shunto" (annual spring wage offensive), for improving wages and

交渉する「春闘」という慣行がある。交渉力を高め、労働者全体の利益の平準化を目ざすものである。2014年から5年間は官製春闘の色彩が強く、政府が経営者団体に強く賃金の引き上げを要求し、2％前後の賃上げが実現している。

5）労働条件
[労働時間・休暇・退職年齢]
　日本人労働者の年間実労働時間は、1980年代初めまで2,100時間程度であったが、1997年までに週40時間制が段階的に実施されたことなどにより減少し、2016年には年間1,713時間であった。

　法定の年次有給休暇は原則として年間10日で、勤続年数によって最大20日まで延長される。ただし、これを超える日数を定める企業も多い。

　女性の産前休暇は6週間、産後休暇は8週間である。有給か否かは企業によって異なるが、無給の場合、健康保険による支給などの措置もある。なお、近年は、夫に育児のための休暇を認める企業、役所が大幅に増えている。

　終身雇用制の場合の退職年齢は、長い間55歳が一般的であったが、人口高齢化を背景とする法令の定めで60歳が基準となり、さらに65歳への段階的な引き上げが進んでいる。さらに日本政府は「生涯現役社会の実現に向け、意欲ある高齢者に働く場を準備する」として、企業に雇用継続を義務づける年齢を65歳から70歳に引き上げる方針を示し、2020年の通常国会への高年齢者雇用安定法の改正案の提出を目指している。

6）賃金水準
　日本の労働者の平均月間給与（諸手当を含む現金支給）は、2016年の調査で男性43.4万円、女性23.3万円で、男女間に約46％の差がある。同一職務での男女差は解消されつつあり、格差は主に昇進の速さによるとみられる。

　企業規模別では、100人未満の企業と1,000人以上の企業で20〜30％の差がある。この差は1995年ごろまで縮小傾向にあったが、その後は横ばい状況にある。

salaries and other basic labor conditions. First the union leaders coordinate their demands and then negotiate with management. Shunto also aims to enhance the unions' bargaining power and equalize benefits for all workers. In the five years from 2014, the Shunto has been notably strong due to taking advantage of government request and demands to management for higher wages have resulted in increases of around 2%.

5) Working Conditions

Working Hours, Vacations, Retirement Age

Up until the beginning of the 1980s, the average Japanese worker worked 2,100 hours per year. The 40-hour week was implemented in steps by 1997, and by 2016, the annual hours worked was 1,713.

In principle, statutory paid leave is 10 days a year, and can increase to a maximum of 20 days according to the years of service. At many companies more days are granted.

Female employees are entitled to six weeks of prenatal leave and eight weeks of postnatal leave. Whether the leave is with or without payment differs depending on the company. If it is non-paid leave, there are also measures such as payment by national health insurance. In recent years, many more companies and government offices are granting father's childcare leave.

In the case of the lifetime employment system, the retirement age was usually 55 years old. With the aging of the population, the law was amended to make 60 years old the standard, and progress is being made to raise it further in steps, to 65 years old. The Japanese government's policy is to raise the age to which companies are obliged to continue employment from 65 years old to 70 years old, "to prepare a work place for elderly people who have the will to work, to realize a lifelong active society." The aim is to submit an amendment to the Stabilization of Employment of Older Persons Act to the Diet in 2020.

6) Wage Levels

The average monthly salary of Japanese workers (cash payment, including allowances) is 434 thousand yen for men and 233.3 thousand for women, according to a 2016 survey, so there is a pay differential of about 46% between the genders. Pay differentials between men and women for the same job are gradually being eliminated. The gap appears to be mainly due to the speed of promotions.

According to the size of company, the wage difference between companies with fewer than 100 employees and companies with at least 1,000 employees is from 20 to 30%. The difference decreased each year until around 1995, after which it hasn't changed.

国際比較のため、2016年の一人あたりGDP比較で見てみると日本は中国の約5倍、インドの約20倍、韓国の1.3倍となっている。
7）働き方改革
　　安倍政権は急速な労働人口の減少、高齢化の進展に対応し、また国際競争力向上の中核として生産性の大幅向上を目指して、働き方改革の実現に向けて努力している。一億総活躍社会実現に向けた最大のチャレンジ、多様な働き方を可能とするとともに、中間層の厚みを増しつつ、格差の固定化を回避し、成長と分配の好循環を実現するため、働く人の立場・視点で取り組んでいる。具体的には〈1〉非正規雇用の処遇改善、〈2〉賃金引上げと労働生産性向上、〈3〉長時間労働の是正、〈4〉柔軟な働き方がしやすい環境整備、〈5〉病気の治療、子育て・介護等と仕事の両立、〈6〉障害者就労の推進、〈7〉外国人材の受入れ、〈8〉女性・若者が活躍しやすい環境整備、〈9〉再就職支援、〈10〉企業の中高年の採用・高齢者の就業促進などである。これらの政策実現のために官民の協調とIoT、人工知能を利用した社会全体のイノベーションが必要となってくる。

　　雇用の流動化の項で述べたように、経営者側および労働者側から、それぞれ時代にあった働き方に対する雇用形態が要求されている（同一労働・同一賃金、裁量労働制）。しかし、両者の主張には相反する点が多く妥協は困難な状況にある。例えば、非正規雇用就業者の立場からは、同一労働・同一賃金という考えに基づき、同じ労働を提供しているのであれば、雇用形態が異なっても、賃金等の処遇に差を設けるべきではないと主張する。雇用主である企業側は、市場競争に勝ち残るためには、時間ではなく効果で評価する高度プロフェショナル制度等の裁量労働制の幅を多くすべきと主張する。経営側と労働側の見解の違いが大きい。国会では2年越しの論争になっている。2018年度の通常国会においても、政権与党は、これら一連の問題解決のための「働き方改革法案」を提出し決議された。しかし裁量労働制については野党からの強い反対にあい、一部継続審議となった。

For an international comparison of GDP per capita in 2016, Japan's is about five times that of China's, about 20 times that of India's, and 1.3 times that of Korea's.

7) Workplace Reforms

The Abe administration is endeavoring to realize workplace reforms in response to the rapid shrink of the working population and the aging of the population, with the aim of greatly improving productivity as a core need for improving international competitiveness. The biggest challenge to achieve the dynamic engagement of all citizens is to enable various ways of working, avoid income disparities while increasing the size of the middle class, realize a virtuous cycle of growth and distribution, and tackling this from the standpoint and perspective of the workers. Specifically, the focus will be on: <1> improving the treatment of those in non full-time employment, <2> increase wages and improve labor productivity, <3> reducing long working hours, <4> provision of an environment that facilitates flexible work styles; <5> treat illnesses and balance work with child rearing and nursing care, <6> promote employment for persons with disabilities, <7> acceptance of foreign human resources, <8> provision of the environment where women and young people can more easily be active, <9> support reemployment, <10> recruit middle-aged and older persons, promote employment of the elderly, and so forth. Realizing these policies requires cooperation between the public and private sectors, and innovation of society as a whole using IoT and artificial intelligence.

As stated in the section regarding employment mobility, different employment forms are required from both, managers and workers, to match the needs of the times (the same wages for the same work, and discretionary labor system). However, there are many points of conflict between the assertions of the two sides, which makes compromise difficult. For example, from the standpoint of non full-time employee, one would claim based on idea that if the content of the work is same, same amount should be paid no matter what the form of employments are. An employer might argue that in order to survive market competition, the range of the discretionary labor system, such as the advanced professional system that evaluates by effect rather than time, should be increased. There are large difference of view between management and labor. In the National Diet, this has been a running dispute for over two years. In the ordinary Diet session in fiscal 2018, the ruling coalition party submitted and passed a "Work style reform bill" to resolve these problems. Regarding the discretionary labor system, however, part of the reform was carried over for further discussion due to strong opposi-

なお、〈7〉外国人材の受入れについては、2018年12月の国会でいわゆる「外国人材拡大法」（出入国管理及び難民認定法の改正）が成立し、2019年4月施行された。この法律は、当面の産業界における人手不足を解消することを目的に、特定の技能を有する外国人に新たな在留資格を与え、そのために法務省に出入国在留管理庁を新設するものである。建設業、介護、農業、産業機械製造業等14の業種に限られ在留期間は最大5年、家族の帯同は不可（例外あり）となっている。

tion from the opposition parties.

With regard to <7> the acceptance of foreign human resources, the so-called "Foreign Human Resources Expansion Law" (a revision of the Immigration Control and Refugee Recognition Act) was enacted in December 2018 and went into effect in April 2019. The purpose of this law is to give foreign residents with specific skills a new status of residence with the aim of resolving the shortage of manpower in the immediate industrial world and to establish an immigration control agency at the Ministry of Justice for that purpose. It is limited to 14 industries such as the construction industry, nursing care, agriculture, the industrial machinery manufacturing industry, etc. The period of stay is up to 5 years, and family membership is not possible (there are exceptions).

5　社会

(1) 人口動態

a) 総人口

　　2018年4月現在の日本の総人口は、1億2,650万人である。日本の人口は、1920年の第1回国勢調査では5,596万人であったが、1970年に1億人を突破し、2008年には1億2,808万人のピークに達した。その後は減少に転じ、2018年までの過去10年間で人口は約149万人減少した。

　　出生数は、1970年半ば以降連続的に減り続け、2017年には94.1万人となった。死亡数は、2000年以降増え続け、2003年に100万人を超え、2017年には134万人であった。

　　国立社会保障・人口問題研究所の調査によれば、今後日本の人口はさらに減少し、2053年には1億人を割り、2065年には8,808万人になり、2016～2065年の約50年間でおよそ3,900万人、率にして30％減少すると推計される。

　　人口推計の前提となる合計特殊出生率（1人の女性が生涯に産む平均的子供の数）は、2015年には1.45であった。今後、2024年までは1.42まで低下して、その後長期的には1.43～1.44に落ち着くと予測される。

b) 平均寿命・死亡原因

　　日本人の平均寿命（その年に生まれたひとが何歳まで生きられるかを示したもの）は、終戦直後の1946年には「人生50年」であったが、1970年以降急速に伸びて、2017年に男性81.09歳、女性87.26歳となった。女性は香港に次いで世界第2位、男性は香港、スイスに次いで第3位である。

　　日本人の平均寿命はこの約70年の間に男性が31年、女性が33年伸びた。その主な要因としては、科学技術の進歩、医学の発展や医療技術の進歩（薬品を含む）、乳児死亡率の低下、健康に関する教育の広まりや、国民皆保険制度により保健・医療・介護のサービスシステムが整備され一般的に高額となりがちな医療費も低くおさえられていること、衛生・生活環境の改善、低脂肪で栄養バランスのとれた日本型食生活などがあげられる。

5 Society

(1) Population Dynamics

a) Total Population

Japan's total population as of April 2018 was 126.5 million. The population went from 55.96 million at the time of the first census in 1920 to rise over 100 million in 1970 and peaked at 128.08 million in 2008. During the following ten years up to 2018, it decreased by 1.49 million.

The number of births per year has continued to decline since the mid-1970s and was 941,000 in 2017. The number of deaths per year has been rising since 2000. It exceeded 1 million in 2003 and reached 1.34 million in 2017.

According to the National Institute of Population and Social Security Research's projects, the population of Japan will drop below 100 million in 2053 and fall to 88.08 million in 2065. If true, the decrease over approximately fifty years between 2016 and 2065 will amount to some 39 million people, a decline of about 30%.

The total fertility rate (average number of children born per woman during lifetime), as derived from the population projection, is expected to decline from the 1.45 level in 2015 to 1.42 by 2024 and then level off at 1.43 to 1.44 over the long term.

b) Average Life Span and Causes of Death

In 1946, just after World War II, "Life is 50 years" was a common expression among Japanese. However, average life expectancy (expected lifespan at birth) began to shoot up rapidly from around 1970. By 2017, it was 81.09 years for males, and 87.26 years for females. Japan ranks second to Hong Kong in female life expectancy, and third behind Hong Kong and Switzerland in male life expectancy.

Average Japanese life expectancy has increased 31 years for males and 33 years for females over the past seventy years. Among the main reasons are advances in science and technology, developments in medical science, advances in health-care technology (including medicine), a decrease in infant mortality, the spread of health-related education, a universal health insurance program providing health and medical care and home nursing services, keeping down medical treatment costs which usually tend to be expensive, improvements in sanitation and life

また、日本人は昔から首までお湯に浸かる入浴スタイルを持ち、血行促進のほかリラックス効果も持っている。さらに、高齢層の肥満率は世界の中でもかなり低く生活習慣病にかかるリスクも低い。
　また意外な理由の一つが冷蔵庫の普及であると言われている。食べ物を保存する際に塩漬けにするなど塩分過多となる食生活が改善され、脳血管疾患系のリスクが大幅に減少した。加えて、老後の生きがいを容易に見つけられる「人とのコミュニケーション」が、お年寄りの集うサークル活動やインターネットの普及などで促進され、これによって孤独を感じる人が少なくなり、高い社会参加意欲が平均寿命の向上につながったのではと見られている。

　今後も日本人の平均寿命はさらに伸びて、2060年には男性84.2歳、女性90.9歳に達すると予測される（国立社会保障・人口問題研究所）。日本人の死亡原因としては、従来からガン（30％）、心臓疾患（16％）、脳血管疾患（11％）が3大死亡原因とされ、次いで肺炎、老衰や交通事故などが上位を占めてきた。しかし、2016年以降、高齢者の増加にともない肺炎が脳血管疾患を上回った。

c) 世帯数・家族構成

　2015年の日本の総世帯数は5,345万世帯で、1世帯当りの人員は2.38人であった（総務省統計局「国勢調査」）。この20年間の全般的傾向をみると、世帯総数は継続的に増加し、1世帯当たりの人員は継続的に減少している。これは世帯の少人数化が進み、世帯の分散化が進んでいることを示す。世帯の少人数化の要因は次のようなものである。

〈1〉 単独世帯が増えた。この類型には結婚をしていない単身者（未婚・離婚シングル）、一人暮らしの高齢者が多く含まれる。孤独な高齢者が大きな問題となってきた（1,352万世帯）。

〈2〉 子供のいない夫婦だけの世帯（2人家族）が増えた（1,187万世帯）。
（アメリカのDINKs：Double Income No Kids 共稼ぎ・子どもなしと同じ風潮）

environment, and a well-balanced, low-fat, Japanese style of eating.

Japanese have long had a bathing style in which they soak in hot water up to their neck, which has a relaxing effect and promotes blood circulation. The obesity rate of elderly people is quite low in global terms, so the risk of contracting lifestyle-related diseases is also low.

One of the surprising reasons for this is said to be the spread of refrigerators, which improved eating habits such as by reducing the excessive use of salt when preserving food, greatly reducing the incidence of cerebrovascular disease. In addition, interpersonal communication, which helps people of advanced age to enjoy their lives, is promoted by group activities among the elderly and the spread of the Internet, helping to reduce feelings of loneliness, all of which are considered to have led to an improvement in life span by generating a strong desire for community and social participation.

Average life expectancy is likely to increase more. One prediction is that by 2060 males can expect to live 84.2 years and females 90.9 years (National Institute of Population and Social Security Research). The three top causes of death among Japanese have long been cancer (30%), heart disease (16%), and cerebrovascular disease (11%). Other leading causes include pneumonia, senility and traffic accidents. In 2016, however, pneumonia overtook cerebrovascular disease as a cause of death, probably because of the increasing number of elderly people.

c) Number of Households and Family Composition

The number of households in Japan as of 2015 was 53.45 million and the average number of persons per household was 2.38 (Statistics Bureau, Ministry of Internal Affairs and Communications). The overall trend during the past 20 years has been for the number of households to increase gradually and the number of persons per household to decrease gradually. This is the result of shrinking household size and a tendency for large households to split into smaller ones. The following are some of the reasons for shrinking household size:

<1> Increase in one-person households. Many of these households with only one member are made up of an unmarried person (never married or divorced) or a live-alone elderly person. The rising number of lonely old people has become a major problem (13.52 million households).

<2> More households consisting of only a childless married couple (two-person families) (11.87 million households). (This is similar to the rise of households called DINKS (Double Income No Kids) in the United States (U.S.).)

⟨3⟩ 夫婦と子供のいる従来の標準型家族はほとんど増えていない（1,482万世帯）。(⟨2⟩、⟨3⟩は従来「核家族」・おじいちゃん、おばあちゃんのいない家族と呼ばれていた)

⟨4⟩ 離婚増加の結果、親一人と子供だけの世帯（母子家庭・父子家庭）が増えた（362万世帯）。

⟨5⟩ おじいちゃん・おばあちゃんのいる3世代家族が減った（327万世帯）。

さらに、2018年1月に国立社会保障・人口問題研究所が公表した「日本の世帯数の将来推計」によると、単身世帯（一人暮らし）は2026年に初めて2,000万世帯を超え、2040年には全世帯のほぼ40％に達すると予測している。特に、65歳以上の高齢者の一人暮らしが急増するとしており、介護や見守りなどの需要が一層高まることが予想される。

d) 結婚・離婚

日本人の平均初婚年齢は、男性は31.1歳、女性は29.4歳（2016年厚生労働省）で、1985年からの30年間に男性2.9歳、女性3.9歳高くなっている。50歳までの未婚者率（生涯未婚率とも呼ばれる）は男性23.4％、女性14.1％と大幅に上昇している。

結婚に対する意識として「いずれ結婚するつもり」と考える未婚者（18～34歳）の割合は、男性85.7％、女性89.3％であり、ここ30年間を見ても男女ともに依然として高水準である。また、25～34歳の未婚者に独身でいる理由を尋ねると、男女ともに「適当な相手にめぐりあわない」（男性45.3％、女性51.2％）が最も多く、次に多いのが男性では「まだ必要性を感じない」（29.5％）や「結婚資金が足りない」（29.1％）であり、女性では「自由や気楽さを失いたくない」（31.2％）や「まだ必要性を感じない」（23.9％）となっている。

日本では、約90％が恋愛結婚であるが、見合結婚という習慣も残っている。見合結婚の場合は、間をとりもつ紹介者（仲人・なこうど）が、結婚希望の男女を引き合わせる。二人はその出会いの場でお互いを観察する（お見合

\<3\> Almost no increase in the number of the traditional standard type of family consisting of a mother, father and their children (14.82 million households). (Type <2> and <3> families, i.e., families not including a grandfather or grandmother, are sometimes called "nuclear families.")

\<4\> Rise in number of families with one parent and a child or children (single-mother and single-father families), resulting from the increasing divorce rate (3.62 million households).

\<5\> Decline in the number of three-generation families with a grandfather and grandmother in the house (3.27 million households).

Furthermore, according to the "Household Projections for Japan" released by the National Institute of Population and Social Security Research in January 2018, the number of single households (living alone) is projected to exceed 20 million for the first time in 2026, and in 2040 is projected to account for almost 40% of all households. The number of elderly people aged 65 and older living alone is expected to rise rapidly, which is expected to further increase demand for services such as nursing care and monitoring.

d) Marriage and Divorce

The mean age at first marriage for Japanese men is 31.1, and for Japanese women is 29.4 (2016, Ministry of Health, Labor and Welfare). This represents an increase of 2.9 years for men and of 3.9 years for women over a period of about 30 years (since1985). The percentage of persons who do not marry by age 50 (sometimes called the lifetime non-marriage rate) is 23.4% for men and 14.1% for women, a major increase.

The proportion of never-married people (18 to 34 years old) who "Intend to marry someday" is 85.7% for men and 89.3% for women, which are high levels in terms of the past 30 years. When never-married persons aged 25 to 34 were asked why they were single, the most frequent answer by both men and women was "Have not met the right person" (45.3% of men and 51.2% of women). In the case of men, this was followed by "I do not feel the need yet" (29.5%) and "Insufficient marriage funds" (29.1%). In the case of women, it was followed by "I want to keep my freedom and comfort" (31.2%) and "I do not feel the need yet" (23.9%).

Although about 90% of all marriages in Japan are now "love marriages," the traditional *omiai* (arranged) marriage custom is still practiced. In an arranged marriage, a man and a woman, both of whom are seeking a marriage partner, are brought together by a go-between (*nakodo*).

い)。このとき双方の親が立ち会うことが多い。その後しばらく交際して、結婚するかどうかをきめる。仲人は、世話好きな年配者が多く、結婚後も相談相手になってくれる。近年では、結婚したい人のために有料の結婚紹介ビジネス以外に、全国の多くの自治体が、出会い・婚活・結婚の支援をしている。

　　当年の離婚件数を結婚件数で割った割合（離婚率）でみると、2016年は34.9％で3組に1組の割合で離婚しているという結果になっている。この算式による離婚率は、この数十年急速に上昇して西ヨーロッパ諸国に近づいたが、2002年の36.9％をピークに、ゆるやかに下降しつつある。2016年の結婚件数は62.1万件で、離婚は21.7万件であった。

(2) 少子高齢社会

a) 少子化の現状と将来

　　一般論として、国の人口構成は経済レベルの向上とともに、多産多死⇒多産少死⇒少産少死という順序で人口転換と呼ばれる過程をたどる。そして、年齢層別人口のプロフィールは、ピラミッド型から釣り鐘型に、さらに壺型に変化していく。日本の人口構成は現在、人口転換の第3段階の壺型にある。

　　日本人の子供の出生数は、終戦直後の第1次ベビーブーム期（1947～1949年）には毎年約270万人で、これが現在の団塊の世代といわれる年齢層である。その後第2次ベビーブーム期（1972～1974年）の210万人の第2ピークを越えて連続的に減り続け、2017年には94.1万人となった。

　　子供が生まれない原因としては未婚化・晩婚化の進行、非婚、晩産、産まないなどがあげられ、またその原因としては、失業・非正規雇用の増加と所得の不安定化、女性の高学歴化と社会進出、子育て後のキャリア再スタートの困難さ（難関突破後に手に入れた職を手放したくない）、女性の仕事と育児両立の困難性、生きがい論の変化（結婚より仕事）、育児・教育費の負担、育児施設の不備、子育て

This first meeting is to allow them to observe each other directly at the place where the meeting is held. The parents of both sides are usually present at the initial meeting. After this, the prospective couple meet each other socially over a period of time and then eventually decide whether to get married or not. Most go-betweens are elderly persons who like to be helpful and are willing to continue offering counsel after the marriage. Recently, it has also become possible for men and women seeking a marriage partner to take advantage of dating, matchmaking and marriage support services offered at many local government offices, and matrimonial agency fee-based services.

One way to calculate the divorce rate is to divide the number of divorces in a given year by the number of marriages in the same year. Japan's divorce rate determined by this method was 34.9% in 2016, meaning one out of three couples divorce. It had been rising sharply for several decades, to a level near that in Western European countries, but went into a gradual decline after peaking at 36.9% in 2002. In 2016, there were 621 thousand marriages and 217 thousand divorces.

(2) Aging Society with Declining Birth Rate

a) Low Birth Rate

Conventional wisdom is that as a country develops economically, the makeup of its population is affected by a series of transitions from a "high birth rate, high death rate phase," through a "high birth rate, low death rate phase" to a "low birth rate, low death rate phase." Along with this, the shape of the population age-profile changes from a pyramid to a bell and then to an urn. The makeup of Japan's population is now in the third phase, an urn.

During Japan's first baby boom in the early postwar years (1947–1949) around 2.7 million babies were born every year. They are today known as the baby-boomer generation. The birth rate peaked again during a second baby boom (1972–1974) when 2.1 million babies were born each year. The number of births has since continued to decline, hitting a low of 941 thousand in 2017.

Japan's birth dearth can be traced to a number of factors, such as lack of opportunity to marry, late marriage, no desire to marry, late pregnancy, and no desire to have children. The reasons behind these are, for example, unstable income because of no job or irregular employment, more women going on to higher education, difficulty of resuming career after raising children (aversion to giving up job that was hard to acquire), difficulty for women to work and rear children at the same

の負担感、パラサイト・シングル（親の家に寄生してお金と時間の自由を楽しみたい独身者）の増加、親の介護、離婚後の生活リスクなどが論じられている。

　社会学者の山田昌弘氏によれば、少子化の主原因は「若年男性の収入の不安定化」と「パラサイト・シングル現象」の合わせ技としている。日本人の若者の多くには「自分はお金がなくてもよいが、子どもには不自由な思いをさせたくない」という思いがあり、お金のせいで子どもにみじめな思いをさせたくないという親心が強い。1990年代半ばから、IT化やグローバル化が進み、雇用のあり方が根本的に変化し非正規雇用が男女とも増大し、男性のパートやアルバイトが増え始めた結果、未婚率も高まった。一方、彼らの親の世代は高度成長期を経験して終身雇用を経て比較的豊かである。その親から独立して、生活水準を下げてまで結婚するというインセンティブが働かない、ということである。

b）高齢化の現状と将来

　一方、高齢化については、総務省の発表によれば、2016年9月現在での日本の高齢者（65歳以上）はおよそ3,461万人、総人口に対する比率は27.3％で世界一である。人口高齢化の原因は、国民の寿命が延びたことである。日本は、平均寿命、健康寿命、高齢者比率、高齢化のスピードのいずれも世界最高水準である。

　一般に、高齢者人口比率が7～13％の社会を高齢化（Aging）社会、14～20％を高齢（Aged）社会、21％以上を超高齢（Ultra-aged）社会と分類している。日本は、1970年に高齢化社会に、1995年に高齢社会に、2007年に21.5％の超高齢社会に入った。国立社会保障・人口問題研究所の推計によれば2016年の年齢層別の人口構成は、年少人口（0～14歳）は12.4％、生産人口（15～64歳）は60.3％、高齢人口（65歳以上）は27.3％であった。さらに、2060年には高齢者が40％に達するものと予測される。その時点では生産人口は51％、年少人口は9％となる。

time, changing perception of fulfilment (job more rewarding than marriage), high cost of childcare and education, shortage of childcare facilities, feeling that childrearing is burdensome, emergence of "parasite singles" (single parents who continue to live with their own parents so they can spend their money and time as they please), need to care for aging parents with health problems, and concern about risks of living alone after possible divorce.

According to Masahiro Yamada, a sociologist, the main cause of the declining birth rate is a combination of income instability among young men and the "parasite single" phenomenon. Many young Japanese cite strong parental feelings, saying that they do not mind if they themselves don't have money, but they would not want their children to feel they have a hard life and are miserable due to a lack of money. The advancement of IT and globalization from the mid-1990s brought fundamental changes to employment practices, increasing temporary employment for both men and women. For men, part-time jobs began to increase, increasing the percentage of never-married people. On the other hand, their parents' generation is relatively affluent after living through the period of high economic growth and life-time employment. Thus, there was no incentive to become independent from such parents and settle for a lower standard of living until they marry.

b) Aging Population

Japan's elderly population, aged 65 or older, was 34.61 million as of September 2016 and accounted for 27.3% of the total population, the highest percentage of any country in the world (figures reported by the Ministry of Internal Affairs and Communications). The reason for this situation is the increasing longevity of the Japanese people. Life expectancy, healthy-life expectancy, percentage of elderly people, and population aging are all increasing faster in Japan than anywhere else.

Societies are generally classified by percentage of elderly people in the population into aging societies (7–13%), aged societies (14–20%) and ultra-aged societies (21% or more). Japan became an aging society in 1970, an aged society in 1995, and an ultra-aged society (with an elderly ratio of 21.5%) in 2007. The National Institute of Population and Social Security Research estimates that in 2016 Japan had a young population (aged 0 to 14) of 12.4%, working population (15 to 64) of 60.3%, and an aged population (65 and older) of 27.3%. It further predicts that the ratio of older people in the population will reach 40% in 2060, at which point the working population will be 51% and the young population 9%.

c）少子高齢社会の問題

1) 国家の生産力の減退

生産人口の減少による労働力の低下は、経済成長を大きく妨げ、経済力を弱体化させる。

2) 若者市場の衰退

幼稚園、学校、大学、結婚式場、住宅、家具、家電、若者アパレル、電子機器（スマートフォンなど）、音楽、映像産業、若者レジャー産業などの若者向け産業が衰退する。

3) 社会保障制度の破たん

扶養係数（高齢者1人を何人の現役が支えるかを表す指標）は、1995年頃までは1：10〜1：5の「おみこし型社会」であったが、2012年には1：2.8の「騎馬戦型」となり、2050年には1：1.2の「肩車型」となると推測されて若い世代にとって大きな負担となる。また、年金制度を支える働き手の数が減れば制度が保てなくなる。

4) 貧困リスクの高まり

生産人口が少数化・弱体化すると、若者にとって自身の老後の貯蓄が難しくなり、年金だけの生活は厳しく、高齢になっても働き続けなければならなくなる。高齢者が貧困に陥る可能性が出てくる。

5) 高齢者介護の問題

高齢化が進むにつれて高齢者数は増加するため介護職の必要性がますます高まるが、必要な介護職の数が確保できないばかりか、介護にかかる費用が高くなる。

6) 地方の疲弊

地方の衰退、若者の都市部への集中により、地方の過疎化と高齢化が加速する。子どもと若者が全くいない地域もできている。

d）少子化社会の対策

政府はこれまで少子化対策として、1994年「今後の子育て支援のための施策の基本的方向について」（エンゼルプラン）以降毎年のように対策案を掲げてきた。2015年には「新たな少子化対策大綱」を同年3月に閣議決定した。これによると従来の対策の枠組みを超えて、新たに結婚の支援を加え、子育て支援の一層の充実、多子世帯への

c) Low Birth Rate Issues

1) Declining National Production Capacity

A decline in the labor force due to a decrease in the working population greatly hinders economic growth and weakens economic strength.

2) Waning Youth Market

Businesses that target young people will lose vitality. Sectors likely to be affected include kindergartens, schools, colleges, wedding services, housing, furniture, electric appliances, youth apparel, electronic devices (smartphones etc.), music, movies, youth-oriented leisure services and other youth-oriented industries.

3) Collapse of the Social Security System

Japan's social security system has experienced a continuing deterioration of the beneficiary-to-worker ratio. It stood between 1:10 and 1:5 in 1995, after which it then fell to 1:2.8 in 2012. It is expected to become 1:1.2 in 2050, which will place a heavy burden on the younger generation. Furthermore, a decrease in the number of workers supporting the pension system makes the system untenable.

4) Greater Risk of Poverty

As the working population shrinks and weakens, it becomes difficult for young people to save for their old age. Living just on a pension is hard, and even when they get older, they have to continue working. There is a possibility that the elderly will descend into poverty.

5) Difficulty of Providing Elderly Care

As the population ages and the number of elderly people increases, so does the cost of nursing care, and just as there is a growing need for more nursing care workers, it is becoming difficult to secure the necessary numbers of such workers.

6) Weakening of Local Communities

The inclination of young people to migrate to big cities will continue to deplete the populations of small towns and villages of everyone but old folks. Some rural regions are actually already void of children and young adults.

d) Efforts to Avoid a Low-Birth-Rate Society

The government has proposed measures to counter the declining birth rate every year since 1994, when it announced its "Basic Direction for Future Child Rearing Support Measures" (Angel Plan). In March 2015, the Cabinet formulated a "New Outline of Declining Birthrate Policy" that went beyond the framework of conventional measures by adding new support for marriage, enhancing child rearing support, giving

一層の配慮、男女の働き方改革、地域の実情に即した取組み強化の5つの重点課題を設けて、長期的視点に立って、きめ細かな対策を総合的に推進することとしている。さらに「子ども・子育て支援新制度の施行」(2015年4月)、「ニッポン一億総活躍プランの策定」(2016年6月)、「働き方改革実行計画の策定」(2017年3月)へ至っている。

　このうち「希望出生率1.8」実現にむけた対応策として「働き方改革」では、同一労働同一賃金、長時間労働の是正、高齢者の就労促進を揚げ、「子育ての環境整備」では保育の受け皿整備、保育士の処遇改善、多様な保育士の確保・育成、放課後児童クラブの整備を、「すべての子どもが希望する教育を受けられる環境の整備」では、学びの機会の提供、奨学金制度の拡充を揚げている。また「希望出生率1.8に向けたその他取組」としては、女性活躍、若者・子育て世帯への支援、三世代同居・近居、子ども・若者等の活躍支援を掲げ、日本の少子化を反転させるための有効な施策として喫緊の要件となっている。いずれにせよ、若者が希望する職につけ、将来にわたり安定した収入が得られる見通しをつけることや、一定水準の教育が受けられることが少子化対策の基本となると考えられる。

　また、親が認可保育園施設に子どもを入れたいと希望しながら入れない「待機児童」が増えている。国は保育サービスを拡充しているが、共働き家庭が増えたことが待機児童の増える最大の理由である。2017年6月には保育所等待機児童数は2.6万人となっている。政府は女性の社会進出を阻む待機児童の解決なしに成長戦略の実現はおぼつかないとして、「待機児童解消加速プラン」を公表し、2020年3月末までに待機児童の受け皿に22万人分の予算を確保することと、2022年3月末までの5年間で、女性の就業率80％にも対応する32万人分の受け皿を整備する目標を掲げた。一方、保育の受け皿となる施設を増やしても、そこで働く保育士が確保できなければ、絵に描いた餅に終わるため、国は保育士の待遇改善のため2017年度から保育士一人あたりの平均給与を6千円程度の上乗せに踏み切った。

further consideration to multi-child households, men's and women's work-style reforms, strengthening efforts to take local circumstances into account, and promoting these detailed measures from a long-term perspective. This was followed by the "Enforcement of a New System for Supporting Children and Child-Rearing" (April 2015), the formulation of a "Plan for Promoting Dynamic Engagement of All Citizens" (June 2016), and the "Action Plan for the Realization of Work Style Reform" (March 2017).

Of these, work style reform measures to realize a desired fertility rate of 1.8 include equal pay for equal work, reductions in long working hours, and promoting employment of the elderly; improving the child rearing environment by enhancing childcare facilities, improving working conditions for nursery teachers, securing and training a diverse range of childcare professionals, and developing after-school clubs for children; and providing opportunities for learning and expanding scholarship programs for an environment that allows all children to receive the education they want. Other efforts towards the desired fertility rate of 1.8 include active support for women, support for young and child-rearing households; support for three-generations living together or nearby, and active support for children and young people, all of which are urgent requirements to reverse Japan's declining birth rate. Fundamental to measures for countering the declining birth rate is the ability for young people to get the work they want to do and to have the expectation that they will have a stable income into the future and be able to receive a sufficient level of education.

Although the government is expanding nursery care facilities, the number of children waiting to get into authorized nursery schools are increasing. The biggest reason for the longer waiting lists is that the number of families in which both parents work is increasing. As of June 2017, 26,000 children were waiting to get into nursery school. Realizing that having children waiting to get into nursery school hinders women's social advancement, making it difficult to realize national growth strategies, the government has announced a plan to accelerate efforts to eliminate the need for such waiting lists. The plan secured a budget that will cover removing 220,000 children from waiting lists by March 2020. Furthermore, the plan had a 5-year target to allow 320,000 children to be removed from waiting lists by March 2022, corresponding to a women's employment rate of 80%. However, it is not enough to just provide more nursery school facilities: it is also essential to secure more nursery teachers. As a start to improve working conditions for nursery teachers, from fiscal 2017 the average monthly salary of each teacher

e) **高齢化社会の対策**
    1) 高齢者雇用の現状
        日本は現在、「高年齢者の雇用の安定等に関する法律」により高齢者全員が 65 歳まで働ける制度の導入が企業に義務づけられている。31 人以上規模企業の 99.5 ％で実施されている。人口の減少と高齢化の進展により労働力人口が大幅に減少することが懸念される中、高齢者が健康で意欲と能力がある限り年齢に関わりなく、生涯現役で働き続けることができる社会の実現に向けた取組みを推進していくこととしている。
    2)「生涯現役社会」の実現
        65 歳以降の定年延長や継続雇用制度の導入、高年齢者の雇用環境の整備や高年齢の有期契約労働者の期限の定めのない雇用への転換を行う事業主に対して、政府は助成金制度で支援をしている。全国の主要なハローワークに「生涯現役支援窓口」を設置して、求職者に対しスキルアップなどのさまざまな就労支援を行っている。
    3) 高齢者介護と福祉
        政府は高齢者が尊厳を保ちながら暮らし続けることができる社会の実現をめざして、質の高い保健医療・福祉サービスの確保を行っている。また、介護が必要になっても、住み慣れた地域や住まいで自立した生活を送ることができるよう、将来にわたって安定した介護保険制度に取り組んでいる。

f) **女性の社会進出**
    日本で専業主婦即ち家事に専念する女性の割合が最も高かったのは 1970 年代である。1950 年代までは農業や自営業に従事する人がまだ多かったので、男性も女性も農作業や家業にさまざまなかたちで関与していた。
    工業化の発展に伴い、電車やバスに乗り工場やオフィスに出勤し、仕事をして自宅に戻る。勤務時間中は仕事に拘束され、そして報酬である賃金を受け取るというかたちが一般的になった。この結果「男性は会社で稼ぎ、女性は家事・育児・介護をする」という働き方のスタイルに移行してきた。
    日本の女性の就業率（15～64 歳までの生産年齢人口に占める就業者の割合）の変遷を見ると、1970 年後半から

was increased by 6,000 yen.

e) Aging-Society Measures
1) Employment of the Elderly

In accordance with the "Law on Stabilization of Employment of Elderly People", Japan now requires companies to introduce a system that allows all elderly people to work until the age of 65. This has been implemented in 99.5% of companies with 31 or more people. While there is concern that the size of the labor force will greatly decrease due to the shrinking and aging of the population, the aim is to realize a society in which, regardless of age, people can continue to work their whole lifetime as long as they are healthy, motivated and capable.

2) Realizing a Lifelong Active Society

The government has a subsidy system for employers who extend the mandatory retirement of 65 and introduce a continuous employment system, improve the employment environment for elderly people and convert to the long-term employment of older fixed-term contract workers. The government is also setting up lifetime work support desks in major Employment Service Centers and providing job seekers with various support services such as skill improvement training.

3) Elderly Care and Welfare

The government is securing high-quality health care and welfare services with the aim of realizing a society where elderly people can continue living while maintaining dignity. It is also working on a stable nursing-care insurance system so that even when nursing care is needed, the recipients can live independently in places and residences with which they are familiar.

f) Social Advancement of Women

In Japan, the proportion of women who are full-time housewives was highest in the 1970s. Until the 1950s there were still many people engaged in agriculture and self-employed, and both men and women were involved in farming work and family business in various ways.

With the progress of industrialization, there was a shift in work style, as men started commuting by train or bus to a factory or office, where they spent the day working, tied to their job, for which they were paid. Thus, men became the wage earners while women did the housekeeping, looked after the children, and did any nursing care that was required.

The employment rate of women in Japan (the proportion of people working in the working-age female population, aged 15 to 64) has been

コンスタントに上昇しており、1986年では53.1％、2016年には66.0％となっている。就業者数の産業別割合を見ると「医療、福祉」(20.5％)が大きく増加し、以下「卸売業、小売業」(20.0％)、「製造業」(11.4％)となっている。

1986年に男女雇用機会均等法が施行され、女性は結婚して夫を支える立場から、働いて自己実現を目指す方向へと大きく踏み出した。この結果女性の就業率は上昇し、共働き世帯の数は、専業主婦世帯を上回った。また、1992年育児休業法が施行され、採用や昇進において男女の差別をなくし、出産・育児・介護によって就業が中断することがないような制度が徐々に整備されてきた。ただし、女性の非正規雇用率が高い。雇用者数の推移を雇用形態別に見ると「雇用者に占める非正規の職員・従業員の割合」は、2016年、男性32.2％、女性67.8％となっている。

今後日本の総人口の減少と高齢化に伴い、労働力人口(15〜64歳)の減少が危惧される中で、高齢者と並んで女性の労働参加に対する期待はますます高まっている。

近年、女性の職場への進出は活発になっている。その背景として女性の高学歴化があげられる。2017年度の大学の進学率は、男性55.6％に対し、女性は48.2％であった。つぎに、出産・育児休暇制度の活用、育児休業からの円滑な復帰への支援、子育てをしながら就職を希望する女性への支援、保育施設の拡充、フレックスタイムの導入など女性が育児と仕事の両立がしやすい条件の整備が徐々に進んできた。女性の進出分野も広がり、企業では経営者・管理職・専門職なども増えてきた。また、女性の閣僚・国会議員・知事・市町村長・上級公務員、大学教授、学校長、医師なども稀ではなくなった。

それでも、世界経済フォーラム(WEF)が2017年に発表した「ジェンダー・ギャップ指数」では、経済・教育・政治・健康の4分野で分析した結果、世界144カ国のうち、日本は114位となっている。これは女性の政治参画が遅れているのが主な原因である。

increasing steadily since the latter half of the 1970s, rising from 53.1% in 1986 to 66.0% in 2016. Looking at the proportion of the number of women employed by industry, there has been a large increase in "medical care and welfare" (20.5%), followed by "wholesale and retail industries" (20.0%), and "manufacturing industry" (11.4%).

With the enactment of the Equal Opportunity in Employment Act in 1986, women took a major step from marrying and being a support to their husband to achieving their own self-realization through work. The women's employment rate rose, until the number of dual-income households surpassed the number of full-time-housewife households. With the enforcement in 1992 of the Childcare Leave Law, systems have been adopted that eliminate discrimination between men and women in hiring and promotion and ensure that employment will not be interrupted by childbirth, childcare or nursing care. However, the female non-regular employment rate is high. According to the number of employees by type of employment, in 2016 the proportion of irregular employees was 32.2% for males and 67.8% for females.

The ongoing contraction and aging of the population is heightening concern about the decreasing size of the working population (aged 15 to 64). Against this backdrop, the need to bring not only more seniors but also more women into the workforce has steadily increased.

Women have been entering the workplace more actively in recent years. One reason is the rising education level of women. In 2017, the ratio of females going on to college or junior college was 48.2%, as compared to 55.6% for males. Another reason is that it has become easier for women to take jobs while also raising children thanks to gradual improvements in the employment environment, including the spread of maternity and child-rearing leave programs, support for a seamless return from childcare leave and for women who wish to find employment while raising children, availability of more child-care facilities, and introduction of flextime work arrangements. Women are also moving into a broader range of fields and into more significant corporate roles as executives, managers, and specialists. Female Cabinet members, National Diet members, governors, mayors, high-level public officials, college professors, school principals, medical doctors and the like are no longer considered rare.

Nonetheless, when in 2017 the World Economic Forum (WEF) announced its Gender Gap Index based on an analysis in the four areas of economic participation and opportunity, educational attainment, political empowerment, and health and survival, Japan was ranked 114 out of 144 countries, with the main reason being the backward status of

g） 単身赴任

日本では、夫が仕事のために単身で赴任することが珍しくない。企業の社員配置・転換の目的は、〈1〉社員の能力・適性を業務効率の向上に生かす、〈2〉社員の多様な能力を開発する、〈3〉組織・事業所の移動・拡大・縮小への対応などがある。しかし、家庭にとっては〈1〉子どもの教育、〈2〉家族の病気・出産、〈3〉両親の介護、〈4〉配偶者の勤務、〈5〉持家の管理などの問題が残る。

中でも大きな問題は、子どもの転校・進学の問題であり、馴染んだ学校や友達と別れたくない・新しい学校に馴染めない・いじめにあうなどのことがあること、外国赴任の場合は言葉の違いから日本語能力や一般学力が低くなり、帰国後苦しむ場合がある。そこで、やむなく社員だけが単身で赴任することになる。

（3） 社会保障

a） 概要

若者もお年寄りも安心できる社会の実現に向けて、年金や医療、福祉などの「社会保障」は、今や生活していく上でなくてはならない存在である。

2017年度の日本の一般会計予算で見ると、社会保障関係費は前年より 0.4 兆円増えて 32.4 兆円で、予算総額 97.4 兆円の 33％である。これは政府の大きな支出項目である公共事業費（5.9 兆円）と文教・科学振興費（5.3 兆円）と防衛費（5.1 兆円）の 3 つを合計しても及ばない規模である。

しかも、これは国家予算の中の額であり、国全体の社会保障費の規模、すなわち 1 年間に国民に対して給付さ

women's political participation.

g) Taking a Post Away from One's Family

In Japan, it is not unusual for a husband to live temporarily apart from his family for business reasons. A company may transfer an employee from one location to another for a number of purposes. The main reasons are <1> to harness the employee's ability and competence toward the improvement of business efficiency, <2> to develop the employee's latent capabilities, and <3> to deal with organizational changes, workplace relocation, and business expansion or contraction. However, such a transfer may have adverse effects on the employee's family with regard to such matters as <1> the children's education, <2> health and maternity issues, <3> caring for the couple's parents, and <4> the spouse's job. If the entire family accompanies the husband or joins him later, there is also the problem of <5> taking care of the empty house.

Probably the biggest problems regarding a family move are those concerning the children's education, especially the transfer to a new school and the move up to a higher level of education when the time comes. Children do not want to leave their familiar school surroundings and friends and have to try and adapt to a new school where they might be bullied. These problems are particularly severe when the family has to move overseas. A child who transfers to a school in another country is likely to fall behind in both Japanese language ability and general studies, and will almost always have difficulty catching up with classmates on returning to Japan. Owing to these concerns, employees often decide the only choice is to leave the family behind.

(3) Social Security

a) Overview

Social security, such as pensions, medical care, and welfare, is essential for life, to realize a society in which both the young and the elderly can have peace of mind.

Among the expenditures included in Japan's 2017 General Account Budget, the social security allocation was 32.4 trillion yen, up 0.4 trillion yen from the preceding year. This amount accounted for 33% of the total budget of 97.4 trillion yen. It is a sum that far exceeded the government's combined expenditures on public works (5.9 trillion yen), education and science (5.3 trillion yen) and defense (5.1 trillion yen).

Moreover, the above 32 trillion yen figure is only the amount included in the national budget. The total value of all monetary and

れる社会保障給付費（給付される金銭とサービスの総額）は 2015 年度は前年度比 2.4％増の 114.9 兆円という巨額にのぼり過去最高である。その内容は年金 55 兆円で全体の 47.8％、最も伸びが大きかった医療 37 兆円で全体の 32.8％、その他の介護・福祉約 19 兆円である。

　社会保障費は過去 40 年間に国民所得の伸びをはるかに上回る勢いで伸びてきた。これは人口の高齢化と給付内容の向上によるものである。

b）社会保障制度を取り巻く状況の変化と問題点

　社会保障費予算の内訳は医療 11.8 兆円、年金 11.8 兆円、介護 3.1 兆円となっている（2018 年度）。高齢化が進んでいることなどから、予算額は年々増え続けている。過去 20 年間では 2 倍超まで膨張している。急速な少子高齢化が進む中、社会保障の費用が急速に増加し社会保障制度を財政的にも仕組み的にも安定させることが必要になってきた。このため社会保障改革の全体像や、必要な財源を確保するための消費税を含む税制抜本改革について検討が進められた。2012 年に成立した「税制抜本改革法」において消費税率の引き上げ等が定められた。その後、2013 年に全ての世代が年齢だけではなく負担能力に応じて負担し合う「全世代型社会保障」を目指すべきとされた。

　2015 年に閣議決定した財政健全化計画で、2016 年度から 2018 年度までの 3 年間で社会保障費の伸びを合計 1 兆 5 千億円（年 5 千億円）程度に押さえ込む目標を掲げた。これまでに、高額薬の薬価引き下げや一定所得のある 70 歳以上の医療費の自己負担の上限の引き上げなどを実施した。この結果 2016 年度と 2017 年度予算ではそれぞれ 5 千億円程度の伸びに抑えられた。

　年金や医療、介護など社会保障制度を通じて、国民が受け取るお金やサービスの財源は、主に国民や事業者が支払う社会保険料と、国や地方自治体からの税金などで賄っている。国が負担する分は、税収だけでは賄いきれないので、巨額の国債を発行しているため将来世代にツケを先送りしている。将来への負担の先送りである財政赤字を含めた社会保障にかかる国民負担率の増加が懸念される。

service benefits provided to citizens during the year amounted to a whopping 114.9 trillion yen in fiscal 2015, an increase of 2.4% compared to the preceding year. This comprised 55 trillion yen for pensions, or 47.8% of the total, 37 trillion yen for medical services, which showed the biggest increase, and about 19 trillion yen for nursing care and other types of welfare.

Over the past 40 years, the pace of the increase in social security costs has far outstripped that of national income. This is due to population aging and improvements in liberal benefit.

b) Problems and Changes in Circumstances Related to the Social Security System

The social security budget comprises 11.8 trillion yen for medical care, 11.8 trillion yen for pensions, and 3.1 trillion yen for nursing care (fiscal 2018). The budget amount continues to increase year after year as the population ages, and has more than doubled over the past 20 years. Against the backdrop of a rapidly declining birthrate and an aging population, social security costs have risen rapidly, making it necessary to stabilize the social security system financially and structurally. With that aim, studies are moving forward on overall reforms to social security and on extensive reforms of the taxation systems, including the consumption tax, to secure the necessary financial resources. The Tax Reform Law enacted in 2012 raised the consumption tax rate, and in 2013 the government said that the aim should be an all-generational type social security, with the burden being shared based not just on age but on the ability to pay.

In a fiscal consolidation plan approved by the Cabinet in 2015, a target was set to limit the growth of social security expenses to about 1.5 trillion yen (500 billion yen a year) for the three fiscal years 2016 to 2018. So far, the cost of high-priced drugs has been reduced and there have been no increases to the ratio of medical expenses shouldered by people aged 70 and older living on fixed incomes. Those and other measures have made it possible to keep the budget for fiscal 2016 and fiscal 2017 to about 500 billion yen each year.

The funding for money and services dispensed to citizens through the social service system in the form of pensions, medical treatment and nursing care and the like are covered by social insurance fees paid by citizens and business operators, and taxes from the national and local governments. Tax revenues alone are not enough to cover the burden assumed by the government, so the gap is bridged by the issuance of huge amounts of government-backed bonds, running up the debt to be

c）社会保障制度の内容

社会保障制度の内容は、下表のとおりである。

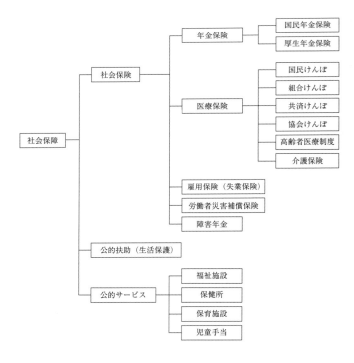

paid by future generations. This gives rise to concerns over increases in the national burden rate on social security, including the fiscal deficit, which is passing the burden onto the future.

c) Elements of the Social Security System

The elements of the social security system are shown in the figure below.

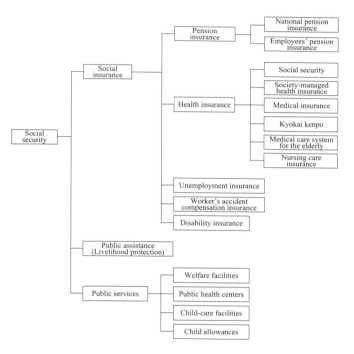

d) 社会保険
    1) 公的年金
        i) 公的年金保険の概要
            日本では1961年以降、公的年金国民皆保険制度が確立している。年金は大別すると、全国民に共通する国民年金と雇われて働く人（企業の社員、公務員）が入る厚生年金からなっている。厚生年金に入ると自動的に国民年金にも入る。2015年の公的年金の加入者は6,712万人で、この内厚生年金の加入者は4,129万人となっている。

            加入者の年金種類別人員は、自営業・農業・学生・フリーター・無職など（国民年金1号加入者）が1,668万人、サラリーマンや公務員など（国民年金2号および厚生年金1〜4号加入者）が4,129万人、サラリーマンや公務員などの配偶者で20〜60歳かつ年収が130万円未満（国民年金3号加入者）が915万人である。

            2017年度の保険料の納付率は66.3％で、1990年代には約85％で推移していたのに比べ直近10年間は低迷している。これは低収入のため払えないとか、年金制度が今後とも維持できるのか、自分の世代では年金を受け取れないのではないか、年金を払ってない人が30％もいるなら自分も払わなくても良いのではなどという理由になっている。
            2017年8月から老後に公的年金を受け取る条件が大幅に緩和された。公的年金は国民年金を基本としている、20歳から60歳になるまでの40年間加入して、これまで最低25年納めれば納付期間に応じた額の年金を原則65歳から受け取ることができる。ただ「25年でも長すぎる」という批判が根強くあり、また無年金者を救済するため、政府は資格期間を10年に縮めることを決定し実施した。
        ii) 国民年金
            国民年金はいわば1階建て構造で、全国民共通の基礎年金である。1号加入者のほとんどは、国民年金だけに加入している。

d) Social Insurance

1) Public Pension

i) Overview of Public Pension Insurance

Since 1961, Japan has had a universal public pension insurance system extending to all citizens. The system can be divided into two parts: the national pension program available to everyone in the country, and the welfare pension program for company employees and public servants. Anyone who enters the welfare pension program also automatically enters the national pension program. As of 2015, the public pension system had 67.12 million subscribers, of which 41.29 million were welfare pension program subscribers.

The number of subscribers to the public pension by type was 16.68 million in the first category comprising self-employed persons, farmers, students, freelancers, the unemployed, and the like, 41.29 million in the second category and the first to fourth welfare pension categories comprising mostly salaried employees and public servants, and 9.15 million in the third category consisting of spouses of salaried employees and public servants aged 20 to 60 having an annual income of less than 1.3 million yen.

The payment rate of premiums in fiscal 2017 was 66.3% and has been sluggish for the last 10 years compared to the fact that it was about 85% in the 1990s. Maybe people can't pay because they have low incomes, or wonder whether the pension system can be maintained, or whether their generation will be able to receive a pension, or think that as 30% of people don't pay into the pension fund, it's all right for oneself not to pay.

Starting in August 2017, the conditions for receiving a public pension in one's old age were greatly relaxed. The public pension is based on the national pension. Pay for at least 25 years of the 40 years from age 20 to 60, and in principle you will receive a pension from the age of 65 according to how long you actually paid into the system. However, in response to persistent criticism that 25 years is too long, the government decided to shorten the qualification period to 10 years in order to help out people who do not have a pension.

ii) National Pension

The national pension program is a single-tier system that provides a basic pension for the entire populace. Almost everyone in the first subscriber category mentioned above belongs to only the national pension program.

iii）厚生年金

会社のサラリーマンや公務員とその家族が加入しており、いわば2階建て構造で、1階の共通基礎年金の上に各人の収入に比例して給付される報酬比例年金が乗っている。保険料率は、標準報酬（給与や賞与などから計算される額）の一定率で、本人と雇用主が折半負担する。

2）医療保険

ⅰ）医療保険体系の概要

医療保険についても日本は1961年以降、国民皆保険が実現している。医療保険は、国民健康保険（国民けんぽ、こくほ）、組合管掌健康保険（組合けんぽ）、全国健康保険協会健康保険（協会けんぽ）、共済組合健康保険（共済けんぽ）、後期高齢者医療保険の5種類に分類される。

ⅱ）国民健康保険

農業、商業などの自営業、退職した75歳未満の高齢者など約3,500万人が加入している（2015年度）。保険者（運営主体）は1,900の各地方自治団体で、保険財源として国は給付費全体の50％を補助している。加入者本人は収入に応じて毎年保険料を納入する。本人は保険料とは別に病院の窓口でその都度医療費の原則30％を支払う。

ⅲ）組合管掌健康保険（組合けんぽ）

比較的大きな企業のサラリーマン（経営者・管理職を含む）が加入している保険である。企業あるいは企業グループごとに社員（組合員）が健康保険組合を設立し、本人および家族を給付対象とする。組合数は約1,400で加入者数は約2,900万人である。財源は年収の一定割合を組合員と企業が折半して拠出する保険料である。社員本人は病院の窓口でその都度別に医療費の30％を支払う。

ⅳ）全国健康保険協会健康保険

中小企業のサラリーマンが加入している保険で、3,700万人が加入している。保険者は国であ

iii) Welfare Pension Program

The members of this program are salaried-employees and public servants, and their families. It is a two-tier system. The lower tier is the basic pension of the national pension program, and the upper tier is a pension geared to each individual's income. The insurance premium is a fixed rate of an individual's standard remuneration (an amount calculated based on salary and bonuses, etc.), with the individual and the employer each bearing half the cost.

2) Medical Insurance

i) Outline of Japanese Medical Insurance

Japan has also had a universal health insurance system since 1961. There are five health insurance programs: National Health Insurance, Society-Managed Health Insurance, Japan Health Insurance Association Program, Mutual Aid Health Insurance, and Medical Care Insurance for the Elderly.

ii) National Health Insurance

Most of the approximately 35 million members of this program are either self-employed people in the agriculture and commerce sectors or retired company employees who are under 75 years old (fiscal year 2015). The program is operated by 1,900 local governments (the insurers) throughout the country. The national government provides assistance covering half of total benefits paid, while each member pays annual premiums in proportion to income. In addition to the premiums, the member also pays 30% of the medical fee to the hospital or clinic on each visit.

iii) Society-Managed Health Insurance

The members of this program are salaried employees of relatively large companies (including executives and managers). The employees of individual companies or corporate groups establish a health insurance society that provides the members (employees) and their family members with health insurance. These societies number around 1,400 and have a total membership of about 29 million. Each society is funded jointly by the members and the companies, at a rate equal to a certain percentage of each member's annual income, with the member and the company each paying half of the total. On receiving medical care, the member pays 30% of the fee to the care provider on each occasion and the remainder is paid by the society.

iv) Japan Health Insurance Association Program

The members of this program are salaried employees of small businesses. Some 37 million persons are covered by this insurance.

る（以前は政府管掌健保と呼んでいた）。給付総額の15％は国の負担。加入者の年収の一定割合の保険料を労使が折半で負担する。給付条件は組合けんぽと同じ。

v）共済組合健康保険

公務員約900万人が加入している健保。保険者は国と地方の85の行政機関。運営、給付条件は、組合けんぽとほぼ同じ。

vi）後期高齢者医療保険

日本人の平均寿命は、世界の中でもトップクラスで、その上75歳以上の後期高齢者層の一人当たり医療費は、現役世代のおよそ5倍かかっているとみられる。少子高齢化が進むなかで、現役世代の後期高齢者医療のための直接的負担を軽減する目的で2008年から導入された制度である。

75歳以上の人は今まで入っていた保険を脱退し、ほかの世代から切り離された「後期高齢者だけの独立した医療保険」に加入する。医療給付をまかなう財源割合は、加入者保険料10％、健保・国保など40％、国・自治体50％である。医療給付費が増加すれば、加入者の保険料も高くなる仕組みとなっている。加入者は約1,646万人（2016年）。給付条件は、組合けんぽとおおむね同じ。

3）介護保険

寝たきりなどで介護を必要とする高齢者を保険制度で支える目的で、2000年にスタートした。原則として65歳以上の人（および40歳以上の重度障害者）が市町村に申請して介護対象者認定を受ければ、在宅サービスまたは施設サービスなどが受けられる。保険料は市町村と40歳以上の人が応分に負担するが、被介護者自身も費用の一部をその都度支払う。

4）雇用保険

労働者が失業した場合に、失業前の給与の一定割合を勤続年数に応じて一定期間給付する制度である。保

The national government is the insurer. (The program used to be called Government-Managed Health Insurance.) The national government bears 15% of total disbursements. The members and their employers each pay half of insurance premiums equivalent to a certain percentage of each member's annual income. The benefit payment conditions are the same as in the case of Society-Managed Health Insurance.

v) Mutual Aid Health Insurance

Around 9 million public servants belong to this program. The insurers are 85 national and local government organizations. The operation and benefit payment conditions of the program are the same as those of the Society-Managed Health Insurance.

vi) Medical Care Insurance for the Elderly

The average lifespan of Japanese is among the highest in the world, and the per capita medical expenses for elderly seniors (75 and over) are believed to be approximately five times as high as those for people of working age. Therefore, against the backdrop of the continuing trend toward an aging population with fewer children, the Medical Care Insurance for the Elderly program was introduced in 2008 in order to mitigate the direct burden of elderly health care costs on people of working age.

In reaching 75, an insured person is transferred from his or her current plan to the new plan, which is operated separately from that of other generations. The funds used to pay these medical benefits comes from those 75 years and older (10%), the society-managed and national insurance plans (40%), and the national and local governments (50%). The plan is set up so that increases in the cost of medical benefits are in part covered by increasing the premiums paid by the insured individuals. The program has about 16.46 million members (2016). The benefit payment conditions are almost the same as in the case of Society-Managed Health Insurance.

3) Nursing Care Insurance

This program was launched in 2000 as an insurance system for assisting bedridden and other elderly persons unable to care for themselves. By applying to their municipal government office, disabled persons 65 and older (40 and older if severely disabled) can, if found eligible, obtain the services they need at home or at specified facilities. While the premiums are paid jointly by the municipalities and citizens aged 40 and over, the care-receiver also has to pay part of the cost each time.

4) Employment Insurance

This insurance program pays benefits to an unemployed worker in proportion to his or her salary before becoming unemployed for a period

険料は会社従業員と会社が、およそ1対2の割合で負担する。育児休業・介護休業の援助、雇用調整助成金制度における休業手当の支給、職業能力の開発などの事業も行う。

5) 労災保険

　労働者が業務上または通勤途上で傷病を被るか死亡した場合に、医療・社会復帰・遺族保護などの費用を補償する制度で1947年に施行された。家族以外の従業員1人以上の事業体は強制加入で、保険料は全額会社負担である。

6) 公的扶助

　公的扶助は、国家が国民の中の生活困窮者と低所得者を救済、支援する制度である。社会保険制度と異なり、財源は全額が国の税金から支出される。

　i) 生活保護

　　いろいろな事情からやむをえず貧困・生活の困窮に陥っている国民に対して、国が「健康で文化的な最低限度の生活を営めるように」(憲法25条) 生活を保障し、自立を援助する制度である。具体的には、生活保護法に基づき、一定の条件下にある困窮者に日常生活、住宅、教育、介護、医療、出産、葬祭などの扶助を行い、その上で受給者が社会的に自立できるように支援する。

　ii) 低所得者対策

　　低所得者の対策としては、社会手当（児童扶養手当、障害者・障害児手当など）、低所得者向け公営住宅、生活福祉資金の貸付けなどの制度がある。

(4) 教育

a) 学校教育制度

　日本の学校教育制度は、小学校6年、中学校3年、高等学校3年、大学4年が基本になっている。この制度は、第二次大戦後、新しい学校教育法（1947年）によって生まれたものである。

that varies with years of employment. The employee and company respectively pay approximately one-third and two-thirds of the premium. The program also assists workers taking leave to care for children or sick family members, provides leave allowances under the employment adjustment subsidy program and conducts worker skill development courses.

5) Worker's Accident Compensation Insurance

This program was launched in 1947. When a worker suffers injury, sickness or death while at work or commuting to and from work, this insurance pays benefits to compensate for medical and rehabilitation expenses and assist surviving family members. Membership is mandatory for all businesses employing one or more non-family members. All the premiums are borne by the worker's employer.

6) Public Assistance

This is a program by which the nation provides assistance and support to needy and low-income citizens. Unlike the social security program, this program is funded entirely from national tax revenue.

i) Livelihood Protection

The livelihood of people who have for any reason unavoidably fallen into poverty or serious living difficulties is secured by the nation as its constitutional responsibility to "maintain the minimum standards of wholesome and cultured living" (Article 25 of the Constitution). Such people are also assisted as they return to self-reliance. Concrete measures are implemented under prescribed conditions in line with the Livelihood Protection Act to provide needy people with assistance in connection with, for example, daily life, housing, education, nursing care, medical care, childbirth, and funerals. Those receiving such assistance are also helped to achieve financial and social independence.

ii) Low-income Earner Assistance

Measures for helping low-income earners under this system include provision of social welfare allowances (child-rearing allowances and allowances for handicapped adults and children), public housing for income-eligible individuals, and low-interest welfare loans.

(4) Education

a) Japanese Educational System

The educational system of Japan is basically comprised of 6 years of elementary school, 3 years of junior high school, 3 years of senior high school and 4 years of college. This system was set up by the new School Education Act enacted in 1947 shortly after the Second World War.

1) 小学校：子供は6歳で小学校に入学する。小学校では、社会における日常生活に必要な基礎科目を学ぶ。この初等教育期間では、1人の先生が全教科を教えることが多い。小学校就学前に、幼稚園（1～3年）や、保育園に入る子供も多い。

2) 中学校：国家および社会の一員として必要な資質を養うために、中学校の生徒には、社会に役立つ職業についての基礎的知識・技能が教えられる。また、個性に応じて将来の進路を選択する能力を養う。科目ごとに違った先生が教える。

この最初の9年間（小学校と中学校）が義務教育になっている。この間の就学率は100％である。憲法26条によって、親は子供に義務教育を受けさせる義務がある。また、市町村は義務教育のために学校を設置しなければならない。

3) 高等学校：中学校卒業生は入学試験に合格して、高校に入学する。高校では、生徒は普通教育科目あるいは専門技能科目を学習する。これらの科目は、国家と社会に有為な人物として必要な資質を伸ばし、さらにそれぞれの使命感を養い、人生の将来の進路を定めさせることを目標にしたものである。専門技能科目は、工業、農業、商業、水産などに分類される。工業はさらに機械・電気・電子・情報通信・化学・土木・建築などに分かれる。ほとんどの高校は都道府県立または私立である。

4) 大学：高校卒業生は入学試験に合格して、大学に入学する。大学での教育科目は、広く知識を授ける一般教養科目と、特定分野の学術を深く学習・研究させるための専門科目からなっている。大学教育の目的は、知識・人格面とともに応用能力を十二分に開発することである。すなわち、大学は教育機関であると同時に学術研究機関としての役割ももっている。

大学教育は一般には4年であるが、医学部・歯学

1) Elementary school: Children enter elementary school at age 6. In elementary school, students learn basic subjects necessary for daily life in society. During the elementary education period, one teacher generally teaches all the subjects in each class. Many children under six go to a kindergarten (for one to three years) or a preschool day-care center before entering elementary school.
2) Junior high school: For cultivating the qualities that young people will need to play useful roles in the nation and society, junior high school students are taught the core knowledge and skills necessary for socially useful occupations. Their ability to choose the future path which best suits their individual characteristics is also nurtured. Each subject is taught by a different teacher.

The first nine years of education (elementary school and junior high school) are compulsory. The rate of school attendance by children during this period is therefore 100%. Under Article 26 of the Constitution, parents are obligated to send their children to school for this compulsory education, and cities, towns and villages are required to establish the schools needed.

3) Senior high school: Junior high school graduates enter senior high schools upon passing entrance examinations. High school students study general academic subjects or specialized technical subjects. The courses are aimed at developing the qualities required of capable members of the country and society, in addition to instilling a sense of mission in every student and helping him or her decide a future course in life. Specialized vocational subjects include such categories as industry, agriculture, commerce, and fishery. Industrial subjects are subdivided into mechanics, electric, electronics, information and communications, chemistry, civil engineering, architecture, etc. Almost all senior high schools are prefectural, municipal, or private.
4) University: Students who want to enter a university after graduation from high school have to pass entrance examinations. Academic pursuits at the university center on a combination of general learning intended to give the student a wide knowledge base and specialized learning intended to allow the student to make deep study and research into a specific field of art or science. The goal of this education is to thoroughly develop the student both in terms of knowledge and character and in terms of practical ability. In other words, the university is an educational organization and at the same time an institution for academic research.

    University education generally lasts 4 years, but medicine,

部・薬学部は6年である。大学院では、修士課程が2年、その上の博士課程が3年である（医学・歯学には修士課程がなく、4年の博士課程だけである）。大学は国立と公立と私立がある。しかし数は、私立大学が他の大学よりもはるかに多い。

上記のほかに、短期大学（2年制）や高等専門学校（中学卒業後5年の課程）がある。

日本の学校の数は、小学校 19,892、中学校 10,270、高等学校 4,897、短期大学 331（公立 17、私立 314）、大学 782（国立 86、公立 93、私立 603）、高等専門学校 57、専修学校 3,160 などである（2018 年 5 月）。

b）教育制度の発展

日本では明治時代以前の江戸時代からすでに国民の間には教育を尊重する気風があった。当時の日本人はすすんで「読み・書き・そろばん」を学習した。その結果、江戸時代末期・明治維新直前の 1867 年当時、農民・町人を含む国民のおよそ半数は読み書きができた。これは国際比較でも当時としては稀に見る高さであった。

当時は、武士階級が軍事担当者であると同時に、行政担当者であった。そのため、その務めに必要な教養・道徳・武芸を、武士の子弟たちに教える学校（藩校）が各地に設置されていた。また、農民や町民のためには、生活に必要な読み・書き・算数（そろばんを使った）を教える寺子屋が、全国に2万箇所もつくられていた（文字通りには「寺の学校」だが、すべてを寺が運営していたわけではない）。この寺子屋への入学はまったく自由で、誰の強制もなく年限も決められていなかった。約 40％の農民や町民が、寺子屋で学んだと推定される。

明治時代に入り、日本の近代化にともなって、政府は西洋の学問を導入して産業・文化を発展させるために、小学校から大学までの一貫した教育制度を整えた。

dentistry and pharmacology require 6 years. In graduate school, the masters (M.A. or M.S.) program requires 2 years, while the subsequent doctoral (Ph.D.) program requires an additional 3 years. (For medicine and dentistry, there is no master's program, but there is a doctoral program which requires 4 years.) There are national, public, and private universities. The number of private universities is by far the greatest.

In addition to the above, there are also junior colleges (2-year curriculum), as well as specialized vocational high schools (with a 5-year curriculum for junior high school graduates).

Japan has 19,892 elementary schools, 10,270 junior high schools, 4,897 senior high schools, 331 junior colleges (17 public, 314 private), 782 universities (86 national, 93 public, 603 private), 57 specialized vocational high schools and 3,160 specialized training schools (as of May 2018).

b) Development of the Educational System

High respect for education had become a characteristic of Japanese society from no later than the Edo period (1603–1867), well before the days of rapid modernization that started with the Meiji Restoration in 1867. Study of reading, writing, and arithmetic was widespread during the Edo period, so that about half of the population, including farmers and ordinary townspeople, could read and write by the time of the Restoration. This level of literacy was rare anywhere in the world at the time.

The military (*samurai*) class was in charge of both military and political affairs. For this reason, schools (*han* schools—schools of the feudal domains) were established all over the country to teach the children of samurai families the cultural, moral, and martial subjects necessary for their duties. There were also 20 thousand *terakoya* (literally "temple schools" though they were not all operated by temples) set up throughout the country to teach reading, writing, and arithmetic (by use of the abacus) to farmers and townspeople who needed such skills in their daily life. Attendance at these temple schools was on a purely voluntary basis; no one was compelled to attend and there was no age limit on those who did. About 40% of the farmers and townspeople are estimated to have studied at such schools, either as children or adults.

Early in the Meiji era, as Japan began undergoing modernization, the government established an integrated educational system from elementary school to university in order to foster the development of industry and culture through the introduction of Western learning.

1900年に日本で初めて6歳からの4年間の初等科義務教育制度が発足した。この年の就学率は90％であった。1907年には6年制の義務教育となり、就学率は99％になった。

それ以降、尋常小学校（6年）・高等小学校（2年）・中学校（5年）・高等女学校・実業学校・高等学校・専門学校・大学などが多くつくられた。このうち小学校の6年間は義務教育とされた。しかし、それ以外は希望者の中から選ばれた者が入学する学校であり、進学率は高くなかった。1935年には、中等教育機関（中学校・高等女学校・実業学校など）への進学率は18.5％で、高等教育機関（高等学校・専門学校・大学など）への進学率は3％であった。

終戦後、1947年に教育制度は全面的に改正され、いわゆる「6・3・3・4制」が実施された。これにより、現在の小学校6年、中学校3年、高校3年、一般大学4年の制度が確立した。そのうち小学校・中学校の9年間は義務教育となった。

c）教育普及率

明治維新の身分制度の廃止以降の日本では、職業につくための条件は能力本位となり、出身階級・家柄・親の財産などは原則として関係がなくなった。能力の端的な尺度として、どんな学校で何を学んだか、すなわち学歴が重視されるようになった。家が貧しくとも、良い学校を出て、良い職業につき、高い社会的地位を得ることが人々の念願となった。また、明治政府も国家近代化のため、教育の普及に非常に力を入れた。

このような背景から、皆が競って進学し、できれば大学まで行こうとする。この気風は戦後の社会にも色濃く残った。そのため、上級校への進学率も高くなった。

2017年における小学校および中学校での義務教育就学率は100％、高等学校への進学率は99％、短期大学および

In 1900, a compulsory education system requiring children to begin 4 years of elementary schooling from age 6 was established in Japan for the first time. In that year, the attendance rate of those required to go to school was 90%. In 1907, when compulsory education was increased to 6 years, the attendance rate was 99%.

After that, many elementary schools (six years), higher elementary schools (two years), middle schools (5 years), girls' high schools, vocational schools, higher schools, colleges, and universities were founded. The six years of elementary school education continued to be compulsory, but the other higher schools admitted only students selected from among applicants. The proportion of students continuing on to higher education was therefore not high. In 1935, the percentage of elementary school students going on to the secondary schools of the time (middle schools, girls' high schools, and vocational schools) was 18.5%, and the percentage going on to receive higher education (higher school, college, university) was 3%.

After the Second World War, in 1947, the educational system was completely revised. The new system, still in effect today, established six years of elementary school, three years of middle (junior high) school, and three years of high school, plus four years of college (the six-three-three-four system). The nine years of elementary and middle school were made compulsory.

c) Education Rate

After the abolishment of the feudal class system with the advent of the Meiji Restoration, the job a person could secure came to depend basically on ability and no longer had much to do with social class at birth, lineage, or parents' wealth. What a person had studied at what school—the person's educational attainment—became the direct measure of this ability. Consequently, all Japanese, even the poor, dreamed of graduating from a prestigious school, finding a good job, and thereby attaining high social status. And the Meiji government, which was bent on modernizing the country, put tremendous effort into promoting education.

Owing to these circumstances, everyone competed for opportunities in higher education, and tried to enter a university if at all possible. This eagerness for education persisted unabated into the post-Second World War period, so that the proportion of students going on to higher education became quite high.

In 2017, the attendance rate at elementary and junior high schools (compulsory education) was 100%. Of those graduating from junior

大学への進学率は57.3％で、大学生数は289万人であった。

d）教育への経済的支援

政府は持続的な経済成長を成し遂げる鍵の一つに「人づくり革命」を揚げ、教育への支出は将来への投資であるとして、子どもたちに大胆に政策資源を投入する内容を2017年12月に閣議決定した。

既に、義務教育段階では国公立学校の授業料や教科書が無償となっているが、学用品費・遠足費・修学旅行費などの学校教育費や給食費が有償になるので、費用を負担することが困難な児童生徒を支援するための修学援助制度がある。

今回決定では、幼児教育・保育の無償化と高等教育の無償化・私立高校の無償化を柱としている。特に高等教育の無償化として、低所得者層の進学を支援し、格差の固定化の解消を目指している。国立大の授業料の免除や私立大の授業料の一定額の支援、入学金の免除や返還不要の給付型奨学金の学生への支払いや、学生生活に必要な生活費を賄えるような措置を講じる等を2020年4月から実施する。また、年収590万円未満世帯を対象として私立高校授業料の実質無償化も実現することとした。

e）大学

日本でもっとも古い大学は、東京大学である。江戸時代、幕府が設立した「開成所」と「医学所」がその前身で、1877年両校が合併して東京大学が設立された。以後戦前の1939年までに、京都大学・東北大学・九州大学・北海道大学・大阪大学・名古屋大学の6つの国立総合大学が設立された。戦後、従来の高等専門学校などが昇格・統合されて大学となり、現在では一橋大学・東京工業大学・東京外国語大学・筑波大学・お茶の水女子大学・奈良女子大学・東京芸術大学・各県の国立大学など合計86校の国立大学がある（2018年5月）。

high school, 99% continued on to senior high school, while 57.3% of senior high school graduates continued on to junior college or university. The number of students attending college or university was 2.89 million.

d) Financial Support for Education

The government intends to make a "revolution in human resource development" which is one of the key factors to achieve sustainable economic growth, and with expenditure on education considered an investment in the future, in December 2017 the Cabinet approved an aggressive commitment of policy resources to children.

Tuition and textbooks at public schools are already free during the compulsory education stage, but there are charges to cover expenses such as for school supplies and school excursions and trips and the like. There are also financial aid programs that provide assistance to families that have difficulty bearing the costs.

The main thrust of the Cabinet decision is the provision of free preschool and childcare education, free higher education, and free private high school education. The objective of providing free higher education is to support the educational advancement of people in lower income brackets, eliminating social polarization. Exempting public university students from having to pay tuition fees. providing a certain level of assistance for private university tuition fees, exemption from entrance fees, providing students with benefit scholarships that do not have to be repaid, covering students' living expenses and other such measures are to be implemented starting in April 2020. In addition, private high schools will be virtually free for students from households with an annual income of less than 5.9 million yen.

e) Colleges and Universities

The oldest national university in Japan is the University of Tokyo. The Kaiseijo and Igakusho (Medical Institute) founded by the Shogunate during the Edo period were the predecessors of the University of Tokyo, which was established in 1877 by the merging of these two schools. The following six national universities were founded between 1877 and 1939: Kyoto University, Tohoku University, Kyushu University, Hokkaido University, Osaka University and Nagoya University. After the Second World War, a number of technical colleges and other institutions were elevated to university status or reestablished as universities through consolidation. These currently include Hitotsubashi University, Tokyo Institute of Technology, Tokyo University of Foreign

公立大学は、首都大学東京、大阪市立大学など93校がある。
　私立大学は603校あり、慶応大学と早稲田大学が「私学の双璧」といわれている。このほかに、331校の短期大学がある。大学・短期大学の在学者総数は約303万人（2018年5月）である。

　2000年以降の出生率の急速な落ち込みの影響で将来は大学進学人口が減少し、大学の収容能力が余ってくることが予想される。2017年度時点で私立大学の39.4％の大学で定員割れが生じ、一部の私学に経営悪化の兆候が見られる。

　大学入学志願者の高等学校段階における基礎的な学習の達成度を判定するため、各大学が大学入試センターと共同して、1990年度入試から大学入試センター試験を実施して、現在非常に大規模な試験として発展し毎年行われている。なお、2020年度からは、センター試験に代わり、「大学入学共通テスト」が実施されることになっている。従来の知識偏重型のテストから、知識を前提にそれを活用する思考力・判断力・表現力を問うテストへ改善するのが狙いである。

　2004年4月、日本の国立大学はすべて独立法人となった。その背景には、まず国の政策が、大学の社会的役割を教育・研究の2本柱から、教育・研究・成果の社会還元の3本柱へと転換したことである。また大学も、大学入学人口の急速な減少に直面し、自主経営による競争力の強化、教育・研究内容の納税者（国民）への開示により、魅力ある個性を積極的にアピールしている。

　法人化に伴い、人事・教科内容・授業料など大学の運用に関し学長の権限が拡大された。さらに、競争原理に基づく民間経営手法の導入、教育・研究に対する第三者評価の実施、教員資質向上プログラムの導入などにより大学の活

Studies, Tsukuba University, Ochanomizu Women's University, Nara Women's University, the Tokyo National University of Fine Arts and Music, and the national universities in each prefecture. The total number of national universities is currently 86 (May 2018).

Prefectural and municipal universities number 93. Two of the best known are Tokyo Metropolitan University and Osaka City University.

There are 603 private universities, among which Keio University and Waseda University are referred to as the "twin jewels of the private universities." The list of junior colleges includes 331 schools. The total enrollment of the universities and junior colleges is 3.03 million (May 2018).

The rapid decline in Japan's birth rate since 2000 is expected eventually to decrease the number of students advancing to the college level, so that many colleges and universities are likely to end up with more capacity than they need. As of fiscal 2017, 39.4% of private universities didn't meet their quota due to shortage of applicants, and there are signs of worsening management conditions in some private institutions.

In order to determine the basic learning achievement of university entrance applicants, each year since the 1990 entrance examinations each university has cooperated with the National Center for University Entrance Examinations to conduct the National Center Test for University Admissions. Over the years, it has developed into a very large-scale examination. In fiscal 2020, the National Center Test will be replaced by the University Admission Common Test, with the aim of improving conventional knowledge-biased tests by using tests that focus on how well students can utilize their knowledge in terms of thinking ability, judgment, and the ability to express themselves.

In April 2004, all of Japan's national universities became independent corporations. Behind this change was a shift in government policies governing universities, which sought to modify the societal role of universities from that of education and research to that of education, research, and contribution to society. At the same time, the universities, faced dramatic declines in the population of people applying to university, sought to become more competitive through autonomous management and to enhance their public appeal by actively selling the merits of their educational approach and research activities to the taxpayer.

With privatization, the authority of the university president over personnel affairs, course content, tuition and fees, and other aspects of university management was expanded. In addition, many universities have been actively endeavoring to revitalize and differentiate them-

性化・個性化を目指す動きも活発化している。

f) 大学院

近年の経済のグローバル化、科学技術の進歩、国家・企業の技術戦略の必要性などを背景に、大学院に対する期待が従来の基礎研究の推進および研究者の養成から社会人の再教育、高度職業人の養成に変わってきた。これを踏まえ、1991 年大学院設置基準が改正され、大学院の多様化が進み、単独大学院大学、大学の基礎学部を持たない独立大学院、複数大学による連合大学院などが設置された。

さらに 2003 年、専門職大学院制度がスタートした。この制度は実務家養成を目的としている。修了者には産業社会実務に直結する専門職学位の資格が与えられる。専門大学院や専門職大学院等の新たな制度が導入され、その分野は、法科大学院、教職大学院、会計大学院、知的財産大学院、公共政策大学院、ICT 専門職大学院、技術経営（MOT）大学院、ビジネススクール（MBA・経営専門職大学院）、社会福祉大学院、公衆衛生大学院、臨床心理大学院で多様である。

卓越した教育研究拠点の整備や産業界との共同研究、受託研究、技術移転といった産学連携の推進など、大学の研究機能の強化に加えて、研究成果の直接的な社会還元が強く求められている。

大学院の修了者数（2017 年度）は修士課程 7.1 万人、博士課程 1.6 万人、専門職学位課程 0.7 万人である。

（5）情報通信社会（ICT）

a) 日本の ICT の現状

近年、インターネット・スマートフォン（略してスマホ

selves by, for example, introducing private sector management methods based on the principles of competition, implementing third-party evaluations of their education and research, and launching programs to improve the skills of teachers.

f) Graduate Schools

Graduate schools have been required to respond to an evolving environment brought by the globalization of the economy, advances in science and technology, and increasing importance of the technological strategies of countries and companies. The anticipated role of graduate schools has therefore become less the promotion of basic research and training of researchers and more the re-education of mid-career professionals and the development of highly skilled workers. Since 1991, when the standards for establishment of graduate schools were revised to deal with the changing times, graduate schools have diversified into various types, such as unaffiliated graduate schools, graduate schools without the basic departments associated with universities, joint graduate schools established by multiple universities, and other non-standard institutions.

The next major move came in 2003, with the establishment of the Professional Graduate School. The objective of this system is to train people in practical business. Those who complete these programs receive a professional degree that directly applies to work in an industrial society. Examples of Professional Graduate Schools and other such post-graduate schools include graduate schools of law, education, accounting, intellectual property, public policy, information and communication technology, management of technology, business (offering MBA and management programs), social welfare, public health, and clinical psychology.

In addition to strengthening university research functions by establishing outstanding educational research bases and promoting industry-academia collaboration such as joint research projects with industry, commissioned research and technology transfers, there is a strong need to return the fruits of research to society.

In fiscal 2017, 71,000 graduate students earned a master's degree, 16,000 a doctorate, and 7,000 a professional degree.

(5) Information and Communication Society

a) Information and Communication Technology (ICT) in Japan

Japan has recently come to see nearly universal Internet accessibility

とも呼ぶことが多い）などが広く普及しており、国民にとってICT（Information and Communication Technology の略で情報通信技術と訳され、IT ともいう）は社会生活を送る上で既に不可欠であり、必要な情報を多様なメディアから入手している。またICTは新たな富の創出や生産活動の効率化に大きく貢献し、国民生活を便利にするものであり、ICTの活用が経済成長のための重要な鍵となっている。少子高齢化が本格化する中、ICTの利活用を定着させ、青少年から高齢者に至るまですべての人々が安全に、安心してICTを利用できることが前提となっている。

通称ダボス会議として有名な世界経済フォーラム（WEF）が、2017年9月に公表した「ICT競争力ランキング（2017〜2018年版）」では、世界137の国・地域を対象に「基礎的要件」、「効率性強化」、「イノベーションと洗練性」の3つを大項目とし、その要素たる12の中項目（「制度」、「インフラ」から「イノベーション」等）、100以上の小項目について調査・評価して順位が算出されている。世界的にみると上位は1位スイス、2位アメリカ、3位シンガポール、4位オランダ、5位ドイツ、6位香港、7位スウェーデン、8位イギリスとなっている。日本の総合順位は前年の8位から9位に順位をさげた。日本は中項目の「ビジネスの洗練度」で3位、「市場規模」と「インフラ整備」で4位、「初等教育・保健衛生」は7位で高位だが、それ以外の項目は低位であった。

b）ICT による日本成長戦略

政府は2013年から開始した「ICT成長戦略会議」で、グローバル展開を視野に入れつつ、ICTを日本経済の成長と国際社会への貢献の切り札として活用する方策等を様々な角度から検討することとしている。

取り組むべき課題としては、復興と防災、経済成長、外交・安全保障を掲げ3つの重要戦略を検討することとしている。
1）社会実装戦略（くらしを変える）
　　資源問題の解決・海底資源確保等（鉱物・石油資源問題、水、食糧、エネルギー問題等への対策）、災害に強い情報インフラの強靭化（新たな街づくりを推進し防災・減災への対策）、ICTを活用した街づくり、超高齢社会への対応等、ICTが社会的課題の解決に寄

and wide proliferation of smartphones. This has made Information and Communication Technology (ICT) an indispensable element in the pursuit of a social life for much of the population. It has also given people the power to obtain the information they need from a broad range of media. ICT greatly contributes to the creation of new wealth and the efficiency of production activities, making life convenient for everyone. The utilization of ICT is an important key for economic growth. In addition, the full-fledged onset of an aging-low-birth-rate society in Japan is drawing attention to ICT as a prerequisite to help ensure the safety and security of people of all ages, from the very young to the elderly.

The *ICT Competitiveness Ranking 2017–2018* issued by the World Economic Forum (WEF), more commonly known as the Davos Forum, in September 2017 determined the rankings of 137 countries and regions based on an survey and assessment of scores in the three main categories of "basic requirements," "efficiency enhancers," and "innovation and sophistication factors," and twelve sub-index items (ranging from "institutions" and "infrastructure" to "innovation," etc.) and over 100 individual items. Topping the rankings was Switzerland, the U.S. came second, followed by Singapore in third place, the Netherlands fourth, Germany fifth, Hong Kong sixth, Sweden seventh, and the UK eighth, Japan's overall ranking dropped from last year's eighth place to ninth. In the sub-index items, Japan placed third in "business sophistication," fourth in "market size" and "infrastructure," and seventh in "primary education and healthcare," but placed low in other items.

b) Japan's ICT-Based Growth Strategy by ICT

Beginning with the "ICT Growth Strategy Conference" that began in 2013, the government is studying from various viewpoints measures to utilize ICT as a key to the growth of the Japanese economy and its contribution to the international community, taking into account global development.

As issues to be addressed, there are three important strategies of reconstruction and disaster prevention, economic growth, and diplomacy and security.

1) Social Implementation Strategy (Change your life)

Resolution of resource problems and securing of seabed resources (measures against mineral and oil resource problems and water, food, and energy problems), toughening information infrastructure resiliency against to disasters (measures to prevent and mitigate disasters by promoting new town development), community development utilizing

　　　　与するための方策。

2) 新産業創出戦略（新しいモノをつくる）
　　　　放送コンテンツの海外展開、放送サービスの高度化（4K、8K、スマートテレビ等）、ICT を活用した「コト」づくり（高付加価値のサービス産業育成）、サイバーセキュリティの強化等、ICT による新産業の創出に向けた方策。

3) 研究開発戦略（世界に貢献する）
　　　　イノベーションの促進（iPS 細胞など再生医療への貢献）、ICT 国際標準への確保の実現に向けた情報通信技術政策の在り方。

　一方、政府は先端 ICT による成長戦略の具体策を立案する官民会議「未来投資会議」を開催し、4分野をテーマとして揚げた。〈1〉第4次産業革命（IoT や AI やロボットなどが産業を大きく変革していく）とイノベーション（技術革新）、〈2〉企業関連制度改革・産業構造改革、〈3〉医療・介護、〈4〉地方経済の活性化。これらの4分野の課題を整理して、国民生活の利便性を抜本的に高め、地方を主役に世界を目指す、また新たな技術革新の芽を社会変革につなげるような産業構造に改革して行くとしている。

c) スマートフォン社会の到来

1) スマートフォンの所有状況

　　　　今やスマートフォンは ICT の中心となっており、インターネットに接続し、膨大なデータが生成されている。スマートフォンの普及状況は、2017年に入り、全世界での利用台数は40億に達していると推計されている。スマートフォンは、今や世界中でインターネット接続され使用されている。スマートフォンの特徴は、パソコンと携帯電話の両方の機能を有し、使い方は個々人・世代によって大きく異なっている。

　　　　日本のスマートフォンの世帯別保有状況は2010年に 9.7% であったが、2012年には 49.5% となり2018年で 72.6% となった。スマートフォンの特徴として、1人が1台持つ情報端末である他、2台目以上では、タブレット端末やウェアラブル端末のメガネ型・腕時計型・リストバンド型・衣類型・アクセサリー型等のさまざまな機種が所有されており、利用する機能、ア

ICT, response to ultra-aged society, measures for ICT to contribute to solving social problems.

2) New Industry Creation Strategy (Creating new things)

With the overseas development of broadcasting content, advanced broadcasting services (4K, 8K, smart television, etc.), using ICT to create intangible "things" (nurturing of high value-added service industry), strengthening of cyber security.

3) Research and Development Strategy (Contributing to the world)

Promoting innovation (contributing to regenerative medicine such as iPS cells), and the state of ICT policy for realizing international ICT standards.

The government's "Future Investment Council" held a conference in collaboration with industry and academia to formulate concrete measures for advanced ICT growth strategies, which came up with themes in four fields. <1> Fourth industrial revolution (IoT, AI and robots, e.g., revolutionize industry) and innovation; <2> Reforms of industry-related systems and structural reforms; <3> Medical and nursing care; <4> Revitalization of regional economies. The elements in these four fields will be organized to drastically increase the convenience of people's lives, aim for the world with outlying regions in Japan taking the lead, and foster the budding of fresh innovations that will lead to reforms in industrial structures that will bring about social change.

c) The Advent of the Smartphone Society

1) Smartphone Ownership

The smartphone is now at the center of ICT, connecting to the Internet and generating enormous amounts of data. Entering 2017, it was estimated that the number of smartphone users worldwide had reached four billion. All the smartphones throughout the world are being used with connection to the Internet. What distinguishes smartphones is that they have the functions of both a personal computer and a mobile phone, and there are big differences in how each person and each generation uses them.

In Japan, 9.7% of households had a smartphone in 2010. By 2012, ownership had risen to 49.5%, and by 2018 to 72.6%. A feature of a smartphone is that it is an information terminal used by one person. Second and subsequent units come in a variety of formats differentiated by function, application, or content: a tablet, or a wearable terminal such as spectacles or a wristwatch or wristband type, or a wearable garment type or accessory.

プリ、コンテンツで使い分けている。

スマートフォンの普及やデータ流通の増加を支えているのが、移動通信の方式の進化である。現在主流である LTE（Long Term Evolution ＝携帯電話の高速通信の規格）の日本における契約数は、2012 年には 230 万件であったが、2018 年 3 月末には 1 億 6,800 万件と普及率は 130％を超えている。

スマートフォンの利用金額は、2018 年の数値で総額の平均で 1 人 5,994 円／月となっている。この月額の内容には、通話料金・パケット料金や利用コンテンツ課金が含まれている。

2) スマートフォンの使用状況

スマートフォン普及のインパクトは、その普及台数のみならず使い方にもある。スマートフォン利用者のインターネット利用時間（2016 年の平日 1 日あたり）を年代別にみると、全体での平均は 82 分であり、10 代及び 20 代がそれぞれ 143 分、129 分と顕著に長くなっている。

スマートフォンの普及と同時に利用が増加してきたのが SNS（ソーシャル・ネットワーキング・サービス）である。日本における代表的な SNS は、LINE、Facebook、Twitter の 3 大ソーシャルメディアを含め 6 つのサービスのいずれかを利用している。特に LINE はこの中で最後発のサービス開始ながらも、現在では最も利用率が高く、社会の基盤サービスとしての地位を確立しつつあるほどである。LINE、Facebook ともに友人登録数を見ると直接面識のある友人数が高くそれぞれ 82.0％と 69.3％となっている。一方 Twitter は、フォロー数、フォロワー数ともに登録自体は多いものの直接面識のある友人数の割合が 12.0％と低い。一方 3 大ソーシャルメディアの平均利用時間は LINE が 51.0 分、Twitter が 26.2 分、Facebook が 13.7 分／日となっている。LINE の日本の登録ユーザー数は 6,800 万人（2017 年 1 月）で、その機能として、利用者間で無料通話できるほか、グループを作って行うメッセージのやり取りや、感情を表現できるイラスト「スタンプ」を使うことができ、多くの若者にとって欠かせない存在となっている。

SNS の活用として豪雨などの災害の際、インターネットの短文投稿サイトを使う人が増え、2011 年の

The spread of smartphones and increases in data distribution are supported by the evolution of mobile communication methods. The current mainstream technology is Long Term Evolution (LTE), a standard for high-speed wireless communication for mobile devices. In Japan, there were 2.3 million LTE subscribers in 2012, and by March 2018 that figure had risen to 168 million, corresponding to a penetration rate of over 130%.

Based on 2018 figures, the average cost of using a smartphone was 5,994 yen per month, which included call charges, packet service charges, and usage content charges.

2) Smartphone Usage

The impact of the spread of smartphones are reflected not just by the number of units but by how they are used. Looking at the internet usage time of smartphone users (per weekday in 2016) by age, the overall average was 82 minutes, but for users aged 10 to 19 the time rose to 143 minutes, and to 129 minutes in the case of users in their 20s.

The use of Social Networking Services (SNS) has increased with the spread of the smartphone. A typical SNS in Japan is one of six services that include the big three social media of LINE, Facebook, and Twitter. Even though LINE was the most recent of the three to be launched, it now has the highest utilization rate and is establishing its position as a basic service of society. On LINE, 82.0% of registered friends are direct friends, and the corresponding figure on Facebook is 69.3%. Twitter users, on the other hand, might have large numbers of people they follow and followers, but the proportion of direct friends is a low 12.0%. The average daily utilization time of the big three is 51.0 minutes for LINE, 26.2 minutes for Twitter, and 13.7 minutes for Facebook. As of January 2017, LINE had 68 million registered users in Japan. LINE's functions include free calling between users, groups can be formed and used to exchange messages; feelings can be expressed using illustrations called "Stamps," which many young people consider indispensable.

Growing numbers of people have used SNS to post short messages on the Internet in the event of disasters such as torrential rain, a tendency

東日本大震災がその流れを一気に加速させた。この経験をもとに政府は自治体向けに「災害対応 SNS 活用ガイドブック」をまとめた。これは臨場感、即時性を有する貴重な情報源であり、情報発信手段として有効である。

通常 SNS に投稿されるのは、個人の思いや主張である。利用者は事実を伝えるというより、感情や意見を他の人と共有するために発信している。伝聞の繰り返しである「拡散」によって情報が共有されることが多いため、デマや誤情報がそのまま広まってしまう恐れもあり、真偽不明な情報の管理を誰が担うかが課題となっている。また、2017 年には、写真共有サービス「Instagram」（インスタグラム）にスマートフォンで撮影した写真をアップロードして、公開した際にひときわ映える・見栄えが良い「インスタ映え」と言う言葉が流行語となるほど人気に火がつき、「拡散」された写真や動画によって特定の商品の売上が上がったり、穴場の観光地には訪日外国人が殺到するなどの現象が顕著となっている。

スマートフォンの利用状況として SNS 以外では、動画共有サイト、知識共有サイト、クチコミサイト、Q&A サイト、ブログ、掲示板、ミニブログとなっている。

また、スマートフォンで情報収集する際の使い方では、ニュース（報道情報）の収集、生活情報（お買い得情報や趣味に関する情報）の収集、世間で話題になっているモノ・コトの把握、有名人など・知人以外の動向の把握、知人の状況把握となっている。

一方、これだけスマートフォンが普及すると、新たに利用・使用のマナーも問題視されている。「歩きスマホ」、「食事中の使用」、「人ごみの中での使用」、「場所・時間をわきまえない撮影」、「マナーモードにせず電車やバスに乗っている」、「手持ちぶさたに端末をいじる」、「授業中や会議中に端末を操作したり着信をチェックする」など、スマートフォンの使用に関わる行動に他者が不快と思うことがありマナーを守り十分な気遣いが必要となる。

d）インターネット

2016 年の日本のインターネット利用人口は 1 億 84 万人で、総人口に占める普及率は 83.5％に達している。イン

that was instantly accelerated by the Great East Japan Earthquake of 2011. With local governments in mind, the government then compiled a guide to using SNS in disaster-response situations. It is an effective way of communicating a valuable source of information having realism and immediacy.

SNS are commonly used to post personal ideas and assertions. Users do not convey facts so much as share emotions and opinions with others. Since the information may often be the sharing and dissemination of repeated hearsay, the result can be the spreading of misinformation or wild rumors. This has given rise to discussion about who is responsible for oversight of the authenticity of the information. "Insta-bae" is a Japanese coinage that refers to photos or videos uploaded to the photo sharing service Instagram that look so outstandingly brilliant and attractive that they boosted sales of the goods photographed and had overseas visitors to Japan flocking to the tourist spots shown. Insta-bae became enormously popular and one of the top buzzwords of 2017.

Smartphones are also used to visit many other kinds of sites, including video sharing sites, knowledge-sharing sites, review sites, Q&A sites, and blogs, bulletin boards, and mini blogs, etc.

Smartphones are also used to collect news (media information) and information on bargains and hobbies, and on current topics and celebrity news, and what people we know are doing.

The widespread use of smartphones also brings questions of usage etiquette and good manners. It is necessary to observe good manners and not use smartphones in ways that may make other people uncomfortable, such as using a smartphone while walking, during meals, in crowded places, taking pictures and videos without regard for time and place, riding on a bus or train without setting the phone to silent mode, operating a phone during classes or meetings and checking for incoming messages.

d) Internet

About 83.5% of Japanese, or 100.84 million people, regularly use the Internet (2016). About 58.6% of people connect to the Internet with

ターネットの利用端末は、パソコンが58.6％、スマートフォンが57.9％となっておりその利用は概ね上昇傾向にある。

インターネット利用の主なものは、電子メールの送受信、SNS、無料電話アプリ、ホームページの閲覧、ネットショッピング、デジタルコンテンツの購入、地図・交通情報提供サービス、天気予報、ニュースサイト、動画投稿・共有サイトの利用、金融取引、就職転職情報、通信教育などである。インターネットの屋外利用端末がスマートフォンやタブレット端末へ移行する中で、「電子書籍」、「音楽・動画エンターテインメント」の他、ソーシャルゲームと呼ばれる「オンラインゲームソフト」、「メッセージ・音声通話」、「スケジュール・手帳・メモ」の利用も顕著となっている。

また、2013年7月の参議院選挙から「ネット選挙」（候補者や政党がホームページ・ブログ・SNS・掲示板・動画・メールなどから情報発信することができる）が解禁となった。

e）ビッグデータ利活用の開始

あらゆるモノがインターネットにつながるIoT（Internet of Things）技術の普及で、スマートフォンのSNSや自動車の位置情報に基づき、人がいつ、どこで、どんな行動をしているかなどを、ある程度把握できるようになった。天気や気温、湿度なども含め、多種多様な電子情報が膨大に集まったものを、ビッグデータと呼んでいるが、その特徴は、デジタル化されたデータの量、種類、そして処理速度である。文書や音声、画像といった情報もデジタル化する機器やサービスが開発され、データとして保存・処理する技術が進化している。また、ICTの進化とともにデータ集積・活用のためのコストは格段に低くなり、インターネット経由でさまざまなサービスを受けられる「クラウド（コンピューティング）」が登場したため、このサービスを利用することで、より低コストでビッグデータを利用可能となった。

日本においては、2016年から2017年にかけて、官民データ活用推進基本法の制定や改正個人情報保護法の全面施行などの法整備がすすめられている。ビッグデータとしては大きく4つに分類できる。

personal computers and about 57.9% with smartphones.

The main reasons for accessing the Internet are to send and receive email, use social networking services (SNS) and free phone applications, view websites, shop, buy digital content, use map and traffic information services, check weather forecasts and news sites, post and share videos, conduct financial transactions, obtain employment and new job information, and take online study courses. The shift to smartphones and tablets as the terminals of choice for connecting to the Internet outdoors has accelerated the use of electronic books, music and video entertainment, programs for playing social games online, messaging and voice communications, scheduling, and taking notes and memos.

The House of Councilors election held in July 2013 was the first election following the repeal of the ban on Internet-based campaigning and marked the start of a new age in which candidates and political parties are free to campaign using websites, blogs, SNS, bulletin boards, videos, and email.

e) The Start of Big Data Utilization

With the spread of the Internet of Things (IoT) technology that connects everything to the Internet, it became possible to know such things as, what someone is doing and when and where, based on a smartphone's SNS activity and car location information. What is called big data is vast collections of diverse electronic information including weather, temperature, humidity, and so forth, that is characterized by the volume, type and processing speed of the digitized data. Devices and services have been developed for digitizing information such as documents, sounds, and images, and techniques for storing and processing the data are evolving. With the evolution of ICT, the cost of collecting and utilizing data has greatly decreased, and the advent of "cloud computing" able to house services via the Internet has made it possible to lower the cost of using the services to utilize big data.

In Japan, the enactment of the Basic Act on the Advancement of Public and Private Sector Data Utilization and the full implementation of the Amended Act on the Protection of Personal Information helped advance the relevant legal framework in 2016 and 2017. Big data can be broadly divided into four types.

〈1〉 政府：国や地方公共団体が提供する「オープンデータ」
政府や地方公共団体などが保有する公共情報について、データとしてオープン化を強力に推進する。
〈2〉 企業：ノウハウをデジタル化・構造化したデータ
農業やインフラ管理からビジネス等に至る産業や企業が持ちうるパーソナルデータ以外のデータとして捉えられる。
〈3〉 企業：M2M（Machine to Machine）から吐き出されるストリーミングデータ
例えば工場等の生産現場における IoT 機器から収集されるデータや橋梁に設置された IoT 機器からのセンシングデータ（歪み、振動、通行車両の形式・重量など）
〈4〉 個人：個人の属性に係る「パーソナルデータ」
個人の属性情報、移動・行動・購買履歴、ウェアラブル機器から収集された個人情報を含む

　データ流通・利活用の促進において重要と考えられるのは多量かつ多様なデータが生成されることだけでなく、これらのデータをその提供者・利用者・受益者となる個人・企業・政府等の間で円滑かつ適正に循環させていくことで、イノベーションを加速させ、経済成長への貢献を高めていくことである。現在、日本企業もビッグデータをどう使うかの勉強に力を入れ始めている段階で、未だ手探りの状態である。自社のデータの価値を見据え、積極的に集め蓄えることが肝要で、システム設計する際にデータを取得する仕組みが必要となる。
　ビッグデータを、AI（人工知能）を使って解析すれば、これまで数値で表しにくかった人々の行動パターンや流行などを発見できるようになる。また、新しいサービスや商品の開発などに生かすことも可能となる。
　具体的な事例としては、経済動向、公共インフラ・防災、電気供給管理、建築物の安全、鉄道の保安、建設機械状況、犯罪の予防、交通事故の減少、自動運転、工場の稼働向上、生産の最適化、購買分析、販促情報、農業のICT化、観光客行動情報、健康管理、医療制度情報、遺伝情報、機械による学習・教育などあらゆる分野への活用が期待される。

<1> Government: "Open data" provided by national and local governments

The government is strongly promoting open access to public information data held by the national and local governments.

<2> Enterprises: Digitized and structured know-how data

This is regarded as data other than personal data held by industries and companies ranging from agriculture and infrastructure management to business, etc.

<3> Enterprises: Data streamed from Machine to Machine (M2M) operations

Examples include data collected from IoT equipment at factories and other production sites, and sensor data (distortion, vibration, type and weight of passing vehicles, etc.) from IoT equipment installed on bridges and the like.

<4> Individual: Personal data related to personal attributes

Personal attribute information, including relating to movement, behavior, and purchase history, including personal information collected from wearable devices.

What is considered important in promoting the distribution and utilization of data is not only to generate a large amount of diverse data but also to achieve smooth and appropriate circulation among the individuals, companies and governments that are the providers, utilizers and beneficiaries to accelerate innovation and enhance the contribution to economic growth. Currently, Japanese companies are still feeling their way as they start to focus on studying how to use big data. Companies' data is valuable and has to be collected and stored, so when designing a system, it needs to have a mechanism for acquiring the data.

Using Artificial Intelligence (AI) to analyze big data reveals patterns and trends in people's behavior that previously were difficult to express numerically. It can also be used to develop new services and products.

Big data technology is expected to be applied in many fields, including economic trends, public infrastructure and disaster prevention, electricity supply management, safety of building structures, railway security, construction machinery status, crime prevention, reduction of traffic accidents, automated operations, improvement of factory operations, production optimization, purchasing analysis, sales promotion data, ICT of agriculture, tourist behavior data, health management, healthcare system information, genetic data, and machine learning and education.

一方、ビッグデータの権利保護も重要で、データへの不正アクセスなどで盗まれた場合のルールがあいまいであるとの指摘がある。政府は不正競争防止法などを改正することにより、ハッキングなどの方法でデータを取得・利用することや、有償で入手した場合でも無断で転売することなどを差し止め請求できるようにすることとしている。

f）ネットワーク利用に伴う問題点

　インターネットがグローバル社会における社会活動に不可欠の基盤となる中で、情報システムへの不正アクセス、世界規模でのコンピュータウィルスのまん延、サイバーテロ、個人情報の流出などの問題が多発している。個人は勿論のこと企業や政府関係機関での情報セキュリティ対策が重要な課題であり、我々を取り巻く情報セキュリティに関する脅威はますます深刻化している。近年のサイバー攻撃は、国家機密を標的とした攻撃から個人の情報・金銭を標的とした攻撃まで多岐にわたっている。

　政府は、防衛産業を狙うような国家安全保障にかかわる深刻な標的型攻撃を想定し、〈1〉国や国の安全に関する重要な情報を扱う企業などに対する高度な脅威への対応強化、〈2〉スマートフォンなどの本格的な普及に伴うリスクの表面化に対応する安全・安心な利用環境の整備、〈3〉国際連携の強化を基本方針とするために国会において「サイバーセキュリティ基本法」が 2014 年 11 月に成立した。

　さらに政府は、IoT／AI 時代に対応したサイバーセキュリティの確立にむけ、IoT 機器セキュリティ対策の実施、セキュリティ人材育成のスピードアップや国際連携等の対策の実施を 2017 年 1 月に公表した。

　また、スマートフォンの青少年への普及を踏まえて、インターネット上の違法・有害情報への対策や個人情報の保護など、青少年が安全に安心してインターネットを利用できる環境の整備のため、情報技術を使いこなす能力であるリテラシーの向上と、不要な情報を遮断するフィルタリングの改善に官民連携で取り組んでいる。

　スマートフォンの利用拡大で違法情報や有害情報の流通

Big data protection rights are also important, but there have been cases of data theft due to unauthorized access to the data where existing rules and regulations are unclear. By amending legislation such as the Unfair Competition Prevention Act, the government is making it possible for parties to request injunctions against the use of data acquired by hacking, or when data, even if purchased, is resold without permission.

f) Network Usage Issues

The expanding role of the Internet as an indispensable instrument underpinning the social activities of Japan and the global community has been accompanied by emergence of many problems, such as unauthorized access of information systems, worldwide spread of computer viruses, cyber terror, and personal data leaks. The threat to Internet user information security is becoming increasingly severe and making the implementation of security measures an urgent issue not only for individuals but also for businesses and government organizations. Cyber-attacks are being aimed at targets ranging from state secrets to personal data and finances.

In November 2014, the Japanese Government passed the "Basic Act on Cybersecurity" that set out the following basic policies for protecting against possible serious attacks against the defense industry or other targets associated with national security: <1> strengthening measures for dealing with sophisticated threats to companies and organizations handling information important to Japan and its security, <2> establishing a secure user environment for countering the emerging risks posed by the full-fledged proliferation of smartphones and other mobile devices, and <3> reinforcing international collaboration.

Furthermore, in January 2017 the government announced the implementation of security measures for IoT equipment, and of measures such as international collaboration to speed up the development of human resources related to security issues for the establishment of cyber security corresponding to the era of IoT and AI.

In light of the spread of smartphones among young people, the government is also addressing the issue of illegal and harmful information on the Internet, moving towards securing personal information, and taking other measures to make the Internet environment safe for the young to use. To this end, it is orchestrating a joint public and private sector effort to increase information technology literacy and improve the performance of filtering for blocking websites with undesirable contents.

The distribution of illegal and harmful information is becoming a

が問題になっている。フィルタリングの対象サイトとしては、喫煙／飲酒、性的表現、性風俗ビジネス、グロテスク、オカルト、出会い・異性紹介、ハッキング、ウィルスの被害・加害、殺人・銃刀・薬物・テロ・中傷・自殺、ギャンブルなどである。

(6) 環境保全

a) 戦後日本の環境問題

日本は戦後の復興期と、これに続く高度成長期における経済発展の過程で、水俣病、第二水俣病（新潟水俣病）、イタイイタイ病、四日市ぜん息をはじめとするいわゆる4大公害のために人の生命・身体に深刻な災厄をもたらしただけでなく、一般住民の生活に重大な損失、不利益を及ぼす公害問題を発生させ、大きな社会問題となった。

しかしこれらの問題は、このほかの大気、水質、土壌汚染、騒音、振動、地盤沈下および悪臭という環境基本法にうたわれている典型7公害を含めて、政府の環境関係の法制整備、企業の公害防止に向けた技術開発や、膨大な公害防止投資などの努力により、おおむね収束した。

こうした経済成長と環境保全の両立を実現させた日本の努力と実績は、1992年のリオデジャネイロでの「地球サミット」以来、国際的に高く評価されている。現在、日本にはこの他国に例を見ない経験と技術を国際社会に還元することが大きく期待されている。

このような状況の中で、2011年3月11日、突然日本は観測史上最大の東日本大震災とこの地震に起因する巨大な津波に見舞われ、広い範囲で人命と生活基盤を失うとともに、東京電力福島第1原子力発電所の崩壊により深刻な放射性物質の汚染被害をもたらした。現在も日本ではこの放射性物質の汚染が依然として深刻な問題となっており、その対策に取り組んでいる。

problem due to the expansion of smartphone usage. Examples of sites targeted for filtering include those related to smoking and drinking, sexual expression, sex business, grotesquerie and the occult, introductions to the opposite sex, hacking, virus perpetration and damage, homicide, guns and swords, drugs, terrorism, slander, suicide, and gambling, etc.

(6) Preservation of the Environment

a) Environmental Problems in Post-War Japan

During the reconstruction period following the Second World War and the ensuing period of rapid economic growth, Japan experienced a number of serious social issues, most notably the so-called Four Major Pollution Issues that led to the Minamata disease, Niigata Minamata disease, the itai-itai (pain-pain) malady, and Yokkaichi asthma outbreaks. In addition to causing serious harm to life and limb of individuals, the pollution problems gave rise to serious losses and disadvantages to the lives of the general population, causing major social problems.

These problems, as well as the other seven typical kinds of pollution identified by Japan's Basic Law for Environmental Pollution Control (air, water, and soil pollution, noise, vibration, ground subsidence, and offensive odors), were substantially overcome through tougher environmental protection legislation and the efforts of the industrial sector, including development of technologies for reducing pollution and huge outlays for implementing pollution control measures.

Japan's success in simultaneously realizing economic growth and environmental preservation, and the effort behind it, has been highly praised internationally, especially since being spoken of favorably at the Earth Summit held in Rio de Janeiro in 1992. The international community today is very eager for Japan to share its unique experience and technology.

The great earthquake and tsunami that struck Japan in 2011, the worst in the country's recorded history, took many lives and devastated the life-supporting infrastructure of people over a wide area. The simultaneous destruction of Tokyo Electric Power Company's Fukushima Daiichi nuclear power station seriously contaminated the region with radioactive material. The contamination by the radioactive material remains a serious problem on which work continues.

b）環境保全に対するグローバルな視点

1）「リオ+20」におけるグリーン経済の拡大に向けて

2012年、リオデジャネイロで「リオ+20」と呼ばれる国連持続可能な開発会議が開かれた。この会議は、1992年に同じリオで開かれた国連環境開発会議（地球サミット）から20年後に開かれたフォローアップ会議で、世界188カ国および3地域（EU・パレスチナ・バチカン）の代表3万人が参加する国連最大の会議であった。

1992年の地球サミットも世界環境保全の歴史に残るもので、環境開発に関する合意文書「リオ宣言」とその行動計画である「アジェンダ21」等が採択され、同時に「気候変動枠組み条約」、「生物多様性条約」の署名が開始された。

これにより「持続可能な開発」という概念が全世界の行動原則へと具体化されるとともに、持続可能な開発が、人類が安全に繁栄する未来への道であることが確認された。

「リオ+20」の主要テーマは「グリーン経済」であった。グリーン経済とは、20世紀後半からの大量生産、大量消費、大量廃棄システムの負の側面（大気・水の汚染、地球の温暖化、森林の破壊、オゾン層の破壊、貧困の拡大など）の反省に立って、経済発展と環境保全の両立をめざそうとする新しい経済システムである。

2）SDGs

2015年9月、国連本部において「持続可能な開発サミット」が開催され、「我々の世界を変革する：持続可能な開発のための2030アジェンダ」が採択された。人間、地球および繁栄のための行動計画として、17の目標と169のターゲットからなる「持続可能な開発目標（Sustainable Development Goals：SDGs）」である。

c）分野別の環境課題

「リオ宣言」および「リオ+20」がかかげる環境保全の課題として、一般的には9つの分野〈1〉地球温暖化、〈2〉オゾン層破壊、〈3〉酸性雨、〈4〉生物多様性、〈5〉森林破壊、〈6〉砂漠化、〈7〉海洋汚染、〈8〉有害物質の越境移動、

b) Preservation of the Environment from a Global Perspective

1) The Expansion of the Rio+20 Green Economy

Japan participated in the United Nations Conference on Sustainable Development, called "Rio+20," held in Rio de Janeiro in 2012. Rio+20 was a 20-year follow-up to the 1992 United Nations Conference on Environment and Development (Earth Summit) also held in Rio de Janeiro and attended by Japan. It was a UN mega-summit that drew 30 thousand representatives from 188 countries and 3 regions (EU, Palestine and the Vatican).

The 1992 Earth Summit was also a conference of considerable significance in the history of global environmental preservation. It led to the adoption of the Rio Declaration on Environment and Development and the action plan "Agenda 21," and marked the opening for signature of the Framework Convention on Climate Change and the Convention on Biological Diversity.

This confirmed that the concept of "sustainable development" is embodied in action principles around the world and is the way to a future where mankind will flourish safely.

One of the core themes of Rio+20 was "Green Economy." The green economy initiative grew out of the lessons learned from the negative side effects (such as air and water pollution, global warming, deforestation, ozone layer depletion, and increased poverty) of the social system of the latter half of the twentieth century that is characterized by mass production, mass consumption, and mass waste disposal. The initiative's goal is to achieve a new economic system capable of growing the economy while also preserving the natural environment.

2) SDGs

In September 2015, the "Sustainable Development Summit" was held at the United Nations Headquarters and "The 2030 Agenda for Sustainable Development" adopted, which will transform our world. It is a set of Sustainable Development Goals consisting of 17 goals and 169 targets that form an action plan for humanity, the Earth, and prosperity.

c) Environmental Issues in Different Fields

Rio+20 and the Rio Declaration listed nine general fields for environmental protection, which are: <1> global warming, <2> ozone depletion, <3> acid rain, <4> biodiversity, <5> deforestation, <6> desertification, <7> marine pollution, <8> transboundary movement

〈9〉開発途上国の環境問題 を含んでいるが、ここでは地球温暖化、生物の多様性、持続可能な循環型社会の3項目について概説する。

1）地球温暖化の防止

　i）地球温暖化問題の特質

　　　地球温暖化は、科学の発達によって「発見された環境問題」である。大気中の二酸化炭素（CO_2）濃度の上昇が地球温暖化の原因になるという理論は19世紀末にアレニウスにより発表された。それから1世紀を経て、人工衛星やコンピューターを使った観測・予測技術により、これが地球の将来を脅かす重大な問題として認識された。

　　　すでに顕在化した現実問題としては、北極の大氷塊が融解・消失する、南極の氷河の崩壊が加速する、北極海の水面の上昇によりイヌイット（エスキモー）が移住を迫られる、アラスカの永久凍土層の氷解により道路の亀裂や建物の傾倒が起る、ヒマラヤの氷河湖の拡大・決壊による洪水の恐れがある、北極海の氷塊が減少してホッキョクグマの数が減少しているなど、多数の事例が報告されている。

　ii）地球温暖化防止の国際的取組み

　　　［1］気候変動に関する政府間パネル（Intergovernmental Panel on Climate Change, 略称 IPCC）

　　　　　最初の国際的な取り組みはIPCCである。これは1988年に設立された政府間機構で、国際的な専門家で構成され、地球温暖化についての科学的な研究の収集・整理のための学術的な機関である。気候変化に関する科学的な判断基準の提供を目的としており、数年おきに地球温暖化に関する「評価報告書」（Assessment Report）などを発行している。

　　　　　次に説明する「気候変動枠組み条約」とは独立した組織であったが、同条約の成立後その実施のために必要な科学的調査業務を代行している。アル・ゴアとともにIPCCは2007年にノーベル平和賞を受賞した。

　　　［2］気候変動枠組み条約と京都議定書およびその問題点

　　　　　1992年のリオ地球サミットにおいて採択された「気候変動枠組み条約」では、世界を先進

of harmful substances, <9> environmental problems of developing countries. Here, global warming, biodiversity, and the sustainable recycling-oriented society are outlined.

1) Preventing Global Warming
i) Nature of the Global Warming Problem

Global warming is an environmental problem unveiled by scientific progress. Late in the nineteenth century, Svante Arrhenius announced that increased levels of carbon dioxide (CO_2) in the atmosphere cause global warming. A century later, artificial satellite observations and computer-based prediction techniques made it evident that global warming is a critical problem that threatens the future of the world.

Some of the apparent dangers already reported include the melting and disappearance of the arctic icecap, accelerated calving of glaciers in Antarctica, Inuit (Eskimos) being forced to relocate because of rising Arctic Ocean levels, cracking of roads and tilting of buildings in Alaska due to melting of the permafrost, swelling and bursting of Himalayan glacial lakes, and decimation of polar bears with the disappearance of ice floes in the Arctic Ocean.

ii) International Efforts to Prevent Global Warming
[1] Intergovernmental Panel on Climate Change (IPCC)

The IPCC was the first international organization to focus on climate change. It was created in 1988 as an intergovernmental panel comprised of experts from around the world for the purpose of collecting and accessing scientific information on global warming. The goal of these assessments is to offer scientific evaluation criteria concerning climate change. The IPCC publishes an Assessment Report on global warming every few years.

Although the Panel is separate from the Framework Convention on Climate Change discussed below, it has managed scientific survey matters for the Framework Convention since it went into effect. The IPCC and Al Gore shared the Nobel Peace Prize in 2007.

[2] Framework Convention on Climate Change, Kyoto Protocol, and their Shortcomings

Under the Framework Convention on Climate Change adopted at the Rio Earth Summit in 1992, which divided the world into developed

国と発展途上国に分け、「共通だが差異ある責任の原則」に基づき、各国が温暖化ガス濃度の安定化に努力することが合意された。

1997年、京都で開かれた第3回の同条約に基づく条約締約国会議(COP3)において「京都議定書」が採択され、その後124の国家とEUが批准して、2005年2月16日に同議定書は発効した。この議定書は、先進各国に数値目標を定め、対策の実施を求めるものであった(対1990年削減率:日本6%、EU8%、アメリカ7%、ロシアおよび途上国ゼロ%)。また、排出量取引など、いわゆる「京都メカニズム」も導入された。

(注) COP:(Conference of the Parties 条約締約国会議)、関係事案の最高決定機関

しかし、京都議定書は採択時点で次のような問題を含んでいた。

〈1〉 日本・EUなどの先進国だけが削減義務を負った。

〈2〉 経済の急激な発展により排出量が急増している中国、インドなどの途上大国が削減義務を負っていない。

〈3〉 日本は長年削減に真剣に取り組んだ結果、削減目標率の基準の1990年に比べて、すでに他国とは段違いの削減実績を達成していたが、議長国として大幅な譲歩を迫られて合意した。

その後、京都議定書採択当時の二酸化炭素の世界最大排出国であるアメリカが2001年に京都議定書から離脱し、さらにオーストラリア・カナダも目標達成を断念した。その結果、削減義務を負う批准国の第1約束期間(2008~2012年)において削減義務を負う批准国の排出量を合計しても世界の総排出量の4分の1に過ぎなくなった。

このような状況から京都議定書参加国からは、アメリカおよび中国、インドほかの途上国にも排出量の規制を求める声が高まった。

[3] パリ協定の採択

この要請を受けて2010年、メキシコのカンクンでのCOP16では、先進国と途上国との区

and developing countries and established the Principle of Common But Differentiated Responsibilities, the individual countries were committed to strive to stabilize greenhouse gas emissions.

The Kyoto Protocol was adopted at the Third Conference of the Parties on Climate Change (COP3) held in Kyoto in December 1997, and, with its subsequent ratification by 124 countries and the EU, went into effect on February 16, 2005. The protocol set numerical reduction targets for developed countries and required the implementation of measures by all countries (the reduction from 1990 levels was 6% for Japan, 8% for the EU, 7% for the U.S., and 0% for Russia and developing countries). The protocol also introduced "emissions trading" and other flexible mechanisms (the Kyoto mechanisms) to facilitate compliance.

Note: The Conference of the Parties (COP) is the highest decision-making organ of the Convention.

However, the Kyoto Protocol had the following problems from the time of adoption:

<1> Only developed countries and regions like Japan and the EU were required to reduce emissions.

<2> China, India, and other developing countries were not obliged to reduce their rapidly increasing emissions.

<3> Although Japan's long-continuing efforts to lower emissions had already achieved a considerably higher reduction rate from the 1990 base year than that of any other country, it made a substantial concession as the host country.

Then in 2001, the world's greatest producer of emissions at the time of the adoption of the Kyoto Protocol, the U.S., withdrew from the Kyoto Protocol, while Australia and Canada abandoned efforts to meet their targets. As a result, the total emissions of all ratifying countries that still abided by the protocol accounted for less than a quarter of total global emissions during the first commitment period (2008 to 2012).

This situation led the Kyoto Protocol participants to intensify calls for the U.S. and the developing nations, particularly China and India, to regulate emissions.

[3] Adoption of the Paris Agreement

In response to such demands, the Cancun Agreement was adopted at COP16 held in Cancun, Mexico in 2010. This abolished the distinction

別を取り払い、すべての国が2015年までに、2020年以降の削減目標を提示する「カンクン合意」が採択された。さらに、2015年12月、フランス・パリでのCOP21において、地球温暖化防止のための国際枠組みであるパリ協定が採択された。

パリ協定の要点は次の3点である。
〈1〉 世界全体の温度目標を設定。世界的な平均気温上昇を産業革命以前に比べて2℃より十分低く保つとともに、1.5℃に抑える努力を追求する。
〈2〉 先進国、途上国を問わず、各締約国が国情に応じて温室効果ガスの削減・抑制目標を策定し、その根拠となる情報を含め、枠組条約事務局に通報し、その進捗状況を定期的に報告し、専門家によるレビューを受ける。なお、目標達成は義務ではない。
〈3〉 5年に一度、各国の削減努力の総計と、長期の温度目標達成に必要な世界全体の許容排出量を比較し、その結果をもって目標値を見直す(このプロセスをグローバル ストックテイクという)。

この協定は、192カ国と欧州連合(EU)が参加し2016年11月4日に発効し、正式なグローバル ストックテイクは2023年から始まることになっている。そのための準備として、2018年に、IPCCが1.5℃安定化に必要な温暖化ガス削減に関する特別報告書を出すことになっている。日本にとっては、エネルギー基本計画における、いわゆるS+3E(Safety, Energy, Security, Economic Efficiency, Environment)に沿ったエネルギーミックスの実現に最大限の努力をする必要があり、そこでカギとなるのは、安全性の確認された原発の着実な再稼働と運転期間の延長である。

このような枠組みが採択されたところで、2017年6月1日、アメリカ大統領のドナルド・トランプはアメリカがパリ協定から離脱すると表明した。ただ、離脱の手続きのためにパリ協定発効の日から4年を要するため、正式な離脱

between developed and developing countries and required every country by 2015 to submit a reduction target for 2020 and beyond. Then in December 2015, at COP21 held in Paris, France, the Paris Agreement, an international framework for the prevention of global warming, was adopted.

The following are the three main points of the Paris Agreement:

<1> Setting the global temperature target. The increase in the global average temperature is to be held to well below 2°C above pre-industrial levels, and efforts pursued to limit the increase to 1.5°C.

<2> Whether a developed country or a developing country, each Party is to formulate its greenhouse gas reduction target according to its national circumstances, notify the secretariat of the Framework Convention, including with information that serves as a basis for the target, report its progress regularly and receive reviews by experts. The target is not obligatory.

<3> Once every five years, total of reduction efforts of each country will be compared with the global allowable emissions necessary to achieve the long-term temperature goal, and the target value will be reviewed based on the results (a process called the global stocktake).

This agreement was scheduled to go into effect on November 4, 2016, with 192 countries and the European Union participating, and the official global stocktake will start from 2023. In preparation for that, in 2018, the IPCC is to issue a special report on the amount of greenhouse gas reduction needed for stabilization of the temperature at 1.5°C. To Japan, it is necessary to make maximum efforts to realize an energy mix in accordance with the so-called S+3E (Safety, Energy security, Economic efficiency, Environment) in the Basic Energy Plan. Key will be a gradual restart of safety-confirmed nuclear power plants and extension of their operational periods.

This was the adopted framework, but on June 1, 2017, President Donald Trump announced that the U.S. will withdraw from the Paris Agreement. Since it takes four years from the date the Paris Agreement come into effect to complete the withdrawal procedure, formal withdrawal will take place no earlier than on the day after November 3,

は最短でも次のアメリカ合衆国大統領選挙が行われる 2020 年 11 月 3 日の翌日以降となる。
iii）低炭素社会への国内の取り組み
　［1］法制度の整備
　　〈1〉地球温暖化対策推進法の改正等

　2013 年 5 月に成立した改正法により、政府は 2012 年度までの京都議定書に代わる、2013 年 4 月から 2020 年に向けて、地球温暖化対策のための新しい目標計画作りとその達成推進を国・地方公共団体に義務付けた。また政府は 2015 年 7 月に、温室効果ガス排出量を 2030 年度に 2013 年度比で 26％削減することを柱とする案を国連に提出するとともに、この目標達成のための必要な国内法改正も行っている（国民一人ひとりへの普及啓発、国際協力を通じた地球温暖化対策の推進、地域における地球温暖化対策の推進のために必要な措置）。
　　〈2〉地球温暖化対策税（温対税）の創設
　2012 年に成立。CO_2 排出税 289 円／CO_2 トンを従来の石油石炭税に上乗せして徴収し、化石燃料使用の抑制と再生可能エネルギー開発を促進する。石炭を例にとると、従来の石油石炭税 700 円／トンに排出税を段階的に加算する。その結果、2012 年から 220 円加算されて 920 円、2014 年からさらに 220 円加算されて 1,140 円、2016 年以降はさらに 230 円加算されて 1,370 円／トンとなった。

　　〈3〉再生可能エネルギー固定価格買取り制度
　2013 年 7 月から、法律に基づき CO_2 を出さないエネルギー（太陽光、風力、中小水力、地熱、バイオマス）により生産された電力を既存電力会社が全量買い取ることを義務付けた制度を実施している。
　［2］産業界の取り組み
　　〈1〉日本経済団体連合会（経団連）が、2009 年 12 月に作成し、2013 年 1 月に改定した「経団連低炭素社会実行計画」に基づき、参加企業は以下の基本方針を実行する。

2020, the date of the next U.S. presidential election.

iii) Domestic Initiatives Toward a Low Carbon Society
[1] Legislative Measures
<1> Amendment of Act on Promotion of Global Warming Countermeasures

The revised law that went into effect in May 2013 stipulates that the national and local governments are to replace efforts related to the Kyoto Protocol, which ended in 2012, with new global warming counter measures which promotes to achieve their goal from April 2013 to 2020. In July 2015, the government submitted a proposal to the United Nations to reduce greenhouse gas emissions by 26% compared to the fiscal 2013 level, and is undertaking the amendment of the requisite laws to achieve this goal (promotion of public awareness, promotion of measures to combat global warming through international cooperation, and measures to promote regional global warming countermeasures).

<2> New Tax for Combating Global Warming

This carbon dioxide emission tax was introduced in 2012. It is collected on top of already existing oil and coal taxes, eventually at the rate of 289 yen per metric ton of emitted carbon dioxide, as a measure for discouraging use of fossil fuels and encouraging development of renewable energy sources. In the case of coal, for example, the new levy is to be added to the usual tax of 700 yen per ton of coal at progressively higher rates until becoming equivalent to 289 yen per ton of emitted carbon dioxide. The additional tax was 220 yen in 2012 for a total of 920 yen/ton, was increased by 220 yen in 2014 for a total of 1,140 yen/ton, and was increased another 230 yen in 2016 for a total of 1,370 yen/ton.

<3> Fixed-Price Renewable Energy Purchase Program

From July 2013, large electric power companies are legally required to buy all carbon-dioxide-free electricity (from solar, wind, medium-scale hydro, geothermal, and biomass energy sources).

[2] Industry Efforts
<1> In December 2009, the Japan Business Federation (Keidanren) announced a program called Commitment to a Low Carbon Society. This initiative, as revised in January 2013, invites participants to implement the following key policies:

・世界最高水準の低炭素技術やエネルギー効率の維持・向上を社会に約束する。特に、国内事業活動から排出される CO_2 の 2020 年における削減目標を設定し、消費者・顧客を含めた主体間連携強化、途上国への環境省エネルギー（低炭素）技術の移転・普及などを通じた国際貢献の推進、革新的低炭素技術の開発を行う。

さらに、2014 年 7 月には、「日本産業界のさらなる挑戦」として、2020 年目標に加え 2030 年の目標等を設定した。この産業界の取り組みは、政府全体の温暖化政策の中でも、重要施策として位置づけられている。

〈2〉 再生可能エネルギー利用技術の開発

浮体式洋上風力発電、海洋エネルギー発電（潮力・波力発電、海流発電、海洋温度差発電）、地熱発電、雪氷熱エネルギーの利用（冷房、冷蔵庫）

〈3〉 低炭素化最新技術の開発

プラグインハイブリッドカー、充電インフラ整備、ワイヤレス送電技術（非接触送電）、次世代自動車（電気自動車、燃料電池自動車〈水素燃料〉）、高効率（全固体）電池など

2）生物多様性の保全

いろいろな野生生物は自然を豊かにするだけではなく、人間にとっても生存基盤を提供してくれており、その保全は非常に重要な取り組みである。

ⅰ）世界の野生生物の現状

世界で確認されている生物（動物・植物）の種の総数は、約 175 万種で、まだ知られていないものを含めると 500 万～3,000 万種と推定される。国際自然保護連合は、絶滅の恐れのある野生生物（絶滅危惧種）をまとめたレッドリストを作って警告している。

ⅱ）日本の野生生物の現状

日本で確認されている生物の種類の総数は約 9 万種で、まだ知られていない生物を含めると 30 万と推定される。38 万 km^2 の小さな国土にしては生物の種類は豊富である。環境省の作成した 2013 年のレッドリストでは、絶滅危惧種が約 3,600 種で 2007 年に比べて 400 種以上増えてい

- Pledge to provide society with world-leading low carbon technologies while maintaining and/or improving levels of energy efficiency. 2020 reduction targets were set for CO_2 emissions from domestic business activities, cooperation will be strengthened among entities including consumers and customers, the Ministry of the Environment will transfer low-carbon energy technology to developing countries to promote international contributions, and innovative low-carbon technologies will be developed.

In July 2014, in addition to the 2020 targets, 2030 targets were set as a "further challenge for Japanese industry." This industry effort is positioned as an important measure even within the government's overall global warming policy.

<2> Renewable Energy Utilization Technology Development

The chief energy sources targeted are wind (floating wind-turbines), sea energy (tidal energy, energy from waves, sea currents, and sea temperature differences), geothermal energy, and snow-and-ice cryogenic energy (for air conditioning and refrigerators).

<3> Development of New Low Carbon Technologies

R&D is focused on fields such as plug-in-hybrid cars, battery-charging infrastructure, wireless power transmission (contactless power transmission), next-generation vehicles (electric cars, fuel-cell cars that use hydrogen fuel), and high-efficiency (solid-state) batteries.

2) Preservation of Biodiversity

The preservation of biological diversity is profoundly important because wild species enrich nature and also underpin human survival.

i) The World's Wild Species

About 1.75 million species of plants and animals have been identified worldwide. The total number including those still unknown is estimated to be between 5 and 30 million. The Red List of Threatened Species compiled by the International Union for Conservation of Nature and Natural Resources enumerates many species in danger of extinction.

ii) Wild Species in Japan

The number of plant and animal species identified in Japan is about 90 thousand, and the total number including still unknown ones is believed to be around 300 thousand. This represents a rich biodiversity for a small country with a combined land and sea area of only 380 thousand square kilometers. The 2013 Red List compiled by the Ministry of the Environment identifies about 3,600 species threatened with extinction,

iii) 自然共生圏の構築

　　日本における「自然共生圏」づくりの政策実現の事例として、「トキ」の野生回復の試みがある。

　　「トキ（朱鷺）」は、ペリカンに類する大型の鳥で、東アジアに広く分布する。日本では、新潟や佐渡地方を代表する鳥であったが、野生のトキは絶滅した。1981年以降、30年以上にわたる野生トキ再生の努力が始まり、2012年に36年ぶりに自然環境でヒナが生まれ巣立った。

3) 持続可能な循環型社会の構築

　「リオ+20」以来、経済発展と環境保全とが両立するような「グリーン経済」社会をめざすことが、世界共通の流れとなった。持続可能な循環型社会の構築は、この流れの一環である。国内で議論されている第4次循環型社会推進基本計画の策定も重要である。ここでは、日本における取組状況について解説する。

ⅰ) 日本の物質フロー

　　2015年の日本の物質総量の流れを大まかにみると、総投入量16.1億トンで、このうち5.0億トンが建物・道路・港湾などの社会インフラとして蓄積され、1.8億トンが製品として輸出され、5.2億トンがエネルギー消費および工業プロセス排出で、5.6億トンが廃棄物等の発生となっている。

　　廃棄物は、大きく産業廃棄物と一般廃棄物の二つに区分されており、産業廃棄物の発生量は3.9億トンで廃棄物のうち2.8億トン（53%）が回収・循環再利用されている。また一般廃棄物の発生量は4千万トンであった。循環再利用量は、総投入量の約16%である。廃棄物の排出量は2015年までの過去25年間はほぼ横ばいであるが、リサイクル率はこの間に10%あまり向上した（2018年環境白書）。

ⅱ) 政府の取り組み（3Rの推進）

　　政府は、「循環型社会形成推進基本法」（2001年1月施行）において、3Rの推進を産業界と国民に呼びかけている。3Rとは生産活動と市民生活における次の3+2の取り組みである。循環型社会の構築には、企業活動や国民のライフスタイルにおいて3Rの取り組みが浸透し、恒常的な活

an increase of more than 400 species from the 2007 list.

iii) Creating a Harmonious Natural Community

One notable Japanese effort to create a "symbiotic community" is the initiative to return the crested ibis to its natural habitat.

The crested ibis (*Nipponia nippon*) is a large bird of the pelican family once seen widely throughout East Asia. Although it used to be a bird representative of the Niigata and Sado regions, it became extinct in the wild. The effort to restore the bird to its natural habitat that began in 1981 made a big step forward in 2012, when a crested ibis chick became the first in Japan in 36 years to hatch in the wild and leave its nest.

3) Building a Sustainable Recycling-Based Society

Since Rio+20, the global tide has turned toward the realization of a "green economy" society that can grow the economy and preserve the environment at the same time. The creation of a sustainable recycling-based society is an essential step toward this goal. It is also important to formulate a basic plan for promoting the fourth recycling-based society under discussion in Japan. This section describes the efforts being made here.

i) Japanese Material Flows

Total Japanese material flows in 2015 can be roughly summarized to total input of 1,610 million tons, of which 500 million tons were accumulated as buildings, roads, ports and other national infrastructure, 180 million tons was exported as products, 520 million tons was used for energy consumption and industrial processes and the like, and 560 million tons was disposed of as waste.

Waste is broadly classified into industrial waste and general waste. Industrial waste amounted to 390 million tons, of which 280 million tons (53%) was recovered and recycled. Forty million tons of general waste was generated. The amount recycled was about 16% of total input. The amount of waste disposal has remained nearly flat over the past 25 years until 2015, but the recycle rate improved about 10% during the same period (2018 Environment White Paper).

ii) Government Efforts (Promoting the 3Rs)

In line with the Basic Act for Establishing a Sound Material-Cycle Society (implemented in January 2001), the government is urging both businesses and individuals to help achieve the 3Rs (since amplified to the following 3Rs+2). To build a recycle-oriented society, the 3Rs efforts have to become a permanent part of corporate activities and citizens' lifestyles and behavior. To that end, there has to be close coop-

動や行動として定着していく必要がある、そのため、国や地方公共団体、民間企業等が密接に連携し、社会行動として定着していくことが必要である。

〈1〉 Reduce：削減・発生抑制。まず生産活動や日常生活の初めの段階で原材料の投入量を抑え、廃棄物やごみを出さないようにする。

〈2〉 Reuse：再使用。使ったものをきれいにして、そのまま繰り返し使う。水、ビール瓶（びん）、中古自動車、中古住宅など。

〈3〉 Recycle：再生利用。廃棄物となった製品を加工して（分解、溶融、使用目的変更）、新しい製品の原料にする。スチール缶やアルミ缶、古紙、きもの、製鉄の廃棄物からそれぞれ新しい缶、ダンボール、ドレス、セメントや炭素繊維を作るなど。

3Rの後はさらに、

〈4〉 排熱回収：ごみ焼却場の排熱で公衆浴場などの湯を沸かす。

〈5〉 適正処分：利用不能な最終廃棄物は、最も環境負荷が少ない方法で処分する。

政府は、上記〈1〉～〈5〉の順序に従って廃棄物処理を進めるよう呼びかけている。

個別には次のような各種の循環関連法制度を整備し、環境負荷の少ない物質循環を目指している。（各法律名は通称）・容器リサイクル法 ・家電リサイクル法 ・食品リサイクル法 ・建設リサイクル法 ・自動車リサイクル法 ・小型家電リサイクル法 ・農林漁業バイオ燃料法 ・PCB特措法など。

iii) 産業界の廃棄物再資源化の取り組み

〈1〉 容器

容器の回収は事業者と市町村（市民）が実施しており、2016年度のペットボトルの回収率は事業系ボトル回収量と全国の市町村分別収集量を合わせて88.8％で、リサイクル率では83.9％あった。プラスチック容器の回収率は84.0％であった。2016年にはアルミ缶

eration between the national and local governments private enterprises so the necessary behavior becomes socially established.

<1> Reduce

Minimize the amount of material used at the initial stage of production and daily life activities to reduce waste and garbage.

<2> Reuse

Keep things in good condition and use them repeatedly (water and beer bottles, cars, houses, and so on).

<3> Recycle

Process discarded products (dismantle, melt, devote to new purpose, etc.) and use as material for new products. Make new cans out of used steel and aluminum cans, cardboard out of waste paper, dresses out of no longer needed *kimonos*, and cement and carbon fiber out of steelmaking waste.

On top of the 3Rs,

<4> Recover Heat

Use heat from garbage incinerators to heat water for public baths and other purposes.

<5> Optimize Disposal

Dispose of unusable final waste in the way that puts the smallest burden on the environment.

For maximum effect, the five steps should be followed in the order mentioned.

In addition, a number of purpose-specific laws and regulations have been enforced to reduce the environmental burden of recycling containers, home appliances, food, buildings, automobiles, and small home appliances, as well as deal with agriculture, forestry and fishery biofuels, and provide special measures regarding PCBs (Polychlorinated biphenyl).

iii) Industrial Efforts to Promote the Recovery of Resources

<1> Containers

Containers are recovered by companies and local governments (residents). In 2016, the PET bottle recovery rate was 88.8%, which includes the amounts of bottles recovered by businesses and the nationwide collection of bottles sorted at the local level, and the recycling rate was 83.9%. Plastic container recovery was 84.0%. In 2016, 20.7 billion, or 92.4%, of 22.4 billion used aluminum cans were recovered. The ratio of

は224億缶使用されて、その内回収されたのは207億缶92.4％であった。また、回収されたアルミ缶を再びアルミ缶にする〈CAN TO CAN〉の割合は62.8％であった。スチール缶は46.3万トン使用され、リサイクル率は93.9％であった。

〈2〉 家電

2001年に本格施行された家電リサイクル法により、家電メーカーは家庭用家電4品目について、種類別に一定割合の廃品再商品化が義務づけられた。2016年の廃品の引き取り総数は1,120万台で、廃品再商品化率は、エアコン92％、テレビ89％、冷蔵庫81％、洗濯機など90％で、いずれも法定の基準を上回った。

〈3〉 自動車

使用済みの自動車は、2002年成立の自動車リサイクル法に従って、廃車引取、エアコンのフロンガスの回収、解体業者でのエンジン、ドアなどの有用部材の回収、破砕業者による鉄などの金属の回収の工程を経て最後に残った破砕残さ（シュレッダーダスト）が廃棄される。2016年度の自動車破砕残さおよびエアバッグ類の再資源化率は、それぞれ97.3～98.7％、93～94％と高達成率となっている。

〈4〉 鉄鋼業の資源循環利用の現状

日本の製鉄業は、副産物の再利用、排熱回収・副生ガス利用などの省エネルギー設備の開発・普及で世界の最先端レベルにある。

例えば・日本製鉄の2018年版「環境・社会報告書」によると、同社の鉄鋼生産プロセスにおける水の循環率は90％、高炉スラグ（溶けて固まった石灰石）などの再資源化率は99％（セメント・路盤材など）、排熱回収による鉄鋼製造エネルギー効率70％などとなっている。この結果、同社の製鉄副産物（排出物）の再資源化率は99％で、最終処分物質（利用不能なごみ）は製品重量の1％である。年産4,000万トンの製鉄会社で最終的に捨てられるものは40万トンだけである。

recovered cans used to make new aluminum cans (can-to-can rate) was 62.8%. Of 463 thousand tons of steel used for steel cans, 93.9% came from recycled steel.

<2> Home Electric Appliances

The Home Appliance Recycle Act that went into effect in 2001 requires home electric appliance manufacturers to reuse four categories of home electric appliances to make new products, at a prescribed recycle rate for each category. The total number of discarded products collected in 2016 was 11.20 million units, and the rate of reuse in new products was 92% for air conditioners, 89% for TVs, 81% for refrigerators, and 90% for washing machines. All of these percentages were higher than legally required.

<3> Automobiles

The Automobile Recycling Act which has been in effect since 2002 stipulates that when an automobile is scrapped, it must be accepted for disposal, any Freon gas is to be recovered from the air conditioner, useful engine, door, and other components must be recovered by the vehicle disassembler, steel and other metals are to be recovered at the demolishing (shredding) station, and finally the remaining shredder dust is to be disposed of as waste. In fiscal 2016, the recycling rates of automobile residual crush and airbags were 97.3 to 98.7% and 93 to 94% respectively, which are high rates.

<4> Recycling Resources in Steel Industry

The Japanese steel industry is a world leader in the reuse of byproducts, the development and deployment of exhaust heat recovery, byproduct gas utilization, and other energy-saving equipment.

According to *Sustainability Report 2018* issued by Nippon Steel Corporation, 90% of the water used in the company's steelmaking processes is recycled, 99% of blast furnace slag (melted and resolidified limestone) and other byproducts are recycled (for use in cement, pavement, and the like), and 70% of the energy exhausted as heat during iron and steel production is reused. On weight basis, Nippon Steel Corporation can therefore convert 99% of its steelmaking byproducts into usable resources and restrict the ratio of final (unusable) waste to 1% of product weight. So while it makes 40 million tons of steel per year, Nippon Steel Corporation throws away only 0.4 million tons of material as unusable waste.

日本の鉄鋼エネルギー効率（鉄1トン当たりに要する石油換算エネルギー消費量）は世界で最も高いことがIEA（国際エネルギー機関）によっても認められている。また製鉄所内の発生エネルギーによる自家発電は78％となっている。

d）国民の取り組み

近年、スーパーでのマイバッグの普及率（レジ袋の使用の遠慮）は60％を超え、家庭ごみの分別収集も全国的に普及した。日本は2012年のアルミ缶、スチール缶、ビールびんなどの回収率でも世界のトップクラスである。他方、家庭ゴミの排出量はまだ削減の余地が大きい。

2015年の全国の食品関連廃棄物は約2,600万トンで、うち肥料化や飼料化など再生利用量は1,500万トンでその他は廃棄された。この内そのまま食べられる弁当やハンバーガーなどの「食品ロス」だけでも約650万トンと推計される。これは重量比較では、日本のコメの年間収穫量に匹敵し、千数百万人分の食事に相当する。そのうち家庭からの「食品ロス」は、国民1人当たり1年で15 kgと試算されているので、国民にも食品の3Rの第1段階で、食材を買いすぎないように努めることが求められている。

e）最近の重要なキーワード

〈1〉カーボン・ディスクロージャー・プロジェクト（CDP：Carbon Disclosure Project）

世界の機関投資家が連携し、企業に対して気候変動への戦略や具体的な温室効果ガスの排出量に関する公表を求める取り組み。2000年に開始され、主要国の時価総額の上位企業に対し、毎年、質問票を送付して回答を回収・集約する。取り組みに対する評価が公表される。企業価値を図る重要な指標になりつつある。

〈2〉エス・ビー・ティー（SBT：Science Based Targets）

2015年のパリ協定の採択を契機に、世界自然保護基金（WWF）、CDP、国連グローバル・コンパクトおよびWRI（世界資源研究所）が共同で設立した国際連携。科学的根拠に基づいた温室効果ガスの排出量削減目標の設定を促すことを目的としている。

The International Energy Agency (IEA) has determined that Japan's steelmaking energy efficiency (petroleum-equivalent energy consumption per ton of crude steel) is the world's highest. In addition, 78% of the self-generated electricity is generated by the energy produced inside the steelworks.

d) Community Efforts

At Japanese supermarkets, over 60% of shoppers are now bringing their own shopping bag (to avoid using a checkout counter bag), and people throughout the country are sorting their household trash and garbage. In 2012, aluminum cans, steel cans, beer bottles, and similar items were recovered at a higher rate in Japan than in most other countries. On the downside, there was plenty of room to reduce household garbage.

In 2015, nationwide food-related waste amounted to around 26 million tons, of which 15 million tons was recycled as fertilizer and feed, and the rest discarded. Some 6.5 million tons of this is estimated to be wasted food in the form of still edible box-lunch items, hamburgers, and other discarded leftovers. This wasted food weighed approximately as much Japan's annual rice harvest and was enough to feed well over 10 million people. The amount of household "food loss" is believed to be 15 kilograms per person per year. People need to abide by the first 3R rule for food—not buy more than they need.

e) Recent Important Keywords

<1> CDP (Carbon Disclosure Project)

The CDP endeavors to get institutional investors around the world to announce corporate strategies for dealing with climate change and specific amount of greenhouse gas emissions. Since 2000 it has sent questionnaires every year to top companies in terms of market capitalization and collected and collated responses. CDP publishes evaluations of corporate endeavors. It is becoming an important indicator of enterprise value.

<2> SBT (Science Based Targets)

An international collaboration jointly established by the World Wildlife Fund (WWF), CDP, the United Nations Global Compact, and WRI (World Resource Institute), with the adoption of the Paris Agreement in 2015. It aims to encourage the setting of greenhouse gas emission reduction targets based on scientific grounds.

〈3〉 イー・エス・ジー（ESG：Environment Social and Governance）

　企業の長期的な成長のためには、環境、社会およびガバナンスの3つの観点が必要という考えが世界的に広まってきている。機関投資家の間で急速に広がってきており、投資の意思決定において、ESGも考慮に入れる手法は「ESG投資」と呼ばれている。

　（注）ESG投資：機関投資家は、気候変動に対する金融市場の社会的責任の観点から、株式を保有することによって企業経営に影響を及ぼしていくという「エンゲージメント」（行動）あるいは一定の投資判断基準に基づいて特定企業の株式を投資対象から除外する「ダイベストメント」という動きが活発になりつつある。

〈4〉 カーボン・プライシング（炭素価格付け：Carbon Pricing）

　炭素の排出量に価格付けを行うこと。「排出量取引」と「炭素税」がある。日本においては、地球温暖化対策税（温対税：289円／CO_2トン）がある。さらにエネルギー税（石油・石炭税、揮発油税、軽油取引税等）なども隠れた「炭素税」として評価できる。日本の炭素税は決して低くはない。

〈5〉 サーキュラー・エコノミー（循環経済：Circular Economy）

　資源の効率的利用および循環型社会を目指した社会

〈6〉 海のプラスチックごみ汚染対策

　世界でプラスチックごみの生産量が増加して年間3億トンを超え、海に流出する量も最大推定量が年間1,200万トンに及んでいる。プラスチックごみをのみ込んだ魚介類を通じて人間の健康を脅かすリスクがある（OECD報告書）。このため、当面は各企業の判断によりプラスチックストローの廃止や紙による代替化、レジ袋の有料化などの対策がとられている。化学メーカーは微生物によって分解される生分解性プラスチック製品の開発を急いでいる。

<3> ESG (Environment, Social and Governance)

The idea that the three perspectives of environmental, society and governance are necessary for corporate long-term growth is globally widespread. It is spreading rapidly among institutional investors, and methods that take ESG into consideration in investment decision-making are called "ESG investing."

(Note) ESG Investing: From the viewpoint of the social responsibility of financial markets vis-à-vis climate change, institutional investors increasingly consider pursuing "engagement" that seeks to influence corporate management by holding shares, or "divestment" in which shares of a specific company are ruled out as an investment target based on certain investment judgment criteria.

<4> Carbon Pricing

The pricing of carbon emissions. There are "emissions trading" and "carbon taxes." In Japan, there is a tax for combating global warming, which is 289 yen per metric ton of emitted carbon dioxide. Energy taxes (oil, coal, and volatile-oil tax, diesel trading tax, etc.) can also be considered as a hidden carbon tax. Japan's carbon taxes are not low.

<5> Circular Economy

Efficient use of resources and a society aiming to be a recycling-oriented society

<6> Measures Against Marine Plastic Waste Contamination

The amount of plastic garbage produced worldwide has increased to over 300 million tons annually, and the amount estimated to enter the ocean is up to 12 million tons per year. Due to ecological food chain, fish and shellfish that have ingested plastic waste is a threat to human health (OECD report). For the time being, therefore, companies are independently deciding to take measures such as abolishing plastic straws, using paper instead of plastic, and charging for plastic bags. Chemical industries are rushing to develop biodegradable plastic products that are degraded by microorganisms.

6 科学技術

　天然資源に恵まれない日本にとっては、人の知的創造力こそが最大の資源である。国民が安心して経済的・文化的に豊かな生活を享受するためは、日本の科学技術の果たす役割は諸外国以上に大きいといえる。
　国際社会においても日本の科学技術は、地球環境、食糧問題、医療、資源、エネルギーなどの人類共通の諸問題について積極的に貢献することが期待されている。

　日本の科学技術は、21世紀の科学技術分野のノーベル賞受賞者がアメリカ、イギリスに次いで世界第3位、特許出願数が第3位など一定の実績をあげている。しかし、産業のグローバル化・ボーダレス化に伴い、発展途上国への技術移転が急速かつ広範囲に進み、日本の国際競争力を支えてきた科学技術のかつての優位性は相対的に後退しつつある。

　国家の国際競争力の優位性を確保するためには、イノベーションの推進、研究成果の経済産業活動への反映、人材育成につき不断の努力が必要とされる。
　また近年では、人口知能（AI）やあらゆるモノをインターネットでつないでやりとりする IoT などの先端技術を組み合わせて活用し、産業の生産性を高めたり、新しい事業・サービスを創出したりする取り組みである「第4次産業革命」を推進して行くことも日本の国際競争力を高める上で欠かすことができない。

(1) 先端科学技術

a) ライフサイエンス分野

1) iPS 細胞の作製

　　近年のこの分野における最も顕著な成果は、京都大学山中伸弥教授のノーベル賞受賞（2012年）の根拠となった iPS 細胞の作製と用途の開発である。

　　山中教授はヒトの体細胞の中に約2万個あるといわれる遺伝子の中のわずか4つの特定遺伝子（山中ファ

6 Science and Technology

As a country with few natural resources, Japan's greatest asset is the intellectual creativity of its people. Role of science and technology plays to help citizens enjoy economically and culturally rich life is greater in Japan than in most of other countries.

The international community expects Japan to vigorously apply its scientific and technological capabilities to solving problems common to all mankind, in areas like the global environment, food, medicine, resources, and energy.

Japanese achievements in science and technology have become more evident in current years. For example, Japan is now in third place behind the United States (U.S.) and the United Kingdom (UK) in number of science-category Nobel Prize winners in the 21st century and ranks third in number of patent applications. However, advances in industrial globalization and borderless competition have rapidly accelerated and expanded the range of technology transfers to emerging nations. For Japan this has meant a decline in the relative technological superiority that has long underpinned its international competitiveness.

In order to ensure national competitive strength, Japan must make persistent efforts to promote innovation, reflect research results in economic and industrial activities, and develop human resources.

The promotion in recent years of the fourth industrial revolution is also indispensable for enhancing Japan's international competitiveness by combining and utilizing advanced technologies such as artificial intelligence (AI) and the Internet of Things (IoT) technology that connects everything to the Internet, to increase industrial productivity and create new businesses and services.

(1) Advanced Science and Technology

a) Life Sciences

1) Generation of iPS Cells

The most notable advance in this field in recent years was the development of techniques for generating and using iPS cells by Yamanaka Shinya, a professor at Kyoto University, for which he received a Nobel Prize (2012).

Yamanaka identified four specific genes (Yamanaka factors) among approximately 20 thousand genes in a human cell, that when introduced

クター）をヒトの皮膚や血液などの成熟した細胞に移して数週間培養すると、この細胞が再び未成熟な状態に戻り（初期化あるいはリプログラミングされ）、ほぼすべての種類の臓器に分化できる能力と、無限に増殖する能力を持ったiPS細胞（induced pluripotents stemcells：人工多能性幹細胞）に変わることを発見し、膨大な回数の実験によってこれを実証した。

　このiPS細胞作製方法は、再現できる確率が高く、別の方法（将来ヒトになれるかもしれない受精卵や胚細胞を利用する方法）のような生命倫理的な問題も少なく拒否反応の少ない画期的な技術であり、幹細胞研究に新しい活路を開いたものと評価された。

　iPS細胞開発の確立は、再生医療（細胞組織移植による臓器の機能回復）および難病や希少疾患の創薬（新たな医薬品が製品となるまでの一連の過程）の可能性をもたらすものとして期待されている。
　具体的な応用例では、再生医療としては、理化学研究所多細胞システム形成研究センター網膜再生医療研究開発プロジェクトの髙橋政代プロジェクトリーダーらは、「滲出型加齢黄斑変性」の患者を対象として眼球の網膜に患者の皮膚から作製したiPS細胞のシートを移植する臨床研究を実施した。また、京都大学iPS細胞研究所の高橋淳教授らは、2018年10月に、健康な人のiPS細胞から脳の神経細胞を作り、パーキンソン病患者に移植する世界初の臨床試験（治験）の手術を京都大学附属病院で行った。保険適用を見据えた治験のため、早期の実用化への期待が高まっている。

・治験（implementation of clinical trials and studies）：新しい薬や医療機器を保険が適用される一般的な診療で使えるよう国に承認してもらうため、データを集める試験のこと。
　一方、創薬分野での応用の第一歩となった対象は、筋肉が骨に変わる難病「進行性骨化性線維異形成症（FOP）」の患者への治験で、患者の細胞から作ったiPS細胞を利用して病気を再現して、約6,800種類の

into mature human skin, blood or other cells and cultured for a few weeks cause these cells to return to their undifferentiated state (that is, to initialize or reprogram them) and change into iPS cells (induced pluripotent stem cells), which have the ability to differentiate into nearly any type of organ and the ability to self-renew without limit. Yamanaka verified his findings by performing a huge number of experiments.

This method of generating iPS cells is a revolutionary technology that offers high reproducibility and involves fewer bioethical issues and rejection risks than other methods (ones using fertilized eggs or embryonic stem cells that had the potential to develop into a human being). It has been applauded as a method that opens new possibilities for stem cell research.

The ability to generate iPS cells is expected to lead to advancements in regenerative medicine (restoration of organ functions by transplanting cells or tissue) and discovery of drugs for intractable and rare diseases.

Examples of specific applications in the field of regenerative medicine include the work of Takahashi Masayo, project leader of the retinal regeneration R&D project in the RIKEN (Japan's largest comprehensive research institution) Center for Developmental Biology (RIKEN CDB). Takahashi is conducting clinical research on transplanting iPS cell sheets generated from the skin of patients to the retina of patients suffering from wet-type age-related macular degeneration (AMD). Also, in October 2018, Takahashi Jun of the Center for iPS Cell Research and Application (CiRA) at Kyoto University created brain nerve cells from the iPS cells of a healthy person and transplanted them into a patient with Parkinson's disease in a surgical procedure as a part of clinical trials conducted at Kyoto University Hospital, which was the first transplant of its kind in the world. Because this clinical trial was conducted for developing a method that can be covered under Japan's health insurance system, many are hoping that it can be quickly adopted for practical use.

- Implementation of clinical trials and studies: conducting of trials that collect data for receiving government approval so that new medicines and medical equipment can be used for general medical care that is covered under health insurance.

On the other hand, in the drug development field, as a first step for practical application, clinical trials were conducted for patients with fibrodysplasia ossificans progressiva (FOP), an intractable disease where muscle tissue turns to bone. In these clinical trials, iPS cells

化合物を個々に細胞にふりかけ、効果のある既存薬を特定し治験を開始した。iPS細胞と既存薬を組み合わせることで、費用の大幅削減と開発効率の向上が期待されている。同様にアルツハイマー型認知症の患者から作ったiPS細胞を使い、発症の原因物質を減らす薬の組み合わせを探し、その結果パーキンソン病とぜんそく、てんかんの3種類の既存薬を同時に加えると最も効果があることをつきとめ臨床試験を進めている。

2）生命プログラムの研究

あらゆる生物は生命の設計図、DNA（染色体はDNAが凝縮したもの）で成り立ち、ヒトであれば37兆個という細胞ひとつひとつの中にある。このDNAの遺伝情報のすべてがゲノムであり、ヒトゲノム（約30億の塩基対）配列の精密解読が完了している。遺伝子はDNAが数千・数万個が集まって一つの遺伝形質を決定する機能をもつ。そして遺伝子はRNAに転写されて伝わる情報で、細胞中で活発な調整機能を担っている。こうした最新の知見によって、細菌やウイルスによる感染症やがんなど様々な慢性疾患に対抗する新しい実験的医薬を作ることが可能になった。

理化学研究所では、ゲノム科学の分野でDNAやRNAがどう調和し、どんな役割を果たしているか、生命情報の三次元ネットワークが時系列でどうなっていくかを研究するために、世界最高速クラスの「分子動力学専用計算機（MDGRAPE-4）」を開発したほか、物質の動きを見ることができるシャッター速度世界一の「超解像蛍光顕微鏡」も開発し研究に取り組んでいる。

・DNA（Deoxyribonucleic Acid・デオキシリボ核酸）：人間や動物、植物、細菌といった生物の遺伝情報の蓄積・保存と伝達を担う遺伝物質
・RNA（Ribonucleic Acid・リボ核酸）：DNAと同様な機能を有するが、常に存在するのではなく、必要に応じて合成・分解され、遺伝子として働く場合には、ウイルスの遺伝情報の保存と伝達を担う

3）動植物のゲノム研究

稲ゲノムの完全解読をもとに、さらに微生物・動物・植物のゲノム研究を進め、狙った遺伝子を効率良

created from patient cells were used to recreate the disease, and about 6,800 compounds were distributed to individual cells for identifying effective existing medicines and starting clinical trials. The process of combining iPS cells and existing medicines is expected to significantly reduce treatment costs and improve development efficiency. Similarly, iPS cells created from patients with Alzheimer-type dementia are used to find combinations of medicines that reduce the substances that trigger onset of the disease, and simultaneous use of existing medicines for Parkinson's disease, asthma, and epilepsy are added to these results to pinpoint the most effective treatment for conducting clinical trials.

2) Human Genome Related Research

All living things are built from DNA, the blueprint of life, (chromosomes contain tightly-packaged DNA) and DNA is found in each cell, which number 37 trillion in humans. All of the genetic information for the DNA is the genome. The sequencing of human genome (consisting of about 3 billion base pairs) has been completed. A gene is a collection of several thousand or several tens of thousands of DNA bases that determine a single hereditary trait. The gene is also information that is transcribed and transferred to RNA, and genes provide active adjustment functions within the cell. These latest finding have enabled the creation of new experimental medicines for infectious diseases caused by bacteria and viruses and for cancer and a wide range of other chronic diseases.

The RIKEN research institute has developed a special-purpose high-speed computer for simulations of molecular dynamics, the MDGRAPE-4, that is among the fastest in the world, to study how to ensure consistency of DNA and RNA in the field of genomics, the roles that DNA and RNA play, and how the 3D network of life information changes over time. RIKEN is also engaged in research and development of a super-resolved fluorescence microscope, which has the world's fastest shutter speed and enables viewing of how matter moves.

- DNA (Deoxyribonucleic Acid): Hereditary material that collects, stores, and transfers genetic information for living things such as humans, animals, plants, and bacteria.
- RNA (Ribonucleic Acid): Although RNA has the same functions as DNA, it is not always present, and it is synthesized and disintegrated when necessary. When acting as a gene, it saves and transfers the genetic information of viruses.

3) Animal and Plant Genome Research

Now that the rice plant genome has been completely determined, researchers are focusing on the genomes of microbes, animals, and

く改変できる新技術「ゲノム編集」を農作物の品種改良に用いる研究が進んでいる。細胞内の4種類の「塩基」を狙い通りに切り貼りし、画期的な新品種の開発・品種改良・育成技術の開発などによる食の安全性・自給率向上に取り組む。

農業・食品産業技術総合研究機構のチームは、「イネ」の試験栽培を始めた。世界的な食料不足の解決には、品種改良が不可欠として、植えたイネはもみの数が増え、米粒も大きくなると期待される。

一方、筑波大学のチームは「トマト」の試験栽培を始め、リラックス効果があるとされるアミノ酸「GABA」が従来の15倍多いトマトができたと発表した。

しかしながら、海外と違い日本国内では、遺伝子組み換え作物の安全性や生態系への影響を懸念する声が強い。観賞用のバラを除き、組み換え作物は商業栽培されていない。

b) 超電導技術

[リニア中央新幹線の起工]

最高設計速度505 km/hの高速走行が可能な超電導磁気浮上式リニアモーターカー（超電導リニア）が、まず、2027年に東京（品川駅）—名古屋駅間を最速40分で結ぶ予定で建設・開業され、さらに、2037年に東京—大阪の全線開業（最速67分）と予定されている。

超電導リニアは、車両に搭載した超電導磁石と地上に取り付けられたコイルとの間の磁力によって、浮上高さが約10 cmに達して走行する輸送システムで、2015年4月には、有人走行で鉄道の世界最高速度となる時速603 kmを記録した。航空機並みのスピードで多くの乗客を一度に輸送できる新しい高速輸送システムである。

鉄道のリニア技術には2種類があり、「常電導方式」と「超電導方式」で、常電導方式では車体を1 cm程度浮上させて走行し、中国の上海に導入されている。また、常電導吸引型リニア（リニモの名称）で日本の名古屋に導入されている。しかしながら高速で安定した走行を目指すには超電導方式が必要となる。

other plants, and are conducting research on the new technology of genome editing, which enables efficient modification of target genes for developing improved varieties of farm crops. The four bases in cells are cut and added in the desired order, with the aim of improving food safety and self-sufficiency through the development of revolutionary new species and advances in selective breeding and cultivation technology.

A team at the National Agriculture and Food Research Organization (NARO) has started test growing of rice plants. Improved varieties of foods are essential for resolving global food shortages, and the planted rice is expected to have an increased number of husks and larger grains.

A team at Tsukuba University reported that they started test growing of tomatoes and have developed a tomato which has up to 15 times the normal amount of the amino acid GABA, which is said to have relaxing effects.

However, in contrast to some other countries, in Japan there is strong concern about the safety of genetically-modified crops and their impact on the ecosystem. Except for roses for ornamental purposes, genetically-modified crops are not raised for commercial purposes.

b) Superconducting Technology
Start of Construction on the Linear Chuo Shinkansen

Plans are underway to construct a high-speed superconductive maglev (SCMaglev) linear motor car which has a maximum design speed of 505 kilometers per hour. Scheduled to open in 2027, it will connect Tokyo (Shinagawa station) and Nagoya station in 40 minutes, and the entire line between Tokyo and Osaka (67 minutes) is expected to open in 2037.

An SCMaglev is a transportation system where train cars are levitated to a height of about 10 cm through the magnetic force between superconductive magnets installed in the train cars and coils installed on the ground. In April 2015, this train system reached a speed of 603 kilometers per hour, which is the world's fastest speed ever recorded for a manned train. It is a new high-speed transportation system capable of mass transportation of large numbers of passengers at speeds rivaling airplanes.

There are two types of railway linear motor maglev technology, a normal conductivity system and a superconductivity system. In a normal conductivity system, the train car runs by levitating at about 1 cm, and this system is currently being used in Shanghai, China. A normal conductivity linear motor maglev train (Linimo) is also operating in Nagoya. However, a superconductivity system is required to achieve

超電導方式では、ある種の金属・合金・酸化物を一定温度以下に冷やすと、電気抵抗がゼロになる「超電導現象」が生まれる。超電導状態になったコイルに一度電流を流せば、電流は永遠に流れ続け、強力なパワーをもつ超電導磁石となる。日本のリニアは超電導材料としてニオブチタン合金を使用し、液体ヘリウムで−269℃まで冷却することで超電導状態を作り出している。この「超電導現象」を生み出すのが技術的に極めて難しい。日本の旧国鉄（JR）でリニアモーターカーの研究が始まったのは1962年で、半世紀以上もかけた研究の蓄積がようやく実を結ぼうとしている。また最近では、超電導臨界温度が−163℃のビスマス系の超電導体をコイルとした超電導磁石が走行試験に採用され、さらなる信頼性の向上を検討している。

c）発光ダイオード（LED）

　発光ダイオードはLEDとも呼ばれるが、これはLight Emitting Diodeの略号である。ダイオードとは昔の2極真空管のことで、LEDは現在、2極端子の発光半導体素子の呼び名になっている。

　発光ダイオードは、一定方向に電圧をかけた場合に光を発する。最初の発明は、1962年であったが、当初は赤色しか出せなかった。この発光原理は、白熱電灯や蛍光灯とは基本的に異なるので、高い発熱や大きな電力の消費を伴わないのが特徴である。

　LEDは、材料の違いでさまざまな色を出すことも知られていた。しかし、1985年ごろまでは赤色だけで青と緑の発光体は使い物にはならなかった。

　その後、日本の3人のノーベル賞（2014年物理学賞）学者の赤崎勇名城大学教授、天野浩名古屋大学教授、中村修二米カリフォルニア大学サンタバーバラ校教授により、青色のLEDが開発され、すべての色を表わすことが可能になった。ノーベル賞の受賞理由は、「明るくエネルギー消費の少ない白色光源を可能にした高効率な青色LEDの発明」で、「20世紀は白熱灯が照らし、21世紀はLEDが照らす」と説明された。

　今日、LEDは、消費電力が少なく、発光させ続けても

stable running at high speeds.

In a superconductivity system, when certain metals, alloys, and oxides are cooled to below a fixed temperature, a state of superconductivity occurs in which their electrical resistance becomes zero. If a current is made to flow through a coil in a superconductive state, the current will continue to flow indefinitely, forming a high-power superconductive magnet. Japan's linear motor maglev trains use niobium-titanium alloy as their superconductive material, and their superconductive state is created by cooling to $-269°C$ using liquid helium. Technically, it is extremely difficult to create this state of superconductivity. Research into maglev linear motor cars started in Japan in 1962 under the former Japan National Railway (present-day "JR"), and the accumulated research from more than half a century is finally leading to the significant results seen today. Recently, superconductive magnets of bismuth superconductor coils having a superconducting critical temperature of $-163°C$ are being used in test runs to study their feasibility for providing even higher reliability.

c) Light-Emitting Diode (LED)

The light-emitting diode or LED is a semiconductor device that emits light. It is called a "diode" because, like the old vacuum tube of the same name, it has two active electrodes.

The LED emits light when a forward bias voltage is applied across the electrodes. The first LED, invented in 1962, emitted only red light. Operating on a fundamentally different principle from those of incandescent and fluorescent lamps, the LED is characterized by low heat emission and low power consumption.

Although it was known that LEDs could be made to emit various colors by using different materials, only the red LED was usable up until around 1985, and those that emitted blue or green light, for example, were useless.

Subsequently, in 2014 Akasaki Isamu of Meijo University, Amano Hiroshi of Nagoya University, and Nakamura Shuji of the University of California, Santa Barbara, were awarded the Nobel Prize in Physics for their development of a blue LED, making it possible to express all colors. The Nobel Prize was awarded "for the invention of efficient blue light-emitting diodes which has enabled bright and energy-saving white light sources." The Nobel Foundation added that "incandescent light bulbs lit the 20th century; the 21st century will be lit by LED lamps."

Nowadays, with their low power consumption, long life, and low

低温で寿命が長いため、スマートフォンや液晶テレビのバックライトを始め、照明、信号機、自動車、自転車、電光掲示板、広告塔など様々なところで利用されている。現在は、省エネルギーの観点からさらに大容量・高輝度LEDの開発が進められている。

d）宇宙開発

1）イプシロンロケット

2013年9月、日本の宇宙航空研究開発機構（JAXA）は、新型ロケット「イプシロン」第1号機を打ち上げた。イプシロンロケットは、直径2.6m、長さ24.4m、重さ91トンの小型ロケットで、日本が独自開発したH-ⅡA以来12年間の研究の集大成である。日本で現在活躍しているロケットはこのほかH-ⅡBがあり、打ち上げの成功率は97％以上で信頼性が極めて高い。イプシロンロケットは、いくつかの革新的特徴を持っている。

〈1〉固体燃料の使用：これは酸素と水素の液体燃料に比べ、ロケットの構造も簡素化でき、燃料の設置も簡単で、打ち上げ時の天候の変化にも即応できる。

〈2〉蓄積技術の活用：1段目はH-ⅡAの補助ブースターを転用し、2、3段目には世界最高性能とされたM-V（ミュー5）ロケットの上段モーターをさらに改良して搭載した。その結果、1回の打ち上げ費用は38億円とM-Vの半分まで削減できた。

〈3〉モバイル管制の開発：イプシロンロケットは内部に人工知能が組み込まれ、1万8,000項目の点検を1秒で完了できる。この結果、今まで100人で40日余りを要していた打ち上げ準備作業を数名のオペレーターで7日で終わることができる革新的システムである。

2）小惑星探査機「はやぶさ」

小惑星探査機の1号機である「はやぶさ」は、2003年5月宇宙科学研究所（JAXAの一部）によって打ち上げられ、2005年夏アポロ群の小惑星「イトカワ」（長径540m）に到達し、表面物質を採取して2010年10月に、7年半で60億kmの旅を終えて、地球に帰還した。

2号機である「はやぶさ2」に与えられた最大の

temperature even when used for an extended period of time, LEDs are used in countless applications ranging from liquid crystal TV backlights, illumination equipment, traffic lights, automobiles, and bicycles to electronic bulletin boards and ad towers. High-output, ultra-bright LEDs are under development as energy savers.

d) Space Exploration
1) Epsilon Rocket

In September 2013, the Japan Aerospace Exploration Agency (JAXA) launched the first new type of rocket called "Epsilon." The Epsilon rocket is a small launch vehicle measuring 2.6 meters in diameter, standing 24.4 meters tall, and weighing 91 tons. It grew out of 12 years of extensive R&D following Japan's development of the H-IIA rocket. Also, H-IIB which is currently in use in Japan is a highly reliable rocket with a successful launch rate of over 97%. The Epsilon rocket has a number of innovative features such as the ones listed below.

<1> Use of Solid Fuel: Advantages of this over the use of liquid oxygen and hydrogen include simpler rocket structure, easier fuel loading, and ability to respond quickly to weather changes at launch time.

<2> Exploitation of Earlier Technologies: The solid rocket booster of the H-IIA was adopted as the first stage, and the upper stage motors of the M-V (Mu-5) rocket, considered the world's top performing rocket, were upgraded and used as the second and third stages. This lowered the cost per launch to 380 million yen, half that of the M-V.

<3> Mobile Launch Control: The Epsilon rocket is equipped with artificial intelligence that can check 18 thousand inspection items in one second. Thanks to this system, the work of preparing for a launch, which used to take 100 people more than 40 days, can be completed by a few operators in 7 days.

2) Hayabusa 2 Asteroid Probe

The first Hayabusa asteroid probe was launched by the Institute of Space and Astronautical Science (part of JAXA) in May 2003, reached and sampled surface material from the Itokawa asteroid (540 meters long) in the Apollo group in the summer of 2005, and returned to earth in October 2010 after a 6 billion kilometer journey that took seven and a half years.

The primary mission assigned to the second probe, Hayabusa2, is to

ミッションは、地球生命誕生の謎を探るべく、直径900 m の太陽系の小惑星「リュウグウ」へ着陸し、そのサンプルを持ち帰ることにある。2014 年 12 月に H-IIA ロケットに乗せられて出発し、約 52 億 4 千万 km を飛行し、2018 年 6 月 27 日に到着した。

　「はやぶさ 2」はイオンエンジンを搭載すると共に、高度な自律航行能力を有し、到着して小型のロボットを投下し細かく調査しながら同年 9 ～ 10 月と 2019 年 2 月に地表の試料採取をした。注目は 2019 年 4 ～ 7 月に予定される 3 回目で、地表に弾丸を撃ち込んで地中の試料を採る難易度の高い試みである。予定通りミッションがすすめば 2020 年に地球に帰還する計画となっている。

- イオンエンジン：電気推進とよばれる方式を採用したロケットエンジンの一種で、マイクロ波を使って生成したプラズマ状イオンを静電場で加速・噴射することで推力を得る。

3）宇宙ステーションに物資を運ぶ無人補給船「こうのとり（HTV）」

　宇宙空間を利用して、地球・天体の観測や、宇宙での実験・研究などを行う国際宇宙ステーション（ISS）計画は 15 カ国が協力する国際プロジェクトである。ISS には、水、食料、衣料などの生活物資や、新しい実験装置、実験用サンプルなどの研究用資材、バッテリのように定期的に交換が必要な機器などを継続的に運ぶ必要がある。これら ISS 運用に必要な物資の輸送は、ISS 計画の参加各国が分担して行っており、日本は、H-IIB ロケットで打ち上げる宇宙ステーション補給機「こうのとり」（HTV：H-II Transfer Vehicle）を開発・運用している。その大きさは直径約 4 m、全長 10 m 弱、観光バスが収まるサイズである。また、実験機器や使用後の衣類などを積み込み、大気圏に再突入して燃やし処理する役目もしている。

　「こうのとり」のミッションは、2009 年 9 月に打ち上げられた 1 号機から 2018 年 9 月打ち上げの 7 号機まで連続してすべて成功し、7 号機には今回初めて ISS で作った実験試料などを地上に持ち帰る小型カプセル（重さ約 180 kg）を搭載し回収された。高い評価を受け、今後さらに 8・9 号機までの打ち上げが計画されている。

land on the 900-meter diameter asteroid Ryugu and collect and bring back samples to Earth for unlocking some of the mysteries about the origin of life on Earth. Hayabusa2 was launched from an H-IIA rocket in December 2014, and after a journey of some 5.24 billion km it arrived at Ryugu on June 27, 2018.

Hayabasa2 has Ion engines and features advanced autonomous navigation capability. After landing and unloading rovers for detailed surveying of the asteroid, the rovers collected surface samples in September and October 2018 and in February 2019. The third sampling scheduled from April to July 2019 has attracted growing attention because it is a high-difficulty attempt to extract subsurface samples from the asteroid by firing an impactor shot into the surface. If the mission proceeds as planned, Hayabusa2 should return to Earth in 2020.

- Ion engine: A type of rocket engine using electric propulsion where plasma-like ions generated using microwaves are accelerated and injected in an electrostatic field to produce thrust.

3) Unmanned Supply Ship "Kounotori (HTV)" Carries Cargo to International Space Station

The International Space Station (ISS) is an international collaboration project between 15 countries for making observations of the Earth and celestial bodies and for conducting research and experiments in space. The ISS requires continual delivery of daily commodities such as water, food, and clothing, research materials and equipment such as new experimental instruments and experimental samples, and items that need periodic replacement such as batteries. Supplies needed for ISS operation are transported by the countries participating in the ISS program. Japan has developed and operates the space station supply ship "Kounotori" (HTV: H-II Transfer Vehicle), which is launched by an H-IIB rocket. The supply ship is about 4 meters in diameter and has a total length of nearly 10 meters, making small enough to fit inside a tourist bus. After unloading, the supply ship is filled with used experimental equipment and used clothes for disposal, which are burned upon reentry into the atmosphere.

From the launch of the first "Kounotori" mission in September 2009 until the launch of the seventh one in September 2018, each mission has been successful. For the first time, the seventh "Kounotori" contained a compact reentry capsule (weighing approximately 180 kg) for bringing back experimental samples and other items from the ISS to the Earth. "Kounotori" has been widely lauded as a successful project, and plans are already underway for the launch of the 8th and 9th ships.

e) ナノテクノロジー

　　ナノテクノロジーとは、物質をナノメートル（10億分の1メートル）という微細な単位で計測・加工など自在に制御する技術をいう。ナノテクノロジーは、あらゆる分野の科学技術の基盤で、いわば21世紀の産業革命ともいうべき科学技術の飛躍的発展を支える技術として期待されており、日本が国際的にも進んだ分野である。以下の事例のほか各分野で実用化され、応用研究が進められている。

〈1〉エレクトロニクス領域：論理演算デバイスとして、シリコンデバイスの限界を破る容量をもつ情報メモリー、画期的情報通信材料の開発など。

〈2〉カーボンナノチューブ：炭素でできた軽くて非常に強いきわめて小さなチューブ状の物質で、形に応じて電気の流れやすさを変える性質があり、日本で発見された。アルミニウムの半分という軽さ、高い強度、弾力性から、建築物、自動車、航空機など工業製品への応用が期待されるほか、エネルギー、バイオ・医療、エレクトロニクスなど幅広い分野での実用化の取り組みが行われている。

〈3〉セルロースナノファイバー：木材の繊維を1ミクロンの数百万分の1以下のナノメートルサイズの太さにまで微細化したバイオマス素材で、重さは鋼鉄の5分の1程度で鋼鉄の5倍程度の強度を有し、熱による変形は石英ガラス並みに少ないなどの特徴を持っている。樹木を原料に低コストで量産できるようになれば、炭素繊維やガラス繊維の代わりにプラスチックに配合し、自動車の部品や車体、建築材料をはじめ、様々な分野で広く利用されると期待されている。

f) 化学分野

　　化学製品は、現在のエネルギー問題へ多大な貢献をしてきた。例えば、太陽光発電や燃料電池などによる創エネ、リチウムイオン電池などによる蓄エネ、断熱材やLEDなどによる省エネ、等々で大きな役割を果たしており、今後もその重要性は高まるであろう。

1) 有機・無機化合物分野

　　有機化合物の有機ELや無機化合物の炭素繊維などは、今までにない新しい機能をもつ素材を産み出し、

e) Nanotechnology

Nanotechnology is the ability to manipulate and engineer matter at the nanometer level (a nanometer is one billionth of a meter). As an interdisciplinary field with the potential to underpin every branch of science and technology, nanotechnology can be expected to drive rapid scientific and industrial advances on the order of a second industrial revolution. Japan is an international leader in nanotechnology. Applications have been achieved and further research is continuing in virtually every scientific field. Three examples follow.

<1> Electronics: Development of logic and memory devices with capacities exceeding the limits of silicon devices, and groundbreaking information and communication materials.

<2> Carbon Nanotubes: These are molecular-scale structures made of carbon that were discovered in Japan. They are light in weight, extraordinarily strong, and have the ability to vary resistance to electrical flow by their shape. Owing to their low weight (half that of aluminum), and high strength and elasticity, carbon nanotubes are being studied for application in a broad range of industrial products, including buildings, automobiles, and airplanes, as well as in the energy, biotechnology, medical, and electronics sectors.

<3> Cellulose Nanofiber: This is a biomass material formed of wood fiber refined to a nanometric thickness of several hundredths of a micron or less. It is one-fifth the weight of steel and five times as strong, and exhibits very low thermal deformation comparable to that of quartz glass. If it can be mass-produced at low cost using trees as the raw material and blended with plastic instead of carbon fiber and glass fiber, it is expected to be widely applied in various fields including car parts, car bodies, and building materials.

f) Chemical Sector

Chemical products have contributed tremendously to recent energy issues. They have, for example, been a major force behind the development of solar cells, fuel cells, and other energy creation equipment, lithium-ion batteries and other energy storage devices, thermal insulation materials, LEDs, and other energy saving advances. Such contributions will continue to increase.

1) Organic and Inorganic Materials

Electro-luminescent (EL) materials and inorganic carbon fibers are among a number of emerging chemical materials that offer new func-

新たな産業をも創出している。
- 〈1〉 有機EL：有機光エレクトロニクスの展開において、有機薄膜に本格的に通電して動作させたデバイスで、既に有機ELディスプレイはスマートフォンに採用されているほか、高精細4K・8K大型テレビにも採用され市場を賑わしている。現在、日本は世界最高水準の輝度と長寿命の新型有機ELの開発を進めているほか、基本素材の生産では世界シェアの過半を占めている。
- 〈2〉 炭素繊維：最近では航空機や自動車産業も、世界各国で強まる燃費規制に対応するため、軽量化に取り組んでいる。日本は炭素繊維の世界最大の生産国であるばかりでなく、これを加工する技術、さらに最終用途となる自動車などの部材一体技術においても最先端を走っている。

2） 高分子化合物分野

各種の高分子先端材料はまったく新しい素材を生み出したり、新しい価値を提供したりすることで、ソリューションプロバイダーとしての貢献が可能である。具体的な2例をあげる。
- 〈1〉 バイオマテリアル：主に医療用材料として用いられ、最近では、再生医療発展の観点から注目されている。なかでも高分子材料は、生体に積極的に働きかける性質を持つバイオマテリアルの研究開発が始まっており、日本では細胞培養の基材として利用したり、細胞の増殖・分化能力を増強する機能を制御したりする方法で、バイオメディカルの一翼として期待されている。
- 〈2〉 ポリウレタン：ウレタン基を有する高分子化合物であり、既に世界で年約1,000万トン生産されているが、日本では新たに機能性材料としてのシートクッションなどの自動車用植物由来ポリウレタンが開発された。石油系由来に比べ環境負荷という点で決定的に異なり注目されている。

g） ロボット
1） 災害現場で活躍するロボット：東日本大震災の復興にロボットが大量に投入されている。解体作業や廃材の

tions and capabilities and are giving rise to new industries.

- <1> Organic EL: The organic photonics and electronics field has already seen the development of a device that operates under full-scale application of electric current to an organic thin film and has been incorporated in smartphones as an organic electroluminescent display, or in high definition 4K and 8K large, flat-screen TVs. Currently under development is a new type of organic EL display that promises to be the world's brightest and most durable. Japan manufactures a majority of the basic materials used in organic EL displays.

- <2> Carbon Fiber: Aircraft and automobile manufacturers are in increasing need of light-weight materials in order to comply with ever more strict fuel efficiency regulations around the globe. This has led Japan, the world's largest producer of carbon fiber, to intensify efforts to develop weight-reducing carbon fibers, and also to take the lead in automobile and other technologies related to the multi parts simultaneous processing of this material.

2) Polymers

High-performance polymers give rise to revolutionary materials that create new value and thereby become a source of innovative solutions. Here are two concrete examples.

- <1> Biomaterials: These are used chiefly as medical materials and have recently come into the spotlight along with advances in regenerative medicine. A start has been made on R&D on polymeric biomaterials that work with living tissue and in Japan are used as cell-culturing substrates and in methods for controlling functions that enhance cell proliferation and differentiation. They are therefore expected to play an important future role in the biomedical field.

- <2> Polyurethane: Although this is a common urethane-base polymer produced worldwide, at the rate of about 10 million tons annually, Japan has developed a new plant-derived variety as a functional material for automotive applications such as seat cushions. The plant-based polyurethane is attracting attention for being decisively superior to conventional petroleum-derived types in terms of burden on the environment.

g) Robotic Process Automation

1) Disaster Site Robots: Robots have been introduced in large numbers in the reconstruction work following the Great East Japan

分別など細かい作業が可能な「双腕作業機」で津波後の瓦礫の撤去に投入された。また福島原発の事故では高濃度の放射線のため人間が入れない箇所が多くあり、事故直後には調査目的用のロボットが投入された。作業用ロボットでは、コンクリート内部でも通信が途絶えないよう WiFi を使い、ロボットが無人のままバッテリ充電ができる機能などを備えており、原子炉建屋内の核燃料デブリ撤去作業を行っている。

2）次世代ロボット：日本のロボット技術はさらに高度化して、運転手が触らなくても安全運転のできる自動車、人の顔を認識できる警備ロボット、人とコミュニケーション（音声の会話や身振りによる交流）のできる介護・生活支援ロボット、幼児の形をしていて乱暴に扱うと泣き出す育児実習用ロボット、人の身体機能を助ける身に着けるロボット（パワースーツ）、人の入れない場所で働く清掃用産業ロボット、地雷探査用ロボット、レスキュー（救助）ロボット、山の斜面を登り樹木を間伐する林業支援ロボットなど、広い分野で人の活動を支援する。また最新の超高速 5G 通信のもとで精細な 4K モニター画面を見ながら無人で操作する建設作業用ロボットの試作などと、この種のサービスロボットの開発はさらに進み、需要も増えることが予測される。

h）エネルギー

メタンハイドレート生産技術の開発：2013 年 1 月、石油天然ガス・金属鉱物機構（JOGMEC）と産業技術総合研究所（AIST）は、世界で初めて海底のメタンハイドレートからメタンガスを取り出すことに成功した（陸上では、2008 年にカナダとの共同生産に成功している）。メタンハイドレートは、メタンガスが高圧・低温の条件下で水の分子に取り囲まれてシャーベット状になった物質で、温度・気圧が変わると水とガスが分離してメタンガスが発生する。深い海底に分布し、日本でも東部南海トラフの海域に、日本の天然ガス消費量の 11 年分の埋蔵があると推定される。今回の実験は、地球深部探査船「ちきゅう」を

Earthquake. Double arm work robots were brought in to remove rubble left by the tsunami. These machines can perform detailed tasks such as dismantling and the separation of waste materials. The Fukushima Nuclear Power Plant accident resulted in many places where humans could not enter due to the high levels of radiation. Investigation robots were deployed immediately after the accident. Work robots used WiFi to ensure that communication was not interrupted even inside the concrete structure and were capable of performing such functions as recharging their batteries without human intervention, as they removed debris from the nuclear reactor buildings.

2) Next-Generation Robots: The increasing sophistication of Japan's robotic technology will lead to the development of robots able to assist humans in a broader range of fields. These include automatically guided vehicles that can safely transport passengers without needing a driver, security robots able to recognize faces, robots for nursing care and living assistance (able to communicate with humans via voice and gestures), robots for learning how to perform child-care that are shaped like infants and start crying if not handled gently, robots in the form of power suits that help the wearer perform physical activities, and robots that can work in places humans cannot enter, such as industrial cleaning robots, mine surveillance robots, rescue robots, and forestry support robots that climb mountain slopes and thin out trees. Trial production of robots for construction work that are remotely operated via 4K monitor screens and the latest ultrahigh-speed 5G communications is part of the steady advance in the development of such service robots that is expected to increase demand for them.

h) Energy

Development of Methane Hydrate Production Technology: In January 2013, Japan Oil, Gas and Metals National Corporation (JOGMEC) and the Institute of Advanced Industrial Science and Technology (AIST) confirmed the world's first offshore production of methane from methane hydrate (terrestrial production had already been achieved in 2008 in collaboration with Canada). Methane hydrate is a sherbet-like substance formed of methane gas captured inside water molecules under high pressure and low temperature conditions. It generates methane gas by separation of the water and gas components under altered temperature and pressure conditions. It is found under deep seabeds, and reserves in Japan's Eastern Nankai Trough region alone are estimated to be equiva-

使って三重県・愛知県の沖合の水深1,000 mの海底のさらに300 m地下にあるメタンハイドレート層に鉄のパイプを通して、メタンガスの採取に成功した。

i) スーパーコンピュータ

現代においては、技術ブレイクスルーを牽引するために「スーパーコンピュータ」の存在が必要不可欠である。医療分野、エネルギー分野、宇宙開発分野において、人類の「夢」を実現する技術を開発するためには、スーパーコンピュータを用いたさまざまな解析やシミュレーションが欠かせない。スーパーコンピュータは、膨大な計算処理を実現するためのハードウェアおよびソフトウェアの総称で、おもに1秒あたりの浮動小数点演算の計算能力で性能が評価されている。

1)「京」

スーパーコンピュータ「京」は、CPUが8万個以上といった超高速並列計算処理装置で、1秒間に1京回即ち10P（ペタ）FLOPS（1京は1兆の1万倍）という計算速度で2011年6月に計算速度世界一となった。2兆個の粒子の重力進化の計算を、1台のコンピュータなら数百年かかるところをわずか3日で完了して、宇宙の解明を大きく前進させた。この他、新しい工業素材や次世代半導体の開発、生命活動の解明、気象予測、医療技術、災害対策、宇宙の解明、新エネルギー源の確保、さらには複雑な社会現象の予測などの分野で活用されている。消費電力は約12.7 MWとなっている。

設置・運用している理化学研究所では、「京」の経験や成果を生かし、100倍程度の実行性能を目指すポスト「京」の開発を進めており、2021年頃の運用開始を予定している。ポスト「京」では、性能競争を絶対視しないで研究成果に重点を置き、研究テーマに合わせて設計することとしている。国は、ポスト「京」の開発・製造に1,100億円の国費を投入する計画である。

lent to 11 years of Japan's natural gas consumption. The test was carried out by the scientific deep-sea drilling vessel Chikyu, which sampled methane gas through a steel pipe sunk 300 meters into the seabed at an underwater depth of 1,000 meters off Mie and Aichi Prefectures.

i) Supercomputers

In this age, supercomputers are indispensable for driving technology breakthroughs. Analyses and simulations using supercomputers are essential for developing technologies that realize the dreams of humankind in the medical, energy, and space development fields. "Supercomputer" is a generic term for a collection of hardware and software for processing calculations on an enormous scale. A supercomputer's performance is mainly evaluated by its computing ability in terms of floating-point calculations a second.

1) K

The K Supercomputer (K is short for Kei, the Japanese word for 10 quadrillion) is an ultrahigh speed parallel computing system equipped with more than 80 thousand CPUs. It became the world's fastest computer in June 2011, with a speed of 10 quadrillion floating-point calculations a second, or 10 PFLOPS (1KFLOPS). The computer simulated the gravitational evolution of two trillion particles of dark matter in three days, a job that would take a single ordinary computer several hundred years to complete and an achievement that helped to accelerate studies into how the universe formed. The K Supercomputer is being used in many fields such as the development of new industrial materials and next generation semiconductors, elucidation of vital activity, climate prediction, medical technology, disaster countermeasures, unravelling the mysteries of the universe, securing new energy sources, and even prediction of complex social phenomena. The K consumes 12.7 megawatts of electricity.

The K Supercomputer is installed and operating at RIKEN, which is using its experience with the K and the results it has obtained to move forward with the development of a post-K computer with around 100 times the execution performance of the K. The post-K is scheduled to start operations around 2021. For the post-K, the emphasis is on the achievement of research results that will make it completely unequalled in terms of performance, with the design being tailored to the research theme. The government plans to commit 110 billion yen in funding for the development and manufacture of the post-K.

2）第3世代「地球シミュレータ」

　　海洋研究開発機構（JAMSTEC）は2015年、第3世代となる「地球シミュレータ」の本格稼働を6月から開始した。今迄よりさらに複雑なパラメータを扱ったり、最先端の予測モデルや大規模なシミュレーション技術の開発により高速実行できるようになった。地球環境問題、気候変動問題、地殻変動、地震発生機構の解明や津波被害予測への貢献が期待されている。

　　地球シミュレータは2002年3月からJAMSTECが運用しているスーパーコンピュータで、当時では圧倒的な能力をもつ世界一のスーパーコンピュータとして世界を驚かせた。その後、2009年3月に131 TFLOPS、メモリー容量20 TBへとアップデート。さらに今回のシステム更新で1.31 PFLOPS、メモリー容量320 TBになり、ベンチマーク結果からおおよそ10倍の実効性能となった。なお消費電力は初代が約5 MWだったのに対して、約2 MW以下に抑えられている。

j）先端医療
1）光免疫療法

　　アメリカ国立衛生研究所（NIH）に勤務する日本人の小林久隆主任研究員は、（テレビのリモコンにも使われる）近赤外線をあてると、細胞を傷つける物質を発見した。がん細胞に集まる抗体と呼ばれるたんぱく質に、この物質を付けて体内に注入し、がん細胞に集まったところで、近赤外線を照射する。すると光が当たった物質が化学反応を起し、がん細胞の膜を破って攻撃する。がん細胞だけを壊す「光免疫療法」への道が開けた。

　　既に、アメリカでは2015年に治験が始まり、手術や放射線療法などで治らなかった患者のうちがんが消えたり、縮小した事例が報告されている。日本では2018年3月から国立がん研究センターで治験開始された。がん治療のつらい副作用を抑え、患者の治療への負担や恐怖心をなくすことが期待されている。

2) Third Generation Earth Simulator

In June 2015 the Japan Agency for Marine-Earth Science and Technology (JAMSTEC) started full-scale operation of the third generation Earth Simulator. It can handle more complex parameters, and with the development of leading-edge prediction models and large-scale simulation technology is capable of high-speed execution. The new Earth Simulator is expected to make a contribution with respect to global environmental problems, climate change issues, diastrophism, understanding earthquake occurrence mechanisms, and tsunami damage prediction.

The original Earth Simulator was a supercomputer that JAMSTEC started operating in March 2002, when it created widespread surprise with its overwhelming capability that ranked it as the world's best supercomputer at that time. In March 2009, its performance was updated to 131 TFLOPS with a memory capacity of 20 terabytes (TB). With this latest system update, the performance has been elevated to 1.31 PFLOPS and the memory capacity to 320 TB, giving a ten-fold increase in its effective performance benchmark. While the power consumption of the first generation was about 5 MW, that of the latest iteration is 2 MW or less.

j) Advanced Medical Treatment

1) Photoimmunotherapy

Kobayashi Hisataka, a Japanese doctor and chief researcher at the National Institutes of Health (NIH) in the U.S., found substances that harm cells when exposed to near-infrared light (also used by TV remote controls). This substance is added to proteins called antibodies that target cancer cells, and after injecting into the body, it collects on the cancer cells, where it is then irradiated by near-infrared light rays. Exposing the substance to this light incites a chemical reaction that ruptures and attacks the membrane of the cancer cell. This discovery opened up the new field of photoimmunotherapy for destroying targeted cancer cells.

Clinical trials were started in the U.S. in 2015, and there have been cases of cancer disappearing or shrinking in patients who did not respond to surgical, radioactive, and other treatments. In Japan, the National Cancer Center (NCC) started clinical trials in March 2018. This treatment is expected to reduce the debilitating side-effects of cancer treatments and eliminate the burden and fear of treatment felt by patients.

2）アルツハイマー病変の早期検出法を血液検査で確立

　認知症で最も多いアルツハイマー病の原因物質の脳内への蓄積を、わずかな血液でしらべることができる検査法を開発したと、国立長寿医療研究センターと島津製作所の研究チームが2018年2月に発表した。

　原因物質は「アミロイドベータ（Aβ）」というタンパク質で、発症の20年ほど前から脳に徐々に蓄積するとされる。Aβ の検査は現在一人あたり十数万円〜数十万円かかる特殊な脳画像検査や、脳脊髄液を採取する検査法が必要で、費用や体への負担が大きい。研究チームは、Aβ の蓄積によって変動する複数の関連物質の比率から脳内の蓄積の度合いを推定する技術を開発し、僅か0.5 cc の血液で測定できる方法を確立した。

3）尿一滴で、「線虫」が早期がんを嗅ぎ分ける

　九州大学大学院生物科学部門の廣津崇亮助教らの研究グループが、がんの匂いに注目し、「線虫」が高い精度でがんの有無を識別できることをつきとめた。
　検査するものは尿。使うのは「線虫」という体長1 mm ほどの生き物で、1滴垂らした尿の匂いに線虫が好んで寄って来れば「がんの疑いあり」、嫌って遠ざかって行けば「がんの心配なし」となる。装置を使った大がかりな診断と違い、線虫を使ったこの方法は簡単かつ数百円と安価である。さらに精度も95.8%と驚きの高さである。しかも、ステージ0〜4まであるがんの進行度のうち、ステージ0や1といった早期がんも発見できるという。現時点ではどんな部位のがんかは診断できていないが、線虫は「がんの有無」を発見し、すい臓がんのように発見が困難ながんをも見逃さないという。したがって、「がん有り」となった人だけが従来の部位別検診を受ければいい。

　現在、この検査を広く普及させるために医工連携で日立製作所と共同で機械化に取り組み、自動解析装置の開発を行っている。手作業の場合、1日に解析できる尿の検体数は3〜5人分程度だが、自動化により

2) Blood Test for Early Detection of Alzheimer's Disease

A collaborative research team from the National Center for Geriatrics and Gerontology (NCGG) and Shimadzu Corporation announced in February 2018 that they had developed a testing method capable of detecting the accumulation of a substance in the brain that causes Alzheimer's disease, which is the most common type of dementia, from only a small sample of blood.

The causative substance is a protein called Aβ-amyloid (Aβ), and it gradually accumulates in the brain from about 20 years before the onset of symptoms. Current Aβ tests require special brain image scans that currently range in cost from one hundred thousand yen up to several hundred thousand yen per person, or testing methods that extract cerebrospinal fluid, which are costly and hard on the patient. The research team developed a technique for predicting the degree of Aβ accumulation in the brain from the ratio of multiple related substances that vary depending on the amount of Aβ that has accumulated, and established a method capable of measuring using only 0.5 cc of blood.

3) Using Nematodes to Detect Early Stage Cancer Odors from a Single Drop of Urine

A research group including Hirotsu Takaaki, a biologist at Kyushu University found that nematodes were able to identify the presence of cancer with high accuracy by its odor.

Tests were conducted using patients' urine. This study used nematodes, which are living organisms about 1 mm in length. A sample was considered as possibly being cancerous when the nematodes were attracted to the smell of a drop of urine, and noncancerous when the nematodes were not attracted to the urine. In contrast to extensive diagnostic tests using medical equipment, the method using nematodes is simple and inexpensive, costing only several hundred yen. Furthermore, it has an astonishingly high detection accuracy of 95.8%. Moreover, for cancer progression from stages 0 to 4, the test was even capable of detecting early-onset cancer in stages 0 and 1. Currently, although the type of cancer cannot be identified by this test, nematodes can indicate the presence of cancer, which can prevent the overlooking of difficult-to-detect cancers such as pancreatic cancer. This would allow only people who test positive for cancer by this test to undergo the conventional cancer screening for specific body parts.

To make the test widespread for general use, researchers are currently collaborating with Hitachi, Ltd. on testing mechanisms for developing automatic analyzers. When performed manually, about 3 to 5 urine samples can be analyzed per day, but researchers hope to automate the

100人以上に増える、2020年までに実用化することを目指している。

4）消化器内視鏡

がんの早期発見に大きく貢献するのが、消化器内視鏡で、日本はこの分野で最先端の技術と7割のシェアを保持している。

2002年、世界で初めて「ハイビジョン内視鏡システム」が生まれ、内視鏡の概念が大きく変わることとなった。医工連携により飛躍的に情報量が増えたハイビジョン画像システムによって、微細な血管や粘膜の表層構造までリアルに観察することができるようになった。胃や大腸等の消化管用の消化器内視鏡では、先端外径がわずか5 mm台の内視鏡や、ハイビジョンタイプの内視鏡、拡大観察用の内視鏡も実用化され、さらには、それまでの内視鏡では挿入が困難だった小腸の検査を目的としたカプセル内視鏡も実用化されている。また、動画や静止画像の電子的拡大が可能となり、挿入性の向上や検査・診断の効率化とあいまって、医師の診断時間の短縮や疲労の軽減、患者の身体的な負担の軽減に大きく貢献している。

5）超微細外科（高解像度立体視顕微鏡と極細手術針）

0.1 mm単位の非常に細い血管や神経をつなぐ手術のことを超微細外科という。ほとんど不可能に見える精緻な作業を実現するのは、日本製の超高倍率の顕微鏡と極細の針である。

三鷹光器製の高解像度立体視顕微鏡は、77倍まで拡大して観察でき、立体カメラで部位を見るとき、明るい視野と高分解能を兼ね備えて、手術しやすい奥行のある映像を得たり、超高倍率化に伴う振動吸収設計やカメラの操作性向上などで、今まで困難だった微細手術も可能となった。

この手術を可能にする世界最小の手術針は、針の直径はわずか0.03 mmで、そこに通す糸は0.012 mmで、日本の千葉県市川市の中小企業である河野製作所が可能にしたスーパーマイクロサージャリー（微少外科）である。この結果、肉体の組織を壊死させる率を減らし、手術の成功率を高めた。また手術後のしびれ

process by 2020 to enable analysis of more than 100 samples per day.

4) Gastrointestinal Endoscope

Gastrointestinal endoscopy is a major contributor to early cancer detection and a field in which Japan boasts advanced technology and a global market share of about 70%.

The emergence of the world's first high-vision (ultrahigh definition) endoscopic system in 2002 radically changed the perception of endoscopy. The high-vision imaging system combined medical and engineering expertise to realize a massive increase in collected data that made it possible to realistically observe down to the minute level of fine blood vessels and the surface structure of mucous membranes. For gastrointestinal applications, such as for the stomach and large intestine, there are endoscopes with a tip outer diameter of just 5 mm, high-vision endoscopes, and endoscopes with magnification observation capabilities. There is also a capsule endoscope for examining the small intestine, into which it has been difficult to insert a conventional endoscope. Moreover, the ability to electronically magnify moving and still images, in combination with improved insertion performance and more efficient examination and diagnosis, is reducing the burden on the patient considerably.

5) Ultrafine Surgery (high-resolution stereoscopic microscope and ultrafine needles)

Ultrafine surgery refers to operations used to connect nerves and blood vessels as fine as 0.1 mm in diameter. It is an ultrahigh magnification microscope and extremely fine needles, both of which are made in Japan, that make it possible to perform what are almost unbelievably finely detailed surgical operations.

A high-resolution stereoscopic microscope made by Mitaka Kohki Co., Ltd. enables observations up to 77x magnification. When a stereoscopic camera is used to view a region, the field of view is bright and high resolution, and the image has depth that facilitates surgery. The instrument has a design that absorbs the vibration that accompanies ultrahigh magnification, and improved camera operability, facilitating microsurgery that was previously too difficult.

The world's smallest surgical needle that enables this microsurgery has a diameter of only 0.03 mm and the thread used is 0.012 mm thick, which are manufactured by Kono Seisakujo Co., Ltd., a small Japanese company located in Ichikawa City, Chiba Prefecture. The result is a reduced rate of necrosis of the body tissue and an increased success rate of the surgery. These products are expanding the horizons of medical

などの後遺症を減らしたり、傷跡がほとんど残らない形成手術を可能とするなど、医療の可能性を押し広げている。

(2) 日本の製造業技術・ものづくりの技の強み

日本は主要な製造業の基礎技術で優れたものを多く保有している。これらの中には伝統的技術の改善であるものもあるし、通常は目立たないところで使われているので一般に知られていないものもある。しかし、これらの技術は世界でナンバーワンあるいはオンリーワンの技術として、広く日本と世界の産業を支えている。

一方、デジタル技術の進展によるデータの利活用によって製造業のビジネスモデルが大きく変化し、日本の製造業においても刻々と変わる状況認識のもと、迅速な対応が求められている。第4次産業革命であるモノとモノがつながるIoTや人と機械・システムの協働・共創、また国境を越えて企業と企業がつながることで様々な付加価値が生まれることで、ソリューション志向の新たな産業が形成されて行くのが、日本の産業が目指すコネクテッド・インダストリーズ（Connected Industries）である。その実現に当たっては、日本の強みである、高い「技術力」や高度な「現場力」を生かして行く必要がある。

以下日本のものづくり技術の中のいくつかを紹介する。

a）高効率大型火力発電所

日本企業は3段階発電方式の大型ガス火力発電所の技術を開発した。この方式は、まず−162℃の液化天然ガスを気体ガスに戻すときに体積が600倍に膨張する力を利用して1回目の発電をする。次に気体ガスをガスタービンで燃やして2回目の、さらにガスタービンから出る高温の排気ガスでボイラーを動かして3回目の発電をする。これにより、エネルギー効率が大幅に向上する。この技術は、2014年に三菱重工と日立製作所が設立した三菱日立パワーシステムズ（MHPS）の大型火力発電設備事業会社で活用されている。

一方、JX日鉱日石開発は、アメリカで石炭火力発電所の燃焼排ガスから二酸化炭素（CO_2）を回収するプラント

treatment, making it possible to reduce surgical problems such as post-operative numbness and enabling plastic surgery that leaves hardly any scars.

(2) Strength of Japanese Manufacturing Technology

Japan has many outstanding basic technologies in the major manufacturing sectors. Some are improvements on traditional crafts and are not widely known because they are usually used inconspicuously. However, these include many that are the world's best or have no counterpart elsewhere, and as such, they help to support a wide range of industries both in Japan and overseas.

At the same time, the business model of the manufacturing industry has undergone dramatic changes wrought by the utilization of data generated by the progress of digital technology, with rapid response being required by the recognition that Japan's manufacturing industry is constantly changing. The fourth industrial revolution, comprising IoT technology that connects everything to the Internet, the collaboration and co-creation of people, machines, and systems, and the creation of added value by connecting companies across national boundaries to form new, solutions-oriented industries is the "Connected Industries" that is the aim of Japanese industry. In order to realize that, it is necessary to make the most of Japan's strengths, which are high technological capabilities and advanced workplace capabilities.

Here are a few examples of Japan's manufacturing technology:

a) High-Efficiency Large-Scale Thermal Power Plants

A Japanese company has developed a large-scale gas-fired power plant that utilizes three-stage power generation. In this system, liquefied natural gas (LNG) at a temperature of minus 162 degrees Celsius is regasified, and the force of the resulting 600-fold expansion in volume is used to generate power in the first stage. The natural gas is then burned in a gas turbine for second stage power generation, and the high-temperature exhaust gas from the gas turbine is used to operate a boiler for third stage power generation. The method greatly improves energy conversion efficiency. In 2014, Hitachi and Mitsubishi Heavy Industries established Mitsubishi Hitachi Power Systems, Ltd. (MHPS), a thermal power plant equipment company for utilizing this technology commercially.

JX Nippon Oil & Gas Exploration Corporation has initiated a project in the U.S. that involves constructing a plant for recovering carbon

を建設し、回収したCO_2の油田への圧入により原油の増産を図るプロジェクトを開始した。老朽化した油田における原油生産量の飛躍的な増加と、石炭火力発電所から大気中へ排出する温暖化ガスの低減を同時に目指している。この技術は発展途上国への移転が期待されている。なお、5 社会（6）環境保全 e）最近の重要なキーワード〈3〉イー・エス・ジー（ESG：Environment Social and Governance）を参照。

b）鉄道関連技術

世界の高速鉄道の運行を支える下部構造には日本の技術が不可欠である。すなわち、車輪とレールである。この2つの製品について日本は他国が追い付けない技術的国際競争力を持っている。

〈1〉車輪：列車の車輪、特に車軸と一体となった車輪を大きな鉄の塊から鍛造する技術は、日本では日本製鉄だけが保有している。一貫した製造工程のもとで清浄度、寸法精度の優れた高品質な車輪の製造が可能となっている。同社の車輪は最も厳しいとされるアメリカの車輪超音波テスト（不純物や気泡のテスト）もパスして、アメリカ、ドイツなど世界各国で広く使用されている。

〈2〉重量レール：時速 300 km 以上の超高速列車の走行では、大きくて重い80キロレール（1 m 当たりの重さが 80 kg のレール）でなければ安全性が保持できない。このレールを 80 m の長さにして均一に焼き入れる技術で日本製鉄のレールは世界一の硬さ、高い直線性、長寿命さらに耐摩耗性・耐表面損傷性が高く、レールの高寿命化でライフサイクルコストに優れている。これは鉄鉱石から鋼材製品までを一貫して製造するため、清浄で均質性の高い、耐久性の良いレールが製造可能となっているからである。日本の新幹線や、ドーバー〈英仏〉海峡の海底トンネル内のレール、また大重量の大型コンテナ貨物列車が走るアメリカのアムトラックの大陸横断鉄道にも日本の 80 キロレールが使われている。

dioxide (CO_2) from the flue gas of a coal-fired power plant and injecting the recovered CO_2 into an oil field to increase the production of crude oil. The aim is to achieve a large increase in crude oil production from aging oil fields while at the same time reducing atmospheric greenhouse gas emissions by coal-fired power plants. Japan's highly sophisticated coal-fired power generation technologies are expected to be transferred to the developing countries.

Note: Refer to Chapter 5 Society, Section (6) Preservation of the Environment, e) Recent important keywords, <3> ESG (Environment, Social and Governance).

b) Railway-Related Technology

Japanese technology is indispensable for the understructures that support the operation of the world's high-speed railways. Japan's competitiveness in two key understructure products, wheels and rails, are unrivaled by any other country.

<1> Wheels: Nippon Steel is the only Japanese company that has the technology needed to forge train wheels, especially unitary wheel-axle assemblies (wheelsets), from large steel ingots. It enables high quality wheels with excellent cleanliness and dimensional accuracy to be produced under a consistent manufacturing process. The company's wheels have passed the U.S. ultrasonic wheel test (for impurities and bubbles), considered the most stringent wheel test, and are used in the U.S., Germany, and many other countries.

<2> Heavy Rails: The safety of an ultrahigh speed train traveling at 300 kilometers per hour or faster cannot be ensured without use of large and heavy rails, typically weighing 80 kilograms per meter length. Nippon Steel is the only company with the technology for uniformly producing and hardening 80-kilogram rails to a length of 80 meters. Nippon Steel's rails are the world's hardest, have high linearity, long service life, high wear and abrasion resistance and surface damage resistance, and with their long service life, have excellent life cycle cost properties, all of which is the result of the consistency of the manufacturing process from iron ore to steel product, enabling the manufacture of rails that are clean, highly homogeneous, and durable. Japanese 80-kilogram rails are also used in the rail tunnel below the Strait of Dover between England and France, and on Amtrak transcontinental routes for heavy-weight container freight trains in the U.S., as well as for the Japanese *Shinkansen* (bullet train) line.

c) 石油・シェールガス生産用のパイプ

　　現在、アメリカはシェールガスの大産出国でエネルギーの構造変革が進んでおり、既にアメリカは天然ガスの輸出国となっている。シェールガスは世界に広く分布しているが、多くは地下の深い岩石の中に埋蔵されている。アメリカの場合は地下 3,000 m ほどの岩石に鋼製のパイプで垂直に穴をあけ、そこから水平の穴を掘り、その先端から超高圧水を噴射させて岩石を振動させてガスを取り出す。この瞬間掘削用パイプには想像を超える力がかかる。日本製のシームレスパイプはこの条件に耐えて何回もくり返して使える実績と信頼性が高く、その結果顧客にとってもコスト的に優位になる。また、石油、一般の天然ガス生産にも日本製のパイプが広く使われている。

d) ミシン

　　世界で使われているミシンの 90％は日本製である。特に工業用ミシンでは、日本のメーカーJUKI が世界シェアの 50％を占め、これに続くジャノメ、ブラザーを加えると 80％に達する。中国は年間膨大な量の衣類を輸出しているが、その製造に使われているのはほぼすべて日本製ミシンである。JUKI の工業用ミシンは毎分 1 万回転で、飾り縫い、千鳥縫い、穴かがり、ボタン付けなど縫製工程ごとの専用機があり、ユニクロのカジュアルウエアからプラダなどの高級ブランドの衣類、靴、バッグなどの品質を支えている。

e) その他のユニークな技術
　〈1〉 2013 年 10 月に、アジアとヨーロッパを結ぶトルコ・イスタンブールのボスポラス海峡の鉄道海底トンネルが完成した。1860 年からのトルコの夢であったこのトンネルを作ったのは、日本の掘削機械と掘削技術であった。日本のトンネル技術はドーバー〈英仏〉海峡海底トンネル完成にも多大な貢献をした。
　〈2〉 人の髪の毛の断面を 22 分割することができる精密研削切断装置と切断技術を日本の企業は開発した。この技術は、パソコンやスマートフォンなどに組み込まれる円形の半導体ウエハーから小さな電子部品チップの加工には欠かせないものである。

c) Pipes for Petroleum and Shale Gas Production

The U.S. is a major shale gas producer, which is driving a restructuring of the country's energy system that has transformed the U.S. into a natural gas exporter. Shale gas reserves are found throughout the world, most often in deep underground rock formations. The extraction process used in the U.S. forms a vertical hole by sinking a steel pipe around 3,000 meters into the ground to the source rock, digs a horizontal hole at this depth, and injects ultrahigh pressure water from the edge of this hole to fracture the rock and release the gas. The drilling pipe is exposed to incredibly high pressures when this happens. Japanese manufacturers produce seamless pipes that have a proven record of being able to withstand these drilling and pressure conditions and are very cost-effective because they can reliably be used repeatedly. Japanese pipes are also widely used in petroleum and ordinary natural gas production.

d) Sewing Machines

Japan makes 90% of the world's sewing machines. In the industrial sewing machine sector, Japan's JUKI Corporation alone holds a 50% share of the global market, and when this is combined with the shares of runner-ups Janome and Brother, the total comes to 80%. Almost all of the tremendous number of garments exported by China every year are made using Japan-made sewing machines. JUKI's industrial sewing machines can do up to ten thousand stitches a minute and are available in dedicated types for embroidery, staggered stitching, button hole stitching, button attachment, and other purposes. JUKI machines help to ensure the quality of clothing, shoes, bags, and other products ranging from Uniqlo's casual wear to the products of Prada and other luxury brands.

e) Other Unique Technologies

<1> A railway tunnel underneath the Bosporus Strait completed in Turkey in October 2013 created a new link between Asia and Europe. The undersea tunnel, which fulfilled a Turkish dream from 1860, was excavated with Japanese machinery and technology. Japanese tunneling technology also contributed immensely to the completion of the Dover Channel Tunnel between England and France.

<2> A Japanese company developed a grinding and cutting system so precise that it can divide the cross-section of a human hair into 22 slices. The related technology has become indispensable in the machining of tiny chips from the round semiconductor wafers and other electronic components incorporated in personal computers,

〈3〉 このほかにも、世界の大手自動車メーカーが使用しているボディ一体成型用の大型プレスの金型、機械の機械といわれるNC旋盤などの工作機械、330トンのダンプトラックなどの建設機械のほか、多くの日本の製造技術が世界に貢献している。

(3) 諸技術の組み合わせによる業務運営効率化のためのシステムの追求

以上のような個別の課題解決のための要素技術の開発のほかに、業務全体の運営について、関連する個々のユニットの課題を相互に有機的にとらえ、異なる複数の技術をシステム化して、豊かさや利便性を追求するというのが今後の技術開発の一つの方向である。こうした内容をビッグデータやIoTという概念が生まれる前から実際に活用して、グローバル経営を成功させてきた建設機械メーカーのコマツ（小松製作所）の事例を紹介する。

コマツでは、同社が製造販売する、鉱山や土木現場等で使用される大型のブルドーザやダンプトラックのような建設機械について、単に車両を製造して顧客に販売するだけでなく、ICT（情報通信技術）を活用して、車両の運行管理方法や、消耗品交換や発生している機械のエラー情報を把握し、保守サービス等も併せた遠隔機械稼働管理システム（KOMTRAX）を商品化し、顧客に提供している。世界中の鉱山や土木現場等で稼働する数多くの車両の運行状況や位置の情報、車両のメンテナンス履歴や作業負荷履歴情報を、インターネットを利用してリアルタイムで同社の担当部門で収受し、現場のオペレーターに対し衛星通信等を利用してリアルタイムで必要な指示を与え、疑問に応える。このことによって、顧客の計画的安定生産、生産コスト低減、機械の故障の撲滅、省燃費運転等に寄与している。

さらに、コマツでは、土地測量専用ドローンに最新のICT技術を使って、人手の何万倍のポイント（約数百万ポイント）を百倍レベルの精度（数センチメートルピッチ）

smartphones, and similar devices.

<3> A list of the many other Japanese manufacturing technologies that are playing key roles in industries everywhere would include the large press dies automakers use to integrally shape car bodies, machine tools such as numerically controlled lathes, sometimes called the "machine of machines," and construction equipment like a 330-ton dump truck.

(3) Combining Technologies to Optimize Operational Efficiency

The technologies discussed in the foregoing section were developed independently to solve specific operational problems. Another emerging direction in technology development is to take a broad view of operations, and with a focus on the interrelations among the different issues at hand, to enhance productivity and convenience by creating systems that combine multiple technologies. Utilizing this, Komatsu Ltd., a manufacturer of construction machinery, succeeded with its global management before there was any such concept as big data and IoT.

Komatsu has taken a new approach in its marketing strategy for construction equipment like the heavy-duty bulldozers and dump trucks used at mines and civil engineering sites. Rather than just selling these vehicles, Komatsu offers customers a remote equipment and fleet monitoring system (KOMTRAX), which uses information-communication technology to collect data on vehicle operation management, expendable part replacement, equipment error messages, and other aspects of equipment operation and performance. The company's KOMTRAX service center receives transmissions through the Internet to collect real-time information on the operating condition and location, maintenance history, workload, and the like of a tremendous amount of construction equipment that is operating at mines, civil engineering sites, and other places around the globe. Using the gathered information, the center can supply the on-site operators with required instructions and answer their questions in real time through satellite or other communication channels. For the customer this means such benefits as being able to move forward with projects and production stably as planned, reduce operating costs, eliminate equipment breakdowns, and increase fuel efficiency.

Komatsu provides a service ("Smart Construction") that uses the latest ICT with specialized land survey drones to conduct point surveys of several million points at a pitch of several centimeters, which is

で測量させ、完成図面を 3D モデル化し、これをクラウドから取得し活用できるサービスを提供している。さらに ICT 装備を施した建機にその測量データを転送し、現場で簡単な設定作業をするだけで、経験の浅いオペレーターでも正確な土地の基礎マウンド等の施工ができる。これによって、最近の深刻な人手不足にも対応が可能となる、というものである（スマートコンストラクション）。

その他の例として、新幹線の安全性やスケジュール管理を守り続けるための車両と信号システムや運行システムの組み合わせ、ハンドルを操作しなくても走行できる自動車の自動運転システムと交通の安全を担保する道路交通システムの組み合わせ、POS（point of sales）システムと、多数の顧客の POS システムの運用によって得られる販売情報から推定する需要予測情報の提供の組み合わせなど、諸方面で研究開発が進められている。

また身近な商品にも AI や IoT が活用されている例もある。福井市に本社のあるセーレンの「ビスコテック」と呼ばれるシステムである。パソコンで作ったデザインデータを、この会社の「ビスコデザイン CAD」に取り込み、タイムラグなしに「ビスコテック CAM」で布地に染めて（1,677 万色まで可能）最終製品にする。布地はポリエステル、ナイロン、綿、ウール、シルク、混紡素材などほとんどすべての繊維素材に対応できる。世界に一着のオーダーメイドから、グローバルオーダーの大量生産まで、短時間で、多品種のあらゆるプロダクションシステムへ応用が可能である。さらに、洋服だけでなく、ガラス、セラミックス、木材、プラスチックなどへの応用が可能である。

（4）日本の科学技術の現状

a）科学技術基本計画

1995 年に制定された「科学技術基本法」に基づき、政府は「科学技術基本計画」を策定し、長期的視野に立って一貫した科学技術政策を実行することになっている。これまで、第 1 期（1996～2000 年度）、第 2 期（2001～2005 年度）、第 3 期（2006～2010 年度）、第 4 期（2011～2015 年度）に基本計画を策定し、科学技術政策を推進してきた。その継続として、2016 年 1 月 22 日、2016～2020 年度の第 5 期基本計画が閣議決定された。

one hundred times the precision obtained by a manual survey, and converts 2D completion drawings into 3D models that can be acquired for use from a cloud-based service. By transferring the survey data to a construction machine equipped with ICT and performing simple setting procedures at the work site, even a somewhat inexperienced operator can construct accurate ground foundation mounds and the like. This is a way of coping with recent serious shortages of manpower.

R&D into combined technology systems is also moving forward in numerous other areas. One example is the combination of the bullet-train railcar and signal systems with an operating system to ensure that safety and scheduling reliability are continuously maintained, another is the combination of a hands-free automatic car driving system and a road traffic management system for ensuring road safety, and still another is the combination of a point-of-sales (POS) system with one for supplying demand forecast information estimated from sales data obtained from many customers through POS system operation.

There are also instances where AI and IoT are utilized for familiar products as well. There is a system called "Viscotecs" of Seiren Co., Ltd., which is based in Fukui city. Design data generated on a personal computer is imported into the company's Visco Design CAD, and without any time lag is dyed onto the required fabric by the Viscotecs CAM in up to 16.77 million colors, to form the final product. The fabric can be almost any fiber material such as polyester, nylon, cotton, wool, and silk, or a fabric blend. It can rapidly be applied to various kinds of production systems, from custom-made single piece to mass production of global orders. In addition to clothes, it can be applied to glass, ceramics, wood, and plastics.

(4) Science and Technology in Japan

a) Science and Technology Basic Plan

In accordance with the Science and Technology Basic Law enacted in 1995, the Japanese government has formulated its Science and Technology Basic Plans for implementing a consistent science and technology policy from a long-term perspective. So far, science and technology policy has been promoted under the 1st Science and Technology Basic Plan (1996 to 2000), the 2nd Basic Plan (2001 to 2005), the 3rd Basic Plan (2006 to 2010), the 4th Basic Plan (2011 to 2015), and following the cabinet's endorsement on January 22, 2016, the 5th Basic Plan (2016 to 2020).

本計画の内容は、まず、ICTの進化等により、社会・経済の構造が日々変革する「大変革時代」が到来したこと、および国内外の課題が増大、複雑化（エネルギー制約、少子高齢化、地域の疲弊、自然災害、安全保障環境の変化、地球規模課題の深刻化など）していることを基本認識している。そのうえで、本計画は、未来の産業創造と社会変革に向けた新たな価値創出の取り組みであるととらえ、世界に先駆けた「超スマート社会」（Society 5.0）を未来の姿として共有すると述べている。「超スマート社会」とは、狩猟社会、農耕社会、工業社会、情報社会に続くような新たな5番目の社会を生み出す変革を科学技術イノベーションが先導していくという意味を持つ。

　即ち、IoT、ビッグデータ、AI、ロボット技術等を活用し、サイバー空間とフィジカル空間（現実空間）とが高度に融合された社会であり、必要なもの・サービスが、必要な人に、必要な時に、必要なだけ提供され、社会の様々なニーズに対応して、あらゆる人が質の高いサービスを受けることを可能とするものである。このような認識の下で以下の3つのテーマの下に全部で13の重要政策課題を設定し、研究開発から社会実装までの取り組みを一体的に推進しようとするものである。なお、研究開発を担う人材力の強化について述べられている。

〈1〉持続的な成長と地域社会の自律的発展
　・エネルギーの安定確保とエネルギー利用の効率化　・資源の安定的確保と循環的な利用　・食料の安定的確保　・世界最先端の医療技術による健康長寿社会の形成　・持続可能な都市および地域のための社会基盤の実現　・効率的、効果的なインフラの長寿命化への対策　・ものづくり、コトづくりの競争力向上
〈2〉国および国民の安全・安心の確保と豊かで質の高い生活の実現
　・自然災害への対応　・食品安全、生活環境、労働衛生等の確保　・サイバーセキュリティの確保　・国家安全保障上の諸課題への対応
〈3〉地球規模課題への対応と世界の発展への貢献
　・地球規模の気候変動への対応　・生物多様性への対応

The contents of the plan are as follows. To begin with, there is a basic recognition that due to the evolution of ICT, the era of drastic change has arrived in which the structure of society and the economy changes day by day, and problems at home and abroad are increasing and becoming more complicated, including energy restrictions, the declining birthrate and aging, exhaustion in local regions, natural disasters, changes in the security environment, and increasingly serious global issues. In addition, with this plan being a new value creation effort for future industrial creativity and social transformation, it involves sharing a vision of the coming "Super Smart Society" (Society 5.0) as a world frontrunner. It is called Super Smart Society to indicate it is the new, fifth-stage society created by transformations led by scientific and technological innovation, following the hunter-gatherer society, agricultural society, industrial society, and information society.

That is, it will be a society in which IoT, big data, AI, and robot technology are utilized to merge the physical space (real world) and cyberspace. Such a society will be one capable of providing the requisite goods and services to the people who need them at the required time and in just the right amount. Society will be able to respond to a wide range of social needs, and it will be one in which all kinds of people will be readily able to obtain high-quality services. Based on this recognition, the 5th Basic Plan sets a total of 13 important policy tasks under the following three themes, and the promotion of integrated efforts from R&D to social implementation. It also describes strengthening human resources that are responsible for research and development.

<1> Sustainable growth and autonomous regional development

Ensuring stable energy and improving energy utilization efficiency; ensuring stable resources and their reusability; securing a stable food supply; establishment of a society in which people enjoy long and healthy lives with world-leading medical technology; building infrastructure for sustainable cities and regions; extending the service life of efficient and effective infrastructure; improving competitiveness in manufacturing and value creation

<2> Ensuring the safety and security of the nation and its citizens and a high-quality, prosperous way of life

Addressing natural disasters; ensuring food safety, living environments, and occupational health; ensuring cybersecurity; addressing national security issues

<3> Addressing global challenges and contributing to global development

Addressing global climate change; responding to biodiversity loss

b) 研究開発費および予算

政府は 2018 年第 5 期基本計画において、5 年間の政府の投資総額目標を 26 兆円とすること、および官民合わせた研究開発投資の年間目標総額を GDP の 4 ％以上、政府投資目標額を GDP の 1 ％とすることを明示した。

直近の実績では、日本の 2015 年の官民を合わせた研究開発費は 18.9 兆円で、アメリカの 51.2 兆円、中国の 41.9 兆円に次いでいる。対 GDP 比率は、3 ％台後半で推移しているが、直近 3 年間は緩やかに減少している。2015 年の GDP に対する割合では、日本は 3.6％で , アメリカ 2.7％、ドイツ 2.9％、フランス 2.3％、中国 2.1％などの欧米、アジア諸国を引き離しているが、近年中国、韓国の伸び率が目立っている (科学技術指標 2018)。

c) ノーベル賞受賞者

21 世紀に入ってから (2001〜2018 年) の自然科学系ノーベル賞受賞者数をみると、アメリカ 73 人、イギリス 18 人、日本 15 人、フランス 8 人、ドイツ 6 人で、日本は第 3 位である。
(注) 南部陽一郎氏、中村修二氏はアメリカとしてカウントした。

d) 自然科学系学位 (博士号) 新規取得者

自然科学系の研究者を代表する学位取得者について、日本はこの 30 年間で約 2 倍の 1.3 万人となった。しかし、国際比較では 2014 年アメリカの取得者は 3 倍の 4.0 万人に、ドイツは 1.8 倍の 1.5 万人となった。

e) 自然科学系論文数

研究活動を定量的に表す方法には、量的指標としての論文数と質的指標としての論文の被引用回数がある。2003〜2005 年頃の日本の論文数は世界第 2 位であったが、2013〜2015 年には約 64,000 とアメリカ、中国、ドイツに次いで世界第 4 位に後退した。

論文の質についても、被引用数がトップ 10 ％以内にある論文の数は、2003〜2005 年頃の第 4 位から、2013〜2015 年には 4,200 と第 9 位に後退した。

各国の研究予算の比較でも、2015 年の日本の研究開発

b) R&D Expenditures and Budget

The government indicated in 2018 that its target for the total five-year 5th Basic Plan investment is 26 trillion yen and the target for combined government and private sector annual R&D investment is 4% or more of gross domestic product (GDP), with the government's share amounting to 1% of GDP.

In 2015, combined government and private sector R&D expenditures in Japan came to 18.9 trillion yen, placing Japan after the U.S. with 51.2 trillion yen, and China with 41.9 trillion yen. Japan's outlays as a percentage of GDP is in the upper half of the 3% range, but has shown a slight decline in the most recent three-year period. In 2015, Japan's outlays as a percentage of GDP amounted to 3.6%, outstripping those of the U.S. at 2.7%, Germany at 2.9%, France at 2.3%, and China at 2.1%. However, China and South Korea stand out in terms of growth rate.

c) Nobel Prize Winners

A breakdown by country of science-category Nobel Prize winners since the beginning of the 21st Century (2001 to 2018) shows the U.S. had 73, the UK 18, Japan 15, France 8, and Germany 6. So Japan is in third place.

Note: Nambu Yoichiro and Nakamura Shuji are included in the U.S. total.

d) Doctorates in the Natural Sciences

The number of natural science researchers in Japan with doctor's degrees, currently 13 thousand, has doubled over the past 30 years. During the same period, the number in the U.S. tripled to 40.0 thousand and in Germany increased 1.8 fold to 15 thousand.

e) Natural Science Research Papers

A common practice is to use number of published research papers as an index of the volume of research activity and number of times papers are cited as an index of research quality. From 2003 to 2005, Japan ranked second in the world in number of published papers but had fallen to fourth place for the 2013 to 2015 period, with about 64 thousand papers, trailing the U.S., China, and Germany.

In terms of citation frequency as a measure of quality, for papers that fall in the top 10%, Japan fell from fourth place in the 2003 to 2005 period to ninth place in 2013 to 2015, with about 4,200 papers meeting this criterion.

In a comparison of the research budgets of each country, the total

費の総額は 18.9 兆円で、アメリカ、中国に次ぐ 3 位だった。しかし、大半は企業が占めており、基礎研究を担う大学の分が少ないことが論文低迷の原因とみられる。予算のほか、修士や博士を目指す若手の減少など複数の要因も絡んでいる可能性があるものと見られる。

f) 特許出願件数

世界で出願された 2017 年の日本の特許出願件数は 48,208 件で、アメリカ 56,624 件、中国 48,882 件で 14 年間守ってきた 2 位を中国に抜かれ世界第 3 位となった。以下 4 位ドイツ 18,982 件、5 位韓国 15,763 件となっている（WIPO：世界知的所有権機関）。日本は前年比 6.6％と伸ばした。出願年別に見た特許登録率（特許出願件数に対する特許登録件数の割合）は増加傾向にあり、知的財産戦略において量から質への転換が進んでいる。

特筆すべきは、中国が急速に伸びて、世界で出願された特許出願件数で WIPO は「3 年以内に 40 年間首位のアメリカを追い越すとみられる」と分析している。一方 2016 年の全世界国別の特許出願件数は約 312.8 万件に達し、7 年間連続で増加したが、国別の特許出願件数をみると、上位 5 カ国では、中国が約 133.9 万件、アメリカが約 60.6 万件、日本が約 31.8 万件、韓国が約 20.9 万件、欧州が約 15.9 万件である。中国の特許出願件数はアメリカ、日本、韓国、欧州の各特許当局が受理した件数の合計を上回っている。

世界がスピードを上げて変革する中、各国は、競争力を高めるために、事業の選択と集中、そして海外展開を進めており、知的財産戦略も高度化・グローバル化している。

g) 技術貿易

技術貿易とはモノの貿易ではなく、特許、商標、意匠、ノウハウ（企業秘密）などの知的財産権のライセンス・ロイヤリティの支払額と受取額を表すものである。技術を輸出すればロイヤリティ（対価）を受取り、輸入すればロイヤリティを支払うことになる。総務省技術研究調査統計

amount of research and development expenditure in Japan in 2015 was 18.9 trillion yen, third behind the U.S. and China. However, most of the spending is accounted for by companies, and the low output from universities carrying out basic research is considered to be the cause of the decrease in the number and quality of papers. Another factor that might play a role is the decrease in the number of young people seeking to study for a master's degree or doctorate.

f) Number of Patent Applications

In 2017 Japan filed 48,208 international patent applications, the U.S. 56,824, and China 48,882. Thus, after 14 years in second place, Japan slipped to third, behind the U.S. and China. In fourth place was Germany, with 18,982 applications, and in fifth place was South Korea, with 15,763 applications. (WIPO: World Intellectual Property Organization). Japan's total represented an increase of 6.6% over the preceding year, and its patent registration rate (proportion of patent registrations to patent applications), by year of application, is increasing, in line with its intellectual property strategy of changing from quantity to quality.

Of particular note is the rapid increase shown by China. According to an analysis of the number of applications by country conducted by WIPO, within three years China will take over the top spot that has been held by the U.S. for 40 years. The number of patent applications filed in all countries in 2016 was about 3.128 million, representing an increase for the seventh consecutive year. The top five countries in terms of the number of filings were China, with 1.339 million, the U.S., with 606 thousand, Japan, with 318 thousand, and South Korea, with 209 thousand, and Europe with 159 thousand. The number of Chinese patent applications has exceeded the combined total filed by the U.S., Japan, South Korea, and Europe.

Amid the increasingly rapid change the world is undergoing, each country is improving its competitiveness by promoting the selection and concentration of business operations, and engaging in overseas development, to improve the sophistication and globalization of their intellectual property strategies.

g) Technology Trade

Technology trade is not a trade in physical goods. Instead, it refers to the amounts of payments and receipts involved in the licensing of, and royalties on, intellectual property rights such as patents, trademarks, designs, knowhow (trade secrets), and so forth. If you export technology you will receive royalties, and if you import it you will pay royalties.

によれば、2016年度の日本の技術輸出額は、3.6兆円であり、技術輸入額は、0.5兆円であり、差し引き、技術貿易収支は、3.1兆円の輸出超過（黒字）で、アメリカに次いで世界第2位である。

産業別技術輸出額では、自動車を中心とする輸送用機械製造業が約60％を占めており、これに医薬品、情報通信機器、電気機械、化学、鉄鋼などが続き、製造業関連が全体の90％以上を占めている。今後は、技術輸出における産業別構成として自動車に次ぐ分野への広がりを持たせることが課題である。

ただし自動車産業の場合は、ほとんどが日本の本社が開発して知財権を取得した技術、車体の設計図、製造技術ノウハウなどを、アメリカで操業する子会社企業・工場に貸与することで得られるロイヤリティが90％となっている。

（5）日本の科学技術の課題と対策

a）イノベーションの産学連携

イノベーションの推進のためには、共同研究等の産学連携が必須である。OECDの2017年2月の調査によれば、日本の大学等における研究費の民間負担率は2.6％で、ドイツの13.9％、韓国の12.3％とは大きな差がある。今後のイノベーションを柱とした経済改革を確実に進めるため、産学連携のスキームが検討されている。

b）科学技術開発の国際化

この10年間の世界各国の科学技術論文の推移をみると、国際共著論文の比率が高くなり、2016年でイギリス66.3％、フランス62.8％、ドイツ59.7％で共著の比率は50％を超え、以下アメリカ43.5％、日本33.4％、中国25.9％となっている。この事実は科学技術活動の国際共同研究などが増加していることを意味し、国のボーダーを越える知識生産や知識の共有が活発化してきていることを示している。

According to a report on technology trade published by the Ministry of Internal Affairs and Communications, in fiscal 2016 Japan's technology exports amounted to 3.6 trillion yen, and imports to 0.5 trillion yen, for a surplus of 3.1 trillion yen, placing Japan second after the U.S.

Looking at technology exports by industry, transportation machinery manufacturers, most notably automakers, accounted for 60%. The remaining top-ranking industries included pharmaceuticals, information-communication equipment, electrical equipment, chemicals, and steel. Manufacturers accounted for over 90% of total technology exports. A future challenge is expanding the role played by sectors other than automobile manufacturing in the industrial makeup of technology exports.

However, in the case of the automakers, 90% of the amount is made up by royalties from loaning to subsidiaries operating in the U.S. of technology, design drawings of car bodies, and manufacturing technology know-how that have nearly all been developed by the Japan headquarters, and on which intellectual property rights have been acquired.

(5) Japanese Science and Technology—Issues and Countermeasures

a) Industry-University Collaborative Innovation

Joint research and other such industry-university collaborations are essential to the promotion of innovation. According to an OECD survey conducted in February 2017, the private sector's share of research funding at Japanese universities is 2.6%, a big difference from the 13.9% in Germany and 12.3% in South Korea. Industry-university collaboration schemes are being considered in order to ensure economic reforms based on future innovations.

b) Internationalizing Science and Technology Research

Over the past ten years, a salient trend in science and technology research papers from countries around the globe has been the increasing ratio of internationally co-authored papers. In 2016, in the UK (66.3%), France (62.8%) and Germany (59.7%), internationally co-authored papers accounted for more than half the total, while the figure was 43.5% for the U.S., 33.4% for Japan, and 25.9% for China. This situation reflects the increasing globalization of scientific and technological research, indicating that knowledge production and sharing across national borders is being pursued more actively.

上記の各国は、物理学、環境・地球科学、臨床医学、化学、材料科学のいずれの分野における国際共著率も上昇傾向である。ただし日本は、いずれ先進国の国際共著論文中においても順位を下げ、各分野においても順位やシェアを低下させている。アメリカの共著相手国として、2003～2005年ではドイツ、イギリス、カナダが拮抗して1～3位を占めていたが、現在は中国が第1位である。中国は日本に比べ国際共著相手としての存在感を増している。

c）博士号取得者の活用

　　日本では博士過剰論もあり、博士号取得者が十分な社会的評価を得ておらず、それにふさわしい地位を得ていないという問題が指摘されている。

　アメリカでは大学院の段階で、若手研究者の長所を伸ばし、積極性、自立心を育み、挑戦を奨励する傾向が強く、このような環境で育成された博士号取得者は学界以外への就職にも有利であり、将来に多様なキャリアパスが確保されている。しかし、日本では、博士課程を終えて大学や研究機関に就職する人のうち、約60%が任期付きの採用で、そのうちの40%超は2年以下の条件で雇われており、身分が不安定で、将来に不安を抱きやすいとの指摘もある。

　　一方世界では、大学や著名な企業の研究職を得ようと思ったら博士号が必須なので、例えばアメリカの場合ではいや応なく博士課程に行くことになるのに対し、日本では企業文化の違いで修士が標準で博士課程に行くと就職しづらくなり早めに職場に入ったほうが優位であるとの考え方が多い。この結果、企業内研究者中の博士号保有者の割合は4%で、オーストリアの16%、ベルギー、ノルウエーの15%、アメリカの13%、ロシアの12%、シガポールの8%より低い。

d）若手・女性・外国人研究者の登用

　　2017年日本の科学技術研究者の中の女性研究者数は14.4万人と過去最多を更新。研究者全体に占める女性の割合は2000年の10%レベルから15.7%と過去最高を更新してきた。しかし、イギリスの37.4%、アメリカの34.3%、ドイツ28.0%、フランスの26.7%レベルに比べると、まだ

In each of the above countries, the international co-authorship rate in the fields of physics, the environment and earth science, clinical medicine, chemistry, and materials science is rising. However, Japan has a lower international co-authorship than most of the other leading countries, and also a falling rank and share in each field. In 2003 to 2005, Germany, the UK, and Canada were the U.S.' top three co-authorship partners, but currently China ranks first. China is increasing its international co-authorship presence more than Japan.

c) Utilizing Graduates with Doctor's Degrees

Some believe Japan has too many people with doctorates, and others complain that a doctorate does not ensure commensurate social status.

At the graduate level in the U.S. there is a strong tendency to develop the strengths of younger researchers, nurture self-initiative and self-reliance, and encourage the taking on of new challenges. Doctoral graduates trained in such an environment are also encouraged to find jobs outside academic circles. Although such an approach is advantageous and ensures a variety of future career paths, in Japan about 60% of doctoral graduates who find employment at universities and research institutions are signed to fixed-term contracts, 40% of which are for terms that don't exceed two years, so their position is insecure and they tend to feel uneasy about the future.

Around the world, a doctoral degree is essential if one wishes to obtain a research position at a university or a famous enterprise. So, in the U.S., for example, graduates will go on to a doctoral course without any qualms. In Japan, however, due to differences in the corporate culture, many think that it is better to just get a master's degree and quickly find employment, as opting for a doctoral course can make it harder to find work later. As a result, the percentage of Japanese corporate researchers who hold doctor's degrees is 4%, lower than Australia's 16%, Belgium's 15%, Norway's 15%, the U.S.' 13%, Russia's 12%, and Singapore's 8%.

d) Creating Opportunities for Junior, Female, and Foreign Researchers

In 2017 Japanese science and technology researchers included 144,000 women, recording highest number ever. The ratio of female researchers rose from around 10% in 2000, to 15.7%, the highest it has been, but remains low compared to the 37.4% in the UK, 34.3% in the U.S., 28% in Germany and 26.7% in France.

かなり低い。

日本が世界に伍して科学技術を発展させていくためには、科学技術の将来を担う優秀な若手研究者の養成とその活躍の促進が不可欠である。若手研究者に自立と活躍の機会を与え、将来につながる研究の基礎を築かせることは、科学技術の振興を図る上でとりわけ重要である。政府は若手研究者ポストの確保や若手研究者の育成システム、若手研究者の自立的環境整備を実施することとしている。

また女性研究者がその能力を最大限発揮できるようにするため、大学や公的研究機関を対象として、研究環境の整備や意識改革など、女性研究者が研究と出産・育児等の両立や、その能力を十分に発揮しつつ研究活動を行える仕組み等を構築するモデルとなる優れた取組を支援している。

さらに優秀な外国の研究者受入れのための支援措置の拡充や、大学等研究機関における外国の研究者の受入れ体制の整備を、日本の研究者の海外派遣と同等に重視し、国として今後、支援措置を拡充する必要がある。

e） 科学技術経営者の育成

日本における特許取得率や研究開発投資額の水準は世界的に高水準であるのに対し、ビジネス効率性の水準は低いという指摘や、ベンチャー企業の立ち上げが容易でないという指摘がある。欧米諸国では、技術と経営の両面に精通した「技術経営（MOT：Management of Technology）」、いわばMBA（経営学修士）の技術版ともいうべき専門的人材が大学や企業で養成されているが、日本はその点では遅れをとっている。

産学連携によるMOT人材育成に国が力を入れ始めてから約10数年が経過した。MOT大学院を卒業した新卒者が現場の経験を積んで30代後半になる今日において、企業におけるMOT活用が新たな段階に入っていくことが期待される。

f） 次の時代を担う人材の育成

子供の「理科離れ」が指摘されて久しい。理科や数学に対する子どもの興味・関心・学力の低下、国民全体の科学技術知識の低下、若者の進路選択時の理工系離れと理工系学生の学力低下など、これらの結果、将来の科学技術人材

It is essential to train excellent young researchers who are responsible for the future of science and technology and to promote their success in order for Japan to develop world-class science and technology. It is particularly important to do this by giving young researchers opportunities to be self-reliant and active, and to allow them to lay the foundation for research that will develop into the future. The government is developing training systems and an environment that allows younger researchers to become self-sufficient and find employment in research positions.

To enable female researchers to exert their research abilities to the full, universities and public research institutions are being supported in their efforts to create model cases for building mechanisms in their work environments and changing people's awareness to enable female researchers to combine their work with childbirth and child-raising.

In addition to emphasizing support measures for accepting outstanding foreign researchers and establishing systems for receiving foreign researchers at universities and other research institutions, equal emphasis is being given to the overseas dispatch of Japanese researchers. Expanded efforts in both of these areas are needed.

e) Training Science and Technology-Minded Business Leaders

While the patent acquisition rate and R&D investment in Japan are high in global terms, business efficiency is low, and most business people agree that it is by no means easy to launch a start-up business in Japan. In the U.S. and European countries, universities and enterprises are training specialists in MOT (Management of Technology), who are well versed in both technology and management. The MOT might be called the technology version of the MBA (Master of Business Administration). Japan lags behind in this regard.

More than ten years have elapsed since Japan began to make an effort to cultivate MOT human resources through industry-university collaboration. Today, as those who first graduated from MOT graduate schools have gained experience in the field and are now in their late thirties, it is expected that efforts to take advantage of MOT in enterprises will enter a new stage.

f) Developing Human Resources for Future Generations

That Japanese school children have lost interest in science is already old news. The decline in children's interest, curiosity, and academic skills with respect to science and mathematics, the decline in the science and technology knowledge of the public as a whole, the turning away

が育たないことなどの問題である。理科離れは先進国に共通の問題であり、各国とも理科離れの阻止、科学技術人材の養成・確保に本腰を入れて取り組んでいる。知的好奇心にあふれた子供の育成には、まず子供の理科的な心を呼びさますような優れたリーダー(教師、ボランティア)の養成が先決である。このために「サイエンス・リーダーズ・キャンプ」などのプログラムが展開されている。

　学校制度としては、「スーパーサイエンス・ハイスクール」の指定制度があり、科学技術振興機構が支援している。高等学校等において、先進的な理数教育を実施するとともに、高校大学接続の在り方について大学との共同研究や、国際性を育むための取組を推進している。また創造性、独創性を高める指導方法、教材の開発等の取組を実施している。

　残された課題として、社会における理系の地位・待遇の向上や国策として息の長い時間軸で科学技術と社会をつなぐ活動の推進が必要である。

from science and engineering when youngsters choose what they want to do in the future, and the declining academic ability of science and engineering students are all problematic when it comes to developing the science and technology personnel of the future and dealing with other issues. The turning away from science is a common problem in developed nations and each country is trying to prevent and putting serious effort to train and secure human resources. The first essential step toward cultivating abundant scientific curiosity in children is to train leaders (teachers and volunteers) skilled in inspiring children to have an interest in science. This thinking is leading to the promotion of science leaders' camps and various other initiatives.

Outstanding public high schools that win a designation of Super Science High School receive special support from the Japan Science and Technology Agency. High schools are implementing advanced science and math education and collaborative research with universities, and promoting the nurturing of internationality. Teaching methods and the development of teaching materials for raising creativity and originality are also being pursued.

As a remaining task, it is necessary to promote activities that connect science and technology with society within a long time frame and improve the status and treatment of science courses in society through national policy.

7 文化

(1) 日本文化の特質

a) 序

　日本は古来より長きにわたり中国文化圏に属し、大陸からの輸入文化・翻訳文化の側面をもちながら、独自の文化を形作っていった。縄文土器で知られる有史以前の土着文化と、その後伝来した水田耕作を営む過程で育（はぐく）まれた文化とが融合し、その後も積極的に摂取された外国の文化が次々とまじりあい、日本化するなかで日本固有の文化が形成されていった。温暖湿潤な気候は水田耕作を可能としたが、その気候そのものも日本の文化を育む要因となった。大陸から遠からず、近からずという島国であることが、言語的にも、民族的にも同質性をほぼ保ってきた要因であり、文化的特徴に影響を与えてきたといえる。

b) 稲作に根ざす日本文化

　文化を人間集団における伝承される生活様式の体系であると定義すれば、文化は農耕社会の成立以降に発生するとされている。

　世界の各地域で農耕社会が成立したのは、紀元前8000～3500年であった。これに対して、日本の農耕社会は紀元前300年以降の弥生時代に成立したとされている。ただし最近の放射性炭素年代測定により、水田稲作は紀元前950年頃日本に伝来したとの分析結果も発表されている。紀元前300年頃の世界各地を見ると、ギリシャのアレクサンダー大王の時代、初期のローマ共和国、エジプトのプトレマイオス朝などの時代であり、インドでは仏教が成立し、中国では孔子が紀元前5世紀に儒家を開き、続いて老子、孟子、孫子などいわゆる諸子百家の学術・思想が発達した時代であった。

　稲作の発達は古代国家成立の基礎となるとともに、日本人の集団帰属意識などの民族的特性の形成に決定的影響を与えた。

7 Culture

(1) Unique Aspects of Japanese Culture

a) Introduction

Dating back to ancient times, Japan was long part of the Chinese cultural sphere and possessed a culture that was in some senses evolved and imported from the continent. But Japan simultaneously built a unique culture of its own. There was a merging of the prehistoric indigenous culture that is known for Jomon pottery and the culture flourished after the introduction of paddy cultivation, and then went through a subsequent merging with a succession of foreign cultures, which were actively assimilated. In the course of this Japanization, a unique Japanese culture was formed. Moreover, the temperate and humid climate of Japan that made rice cultivation possible was a major factor in shaping the country's culture. And Japan's geographical situation as an island nation near, but not too near, the Asian continent was the primary reason for the country being able to essentially preserve its linguistic and ethnic homogeneity, and thus markedly influenced the nature of Japanese culture.

b) Japanese Culture, Rooted in Rice Cultivation

If culture is defined as a system for passing on a way of life within a group of people, it is considered that culture appears after the emergence of an agrarian society.

Agrarian societies are said to have emerged in the various regions of the world between 8000 and 3500 BC. By comparison, agrarian society in Japan is said to have begun with the Yayoi period starting in 300 BC. However, by the use of radiocarbon dating, it was recently determined that irrigated paddy farming was introduced to Japan around 950 BC. This was around the third century BC, the time of Alexander the Great, the establishment of the Roman Empire, and the Ptolemy Dynasty in Egypt. Around the fifth century BC, Buddhism was founded in India, while in China Confucius established the Ru School, which fostered the philosophies of many great thinkers including Lao-tzu, Mencius, and Sun Tzu.

While development of rice cultivation provided the foundation for the formation of the ancient nation of Japan, it was also a decisive influence in shaping group consciousness and other special characteristics of

日本列島の大部分は温帯モンスーン地帯に属し水田稲作農業に適している。日本の水田稲作は、田植え、稲刈りなど限られた期間内の共同作業を必要とした。また、田に引く水の配分にも村落全体の「秩序」が重要である。こうした事情から日本人には仕事も遊びも村ぐるみでという集団重視の生活習慣と、勤勉、時間厳守などの民族的特性が育まれた。

　古来日本は「瑞穂の国」（みずほ＝稲の穂）と呼ばれ、米は食糧であるにとどまらず、日本人の生活文化の基盤であった。古代の律令制度の土地の配分は米の生産量を基準として行われた。また戦国から江戸時代の大名の領地（石高）、武士の給与（禄高）も米の量によって決められた。また江戸時代の庶民生活では米は通貨の役割も持っていた（大工の日当が米5升など）。

　稲作文化はもはや外来文化というよりは、日本人の体質に沁みこんだ固有の文化となっていった。

c) 自然に対する感性・繊細な芸術描写

　日本はヒマラヤから連なる照葉樹林帯の北限にあり、四季の区別、温暖の差がはっきりしている。自然の色彩・景観も美しく多様である。

　日本人は気候の変化にことのほか敏感で、行き会うとまず「暑いですね」、「涼しいですね」、「よく降りますね」などと気候の挨拶を交わすのがごく普通である。

　また、日本の自然は雨と水が豊富で、陰影に富んでいる。この特徴が日本語にも表われている。言語学者の金田一春彦によれば、日本語には春雨、時雨、夕立、雷雨、五月雨、梅雨、秋雨など雨の表現が40以上ある。しっとり、びしょびしょ、しとしと、ざあざあなど、湿潤と水の状態を表わす言葉も非常に多い。また、そよそよ、びゅうびゅうなどのことばで、風の状態が正確に伝わるのも、日本語の特徴である。

Japanese ethnicity.

Most of the Japanese archipelago falls in the temperate monsoon belt and so is ideally situated for irrigated paddy farming. Rice cultivation in Japan requires farming villagers to cooperate in planting and harvesting during specific time frames. And the allocation of irrigation water to the paddies requires good organization village-wide. This village aspect of ancient life has amplified the importance of the group in daily life, whether at work or at play, and has fostered the attitude towards study, strict punctuality, and other characteristics particular to the Japanese.

In ancient times, people spoke of their country as the "land blessed with rice," reflecting the important role of rice not only as a staple food but also as the foundation of Japanese life and culture. Under the ancient *ritsuryo* legal codes, the capacity for rice production was used as the standard for parceling land. From the feudal period to the Edo period, the fiefs of the *daimyo* and the pay of the samurai were determined in volumes of rice. Throughout the Edo period, rice served as currency among the common people. For example, a carpenter would receive 5 *sho* (equal to about nine liters or roughly two gallons) of rice per day.

Although initially imported, this culture based on rice cultivation has become part of the very fiber of the Japanese identity and makes up part of a uniquely Japanese culture.

c) Sensitivity to Nature and Subtleties of Depictions in Art

Japan is located at the northern extreme of the evergreen broad-leaved forest zone stretching out from the Himalayas and has four distinct seasons with wide differences in temperature. The colors and natural scenery are as beautiful as they are varied.

The Japanese are extremely sensitive to changes in climate, and phrases about the climate such as "it's quite hot today, "it's a bit cool, don't you think," and "it's been raining a lot, hasn't it" are regularly exchanged as greetings.

In Japan, nature abounds in rain and water, with fine variations in light and shade. This feature is reflected in the Japanese language. According to Kindaichi Haruhiko, a linguist, there are more than forty different expressions for rain in Japanese: *harusame* (drizzles of early springtime), *shigure* (light showers in late autumn or early winter), *yudachi* (a shower in the late afternoon to early evening, often in the summer), *raiu* (thunderstorms), *samidare* (a long spell of passing showers in May by the lunar calendar), *tsuyu* (the rainy season in early summer), and *akisame* (long autumn rains) to name but a few. There also are many, often onomatopoeic, phrases expressing wetness or

日本の文化には、簡素さ、静寂、余韻を尊ぶ傾向がある。和食の繊細な盛り付け、日本画の淡い色調、細やかな自然描写などは、多くの日本人の感性の表れといえよう。俳句・和歌の短い言葉や能・歌舞伎・人形浄瑠璃・茶道・華道のなかの、微妙な仕草で独特の深い世界を象徴しているのも日本文化の特徴である。

　日本人は自然の豊かな恵みをすなおに受け入れて、自然に対して畏敬と感謝と調和の態度で接してきた。日本人の伝統的信仰はアニミズム・自然崇拝であり、仏教の受入にも大きな抵抗がなかった。
　日本人が長い間培（つちか）ってきた美意識を表わす言葉に「もののあわれ」と「無常」がある。「もののあわれ」は、平安王朝文学の美的理念の一つとされるもので、対象に同情・同感し、その風情や情趣にしみじみと心が動かされるさまを言う。また、「無常」は、仏教思想の影響を受けながら中世以降日本人独特の価値観へと昇華されたもので、移ろいゆくもの、はかないものをいとおしく思い、そこに美を感じるさまを言う。日本人が桜を好むのはその一例ともいわれる。

　また、工芸品・絵画などの微細で繊細な仕上げや、幕の内弁当、ミニ庭園、盆栽など多くの種類のものを小さな空間にまとめることも日本人の得意技である。

d）外国文化の吸収と融合
　日本は、独自の文化を作りあげる 2,000 年余りの歴史のなかで、さまざまな外国の文化を吸収してきた。古くは中国や朝鮮半島から文字・仏教をはじめとする優れた文化が流入し、近くは明治維新から 20 世紀初めにかけて、主としてヨーロッパから合理主義・平等思想とともに近代的文物・諸制度などが積極的に導入された。戦後にはアメリカ文化の圧倒的な影響下に置かれた。

conditions of water, like *shittori* (moist), *bisho-bisho* (dripping wet), *shito-shito* (the sound of gently falling rain), and *zah-zah* (the sound of pouring rain). Also characteristic of Japanese is the state of wind being precisely conveyed by such phrases as *soyo-soyo* (for breeze) and *byu-byu* (for gale).

Japanese culture tends to respect simplicity, silence, and reverberation. The delicate arrangement of Japanese food, the faint colors of traditional Japanese painting, the detailed descriptions of nature—these all express the sensitivities of many Japanese. The brevity of *haiku* and *waka*, the delicate gestures of *noh*, *kabuki*, *ningyo joruri* (puppet theater), the tea ceremony, and flower arrangement—these symbolize a unique and profound world and are also characteristic of Japanese culture.

The Japanese have internalized the rich blessings of nature and approach it with respect, gratefulness, and harmony. The traditional faith of Japan is a blend of animism and nature worship, and there was no great resistance to Buddhism.

Among the words expressive of the aesthetic sense acquired by the Japanese over a long period of time, there are "*mononoaware*" and "*mujo*. "Mononoaware" is said to be one of the aesthetic notions of Heian dynasty literature and denotes the state of mind that feels sympathy and empathy towards the subject and becomes profoundly moved by its elegance and charms. "Mujo" is a Japanese tendency to love and appreciate the beauty of things which are transient and ephemeral in nature, which, under the influence of Buddhist thought since the medieval ages, became sublimed in a peculiarly Japanese sense of values. The Japanese fondness for the short-lived cherry blossoms might be an example of this.

Other characteristic techniques of the Japanese include meticulously fine finishing touches seen in crafts and drawings, *makunouchi-bento* (box lunches containing many small portions of various foods), garden miniatures, and *bonsai*.

d) Absorbing and Assimilating Foreign Cultures

In the process of developing its unique culture over the last 2000 years, Japan has absorbed elements from a number of foreign cultures. In ancient times, there was an influx of major cultural elements from China and the Korean Peninsula, such as Buddhism and writing systems. Then, in modern times (from the Meiji Restoration to the early years of the twentieth century) Japan actively adopted modern social systems, mainly products of Western civilization, and the ideas of rationalism and egalitarianism mainly from Europe. After World War II,

しかし、中国・ヨーロッパ・アメリカの文化を吸収しつつも、長い歴史過程のなかで、民族固有の感性と工夫によってこれらを醸成・融合して、国際的に認められる独自の文化を築き上げてきた。これが、日本文化の最も大きな特質である。このような歴史的背景から日本文化は極めて多彩な要素をもつようになった。

(2) 文字・言語・文学

a) 日本語

日本語は独特の文章構造をとり、固有の文字をもっているため、ほかの言語とあまり類似していない。系統的には、朝鮮語・アルタイ諸語との同系説が有力であるが、その証明はまだされていない。

今日では日本全国で標準語が通用するが、各地には多種多様の方言があり、互いの方言を理解できないこともある。ただし、文字や文法は基本的に同一である。

現代日本語の特徴のいくつかをあげると、次のとおりである。

〈1〉 漢字・平仮名・片仮名・ローマ字など異なった種類の文字をまじえて用いる。

〈2〉 使用する文字の数が多い(一般通用漢字約 3,000 字、そのうち常用漢字 2,136 字、および平仮名・片仮名各 46 字)。

〈3〉 文章は、縦書きも横書きも行われる。

〈4〉 音韻組織が単純で、音節の種類が少ない。標準母音は、ア・イ・ウ・エ・オの五つ、音節は母音または子音と母音とからなり、母音で終わる。単独使用の子音はンのみ。

〈5〉 同じ事物を指すのに、いくつもの単語が用いられる。特に一・二人称代名詞は種類が多い(わたし・ぼく・おれ・じぶん、あなた・きみ・おまえ、など)。

〈6〉 同じ音で異なった意味を表わす単語が多い(対象・

Japan was under overwhelming influence of American culture.

Although Japan has absorbed cultural elements from China, Europe, and America, these elements have evolved and been assimilated over a long period of time through the unique ethnic sensibilities and methods of the Japanese to create a unique culture that is recognized internationally. This is probably the most distinct aspect of Japanese culture. From this historical background, Japan has developed a multi-faceted culture.

(2) Writing System, Language and Literature

a) The Japanese Language

The Japanese language has its own peculiar sentence structure and writing system and has little in common with other languages of the world. Although the theory that Japanese belongs to the Altaic and Korean family of languages is widely accepted, this has never been fully substantiated.

Although standard Japanese is today used throughout the country, a variety of dialects are also used in different regions. These dialects are mutually unintelligible in some instances. However, the writing system and grammar are essentially the same.

Few of the characteristic features of modern Japanese are listed below.

<1> It uses a mixture of different types of characters, namely, *kanji* characters, *hiragana* characters, *katakana* characters and Roman letters.

<2> The number of characters used is large. (There are about 3,000 commonly used kanji characters including the 2,136 "daily use characters," 46 hiragana characters and 46 katakana characters.)

<3> Sentences can be written either vertically or horizontally.

<4> Having few sounds, it is phonetically simple. It has only five standard vowels: "*a*" as in father, "*i*" as in piano, "*u*" as in flute, "*e*" as in red and "*o*" as in cord. Syllables are formed by a single vowel or a combination of a consonant and a vowel in the order mentioned, "*n*" (as in can) being the only consonant that can stand alone.

<5> The same thing or idea can often be expressed with a number of different words. This is especially true of first and second person pronouns. For example, there are a number of words that would translate into English as "I" (*watashi, boku, ore, jibun,* etc.) or "you" (*anata, kimi, omae,* etc.)

<6> There are many words having the same sound but expressing

　　　　　対照・対称・大将・大正・大勝、公正・厚生・構成・攻勢・更生、保障・保証・補償など)。
〈7〉 職業・年齢・性別などによる用語の違いが著しい。

〈8〉 助詞(が・を、など)、助動詞(ない・だろう、など)が文の成立に大切な機能を果たしている。
〈9〉 主語は述語の前におき、述語は文の終わりにおくが、文節の順序はかなり自由である。主語は述語の使い方で省略されることも多い。

〈10〉敬語が発達していて、複雑である。
〈11〉オノマトペ(「擬音語」と「擬態語」を包括的に指した言葉)を効果的に使う。生物・自然の発する声や音・様子・動作・感情などを簡略的に表し、情景をより感情的に表現させることのできる手段として用いられており、生活の中でしばしばオノマトペを利用する(例:グングン、ジャンジャン、スゴスゴ、ビクビク)。

b) 文字
1) 概要

　日本語の表記方法には、漢字・平仮名・片仮名の3種類の文字を使うが、このほか、ローマ字も使われることがある。

　日本語を書くとき名詞・動詞・形容詞など多くは漢字で書き、動詞および形容詞の活用変化の部分や助動詞・助詞は仮名で書く。副詞は漢字でも仮名でも書く。現在は平仮名が広く使われ、片仮名は主に外国の地名、人名や外来語を表す場合に用いられる。

　学校で最初に教えられる文字は平仮名である。しかし現在は、学校へ入学する前に仮名の読み書きのできる子供が多い。

　日本の文字は縦書き用にできているが、横書きもできる。縦書きの場合は右から左へ行を移す。昔は縦書きが多かったが、数字の表記や外国語の引用に便利な

different ideas.

<7> There are marked differences in usage of words and expressions used by persons of different occupation, age, sex etc.
<8> Particles are used to indicate part of speech (subject, object etc.) and auxiliary verbs play an important role in sentence structure.
<9> Aside from the restriction that the subject must come before the predicate (which comes last), the speaker has considerable freedom in choosing the order of the phrases. The subject is often omitted when the meaning is clear from the predicate alone.
<10> It has a complicated system of honorific expression.
<11> Onomatopoeic words are used effectively. These include both simple sound imitations and mimicking of non-auditory phenomena. Japanese is rich in expressions that capture and succinctly express the sounds, appearances, actions and auras of both animate and inanimate things and that speakers and writers can easily use to convey scenes, situations and perceptions with sensory impact. Japanese frequently use onomatopoeia in everyday life. Examples: *gungun* (rapidly, by leaps and bounds, steadily), *janjan* (jingle-jangle, repeatedly and vigorously), *sugosugo* (dejectedly), *bikubiku* (gingerly).

b) Writing System
1) Overview

Japanese is written using mainly three types of characters: *kanji*, *hiragana* and *katakana*. Roman letters are also used, but to a much lesser extent.

In writing Japanese, most nouns, verb roots, and adjectives are represented by kanji while the verb and adjective endings indicating the various tenses etc., the auxiliary verbs, and the particles are written in one of the *kana* systems (hiragana or katakana). Adverbs can be written in either kanji or kana characters. Of the two kana systems, hiragana has by far the wider usage in modern times. Katakana characters are used mostly for the spelling of foreign place and personal names and loanwords brought into Japanese from other languages.

The first characters taught at primary school are those of the hiragana system. In fact, however, a fairly large percentage of Japanese children are able to read and write kana characters even before they enter school.

All three types of Japanese characters are designed to be written in vertical lines, though they can also be written horizontally. When written vertically, the first line comes on the right of the page and

横書きが徐々に普及し、ビジネス文書においては一般的なものとなっている。しかし、読みやすいのは縦書きの方なので、新聞・雑誌・書籍は、縦書きのものが多い。

2）漢字

　漢字は紀元前十数世紀からすでに中国で用いられていた象形文字・指事文字から発達した表意文字である。太陽を表わす文字「日」は太陽の形から、樹木を表わす文字「木」は樹木の形に似せてつくられた。また、林を表わす文字は木を二つ並べてつくられ、森を表わす文字は木を重ねてつくられている。漢字は中国から朝鮮・日本・ベトナムに伝えられた。わが国には2,000年ほど前に朝鮮半島を経由して、伝えられたとされている。

　文字の伝来は日本人の文化・社会生活に画期的な影響を与えた。文字の記録性により文化・歴史の伝承が可能となった。『古事記』が稗田阿礼（ひえだのあれ）の暗誦を太安万侶（おおのやすまろ）が筆録したことにより、はじめて書物となった。
　漢字はその数10万字を超えるといわれる。これは「字」数であり、「語」数はこれの数倍に達する。日本では一般の社会生活で使用する漢字の目安として常用漢字2,136字を選定している（2010年内閣告示第2号）。しかし、人の姓や地名にはこれ以外にもたくさん使われているため、これよりはるかに多くの漢字を知らないと新聞や書籍を読むときに不都合が生じる場合もある。

　なお、日本でつくられた漢字（国字）も多い（働、峠、辻、畑など）。
　中国から伝わった漢字の読み方には、中国式に読む音読みと日本式に読む訓読みがある。
3）ひらがな（平仮名）・カタカナ（片仮名）

　ひらがなは、中国伝来の漢字と日本人の創意との合作の音節文字である。ひらがなの発明は、日本の文化の発達に決定的といえるほど大きな役割を果たした。ひらがなは、漢字の草書体をさらに簡略化した文字で

succeeding lines follow it to the left. Years ago, almost all writing was vertical but the horizontal style has gradually become more popular since it is more adaptable to inclusion of Arabic numerals and passages in foreign languages, and business documents are also generally written horizontally. From the reader's point of view, however, vertically written sentences are easier to assimilate and for this reason most newspapers, magazines, and popular books are printed in this style.

2) Kanji

Kanji characters were already in use in China more than three thousand years ago. They are ideograms developed from pictograms and signs. For example, the character meaning the sun was drawn in the form of the sun, and the character meaning a tree was made to resemble the shape of a tree. Going a step further, two trees were combined in a single character to indicate a wood and three trees were combined to represent a forest. The kanji characters developed in China gradually began to be used in Korea, Japan, and Vietnam. Kanji are considered to have been introduced to Japan some 2000 years ago, via the Korean Peninsula.

Writing had an immense influence on the cultural and social life of the Japanese, making it possible to record cultural and historical events. The *Kojiki* (Records of Ancient Matters) was first compiled as a book by Oo-no-Yasumaro writing the text recited by Hieda-no-Are.

There are said to be several hundred thousand kanji characters. This is only the number of characters; the number of words that can be formed by combining characters is many times this. In Japan, 2,136 kanji characters have been selected as those most suitable for ordinary purposes (number selected as of 2010 Cabinet Notification No. 2). Still one must know considerably more characters than this in order to read even the newspapers and ordinary books since the characters for many personal and place names are not included in this limited number, which can be quite inconvenient.

The Japanese have also invented a fair number of kanji characters (called Japan-originated kanji) for their own use.

Most of the kanji introduced from China can be read in two ways: in the "*on*" or Chinese reading and in the "*kun*" or Japanese reading.

3) Hiragana and Katakana

Hiragana is a phonetic script created by applying Japanese ingenuity to *kanji* characters imported from China. The invention of hiragana played a pivotal role in the development of Japanese culture. The characters of hiragana were crafted by further simplification of already ab-

ある。『万葉集』の時代（5～8世紀）までは、日本語の表記にはその発音に似た漢字（万葉仮名）が用いられていたが、平安時代になるとひらがなが作られた。ひらがなは当時の女性のあいだから広がり、『土佐日記』、『蜻蛉日記』などの日記文学、世界最古の長編小説とされる『源氏物語』、また日本的情趣あふれる和歌の世界もひらがなとともに開花した。

　カタカナもひらがなと同じ時代に発明された音節文字であり、日本語と発音の似た漢字の一部分をとって簡略な文字にしたものである。諸外国の言葉を、その発音に近い形で表現することができ、現代では外来文化・技術の導入に絶大な威力を発揮している。

c）外国人の日本語学習
　日本語は、学びはじめるのに容易な言語の一つであるとされている。発音が簡単で、文法規制も例外が少なく、構文上の制約もゆるい。難しさは主として漢字の読み書きにある。

　日本語は他の言語と異なったところが多いため、難しいと思われがちであるが、基礎的な会話は決して難しくない。日本に来ている外国人は、1年もすると日常会話は一通りできるようになる人が多い。
　しかし、日本語を正しく話すには、かなりの経験が必要である。
　日本語は話す主人公が男であるか女であるか、大人であるか子供であるか、によって用法が少しずつ異なる。たとえば「私」を意味する言葉も、話者の年齢、性別、社会的立場などによって幾通りかに使い分けられる（わたし、ぼく、おれ、じぶん、など）。さらに面倒なことは、相手との関係によっても使い分けられる（お兄ちゃん、お姉ちゃんとはいうが、弟ちゃん、妹ちゃんとは言わない）。そのほか、同じ音で違う意味の言葉（意義・異義・威儀・異議など）が多く、外国人にはすぐ理解しにくい面がある。

　また敬語といわれる用法がかなり広く使われている。こ

breviated cursive-style kanji characters. Until the time of the *Manyoshu* (between fifth to eighth century), the Japanese writing system used kanji with pronunciations similar to those of Japanese syllables. These were called "*manyogana*". Entering the Heian period, hiragana was born. Hiragana became popular among the women of that age, which resulted in the blossoming of Japanese literature—such diary literature as *Tosa Nikki* (The Tosa Diary) and *Kagerou Nikki* (The Kagerou Diary), and *Genji Monogatari* (The Tale of Genji), said to be the world's oldest novel. *Waka* poetry, which is said to exemplify Japanese sensibilities, also came into its own at this time.

Hiragana and its cousin katakana, invented in the same period, are phonetic alphabets that were created as simplified forms of certain kanji that had a similar pronunciation to Japanese syllables. These alphabets, called *kana*, can be used to give a close rendition of the pronunciation of foreign words, so that kana today serves as a powerful tool for the introduction of foreign cultures and technology.

c) Learning Japanese by Foreigners

Purely from the linguistic point of view, Japanese is generally considered as one of the easier languages for a beginner to approach. It has a simple pronunciation scheme and few exceptions to grammatical rules. Restrictions on sentence structure are not severe. Probably the most difficult aspect of the language is the reading and writing of *kanji* characters.

Still, Japanese differs so much from other languages that many tend to think it is very hard to learn, but basic conversation is not terribly difficult. Foreigners who come to Japan can often carry on everyday conversations after being here for only one year.

However, it does take a considerable amount of experience to speak Japanese correctly.

The way Japanese is spoken differs somewhat depending on whether the speaker is a man or a woman, an adult or a child. For example, there are numerous words meaning "I" and each speaker refers to himself or herself using the one that is most appropriate for his or her situation (*watashi*, *boku*, *ore*, *jibun*, etc.). What is even more troublesome is that the speaker must choose his or her words considering the relationship between himself or herself and the person to which he or she is speaking. Another aspect of the language that makes it difficult for foreigners to grasp quickly is the presence of many words which are pronounced the same but have different meanings.

Still another is the relatively common use of especially polite

れには三つのタイプがある。ひとつは相手のものや行為に尊敬語（接頭語）をつける用法で（お荷物、ご好意、ご覧になる）、もうひとつは自分のことを謙遜して表現する用法（申す、まいる、伺う、さしあげる）、そして述語に丁寧な言い回しをする用法（です、ます、ございます）である。敬語を正しく使うには、日本人でもかなりの訓練がいる。日本人は自分達が外国語を話すことが苦手なことから、外国人が日本語を間違えて話しても、できるだけよく理解しようと努める。

国際交流基金は、3年に一度「海外日本語教育機関調査」を実施している。2015年の調査では、137カ国・地域において日本語教育が実施されている。前回調査（2012年）と比べると、受講者の数は中国、インドネシア、韓国および台湾で減少傾向であるが、オーストラリア、タイ、ベトナム、フィリピンでは大幅に増加している。現在、世界各国における日本語学習者は、約365万人（2015年）である。

d）日本語のなかの外来語

日本語には多くの外来語が取り入れられている。このうちもっとも古く、多いのが中国伝来の漢語である。しかも、その大部分は漢語本来の意味とは別に、日本語としての意味が与えられた。したがって、この場合漢語は外来語とはいいがたい。

〈1〉 韓国語から
古代の日本語と韓国語との間には密接な相互関連性があり、類似点も多かったのではないかと推測されている。しかし中世以降は、韓国語を語源とする日本語は非常に少ない。
（例）明太子、チョンガー、パッチ

〈2〉 梵語（サンスクリット語）から
梵語起源の仏教用語は多数ある。
（例）瓦、旦那、世話、袈裟、菩提、舎利、奈落

〈3〉 マレーシア語から
（例）ペケ、トンカチ

〈4〉 その他のアジア諸国語から
（例）シェルパ（チベット語）、キセル（カンボジア

(honorific) speech forms. These are of three types: one which uses special words of respect in connection with the acts and possessions of the person or persons one is speaking to, one which uses special words of modesty regarding oneself, and one which uses special verb endings and prefixes to create polite speech with respect to any subject. Even native speakers require training and practice before they can use honorifics properly. The Japanese themselves are not good at speaking foreign languages, and therefore they understand the problems of the foreigner and will make every effort to understand him or her even if he or she makes mistakes.

The Japan Foundation releases a Survey Report on Japanese-Language Education Abroad every three years. According to the 2015 survey, Japanese language education is being conducted in 137 countries. Compared with the previous survey (2012), the number of students showed a decrease in China, Indonesia, South Korea, and Taiwan, but a significant increase in Australia, Thailand, Vietnam, and the Philippines. The number of people studying Japanese worldwide is about 3.65 million (2015).

d) Loanwords

Japanese has borrowed a large number of words from other languages. The oldest and largest group of borrowed words is from China. However, as the meanings assigned to most of the Chinese words used in Japanese are different from the original Chinese meanings, it does not seem quite proper to call them loanwords.

<1> Korean

Ancient Japanese and Korean are thought to have been closely related and to have had many similarities. However, the number of Japanese words originating from Korean has been very small at least from the Middle Ages.

Examples: *mentaiko* (salted cod roe spiced with red pepper), *chonga* (bachelor), *pacchi* (men's long underpants)

<2> Sanskrit

There are many Buddhist words originating from Sanskrit.

Examples: *kawara* (roof tile), *danna* (master), *sewa* (care), *kesa* (surplice), *bodai* (state of supreme enlightenment), *shari* (the relics of Buddha), *naraku* (hell)

<3> Malay

Examples: *peke* (no good), *tonkachi* (a hammer)

<4> Other Asian languages

Examples: *sherupa* (sherpa, Tibet), *kiseru* (a pipe consisting of a

語)
⟨5⟩ 英語から
19世紀以降数多く流入しており、とくに近年は氾濫気味であるが、一時期を過ぎると使われなくなるものも少なくない。以下は、日本語の一部として定着して久しいものの一例。
(例) ジョッキ、ワイシャツ、スプーン、ポスト、プール

⟨6⟩ オランダ語から
17世紀から19世紀まで、日本はヨーロッパの国としてはオランダとのみ貿易していたため、オランダ語からきたものも多い。
(例) オルゴール、ガラス、コップ、ゴム、ビール、ホース、ポンプ、ランドセル

⟨7⟩ ポルトガル語から
日本に初めて来たヨーロッパ人がポルトガル人であったため、ポルトガル語からも多い。
(例) カステラ、カボチャ、カッパ、タバコ、天ぷら、ボタン

⟨8⟩ イタリア語から
音楽用語・料理用語を中心に比較的多い。
(例) ピアノ、フォルテ、オペラ、ソナタ、パスタ

⟨9⟩ フランス語から
度量衡、美術、ファッション関係はフランス語由来のものが多い。
(例) メートル、リットル、ズボン、デッサン、メニュー

⟨10⟩ ドイツ語から
医療、登山用語などはドイツ語由来のものが多い。

(例) アレルギー、カルテ、レントゲン、ザイル、アルバイト

⟨11⟩ ロシア語から
(例) アジト、イクラ、インテリ、カンパ、ノルマ

e) 日本の文学

8世紀の初め、皇室を中心とした国家体制が完成すると、日本古代の神話と歴史が『古事記』と『日本書紀』に

metal bowl, a bamboo stem, and a metal mouthpiece, Cambodia)

<5> English

Many words have come into Japanese from English since the nineteenth century, and in recent years there has been a veritable flood of English, but many of these words fade out after a short time. Below are some that have become firmly fixed in the Japanese language.

Examples: *jokki* (jug), *waishatsu* (white shirt), *supun* (spoon), *posuto* (post), *puru* (pool)

<6> Dutch

From the seventeenth to nineteenth centuries Japan traded solely with Holland, so there are many words that originated from Dutch.

Examples: *orugooru* (music box), *garasu* (glass), *koppu* (cup), *gomu* (rubber), *biiru* (beer), *hosu* (hose), *ponpu* (pump), *randoseru* (satchel)

<7> Portuguese

The first Europeans to visit Japan were Portuguese, so there are many words from Portuguese.

Examples: *kasutera* (a type of sponge cake), *kabocha* (pumpkin), *kappa* (raincoat), *tabako* (cigarettes), *tempura* (battered and deep-fried foods), *botan* (button)

<8> Italian

Many words of Italian origin are found in music and cooking.

Examples: *piano* (piano), *forute* (forte), *opera* (opera), *sonata* (sonata), *pasuta* (pasta)

<9> French

Many words of French origin are found in weights and measures, art, and fashion.

Examples: *metoru* (meter), *rittoru* (liter), *zubon* (trousers), *dessan* (sketch), *menyu* (menu)

<10> German

Many words of German origin can be found in medicine and mountain climbing terminology.

Examples: *arerugi* (allergy), *karute* (clinical chart), *rentogen* (x-ray), *zairu* (climbing rope), *arubaito* (part-time job)

<11> Russian

Examples: *ajito* (hideout for political troublemakers), *ikura* (salmon caviar), *interi* (intelligentsia), *kanpa* (campaign), *noruma* (quota)

e) **Japanese Literature**

Once Japan had been consolidated as a single nation around the imperial family, the country's ancient myths and history were gathered

まとめられた。

　『古事記』は、故事を記憶することを職としていた宮廷の役人が暗唱していたものをまとめた記録である。和漢折衷的な漢文体で書かれ、天皇を中心としたより強力な国家を形成しようという意図で編纂されたものだが、日本最古の文学と考えられている。
　『日本書紀』は、本格的な史書である。純粋な漢文体で書かれている。
　また8世紀の後半には、現存する最古の歌集『万葉集』が登場した。これは、20巻からなり、450年にわたって天皇から庶民まで各階層の作者がつくった約4,500首もの歌が含まれている。その歌の約9割が万葉仮名で書かれた短歌である。万葉仮名は、日本語の音を表すために、漢字（中国の表意文字）の中国語と日本語の読み方を利用した表現法である。

　9世紀末の仮名文字の発明によって、多くの物語が生み出されるようになった（「仮名」は音節文字で、書くのがやさしく、数も限られているので、日本語を表記するのがたいへん楽になった）。政治の権力が貴族に移ったこととあいまって、女性の日記文学をはじめとして、多彩な平安文学の時代の基盤ができあがった。11世紀の初めに、この時代の文学は紫式部の作品『源氏物語』によって、最盛期を迎えた。この物語のなかで、紫式部は皇子として生まれながら天皇になれなかった主人公、光源氏の華やかな宮廷生活を描いている。『源氏物語』は、和歌をまじえた和文体で書かれており、登場人物たちの心理描写は見事である。『源氏物語』は54帖におよび、世界最古の長編小説である。

　12世紀、武士階級が台頭し、動乱のなかで人々は宗教に救いを求めるようになった。こうして仏教が武士や庶民の間に広まった。これを反映して、この時代の文学は仏教的無常観から描かれた作品が多い。その代表作が『平家物語』だが、作者は不明である。この物語は13世紀に登場し、琵琶の音楽を伴奏として語り継がれ民衆の中に広まった（平曲という）。作品の内容は、12世紀後半の平家一門の繁栄と滅亡を描いた物語であり、作品の根底には、奢（おご）れる者は必ず滅びるという仏教の無常観が貫かれている。

together in the *Kojiki* (Records of Ancient Matters) and the *Nihonshoki* (Chronicles of Japan) in the early eighth century.

The *Kojiki* is a record of ancient events as recited by a court official responsible for memorizing such matters. Written in a blend of Japanese and classical Chinese (*kanbun*), it is considered Japan's earliest literary work, despite being compiled with the political motive of building a stronger nation around the emperor.

The *Nihonshoki* is a straightforward historical record. It is written in pure *kanbun* with deference to China as an advanced neighbor.

Also in the late eighth century, there appeared what is now the oldest existing anthology of poetry, the *Manyoshu* (Collection of Ten Thousand Leaves), which consists of 20 scrolls and includes approximately 4,500 poems written by poets in all walks of life, from emperors to common people, over a period of about 450 years. Around 90% of the poems are *tanka* written in *manyogana*, a style that uses the Chinese and Japanese readings of *kanji* characters (Chinese ideograms) to represent Japanese phonetically.

The invention and spread of *kana* characters toward the end of the ninth century led to the emergence of many stories. (As kana are phonetic with each representing a single syllable, easy to write and of limited number, they greatly simplified the writing of Japanese.) The advent of kana, together with the shift of the center of political power to the nobility, laid the foundation for the productive Heian literary period, such as women's diary literature, which peaked in the early eleventh century with the writing of *Genji Monogatari* (The Tale of Genji) by Murasaki Shikibu. In her story, she depicts the brilliant court life of the hero Hikaru Genji, who, although a prince by birth, fails to become emperor. *Genji Monogatari* is written in Japanese style, intermixed with *waka* poetry. Its portrayal of the thoughts and feelings of the characters is exquisite. Running to 54 books, this is the world's first full-length novel.

In the twelfth century, in the midst of the incessant conflicts that accompanied the rise of the warrior class to power, people turned to religion. Buddhism spread among both the warriors and the common people. Reflecting this, the literature of the period is dominated by works with an underlying tone that derives from the Buddhist concept of the impermanence of worldly things. The best work from the period is *Heike Monogatari* (The Tale of the Heike), whose author is unknown. The story appeared in the thirteenth century and was spread among the people of the time in the form of *heikyoku*, a narration accompanied by the music of the *biwa*, a stringed instrument. It tells the story of the

17世紀初めに江戸幕府の創設とともに、動乱の世が終わりを告げた。平和な年月の間に商業の発展に伴い町人が経済力を身につけるようになり、町人中心の文化が誕生した。その代表的な作家が、井原西鶴と近松門左衛門であった。井原西鶴の代表作は『好色一代男』で、11世紀に書かれた『源氏物語』にならって、世之介という好色の男の生涯が54章にわたって描かれている。近松門左衛門は人形浄瑠璃や歌舞伎の脚本をたくさん執筆し、当時の庶民の姿を巧みに描いた。義理と人情との葛藤に苦しんだ末に心中した、徳兵衛とお初という若い男女を描いた『曾根崎心中』は、特に有名である。また、俳句を優れた芸術にまで高めた松尾芭蕉が活躍したのも、この時代である。芭蕉は、俳句以外にも作品を残しているが、なかでも奥州各地・北陸の大旅行を題材とした『おくのほそ道』は、日本の紀行文学の代表作である。

19世紀後半の明治維新以降、日本は西洋との交流を深め、その影響を受けてさまざまな文芸思潮や新しい作品が生み出された。近代文学の二大巨峰といわれるのが、森鴎外と夏目漱石である。ともに、西欧への留学を経験し、東西文化に精通して、鴎外と漱石は、どこの派にも属さず、独自の立場を守って多くの作品を生み出した。

『舞姫』は、鴎外の処女作である。ドイツ留学中に真の自我に目覚めた官吏、太田豊太郎にかかわる小説である。ドイツ滞在中に踊り子エリスとの恋愛におちいり、免官されてしまう。親友のはからいで帰国することになるが、そのため自由と発狂した恋人を棄てざるをえなくなる。こうした胸中の苦悩を描いた、自伝的な色彩の強い作品である。

また、『吾輩は猫である』は漱石の処女作である。中学校教師、苦沙弥（くしゃみ）先生の飼い猫を語り手とした文体で書かれている。飼い主の家族、周囲の人物とそこに起きるさまざまな事件が、飼い猫の目から、鋭い風刺と

rise to glory and eventual downfall of the Heike clan in the late twelfth century, a theme based on the Buddhist concept of impermanence, that the proud will surely be destroyed.

The period of war-torn turbulence came to an end with the establishment of the Edo Shogunate at the beginning of the seventeenth century. As commerce flourished and the merchant class gradually gained economic power during these peaceful years, a new urban culture developed. The leading writers to emerge were Ihara Saikaku and Chikamatsu Monzaemon. Saikaku's best-known work is *Koshoku Ichidaiotoko* (Life of an Amorous Man) which, in the style of the eleventh-century *Genji Monogatari*, devoted 54 chapters to the lifetime escapades of the lecherous Yonosuke. Monzaemon wrote a large number of *joruri* and *kabuki* plays which are especially notable for their superb portrayal of the common people. Probably his most famous work is *Sonezaki Shinju* (Love Suicides at Sonezaki), the story of young lovers, Tokubei and Hatsu, who, torn between their love and their obligations, find suicide the only solution. Also of this period is Matsuo Basho, the poet who elevated *haiku* to a major poetic genre. While Basho is best known for his poems, he also produced a number of other works, most notably *Oku no Hosomichi* (The Narrow Road to the Deep North), a diary of his extensive travels through northern Honshu which is a classic among Japanese travelogues.

The deepening exchanges between Japan and the West following the Meiji Restoration in the late nineteenth century gave rise to various literary trends and new works. The two masters of this modern literature period were Mori Ogai and Natsume Soseki. Both studied abroad, were deeply versed in Western as well as Eastern cultures, avoided involvement in any particular school, and produced many works that reflected their own independent views.

Ogai's first work was *Maihime* (The Dancing Girl), a novel about Ota Toyotaro, a government official who discovers his true self while studying in Germany. While there, he falls in love with a dancer named Elise, at the cost of losing his post. Although he manages to return to Japan with the help of a friend, he is forced to abandon both his freedom and his now crazed sweetheart. The story, which centers on Ota's anguish, has strong autobiographic overtones.

Soseki's first work was *Wagahai wa Neko de Aru* (I Am a Cat). It is written in such a style that a cat, the pet of a middle school teacher named Kushami, takes the role of narrator. The story about this teacher, his family, and the other characters and the incidents that occur, as seen

ユーモアによって描かれている。

　そのほかに、翻訳版によって海外でよく知られている作家・作品としては、次のようなものがある。大阪の豪商一家の四人姉妹を題材に源氏物語的世界を描いた『細雪（さざめゆき）』の谷崎潤一郎。近代叙情文学の古典といわれる『雪国』を書いた川端康成。金閣寺に放火する青年の心理的過程を描いた『金閣寺』の三島由紀夫。作者の内的な芸術的自叙伝とされる『人間失格』の太宰治。砂の穴に落ち込んだ中学教師が、穴に住む女と共同生活をする話を描いた『砂の女』の安部公房。障害をもった子供の誕生に対する青年の葛藤を描いた『個人的な体験』の大江健三郎。

　近年では1987年『ノルウェイの森』の発刊以降村上春樹ブームが続いているが、経済成長後の先進国共通のライフスタイルの変化を、男（または女）がどう克服し自分を知るか、そして幸せや充実とは何かを描いたテーマは、場面の移り変わりが明確で日本のみならず世界50カ国以上に翻訳されファンを増やしている。

f）短歌・俳句

　短歌は和歌の一形式で、5・7・5・7・7の5句31音の形式をもつ。この定型は、感情を表現する抒情詩として、日本人の呼吸に極めて自然な長さであるといわれている。最初の5・7・5を上（かみ）の句、続く7・7を下（しも）の句という。

　和歌の形式は、もとは長歌・短歌・旋頭歌（せどうか）など多様であったが、やがて短歌のみが優勢となり、平安時代以降（8世紀末以降）は、和歌すなわち短歌と考えられるようになった。ひらがなによって記述され、日本人らしい情趣・情感を表現してきた和歌は、平安時代以降現代にいたるまで、宮廷・僧侶・武家・庶民などに連綿として引き継がれてきた。平安時代には『古今和歌集』が、また鎌倉時代には『新古今和歌集』が、ともに天皇の命を受け

through the eyes of the cat, is told with biting satire and considerable humor.

A short list of Japanese literary works that have become well known overseas in their translated versions would include the following. Tanizaki Jun'ichiro's *Sasame Yuki* (The Makioka Sisters), which paints a *Genji Monogatari*-like world around four sisters belonging to a great Osaka merchant family. Kawabata Yasunari's *Yukiguni* (Snow Country), often called a classic of modern lyric literature. Mishima Yukio's *Kinkakuji* (The Temple of the Golden Pavilion), which follows the mental processes of a young man who sets fire to a famous temple in Kyoto. Dazai Osamu's *Ningen Shikkaku* (No Longer Human), considered a revealing of the writer's inner artistic sensibilities. Abe Kobo's *Suna no Onna* (The Woman in the Dunes), the story of a middle school teacher who falls into a hole in the sand and takes up life with a woman who lives there. Oe Kenzaburo's *Kojinteki na Taiken* (A Personal Matter), which describes a young father's preoccupation with the birth of his handicapped son.

Murakami Haruki's *Norwegian Wood*, published 1987, has since made Murakami one of Japan's best-selling writers. His theme of how men and women can truly know themselves by overcoming the changed lifestyle common among advanced nations following economic development, and the meaning of happiness and fulfillment, with its transition of scenes, is striking a chord among readers not only in Japan but also in the growing numbers of fans in the more than 50 countries in which translations of the book have been published.

f) Tanka and Haiku

Tanka is one form of *waka* (Japanese poetry), consisting of five lines of 5, 7, 5, 7, and 7 syllables. It is said that for a Japanese this is the most natural length for a lyric poem expressing emotion. The first three lines of 5, 7, and 5 syllables are termed the *kami no ku* ("upper poem") and the remaining two lines of 7 and 7 syllables the *shimo no ku* ("lower poem").

Waka originally encompassed a variety of forms, such as *choka*, tanka and *sedoka*, but tanka gradually became the predominant form until, from the Heian Era (late eighth century), the term waka came to be considered synonymous with tanka. Written in *hiragana* and expressing a very Japanese charm and feeling, waka has been carried on in an unbroken line from the Heian period to the present, in the Imperial court, by Buddhist priests, and by samurai and the common people. The *Kokin Wakashu* (Collection of Ancient and Modern Japanese Poetry),

て編さんされた。

　短歌は短詩型抒情詩であるため、自然や人間生活の美を尊重し、あこがれる心が重要な要素である。このあこがれの心の本質を、単純な形式のなかに、喜怒哀楽の諸感情が交錯した深みのあるものとして表現することが求められるのである。こうして心に感ずることをいきいきとうたいあげたものは、豊かな連想を呼ぶ力をもつ。このように、31音の言外に感じられるものを余情といい、短歌一首の内容は、この余情をも含めたものというべきである。
　俳句は5・7・5の17音による定型詩であり、俳諧の連歌の発句（ほっく）を独立させてできたものである。

　連歌というのは、短歌の形式を使ったもともと宮廷での優雅な言葉遊びの中から生まれたものであった。複数の者が集まって、あらかじめ示された先行句に自分の句をつける。長句には短句を、短句には長句をと相互に付け合う即興の味、機知、頓才が連歌の真骨頂である。これが俳諧（たわむれ、滑稽の意）の連歌と言われるものだが、15世紀から16世紀にかけて連歌の名人（例えば山崎宗鑑）が何人も出たことにより、文芸的なものに発展する。

　これをさらに進めて連歌の発句を独立させて俳句を確立させたのは、江戸時代初期の松永貞徳とその門弟たちと言われている。さらに江戸時代の中ごろ（17世紀末）、俳聖（俳句の聖人）といわれる松尾芭蕉が出て、俳句に「さび」（枯れた渋み）、「しおり」（おのずから句に表れた繊細な余情）、「軽み」（題材を日常的な事物の中に求め、そこにあか抜けした面白みを見出そうとするもの）を理念とする人世詩・自然詩の情趣を取り入れ、俳句の芸術性を確立した。
　俳句という呼び名が一般に用いられるようになったのは、明治20年代（19世紀末）になって、正岡子規に始まる。俳句の特色として、季節にあらわれる動物や植物、生活のなかの行事や風習などを用いた季語である。たとえば、「すみれ草」という季語によって、春の暖かさや、すみれ草の咲く山道の自然の情景の連想を呼びおこし、最短詩型でありながら、句に広がりと深さをかもし出す。俳

in the Heian period, and the *Shin Kokin Wakashu* (New Collection of Ancient and Modern Japanese Poetry), in the Kamakura period, are both waka anthologies that were compiled by Imperial order.

As a short form of lyric poetry, tanka stresses the beauty of life and nature, and a feeling of yearning is an important element. What is sought within this simple form is to express the essence of this yearning with a depth in which all the emotions are intermingled. The vivid expression of that which has touched the heart has the power to evoke a wealth of associations. This allusive feeling contained in these thirty-one syllables is referred to as *yojo*. In content, a tanka poem should include this yojo.

Haiku is a fixed verse form of seventeen syllables arranged in a five-seven-five pattern. It was created by developing the opening verse of *haikai-no-renga* (a classical form of linked verse) into an independent poem.

Renga grew out of a sophisticated word game originally played at the Imperial Court using the *tanka* poetry format. A number of players would add their own verses to a preceding one, starting from a leading verse decided beforehand. The pleasure of the game came from its extempore nature, and the resourcefulness and quick wit it required. The poetry produced by this form of entertainment came to be known as "comical linked verse" (haikai-no-renga). It nevertheless developed into a serious genre thanks to the emergence of brilliant renga poets (for example, Yamazaki Sokan) in the late fifteenth and early sixteenth centuries.

Matsunaga Teitoku and his disciples are credited with further advancing this poetry by giving independent life to the opening verse (*hokku*) of renga early in the Edo Period. Matsuo Basho, who appeared around the middle of the Edo Period (late seventeenth century) and came to be known as the Master of Haiku, established Haiku as an art form by infusing it with charming touches of life and nature expressed through concepts like *sabi* (elegant simplicity enhanced by age), *shiori* (delicate suggested feeling that arises naturally from the poem), and *karumi* (seeking a refined charm in plain everyday material).

General use of the name "haiku" for this form began with Masaoka Shiki, in the third decade of the Meiji Era (end of the nineteenth century). A feature of haiku is inclusion of a "season word," referring to an animal, plant, event, or custom of the season. For example, the season word *sumireso* (violets) will bring to mind the warmth of spring and violets in bloom along a mountain path. Thus, breadth and depth is given to haiku, the shortest of poems. Haiku gives an objective, fleeting

句はその対象を客観的・即物的に描き出すが、実景をそのまま細かく描写することは不可能で、対象のかなめをおさえながらの省略が不可欠であり、季語もその一つである。

　短歌・俳句は、現在も国民の間に広く愛好されており、いわば国民的文芸となっている。

(3) 日本美術の歴史

　日本の美術は、中国・朝鮮半島からの影響が大きく、広い視野で見ればインド・中国を含む仏教圏の美術と見ることができる。近代では、明治時代に入って、洋画の技法が習得される一方、伝統への志向が生まれ近代日本画が誕生した。また、西欧では日本美術の独自性が注目され、ジャポニズムがブームとなり、印象派やアール・ヌーボーへの刺激を与えた。

a) 縄文時代（紀元前1万年頃～紀元前4～3世紀頃）

　縄文時代は日本列島が外部からの影響を受けずに、独自の発展をとげた。縄文土器は世界最古の土器で、縄目や火焔などの文様がある。ハート形、ミミズク形などさまざまな形態の土偶や、妊娠した女性を表現した土偶は呪術や豊穣祈願の意図で作成されたといわれている。

　　土器：十日町市博物館（深鉢形［火焔型］土器）

b) 弥生時代（紀元前10世紀頃～紀元後3世紀中頃）

　弥生時代になると、稲作農耕を代表とする外来の文化や技術の影響を受けるようになった。土器は、器形も洗練され、装飾も控えめな弥生土器となる。金属器ももたらされ、代表的遺物は銅鐸である。製作当初は金色に輝き、所有者の富と威厳を誇示する役割があったものと想像される。銅剣なども武器としての本来の用途から離れ、祭器化したものと思われる。

picture of its subject. As it is impossible to depict an actual scene in detail, it is necessary to abbreviate to the essentials, and the season word is one such abbreviation.

Tanka and haiku are still very popular, and can be said to have become literary art for Japanese people.

(3) History of Japanese Art

Japanese art was largely influenced by art from China and the Korean Peninsula, and from a wider perspective, it can be seen as part of the art from the Buddhist sphere, which includes India and China. In modern times, from the beginning of the Meiji era, Western art techniques were learned, and a taste for the traditional was born, resulting in the emergence of modern Japanese painting. The unique qualities of Japanese art gained attention in the West, and Japonism became popular and stimulated the Impressionism and Art Nouveau movements.

a) Jomon Period (10,000 B.C. to 400 or 300 B.C.)

During the Jomon period, the Japanese archipelago was as yet uninfluenced by foreign cultures and developed independently. Jomon pottery, with its impressed-rope and flame patterns, is the world's oldest earthenware. *Dogu* earthenware figures in many shapes (such as hearts and owls) and some representing pregnant women are said to have been made for the purpose of magic or as charms to bring about a good harvest.

Earthenware: Tokamachi City Museum (deep pot form (flame type) earthenware)

b) Yayoi Period (10th century B.C. to mid-3rd century A.D.)

In the Yayoi period, the influences of foreign cultures and technology appeared, typify among them being rice cultivation. Earthenware became more sophisticated in form, and their decoration became more reserved, a signature of Yayoi earthenware. Metal vessels were also introduced, with bronze bell-shaped vessels called *dotaku* being a typical example. When first produced, they were polished so that they shined, and it is thought that they were symbols of the wealth and majesty of their owners. As with bronze swords and other weapons, it is believed that these came to be used in rituals and in ways that were different from their originally intended purposes.

c) 古墳時代（3世紀中頃～7世紀末頃）

　古墳時代になると、前方後円墳と呼ばれ日本独特の形式の大規模な墳墓が営まれるようになった。大阪府堺市の大仙陵古墳または大山古墳（伝・仁徳天皇陵）は典型的な例である。

　1972年に奈良県明日香村で発掘された高松塚古墳の石室に描かれている四神（東の青龍・南の朱雀・西の白虎・北の玄武）、男女群像の大陸文化の影響を受けた彩色壁画は、日本史上はじめての本格的絵画といわれている。

　　埴輪（はにわ）は古墳の墳丘の周囲などに立てられた素焼きの土製品で、人物や動物などを素朴な表現と単純な技法で巧みにとらえ、芸術的に高く評価される作品が多い。

d) 飛鳥白鳳時代（592～710年）

　仏教が百済経由で伝えられ、6世紀末には日本最初の本格的仏教寺院である法興寺（飛鳥寺）が建てられた。聖徳太子は仏教に深く帰依し、四天王寺、法隆寺を建立した。現在の法隆寺はその後奈良時代に再建されたものであるが、西院伽藍は現存する世界最古の木造建築として著名である。

　　彫刻：法隆寺釈迦如来および両脇侍像、法隆寺観音菩薩
　　　　　立像（百済観音）、薬師寺薬師三尊像

　　工芸：法隆寺玉虫厨子、中宮寺天寿国繡帳

e) 奈良時代（710～794年）

　710年、奈良の平城京に遷都され、聖武天皇は仏教に深く帰依し、東大寺に大仏を造立した。飛鳥・白鳳時代様式の仏像を経て、奈良時代には天平仏が製作された。東大寺には正倉院という校倉造り（あぜくらづくり）の特殊な防湿構造の木造宝物殿がある。ここには、当時の天皇の遺愛品、寺宝・文書など奈良時代の美術品のほか、中国やペルシャなどからの伝来品9,000余点が収められている。

c) Tumulus Period (Mid-3rd century to late 7th century)

In the Tumulus period, burial mounds of immense size called *zenpokoenfun* were built, and these uniquely Japanese tombs were circular with a rectangular frontage. The Daisen Tumulus (called the tomb of the Emperor Nintoku) in Sakai City, Osaka, is an example of these tombs.

In 1972 the Takamatsuzuka Tumulus was discovered in Asuka Village, Nara Prefecture. Its various murals of the four sacred animals, or *shijin* (the blue dragon of the east, the red phoenix of the south, the white tiger of the west, the black turtle-snake of the north), and male and female sculptures in the stone chamber were influenced by culture from the continent. These are said to be the first serious paintings in Japanese history.

Haniwa are unglazed clay figures that were placed around burial mounds. They were created in the image of people and animals with unsophisticated expressions but were ingeniously crafted using simple methods, and many of these are highly valued for their artistry.

d) Asuka Hakuho Period (592 to 710)

Buddhism came to Japan via the ancient country of Kudara on the Korean Peninsula, and at the end of the sixth century, Hokoji (Asukadera) Temple was built as the first true Buddhist temple in Japan. Prince Shotoku was a devout Buddhist and built the Shitennouji Temple and Horyuji Temple. However, the Horyuji Temple buildings existing today are ones rebuilt in the Nara Period. Nevertheless, the Saiin Garan (the Western Precinct) of Horyuji is famous for being the world's oldest wooden structure.

Sculptures: *Shaka with Attendants*; *akyamuni and Bodhisattvas* (belonging to Horyuji), *Kannon Bosatsu* (Kudara Kannon; Avalokite vara) (belonging to Horyuji), *Yakushi-sanzon* (Medicine Buddha Trinity) (belonging to Yakushiji)

Crafts: *Tamamushi no Zushi* (Jewel Beetle Portable Shrine) (belonging to Horyuji), *Tenjukoku-Shucho* (belonging to Chuguji)

e) Nara Period (710 to 794)

In 710, the capital was transferred to Heijokyo in Nara, and Emperor Shoumu, a devout adherent of Buddhism, had the Great Buddha built at Todaiji Temple. Evolving from the Buddhist images of the Asuka and Hakuho periods were the Tenpyo Buddhist images. At Todaiji Temple there was a special damp-proof treasure house called the Shosoin Storehouse, which was made of logs. This houses the works of art used by the emperor at that time, the Temple's treasures, and documents of

絵画：薬師寺吉祥天像、高松塚古墳壁画

彫刻：中宮寺菩薩半跏像、唐招提寺鑑真和上坐像、興福寺阿修羅立像、東大寺大仏

建築：法隆寺西院伽藍、正倉院校倉造り宝庫、唐招提寺金堂

工芸：正倉院宝物（金工、漆工、楽器、染織、三彩陶器、刀剣など。渡来品を多く含む）

f）平安時代（794〜1185年）

平安時代前期は、密教の仏教思想により、密教曼荼羅や密教彫像がつくられた。遣唐使が中止された9世紀末以降、文化の和風化（和様）が進展し、絵画や書道作品、工芸品のデザインにも大いに反映している。後期には、末法思想（「末法」の年、1052年以後、釈迦の唱えた正しい仏法が行われなくなると信じられた）が流布し、各地に阿弥陀堂や阿弥陀如来像が造立された。

絵画：教王護国寺両界曼荼羅、源氏物語絵巻、伴大納言絵巻、高山寺鳥獣人物戯画、曼殊院不動明王像

彫刻：観心寺如意輪観音坐像、平等院阿弥陀如来坐像、慈尊院弥勒仏坐像

装飾経：厳島神社平家納経
建築：平等院鳳凰堂、平泉中尊寺金色堂、厳島神社修造

g）鎌倉時代・南北朝時代（1185〜1392年）

1180年、奈良の東大寺と興福寺が炎上し、ただちに再建計画が進められた。宋から伝来の、新建築様式の大仏像が導入され、仏像再興には、東大寺南大門金剛力士立像で

the Nara period, as well as more than 9,000 articles of Chinese, Persian, and other origin.

Paintings: *Portrait of Kichijo-ten* (Maha ri) (belonging to Yakushiji), Takamatsuzuka tumulus mural

Sculptures: *Bosatsu* (Bodhisattva) *Seated in Half-cross-legged Posture Bosatsu* (Bodhisattva) (belonging to Chuguji), *Seated Statue of Abbot Ganjin* (Jian-zhen) (belonging to Toshodaiji), *Asura* (belonging to Kofukuji), Great Buddha (Daibutsu) (belonging to Todaiji)

Architecture: Saiin Garan (the Western Precinct) of Horyuji, The Shosoin Repository in the Azekura style of architecture, Kondo (Main Hall) of Toshodaiji

Crafts: Shosoin Treasures (metalwork, lacquer ware, musical instruments, textiles, three-colored glazed potteries, swords, etc., including many imported pieces)

f) Heian Period (794 to 1185)

In the early part of the Heian period, esoteric Buddhist teachings gave rise to esoteric mandala and Buddhist sculptures. After the dispatch of envoys to China was discontinued at the end of the ninth century, the culture became more Japanized, and this was prominently reflected in the paintings, calligraphy, and design of handicrafts. In the latter half of this period, *mappo shiso*, or the doctrine that correct Buddhist teaching would decline after the first year of mappo (calculated to be 1052 by Japanese Buddhists), became widespread, and Amitabha halls and Amitabha Tathagata statues were built in many regions.

Paintings: *Mandala of Both Realms* (belonging to Kyoogokuji), *Tale of Genji Picture Scroll*, *Ban Dainagon Picture Scroll*, *Caricatures of Animals and Humans* (belonging to Kozanji), *Portrait of Acala* (Fudo-Myo-o) (belonging to Manshuin)

Sculptures: *Seated Nyoirin Kannon* (Cintamanicakra) (belonging to Kanshinji), *Seated Amida Nyorai* (Amitabha Buddha) (belonging to Byodoin), *Seated Miro* (Bodhisattva) *Maitreya* (belonging to Jisonin)

Sutras: *Heike Nokyo* (narrative scroll) (belonging to Itsukushima Shrine)

Architecture: Byodoin Hoohdo (Phoenix Hall), Konjikido (Golden Hall) of Chusonji in Hiraizumi, Itsukushima Shrine repairs

g) Kamakura Period and the Period of North and South Dynasties (1185 to 1392)

In 1180, Todaiji Temple and Kofukuji Temple in Nara were damaged in fires, and a plan to rebuild them was immediately put into motion. For this, an architectural style with roots in the Song Dynasty in China,

知られる運慶、快慶らの仏師が登用された。

政治・文化の中心は鎌倉に移り、美術の主要な享受者も武士へと移っていった。13世紀に京都の建仁寺を皮切りに、鎌倉にも建長寺、円覚寺などの禅寺が建立された。

絵画：神護寺伝源頼朝像、平治物語絵詞

彫刻：東大寺南大門金剛力士立像（運慶、快慶）、長谷の大仏

h) 室町時代（1338～1573年）

室町時代には、文化の中心は再び京都へ戻った。足利義満は京都の北山に山荘（後の鹿苑寺・金閣）、足利義政は東山に山荘（後の慈照寺・銀閣）を営んだ。東山山荘は、後の書院造の原型で、日本の伝統的住宅建築のルーツである。京都を中心に禅宗寺院が隆盛し、枯山水や龍安寺石庭などの庭園、茶道、水墨画などさまざまな文化・美術が生まれ、能もこの時代に観阿弥・世阿弥により完成された。

絵画：水墨画秋冬山水図（雪舟）
庭園：枯山水　龍安寺石庭など
建築：天龍寺、金閣、銀閣など

i) 安土桃山時代（1573～1603年）

長い間の戦国騒乱の状態から急速に統一が達成され、自由闊達な気風がみなぎり新鮮で豪華な文化が生まれた。これまでの仏教的な色彩がほとんど影を潜め、これに代わって世俗的な色彩が濃くなり、おおらかで明るい躍動的な文化が創造された。建築と絵画はこの時代の文化を代表するものである。

城郭建築が発達した。権力のシンボル的な天守閣を持つ大阪城（豊臣秀吉築城）や華麗な障壁画で装飾された聚楽

known as the *daibutsu-yo* style, was introduced, and the remaking of the Buddhist statues was put in the hands of Unkei, Kaikei and other sculptors today especially remembered for sculpting the Todaiji Nandaimon Kongo-Rikishi (Guardian of the Great South Gate).

The political and cultural center shifted to Kamakura, and the samurai became the primary patrons of art. In the thirteenth century, the Kenninji Temple in Kyoto was established, and Zen temples such as the Kenchoji Temple and Engakuji Temple in Kamakura were built.

Paintings: Portrait Thought to Depict Minamoto no Yoritomo (belonging to Jingoji), *Tale of Heiji Picture Scroll*

Sculptures: *Standing Kongo Rikishi* (Vajra-vira) by Unkei and Kaikei (belonging to Todaiji and installed within its Nandaimon (Great South Gate)), Great Buddha of Hase (Kamakura)

h) Muromachi Period (1338 to 1573)

In the Muromachi period, the center of culture returned to Kyoto. Ashikaga Yoshimitsu built a mountain retreat (later called Rokuonji Kinkaku; the Temple of the Golden Pavilion) at Kitayama, and Ashikaga Yoshimasa built a mountain retreat at Higashiyama (later Jishoji Ginkaku; the Temple of the Silver Pavilion). The retreat at Higashiyama would later become the model for *shoinzukuri* (traditional residential architectural style), and it represents the roots of traditional Japanese house construction. The Zen temples (which were found mostly in Kyoto) prospered and gave rise to distinctive Japanese garden styles like the dry landscape (raked) garden and the Ryoanji Temple rock garden, the tea ceremony, and other cultural and artistic disciplines. Noh was fully developed during this period by Kan'ami and Zeami.

Pictures: *Landscape in Autumn and Winter* (a *sumie* painted) by Sesshu
Gardens: *Karesansui* (dry landscape garden) including Ryoanji Sekitei
Architecture: Tenryuji, Kinkaku (Golden Pavilion), Ginkaku (Silver Pavilion), etc.

i) Azuchi-Momoyama Period (1573 to 1603)

Unification made rapid progress after the long period of war-torn turbulence, leading to a more liberal, open-minded atmosphere from which arose a culture that was both fresh and magnificent. Up to that point, Buddhist colors had largely dominated and in lieu of this secular hues became stronger, creating a bright and lively culture. The representation of this cultural era is in its architecture and paintings.

The construction of castles flourished. Some, like Osaka Castle (Toyotomi Hideyoshi's castle), were built with magnificent central

第などがある。茶の湯は千利休によって大成され、茶道具としては、唐物と呼ばれる中国製の天目茶碗なども珍重された。

　　絵画：唐獅子図屏風（狩野永徳）、洛中洛外図屏風（狩野永徳）、松林図（長谷川等伯）

　　城郭建築：熊本城、松本城
　　（注）城郭建築のもっとも有名なものは、安土城、大阪城、聚楽第、伏見城（桃山城）であるが、これらはいずれも現存しない。その遺構といわれるものである。

j）江戸時代（1603〜1868年）

　古代・中世の美術が仏教中心であったのに比べ、安土桃山時代よりもさらに世俗化の傾向が強まった。美術の享受者層も裕福な町人層など広がりをみせた。さらに、同じ作品を複数生産できる版画の普及により、浮世絵のような、庶民の手に届く芸術も生まれた。

　文化の中心は上方（京都・大阪）と江戸であったが、幕藩体制のもと、地方の各藩で、陶磁、工芸など独自の美術品が生産されるようになった。
　　絵画：風神雷神図屏風（俵屋宗達）、燕子花図屏風・紅白梅図（尾形光琳）、動植綵絵（伊藤若冲）、雪松図屏風（円山応挙）

　　浮世絵：美人大首絵（喜多川歌麿）、富嶽三十六景（葛飾北斎）、三世大谷鬼次の奴江戸兵衛（東洲斎写楽）、東海道五十三次（歌川広重）

　　工芸：舟橋蒔絵硯箱（本阿弥光悦）、伊万里焼色絵花鳥文大深鉢（柿右衛門様式）

　　建築：日光東照宮、桂離宮、姫路城天守閣、二条城御殿、彦根城、名古屋城

towers symbolizing great power, while others, like Jurakudai Castle, were constructed as gorgeous palaces adorned with splendid murals. Sen no Rikyu perfected the tea ceremony, and Chinese-made *tenmoku* tea bowls became highly valued as utensils used in the tea ceremony.

Pictures: *Chinese Lions* (painted on six-fold standing screen) by Kano Eitoku, *Grand View of Kyoto* (painted on a six-fold standing screen) by Kano Eitoku, *A Pine Grove* (painted on a pair of six-fold standing screens) by Hasegawa Tohaku

Castellation: Kumamoto Castle, Matsumoto Castle

Note: The most famous examples of castellation are Azuchi Castle, Osaka Castle, Jurakudai, and Fushimi Castle (Momoyama Castle), but none of these exist today. All that survive are parts and remnants.

j) Edo Period (1603 to 1868)

Unlike art in ancient times and the Middle Ages, art in the Edo period, with its focus on Buddhism, exhibited a stronger secular trend than in the Azuchi-Momoyama period. Patrons of the arts came from the affluent merchant class in increasing numbers. In addition, with the introduction and popularization of woodblock prints, which allowed the production of multiple copies of a work, art such as *ukiyo-e* became accessible to the common people.

The cultural centers were Edo and the Kyoto-Osaka area, and under the shogunate system, ceramics, handicrafts, and other original works of art began to be produced in the rural feudal domains.

Paintings: *Wind and Thunder Gods* (painted on a folding screen) by Tawaraya Sotatsu, *Irises* and *Red and White Plum Blossoms* (painted on folding screens) by Ogata Korin, *Doshokusai-e* (colored pictures of animals and plants) by Ito Jakuchu, *Pine Trees in Snow* (painted on a folding screen) by Maruyama Okyo

Ukiyo-e: *Ookubi-e* (bust portraits) of beautiful women by Kitagawa Utamaro, *Fugaku Sanju Rokkei* (Thirty-six views of Mount Fuji) by Katsushika Hokusai, *The Actor Otani Oniji III as Edobei* by Toshusai Sharaku, *The Fifty-three Stations of the Tokaido* by Utagawa Hiroshige

Crafts: Writing Box with Design of a Pontoon Bridge by Hon'ami Koetsu, Large Deep Bowl with Design of Flowers and Birds (Imari ware in Kakiemon style)

Architecture: Nikko Tosho-gu (Shinto shrine), Katsura Rikyu (Imperial Villa), Himeji Castle's main keep (*ten-shu-kaku*), Nijo Castle's residential architecture, Hikone Castle, Nagoya Castle

k) 近代・現代（明治時代・大正時代・昭和時代・平成時代）
（1868年〜）

　江戸時代末期、パリの万国博覧会に出展した幕府や各藩の美術・工芸品はすぐれた装飾品として絶賛された。当時、ヨーロッパでは日本の美術・工芸への関心が高まり、前衛的な芸術家たちにジャポニズムという強力な影響を与えていた。

　明治維新後、政府は西洋式の「ファイン・アート」（純粋美術）を導入してヨーロッパ諸国に恥じない芸術の体裁を整えようとし、日本の諸派の絵画などは旧弊なものとみなされ存続の危機に陥った。また廃仏毀釈や大名家の没落にともない、多くの優れた美術品が古道具市場にあふれ、欧米に流出した。

　一方、フェノロサ・岡倉天心らは日本の美術の優秀性を説き、東京美術学校を開校した。黒田清輝らは海外に留学し、ヨーロッパの最新の絵画運動を取り入れた西洋画の活発な活動を行った。また京都画壇の竹内栖鳳ら多くの日本絵画の作家も留学し、諸派の絵画や西洋画の影響も取り入れた新しい近代日本画が誕生した。日本画においては、その題材から美人画、風景画、仏画があるほか、歴史上の人物や事件を描いた歴史画は、花鳥画と並びもっとも日本画らしさを表す重要なジャンルである。

　　日本画：悲母観音（狩野芳崖）、斑猫（竹内栖鳳）、生々流転（横山大観）、落葉（菱田春草）、炎舞（速水御舟）、薬師寺大唐西域壁画（平山郁夫）

　　洋画：湖畔（黒田清輝）、わだつみのいろこの宮（青木繁）、五人の裸婦（藤田嗣治）

　　版画：釈迦の十大弟子（棟方志功）

　　彫刻：女（荻原守衛）、老猿（高村光雲）、長崎平和祈念像（北村西望）
　　建築物：東京駅駅舎（辰野金吾）、代々木体育館・東京都庁舎（丹下健三）、国立新美術館（黒川紀章）

k) Modern Period and Today (Meiji era, Taisho era, Showa era, and Heisei era) (from 1868)

At the end of the Edo period, arts and crafts of the shogunate and feudal clans displayed at the World's Fair in Paris won high praise as decorative ornaments. At the time, there was great interest in Japanese arts and crafts in Europe, and many avant-garde artists were strongly influenced by Japonism.

After the Meiji Restoration, the government introduced Western-style fine arts and tried to encourage art that appealed to European sensibilities. Japanese schools of painting and other arts were considered anachronistic and their continued existence was in danger. Along with the anti-Buddhist movement and the decline of the feudal families, superior works of art flooded the second-hand market and found their way to collectors in the West.

In contrast, Ernest F. Fenollosa and Okakura Tenshin, among others, understood the value of Japanese art and opened the Tokyo School of Art. Kuroda Seiki and his associates studied overseas, and were very active in Western art, incorporating the latest art movements in Europe. Takeuchi Seiho and many of his associates, active in Kyoto art circles, also studied overseas and their efforts, incorporating influences from many art movements and Western art, gave birth to modern Japanese painting. The subjects of traditional Japanese painting include beautiful people, scenery, Buddhism, and historical people and events. Taken together, these subjects represent an important genre, which is as expressive of the essence of Japanese painting as the bird-and-flower genre.

Japanese Painting: *Merciful Mother Kannon* by Kano Hogai, *Tabby Cat* by Takeuchi Seiho, *Wheel of Life* by Yokoyama Taikan, *Fallen Leaves* by Hishida Shunso, *Fire Dance* by Hayami Gyoshu, *the Daito Saiiki Murals of the Yakushi-ji Temple* by Hirayama Ikuo

Western Painting: *Lakeside* by Kuroda Seiki, *Paradise under the Sea* by Aoki Shigeru, *Five Nudes* by Fujita Tsuguharu, Yakushiji Mural of the Western Regions of the Great Tang Dynasty by Hirayama Ikuo

Woodblock Print: *The Ten Great Disciples of Sakyamuni* by Munakata Shiko

Sculpture: *Woman* by Ogiwara Morie, *The Aged Monkey* by Takamura Koun, *Nagasaki Peace Statue* by Kitamura Seibo

Architecture: Tokyo Station designed by Tatsuno Kingo, Yoyogi National Gymnasium and Tokyo Metropolitan Government Building designed by Tange Kenzo, National Art Center designed by Kurokawa Kisho

l) 国宝・重要文化財

日本では、縄文時代から現代にいたるまでの2,000年を超えて、脈々として受け継がれてきたさまざまな有形文化遺産が保存されている。その中で、世界文化の見地からも価値が高く、類（たぐい）ない国民の宝と認定されたものは、国宝をはじめとする重要文化財に指定されている。

国宝には、美術工芸品885件（絵画・彫刻・工芸品・書跡・典籍・古文書・考古資料・歴史資料が含まれる）、建造物225件が指定されている（2018年5月）。美術工芸品の多くは、東京・奈良・京都・九州の四つの国立博物館、その他の博物館・美術館、寺院、神社に展示・保管されている。また建造物については、奈良・京都をはじめとして、寺院、神社、城郭などが全国各地にあり、観覧することができる。

m) クローン文化財

東京芸術大学では、芸術と科学技術の融合による高精度な文化財複製「クローン文化財」の技術を開発し、特許を取得した。この技術発明は2017年「21世紀発明奨励賞」に輝いた。劣化が進行しつつある、あるいは永遠に失われてしまった文化財の本来の姿を現代に甦らせるために、文化財をクローンとして復元する技術である。2017年、東京芸術大学美術館で複製された文化財の一部の展示会「素心伝心―クローン文化財　失われた刻の再生」が開かれた。展示されたクローン文化財は、シルクロードで文化財を育んだ7つの地域のクローン文化財―法隆寺金堂の壁画と釈迦三尊像（日本）、高句麗古墳群江西大墓の壁画（北朝鮮）、敦煌莫高窟第57窟の壁画と仏像（中国）、キジル石窟航海者窟の壁画（中国・新疆ウイグル自治区）、ペンジケント遺跡発掘区6広間1の壁画（タジキスタン）、バガン遺跡の壁画（ミャンマー）、バーミヤン東大仏天井壁画（アフガニスタン）―である。展示物は、3Dプリンタといった最先端のデジタル技術と、人の手による複製画などの伝統的なアナログ技術を融合して作り上げられている。

クローン文化財の価値は次の3点にあるとされる。
〈1〉オリジナル作品が生まれた時の鮮やかな色彩を復元

l) National Treasures and Important Cultural Assets

Japan possesses an abundance of tangible cultural treasures that span an unbroken 2000-year history from the Jomon period to today. Some of these are highly regarded on the world's cultural stage, and those that are recognized as priceless treasures belonging to the Japanese people have been designated as national treasures or important cultural property.

National treasures include 885 art objects (paintings, sculptures, handicrafts, calligraphy, books of classical literature, archeological documents, and historical documents) and 225 building structures (May, 2018). Many of the art objects are kept at four national museums located in Tokyo, Nara, Kyoto, and Kyushu, and others are on display or stored at temples, shrines, and other museums. The building structures can be seen in Nara and Kyoto, and at temples, shrines, and castles located throughout the country.

m) Cloned Cultural Properties

Tokyo University of the Arts (TUA) developed a technology called "cloned cultural properties," which uses a fusion of art and technology to create highly accurate reproductions of cultural properties. The university obtained patent over the invented technology, and in 2017 the invention was the recipient of a "21st Century Invention Encouragement Award." The technology makes it possible to reproduce or duplicate a cultural property, restoring it to its original appearance, even when it has undergone deterioration or even been lost forever. In 2017, some of the cultural properties that have been duplicated were exhibited at the TUA Fine Arts Museum ("Clone Cultural Property: Revitalization of Lost Time"). The cultural properties displayed were "clones" of cultural properties from seven regions along the Silk Road where such cultural treasures were cultivated. These were: Horyuji Kondo murals and Shaka Triad statue (Japan); complex of Koguryo tombs, Kangso Great Tomb mural (North Korea); Dunhuang Mogao grottoes cave 57 mural and Buddharupa (China); murals from the Seafarers cavern, Kizil caves (Xinjiang Uyghur region, China); murals from the Penjikent archaeological site excavation area 6, Hall 1 (Tajikistan); murals from the Bagan site (Myanmar); and the ceiling mural from the Great Eastern Buddha of Bamiyan (Afghanistan). Exhibits are created by combining state-of-the-art digital technology such as 3D printing with traditional analog technology such as duplication by hand.

The value of the cloned cultural properties technology is threefold. <1> It makes it possible to reconstruct the vivid colors the original

　　　　できる。
　　〈2〉オリジナル作品保護のため、世界中の美術館や博物館が公開展示用にクローン文化財を必要とする。日本でも、国宝は年に2週間しか展示できない。

　　〈3〉戦争や災害で失われた文化財をクローンという形で蘇らせることができる。

(4) 演劇・芸能
a) 伝統的な演劇・芸能
　　日本の演劇には長い歴史があるが、過去のものがしだいに発展変化して現在の演劇になったのではない。過去のものはそのままの形で伝わり、他方、つぎつぎに新しいものが加わって、現在の多種多様な演劇が共存しているのである。

　　伝統的な演劇として、14世紀からの「能」・「狂言」、17世紀からの「文楽」・「歌舞伎」が知られている。これらには現在も熱心な愛好者がいる。一方、伝統的な芸能として「浪花節」・「落語」・「民謡」・「小唄」などがある。

b) 能・狂言
　　能は日本の伝統芸能の一つで、狂言とともに南北朝時代から現代に演じ継がれている。

　　「歌舞伎」や「文楽」が庶民の演劇であるのに対して、能は武士階級のものとされ、舞台の上で、謡曲につれて舞を演じる歌舞劇である。

　　能には「シテ方」「ワキ方」「囃子（はやし）方」「狂言方」という役割分担がある。シテは主役（主人公）、シテの相手役はワキ。囃子方は笛・小鼓（こつづみ）・大鼓（おおつづみ）・太鼓（たいこ）の4種類で音楽を受け持つ。狂言方は能の中で「アイ」を受け持つ。アイとは間狂言のことで、能の前場と後場のつなぎに登場して、物語の状況説明などをする役のこと。狂言だけでも独立して演じられ、能と異なった滑稽味が特徴である。

work had at the time of creation.
<2> Museums around the world can protect original items and exhibit the cloned cultural property instead. In Japan, for example, designated national treasures can only be displayed for two weeks each year.
<3> It can reconstruct cultural assets lost in wars and disasters.

(4) Dramas and Entertainments

a) Traditional Theater and Entertainments

Theater in Japan has a long history. However, the forms of theater today are not result of gradual change and development over the years. Rather, many new forms were consecutively added and variety of forms coexists today.

The well-known traditional forms of theater are *noh* and *kyogen*, dating from the fourteenth century, and *bunraku* and *kabuki*, dating from the seventeenth century. All still have ardent followers. Traditional forms of entertainment include *naniwabushi* (ballads), *rakugo* (comic story-telling), *minyo* (folk songs), and *kouta* (short songs accompanied by the *shamisen*, a Japanese string instrument).

b) Noh and Kyogen

Noh and *kyogen* are Japanese traditional performance arts that have been performed together from the Period of North and South Dynasties (latter half of the fourteenth century) up to modern times.

Whereas *kabuki* and *bunraku* were theater arts for the common people, noh was for members of the warrior or samurai class. Noh is a lyric dance-drama, performed on a stage to the accompaniment of vocal music.

In Noh, the roles of the performers are divided into four distinct categories: shite-kata, waki-kata, hayashi-kata and kyogen-kata. The shite-kata are the main actors (protagonists), and the waki-kata are the shites' supporting actors. The hayashi-kata are the musicians and are divided into four instrument categories: flute, shoulder-drum, hip-drum and stick-drum. The kyogen-kata appears in the middle of the noh to perform the *ai* (*ai-kyogen*), an interlude between the first and second acts of the noh that the kyogen-kata uses, for example, to give the audience a better understanding of how the story is unfolding. The interlude may also be used for an independent performance called *hon-kyogen*,

能で用いられる面は「能面」あるいは「面（おもて）」と呼ばれ、シテを演じる役者が用いるが、面を用いない場合もある。面の目的は変身のためで、この世の存在ではない霊、神、精などの役柄やいろいろな年齢層にわたる女性の面がたくさんある。衣装も面とともに、能の味わい深さを構成する重要な要素となっている。

　謡曲は能の台本ともいえる性格を持つが、謡曲の大部分は15～16世紀ごろにつくられたもので、ことに観阿弥・世阿弥父子によるものが多い。その多くは『源氏物語』、『平家物語』や鎌倉・室町時代の説話集などに題材を求めている。舞と囃子を省略して謡曲のみで独立して演じる場合もあり、これを素謡（すうたい）という。

　能楽の保存と普及を図ることを目的として、1983年9月、東京千駄ヶ谷に国立能楽堂が開場した。能は2001年、ユネスコ無形文化遺産に指定された。

c) 歌舞伎

　歌舞伎は17世紀から盛んになった日本の代表的な庶民演劇である。現在、能や文楽よりも愛好者が多い。能や文楽の要素も取り入れているので、日本の伝統芸能の集大成的なものといえる。

　歌舞伎の舞台装置には、花道や回り舞台など独特のものがある。花道は、舞台に向かって観客席を貫いて設けられた通路である。これは俳優が登場・退場するためだけでなく、俳優と観客との交流をも目的とするものである。

　演劇としての性格からいえば、歌舞伎は音楽劇であり、舞踊劇の要素が多い。純粋の「踊り」の他、貴族階級や武士の世界が中心の「時代物」、庶民・町人の世界が中心の「世話物」などに分けられるが、多くの作品が三味線などによる日本固有の音曲を伴奏とし、台詞にも動作にも独特の音楽的リズム感が要求される。そして、省略・誇張・形式化された動きが一つの様式を生み出し、近代的リアリズムに立脚する演劇とは大きく異なっている。しかし江戸末期から明治にかけて盛んになった「世話物」は現代劇に通ずるリアリズムに立脚している。

that offers a comical contrast to the noh.

A performer in the role of a shite-kata may or may not wear a mask called a *nohmen* or *omote*. The mask is for transforming the shite-kata into the role of a spirt, god, nymph, or other imaginary being. Masks representing women of various ages are also used. The masks and the performers' costumes combine as key elements contributing to the depth of the noh experience.

The vocal music of noh, called *yokyoku*, is substantially the script of the play. Most yokyoku pieces were composed between the fifteenth and sixteenth centuries. Many are the work of Kannami and his son Zeami. The subject is usually a tale from *Genji Monogatari* or *Heike Monogatari*, or a story from the Kamakura or Muromachi era. Sometimes yokyoku is performed independently, without dancing or instrumental music, in what is called *su-utai*.

The National Noh Theatre was launched in the Sendagaya district of Tokyo in 1983 in order to preserve and popularize noh. In 2001, UNESCO designated noh as an intangible cultural heritage of humanity.

c) Kabuki

Kabuki is a popular dramatic art form that has been a favorite among the Japanese people since the seventeenth century. Today, kabuki is more popular than *noh* or *bunraku*. Because of its assimilation of various aspects of the other dramatic art forms, kabuki might well be called a summarization of traditional Japanese theatrical art.

Kabuki has a number of unique points. One of these are the *mawari butai* (revolving stage) which permits almost instantaneous changes of scene. Another is the *hanamichi*, which is a long, narrow, walk-like extension of the stage that runs through the audience to the back of the theater. Although the actors often enter and exit via the hanamichi, it is not primarily a passageway but a device for permitting the actors to come into closer contact with their audience.

Music and dancing are fundamental to most historical kabuki dramas. Most kabuki plays are performed to the accompaniment of typical Japanese melodies played on several *shamisen* (a three-stringed instrument of the lute family) and other instruments unique to Japan. The actors are required to follow a distinctive "kabuki rhythm" in both their speech and their movements. Differing greatly from modern drama, which lays primary emphasis on realism, kabuki is a formalized art in which the significance of omissions, exaggerations, and many of the actors' movements are pre-defined. However, dramas of contemporary life, grounded in the realism of modern theater, flourished from the end

歌舞伎では、男優が女性の役に扮することや、瞬間的な衣装替えの技巧なども特色の一つである。歌舞伎の俳優は、先祖の芸を受け継ぐよう幼少から育てられ、脚本にしたがって演ずるというよりは、俳優の芸を中心に演出される。

歌舞伎は、2005 年ユネスコ無形文化遺産に指定された。なお東京の歌舞伎座は建て替えられて 2013 年 4 月にオープンした。

d) 組踊（くみおどり）

組踊とは、琉球王国時代の沖縄で玉城朝薫（たまぐすくちょうくん、中国名は向受祐・しょうじゅゆう）によって創（はじ）められた踊念仏・能・狂言の組み合わせにより発展した芸能の一種であり、音楽・舞踊・台詞からなり、一般に「舞踊劇」、「音楽劇」などと呼ばれる。そのスタイルは、能や狂言に近いが、音楽に琉球音楽、台詞に琉球語首里方言を使うのが特徴である。筋立ての多くは、勧善懲悪（かんぜんちょうあく・善を勧め悪をこらす）をテーマとしていて、能や狂言と類似する筋書きを多く見つけることもできる。たとえば、「執心鐘入（しゅうしんかにいり）」は能の「道成寺もの」と呼ばれる筋書きを取っている。

組踊は、1972 年沖縄が日本に復帰した 5 月 15 日に重要無形文化財に指定され、2010 年にユネスコ無形文化遺産に登録された。また、沖縄には「国立劇場おきなわ」も設立されている。

e) 文楽（人形浄瑠璃）

「文楽」は一種の人形劇である。能・歌舞伎と並んで日本三大古典演劇の一つで、17 世紀から盛んになった。浄瑠璃の語り、伴奏の三味線、人形の 3 役がひとつになって上演される。語りは大阪弁を使うのが特色である。浄瑠璃は、元禄時代に竹本義太夫が完成させた平曲、謡曲などか

of the Edo era to the Meiji period.

Anyone watching kabuki for the first time will no doubt be surprised to learn that all roles, including those of female characters, are played by men. One will also be amazed by the rapidity with which the actors change costumes, often transforming themselves into totally different characters in a matter of seconds. By subject matter, kabuki plays fall into two categories: those which deal with the fortunes of the noble and warrior classes and those which depict the lives of the common people. The art of kabuki acting is passed on from father to son and training begins at a very early age. The actor is considered more important than the play; he does not change his acting style to fit the play but the play is changed to fit his particular skills.

In 2005, UNESCO designated kabuki as a "masterpiece of the oral and intangible cultural heritage of humanity." The Kabuki-za Theater in Tokyo reopened in April 2013 following three years of reconstruction.

d) Kumi-odori

Kumi-odori is a dance-drama that developed in Okinawa during the era of the Ryukyu Kingdom. Tamagusuku Chokun, a magistrate in the Ryukyuan Royal court, also known by the Chinese name Sho Juyu, is credited with creating kumi-odori in 1719 by combining elements of *odorinenbutsu* (Buddhist invocation with dance), *noh*, and *kyogen*. An ensemble of music, dance and story, kumi-odori is generally classified as dance drama or musical drama. Although it is performed in a style similar to noh and kyogen, the music is Ryukyuan and the story is told in the Ryukyuan (Okinawan) Shuri dialect. The theme usually centers on rewarding good and punishing evil, and many similarities to the stories of noh and kyogen can be seen. For example, the kumi-odori titled Shushin Kaniiri (Passion and the Bell) takes after the *dojoji* genre of noh.

On May 15, 1972, the day of Okinawa's post-World War restoration to Japanese sovereignty, kumi-odori was declared an important intangible cultural property, and in 2010, it was included in UNESCO's list of intangible cultural heritage.

e) Bunraku (Joruri Puppet Theater)

Bunraku is one form of puppet theater. It has flourished since the seventeenth century and now stands with *noh* and *kabuki* as one of the three great classical forms of theater in Japan. A bunraku performance comprises the story related in a special chant, called *joruri*, a *shamisen* musical accompaniment, and the puppets. A feature of the narration

ら派生したものである。なお、平曲とは、平家物語を琵琶の伴奏で語るものである。

　文楽で使う人形は首（かしら）・胴・手・足・衣装からなっていて、1 m から 1.5 m の大きさである。
　舞台の上で、人形遣いが人形を、主な役については1体につき3人で動かす。それぞれ首と右手・左手・足の動きを分担している。女の人形には足がなく、人形の衣装の裾さばきで巧みに表現する。人形は、三味線の伴奏と、独特の節まわしで太夫によって語られる浄瑠璃にあわせて、さまざまな仕草をする。このため、文楽のことを人形浄瑠璃ともいう。

　人形の首は約 60 種類あり、そのうち 40 種類は、一つの首をいろいろの役に使う。そのほかに一首一役の特殊な首がある。目や口が開閉するもの、眉が上下するもの、指の動くものもある。感情の動きなども、人形の微妙な動作で表現される。
　文楽は 2003 年ユネスコ無形文化遺産に指定された。また、大阪には国立文楽劇場もある。

f）邦楽

　日本古来の邦楽には、その発生時期にしたがって、古代の「雅楽」、中世の「能楽」、近世の「三味線」・「箏」の音楽があるが、各種の邦楽のうち、現在も比較的愛好者が多いのは「箏曲（そうきょく）」・「長唄」・「小唄」などである。
　箏曲は、中国の古い琴（きん）を日本化した楽器である箏（こと）を演奏する音楽の総称で、16 世紀後半に発展し、三味線・胡弓・尺八とも合奏されるようになった。現在は西洋音楽との交流も試みられている。

　長唄は、三味線音楽による長編のうたいもので、17 世紀後半に歌舞伎舞踊とともに発達し、その過程で謡曲・地歌・浄瑠璃・民謡などの、歌詞や曲節が取り入れられたため、多様性があり、伴奏に笛・小鼓・大鼓・太鼓の囃子などを用いるので、曲詞が爽快で、はでなことが特徴である。

is that it is performed in the Osaka dialect. Joruri was derived from *heikyoku* and *yokyoku* perfected by Takemoto Gidayu in the Genroku period. Heikyoku is a narration of the *Heike Monogatari* accompanied by the music of the biwa.

Bunraku puppets consist of a head, trunk, hands, feet, and costume, and range in size from about a meter to a meter and a half.

On the stage, puppet is manipulated by puppeteers. For a main character, three puppeteers respectively manipulates head and right hand, left hand, and feet. In the case of female dolls, which have no feet, the third puppeteer skillfully manipulates the skirts of the doll to give the impression of walking and other leg movements. The puppets perform the actions as the story is related in the joruri, to the accompaniment of shamisen music. Because of this, bunraku is also called *ningyojoruri* (puppet ballad-drama).

Altogether there are about 60 puppet heads. Around 40 of these are multi-role heads, while the others are limited to a single role. There are puppets with eyes and mouth that can be opened and shut, with eyebrows that moves up and down, and fingers that moves. Emotions are expressed by subtle movements.

In 2003, UNESCO designated bunraku as a "masterpiece of the oral and intangible cultural heritage of humanity." There is a National Bunraku Theater in Osaka.

f) Japanese Music

Traditional Japanese music is classified by period of origin into *gagaku* (ancient), *nogaku* (medieval), and the music of the *shamisen* and *koto* (recent). Among the various subclasses of Japanese music, those having relatively large followings today are *sokyoku*, *nagauta* and *kouta*.

Sokyoku is the general name for music played on the koto (a kind of harp). This musical form, which developed in the second half of the sixteenth century, later came to be played in concert with the shamisen (three-stringed lute), the *kokyu* (Chinese fiddle), and the *shakuhachi* (five-holed bamboo clarinet). Present-day attempts have been made to blend sokyoku with Occidental music.

Nagauta is a kind of long epic song based on shamisen music which evolved together with *kabuki* dancing in the latter half of the seventeenth century. Having absorbed the lyrics and melodies of yokyoku, *jiuta* (regional music), *joruri* (puppet ballad-drama music), and *minyo* (folk music) in the course of its development, nagauta has become very diverse in form. It is performed in a lively, florid style to

小唄は、15〜16世紀ごろ行われた庶民的な短い歌謡である小歌の流れをくみ、19世紀初めごろに生まれた小歌曲で、テンポが早く、声をおさえる発声法でうたわれ、伴奏の三味線は「ばち」を使わず「つまびき」をする。19世紀終わりごろに、個性的な作詩・作曲、独特な伴奏が行われるようになって様式が確立した。

g） 日本舞踊

　日本舞踊は、一般に「能」以前のものが「舞」、歌舞伎以後のものが「踊」と呼ばれてきた。

　「歌舞伎踊」は今日も盛んに行われており、日本舞踊といえば、この歌舞伎踊を指すことも多い。踊は15〜16世紀ごろから、民俗舞踊として庶民の間で広く行われ、やがてそのなかから歌舞伎踊が生まれた。その発展過程で舞の要素も取り入れられ、さらにたとえば、富士山の形を描いてみせるというような、演劇的表現の強い「振り」といわれる要素も加えられた。

　女歌舞伎が禁止されて以後、専門の舞踊家は男子ばかりだったが、18世紀ごろからしだいに芸者などの間に広まり、庶民の愛好者も増加した。踊の流派も、「西川」・「花柳」・「若柳」・「藤間」など多くのものが生まれ、また20世紀初めごろからは西洋舞踊の影響を受けて、新舞踊運動が起こった。現在では、主として女性が趣味として日本舞踊を習っている。

　「舞」は大阪・京都で行われたので「上方舞」ともいう。京都の祇園だけで行われる「井上流」のほか、大阪を中心とする「山村流」などがある。

　なお、沖縄には独特の琉球舞踊がある。

h） 大衆芸能

　現在多くの日本人に親しまれている、伝統的な大衆芸能

the accompaniment of flutes and full-sized drums.

Kouta is a form of short song or ditty which appeared in the early nineteenth century which derives from popular short songs of the fifteenth and sixteenth centuries. The songs are sung at a quick tempo in a suppressed voice to the accompaniment of a shamisen plucked with the fingers instead of a plectrum, as is more common in other types of music. Kouta became established in its present form near the end of the nineteenth century as its devotees provided it with its own individual lyrics, melodies, and style of shamisen accompaniment.

g) **Japanese Dancing**

There are two main types of Japanese dancing: *mai* and *odori*. Generally, Japanese dance before *noh* is considered mai, and dance after *kabuki* is called mai.

Kabukiodori (kabuki dancing) is by far the more popular today, so much so that when people refer to Japanese dancing today, they almost always mean kabuki dancing. Kabuki dancing grew out of various folk dances that became popular from around the fifteenth to sixteenth century. As it developed, kabuki dancing borrowed certain aspects of mai (noh dancing). It also developed its own dramatic form of expression through gestures and postures. For example, if Mt. Fuji is mentioned in the accompanying song, the dancer may use the hands to suggest the shape of the mountain.

For many years following the prohibition of kabuki acting by women, all professional Japanese dancers were men. From around the middle of the eighteenth century, however, kabuki dancing became increasingly popular among *geisha* and was also taken up more by the general populace. Today there are many different schools of Japanese dancing. A few of the better known are Nishikawa, Hanayagi, Wakayagi, and Fujima. There is also a neo-Japanese dancing movement which arose in the early 1900s under the influence of Western dance. Nowadays, more women practice Japanese dancing as a pastime.

Mai, or traditional Japanese dance, was performed in Osaka and Kyoto, and was also called *kamigatamai*, since the term "Kamigata" referred to the Osaka-Kyoto area. There are variations of this dance, such as the Inoue style which was performed only in the Gion district of Kyoto, and the Yamamura style, which is found primarily in Osaka.

There is also the unique Ryukyu dance, which is found in Okinawa.

h) **Popular Entertainment**

Some traditional popular Japanese entertainments are listed below.

をいくつかあげてみよう。
〈1〉 落語は、対話を主とした滑稽な話を独演し、聴衆を笑わせる大衆芸能の一つである。落語の源流は16世紀にみられ、17世紀中ごろには、身ぶりもまじえて話すようになり、おかしさを効果的に盛り上げる方法として、話の終わりに「落ち」がつけられるようになった。かけだしの落語家のことを「前座」というが、これは寄席（よせ）で客が出揃うまでの時間を埋めるために、プログラムの初めの方に出演するということから出た呼び名である。一座でもっとも芸の優れた落語家のことを「真打ち」といい、寄席では最後に出演する。

〈2〉 講談は、武勇伝・政談・人情話などを語り聞かせるもので、落語とともに日本特有の話術芸能の一種である。起源は17世紀で、はじめは棒読みだったが、その後調子をつけて独特なテンポで語るようになった。

〈3〉 浪花節（浪曲）は、三味線の伴奏に合わせて渋みのある独特の節まわしでうたう部分と、対話を主とした語りの部分からなり、これを独演する。義理・人情や勧善・懲悪を内容とするものが多く、愛好者は年輩者に多い。「浪花節的」という言葉があるが、これは義理・人情に安易に傾きすぎていることをいう。

〈4〉 漫才は、2人のコンビで滑稽な軽口の掛け合いを行う演芸である。13〜14世紀ごろから伝わる伝統的な万歳（初春に悪魔をはらい、祝福をもたらすという習俗を演芸化したもので、2人で演ずる）を現代化したもので、19世紀末に大阪で生まれ、その後全国に広まった。現在はコント（2人または若干名で行う滑稽な寸劇）、漫談（1人または3名以上で行う滑稽な話芸で、楽器を持ち込むものもある）などとともに「お笑い芸」の一ジャンルであり、軽妙でテンポの速いものに特に人気がある。

〈5〉 日本民謡には、農村の田植歌や馬子唄などの仕事

<1> *Rakugo*, the telling of long comic stories, mainly in the form of one-person dialogs. Rakugo has its beginnings in the sixteenth century. By the middle of the seventeenth, the use of gestures and facial expression to bring excitement to the stories had become common and it had become the custom to include a "punch line," called the *ochi*, at the end of the story for additional effect. The storytellers are ranked according to their skill and experience. A beginner, for example, is referred to as a *zenza* (curtain raiser) from the fact that he is placed at the beginning of the program and performs while the audience is being seated. On the other hand, a rakugo master, the central performer, is called a *shin'uchi* and is of course the last to perform.

<2> *Kodan*, also a kind of storytelling but in this case the subject is a heroic tale, famous historical episode, or human interest story. Kodan has its origins in the seventeenth century. Although in the early days the deliveries were flat and monotonous, the storytellers later began to chant their stories in a unique rhythm which remains a feature of the art right up to today. Rakugo and kodan stand together as two unique narrative forms.

<3> *Naniwabushi* (also called *rokyoku*), a solo recitation partly sung in a special, sober intonation to the accompaniment of a *shamisen* and partly narrated in the form of a dialog. The theme is usually one of love versus duty or good versus evil. Naniwabushi is popular mostly among older people. Naniwabushi has also given the Japanese language the word "naniwabushiteki" (naniwabushi-like) which means to be overly susceptible to the feelings of love and duty.

<4> *Manzai*, slapstick and wisecracks by a comedy duo. Today's manzai developed originally in Osaka towards the end of the nineteenth century as a modernized version of a dramatic form going back to the thirteenth or fourteenth century. (This traditional manzai, also performed by two persons, was based on a ritual for driving away demons and ushering in good fortune at the beginning of the new year.) It is now a comic genre that includes a number of sub-genres, such as "*konto*" (funny skits by two or more performers), and *mandan* (witty monologues, or patter by three or more performers, sometimes including the use of musical instruments). Manzai performed in a breezy, fast-paced style is especially popular.

<5> Japanese folk music covers a large number of types: work songs,

歌、婚礼や新築を祝う祝賀歌、子守歌などさまざまの種類がある。しかし、文明の発達とともに労働の機械化や生活そのものの均質化が進む中、その土地土地で歌い継がれてきた民謡も、現在は宴席用の娯楽歌、あるいは盆踊り歌として変質を遂げつつ、一部だけが生き残っているのが実情である。

(5) 伝統芸術・工芸

a) いけばな

日本のいけばなは、切花を使った伝統的生活芸術で、16世紀ごろから盛んになった。

初期のいけばなは自然のままの素材と姿を重んじていたが、しだいに素材は自然のものを用いながら、構成について理念的な意味づけが行われるようになった。すなわち、いけばなの基本となる枝を天（宇宙）・地（地球）・人の3本とし、これらが調和のとれた大自然を表現する。

しかし伝統的ないけばなに対し、第二次大戦後、生命のない鉄片・石膏・ガラスなども素材にしてそれに生命感を与え、生きた形として表現しようとする前衛的ないけばなが生まれた。

いけばなの基礎技術としては、一つには素材を花器に定着させる方法、余分な枝葉の切り落とし方、素材の曲げ方、ゆがみの直し方など、造形上の技法がある。現在では室内装飾の一つとして、また生活を楽しむ趣味として、気軽に生活のなかに浸透している。

b) 茶道

「茶道」は一定の作法にしたがって、主人と客が心の共感をもってお茶を飲む日本伝統のもので、安土桃山時代（16世紀後半）に千利休によって大成された。

現在も千利休の子孫が表千家・裏千家・武者小路千家として京都に住み、全国的に盛んな活動をしている。

茶道では、抹茶という粉末状の精製された茶の葉を茶碗に入れて湯を注ぎ、茶筅（ちゃせん—竹の攪拌具）でかきまわして泡立てて飲む。

such as rice-planting songs and horse-driver songs, songs celebrating an event such as a wedding or the construction of a new house, and lullabies. However, with the increasing mechanization of labor and the homogenization of everyday life, songs that were originally associated with particular places were readapted as party songs or for community dancing and, as a result of this process, only a few dozens of the tunes have survived.

(5) Traditional Arts and Crafts

a) Ikebana

Ikebana, the Japanese traditional art of arranging cut flowers, started to flourish in the sixteenth century.

At first, the emphasis in ikebana was on the materials and forms as they existed in their natural state; gradually, though, while continuing to employ natural materials, ideological significance became attached to the compositions. That is, main branches each represent sky (universe), land (earth) and mankind and express harmonic balance of nature.

Since the Second World War, however, an avant-garde school of ikebana has appeared, the exponents of which, unlike those of the traditional schools, use lifeless materials such as iron, plaster, glass and the like arranged so as to give an impression of life through the vitality of form.

Many of the fundamental ikebana techniques are concerned with structure, such as how to fix the materials in the vase, cutting off unnecessary leaves and twigs, curving the materials, correcting kinks, and so forth. Nowadays, ikebana is practiced as a form of interior decoration, or just as an enjoyable pastime.

b) Tea Cult

Called *cha-no-yu* or *sado*, the tea cult is the traditional Japanese way of drinking tea in accordance with set rules of etiquette. Both the host and guests share a sense of togetherness during the ceremony. The cult was perfected by Sen no Rikyu in the Azuchi-Momoyama period in the latter half of the sixteenth century.

Sen no Rikyu's descendants, the houses of Omotesenke, Urasenke, and Mushakojisenke, live in Kyoto and are very active throughout Japan.

In the tea ceremony, tea is made by putting powdered tea leaves into a cup and then hot water is added. Then, it is stirred with a tool called *chasen* until it gets foamy to be drunk.

茶道の礼法は、そのためにつくられた観賞価値のある独特の茶碗に、香り高い茶をたてて客にすすめる方法や、客がこれをいただく心得からなる。茶道の礼法には、武士の礼法や能の影響がみられ、これは日本の伝統的な礼儀作法に強い影響を与えた。形のみならず心も重んじ、おのれをむなしくして客をもてなすのが茶道の心といわれている。

　茶室（茶をたてるためにつくられた専門の部屋）・露地（茶室の庭）・懐石料理（茶席で出す料理）・茶道具さらに茶菓子の取り合わせなど、すべてにわたり「客をもてなす」という主人の細心の注意が払われる。茶菓子は、抹茶の味を引き立てるために添えられるもので、季節感があり見た目にも美しいものが好まれる。多くは花鳥風月などの自然にちなんだ名前が付けられている。
　単にお茶を飲むという日常行為を、形式美をともなった一種の芸術に仕上げたところに茶道の特色がある。岡倉天心が英語で書いた『茶の本』は、日本の茶道を世界に紹介した本として有名である。

c）書道

　書道は、漢字や仮名文字を、毛筆と墨で書くことによって、精神的な深さ、美しさを表わそうとする造形芸術である。

　西洋でも文字を美しく書くことは行われているが、中国・朝鮮・日本では漢字が複雑で一字一字に意味があること、軟らかくも硬くも、太くも細くも書ける毛筆があったことにより、芸術として発達した。

　作品の鑑賞は表現美（運筆・構成・墨色・配置など）と内容美（風格・意味）によるが、書道は書家の人格の表現であるから、鑑賞者の心を打つものがよいとされる。

　正月２日に、めでたい言葉や縁起のよい詩歌などを毛筆で書く「書き初め」の風習もあるが、現在の一般家庭ではあまり見られなくなってきている。

d）日本画

　日本画は、日本家屋に飾る絵としてふさわしく、その愛

The "etiquette" of the tea ceremony concerns the manner in which the host serves the guests fine aromatic tea in a traditional tea cup of exquisite beauty and the manner in which guests show their appreciation to the host in the way they accept the tea. The tea ceremony etiquette has been influenced by the etiquette observed by the *samurai* classes as well as by the form of *noh* dances. In turn, the tea cult has greatly influenced traditional Japanese customs and manners. In the tea cult, inner spirit is emphasized as well as the ritual form, and the heart of the ceremony lies in the "selfless manner" in which the host serves tea to the guests.

In inviting the guests to a ceremony, the host always takes the greatest care in the preparation of the tea room, the adjacent garden, the tea utensils, and the cakes served with the tea, and in the provision of simple dishes, to ensure the guests are shown the utmost hospitality. The cakes, which are designed to bring out the taste of the powdered tea, preferably convey a sense of the season and look pleasing to the eye. They are usually adorned with names that evoke the beauty of nature.

The tea ceremony is distinguished from other art forms in that it has taken a simple, everyday activity (tea drinking) and elevated it to the level of an art embodying the beauty of form. *The Book of Tea*, written in English by Okakura Tenshin, is well known as the book that introduced the Japanese tea ceremony to the world.

c) Calligraphy

Calligraphy is a creative art form which attempts to express spiritual depth and beauty by means of *kanji* and *kana* characters written with a brush and *sumi* (ink).

The art of beautiful handwriting is practiced in the West, too; but because of the complexity of the kanji character, each of which has a meaning, and the use of a brush which allows the strokes to be made softly or firmly, thick or fine, calligraphy as an art is more highly developed in China, Korea, and Japan.

Although appreciation of a work of calligraphy depends on the beauty of expression (brush strokes, structure, color of sumi, arrangement, etc.) and content (style, meaning), as the writing expresses the personality of the writer, a good work is considered to be one that moves the observer.

January 2nd has long been a day for writing auspicious words and poems in what is called the "First Writing of the New Year." However, this custom is no longer observed in most ordinary households.

d) Japanese Painting

Japanese-style paintings are suitable for the traditional Japanese

好者も多い。絹地または和紙の上に毛筆で、墨や岩絵具（群青・緑青・黄土などの鉱物を砕いたもの）を膠（にかわ）などで溶いて画く。

日本の絵画は、当初仏画として中国から伝わったが、10世紀ごろになると日本の風景や風俗も描かれるようになり、大和絵が発生して日本画の基礎が築かれた。

水墨画は、禅宗とともに中国からもたらされ、15世紀ごろには、日本画としても独自の発達をとげた。墨の濃淡を用い、簡素・素朴で暗示的な表現を特徴としている。

その後、水墨画に大和絵の手法を取り入れるなどいろいろな変遷をたどり、さらに近代以降は油絵の影響も受けて、現代の日本画に至っている。

江戸時代の絵画で、現在でも広く鑑賞されているものに浮世絵がある。民衆的風俗画の一様式で、肉筆画も行われたが、とくに版画として普及した。その画題は、芝居の情景・美女・役者・力士の似顔絵を主とし、歴史画や風景・花鳥におよぶ。18世紀中ごろに、多色刷版画が鈴木春信により創始され黄金期を迎えた。代表的な浮世絵師には、美人画の喜多川歌麿、役者絵の東洲斎写楽、風景画の葛飾北斎、歌川広重などがあげられる。浮世絵の画法が印象派の画家たち（モネ、ゴッホなど）に大きな影響を与え、新しい写実技法が展開したといわれている。

e）陶磁器

日本の先史時代を縄文時代・弥生時代などその当時の土器の名称で呼ぶことから分かるように、日本の陶器の起源は古く原始時代に始まる。その後5～6世紀ごろ朝鮮・中国からすぐれた陶工とともに技術が渡来し、日本各地で独特のものを産出するようになった。

陶磁器とは陶器と磁器の総称で、「やきもの」または

house, and thus have many devotees. Japanese paintings are done on silk or Japanese paper with a brush, using *sumi* and natural mineral pigments (pulverized lapis lazuli, malachite, ocher, etc.) dissolved in liquid glue, etc.

The Japanese style of painting has its origin in Buddhist painting introduced from China. From this beginning, there had, by around the tenth century, evolved the *yamato-e* painting style which dealt with Japanese scenes and themes. This style served as the foundation for what has come to be known as "Japanese painting."

The black-and-white *suiboku-ga* style came into Japan from China together with *Zen* Buddhism and became established as an independent art form in about the fifteenth century. The suiboku-ga of that time were characterized by an allusive mode of expression that, based on lines and shades of sumi, was simple and unsophisticated.

Before reaching its present form, this style of painting underwent considerable change and development through the adoption of Yamato-e techniques and under various other influences such as modern oil painting.

The *ukiyo-e* paintings of the Edo Period are very popular even today. A form of genre picture, some were painted by hand, but it is as woodblock prints that they became widely known. The most common subjects were scenes from the theater, and portraits of famous beauties, actors, and *sumo* wrestlers, but historical themes, landscapes, birds, and flowers were also depicted. The development by Suzuki Harunobu of multi-color printing in the mid-eighteenth century gave rise to the golden age of color prints. The studies of women by Kitagawa Utamaro, the portraits of Kabuki actors by Toshusai Sharaku, and the landscapes by Katsushika Hokusai and Utagawa Hiroshige are representative examples of the ukiyo-e genre. It is said that the ukiyo-e art of drawing had a strong influence on such impressionists as Monet and van Gogh, and resulted in the development of the new techniques of realism.

e) Ceramic Ware

From the fact that Japan's prehistoric periods are referred to by the name of the earthenware of the time, such as the Jomon or Yayoi period, it can be seen that Japan has a long tradition of ceramics going back to primitive times. In the fifth and sixth centuries, skilled craftsmen visiting Japan from Korea and China introduced the techniques of these countries. This led to the appearance of distinctive ceramic products in numerous localities.

Japanese commonly lump pottery and porcelain (china) together

「瀬戸物」とも呼ばれている。これは中部地方の瀬戸市付近が長い間有名な産地であったからである（平安後期の11世紀〜江戸中期の18世紀）。

しかし、陶器と磁器とは別のもので、その間にはかなりはっきりした違いがある。その主な違いは、素材、焼く温度、固さ、厚さ、色、たたいたときの音、などによるものである。

陶器は「土もの」といわれ、ガラス質を含まない土（粘土）を素材とし、低い温度で焼くので多孔性で吸水性があり、余り硬くない。また肉厚で色は一般に茶系統の不透明色である。たたくと、にぶく低い音がする。「轆轤（ろくろ）」を回しながら手で作ったものは、表面が滑らかではなく形も不整形で温か味がある。日本の芸術的・伝統的な陶器の有名なものには、信楽焼、京焼、薩摩焼、楽焼、栗田焼、織部焼、萩焼、志野焼、備前焼などがある。

他方、磁器は「石もの」と呼ばれ、素材はガラスの光沢をもつ岩石（長石）を含む石の粉で、高温で焼くため非常に硬く水を通さない。肉は一般に陶器より薄く、表面はガラスのように滑らかである。内部の色は半透明の乳白色である。たたくと高く澄んだ金属音がする。工業的に成形するので形は整っていて、量産も可能である。日常生活で使われるのは大部分が磁器である。日本の磁器で伝統的に有名なものには、有田焼、伊万里焼、清水焼、九谷焼、美濃焼などがある。

中国の青磁、朝鮮の白磁も磁器の代表である。西洋に磁器の製法が伝わったのは比較的新しく18世紀初めで、日本、中国からである。当初ヨーロッパでは磁器は宝石並みに高価で、王室では「磁器の間」などに飾られていた。今日世界的に有名なドイツのマイセンなどの製品が東洋の磁器に似ているのはこのような歴史的背景による。

f) 漆器

漆器とは漆を塗った器などの美術工芸品である。漆が東洋特産のため、漆器は日本・中国・朝鮮・ベトナム・タイ・ミャンマーなどで発達した。とりわけ日本のものは世界的に名高い。英語で漆器のことを japan（ジャパン）というが、これは漆器が、日本から欧米に紹介されたからである。

漆とは、ウルシの木の樹皮の下から浸み出てくる粘液で

under a common term like *tojiki* (ceramic ware), *yakimono* (fired ware), or *seto-mono* (a name taken from the area around Seto City in the Chubu region which was famous for ceramic products between the eleventh and eighteenth centuries).

But pottery and porcelain are markedly dissimilar in a number of respects. The most notable differences are in the starting materials, firing temperature, hardness, thickness, color, and sound when tapped.

Pottery, also called "earthenware," is made by firing clay containing no vitreous (glassy) material at a low temperature. It is porous, absorbs water, and is not very hard. It is thick and generally of an opaque, brownish color, and produces a dull sound when tapped. Pottery shaped by hand while turning on a potter's wheel has a rough surface and uneven shape, qualities that give it a warm feeling. Famous traditional artistic potteries include *shigarakiyaki*, *kyoyaki*, *satsumayaki*, *rakuyaki*, *kuritayaki*, *oribeyaki*, *hagiyaki*, *shinoyaki*, and *bizenyaki*.

Porcelain, also called "stoneware," is made by firing a stone powder containing lustrous rock of vitreous nature (feldspar) at a high temperature, so it is very hard and impervious to water. It is generally thinner than pottery and has a smooth glasslike surface and a milky translucent interior. Porcelain produces a metallic sound when tapped. China and other porcelain wares are manufactured industrially, so they are well-shaped and amenable to mass production. Most ceramic wares used in daily life are porcelain. Famous Japanese porcelain wares include *aritayaki*, *imariyaki*, *kiyomizuyaki*, *kutaniyaki*, and *minoyaki*.

Chinese celadon porcelain and Korean white porcelain are also well known. The secret of porcelain manufacture reached the West only fairly recently, from Japan and China in the early eighteenth century. In Europe, porcelain products at first were as valuable as gems, and the royal palaces had "porcelain rooms" for displaying them. Dresden and other world-famous European porcelain products resemble Oriental products because the underlying techniques came from the East.

f) Lacquer Ware

The term "lacquer ware" means any artistically-crafted article which has a lacquer finish. Because lacquer is a product of the Orient, the best lacquer ware has developed in Asian countries such as Japan, China, Korea, Vietnam, Thailand, and Myanmar. Japanese lacquer ware has high international reputation. In English, lacquer ware is also called "japan" from the fact that it was first introduced to the West by Japan.

Lacquer is a viscous liquid that exudes from under the bark of the

ある。これを精製して顔料を加えたものを塗って、ほどよい湿度で乾燥させると、接着性や防蝕・防湿性の強い被膜が得られる。通常、薄く塗っては乾かすことを何回も繰り返す。

漆器を彩る加飾はさまざまで、伝統的なものとして蒔絵（まきえ）と沈金（ちんきん）および螺鈿（らでん）がある。蒔絵は、筆に漆を含ませて模様を描き、そこに金粉・銀粉などを蒔（ま）きつけ、研ぎ・磨きを繰り返してつくりあげる。沈金は、刃物で絵柄を彫り、その彫り跡に金箔・銀箔、金粉・銀粉、顔料等を漆で接着させて仕上げる。そして螺鈿は、夜光貝や白蝶貝などの貝殻の内側の真珠層の部分を薄く削り、漆地や木地の彫刻された部分にはめ込む技法を使って制作される。

漆の利用は古くから行われ、原始時代のものも発見されているが、芸術品としては法隆寺に残されている玉虫厨子（桧造りの上に黒漆が塗ってある。玉虫の羽根は漆塗りの上に張ってある）がもっとも古い。

7世紀以後、中国の技術も導入されて、箱・食器そのほかの家具・仏像・建築などの、美術工芸品に用いられている。現在では、日本食に必須の汁ものには、漆のお椀が食器として用いられている。

日本の漆器で伝統的に有名なものには、津軽塗、会津塗、秀衡塗、高岡漆器、飛騨春慶塗、輪島塗、山中漆器などがある。

g）日本刀

日本刀は片刃で反りがあり、加熱した玉鋼を槌で打ってよく鍛練し、焼き入れを行うなど独特の製法によってつくられるので、折れたり曲がったりせず、切れ味の鋭いのが特徴である。

日本には中国・朝鮮などから刀剣の製法が伝えられたが、9世紀ごろになって反（そ）りのある日本刀がつくられるまでは、ほとんど直刀（両刃のものもある）で、これは古代刀と呼ばれている。

9世紀から12世紀にかけてつくられたものは、刀身の元幅と先幅の差が大きく、腰もとでの反りが強く、またこ

lacquer tree. This liquid is refined and mixed with pigment. By applying a layer of the mixture to the surface of an object and then drying it in air of an appropriate humidity, a coating is obtained that is highly adhesive and resistant to damp and corrosion. Usually, a number of thin layers are applied, each layer being dried before the next application.

Lacquer ware is decorated in various ways, with traditional methods including *makie*, *chinkin*, and *raden*. In makie, a pattern is painted in lacquer, on which gold or silver or other metal powder is sprinkled, which is followed by repeated burnishing and polishing. In chinkin, a chisel is used to engrave a design, lacquer is applied to the carved surface, and this is followed by the adhering of gold or silver leaf and powder or pigment to the lacquer. Raden is a technique in which thin pieces of the lining of mother-of-pearl or other shells are set into a lacquer ground coating or into shapes carved in a wood surface.

Lacquer has been utilized since early times, and some examples of its use in primitive times have been discovered. The oldest object that displays an artistic use of lacquer, however, is the *Tamamushi no Zushi* (a black lacquered miniature shrine made of Japanese cypress, the lacquer being overlaid with the wings of the jewel beetle) preserved in Horyuji Temple.

Starting with the introduction of Chinese techniques from the seventh century, lacquer was used on artistically crafted items such as furniture, Buddhist images, buildings, etc. as well as on boxes and eating utensils. Today, lacquer-ware bowls are often used to serve the soups that are an indispensable part of Japanese meals.

Famous traditional Japanese lacquer wares include *tsugarunuri*, *aizunuri*, *hidehiranuri*, *takaokashikki*, *hidashunkeinuri*, *wajimanuri*, and *yamanakashikki*.

g) Japanese Swords

The Japanese sword has a curved blade with a single cutting edge. Made by a special process that includes hammer-forging, hardening and quenching hot raw steel made by smelting sand iron, the sword is characterized by its great spring-like toughness and its extremely sharp cutting edge.

The art of swordmaking came to Japan from China and Korea. The early swords, what are today called ancient swords, were straight (and sometimes double edged), the curved blade did not appear until the ninth century.

Swords made between the ninth and twelfth centuries were much wider across the base than the tip and were curved sharply near the

の時代から刀に作者の銘がきざまれるようになった。無銘のものも少なくないが、刀の特徴によって、現在では作者が確かめられているものが多い。

　13世紀初めごろから日本刀は武家の需要により、刀身の身幅が広くなるとともに元幅と先幅の差が縮まり、切っ先が短くなって豪壮さを加え、その黄金時代を迎えた。

　一般に、16世紀末ごろまでにつくられたものは古刀、それより新しいものは新刀と呼ばれている。新刀は身幅が広く、反りが少なく、先幅が細く、切っ先が長いのが特徴である。
　刀は武士の魂とみなされ、武家社会の象徴だったので、工芸品としても優れた名刀も多い。

　第二次世界大戦後は、日本刀はもっぱら美術品として鑑賞の対象となり、清く澄み切った冷たい美しさから、心の落ち着きを得るために、一部の人によって珍重されている。日本では日本刀を所持するには、許可証をとる必要がある。

h）人形
　日本の原始時代の遺跡から土の人形（土偶）が発見され、古代の古墳から埴輪人形が出土するなど、大昔から日本人と人形の関係は切り離せない。

　日本の伝統芸術の一つである文楽は、大きな人形をあやつりながら演ずる大規模な人形劇である。

　男の子の節句（5月5日）には武者人形を飾り、女の子の節句（3月3日）には華美な雛人形を飾る。
　日本で現在つくられている人形の種類は、ヨーロッパ式も含め非常に多い。もっともポピュラーなものは「博多人形」と「こけし」であろう。
　「博多人形」は、土で形をつくり、素焼にしてから彩色するもので、福岡県の特産である。写実的で繊細な姿態と彩色が特徴であり、模写に優れ、世界各国の風俗、古今の美人画、歌舞伎役者などの題材をこなしている。

base. It was also during this period that swordmakers began stamping their names onto the swords they made. Today, while there are many unmarked swords from this period, in many cases they are accredited to specific swordmakers on the basis of distinguishing features in the craftsmanship.

Early in the thirteenth century, swords began to undergo modifications to meet the needs of the *samurai*. The blade was made broader and the difference in breadth between the base and the tip was reduced. The tip was given a sharper angle and made shorter. These changes enhanced the splendor of the weapon and marked the beginning of the golden age of the Japanese sword.

Swords made until the sixteenth century are classified as "old swords" and those after are referred to as "new swords." New swords have a broader blade that is only slightly curved, and a long, narrow tip.

As the sword was considered to be the very soul of the samurai and became the symbol of the warrior class, many specimens show superb craftsmanship.

Since the end of World War II, the Japanese sword has come to be regarded solely as an object of art, often to be treasured for a sense of tranquility found in its cold, serene beauty. One has to obtain a permit to own a sword in Japan.

h) Dolls

Dolls have played a part in Japanese people's life since time immemorial. Clay figurines have been discovered among protohistoric relics and *haniwa* clay images have been unearthed from ancient burial mounds.

Bunraku, one of the traditional theater arts of Japan, is a large-scale puppet drama in which big dolls are manipulated to show the action of the play.

Warrior-dolls are displayed during the Boy's Festival (May 5), and beautifully attired dolls during the Girl's Festival (March 3).

A tremendous variety of dolls, of both Japanese and European style, are manufactured in Japan today. The most popular are the *Hakata* dolls and *kokeshi*.

Hakata dolls, which are molded from clay, fired, then painted, are the specialty of Fukuoka Prefecture in Kyushu, the southern island. Hakata dolls, which are characterized by a finely detailed realism and by the colors used, depict subjects old and new and from every land, such as

「こけし」は、東北地方伝統の木製人形である。ろくろでひいた円筒形の胴体に、丸い頭をつけて女の子の顔を描き、胴体に赤・青・黄など2〜3色で線や菊の花などの模様を描く。素朴なものであるが、面相や彩色にひなびた味わいがある。

i) 扇子（せんす）

　扇子は日本で発明されたもので、もともと暑さをしのぐためのものであったが、その後、儀礼用や舞踊の用具として用いられるようになった。

　はじめに桧の薄片を綴り合わせた桧扇がつくられ、その後、紙扇がつくられた。桧扇は7世紀ごろから宮廷で使われ、8世紀には、宮廷内での装束になくてはならないものとなった。やがて紙扇もつくられるようになり、能や歌舞伎の用具としても取り入れられ、また宗教行事や庶民の日常生活のなかにも、盛んに用いられるようになった。

　能や歌舞伎に用いられる扇子にはそれぞれきまりの文様があるが、庶民がふだん使用する扇子には自由に歌や書や絵が描かれた。桧扇や紙扇は中国や朝鮮にわたり、朝鮮扇は扇骨の数が増加し、中国では扇骨に彫刻をほどこすようになった。西欧の扇が日本の方式にならって折りたたみ式になったのは、17世紀中ごろからである。

j) 羽子板

　羽子板は正月などに遊ぶゲームで使う板で、長方形の柄がついている。遊び方はバドミントンに似ており、ふつうは着物をきた若い女性2人が「羽根」（黒くて固い種子に鳥の羽毛を植えつけたもの）を高く打ちあげて遊ぶ。「羽根」を地上に落とした方が負けになる。この遊びが最初に出てくるのは、室町時代（14〜15世紀）の文献である。

　羽根は、蚊を食うトンボに似せたもので、この遊びは子供の蚊よけ、厄病よけのまじないから生まれたともいわれる。室町時代には宮中の公家や女官の遊びであったが、江

beautiful women from all periods of history, and *kabuki* actors.

Kokeshi are the traditional wooden dolls made in the northeastern region of Japan. The dolls consist of a cylindrical torso, turned out on a lathe. A round head is fitted on the torso and a girl's face drawn in. Two or three colors, such as red, blue or yellow, are used to paint lines or a chrysanthemum design on the body. While unsophisticated, the face and colors give kokeshi dolls a certain rustic charm.

i) Folding Fans

The folding fan is a Japanese invention. Originally it was purely used to cool down, but it later became important in Japanese etiquette and dancing.

The first folding fans consisted just of thin sticks of Japanese cypress held together by ribbons. It was only later the sticks were covered with paper. The cypress stick fans first appeared at the Imperial Court in the seventh century and by the eighth century they had become an indispensable part of Court attire. Later, the paper fans came to be used extensively—in *noh* and *kabuki*, in religious ceremonies, and in everyday life.

Although noh and kabuki fans are decorated with certain fixed painted or printed patterns, those for daily use come in all manner of designs, the most popular types being handwritten poems, artistically executed *kanji* characters, and various painted patterns, landscapes, and portraits. The Japanese folding fan served as a model for similar fans in China, where the embellishment of elaborately carved ribs was added, and Korea, where the number of ribs was greatly increased. The folding fans that first appeared in Europe around the middle of the seventeenth century were also derived from the Japanese fan.

j) Hagoita

The *hagoita* is a paddle used in a game played typically at the beginning of the new year. It consists of a board with a rectangular handle. The game is played somewhat in the manner of badminton, typically by two kimono-clad girls, with the players taking turns at hitting a shuttlecock (a hard black seed to which feathers have been attached) high into the air. The player who allows the shuttlecock to fall on the ground is the loser. The first references to the game are found in literary works of the Muromachi period (fourteenth and fifteenth centuries).

The shuttlecock is modeled after a mosquito-eating dragonfly, and the game is thought to have grown out of a magical rite for protecting children from mosquitoes and sickness. In the Muromachi period, the

戸時代に一般庶民の遊びとなった。

　羽子板は、江戸時代には飾りものとしても使われるようになった。大形の羽子板には、船・美人・初日の出・花・鳥など豪華な絵柄を飾りたてたものもある。現在でも正月には、東京をはじめ各地で羽子板市が開かれている。

k) 庭園

　日本・中国・朝鮮の庭園は、自然の景観美を主とするものであって、幾何学的な美しさを重視する西洋の庭園とは対照的である。自然の景観美といっても、自然そのままの姿ではない。樹木・石など自然の材料を用いて自然の山水のたたずまいを象徴化し、あるいは強調して、一つのまとまりのある調和した人工的空間美を形成する。

　1,000年にわたる庭園の歴史のなかで、時代の推移とともにその様式も変化する。大別して、中心の池で大海を表わし、土を盛り岩を配して山を表わす形式（築山式）と、水を使用せず、白砂を敷いて大海を、砂紋によって流れを表現し、青石を立てて滝を象徴させる方式（枯山水式）がある。

　京都の天龍寺や西芳寺の庭園が前者の、龍安寺や大徳寺大仙院の庭園が後者の例である。

　こうした日本庭園のそれぞれの特徴をすべて取り入れたうえ、庭園外の山や樹木をも遠景として活用した借景庭園としては、京都の円通寺が有名である。

l) 盆栽

　盆栽は陶磁器の鉢に樹木を植え、その生育する力を利用して適切な手入れを行い、自然の雅趣をかもし出すように姿を整えて観賞するものである。中国で生まれ、隋・唐の時代（日本の奈良・平安時代）に日本に伝えられ、日本で独自の発展を見た。

　短期間観賞する鉢植えとは異なり、盆栽は数十年から数

game was played only by nobles and ladies of the Imperial Court, but by the Edo period it had become an amusement of the common people.

The Edo Period also saw the hagoita as a decorative object. Huge specimens embellished with fancy pictures of ships, beautiful women, New Year's Day sunrises, flowers, birds, and the like came into fashion. In early January even today, stalls selling decorative hagoitas can be found around Tokyo and other parts of the country.

k) Gardens

The main consideration in the gardens of Japan, China, and Korea is on natural scenic beauty, which is in contrast to the gardens of the West in which the emphasis is on beauty of geometrical form. However, "natural scenic beauty" does not mean nature in its original, unchanged forms. Rather, natural materials such as trees, shrubs, and rocks are used to symbolize or emphasize the forms and features of the natural landscape, thereby creating an artificial spatial beauty that has a harmonic unity.

The history of landscape gardening spans a thousand years, during which styles changed as one age gave way to the next. Broadly speaking, there are the miniature artificial hill style (*tsukiyama*), where a central pond symbolizes the sea, and mountains are represented by banks of earth and arrangements of rocks; and the dry landscape style (*karesansui*), in which the sea is symbolized not by water but by a layer of white sand, which is given a pattern of furrows to represent the rippling movement of the water, and waterfalls are symbolized by an arrangement of blue rocks.

The gardens of Tenryuji Temple and Saihoji Temple in Kyoto are examples of the former style, and those of Ryoanji Temple and Daitokuji Temple's Daisen-in, also in Kyoto, are examples of the latter style.

Famous examples of gardens which, in addition to incorporating the above features, utilize the views of surrounding mountains and woods (*shakkei*) include Entsuji Temple in Kyoto.

l) Bonsai

Bonsai (dwarf trees) is an art form that consists of planting a tree in a ceramic pot and then, through a process of cultivation that draws on and accents the plant's vital powers, producing a natural elegance of form pleasing to the eye. It originated in China and was introduced to Japan during the Sui and Tang Dynasties (the Nara and Heian periods of Japan), whereafter it developed independently in Japan.

Ordinary potted plants can only be appreciated for a short time, but

百年もの長期にわたって育て、しだいに古木の風格をつくり出していくものであり、そのために、特殊な培養を行う。

　盆栽の素材の代表格は松であるが、常緑樹、落葉樹、花や実のなる樹など多くのものを盆栽に仕上げることができ、それぞれに独特の趣があるとされる。

　盆栽は、自然の美を愛し、それを身近な生活に取り入れようとした日本人の生活の知恵の所産といえよう。

　近年盆栽は自然を凝縮したアートとしてアジアや欧米で楽しまれ、日本からの輸出も飛躍的に伸びている。

　なお、2010年3月に「さいたま市大宮盆栽美術館」が開館し、世界に誇る盆栽の名品の展示などによる盆栽文化の紹介などをしており、盆栽に親しむ機会を提供することにより関心を高め、盆栽文化の振興を図り、盆栽を介して国際交流や愛好家などと交流促進を図る施設となっている。

(6) 建築・住居

a) 家屋

　日本の個人住宅は木造が多く、2階または平屋である。木造は火災や地震に弱いが、通風採光がよく、高温多湿な日本の風土に適している。また、材料である木の落ち着いた感触が日本人の好みに適合している。

　現在は、耐震性を重視したコンクリート造りあるいは鉄骨造りの住宅も増えているほか、家屋の形にヨーロッパ風も取り入れられている。また、都市およびその周辺には、3階建から40階建以上のアパートがある。このような集合形式の住宅はマンションと呼ばれ、戸建住宅と区別されている。マンションも和室を備えているところが多い。

　和室の内装は、一般に天井は木の板であり、壁は塗り壁、床は板を張った上に畳を敷いてある。畳の本体は米作の副産物であるワラでつくったマットであり、表にいぐさで織ったシートが張ってある。和室の境界には木の枠に紙を張りつけた襖や障子がある。これは敷居という横木に刻まれた溝の上を、左右に滑らせることにより開閉する建具

bonsai last for periods ranging from decades to centuries, gradually gaining in character as they age. Special cultivation methods are used for this.

Pine trees are typical bonsai subjects; but many other types of trees can be used, such as various evergreens and deciduous trees, and trees that blossom and bear fruit, and each has its own unique attractiveness.

The ability to produce bonsai can be said to spring from the resourcefulness of the Japanese people who, in their love of natural beauty, have tried to bring it closer to their lives.

Nowadays, bonsai is also being more widely enjoyed in other Asian and Western countries as an art that concentrates the beauty of nature. Japanese bonsai exports are increasing rapidly.

The Omiya Bonsai Art Museum, Saitama opened in March 2010. The museum gives people an opportunity to get to know more about the culture of bonsai by exhibiting masterpieces of the art, raising interest in bonsai, promoting related international exchanges, and attracting enthusiasts.

(6) Buildings

a) Houses

Most private houses in Japan are made of wood and are of one or two stories. While wooden houses are easily damaged by fires and earthquakes, they are airy and bright and, therefore, suited to the hot, humid climate of Japan. Moreover, Japanese people feel more settled and relaxed in a house made of wood.

Recent years have seen an increase in the use of other materials, such as concrete, with its earthquake resistance, and, for the framework, steel; there has also been greater incorporation of Western styles. Apartment houses, ranging in height from three to forty or more stories, can be seen in urban centers and their environs. The apartments in such multiple-unit residential buildings are called "*manshon*" (coined from the English word "mansion") and are differentiated from detached houses. Many "manshon" have one or more Japanese-style rooms.

The interiors of Japanese-style rooms follow fairly fixed patterns: ceiling of wooden boards, plaster-covered walls, and *tatami* laid on wooden floorboards. Tatami are thick mats made of rice straw and are thus a by-product of the cultivation of rice. They are finished with a cover of woven rush (*igusa*). In a Japanese-style house, the rooms are partitioned by *fusuma* and *shoji*, sliding doors and screens made of a

である。障子は採光を考慮したものであり、襖は遮蔽を主目的とし、採光は考慮されていない。これらの素材は日本の多湿の風土によく適合しており（湿気を吸うので湿度を調整する機能がある）、長い間の生活の知恵から生まれたものである。

　洋間のつくりは、おおむね欧米の部屋と変わりはない。家に入るときには、玄関で靴を脱ぐ。ここで、スリッパにはきかえることもあるが、これも和室に入る前には必ず脱ぐ。

b）建築物

　日本では19世紀以前の建築物は、ほとんど木造であった。それは良質な木材が豊富に採取できたこと、高温多湿の気候に適していること、地震や風に対しても構造を工夫すれば、かなり強い建物が造れることなどの事情による。

　7世紀後半の建物といわれる法隆寺は、現存する世界最古の木造建築であり、また奈良の大仏のある東大寺は、世界最大（東西57.3 m、南北50.4 m、高さ48.6 m）の木造建築である。なお、寺院建築の多くは中国・朝鮮の建築様式に倣ったものである

　19世紀にヨーロッパの建築技術が導入されて以来、レンガ造りや鉄筋コンクリート造りで大学・官庁・事務所などが建てられた。とくに鉄骨については、使用鋼材の改良と従来の剛構造から柔構造への設計思想の進歩、また免震および耐震技術の進化により、1960年代半ば以降は都市部には40階以上の高層建築物がたくさん建てられるようになった。現在では、70階以上の建物もある。

　こうして、昔から日本の建築界を悩ましてきた地震に対する問題も一応克服できた。しかし、新技法による高層建築は、現実の試練に直面した経験が少ないので、倒壊・火災以外のトラブルに対する配慮が要望されている。

wooden frame with paper stretched over it. They are set in grooved beams (called *shikii*) so they can be slid to one side or the other. Shoji permit the passage of light, whereas the purpose of fusuma is to act as a partition. Shoji and fusuma are eminently suited to the highly humid Japanese climate (they absorb and release moisture and thus even out humidity fluctuations), and were developed over a long period from the experience of the people in their everyday life.

Western-style rooms are built substantially the same as their counterparts in Europe and America. When entering a Japanese house, whether of Japanese or Western style, one removes one's shoes at the entrance and, generally, puts on slippers. The slippers are removed on entering a Japanese-style (tatami-matted) room.

b) Large Buildings

Up to the nineteenth century, most buildings in Japan were made of wood. This was because, among other reasons, a plentiful supply of good wood could be obtained, and wood was suitable for the hot and humid climate. Also, with skillful technique, structures could be built that would stand up fairly well to earthquakes and strong winds.

The world's oldest wooden structure still standing is Horyuji Temple, which is said to date from the latter half of the seventh century; and the world's largest wooden structure is Todaiji Temple, which houses a large statue of Buddha, and is situated in Nara. Todaiji Temple measures 57.3 meters (188 feet) from east to west, 50.4 meters (165.35 feet) from north to south, and is 48.6 meters (159.45 feet) high. The structures of most temples are modeled after Chinese and Korean architectural styles.

After European building techniques began to be introduced in the nineteenth century, universities, government buildings, business offices and the like started to be constructed of brick or reinforced concrete. The use of steel frames, in particular, has shown a considerable increase, and with the improvements in the steel used, together with the advance in design concept from rigid structures to flexible structures, due to the evolution of seismic isolation and earthquake resistance technology, many high-rise buildings of more than 40 stories have been constructed in cities since the mid-1960s. At present there are a few buildings of more than 70 stories.

It would therefore seem that the Japanese construction industry has managed to overcome the problem that has always existed in Japan— that of earthquakes. However, such high buildings constructed with these new methods have been little tested in actual circumstances, and though probably quite safe from collapse and fire, they may be

(7) スポーツ

a) 概要

スポーツで人気があるのは、野球・サッカー・相撲・ラグビー・バレーボール・バスケットボール・テニス・ゴルフ・卓球・水泳・柔道・剣道・弓道（アーチェリーを含む）・空手道・マラソン（駅伝マラソンを含む）・登山・釣などである。ウィンタースポーツとしてスキー・スノーボード・スケート・アイスホッケーが盛んである。

野球やサッカーなどにはプロのチームがあり、相撲・ゴルフ・ボクシング・レスリング・テニスなどには、プロの選手がいる。試合は、テレビで放映されてファンが多い。

b) 相撲

相撲は日本の国技である。その歴史は古代にまでさかのぼることができる。相撲は単にスポーツとしてだけではなく、農業生活の吉凶を占い、神の心を伺う行事として行われてきた。16世紀ごろからは見るスポーツとしても発展してきた。

現在の相撲は、直径 4.55 m（日本の古い尺という単位で 15 尺、14.9 フィート）の円形の土俵の中で力士 2 人が技を競う。力士は、素手で腰に「まわし」を締めただけの裸体で登場する。

2 人は呼吸の合ったところで同時に立ち合い、押し合い、突き合い、組み合って闘う。土俵の中で足の裏以外の部分が土につくか、土俵の外に体の一部がつくか大勢が土俵の外に出た方が負けになる。

プロの相撲団体が一つあり、年に 6 回、1 回 15 日間の興業（「大相撲」と呼ばれる）を東京で 3 回、大阪・名古屋・福岡で各 1 回行っている。各場所ごとに、勝率によって各力士の地位の入れ替え（番付編成：ばんづけへんせい）が行われる。

力士の最高位は横綱で、過去 300 年間に 72 人（2017 年）しかこの地位に上っていない。1990 年代から外国人力士の進出が目立ち、曙、武蔵丸、朝青龍、白鵬、日馬富士、鶴竜などハワイ、モンゴル出身の横綱が誕生し、2017 年に 19 年ぶりに稀勢の里が日本出身横綱となった。優勝す

susceptible to other troubles which must now be taken into account.

(7) Sports

a) Overview

Popular sports include baseball, soccer, *sumo*, rugby, volleyball, basketball, tennis, golf, table tennis, swimming, *judo*, *kendo*, archery (both Japanese- and Western-style), *karatedo*, marathons (including road relay races), mountain climbing, and fishing. The most popular winter sports are skiing, snowboarding, skating, and ice hockey.

Professional team sports include baseball and soccer. Sumo, golf, boxing, wrestling, and tennis are also practiced by professionals, with competitions broadcasted on television with many fans.

b) Sumo

Sumo is Japan's national sport; its history goes back to ancient times. Originally, sumo was not just a sport, but an event used to tell whether crops would be good or not by seeking the divine intention of the gods. From about the sixteenth century it developed into a spectator sport.

In modern sumo, two wrestlers at a time, pit their skills against each other in the round sumo ring which is 4.55 meters in diameter (or 15 *shaku*—14.9 feet—using the old Japanese unit of measurement). The wrestlers are bare-handed in their bouts and wear only a loincloth, called a *mawashi*.

When both are ready they charge and start pushing, thrusting, and grappling. The first one who touches the ground with any part of his body except the soles of his feet, or who is pushed out of the ring, is the loser.

There is just one professional sumo organization, which holds six tournaments (called *ozumo*) a year: three in Tokyo, and one each in Osaka, Nagoya and Fukuoka. Each tournament lasts fifteen days. The individual sumo wrestlers are moved up or down in rank according to how many victories they obtain in each of these tournaments (banzukei-hensei: ranking organization).

Top of the ranks are the *yokozuna*, or grand champions: in the past three hundred years only 72 have reached this grade (as of 2017). Since the 1990s, foreign wrestlers have been prominent among those rising to high ranks. Two Hawaiians (Akebono and Musashimaru) and four Mongolians (Asashoryu, Hakuho, Harumafuji and Kakuryu) made it

ると天皇杯を賜るほか、外国大使館やいろいろの団体から賞をもらう。

相撲は国技として人気があり、テレビ中継やラジオ放送によって全国民が楽しんでいる。プロの相撲のほか学生相撲もあり、また少年達は、かつては相撲で遊ぶことも多かった。

c）柔道

日本には古来、柔術（じゅうじゅつ）という徒手による攻防の技法を中心とした武術があった。相手を殺傷せずに捕らえたり、護身として身を護ることを重視し、このような技法は広く研究され、流派が多数存在した。柔道はこれら流派をもとに嘉納治五郎が創始した。

嘉納治五郎は、教育者（東京高等師範学校長になった人）で、私費を投じて講道館を1882年に開き、柔道の研究と指導を行った。ここで古来の武術である柔術から、近代柔道としての発展の基礎をつくったのである。

柔道は単に勝負を競うのみでなく、これにより心身を錬磨するものである。20世紀になってから男子の中等学校以上の教育にも取り入れられ、大いに普及した。

柔道の競技方法は、上衣・下袴・帯から成る柔道着を着けた2人が、5間（9m）四方（50枚の畳を敷いてある）の中で、互いに組み合い、投げ技と固め技によって勝負を競う。

柔道の柔とは「やわらかい」という意味であり、「柔よく剛を制す」という原理により名付けられた。

各人の力量を段と級で表わし、段のなかでは10段が最高、初段が最低である。級は段に至らないもので、1級が最高、5級が最低である。そして段と級の区分により帯の色をかえる。10〜9段は紅、8〜6段は紅白のだんだら、5〜初段は黒、1〜3級は茶、4〜5級は白、初心者は水色になっている。

1964年以来男子柔道が、1992年以来女子柔道が、国際

to the rank of yokozuna. (All sumo wrestlers use professional names.) In 2017 Kisenosato became the first wrestler of Japanese descent to be promoted to Yokozuna in 19 years. The winner of a tournament receives the Emperor's Cup, the top award, plus a number of prizes from foreign embassies and various organizations.

Sumo, as the national sport, is highly popular, and is enjoyed by people all over the country through television and radio broadcasts. In addition to professional sumo, the sport is also practiced in universities. Many children used to like to play sumo.

c) Judo

Jujutsu is a martial art involving bare-handed combat with a history that goes back to olden times. It placed emphasis on being able to protect oneself and capture an opponent without killing him. It was widely studied and practiced in many schools. The system of *judo* founded by the educator Kano Jigoro was based on the jujutsu techniques of the various schools.

In 1882, Kano Jigoro (who later became head of the Tokyo Higher Normal School) personally financed and opened the Kodokan for the study and instruction of judo. This formed the starting point of the development of modern judo from jujutsu.

The aim in judo is not just to win contests; rather, it is to train the mind and body. At the beginning of the twentieth century judo became part of the educational curriculum for boys from middle school, and since then it has become very widespread.

In a judo match two participants, each wearing jacket, trousers, and belt, contest in an area 9 meters square (on 50 *tatami* mats), and each tries to win by using throwing techniques or grappling techniques.

The *ju* of judo means "soft" or "pliant," and the sport was named after the principle shown in the saying *ju yoku go o seisu*—"flexibility overcomes stiffness."

The ability of judo practitioners is indicated by *dan* and *kyu* grades. Tenth dan is the highest of the dan grades, and *shodan* (first dan) the lowest. Kyu grades rank below dan, and first kyu is the highest and fifth kyu the lowest of the kyu grades. These various grades are indicated by the color of the belts worn: red for ninth and tenth dan, red and white for sixth to eighth dan, and black for first to fifth dan. First to third kyu wear brown belts, fourth and fifth kyu white belts, and beginners blue belts.

Judo has been recognized as an international sport and designated

スポーツとしてオリンピック正式種目になっている。これと共に柔道が外国で広く普及し国際化されて、今や日本以上の柔道人口をもつフランスのような国も出現している。

d) 剣道・弓道・薙刀（なぎなた）・空手道

剣道・弓道・空手道は日本の伝統的な武道であるが、現在はスポーツとして親しまれている。最近では外国人の愛好者も非常に増加している。

剣道は、剣で身を守り、敵をたおす道である。7～8世紀ごろから行われ、16世紀ごろに急速に発展して、いろいろな流派が生まれた。17世紀以降、剣道は技術とともに精神を練ることに重きがおかれ、仏教や儒教、とくに禅宗の影響によって、道徳的に修練されるようになった。昔は木刀を多く用いたが、18世紀に竹刀と面・胴・小手・たれ、などの防具が考案され、今日に至っている。

面打ち・小手打ち・胴打ち・突きを技の基本とし、いろいろな連続わざ、応用わざや構え方がある。競技は通常3本勝負で行われ、3人の審判員のうち2人以上が有効な打ち・突きを認めれば1本となる。

弓は狩猟や武器に使われ発達したが、鉄砲の伝来（1543年）以来、薙刀と同じく、しだいに武器としての効用を失った。弓道は、その後禅や儒教の思想を取り入れて、心身鍛練のための武道の一つとして発展した。競技方法は、的中を競うだけではなく、射形、射品、態度などを総合して審査員が採点するもので、ヨーロッパで生まれたアーチェリーなどの同種のスポーツとの相違がある。

薙刀は、堅い木で作られた長い柄の先に反りのある刀身を装着した武具であり、江戸時代以降、武家の婦女子の精神鍛練である武道として発展をみた。武士の家であれば嫁入りの際には薙刀を必ず持参したという。大正から戦後にかけて、主に女性のたしなむ武道となり、「なぎなた」として現代も競技が盛んである。

as an official Olympic event since 1964 for men and 1992 for women. Along with this, judo has become increasingly widespread in many countries. In fact, there are some countries, such as France, that now have a larger judo population than Japan.

d) Kendo, Kyudo, Naginata, and Karatedo

Kendo, *kyudo*, and *karatedo* are traditional Japanese martial arts, but today they are popularly practiced as sports. In recent times these sports have found many ardent followers overseas as well.

In kendo, a competitor uses a sword to protect him or herself while trying to defeat an opponent. Originating around the seventh or eighth century, kendo became widely popular in the sixteenth century, when many different styles were created. In the seventeenth century kendo began to focus on the spiritual aspects of training as well as the technical, and with influences from Buddhism, Confucianism, and (in particular) *Zen*, it became a type of moral training. Initially, a wooden sword was commonly used, but the bamboo sword and *bogu* (protective gear), which includes the *men* (mask), *do* (breastplate), *kote* (gloves), and *tare* (groin protector), were introduced in the eighteenth century.

The basic techniques are the men (face) strike, kote (hand) strike, do (torso) strike, and *tsuki* thrust (frontal thrust to the neck), which are used in combination with various consecutive attack, counter attack, and guard stance techniques. A match is usually the best of three points, and at least two of the three judges must agree for a point to be awarded for a strike or thrust.

Kyudo was developed for use in hunting and fighting, but with the arrival of rifles (in 1543) the bow went the way of the *naginata* halberd, with both losing their effectiveness as weapons. Thereafter, Japanese archery began to take in the concepts of Zen and Confucianism, and developed as a martial art whose main focus was mental and physical discipline. Competitions involve getting as close as possible to the center of the target, but judges also award points for form, grace, and attitude, which sets it apart from the sport of archery as practiced in Europe.

The naginata is a weapon consisting of a long pole made of hardwood with a curved blade attached to one end. Starting in the Edo period, "naginata" also came to mean a martial art centered on training in the use of the weapon and aimed mainly at developing the mental discipline of the women of samurai families. It is said that a naginata was always included in the dowry of a samurai wedding. During the period from the Taisho era until just after the war, naginata became the preferred martial

空手道は、手の突きや足のけりを主体に、体の各部位を有効に使って身を防ぎ、相手を制する技をきわめるものである。7世紀ごろ中国に発生し、14世紀に沖縄に伝えられた。試合には、型と組手の2種類がある。型の試合は、基本動作と移動転身による正しい姿勢、正確な突き・けり、気合の充実、動作の緩急などにより勝負を決する。組手試合は、気合の充実した正確な突き・けり・間合い・残心などを重要な要素として、相手を倒しえたと判定される技をもって優劣を決める。

e）野球

　日本はアメリカに次いで野球が普及している。アマチュア野球は、むしろ本家のアメリカをしのぐ隆盛を示している。

　日本に野球が伝えられたのは1873年である。1934年にプロ野球ができるまでは、学生野球を中心として発展普及した。現在も、東京6大学（早稲田・慶応・明治・法政・立教・東大）のリーグ戦や、春夏の全国高等学校野球大会が多くのファンを湧かせている。2018年夏の高等学校野球大会には、3,781校が参加した。

　プロ野球は第二次世界大戦後非常に人気を高め、今日に至っている。現在のプロ野球は、セントラルリーグとパシフィックリーグの2リーグ制で、各6球団計12球団がある。シーズン末には、両リーグの優勝チーム同士で日本シリーズが行われる。2018年の観客動員数はセ・パ両リーグ合計で年間2,555万人であった。

　日本の代表的プロ野球選手であった王貞治は、1977年にホームラン756本の世界記録を達成し、1980年に引退するまで、通算868本のホームラン記録を樹立した。

　1995年、野茂英雄投手が先鞭をつけて以来、多くの日本人選手がアメリカ大リーグで活躍するようになった。イチロー（鈴木一朗）はアメリカの年間安打最多記録を84年ぶりに更新して262本（2004年）とし、日米通算で4,000本安打（2013年）を達成した。2018年時点で、各

art for women, and even today naginata competitions are thriving.

Karatedo involves mastering techniques for effectively using the body to protect oneself and subdue one's opponent, and consists mostly of hand strikes and kicks. It originated in the seventh century in China, and was brought to Okinawa in the fourteenth century. Karatedo competitions include two disciplines: forms and sparring. In forms competition, participants compete to demonstrate correctness of posture while performing basic techniques and movements. They are judged on their punches, kicks, and show of determination, as well as on the speed with which they perform the techniques. In sparring competition, participants are judged on the execution and correctness of their punches and kicks, on their distance and readiness, and on whether or not their technique would have effectively defeated the opponent.

e) Baseball

The United States (U.S.) is the only country other than Japan where baseball is more popular among people. Amateur baseball may be even more popular here than in the U.S., which is home for baseball.

Baseball was introduced into Japan in 1873. Its development centered mainly on baseball played at schools and universities until the advent in 1934 of Japanese professional baseball. Today, the league competition of Tokyo's "Big Six" universities (Waseda, Keio, Meiji, Hosei, Rikkyo, and Tokyo) and the spring and summer all-Japan high school baseball tournament are followed avidly by many fans; in 2018, 3,781 schools participated in the high school baseball meets.

Professional baseball became extremely popular just after the Second World War, and this popularity has continued up to the present day. There are two leagues, the Central League and the Pacific League, each league consisting of six teams, giving a total for the two leagues of twelve teams. At the end of the season the two league winners compete in the Japan Series. In 2018 the two leagues drew a grand total of 25.55 million audience to the game.

In 1977 Oh Sadaharu, then the most famous professional in Japanese baseball, hit the 756th home-run of his career, for a new world record. At the time of his retirement in 1980, he had improved his home-run record to 868.

In 1995, pitcher Nomo Hideo became the first Japanese player in U.S. major league baseball in many years. He has since been followed by many others. These include (Suzuki) Ichiro, who in 2004 broke the 84-year-old major league record for hits in one season (with 262 hits) and in 2013 reached a Japan-US career total of 4,000 hits. Other

チームの主力選手として活躍しているダルビッシュ有、田中将大、平野佳寿、前田健太や、投打の二刀流で活躍し話題となっている大谷翔平などがいる。

f) サッカー

　サッカーは野球と並んで人気のあるスポーツであり、子供から成人まで多くの人々に親しまれている。小学生・中学生・高校生・大学生・社会人など各層レベルの全国大会がある。

　1993年、プロの競技団体としての「日本プロサッカーリーグ」（Jリーグ）が設立された。2018年一部リーグ（J1）は18チーム、二部リーグ（J2）は22チームあり、世界のトップレベルへの仲間入りを目ざしている。J1の2018年の年間観客動員数は583万人であった。ワールドカップには1998年から2018年で6回出場し、2002年、2010年と2018年に最高成績となるベスト16に入った。

　最近ではイングランド・プレミアリーグに所属する吉田麻也やドイツ・ブンデスリーガの長谷部誠、大迫勇也、スペイン・リーガエスパニョーラの乾貴士ほか、長友佑都、香川真司など海外リーグで多数の選手が活躍している。

g) マラソン・駅伝マラソン

　一般市民が参加するマラソン大会は、全国各地でそれぞれ定期的に開催されている。42.195キロメートルのフルマラソンから、ハーフマラソン、10キロマラソンが一般的であるが、5キロ、3キロなどのマラソン大会もある。1920年から始まり、毎年1月の1日と2日にわたって、東京大手町と箱根芦ノ湖畔との往復コース（片道110キロ程度）で行われる大学対抗の「箱根駅伝」は、テレビの実況放送が行われ、正月の風物詩として多くの国民を沸かせている。また、2007年から毎年2月もしくは3月に行われる東京マラソンは、一般市民からオリンピックの候補選手まで3万人もの参加者がある。2019年は3月3日（日）に東京都庁を出発し、都内の観光名所を経由して東京駅前行幸通りにゴールするコースで行われた。一般市民の出場者は30万人以上の応募者の中から抽選で選ばれる。

Japanese currently active as leading players on Major League teams include Darvish Yu, Tanaka Masahiro, Hirano Yoshihisa, Maeda Kenta, and Otani Shohei, who is a pitcher as well as a batter.

f) Soccer

Soccer is as popular as baseball and is enjoyed by large number of both children and adults. National soccer tournaments are held at the elementary school, junior high school, high school, university, and company levels.

The Japan Professional Football League (J. League) was established as a professional sports association in 1993. In 2018, Division 1 (J1) had 18 teams and Division 2 (J2) had 22 teams all aiming to place themselves among the world's best. In 2018 J1 teams had an audience of 5.83 million. The Japan team has participated in FIFA World Cup Games six times between 1998 and 2018.

Many Japanese soccer players have recently become active in oversea leagues. Among the best known are English Premier League players Yoshida Maya, German Bundesliga players Hasebe Makoto and Osako Yuya, Spanish La Liga player Inui Takashi, and other players active in overseas leagues include Nagatomo Yuto and Kagawa Shinji.

g) Marathons and Road Relay Races

Marathon tournaments which anyone can enter are held regularly throughout the country. In addition to full marathons of 42.195 kilometers, these include half marathons. There are also many 10 kilometer, 5 kilometer, and 3 kilometer races, and road relay races. In 1920 the first "Hakone Ekiden (road relay race)" was held as a college competition on a round-trip course between Otemachi in Tokyo and Hakone Ashinoko lake (about 110 kilometers each way), and it is now held every January. It is televised live and is a featured event of the new year, with an enthusiastic following. Since 2007, the Tokyo Marathon has been held every February or March. It has 30,000 participants, ranging from members of the general public to potential Olympic competitors. In 2019, the race took place on Sunday March 3, starting off from the Tokyo Metropolitan Government Building. The course included tourist attractions along the route to Tokyo Station and Gyoko-dori Avenue. Ordinary participants were selected by lottery from more than 300,000 applicants.

(8) オリンピック

a) 概説

　　オリンピックは4年に一度開催される世界的なスポーツの祭典で、スポーツを通した人間育成と世界平和を究極の目的とし、夏季大会と冬季大会を行っている。オリンピックの歴史は、今から約2800年前にさかのぼる。古代ギリシャのオリンピア地方で行われていた神々をあがめる体育や芸術を競う「オリンピア祭典競技」といわれている。しかしその後、数々の戦乱に巻き込まれた古代オリンピックは、393年を最後に幕を閉じていた。1894年、パリ国際会議においてフランスの教育者であったピエール・ド・クーベルタン男爵の提唱した「オリンピック復興」は満場一致で可決され、2年後の1896年、ギリシャのアテネで記念すべき第1回オリンピック競技大会が開催された。大会のシンボルとしてなじみ深い五輪のマークも彼が考案したもので、世界五大陸の団結を表している。またオリンピックの精神は「スポーツを通して心身を向上させ、文化・国籍などさまざまな違いを乗り越え、友情・連帯感・フェアプレーの精神をもって、平和でよりよい世界の実現に貢献すること」であり、この精神は今も変わらず受け継がれている。

　　日本は、1912年の第5回ストックホルム大会に初参加して以来2016年の第31回リオネジャネイロ大会まで、また冬季オリンピックも1928年の第2回サンモリッツ大会から2018年の第23回平昌大会まで、ほとんど毎回参加している。

b) 2020年夏季オリンピック・パラリンピック競技東京大会（概要）

　　2013年9月ブエノスアイレスで行われた第125回IOC総会で、イスタンブール、マドリードを抑えて2020年夏季オリンピック・パラリンピック競技大会の開催都市に東京が選出された。1964年10月に行われた第18回夏季オリンピック競技東京大会から56年振りの開催となる。東京オリンピック1964年大会は、第二次世界大戦後の日本を大きく変え、日本の戦後復興を世界に強く印象づける契機になるとともに、その後の高度経済成長の弾みとなる大会となった。東京オリンピック・パラリンピック2020年大会は、成熟国家となった日本が、今度は世界にポジティ

(8) The Olympics

a) Outline

The Olympic Games is an international sports event held once every four years, with the ultimate goal being the achievement of human development and world peace through sports, and features summer and winter sports competitions. The Olympic Games were first started some 2800 years ago as an athletic and artistic festival held in the Olympia region of ancient Greece to honor the gods. After a number of wars and conflicts, the last of the ancient Olympic Games was held in 393. In 1894, a resolution to revive the Olympic games advocated by the French educator Baron Pierre de Coubertin was passed unanimously at the Paris Congress. Two years later, in 1896, the first modern Olympic Games was held at Athens, in Greece. The familiar Olympic symbol of five rings was Coubertin's idea, representing the unity of the five continents of the world. The Olympic spirit was "to improve mind and body through sports, to overcome various differences of culture and nationality, to contribute to the realization of a better world of peace with a spirit of friendship, solidarity and fair play." That same spirit is still carried forward today.

Japan first participated in the 1912 Stockholm Olympic Games, the 5th Olympiad, and has been represented in almost all Olympics since, up to the 31st held in Rio de Janeiro in 2016. Similarly, since Japan first participated in the second Olympic Winter Games, held in San Moritz in 1928, it has participated in nearly all, up to the 23rd Winter Olympics held in Pyeongchang in 2018.

b) Overview of the Tokyo 2020 Summer Olympics and Paralympics

At the 125th IOC session in Buenos Aires in September 2013, Tokyo was selected as the host city of the 2020 Summer Olympic and Paralympic Games, holding off Istanbul and Madrid. It will be 56 years since the 18th Summer Olympic Games were held in Tokyo in October 1964. The Tokyo Olympics marked a great change in post-World War II Japan and became an opportunity for Japan's postwar reconstruction to make a strong impression on the world and for the economy to rebound and grow at a high rate. The aim of the Tokyo 2020 Olympics and Paralympics is to promote positive international changes, and for Japan, as a mature state, to pass on this legacy for the future. In 2020, there will

ブな変革を促し、それらをレガシーとして未来へ継承していくことを目標としている。1964年東京大会に比べ2020年東京大会は、参加国・地域数は93から207（予定）、参加人数は5,133人から12,000人以上（予定）、競技種目数は20競技163種目から33競技339種目と2倍以上の規模に拡大すると予想されている。また、1964年のパラリンピック競技では21カ国375名のアスリートが9競技143種目に於いて競い合ったが、2020年大会は22競技537種目と競技種目数が約4倍に大幅増加するため、参加者も比例して大幅増加するものと予想されている。

c）2020年夏季オリンピック・パラリンピック競技東京大会（全体像と課題）

　この大会の理念は、「すべての人が自己ベストを目指し（全員が自己ベスト）」、「一人ひとりが互いを認め合い（多様性と調和）」、「そして、未来につなげよう（未来への継承）」を3つの基本コンセプトとし、史上最もイノベーティブで、世界にポジティブな改革をもたらそうというものである。

　大会招致時のコンセプトとして「都市の中心で開催するコンパクトな大会」を掲げ、東京都心で開催することによるダイナミックな祭典、かつ選手村を会場配置計画の中心に設置して約9割の競技会場が8km圏内に配置されるなど、移動時間の短縮が可能なコンパクトな配置計画となっている。メインスタジアムは、1964年東京オリンピックでメインスタジアムとなった国立霞ヶ丘陸上競技場を建て直して建設される新国立競技場（オリンピックスタジアム）となる。その他、主に内陸部の「ヘリテッジゾーン」と臨海部の「東京ベイゾーン」に分けられる各会場群にて競技が行われる予定である。

　また、半径8km圏外ゾーンでは馬術会場として「馬事公苑」（世田谷区）が使用される。東京23区外に配置される競技場は、サッカーの会場として札幌ドーム（北海道札幌市）、宮城スタジアム（宮城県宮城郡利府町）、カシマスタジアム（茨城県鹿嶋市）、埼玉スタジアム2002（埼玉県さいたま市）、東京スタジアム（東京都調布市）、横浜国際総合競技場（神奈川県横浜市）が使用される。ゴルフの会場として霞ヶ関カンツリー倶楽部（埼玉県川越市）、近代五種の会場として武蔵野の森総合スポーツプラザ（東京都調布市）、セーリングの会場として江の島ヨットハーバー（神奈川県藤沢市）、射撃の会場として陸上自衛隊朝霞駐屯

be over twelve thousand competitors from an estimated 207 countries (and regions) participating, compared to the 5,133 competitors from 93 countries in 1964, and the 339 events in 33 sports will be more than twice the 163 events in 20 sports in 1964. In the 1964 Paralympics, 375 athletes from 21 countries competed in 143 events in nine sports, which in 2020 will undergo a fourfold increase to 537 events in 22 sports, with a proportionally major increase in the number of participants also expected.

c) Overall Theme and the Issues Facing the Tokyo 2020 Summer Games

The philosophy of the Tokyo 2020 Games, as the most innovative in history, is expressed as bringing positive reform to the world by building on the three core concepts of "striving for your personal best (achieving personal best)," "accepting one another (unity in diversity)," and "passing the torch forward (connecting to tomorrow)."

A concept behind the invitation bid was that it would be a compact Games held in the heart of the city, a dynamic Olympics in the center of Tokyo, with nine-tenths of the competition venues located within 8 km of the Olympic Village, reducing travelling time. The National Stadium at Kasumigaoka, which was the main venue at the 1964 Olympics, is being redeveloped into a new National Olympic Stadium that will be the main venue for the 2020 Games. Most of the sports venues will be located in the inland "Heritage Zone" or the coastal "Tokyo Bay Zone."

Located outside the 8 km radius zone is Equestrian Park (Baji Kouen, Setagaya), the equestrian event venue. Outside the 23 wards of Tokyo, the soccer venues are Sapporo Dome (Sapporo, Hokkaido), Miyagi Stadium (Rifu, Miyagi), Kashima Soccer Stadium (Kashima, Ibaraki), Saitama Stadium 2002 (Saitama, Saitama), Tokyo Stadium (Chofu, Tokyo), and International Stadium Yokohama (Yokohama, Kanagawa). The golf venue is Kasumigaseki Country Club (Kawagoe, Saitama), and Musashino Forest Sports Plaza (Chofu) is the venue for the modern pentathlon. Enoshima Yacht Harbour (Fujisawa, Kanagawa) is the sailing venue, and the shooting venue is the Asaka Shooting Range (Asaka, Saitama).

地（埼玉県朝霞市）などが使用される予定となっている。

開催時期が8月と真夏の開催のため、マラソン・屋外スポーツなどへの暑さ対策も検討されている。2016年には国土交通省がマラソン・競歩・自転車のコースを新たな特殊技術で舗装することで、路面温度を4.8℃下げるなどの技術開発に成功している。また移動式の樹木を利用した日蔭づくり、道路への散水やミストを吹きかけ、体温の上昇を抑制し、選手・観客への給水補給および試合時間の早朝・夜間への移動など対策に取り組んでいる。

本大会では、5つの競技が追加種目として決定した。野球・ソフトボールが復活し、新たに空手、スケートボード、スポーツクライミング、サーフィンの4競技16種目が初めて採用される。

なお、大会費用については、2018年には2.16兆円と試算されているが、大幅な増加が予想されている。

外国人観光客のさらなる増加に対応し、1964年東京オリンピックにて発案されたピクトグラム（案内用図記号）について、日本人だけでなく外国人観光客にもより分かりやすくするため、駐車場、手荷物受取所、救護所、乳幼児用設備（ベビーケアルーム）、乗り継ぎ（飛行機）、案内所・情報コーナー、温泉のピクトグラムの変更および追加を決めている。

(9) 宗教

a) 概説

日本でのおもな宗教には、神道・仏教・キリスト教がある。統計によると、特定の宗教を熱心に信仰しているとする日本人は少なく、宗教には無関心とみずからいう者が多い。

元来多神教的であった日本古来の神道の影響から、どの宗教に対しても伝統的に寛容であった。多くの日本人は誕生や結婚の儀式は神道やキリスト教により、葬式は仏教により行う。同じ人間が神社に初詣でもするし、お盆の寺参りもするし、クリスマスも祝う。

各宗教が自宗の信徒数として発表している数は、神道系8,953万人・仏教系8,872万人・キリスト教系193万人・

As events will take place at the height of summer in August, measures against the heat are being considered for the marathon and other outdoor events. In 2016, the Ministry of Land, Infrastructure and Transport succeeded in developing paving technology that can lower road surface temperature by 4.8°C, which will be used to coat the marathon, race walking, and bicycle courses. Trees will be made transportable to provide strategic shade, and mist sprayers will be mobilized to cool people down. Spectators as well as competitors will be provided with water, and events will be started earlier in the morning and later in the evening.

Five sports have been added, including baseball and softball, which are being reinstated. There will be 16 events in the four new sports of karate, skateboarding, sport climbing, and surfing.

In 2018 it was estimated that the cost of the Games would be 2.16 trillion yen, a figure that is expected to increase significantly.

In response to the expected further increase in the number of foreign tourists, pictograms (guide symbols) devised at the time of the Tokyo Olympics in 1964 will be made easier to understand by Japanese as well as by foreigners. There will be new or amended pictograms to indicate parking lots, baggage handling services, first aid stations, infant care facilities, airline connecting flights, information desks, and hot springs.

(9) Religion

a) Overview

The major religions in Japan are Shinto, Buddhism, and Christianity. Statistics show that few Japanese are deeply devoted to a specific religion and that, in fact, many profess to have no interest in religion at all.

Shintoism, the religion of Japan from time untold, is polytheistic, and because of this the Japanese people have traditionally been tolerant of all religious sects. The birth and marriage ceremonies of most Japanese are Shinto or Christian, while funerals are conducted according to Buddhist rites. The same person will pay his respects to a Shinto shrine at the beginning of the year, visit a Buddhist temple during the Festival of the Souls in summer, and celebrate Christmas at the end of the year.

The number of followers claimed by different religions are: Shinto, 89.53 million; Buddhism, 88.72 million; and Christianity, 1.93 million,

諸派872万人（2015年、文化庁）である。宗教人口を合計すると、日本の人口をはるかにオーバーするという事実は、外国には例がない。

日本では憲法で宗教の自由が保障され、厳格に実行されている。したがって国教というものはなく、国の行事も宗教とは一切無関係である。国公立の学校では、宗教教育が禁じられている。

b）神道

神道は日本固有の自然宗教であり、神道の神を祭るところが神社である。田舎の町や村の中心には、鎮守の神がまつられている。神道でいう神は無数にあり、初めは自然物や自然現象を神としていた。そしてしだいに先祖をも祭るようになった。したがって神道には特定の教祖はなく教典もない。

日本神話では「八百万（やおよろず）の神」という言葉があるように、神々の数は極めて多かった。のち神道は仏教・儒教の影響を受け理論化もされてきた。19世紀以後は国教のような扱いを受け、天皇が神格化された。第二次世界大戦後は国家との関係を断ち切り、各地の神社ごとの信仰となっている。

伊勢神宮は全国の神社の中心的な地位を占めており、2013年には20年に一度の神社の正殿を新たに建て替える式年遷宮が行われた。

日本人は誕生のときお宮参りをし、結婚式を神前で行う。さらに神社に入学試験合格を願ったり、自動車を運転する人が交通安全のお札を受けたりする。家や事務所の中に神棚を祭ることが多い。正月には神社に一家そろってお参りし、また神社ごとに定めているお祭りには、その地域の住民が多く集まり、出店なども繁盛する。

このように神社との縁は深いが、大部分の国民は神道の教義に無関心であり、現代日本人に対する思想的影響は少ない。

with others at a combined 8.72 million (2015, Agency for Cultural Affairs). The sum of these figures are roughly twice Japan's population, a condition which can't be observed in other countries.

The Japanese constitution guarantees religious freedom, and this guarantee is strictly maintained. Therefore, there is no state religion, and no connection between national and religious functions. Religious instruction is forbidden at public schools.

b) Shinto

Shinto is the natural indigenous religion of Japan. Shinto gods, or *kami*, are worshipped at shrines (*jinja*). Country towns and villages worship guardian gods. All natural objects and phenomena used to be considered as having kami, so the gods of Shinto were uncountably numerous. Gradually, Shinto practice extended to the worship of ancestors. Thus, there are no specific leaders in Shinto religion, nor any books of scripture.

To understand how large in number Shinto gods were, there is an expression *yaoyorozu no kami*, meaning "eight million gods" in Japanese mythology. Later, influenced by Buddhism and Confucianism, Shinto became ideologized. From the nineteenth century it came to be regarded as the national religion of Japan, and the Emperor became deified. However, after World War II the practice of religion was separated from the functions of state, and worship became limited to the shrines in each locality.

Ise Shrine holds a prestigious position among the nation's shrines, and 2013 was an especially important year for the shrine as it was the occasion of the Shikinen Sengu, an ancient tradition dictating that the main sanctuary must be rebuilt once every twenty years.

People go to shrines when a child is born, and marriage ceremonies are also conducted according to Shinto rites. Further, people offer prayers at shrines for success in passing university entrance examinations and motorists visit shrines to receive charms they hope will keep them from automobile accidents. Small Shinto altars are found in many homes and offices. Families go to shrines at the beginning of the new year. Each shrine has its own festival, attended by the people in the area and served by numerous stalls selling a variety of things.

Thus, the people have a deep relationship with shrines, but the majority of Japanese have no interest in the tenets of Shinto, and the influence of the religion on the thought of the Japanese of today is small.

c）仏教

　仏教は紀元前5世紀にインドで起こり、1世紀に中国に伝わり、のち朝鮮半島を経由して6世紀に日本に伝わった。奈良時代・平安時代を通して、仏教は日本国家の政治的統一と日本文化の発達に大きな役割を果たした。9世紀はじめに遣唐使として唐で学んだ最澄（伝教大師）が帰国後開いた天台宗とその本山・比叡山延暦寺は次の鎌倉仏教に多大の影響を与え、現在も多くの信徒を集めている。同じく9世紀に唐に渡り密教を学んだ空海（弘法大師）は帰国して真言宗と本山・高野山金剛峯寺を開き、平安貴族社会に生活実践の宗教として浸透した。また、空海の修行の遺跡である四国88箇所の霊場を巡る「遍路」の信仰習慣は今も人々により継承されている。

　その後、鎌倉時代には鎌倉仏教と総称される日本独自の諸宗派が生まれた。それらは平安時代までの貴族対象の鎮護国家思想から独立し、戦乱期の厭世観と末法思想を背景に大衆の魂の救済をめざすものであった。

　「南無阿弥陀仏」の念仏を唱える法然の浄土宗と親鸞の浄土真宗、「南無妙法蓮華経」の題目を唱える日蓮の法華宗（日蓮宗）などは、庶民の間でも非常に盛んになり、同時にこれらは現在まで引き続いて日本人の宗教の中心になっている。一方、栄西の臨済宗や道元の曹洞宗などの禅宗は武士階級に普及した。

　「仏教はみずから真理に目覚めることによってえられる悟り」を究極の境地とする。また「あらゆるものが無常であるにもかかわらず恒常のものと考え、すべてのものは実体を持たないにもかかわらず実体あるものと考える執着を絶つことを眼目とする」。
　仏教では神がなく、無限の愛をもって憎しみや怨みを捨てることを強調する。一般に狂信を排して寛容であり、同時に平等を貫こうとする。
　日本人の生活では仏教とのつながりが非常に強く、信徒でなくともお寺に参詣し、葬式を仏教式で行い、死後は仏

c) Buddhism

Buddhism originated in the fifth century BC in India, and was transmitted to China in the first century, and then to Japan in the sixth century via the Korean Peninsula. During the Nara and Heian periods, Buddhism played a pivotal role in the political unification of the Japanese nation and the development of Japanese culture. At the beginning of the ninth century, Saicho (Dengyo Daishi) studied at the Tang court in China as an envoy. Upon his return to Japan, he founded the Tendai sect of Buddhism with the Hieizan Enryakuji as its head temple. This was a major influence on Kamakura Buddhism and even today the sect still has many adherents. Kukai (Kobo Daishi) also went to China as an envoy in the ninth century and studied esoteric Buddhism. Upon his return to Japan, he founded the Shingon sect of Buddhism, with Koyasan Kongobuji as its head temple. This type of Buddhism became popular as a practical religion among the Heian aristocrats. Even today, people still undertake the pilgrimage to the 88 sacred sites (temples) in Shikoku which Kukai is said to have visited.

During the following Kamakura period, Kamakura Buddhism (as it came to be known) emerged as a unique Japanese form of Buddhism. This school of Buddhism broke away from the ideology of the protection of the state (*chingo kokka*), which favored the aristocracy, and sought to succor the souls of the common people, who had become pessimistic due to prolonged war and the *mappo* doctrine.

Honen's Pure Land sect as well as Shinran's True Pure Land sect, whose adherents chant a prayer "*Namu amidabutsu*" to Amitabha, and Nichiren's Nichiren sect, whose adherents chant the Nichiren prayer of "*Namu myoho rengekyo*," were very popular, even among the general population. Even today they continue to constitute the principal Buddhist sects among the Japanese people. In contrast, Zen sects such as Eisai's Rinzai sect and Dogen's Soto sect spread among the samurai elite.

Buddhism holds that the ultimate state is one of self-enlightenment attained by awakening to the truth. It is an objective, too, to rid oneself of the tenacious idea that everything is everlasting, although all is transitory, that everything has substance, although all is insubstantial.

There is no God in Buddhism; the emphasis is on ridding oneself of hate and jealousy through infinite love. Fanaticism is rejected; one should be tolerant and strive for equality.

Buddhism is a major presence in the life of the Japanese people. Even if they are non-believers they go to temples, are buried according to

教上の名前（戒名）をつけ、ほとんどの家庭が、自分の家に仏壇を設け、供物を置き、線香をたき、先祖の冥福を祈っている。仏教は、日本の美術・文学・建築あるいは日本人の思想・道徳など、文化全般にわたり非常に強く影響を与えている。

d) 禅

禅宗は仏教の一つである。禅とは、悟りを求め、心を静めることによって得られる高次の宗教的・内面的体験である。心を静めるために座って静かに思いをこらすことが坐禅である。

禅宗は 12〜13 世紀に、中国から帰国した日本人僧侶（栄西・道元）によって伝えられた。

禅宗では、真理は我々の言語・文字による表現を超えているとされ、坐禅修道によって直接に自証体得することによってのみ把握されるものだとする。禅宗は武士道や茶道・いけばな、などのバックボーンになり、日本の思想や文化・生活全般に影響を与えた。

現在の日本では、禅宗の僧侶以外で、みずから坐禅をして真理を追求している人は少ないが、精神修養の方法として、短期間、禅寺に坐禅をしにいくことは一部に行われている。

e) キリスト教

日本に最初にキリスト教が伝えられたのは、1549 年にカトリック教会のイエズス会士フランシスコ・ザビエルが鹿児島に渡来したときである。

はじめは、支配層のなかには西洋の文物に対する関心もあって、イエズス会のカトリック布教に好意的な者もあった。17 世紀初めの最盛期には、信徒が約 75 万人いたとされる。のち、封建秩序に有害であると考えられ、しだいに抑圧禁止されるようになった。信者は迫害を受け、1613 年には外国人宣教師は国外に追放された。カトリック禁止後も、秘密に信仰を持ち続ける人々も少なくなかった。これらの人々は「隠れキリシタン」と呼ばれた（世界遺産では「潜伏キリシタン」として登録）。

19 世紀後半、日本が欧米と国交を開いてから、再びキ

Buddhist rites and, after death, are given posthumous Buddhist names. Most families have a Buddhist altar in their homes, where they place offerings, burn incense and pray for the repose of their ancestors. Buddhism has exerted a tremendous influence on every aspect of Japanese culture, including art, literature and architecture, and on the morals and way of thought of the people.

d) Zen Buddhism

The Zen sect is one of the denominations of Buddhism. "Zen" is defined as an enlightened religious and mental state attained by striving to achieve spiritual awakening and serenity of mind. One of the practices used to obtain this serenity of mind is called *zazen* or "sitting in silent meditation."

Eisai, Dogen, and other Japanese priests introduced the Zen sect to Japan in the twelfth and thirteenth centuries after studying in China.

According to the Zen sect, truth is something which transcends the expressions of language and letters. It can only be grasped through the direct proof of experience obtained in the practice of zazen. The Zen sect has become the backbone of the samurai spirit, tea cult, and *ikebana* or Japanese flower arrangement. It has exerted great influence on Japanese thought, culture, and literally all aspects of Japanese life.

In Japan today there are few people, besides the Zen priests, who pursue truth by practicing zazen. However, as a method of spiritual training, some people pay visits to Zen temples for short sessions of zazen.

e) Christianity

Christianity first reached Japan in 1549 with the arrival of Francis Xavier, a Catholic missionary belonging to the Society of Jesus, to Kagoshima.

At first, there were some members of the ruling class in Japan who were interested in Western culture and institutions and therefore acted friendly towards the propagation of the Catholic religion by the Jesuits. At its peak, in the early seventeenth century, it is estimated that there were about 750 thousand Christians in Japan. Later, though, it came to be considered a danger to the feudal order and was eventually repressed and banned. Christians were persecuted, and in 1613 foreign missionaries banished from the country. Even after Christianity was prohibited, quite a few believers carried on practicing their faith, secretly. Such believers were referred to as "Hidden Christians."

After Japan established diplomatic relations with Europe and America

リスト教布教が盛んになった。1859年以降、プロテスタント宣教師がアメリカから派遣され、またカトリック、ロシア正教も布教活動を行った。これらの外国人宣教師は、日本で社会事業や教育事業にも従事し、日本におけるヨーロッパ・アメリカの文化導入に貢献した。

日本における近代文化とは、ほとんど欧米文化を意味したが、欧米文化の中心をなすキリスト教的思考・生活方式の一部、道徳なども日本に取り入れられた。現在の一夫一婦制などもその一例とされている。

現在日本のキリスト教信者は、プロテスタントなどの新教51万人、カトリック45万人といわれている（2015年文化庁）。各派がつくった大学もある。また、宗派を超越した国際基督教大学も設立されている。

(10) 風俗・習慣・娯楽

a) 着物（和服）

現在日本人は、日常ほとんど洋服を着て生活しているが、和服は正装として、あるいは室内着として現在でも愛好されている。

今では、この着物は日本の独自の様式と考えられているが、その起源は平安時代の十二単の下着に発している。飛鳥・奈良時代には当時の唐風の服装をそのまま受け入れていたが、平安時代の国風文化の流れの中で十二単が貴族社会の女性の間に定着した。十二単は色彩の衣装といわれるように、色の組合せに四季折々の季節感を表わすという当時の貴族の繊細優美な美意識がうかがえる。十二単は日本人の感性と創意が造り出した日中融合文化の典型であり、平安王朝文化の華でもある。鎌倉時代になると、十二単の外側の衣と袴を脱ぎ、下着である小袖を表着として着るようになった。その後、江戸時代に絹・木綿の素材が一般に普及し、華やかな元禄時代を通じて現在の着物が完成した。

現代の女性の着る着物は、一番豪華なものは、花嫁が着る打掛けである。これは絹の布地に金銀の箔を織り込んだ

in the latter half of the nineteenth century, propagation of Christian faith again began to flourish. From 1859, Protestant missionaries from America started to arrive, and the Catholic and Russian Orthodox churches also became actively involved in missionary work. These foreign missionaries also engaged in social and educational activities, contributing to the introduction of American and European culture into Japan.

The term "modern culture" in Japan was mostly referred as Western culture. Christian moral, modes of life and thoughts which centers in Western culture were also introduced. The present monogamous system of marriage is considered an example of such influences.

At present there are in Japan about 510 thousand Protestants and 450 thousand Catholics (2015, Agency for Cultural Affairs). There are universities that have been established by each of the various church denominations. There is also a university, International Christian University, which is ecumenical.

(10) Customs, Manners and Pastimes

a) Kimono (Japanese Dress)

For the most part, Japanese people today wear Western clothing in their everyday life, but the traditional *kimono* is still popular both as formal attire and as clothing for the home.

Today the kimono is known as a form of dress unique to Japan, and it has its origins as the undergarments of the *junihitoe* (ceremonial attire of Japanese court ladies) in the Heian period. During the Asuka and Nara periods, the Tang dynasty clothing of the time was adopted without modification, but with the rise of Japanese culture during the Heian period, the junihitoe became a popular mode of dress among the ladies of aristocratic society. The junihitoe were termed "color clothes" because the aristocrats of the day matched the color of the junihitoe with the season, thereby demonstrating their delicate sense of aesthetics. The junihitoe is a typical fusion of Japanese and Chinese culture that shows Japanese sensibility and ingenuity, and it was also the flower of Heian dynasty culture. In the Kamakura period, they removed the outer *hakama* skirt of the junihitoe and wore the short-sleeved inner kimono as the outer layer. Then, during the Edo period, silk and cotton material became generally available, and during the flamboyant Genroku era, the kimono developed into its current form.

The kimonos worn by Japanese women today are well known abroad for their beauty. By far the most gorgeous is the *uchikake*, a long

金糸・銀糸で刺繡を施し、多くは花鳥の図案模様を描いたものが用いられる。このほか、未婚の女性と既婚の女性では着物の模様・色合いや袖丈の長さなどが異なり、正式訪問用、遊楽用など外出の目的によっても、布地・模様・色合い・仕立て方などが異なる。着物の染めの代表的なものには4種類あり、友禅、江戸小紋・辻が花、絞り・草木染め、更紗である。

一般の女性が着物を着るのは、正月・成人式・大学卒業式・結婚式・同披露宴・葬儀・祝賀会などである。男性の場合の正式な和服姿は羽織袴（はおりはかま）で、主に正月・成人式・結婚式などである。

最も軽便な室内着として、木綿地の浴衣（ゆかた）がある。これはとくに夏期には、入浴後に着て室内の風通しのよいところで涼をとり、くつろぐのには、最適の着物である。京都では、訪れた外国人観光客が、浴衣を着て街を歩くのが流行っており、浴衣や着物を貸す商売が繁盛している。

b）主な年中行事

○元日（1月1日）：新年の門出を祝う日である。元日から1月3日までの3日間を、「お正月」または「三が日」といって完全に仕事を休む。「正月」とは本来「1月」のことであるが、慣習的にこの3日間を指すようになっている。神社やお寺に参詣して、おみくじ（神仏に祈って吉凶を知るために引くくじ）を引き、破魔矢（昔、正月に悪魔を射ると言って男の子が持って遊んだ弓の矢）や種々のお守りを買う。神社や寺の境内には縁日（神社や寺で、供養や祭りが行われる日）に設置される屋台が並び、焼きそばや綿菓子（わたあめ、ともいう）などの駄菓子が売られ、金魚釣りなどを楽しむことができる。手相見（手筋で吉凶・運命などを占う人）も威厳のあるいでたちで、小ぢんまりと店を出していることもある。また、知人宅を訪問して新年のあいさつを交わし、酒を飲み酌み交わし、正月独特の料理（おせち料理）を食べたりして楽しむ。正月には、門には注連縄（しめなわ）を張り、松飾りをつけ、または門松をたてる。門松は、神が降臨するための樹木をたてるという意味がある。松

overgarment worn by the bride in a wedding ceremony. The silk fabric is embroidered with gold and silver threads, most commonly in patterns of flowers or birds. There are various types of kimonos. Those of married and unmarried women differ in design, color, sleeve length, and other aspects. Women also wear kimonos of different fabrics, designs, patterns, and cuts in accordance with the occasion, for example, whether for a formal visit or for pleasure. There are four typical kinds of kimono dyeing methods, <1> Yuzen, <2> Edo Komon, Tsujigahana, <3> Shibori, Kusakizome, and <4> Sarasa.

Japanese women ordinarily wear kimonos during the New Year holidays, or on such occasions as the coming-of-age ceremony, college graduation ceremonies, wedding ceremonies, receptions, funeral services, and celebrations. A formal kimono garb in the case of men is a haori and hakama, mainly for New Year's holidays, coming-of-age ceremony, and wedding ceremonies.

The cotton *yukata* is an informal kimono and is popular as a home garment especially for summer wear. It is an ideal kimono to wear while cooling off in a breezy part of the house after a bath in the summer. In Kyoto, where foreign visitors like to walk around wearing yukata, shops that rent out yukata and kimono are flourishing.

b) Main Annual Festivals

○ *Ganjitsu* (January 1): The day on which the birth of the New Year is celebrated. Offices and factories are commonly closed during the first three days of the new year, the period called *sanga nichi* or *shogatsu*. Shogatsu originally referred to the whole of January, but now is used just to refer to these three days. On these days, the people go to shrines or temples and draw an omikuji (a piece of paper on which your fortune is written, good or bad), and buy a hamaya (a sacred arrow played with by boys in the old days for shooting a devil) or an amulet. At shrines and temples, stalls are set up on ennichi (days when festivals and memorial services are held) to sell fried noodles (*yakisoba*), confectionaries such as cotton candy (*wata-ame*), and to let people fish for goldfish. There are also palm readers to tell your fortune, dressed up and sitting at a tiny stall. They also visit friends and relatives, drinking *sake*, and eating special new-year dishes, called *osechi*, are also commonly enjoyed. *Shimenawa*, sacred rice-straw ropes, are hung across the top of the gateway, which is also decorated with pine boughs or *kadomatsu* (gate pines). The kadomatsu symbolizes a tree provided for the descent of the gods.

飾りのある期間は元日から7日まで（昔は15日まで）で、この期間を「松の内」ともいう。

○節分（2月3日または4日）：太陰太陽暦の立春の前日をいい、節分の夜に各家庭では「鬼は外、福は内」と掛け声をかけながら家の内外に大豆をまき、鬼（災い）を追い払って戸口を閉ざす行事が行われる。成田山新勝寺（千葉県成田市）では、毎年大相撲力士や名士が参加しているが、掛け声は「福は内」だけで「鬼は外」とは言わない。これは本尊の不動明王の力が強力なので鬼を外に払う必要がないからだとされる。また奈良の元興寺では「福は内、鬼は内」と言うとのこと。

○ひなまつり（3月3日）：女の子の将来の幸福を願うお祭りである。昔の宮廷の風俗を模したきれいなひな人形を桃の花と一緒に飾る。もち米の粥に麹をまぜて醸造した白酒（甘酒）を飲んで楽しむ。

○花見（各地の桜の開花期）全国各地の桜の名所で、桜の開花期に人々が集まって花を見て遊び楽しむ。東京では北の丸公園、上野公園などには大勢の人が訪れる。京都では豊臣秀吉が、1598年（慶長3年）3月15日、京都醍醐寺の三宝院で催した「醍醐の花見」は豪華な花見の宴として歴史に残る。

○端午の節句（5月5日）：男の子が健やかに育つことを願うお祭である。武士の人形を飾り、邪気を払うための菖蒲を軒に差し、鯉のぼりをたて、柏餅を食べて楽しむ。

○七夕（7月7日）：中国伝来の風習と、わが国固有の信仰とが結合したものといわれている。天の川（銀河）の両岸にある牽牛星と織女星とが、年に一度出会うことを祝うお祭りである。庭前に供物（とうもろこし、なす、など）をし、歌や字を書いた5色の短冊を笹竹につけて

This pine decoration is left in place from January the first to the seventh (until the fifteenth in olden times), the period referred to as *matsu no uchi*.

- *Setsubun* (February 3 or 4): The day before the beginning of spring according to the lunisolar calendar. On the evening of this day, people open the doors of their houses and drive the demons (i.e., bad luck) out of their homes and gardens by throwing handfuls of beans and shouting, "Demons out! Good luck in!" At the Naritasan Shinshoji Temple (in Narita, Chiba Prefecture), sumo wrestlers and celebrities participate every year, but they only shout "Good luck in," not "Demons out." It is said that it is because you do not have to drive the demons out, as the power of the principal image of worship, Acala (Fudo myo-o: "unmovable wisdom king"), is so strong. In addition, in Gangoji Temple in Nara it is said the shout is "Good luck in, Demons in."
- *Hina matsuri* (March 3): The Festival of Dolls. Also called Girls' Day Festival, this is the day on which wishes are expressed for the future happiness of girls. A set of dolls dressed in costumes which were worn in the royal court in ancient times are displayed together with peach blossoms as decoration. A sweet drink called *shirozake* (or *amazake*), brewed from rice gruel mixed with fermented rice, is partaken of on this day.
- *Hanami* (Cherry blossom season in each region): Cherry blossom viewing. When the cherry trees are in full blossom at various locations throughout the country, people get together to view the blossoms and have a good time. In Tokyo, Kitanomaru Park and Ueno Park are popular destinations for hanami. In Kyoto, there is the Daigoji Temple, in which on March 15, 1598, Toyotomi Hideyoshi held the "Daigo hanami," a historic gorgeous cherry blossom viewing party in the Sanboin Temple.
- *Tango no sekku* (May 5): The Boys' Festival for expressing the hope that each boy in the family will grow up healthy and strong. Warrior figures are set up in the house during this festival, iris leaves are placed under the eaves to fend off evil, and huge fish-like streamers are fastened to poles. Special rice cakes wrapped in oak leaves are eaten on this day.
- *Tanabata* (July 7): The Star Festival, which is said to be a combination of Chinese tradition with beliefs peculiar to Japan. This festival celebrates the meeting, just once a year, of two lovers, Kengyu (the star Altair, personified as a cowherd) and Shokujo (Vega, as a weaving girl), who are separated by the Milky Way on the other days

飾り、織女星にあやかって女児の手芸の上達を祈る。なお、日本各地では、それぞれ趣向を凝らした祭りが催されているが、必ずしも7月7日に開催されているわけではない。例えば、東京の阿佐ヶ谷七夕まつりは8月の初旬の5日間、下町七夕まつり（浅草合羽橋）は7月7日の前後数日間、有名な宮城県仙台市の七夕祭りは、8月6日から8日まで、となっている。

○お盆（8月15日の前後数日）：種々の食物を祖先の霊に供えてその冥福を祈る。都会に働きに行っている者は郷里に帰る。なお、東京などの大都市では7月に行うところもある。各地の町や村で盆踊りが行われ、浴衣（ゆかた）姿で多くの人が参加するが、これは日本の夏の風物詩の一つである。

○月見（太陰暦8月15日夜および9月13日夜〔満月の夜〕）：すすきを飾り、お酒とだんごを月に供え、月を見ながら秋の夜を楽しむ。

○お彼岸（春分の日と秋分の日を中心とした前後7日間）：彼岸とは向こう岸の意味で、仏教ではさとりの世界（涅槃〔ねはん〕）のことである。先祖の霊を呼び、仏事を行い、墓にお参りする。

○七五三：男の子は（3歳と）5歳、女の子は3歳と7歳にあたる年の11月15日に、子供の成長を祝い、晴着を着せて神社に詣でる。奇数をめでたい数とし、そのうちから三つを取ったものである。

○クリスマス：日本には洗礼をうけたクリスチャンの数は多くないが、かなりの人が一種のお祭り的なものとして、クリスマスイブを楽しむ。子供にとってはサンタクロースのプレゼントが楽しみである。

c）国民の祝日

　法律で16（2018年6月時点）の国民の祝日が定まっており、学校・官庁・会社が休日になる。

of the year. Pieces of bamboo are set up in the garden and adorned with strips of paper of five different colors on which are written poems associated with the legend, and offerings of food, such as corn and eggplant, are made. Also, young girls pray that their handicraft will become as proficient as Vega's is supposed to be. In various places in Japan, festivals are held that also have a local appeal and are not necessarily held on July 7. These include the Asagaya Tanabata Festival in Tokyo held for five days in early August, the Shitamachi Tanabata Festival (Asakusa Kappa Bridge) is held for several days around July 7, and the famous Tanabata Festival in Sendai City, Miyagi Prefecture, from August 6 to 8.

- *Obon* (around mid-August): The Festival of Souls. In this festival a variety of foods are offered to the spirits of ancestors, and their repose prayed for. People who have moved to the cities to work return to their home towns during this period. In Tokyo and other major cities this festival is celebrated in July. In towns and villages across the country people in *yukata* (light cotton *kimono*) gather for outdoor dances known as *bon-odori*. For some Japanese, summer wouldn't be summer without a bon-odori.
- *Tsukimi* (night of the full moon on August 15 and September 13 of the lunar calendar): The days for "moon-viewing." Decorations of Japanese pampas grass are used, and moon-offerings of *sake* and *dango* (a kind of dumpling) are made as the people view and admire the full moon (harvest moon), enjoying the air of an autumn evening.
- *Higan* (two periods of seven days with the middle day falling on the spring or autumn equinox): The word "higan" meaning "the other shore," or, in Buddhism, nirvana. During higan the spirits of ancestors are recalled, Buddhist rites carried out, and family graves visited.
- *Shichi-go-san* (November 15): The seven-five-three festival when parents with boys of five, girls of seven, and either boys or girls of three dress their children in formal best clothes and take them to shrines where they pray for their children's future. These three numbers were chosen since odd numbers are considered lucky.
- Christmas: There are not many baptized Christians in Japan, but many people engage in festive activities on Christmas Eve. Children, especially, enjoy receiving presents from "Santa Claus."

c) National Holidays

Schools, companies, and government offices close on these sixteen legally-established national holidays:

○元日（1月1日）：年のはじめを祝う。

○成人の日（1月の第2月曜日）：大人になったことを自覚し、自ら生き抜こうとする青年を祝い励ます。各市町村は、その年成人になる人を集めて祝いの式を行う。

○建国記念の日（2月11日）：建国をしのび、国を愛する心を養う（紀元前660年に初代の神武天皇が即位したと伝えられる日を記念する）。

○天皇誕生日（2月23日）：今上天皇の誕生日（1960年2月23日）を祝う。皇居で天皇・皇后両陛下が国民の参賀を受ける。

○春分の日（暦の上での春分日）：自然をたたえ、生物をいつくしむ（古来より仏教上のお祭りの日であった）。

○昭和の日（4月29日）：激動の日々を経て、復興を遂げた昭和の時代を顧み、国の将来に思いをいたす（1988年までは昭和天皇の誕生日、また1989年から2006年までは、みどりの日として祝っていた）。

○憲法記念日（5月3日）：日本国憲法の施行を記念し、国の成長を期する（1947年5月3日施行）。

○みどりの日（5月4日）：自然に親しむとともにその恩恵に感謝し、豊かな心をはぐくむ（2007年より、当初の4月29日からこの日に移された）。

○こどもの日（5月5日）：子供の人格を重んじ、子供の幸福をはかるとともに、母に感謝する（古来より5月5日が男の子のお祝いの日であった）。

○海の日（7月の第3月曜日）：海に囲まれた国として、日本が海から受けているさまざまの恩恵に感謝するとともに、海洋国としての繁栄を願う。

○山の日（8月11日）：山に親しむ機会を得て、山の恩恵に感謝する。

○敬老の日（9月の第3月曜日）：多年にわたり社会に尽くしてきた老人を敬愛し、長寿を祝う。各市町村では、高齢者を招いて演芸会などを開いたり、記念品を贈呈し

- New Year's Day (January 1): day on which the start of the new year is celebrated.
- Coming-of-Age Day (second Monday of January): day for congratulating those who have reached their majority and are now ready to make their own way in the world. Each city, town, and village holds a congratulatory ceremony for those who come of age in that particular year.
- National Foundation Day (February 11): day for commemorating the founding of the nation and for fostering patriotic feelings. (Marks the anniversary of the accession to the throne of the first emperor, in the year 660 B.C.)
- Emperor's Birthday (February 23): on this day the Emperor, with the Empress, receives the congratulations of the people at the Imperial Palace.
- Vernal Equinox Day (on the day of the spring equinox according to the calendar): day for praising nature and showing love of all living things. (This has been a Buddhist festival day from ancient times.)
- Showa Day (April 29): day for reflecting on Japan's Showa period when recovery was made following turbulent times, and for thinking of the country's future. (This day was celebrated as the birthday of the Emperor Showa up to 1988, and thereafter as Greenery Day between 1989 and 2006.)
- Constitution Memorial Day (May 3): day for commemorating the enforcement of the Constitution and reaffirming hope in the growth of the nation. (The Constitution was enforced on May 3, 1947.)
- Greenery Day (May 4): day to enrich one's spirit by communing with nature and giving thanks for nature's blessings (first observed on its current date in 2007, having been moved from April 29).
- Children's Day (May 5): day on which wishes are expressed that the children will grow up good and find happiness; it is also for expressing thanks to mothers. (May 5 has long been the celebratory day for boys.)
- Marine Day (third Monday of July): day for giving thanks for the many blessings Japan receives from the ocean as a country completely surrounded by water and also for reaffirming the people's desire to prosper as a maritime country.
- Mountain Day (August 11): day for an opportunity to get familiar with mountains and appreciate the blessings of mountains.
- Respect-for-the-Aged Day (third Monday of September): day for showing respect and affection for the elderly who have devoted themselves to the society for so many years, and for celebrating their

たりする。

○秋分の日（暦の上での秋分日）：祖先を敬い、亡くなった人々をしのぶ（古来より仏教上のお祭りの日であった）。

○体育の日（10月の第2月曜日）：スポーツに親しみ、健康な心身を培（つちか）う（1964年10月10日の東京オリンピック開会を記念する）。体育振興の行事が開かれることが多い。

○文化の日（11月3日）：自由と平和を愛し、文化をすすめる（1946年11月3日、日本国憲法公布の日を記念する。ちなみに1945年以前には、明治天皇誕生の日として祝っていた）。

○勤労感謝の日（11月23日）：勤労を尊び、生産を祝い国民互いに感謝しあう（天皇が新しく収穫した米を神に捧げる日を記念する）。

d) 郷土色豊かな祭りや伝統的行事

○秋田県横手地方の「かまくら」（正月行事の一つ）：縦横2m位の雪室をつくり、中に祭壇を設け水神を祭る。夜、数人の子供達が雪室の中に集まり、甘酒を飲み餅などを食べる。昔は、正月小屋にこもって飲食を慎み、不浄を避けた生活を送る風習が、日本の中部以東でかなり広く行われていた。その変形として、今は、子供の楽しい行事となっている。

○札幌の雪祭（2月の第1月曜日〜第2月曜日）：動物・神話・伝説・人気マンガのキャラクター・有名な建物などを題材にした、大小さまざまの雪像が立ち並ぶ雪の祭典である。札幌の大通り公園で行われる。

○博多の「どんたく」（5月3日〜4日）：「どんたく」とは、オランダ語のZondagのなまりで、休日の意である。馬に乗った神話の神様の仮装行列や、屋台に乗った着飾った子供の行列がにぎやかに市内をねり歩くほか、種々の芸能大会が催される。

○京都の葵祭（5月15日）：わが国の祭りのうち最も優雅

long life. In cities, towns, and villages, the elderly are invited to entertainments and given gifts to mark the occasion.
- Autumnal Equinox Day (on the day of the autumnal equinox according to the calendar): day on which ancestors are honored, and the deceased remembered. (This has been a Buddhist festival day from ancient times.)
- Health-Sports Day (second Monday of October): day for sports and to foster a sound mind and body. (Commemorates the 1964 Tokyo Olympiad, the opening ceremony of which took place on October 10.) Many sporting events are held on this day.
- Culture Day (November 3): day for celebrating love of freedom and peace, and promoting culture. (Commemorates the promulgation, on November 3, 1946, of the Japanese Constitution. Prior to 1945, this day was celebrated as the birthday of the Emperor Meiji.)
- Labor Thanksgiving Day (November 23): day for praise and celebration of labor and production. The people give thanks for the benefits of labor. (It is on this day that the Emperor makes an offering of newly harvested rice to the Shinto gods.)

d) Local Festivals and Traditional Events
- Kamakura Festival at Yokote in Akita Prefecture (one of the New Year holiday events): A "*kamakura*" is an igloo-like snow house, about 2 meters square, which shelters an altar dedicated to the God of Water. At night, children gather in the kamakura to enjoy rice cakes and a sweet mild *sake* called *amazake*. In olden times, it was a widespread custom among people in central and eastern Japan to build a small New Year's hut in which to spend a few days refraining from the pleasures of eating and drinking in order to purify themselves. This has now turned into a happy event for children.
- Snow Festival in Sapporo (From the first to the second Monday in February): winter carnival at which an array of huge snow sculptures of animals, figures from mythology and legends, popular cartoon characters, and famous buildings is exhibited in Sapporo's Odori Park.
- Dontaku Festival in Hakata, Fukuoka Prefecture (May 3 to 4): The word "*dontaku*" deriving from the Dutch "zondag" meaning "holiday." The Dontaku Festival is marked by a gala procession of figures on horseback masquerading as deities from Japanese mythology and of floats with *kimono*-clad children aboard. Many different shows are also held during the festival period.
- Aoi Festival in Kyoto (May 15): Renowned as Japan's most elegant

で古趣に富んだ祭りとして知られている。平安朝の優雅古典行列は平安貴族そのままの姿で列をつくり、総勢500人が京都御所から下鴨神社を経て上賀茂神社へ向かう。

○東京の山王祭と神田祭（6月15日）：日枝神社の祭礼である。山王祭と神田祭はともに江戸（現在の東京）の二大祭とされた。しかし、しだいに豪華になり、氏子の負担がますます大きくなった。このため氏子の負担を軽減するために、1615年以来、双方が隔年に行われるようになった。現在もこの伝統によって隔年に行われる。

○京都の祇園祭（7月1日〜31日）：八坂神社の祭礼で、9世紀末に疫病退散を願ったのが起源とされる。16日の夜には、町の旧家は軒に神灯や青簾をかけ、敷物をのべて花を飾り、屏風を立てて祭りに色彩をそえる。また、山鉾には、提灯が明々とともり、祇園囃子が奏でられる。17日の豪華壮麗な山鉾の巡行で、祭りの雰囲気は最高潮に達する。

○大阪の天神祭（7月25日）：天満宮の祭礼。神輿が堂島川を下る神幸式が中心である。お迎え人形船・ドンドコ船・かがり船・はやし船などが川いっぱいに豪華な船祭りをくりひろげる。

○相馬野馬追（7月末の土・日・月曜日）：一千有余年の昔、相馬氏の祖といわれる平将門が野馬を放ち、敵兵に見立てて軍事訓練を行ったのが始まりと伝えられ、甲冑に身を固めた500余騎の騎馬武者が腰に太刀、背に旗指物をつけて疾走する豪華絢爛で勇壮な戦国絵巻をくりひろげる（福島県雲雀ヶ原祭場地）。

○青森の「ねぶた」祭（8月3日〜7日）：大きな張り

festival and an event brimming with the charm of past times. A grand procession in the elegant style of the Heian period brings to life the nobility of the era just as they appeared in their day. The pageant involves all of 500 participants who wind their way from the Kyoto Imperial Palace through the Shimokamo Shrine to the Kamigamo Shrine.

- Sanno Festival and Kanda Festival in Tokyo (June 15): The Hie Shrine Festival. The Sanno Festival and the Kanda Festival were formerly considered to be the two major festivals of Edo (present-day Tokyo). Year by year, however, these festivals became more and more extravagant, and more burdensome for the shrine parishioners, until it was decided in 1615 to hold them in alternate years. The practice of holding the festivals alternately continues to this day.
- Gion Festival in Kyoto (July 1 to 31): Festival of Yasaka Shrine said to have originated in an attempt to secure protection from a plague toward the end of the ninth century. On the evening of July 16, lanterns are hung from the eaves of the houses in the old sections of the city, special blue curtains are hung in the doorways, flowers are set out on cloth spreads, and decorative screens are displayed, thus adding color to the festival. It is also on this evening that the float lanterns are lighted to the accompaniment of Gion festival music. The climax comes on July 17, when a fleet of gorgeously decorated floats parade through the boulevards.
- Tenjin Festival in Osaka (July 25): Festival of the Tenman Shrine, the main event of which is the Shinkoshiki or the descent of Dojimagawa River by a *mikoshi* (portable shrine). Numerous boats, some decked out with life-size dolls, others with blazing torches suspended over the sides and still others carrying drummers and other musicians who provide lively music for the occasion, create a gorgeous scene as they spread across the river to greet the mikoshi.
- Soma Nomaoi (Wild Horse Chasing) in Hibarigahara, Haramachi, Fukushima Prefecture (last Saturday, Sunday, and Monday in July): More than a thousand years ago Taira Masakado, believed to be the founder of the Soma Clan, is said to have released wild horses and used them to represent enemy forces in a military training exercise. Today's horse chasing spectacle is thought to have grown out of this episode. More than 500 horse-mounted Soma warriors clad in armor, with swords at the waist and battle flags on their backs, put on a spectacular, valiant show as they charge across the Hibarigahara Plain.
- Nebuta Festival in Aomori (August 3 to 7): A festival featuring as

子（はりこ）の人形・魚・鳥獣などを担いだり、車に乗せ、笛や太鼓の囃子にあわせて「らっせ・らっせ」の掛声にぎやかに市中をひきまわす。夜はねぶたの中から照明を照らし、幻想的な雰囲気につつみ込む。6日夜から7日にかけて、これらを船に乗せて海上をねるのが見ものである。青森地方の夏を彩る風物詩である。ねむいことを「ねぶたい」ともいうが、この語幹の「ねぶた」をとって、睡魔のことをいうらしい。この睡魔を払う行事が発端である。

○仙台の七夕祭（8月6日〜8日）：七夕の伝説にちなんでの祭りで、全国で行われるが、とくに仙台のものが有名である。各戸に種々意匠をこらした短冊や吹流しを飾りつけた竹を立てて優美を競うが、ことに商店街では、軒並みに趣向をこらした豪華な飾りつけをして雰囲気を盛り上げる。

○秋田の竿灯（かんとう）祭（8月5日〜7日）：秋田市で行われる七夕祭りの行事である。仕事の妨げとなる一年中の睡魔をはらうことを願うものである。1本の長い親竹に横竹を結びつけ、それに46個または48個の提灯をぶらさげたものを、バランスをとって頭上・肩先・掌上などに立てる。若者が太鼓の囃子につれて、倒さないように扱う技を競う。

○徳島の阿波踊り（8月12日〜15日）：16世紀末に、時の大名がこの地方に入城したのを祝って、住民が踊ったのがはじまりといわれる。三味線・太鼓・笛などの伴奏につれて、老若男女を問わず、ゆかたがけで踊る。踊りは単純活発で、手びょうし・足どりも面白く、全市をあげて夜を明かして踊り抜く。

○長崎の「おくんち」（10月7日〜9日）：諏訪神社の祭礼である。「おくんち」とは、太陰暦9月9日のことで、中国の重陽の節句（中国では、9は陽の数とされ、これを二つ重ねた月日にあたる）にちなんでいる。中国風の蛇踊りなどがあり、鎖国時代も唯一の開港地だった

its main attraction a parade of huge papier-mâché dolls, fish, birds, and animals which are carried through the city on shoulder or aboard wagons to the accompaniment of flute and drum music and the chants of the participants shouting, "*Rasse! Rasse!*" At night the papier-mâché figures are lighted from the inside, creating a fantastic atmosphere. From the night of August 6 into the morning of August 7, the figures are loaded on boats for a spectacular sea parade. This summer festival is the biggest annual event in the Aomori district.

The word "*nebuta*" is derived from "*nebutai*" which in the local dialect means "sleepy." It apparently refers to the demon of sleep, and the festival originated from a local ritual aimed at chasing off this demon.

- Tanabata Festival in Sendai (August 6 to 8): One of numerous Tanabata festivals held throughout the country. The one held in Sendai is, however, especially famous. Each family in the city tries to outdo its neighbors in putting up bamboo poles colorfully decorated with streamers and strips of fancy paper. The decorations are by far the most gorgeous and colorful in the shopping centers where elaborate adornments continue block after block and help to raise the festive mood to a high pitch.

- Kanto Festival in Akita (August 5 to 7): Akita City's version of the Tanabata festival. It is held to drive off the demon of drowsiness that hampers the people's work throughout the year. A "*kanto*" is a long bamboo pole with numerous cross bars on which forty-six or forty-eight lanterns are hung. The highlight of the festival is a competition among local youths who vie with each other in balancing the kantos on their heads, shoulders, and hands as they dance to the accompaniment of drums.

- Awa Odori Dancing Festival in Tokushima (August 12 to 15): A festival dating back to the end of the sixteenth century when residents danced in the streets in celebration of their new warlord's move into the city's castle. Men and women, young and old, don their *yukata* (a traditional Japanese summer garment) and dance through the night to the music of *shamisen* (a three-stringed musical instrument), drums, and flutes. The dance itself is simple, but very lively, and involves interesting hand and foot movements.

- Okunchi Festival in Nagasaki (October 7 to 9): The festival of the Suwa Shrine in Nagasaki. "*Okunchi*" means ninth day of the ninth month according to the lunar calendar and the festival originated from one in China falling on the same day. (Nine is considered a lucky number in China and the double nine especially so.) The

土地柄をしのばせる。

○京都の時代祭（10月22日）：平安神宮の祭礼である。京都に都がおかれていた、一千余年にわたる風俗・習慣などを、時代別にかたどった行列がくりひろげられ、日本歴史の絵巻物を、目のあたりに見るような美しさである。

○秩父の夜祭り（12月3日）：埼玉の秩父神社の祭礼で、夜祭りとして有名である。神輿に続いて、ぼんぼりを無数にともした屋台と山車（だし）が行進する。はげしいリズムをもつ祭囃子は、秩父屋台囃子として知られている。

○男鹿半島の「なまはげ」（12月31日）：古くから男鹿半島に伝わる行事である。面をかぶり、わらや海草でつくった腰みのをつけて、鬼に仮装した青年達が、張子の出刃包丁・棒・かますなどを持って各家を訪れ、怠け者をいましめて歩く。「なまはげ」は「なまみはぎ」（生身剥ぎ）の転訛であるが、なまみとは炉端で火にあたってばかりいるときにできる皮膚の火だこのことで、これができるような怠け者を指す。

e）日本の代表的ペット
1）日本猫（にほんねこ）

　　日本猫は奈良時代頃に中国から輸入されたのが始まりと言われている。日本人に長く親しまれてきた猫で、その特徴は、顔は鼻筋が通り、耳の毛は短い。全身の毛はそれほど長くない。尾は細長いものと極端に短いものがあるが、細長くても先だけが折れ曲がっているものもある。毛並みが美しく、またその色分けも外国人から珍しがられている。白・黒の一色または二色、濃淡帯状の縞模様、白地に黒ぶちや茶ぶち、そして三毛猫と呼ばれる白・茶・黒の三色に色分けされているものなどがいる。

2）日本犬（にほんいぬ）

　　日本犬は、古くから日本に住んでいる犬の総称で、日本犬保存会によって定められたスタンダードである

festival features dragon dances in the traditional Chinese fashion and is reminiscent of the days of isolation when Nagasaki was the only port open to foreign countries.

- Jidai Festival in Kyoto (October 22): The festival of the Heian Shrine highlighted by a unique procession of historical figures clad in costumes representing each of the historical periods of the ten centuries during which Kyoto was the capital. The parade is a beautiful reproduction of the history of Japan.
- Chichibu Night Festival in Saitama (December 3): The festival of the Chichibu Shrine and one of the most famous to be held at night. The *mikoshi* (portable shrine) at the head of the parade is followed by floats lit up with countless paper lanterns. The parade progresses to the strong beat of the festival song, the well known Chichibu Yataibayashi.
- Namahage Festival of the Oga Peninsula in Akita Prefecture (December 31): A unique event observed from ancient times in the Oga Peninsula. Young men dressed as dreadful demons and bearing big papier-mache knives, clubs, and straw bags go from house to house admonishing sluggards to mend their ways. The costume includes a demon's mask and a skirt of straw or seaweed.

  "*Namahage*" is a corruption of "*namami-hagi*" which literally means "getting rid of calluses formed by excessive exposure of the skin to heat." The term is used to indicate the treatment required by a person so lazy as to sit warming himself at the fire long enough for such a callus to form.

e) Japanese Pets

1) Japanese Cats

It is thought that Japanese cats were first imported from China around the Nara period (710 to 794). This is a cat that has long been familiar to the Japanese. It has a long nose ridge and short ear hairs, and overall, its fur is not that long. Some of the cats have long, thin tails that sometimes have a bend at the tip, and others have extremely short tails. They have beautiful fur and its coloring is unusual to the foreign eye. They can be black or white, or both. There are cats with light and dark stripes, or that are white with black or brown patches, and calico cats that are predominantly white with patches of brown and black.

2) Japanese Dogs

This is a generic term for dogs that have been known in Japan since ancient times. It particularly refers to the six standard native dog species

「日本犬標準」に名前の挙げられている6つの在来犬種を特に指定している。大型犬の秋田犬、中型犬の甲斐犬・紀州犬・柴犬・四国犬・北海道犬で、それぞれ天然記念物に指定され保存活動が続けられている。この内、秋田犬と柴犬は海外でもよく知られ愛好家がいる。

特徴は素朴で主人には非常に忠実かつ勇敢といった性質が日本犬らしいとされ、もともと狩猟犬として、人間と協力して狩猟およびそれに伴う諸作業に従事してきたので、高い身体能力を持っている。体型は、数千年前の犬の姿とほとんど変わっておらず、犬そのものの原型を色濃く残していると言われている。

（注）天然記念物：日本の自然を理解するうえで欠くことのできない自然および自然現象をいい、文化財保護法によって指定される記念物のうち、学術上貴重な動物、植物、地質鉱物。

3）鑑賞魚

ⅰ）錦鯉（にしきごい）は日本を代表する鑑賞魚で、色彩や斑点など、体色を改良されたものを錦鯉という。錦鯉にはその模様によって多くの品種があり、飼育用として人気が高く、斑点模様、色彩の鮮やかさ、大きさ、体型を価値基準として高額で取引されている。新潟県小千谷市と旧山古志村で錦鯉の養殖が盛んになり、錦鯉の交配が進み、質の良い個体が売買されるようになった。プラスチック袋の出現や航空機の利用で錦鯉の輸出が速く安全なものとなり世界中へ輸出できるようになった。その美しく優雅に泳ぐ姿に世界中に愛好家がいて一匹で100万円以上の値がつく高価な固体も珍しくない。

ⅱ）金魚（きんぎょ）も観賞魚として世界中で親しまれている。金魚の原産地は中国で、緋鮒（ヒブナ）を改良したものである。1500年頃に日本に渡来し人為的に様々な品種が作りだされてきた。比較的フナの体型に近い和金、ずんぐりした体に長いひれを持つ琉金、眼球が左右に飛び出した出目金などは、在来種として古くから親しまれてきた。これらをさらに品種改良して高級な金魚を生産している。有名な日本の産地は奈良県の大和郡

prescribed by the Association for the Preservation of the Japanese Dog. These are the Akita, a large dog, and the medium-sized Kai, Kishu, Shiba, Shikoku, and Hokkaido, each designated as a natural monument and subject to continuing preservation activities. The Akita and Shiba are also known and have many fans in other countries.

The Japanese dog is considered to be rustic, courageous and very faithful to its owner. Since it was originally a hunting dog in which role it accompanied humans, it has high physical capabilities. In appearance, they are said to have undergone little change over the past several thousand years, so they are very much the archetype of what a dog is.

(Note) Natural monument: refers to nature and natural phenomena indispensable for understanding the nature of Japan; of monuments designated by the Cultural Properties Protection Law of which there are scientifically valuable animals, plants, and geological minerals.

3) Aquarium Fish

i) Nishikigoi (brocaded koi) is a term for koi (carp) which are a well-known fish raised in Japan for appreciation whose body colors and patches have been improved over time. There are many varieties of nishikigoi differentiated by pattern, and which are popular for breeding purposes. These are traded at high prices that are based on speckle pattern, vividness of color, size, and body type. Nishikigoi cultivation became popular in Ojiya City in Niigata, and in what was formerly Yamakoshi village, where the breeding of nishikigoi made advances, resulting in good quality examples that could be traded. With the advent of plastic bags and the use of aircraft, enabling nishikigoi to be safely transported, exports to all over the world grew rapidly. Enthusiasts the world over can now enjoy the sight of the elegant swimming of beautiful koi, and it is not unusual for an individual koi to be valued at one million yen or more.

ii) The goldfish is a familiar aquarium fish around the world. Goldfish originated in China, where they were derived from the common goldfish. After being brought to Japan around 1500 they were artificially bred to develop a number of varieties. Popular types included the wakin goldfish having a body type relatively similar to that of the Prussian carp, the ryukin, a deep-bodied goldfish with long fins, and the telescope goldfish which had protruding eyes, all long-established varieties. These were further improved to derive high-quality goldfish. Notable production areas in Japan

山、愛知県の弥富、熊本県の長洲町などがあげられる。金魚は明治時代に初めて日本からアメリカに輸出され、1910年の日英博覧会に出展されヨーロッパの人たちが初めて金魚を見たことで、金魚イコール日本のイメージとなった。しかし最近では、中国が安価に輸出して輸出大国となっている。

f) 外国と異なる日本の習慣

○入浴：日本人は入浴により体を洗うだけでなく、湯槽につかってゆっくり温まる習慣がある。体を洗い、汚れを流すのは湯槽の外で行う。最近の風呂は好みの温度設定で湯張りができるようになっており、湯の減った分は湯を追加したり、ぬるくなった分は再加熱して温めることもできる。数人が順次同じ湯槽に入る。

各家庭だけでなく、代金を支払って入る公衆浴場の銭湯も同様である。現在の銭湯の軒数は、最盛期の約4分の1以下の4,000軒を切るまで減少してしまったが、最近になり、一般銭湯のリニューアルが増えてきた。それらの新しい銭湯は、外観はモダンなデザインで、スーパー銭湯的な設備となり多くの客で連日賑わっているが、入浴時のマナーは同様である。

○家に入るときは靴を脱ぐ：日本の家の中では靴を脱ぐというルールがあり、玄関の靴脱ぎ場で、スリッパなどに履き替え、家の中履きと外履きを明確に区別して生活する。日本式の旅館などを利用する時も同様に、宿や部屋の玄関で靴を脱ぎ、館内でスリッパなどの中履きで滞在する。

g) 名刺

日本でも名刺は広く使われており、とくにビジネスマンが初対面のときに、姓名のほかに、勤務先企業・団体名・所属名・役職名・住所・電話番号・メールアドレスが印刷されている名刺を、相互に交換する習慣がある。名刺の交換は、地位の低い人や若い人の方から先に相手に渡すのがエチケットとされている。

include Yamatokoriyama in Nara Prefecture, Yatomi in Aichi Prefecture, and Nagasu in Kumamoto Prefecture. Japan started exporting goldfish to the U.S. in the Meiji period (1868 to 1912) and exhibited goldfish at the Japan-British Exhibition of 1910, giving Europeans their first view of the fish and leading to people associating goldfish with Japan. Recently, however, China has used low prices to become a major goldfish exporter.

f) Customs and Beliefs Peculiar to Japan

- Baths: Japanese people do not use baths just to wash themselves; they also like to warm themselves by soaking slowly in a deep tub full of hot water. The actual washing and rinsing is done outside the tub. Today's baths are designed to automatically fill the tub with hot water of a preset temperature. The water can be reheated directly in the tub, so when the level of the water drops, the tub is topped up with fresh water and reheated. All family members use the same bath in turn without changing the water. This use of the same bath water by a number of people applies not only to home baths but also to public baths (baths open to anyone for a fee).

  The current number of public baths has decreased to under 4,000, which is less than a quarter of what it was at its peak. However, recently a growing number of public baths are being refurbished. These new public baths look modern, have superb facilities, and are crowded with customers every day, but once inside, bathing etiquette and manners are the same.

- Removing shoes at house entrance: Shoes are not worn inside rooms of a Japanese house but left at the entrance (*genkan*). Slippers or similar are worn inside. So Japanese footwear is distinctly different between inside and outside the home. Similarly, when using a Japanese-style hotel or other facilities, shoes are removed at the entrance of the hotel or when entering the room, and slippers are used instead.

g) Name Cards

Name cards (calling and business cards) are used extensively in Japan. When business people meet for the first time, each invariably gives the other a card printed with his or her name as well as the name, address, telephone number, and e-mail address of one's company, the department one works in, and one's position. Etiquette calls for the lower ranking or younger person to offer his card first.

h）判子（はんこ：印鑑ともいう）

　日本では、西欧式のサインと同じような意味で、自分の姓や名を彫った判子による押印が用いられる。

　市町村の役所に登録してある印を「実印」と呼び、それ以外の「認め印」と区別する。この実印の印鑑証明によって、本人に相違ないことを確認することが法律上定められている。したがって、主要な取引や契約書作成には印鑑証明が必要になる。

　このように判子は、ビジネス社会に限らず一般市民生活にも、極めて重要である。たとえば、日本では近年、銀行預金の出し入れのさいの「キャッシュカード」の利用が盛んになっている。しかし、この「カード」によらない銀行からの預金払い戻しや、郵便書留の受取証、領収書発行などにも判子が必要である。

i）風呂敷

　風呂敷は、日本で古くから物品の持ち運びや保存などに使用されている四角形の布である。風呂敷の名称が一般に用いられるようになったのは、江戸時代前期（17世紀ごろ）である。共同風呂である銭湯の発達にともない、衣料をこの布に包んで運び、更衣をこの布の上で行ったため、風呂敷と呼ばれるようになった。

　風呂敷は、物品の形・大きさなどにあまり関係なく自由に包装できる。また何も包まないときは、小さく折りたたんで持ち歩ける。物品を包装するさい、四角の布の対角線上の端を相互に結ぶ。

　風呂敷の大きさや材質は、用途に応じていろいろなものがある。ふとんを包むための木綿で唐草模様の実用一点張りのものや、絹織物に紋様や花鳥の模様をあしらった美しいものまである。

j）そろばん

　日本古来よりの計算器であり、電卓やコンピュータが普及した現在でも、算数の基礎学習のために利用されている。横長浅底の木枠の内側に、上方に横に梁を設け、これを貫いて縦に木枠の上辺と下辺に竹串を等間隔に渡し、梁

h) Seal Stamps (Seal Impressions)

Where a Westerner would put his signature on something, a Japanese will stamp it with a seal (stamp) engraved with his or her name.

A Japanese may have more than one seal. The one registered at the local government office is called his *jitsuin* and the others *mitomein*. Under Japanese law, a person who has registered a seal impression can obtain a certificate of seal impression which he can use to prove one's identity. Such a certificate is necessary whenever one makes a major transaction or concludes a contract.

Seals are very important not only in the business world but also in everyday life. For example, although the use of cash cards for making deposits and withdrawals at Automated Teller Machines (ATMs) is now widespread in Japan, a person who wants to withdraw money from a bank or postal savings account over the counter without his card will have to use his or her seal. The seal is also needed for receiving registered letters and making out receipts.

i) Furoshiki

A *furoshiki* (literally a "bath spread") is a square piece of cloth for bundling up various articles that one wishes to carry or store away. Furoshiki have long been used in Japan. The word itself dates back to the early part of the Edo Era (around the 17th century) when public, communal bath houses became popular. The name comes from one of the first uses for this cloth—to carry a change of clothes in it to a public bath house and to change clothes on it.

The furoshiki is very handy since it is so freely adaptable to the size and shape of the article being wrapped, and when not in use it can be folded up and easily carried in the hand or pocket. The usual way of wrapping an article is to place it in the center of the furoshiki, and tie first one pair of diagonally opposite corners together over the article, followed by the other pair.

Furoshiki come in various sizes and materials. There are large cotton ones with arabesque patterns for binding up quilts and dainty silk ones patterned with decorative designs, flowers, and birds.

j) Abacus

The Japanese have been using the abacus for hundreds of years. Even today, in the age of the ubiquitous electronic calculator and personal computer, this traditional calculating device continues to be used for teaching basic arithmetic skills. The Japanese abacus consists of a rec-

を隔てて各串の上部に珠を1箇おいて数字の5を、下部に珠を4箇おいて、1箇で1を表わす。この珠を上下して加減乗除を行う。

そろばんは16世紀ごろ中国から日本に伝わったといわれている。その後現在の形に改良が加えられた。
そろばんの技術を示す段や級が設けられており、その認定を受けたい者は検定試験を受ける。

k）賭け事

日本では賭博は禁止されており、2018年まではカジノはないが、今後は解禁される。競馬・競輪・競艇・オートレース・宝くじは公営で行われている。

競馬は、全国規模の26のG1重賞レースがある（2018年）。競馬の年間の売上げは2兆7,477億円（2017年）である。

宝くじは、地方自治体の財政資金を調達するために1946年以来発売されており、夢を買うということで、国民の間に根強い人気がある。現在の最高賞金は前後賞を含め10億円（2017年）である。この他に、ロト・ナンバーズという購入者が数字を選び、発売額と当せん口数によって賞金額が変動するものもあり、ロト7の1等賞金は最大8億円となっている。

2001年3月に、サッカーくじ（愛称トト）の販売も開始された。これは、購入者が各試合の勝ち負けを予想し投票する仕組みである。2006年には新しくコンピュータが勝ち負けをランダムに選択する方法のサッカーくじ（愛称ビッグ）も発売された。最高賞金金額はキャリーオーバー発生時に6億円となっている。

l）パチンコ・パチスロ

パチンコは日本の社会に広く普及した庶民の遊びである。その愛好者は現在およそ940万人と見られている

tangular wooden frame having a crosspiece running lengthwise slightly below the upper edge of the frame. Evenly spaced thin bamboo rods run vertically from the upper edge of the frame to the lower, passing through small holes in the crosspiece. Each of the rods carries beads, a single bead above the crosspiece which counts as five, and four beads below the crosspiece, each counting as one. These beads are moved up and down on the rods to carry out addition, subtraction, multiplication and division.

The Japanese abacus is believed to have been developed from one brought in from China in the 16th century.

Tests are held periodically to rank abacus operators by skill and speed. Anyone interested can take one of these tests.

k) Betting

In Japan, serious gambling is forbidden, so up to 2018 there have been no casinos, but they will be allowed in future. There are, however, publicly operated horse, bicycle, boat, and motorcycle races as well as lotteries.

There are 26 Grade One (GI) "big-prize" horse races which attract the interest of fans throughout the country (2018). Annual takings from horse races amount to some 2.7477 trillion yen (2017).

Publicly operated lotteries begun in 1946 as a way of raising funds for local governments. As they offer a chance to become rich on a very modest investment, these lotteries have remained popular. At present (2017), a lucky ticket holder can win up to one billion yen if he holds the winning number and the ones before and after. There are other lotteries in which the amount that can be won also depends on what is called the Loto numbers chosen by the purchaser, the amount of tickets sold, and the number of winners. The highest prize in the Lotto 7 lottery, for example, is 800 million yen.

Soccer pari-mutuel tickets (popularly called "Toto" tickets) went on sale from March 2001. This is an arrangement in which ticket purchasers forecast the outcomes of matches. In 2006, a new kind of soccer pari-mutuel tickets (popularly called "Toto Big" tickets) went on sale. In the Toto Big system, the outcomes of matches are randomly selected by computer. In the case of a carry-over, the maximum amount that can be won is 600 million yen.

l) Pachinko and Pachisuro

A pinball game called *pachinko* is enjoyed as a pastime throughout Japan. Enthusiasts are thought to number around 9.4 million (2016

(2016年レジャー白書2017)。パチンコ・パチスロの市場規模は2016年で売上高21兆6,260億円、全国の店舗数11,000軒、機械台数452万台である。

パチンコの原型は1920年頃アメリカから渡来し戦前はコリントゲームの名前で知られていた。パチンコの機械は一種の縦型のピンボールゲームで、前面がガラス張りの盤の中央の少し下にポケットと呼ばれる穴があいていて、穴は多くの釘で周囲をガードされている。プレーヤーは電動レバーを操作して直径11 mmの鋼球を連続的に盤の上方に向けて打ち出す。釘の間を落ちてくる球がポケットに入ると機械の下の出口から15個以内の玉が出てくる。

現在では、ハイテク技術が加えられた新機種が次々と開発され、玉が入ると同時に遊戯機械の複雑な電子機構が働いたり、盤の中央の派手な液晶画面のさまざまなキャラクターや数字が動き出してゲームを演じ、同じものが揃うと「大当たり」となって、場合によっては最大数千個の玉が1度に出てくるようなギャンブル性の強いものもある。この他にパチスロという一種のスロットマシーンも人気がありパチンコと並ぶ大衆娯楽となっている。

m) カルタ

日本の家庭で親しまれているカード遊びとして、カルタ取りがある。

カルタ取りのうち、古くから行われているものに小倉百人一首がある。これは、13世紀に新古今和歌集の選者である藤原定家が、7世紀以来の代表的な和歌百首を集めたものである。その後歌ガルタとなって普及し、今日もカルタ遊びとして広く親しまれている。

和歌は、5音7音5音の上の句と、7音7音の下の句から成っている。遊び方としては、まず下の句だけを書いたカードを広げておく。何人かでこれを囲み、一人の人が和歌を読み上げるのを聞いて、対応するカードを拾う。たくさん拾った人が勝ちである。

上手な人は上の句を読み始めるとすぐカードを拾ってし

Leisure White Paper 2017). The 11,000 pachinko and *pachisuro* (a type of slot machine) game centers (called "parlors") located throughout the country have a total of about 4.52 million machines and take in around 21.626 trillion yen per year (2016).

The precursor of pachinko was the Corinthian Game brought in from the U.S. in about 1920. The pachinko pinball machine stands upright. It has a vertical, glass-covered panel with target holes (pockets) located here and there on its lower half. The holes are guarded by many protruding pins. The player operates an electric lever to shoot 11-millimeter (0.4-inch) steel balls one after another to the top of the panel, from where they filter down through the pins. If a ball enters a pocket, the machine dispenses up to fifteen balls. The balls can be reused or exchanged for a prize.

New model machines including the latest technical advances come out at frequent intervals. Recent ones are often equipped with a complex electronic system that comes into action as soon as loaded with balls. Some of these have a gaudy LCD at the center of the panel that displays moving characters or numerals that line up in different patterns. If a pattern made up of only one kind of character or numeral appears, the player hits the jackpot, which may amount to several thousand balls. This kind of pachinko borders on gambling. The pachisuro (also spelled *pachislo*) slot machines have also attracted many devotees and offer a popular pastime on a par with pachinko.

m) Japanese Card Games

Some of the card games played in the Japanese home use cards unique to Japan.

One of the oldest such games is that of "one hundred *waka* poems." These waka, which are representative of this form of poetry, date back as early as the seventh century and were assembled together in the thirteenth century by Fujiwara no Teika, a compiler of the *Shin Kokin Wakashu*. Subsequently these became popular through the *uta-garuta* card game played even today.

Each of these waka consists of 31 syllables arranged in three lines of 5, 7 and 5 syllables respectively in the first part and two lines of 7 syllables each in the second part. To play the game, first the cards that have only the second part of the waka printed on them are laid face up. A number of people sit around these cards, listen to one person read out the waka and try to pick up the matching card. The winner is the one who picks up the most.

An expert is able to pick up the correct card as soon as he hears the

まう。したがって、100の和歌を全部記憶しておかなければ勝負に勝てない。和歌の記憶を通じて、文化の伝承を行った古人の知恵といえよう。この遊びはおもに正月に行われ、家庭のみでなく、全国的な競技大会もある。

このほか、子供用にことわざなどを読み上げ、そのことわざの最初の文字および関係ある絵を書いたカードを拾うイロハカルタもある。

n）碁（囲碁）・将棋・麻雀

日本でもっとも普及している室内の娯楽には、碁・将棋・麻雀などがある。

碁は361箇の目（交点）のある正方形の碁盤の上で、2人の対局者が白と黒の碁石を交互に並べて、囲み取った目の数で勝負を決めるゲームである。

上手の者が白石を持ち、黒石を持った者が先手となる。対局者の実力の差に応じて、いくつかの黒石を碁盤の目の一定の場所にあらかじめ並べておくというルールがあり、こうしてハンディキャップをつけることにより、実力に差のある者同士でも互角に戦うことができる。

碁は8世紀に中国から伝わり、初めは当時の貴族の遊びであった。13世紀ごろから貴族以外にもしだいに広まり今日におよんでいる。

将棋はチェスに似て、2名の対局者が81箇の区画が描かれた将棋盤の上で交互に駒を動かして、相手の王将を早く追い詰めた方が勝ちとなるゲームである。駒は8種類あり、それぞれが合計20枚を持ち、最初に将棋盤の所定の位置に並べる。

将棋は8世紀に中国から渡来し、しだいに改良が加えられて日本将棋として発展し、相手からとった駒を自分の持ち駒として再び使用できる独特のルールが生まれ、ゲームが変化に富んだものとなった。

段位の差のある人同士の対戦では、上位の人が、自陣の

beginning of the first part. So it means that if you want to win you have to memorize the whole of the one hundred waka. Devising this method of transmitting the culture of Japan in this way, through the memorization of waka, shows the wisdom of our ancestors. This game is played not only in the home but also in tournaments across the country, with both adults and children taking part. It is mostly played around New Year.

There is a similar game for children where the reader reads a proverb, for example, and the players compete to pick up the card showing the first letter or word of the proverb and a matching picture. There are also various other Japanese card games based on this same idea.

n) Go (Igo), Shogi, Mah-jong

Go, *shogi* and mah-jong are among the most popular indoor games in Japan.

Go, also called *igo*, is played by two players on a square board marked with a grid having 361 intersections. The players take turns placing stones (black for one, white for the other) on the intersections in such a way as to surround as much territory as possible. The player who encloses the greater area is the winner.

The more skillful player has the white stones, and black moves first. Rules allow for the use of handicaps to even out the effect of differences in skill, thereby allowing a more evenly matched game even when the levels of two players are considerably different. The handicap consists in black being able to put stones at specified locations on the board prior to the start of the game. How many stones he is allowed to place naturally depends on how much better the other player is.

Go was introduced to Japan from China in the eighth century. At first it was played only by the aristocracy, but from the thirteenth century it spread beyond the upper class to become the widely popular game it is today.

Shogi is played by two players, moving in turns, on a board of 81 squares. As with chess, the object of the game is to immobilize the opposing King so that he cannot evade capture. Each player has twenty pieces, of eight different ranks, set up in accordance with the rules.

The shogi now played in Japan has developed from the game originally brought from China in the eighth century. One of the changes made is that captured pieces can be re-used, providing complex variation in the game.

A player who is considerably better than his opponent may remove

駒の一部を落として、戦力のバランスをとることになっている。

　碁・将棋の段位は実力に応じて上位に向かって初段から九段まである。さらに名人・棋聖・十段位などのタイトルがある。初段の下は1級で、2級、3級となるほど下位になる。

　碁・将棋いずれの場合もプロにとっては厳しい勝負の世界であり、人間形成の場でもある。したがって昇段基準も厳しく、アマチュアとの対比では、同じ段位でも、実力の差はかなりあるようである。

　しかし2017年には前年にプロ入りした中学生の藤井聡太（15歳）が、将棋公式戦で29連勝して、デビューから無敗のまま歴代最多連勝記録を更新し世間の話題をさらった。さらに2018年5月に15歳9カ月で7段昇段となり、12月には公式戦通算100勝目をあげ最年少記録となった。

　麻雀は136個の牌（パイ）を用いて4人で得点を争うゲームである。4人がそれぞれ13個ずつの牌を持ってゲームを開始し、牌に刻まれた記号が相手に見えないように裏返しに並べられた残りの牌を順番に1個ずつ引き、代わりに不要の牌を1個ずつ捨てながら、手持ちの牌の組み合わせを定められた形に整えていく。もっとも早くその形ができ上がった者を勝ちとし、でき上がった形の種類によって得点が計算される。

　日本には1920年代に、中国からの帰国者によって伝えられ、第二次世界大戦後は麻雀人口が急速に増加した。しかし、近年麻雀人口はかなり減少している。

o) **日本の流行歌とクラシック音楽**
　1) 流行歌
　　　　西洋音楽の影響を受けて、日本の伝統的なうたである詩吟・音曲・民謡などとは異なる独特なふしまわしの歌謡曲が生まれ、いわゆる流行歌として国民大衆に愛好されるようになった。

one or more of his own pieces from the board before starting to play, in order to ensure a more balanced contest.

Go and shogi players are ranked according to ability. For advanced players these rankings range from first *dan* (grade) up to ninth dan. In addition, tournament winners are awarded such titles as *meijin*, *kisei*, tenth dan, etc. Below the dans are a number of grades for novices called *kyu*. The highest kyu is first kyu, so the higher the number of the kyu grade a person holds, the less skillful he is.

In the professional world of both go and shogi, there is a cutthroat competition which leads to character building of players. The standards by which promotion is made are correspondingly rigorous and because of this a professional player is usually considerably stronger than an amateur, even when they both possess the same dan ranking.

But in 2017, a 15-year-old junior high school student, Fujii Sota, who had entered the professional ranks the previous year, won his first 29 official games of shogi, setting a new record for the most consecutive wins, and instantly becoming the number one story. In May 2018, he was promoted to seventh dan at the age of 15 years, 9 months, and in December became the youngest player to achieve 100 victories in official games.

Mah-jong is usually played by four people with 136 pieces shaped like small tiles, each identified by a *kanji* character inscribed on the face. At the start of the game each player has a "hand" of thirteen pieces. The remaining pieces are placed in the middle of the table, face down. The players take turns at picking up a piece from the center pool and discarding an unwanted piece from their hand, as each tries to build up various combinations. The first player to meld wins the hand, and is credited with a certain number of points calculated on the basis of the particular combination of pieces making up the hand.

Mah-jong first started to be played in Japan in the 1920's, when it was introduced by Japanese returning from China, but it was following the Second World War that the game attained its immense popularity as the numbers of players grew by leaps and bounds. However, the number of devotees has declined considerably in recent years.

o) **Japanese Popular Songs and Classical Music**
1) Japanese Popular Songs

Japanese popular songs, known as *kayokyoku* or *ryukoka*, evolved under the influence of Western music. Their melodies are therefore quite unlike those of traditional *shigin* (chanting of classical Chinese-style poems), *ongyoku* (old-style ballads accompanied by *shamisen*), folk

日本の歌謡曲の発生は、1914年にトルストイ原作の『復活』の劇中でうたわれた「カチューシャのうた」がはじまりといわれている。その後、毎年多くのヒット曲がつくられ、ひろくうたわれ、大衆の心のいこいとなってきた。

　テレビやラジオでの歌謡曲の放送は、根強い人気があるが、プロの歌手のみでなく、一般視聴者が出演する素人のど自慢の放送もたびたび行われている。

　毎年末には、その年にもっともヒットし評価の高かった歌謡曲の歌手や作詞・作曲者を選ぶレコード大賞や歌謡大賞の選定がある。

　その年の人気歌手が、男性と女性のチームに分かれて各自のヒット曲をうたい、チームの総合評価を競い合う「紅白歌合戦」は、毎年12月31日にNHKで放映される。年末をしめくくる恒例の番組として親しまれている。このテレビ番組は海外にも放送されている。

　カラオケは依然高い人気を保っているものの市場規模は漸減傾向となっている。メロディだけで歌詞が入っていないディスクなどの伴奏に合わせて各人が歌い、歌手気分を味わって楽しむことが、気安い仲間同士の宴会や家庭で一般化している。「カラオケ」とは、歌の入っていないオーケストラ（空のオーケストラ）という意味の日本語の略称である。このシステムは、東南アジアをはじめ諸外国にもかなり広がっている。

　歌謡曲の多岐にわたるジャンルの中で、演歌は1960年代から1980年代まで日本の流行歌の主流の一角を占めていた。小節（こぶし）を利かせた特有の歌唱法とあいまって、もの悲しく、暗く、どこか哀愁を帯びた演歌のメロディは日本人の感情に深く訴えるものであった。しかし、近年では演歌の新しいヒット曲は数少なくなってきており、往年を懐かしむ年配者などの愛好者が主体となっている。歌謡界の女王といわれた美空ひばりは、1989年女性として初の国民栄誉賞を受賞した。

　一方、若い世代は軽快でポップな曲調を好み、海外ミュージシャン（代表例はプレスリーやビートルズなど）の影響も取り入れながら、戦後から今日に至る

songs, etc.

Some trace the beginnings of kayokyoku to a 1914 song, "Song of Katyusha," which was sung during a stage performance that year of Tolstoy's "Resurrection." Since that time such popular songs have appeared in great numbers every year and enjoyed widespread popularity among the people.

Kayokyoku programs on television and radio are immensely popular. Amateur singing contest programs are also frequently aired for general viewers and listeners.

At the end of each year, awards are presented to singers, lyricists, and composers of songs which have enjoyed the greatest popularity and critical success during the year.

The singers who have been chosen as the year's most popular appear in the *Kohaku Uta Gassen* (Red and White Singing Contest), which is aired by NHK on the evening of the thirty-first of December. The singers are divided into two teams, the women as the "Red" team and the men as the "White" team. For many Japanese the show is the traditional way of seeing out the old year and welcoming in the new. The show is also broadcast overseas.

Karaoke is still very popular in Japan, but the scale of the karaoke market is declining. Karaoke systems are CD or other media players with voice mixing facilities used to play an accompaniment to singing that evokes a professional's stage performance, at drinking parties or at home. "*Kara*" of "karaoke" means "empty"—empty of singing and words—and "*oke*" is a Japanese shortened form of "orchestra." The combination is intended to imply an orchestra without a vocalist. Karaoke systems have also come into fairly wide use in Southeast Asia and other parts of the world.

Among various genres of today's popular music in Japan, *enka* was one of the mainstreams from the 1960s into the 1980s. The enka singer puts the emotional content of the song across by using distinctive vocalization spiced with *kobushi* (similar to vibrato) to create a sad, melancholic, sorrowful mood that tugs at the listener's heartstrings. Recently, however, the number of enka songs that make it into the charts has declined noticeably. The majority of enka fans today are older people who reminisce about the good old days. In 1989 Misora Hibari, called the queen of popular song, was the first woman to receive the People's Honour Award.

The younger generation tends to prefer lighter and faster music. Reflecting their tastes, new genres with names like "*wasei* pops" (pops made in Japan) and "group sounds" emerged in succession, often under

まで、和製ポップス、グループ・サウンズ、ニューミュージック、J-POP など、時代時代で新たなジャンルを切り開いてきた。J-POP の多くの曲が、日本国内だけでなく海外、特に東アジア諸国でも広く受け入れられている。身近なアイドルとして東京で作られた AKB48 というグループが高い人気を博しており、同様なグループが国内 5 都市および国外の都市にも展開されている。

また、「ボーカロイド」という日本企業が 2004 年に開発した、歌声をコンピュータ上で人工的に合成する歌唱合成システムをベースに、別の各企業が製品化して複数のソフトウェアとして販売されている。2007 年にこれを利用した製品「初音ミク」が日本の企業から発売されると、音楽制作ソフトウェアとしては異例のヒット商品となった。バーチャルなキャラクターを設定し、ユーザーによる創作活動を刺激してユーザー自身がコンテンツを制作し、メディアの中で流通することとなり、世界中にファンを増やしている。

2）クラシック音楽

日本におけるクラシック音楽の源流は明治時代に遡る。当初は、原歌の旋律に日本語訳詞を乗せた、翻訳唱歌の域を出なかったが、1879 年に国の音楽専門教育機関（1887 年に東京音楽学校と命名。現・東京芸術大学の前身）が設立されて以降、主に学校教育の場を通じて根付くようになり、多くの英才を輩出してきた。

その先駆的存在でドイツにも留学した作曲家・瀧廉太郎は、その短い生涯で「荒城の月」「箱根八里」「花」「お正月」など現代も多くの日本人に親しまれる数々の名曲を残した。

その後、ラジオやレコードの普及により、学校における音楽だけでなく、古典派を中心としたオーケストラによる西洋音楽の愛好家が増加した。

日本のプロのオーケストラの数は現在 36 あり、公演数は約 3,900 回で、総入場者数は 423 万人となっている（2015 年）。また海外からも本場ヨーロッパを中心に毎年何十ものオーケストラが来日し、全国で 150

the influence of foreign musicians of the time (like Elvis Presley and the Beatles). These genres, collectively called J-pop music, have also won a considerable following outside Japan, particularly in East Asian countries. A girls' group named AKB48 (pronounced a．k．b forty-eight) that was formed in Tokyo on the concept of "idols whose fans can easily meet" has achieved exceptional popularity. The success of AKB48 has prompted the creation of similar groups both in five cities in Japan and overseas.

Based on a singing synthesis system that artificially synthesizes singing voices on a computer, Vocaloids, developed by a Japanese company in 2004, are commercially produced by other companies and sold as multiple sets of software. When in 2007 a Japanese company released "Hatsune Miku," a product utilizing the Vocaloid technology, it became a hit, which was unusual for music production software. Users can create contents by themselves by setting virtual characters and stimulating creative activities. The results are circulated in the media, increasing the number of fans around the world.

2) Classical Music

To find the roots of classical music in Japan we must look back to the Meiji era. At that time, lyrics from overseas songs were translated into Japanese and put to the melody of the original song, but these translated songs never became popular in their own right. Then in 1879, a national institute of music education (named the Tokyo Music School in 1887, which is the predecessor of today's Tokyo University of the Arts) was established. Thereafter, classical music started to take root, primarily through education in school, and many great talents have since been produced.

One of Japan's pioneers in this area was the composer Taki Rentaro, who studied abroad in Germany. During his short life, he left us many famous pieces that are still recognized by many Japanese today, such as *Kojo no Tsuki* (The Moon Over a Ruined Castle), *Hakone Hachiri* (The Eight-*Ri* Hakone Mountain Trail), *Hana* (Cherry Blossoms), and *Oshogatsu* (New Year's Day is Coming).

Then, with the spread of radio and records, people were able to enjoy music outside school. The number of Western music lovers grew, centering on classical music played by an orchestra.

Japan now has 36 professional orchestras which have given some 3,900 public performances to audiences totaling 4.23 million people (2015). Numerous orchestras from overseas, particularly from Europe, the birthplace of classical music, come to Japan each year. There are

以上のコンサートホールが演奏会用に供されている。

音楽家の育成については、音楽大学、音楽専攻学部が約40校あり、ピアノ教室など楽器や歌唱のレッスンを提供する場も全国各地に多数存在する。海外で活躍する日本人演奏家、歌手、指揮者も多い。

エリザベート王妃国際コンクール、ショパン国際ピアノコンクール、チャイコフスキー国際コンクールなどの世界三大音楽コンクールにおいてこれまでに、堀米ゆず子、戸田弥生、諏訪内晶子、佐藤美枝子、上原彩子、神尾真由子が優勝し、日本人の音楽家が国際的にも認められようになった。

最近では2018年にエリザベート王妃国際コンクールのバイオリン部門で、成田達輝が2位になったほか、作曲部門では酒井健治がグランプリを受賞した。
一方、外国の一流歌劇団が日本でオペラを上演することが増え、オペラ専用の新国立劇場が完成し、日本国内でもオペラを愛好する人が近年めざましく増えてきた。日本人のみによるオペラも上演される。

p）日本映画（邦画とも呼ぶ）

第二次世界大戦後、日本映画は、国際的に高い評価を受けるようになった。そのきっかけとなったのは、1951年に黒沢明の『羅生門』が、ベネチア国際映画祭で最高賞の金獅子賞を獲得したことである。

（注）世界三大映画祭：カンヌ、ベネチア、ベルリン国際映画祭

その後日本映画は、各地の国際映画祭で多くの賞を得ているが、そのいくつかを紹介すると、衣笠貞之助の『地獄門』が、1954年のカンヌ国際映画祭で当時最高賞のグランプリを受賞するとともに、ニューヨーク映画批評家賞で外国映画賞首位に輝いている。1958年には稲垣浩の『無法松の一生』がベネチア国際映画祭で金獅子賞を獲得し、1961年には新藤兼人の『裸の島』がモスクワ国際映画祭のグランプリを獲得、また1963年には今井正の『武士道残酷物語』がベルリン国際映画祭で最高賞の金熊賞を獲得した。

also more than 150 concert halls nationwide that are suitable for classical performances.

For training musicians, there are more than 40 music universities and schools with music departments, and there are many places all over the country where one can receive instruction in musical instruments or in singing. There are many Japanese performers, singers, and conductors who are active overseas.

Japanese musicians have often won notable music competitions around the world, such as the Queen Elisabeth International Music Competition of Belgium, the International Frederic Chopin Piano Competition, and the International Tchaikovsky Competition. Competition winners have included Horigome Yuzuko, Toda Yayoi, Suwanai Akiko, Sato Mieko, Uehara Ayako, and Kamio Mayuko, and young Japanese musicians are starting to be recognized internationally.

In 2018, in the violin category of the Queen Elisabeth International Music Competition, Narita Tatsuki took second place and Sakai Kenji won the Grand Prix in the composition category.

World-class opera troupes are coming to perform in Japan in increasing numbers. With the completion of the New National Theatre, Tokyo, which was designed especially for opera, the number of opera lovers in Japan has also been increasing steeply in recent years. Some operas have even been performed by an entirely Japanese cast.

p) Japanese Films

Japanese films first received international critical acclaim in 1951, when *Rashomon*, directed by Kurosawa Akira, was awarded the Golden Lion, the highest award, at the Venice International Film Festival. In the following years Japanese films received many awards at international film festivals around the world.

Note: The major film festivals are the Cannes Film Festival, the Venice Film Festival, and the Berlin International Film Festival.

Some of the most famous of these films are Kinugasa Teinosuke's *Gate of Hell*—which in 1954 received the Grand Prix, the highest award at that time, at the Cannes International Film Festival and also won the New York Film Critics Circle Awards for best foreign film of the year; Inagaki Hiroshi's *Wild Matsu the Rickshaw Man*, the 1958 Golden Lion winner at the Venice International Film Festival; Shindo Kaneto's *Naked Island*, the 1961 Grand Prix winner at the Moscow International Film Festival; Imai Tadashi's *Bushido, Samurai Saga*, the 1963 Golden Bear, the highest award, winner at the Berlin International Film Festival.

黒沢明の『七人の侍』は1954年にベネチア国際映画祭で銀獅子賞を、『隠し砦の三悪人』は1959年にベルリン国際映画祭で銀熊賞を、『影武者』は1980年にカンヌ国際映画祭で最高賞のパルムドールを受賞している。さらに1982年、ベネチア国際映画祭50周年記念行事で歴代グランプリ作品中最高の作品「獅子の中の獅子」栄誉金獅子賞（Career Golden Lion）に『羅生門』が選ばれた。
　またカンヌ国際映画祭では、今村昌平が1983年に『楢山節考』で、1997年に『うなぎ』で二度のパルムドールを受賞した。同年の1997年、ベネチア国際映画祭で北野武の『HANA-BI』が金獅子賞を受賞した。
　さらに、宮崎駿の『千と千尋の神隠し』は、2002年ベルリン国際映画祭で金熊賞を受賞した。

　2009年に滝田洋二郎の『おくりびと』がアメリカのアカデミー賞・外国語映画賞に輝いた。遺体を棺におさめる納棺師の仕事が描かれ、生と死、家族の絆（きずな）という普遍的なテーマを、日本文化の美を通して描いたことが高く評価された。

　2018年のカンヌ国際映画祭で是枝裕和の『万引き家族』が最高賞のパルムドールを受賞した。日本作品の最高賞受賞は1997年の『うなぎ』以来21年ぶりの受賞となった。東京の下町を舞台に、生きていくために祖母の年金と万引きなどの犯罪を重ね食いつなぐ家族の姿を通し、真の家族とは、人間の絆とは何かを描きつつ、「格差社会」のひずみを浮き彫りにしている。

　一方、日本の特撮（特殊撮影）映画も1950年代以降に円谷英二が創始し日本独自の映像技術として、『ゴジラ』シリーズなど特撮作品と呼ばれる映画や『ウルトラマン』シリーズなどのテレビ番組が大きなジャンルを形成するほど発展し、その後のSF映画・怪獣映画・特撮テレビシリーズといった日本の特撮の礎を築いた。1990年代以降になると、コンピュータグラフィックス（CG）による、デジタル技術を活用したSFXが普及し始め、現在、ほぼ全ての商業映画において映像素材に手が加えられており、こうした技術を前面に出した呼称で作品を売ることは少なくなっている。

Kurosawa Akira's *Seven Samurai* was the Silver Bear winner at the Venice Film Festival of 1954, his *Hidden Fortress* was the Silver Bear winner at the Berlin festival of 1959; and his *Kagemusha*, won the Golden Palm, the highest award, at the 1980 Cannes festival. At the 50th year commemorative Venice International Film Festival held in 1982, *Rashomon* was awarded the Career Golden Lion, the "Lion of Lions," as the best film of previous Golden Lion winners.

At the Canners Festival, Imamura Shohei's *The Ballad of Narayama* won the Golden Palm in 1983 and his *The Eel* won the same prize in 1997. Also in 1997, Kitano Takeshi was awarded the Venice Festival's Golden Lion for *Hana-bi*.

Sen to Chihiro no Kamikakushi (Spirited Away), directed by Miyazaki Hayao, won the Golden Bear at the 2002 Berlin International Film Festival.

At the 81st Academy Awards in 2009, *Departures*, directed by Takita Yojiro, won the award for Best Foreign Language Film. The film depicted the work of an encoffinment apprentice, the task of placing a corpse in a coffin. It was widely praised for depicting the universal themes of life and death, and family bonds, through the grace and beauty of the Japanese culture.

At the 2018 Cannes Film Festival, "*Shoplifters*" by Kore-eda Hirokazu won the highest award, the Palme d'Or. The last time a Japanese film won the highest award was 21 years ago, in 1997, for "*The Eel*." The setting for Shoplifters is Shitamachi (formerly a lower-class part of Tokyo), and through the depiction of the family who get by the grandmother's pension and committing crimes such as shoplifting in order to eat, showing what being a true family means, and the meaning of human ties, while bringing the strains of socio-economic polarization into stark relief.

Japanese special effects movies started to be made in the 1950s by Tsuburaya Eiji, Examples of Japan's unique film technology included movies such as the "*Godzilla*" series, and TV programs such as the "*Ultraman*" series, creating a major genre that laid the foundation for the science fiction and monster movies and special effects TV series that came later. Starting in the 1990s, special effects utilizing digital technology based on computer graphics began to spread, and today are applied to video footage of virtually all commercial movies. Emphasizing these technologies out front to sell a film is not done much now.

q) **日本のマンガ**

今日の日本で見られるマンガが生まれたのは、明治時代（1800年代後半）で、新聞マンガが最初である。風刺絵に近いマンガから始まり、現在でもほとんどの日刊新聞に掲載されている4コママンガに発展した。

ストーリー性を重視したマンガも第二次世界大戦前に生まれ、主として少年向きの人気キャラクターが活躍するマンガが呼び物になった。この分野のマンガで、第二次世界大戦後もっとも広く国民に親しまれているのは、長谷川町子の『サザエさん』である。

戦後のマンガブームの先駆者は、手塚治虫である。彼は映画的手法を初めて日本のマンガに導入した。マンガの読み手は、はじめは主として子供であったが、1960年代になると「劇画」が生まれ、そのリアルな絵と社会的なテーマによって、大学生を中心に大人の読者を増やして行った。その後も多くのマンガ家が多彩な表現に挑戦し、娯楽性をもったものだけではなく、芸術的・文学的価値をもつ作品が生み出された。これらの中には翻訳され、海外で楽しまれているものも多い。特にヨーロッパではイギリス、フランス、イタリアなど、アジアでは韓国、中国、香港、台湾、タイで広く読まれている。また、アメリカのアニメーション『ライオン・キング』は手塚治虫の『ジャングル大帝』がもとになっているといわれ、その他『ターミネーター2』、『ロボコップ3』など日本のマンガはハリウッドのエンタテイメントのアイディアの種を与えている。

長年愛されているマンガとしては『サザエさん』、『鉄腕アトム』や『ドラえもん』が特に著名であり、近年では『ONE PIECE』が爆発的人気となっている。ほかにも『名探偵コナン』、『ゴルゴ13』、『NARUTO』や『HUNTER × HUNTER』なども人気を集めている。

2016年のマンガ市場の規模はマンガ単行本の売上が前年比7.4％減の1,947億円、マンガ雑誌の売上が12.9％減の1,016億円と引き続き縮小傾向にある。近年では、スマートフォンを中心としたデジタルマンガ市場が急激に伸長し27.5％増の1,491億円となった。紙の落ち込みをデジタルの成長で補ったかたちで、市場の縮小というよりも市場の変化と言える。

q) Japanese Comics (manga)

Cartoons and comic strips of the kind seen in Japan today got their start in the newspapers of the Meiji Era (late 1800s). Began with a taste of caricature-like cartoons, they evolved into the four-frame comic strips that can be seen in almost every daily newspaper today.

Comics with a story line appeared before the Second World War and in most cases featured the escapades of characters that appealed to boys. The most popular of the story comics in the postwar years was *Sazae-san*, created by Hasegawa Machiko and loved by readers of all ages.

The postwar comic book boom was pioneered by Tezuka Osamu, the first cartoonist to apply motion picture techniques to Japanese comics. With the advent in the 1960s of a style (the *gekiga* style) that used realistic pictures to tell stories dealing with topics of social import, comic book readership expanded beyond boys, the main readers up to then, to college students and other adults. Once adults had been brought into the fold of comic book aficionados, numerous other cartoonists began experimenting with a wide range of cartooning genres and techniques, creating not only comics that entertained but also works with artistic and literary value. Many of these have been made available in translation for the enjoyment of readers in other countries. In Europe, readership is largest in the UK (United Kingdom), France, and Italy, while in Asia it is largest in South Korea, China, Hong Kong, Taiwan, and Thailand. Japanese comics have also sown seeds in Hollywood. Examples include the animated movie *The Lion King* (which shows influence from Tezuka Osamu's comic book *Kimba the White Lion*), *Terminator 2*, and *RoboCop 3*.

Sazae-san, *Astro Boy* and *Doraemon* are particularly famous as long-running and much loved comics. The popularity of the *manga* series *ONE PIECE* has skyrocketed in recent years. Other comics that are rapidly attracting fans include *Detective Conan* (Cased Closed), *Golgo 13*, *NARUTO* and *HUNTER × HUNTER*.

Annual sales of manga books in 2016 amounted about 194.7 billion yen, 7.4% less than the previous year, and sales of manga magazines declined 12.9%, to 101.6 billion, so the market continues to shrink. However, rapid growth of digital manga market has drawn attention in recent years, centering on smartphones, which registered a rapid growth of 27.5%, to 149.1 billion yen. The drop in sales of paper product is being made up for by the growth of digital, so the market can be better described as changing rather than shrinking.

r) メディアコンテンツ

　メディアコンテンツを知的財産立国の一つの柱とする日本では、現在世界的に優位に立っているアニメ・ゲームソフト・映画などを活用したビジネスを飛躍的に発展・拡大させることに関心が高まっている。コンテンツ産業は世界的にも最も高い成長率が期待され、新たな成長主導産業ともなりうると見られている。

　メディアコンテンツはその国の文化的土壌を背景として育まれたもので、日本のコンテンツの基盤には、日本の文化が連綿と流れており、より良いコンテンツを世界に問うことは、世界に日本の文化を発信すること、つまりソフトパワーを発揮することとなる。即ち、日本発コンテンツの普及により、海外の人たちの間で日本および日本文化への関心が高まり、それによって相互交流や相互理解が深まる契機になるのではとの期待も寄せられている。実際に外国人訪日客の来日の理由の一つに、日本のアニメやゲームが人気を集めていることが挙げられている。また、「東京ゲームショウ」や「東京国際アニメ祭」など日本が誇るコンテンツと関わり深いイベントを開催し毎回内外から多数の集客となっている。

1) アニメ

　マンガの静止画像に映像メディア工学の技術が結合したものがアニメである。世界最初の長編アニメであるディズニーの『白雪姫』が日本で公開されたのは1950年のことである。

　1963年、日本アニメの草分けとして手塚治虫の『鉄腕アトム』がテレビシリーズ化されたが、その成功はその後の日本アニメ界に大きな影響を与えた。1977年に松本零士の劇場用アニメ『宇宙戦艦ヤマト』が大ヒットし、それ以降、劇場用アニメも盛んにつくられるようになった。また、藤子・F・不二雄の『ドラえもん』は、時代によって変化しない子供の気持ちを代弁したアニメと言われ、主人公をキャラクターとした関連商品の売上もビジネスとなっている。

　日本のアニメは、その画面の美しさや物語性に加えて、地球エコなどのテーマ性で大人をも惹きつける魅力をもっており、世界でも広く受け入れられている。

　現在世界で放映されるアニメの6割は日本のアニメ

r) Media Content

As a country endeavoring to make intellectual property (inventions, software, and other products of the human intellect) a key driving force behind national prosperity, interest has increased among Japanese in dramatically developing and expanding businesses that capitalize on its current world-leading position in media content like animation, game software, and motion pictures. The media content industry is expected to grow faster than any other, both in Japan and worldwide, and is viewed as having the potential to become a new growth-driving industry.

Media content is nurtured against the backdrop of a country's cultural landscape. Japanese culture has been flowing non-stop through the under-layer of Japanese media content, and asking the outside world to accept such content, in effect means spreading Japanese culture to the world; that is, it means the wielding of soft power. The popularity of media content made in Japan will help to increase interest in Japan and Japanese culture abroad, leading to a deepening of mutual exchanges and understanding. One of the reasons why foreign visitors come here is that Japanese animation and games are gaining popularity. And, Japan hosts events related to content it can boast such as "Tokyo Game Show" and "Tokyo International Anime Fair," which each time have attracted large numbers of visitors from home and abroad.

1) Animation (*anime*)

Animation is a union between the still cartoon images of comics and video media engineering technology. The world's first feature length animation, Disney's *Snow White*, was first shown in Japan in 1950.

In 1963, *Astro Boy* by Tezuka Osamu, the pioneer of Japanese anime, was made into a TV series, and the success of the program had a profound effect on the Japanese anime world. In 1977 Matsumoto Leiji's *Space Battleship Yamato* was a big hit at the box office, and triggered a boom in made-for-cinema anime. *Doraemon* by Fujiko F. Fujio, is said to represent the universal feelings of children, and with an animated character in the starring role, the related merchandising is big business.

As well as featuring beautiful art and interesting stories, Japanese anime also addresses topics that interest adults, such as the global environment. Because of this, it is well accepted around the world.

Today, 60% of the anime shown around the world comes from Japan.

である。人気アニメとしては、『ルパンⅢ世』、『機動戦士ガンダム』、『キャプテン翼』、『ちびまる子ちゃん』、『美少女戦士セーラームーン』、『ドラえもん』、『ONE PIECE』、『ドラゴンボールZ』、『ポケットモンスター』、『クレヨンしんちゃん』、『名探偵コナン』などが著名である。

また長編アニメ映画も個性的で見ごたえある作品が並び、劇場用作品ならではの骨太なストーリーや、力の入った作画など見所も満載で、日本のみならず世界中で大きな話題を呼んでいる。宮崎駿の『千と千尋の神隠し』を始めとして『もののけ姫』、『ハウルの動く城』、『崖の上のポニョ』、『風立ちぬ』や、高畑勲の『かぐや姫』などこれらのスタジオジブリ作品のほか、2016年にブームとなった新海誠の『君の名は。』など興行収入面でも大ヒットを飛ばしている。

2016年度における日本の放送コンテンツ輸出は393億5千万円で、このうちアニメの輸出額は77.1％の225億1千万円となっている。

海外において日本文化は「クールジャパン」(かっこいい日本)と呼ばれるようになり、親しみ賞賛されているが、特に欧米では日本のポップカルチャーに対してこの言葉が使われている。中でも人気なのがマンガとアニメで、これらの主人公に扮したコスプレが人気となっている。

2) ゲーム

マンガ、映画、アニメなどは鑑賞作品で、情報発信は一方向的であり、作品と鑑賞者は分離されている。しかし、メディアアートとしてのゲームは、鑑賞者がゲームに参入することができるインターラクティブ性(双方向性・相互作用性)をもつので、ゲームの参加者が自分でストーリーの筋を変化させたり、自分のキャラクターを成長させたりすることができる。

さらにインターネットによるオンラインゲームの登場により、遠隔地の未知の人々同志が競争したり、戦ったりするバーチャルリアリティー(仮想現実)の世界を体験することができる。これによってメディアアートとしてのゲームは従来になかった新次元の魅力を有するものとなった。オンラインのゲームでも専用のハードやソフトを必要とせず、汎用のWebブラウザーで遊べるゲームをWebゲームと呼び、さらにこうしたWebゲームがソーシャル・ネットワーク上で

Some famous anime include *Lupin III*, *Mobile Suit Gundam*, *Captain Tsubasa*, *Chibi Maruko-chan*, *Sailor Moon*, *Doraemon*, *ONE PIECE*, *Dragon Ball Z*, *Pocket Monsters*, *Crayon Shin-chan*, and *Detective Conan*.

Moreover, feature length animated films are also unique works well worth seeing, packed with solid stories and powerful images that theaters can show to the best effect, plus stories with great plot attracts attention in Japan and throughout the world. These include the Sutudio Ghibli works, that are Miyazaki Hayao's "*Spirited Away*" and "*Princess Mononoke,*" "*Howl's Moving Castle,*" "*Ponyo on the Cliff,*" "*Wind Standing,*" and Takahata Isao's "*Kaguya Hime.*" In addition to the Studio Ghibli works, there is "*Your Name,*" the 2016 massive box-office hit by Shinkai Makoto, and other big hits.

Exports of Japanese broadcasting content in 2016 came to 39.35 billion yen, of which animation accounted for 77.1%, or 22.51 billion yen.

Overseas, people have praised the easy accessibility of Japanese culture and coined the term "cool Japan". Europeans and Americans in particular have used the term to refer to pop culture in Japan. Cosplay is the term used to describe the popular pastime of dressing up in outfits that are made to look like those worn by the fictional main characters in manga and anime.

2) Video Games

Cartoons, motion pictures, and animated films convey information in only one direction, with no interaction between the work and the viewer. However, video games are a form of interactive media art that allows the viewer to intervene in the action by, for example, modifying the story line or molding the development of the characters.

And with the advent of online games on the Internet, strangers separated by great distances can gather in a world of virtual reality to engage one another in contests and battles of every description. For the first time, this gives these media games the allure of a new dimension. Some online games do not require special hardware or software and can be played with an ordinary web browser. These are called web games. Such games are also being made available on web-based social networks as social games.

提供されるようになり、これをソーシャルゲームと呼ぶようになった。
　ゲームソフトとしては、1985年任天堂のファミリーコンピュータ用ゲームソフトとして発売された『スーパーマリオ』は家庭用ゲームの認知度を高めるのに最も貢献したソフトであると言われている。このほか『ファイナル・ファンタジー』、『ドラゴンクエスト』、『妖怪ウォッチ』などが著名である。
　日本のゲーム市場は2009年を底に市場が急拡大して、2017年に1兆6千億円に達し、中でもスマートフォンの普及とともにオンラインゲームが急成長している。
　特に、日本のメディアゲームソフトの代表作『ポケットモンスター（ポケモン）』は大ヒットし、日本のみならず、東南アジア、アメリカその他世界各地で多くのファンを魅了した。ポケモンソフト76タイトルの1996年2月からの総売上本数は2017年11月に世界累計3億本を突破し、アニメ・映画・カードゲーム・ハードウェア（ゲーム機）および4,000件におよぶ関連商品の累計売上は2017年約6兆円（580億ドル）と見られる。
　2016年7月配信スタートした『ポケモンGO』は、アメリカの会社が開発・発売したものである。キャラクター使用権を提供されたポケモンを使って遊ぶスマートフォン（スマホ）用ゲームソフトで、街や公園などを歩きながら、ゲームや映画の世界観そのままにスマホ画面上でポケモンを収集・育成・対戦・交換できる体験型ゲームである。人工衛星の電波を使いスマホを持つ人の位置を特定する全地球測位システム（GPS）技術と、スマホのカメラで写した実風景にコンピュータ・グラフィクスによるポケモン映像を重ねる拡張現実（AR）技術を駆使している。世界200カ国で配信され爆発的な人気となり、社会現象となった。

（11）食物・飲み物

a）食生活

　日本人の食生活には、伝統的に主食と副食という考えがあって、米を主食とし、野菜や魚などを副食としてきた。肉食も相当古くから行われていたが、仏教の普及により肉

"*Super Mario Bros.*" was released as a video game for the Nintendo Family Computer in 1985, and is said to be the software that made the biggest contribution to boosting awareness of home video games. Other prominent games were "*Final Fantasy*," "*Dragon Quest*," and "*Yo-kai Watch*."

After bottoming out in 2009 the Japanese video game market rapidly expanded, reaching 1.6 trillion yen in 2017. Some of that is due to online games, which grew rapidly with the spread of smartphones.

The highly popular *Pokemon* (*Pocket Monster*) is a typical Japanese media game that has gathered a huge following not only in Japan but also in Southeast Asia, the U.S., and other regions around the globe. Total Pokemon software sales for the 76 titles from February 1996 to November 2017 amount to some 300 million units. It is estimated that the game's overall sales are in the order of six trillion yen ($58 billion) (2017) when sales of animated products, motion pictures, card games, game machines, and as many as 4,000 other related products are taken into account.

"*Pokemon GO*," distribution of which started in July 2016, was developed and released by an American company. It is a mobile game for playing on smartphones, using Pokemon with character usage rights. It is an experience game in which players walk around towns and parks and other places to collect, train, battle, and exchange Pokemons on the smartphone screen as if they are in the player's real-world location in a game or movie. It utilizes Global Positioning System (GPS) technology that determines the location of people with smartphones using satellite radio waves and Augmented Reality (AR) technology and computer graphics to superimpose Pokemon images on real-world landscapes photographed by the smartphone camera. It was distributed in 200 countries and enjoyed explosive popularity, becoming a social phenomenon.

(11) Food and Drink

a) The Japanese Diet

The daily diet in Japan has traditionally been considered as consisting of a main dish or staple, where staple is supplemented as side dish. Rice has long been the staple, and vegetables, fish and so forth are the side

食を禁忌するようになり、中世以降すたれ、明治以後復活した。

第二次世界大戦後、学校給食の影響でパン食が普及し、経済成長とともに、肉類や乳製品などの摂取も大幅に増加した。

米食には、副食として野菜や魚または肉などの煮物・揚げ物・焼き物などに、味噌汁・漬物をそえる。副食には、西洋風あるいは中華風の料理もたくさん取り入れられている。

日本の食生活では、節約、もったいないという観念が古くから定着している。たとえば、魚の利用にあたっては、「身は刺身（または焼物）に、アラ（頭部）は煮物に、骨は汁に」というならわしがある。

また、不作のときに備えるための保存食として、野菜の漬物、魚・肉の塩蔵物、乾物などが、古くから定着している。

食事をするには、一般に箸（多くの場合は木製）を用いる。朝食は簡素で、昼食も比較的軽く、夕食にもっとも重点をおく傾向が見られる。

最近は、社会構造・生活様式の変化にともないグルメ指向、外食の利用、さらにインスタント食品の普及もあり食生活は一層多様化してきている。

外食産業の市場規模は 25.4 兆円（2016 年）であり、食堂・レストランの飲食業は 13.9 兆円となっている。この中で、短時間で作れる、あるいは短時間で食べられる手軽な食品・食事を「ファストフード」と呼び、このチェーン店は日本中の盛り場や、交通量の多い道沿いに進出している。

ファストフードと呼ぶ場合は、元来アメリカ資本のフードチェーンが作り出した安価な手軽に食べられる食事というイメージがあり、ハンバーガーなどのチェーン店を指しているが、加えて日本式の牛丼や立ち食いうどん・そば、などもこの仲間とされ庶民に親しまれている。

インスタント食品は、簡単にしかも短時間であまり手間をかけないで調理できる保存性食品の総称で、昔からある粉末、乾燥、濃縮の各食品や冷凍、缶詰、レトルト食品な

dishes. Meat has been eaten in Japan since fairly early times, but with the rise of Buddhism the eating of meat became taboo, and consequently meat disappeared from the table from the Middle Ages only reappeared during the Meiji Era (from 1868).

After the Second World War bread became part of the diet, an effect of its inclusion in school meals. With the growth of the economy there was also a great upsurge in the consumption of different kinds of meat and dairy products.

A Japanese meal with rice as the staple will include vegetables and boiled, fried, or roasted fish or meat as well as *miso* (mixture of fermented beans, barley, and rice) soup and pickled vegetables. Many supplementary dishes cooked in Western or Chinese styles have now also become part of the meals in Japan.

In the preparation and eating food, the Japanese have long emphasized thrift and avoided waste. The custom is, for instance, to try to use every part of a fish—the meat for *sashimi* (sliced raw), the bony parts (head) for stew, and the bones for soup stock.

Also, preserved foods have been used since long ago to make up for shortages in lean years; preservation methods include pickling for vegetables, and salting or drying for fish and meat.

The food is generally eaten using chopsticks (nearly always made of wood). Breakfast is rather plain and simple, and lunch fairly light, with the main emphasis tending to be on the evening meal.

In recent years, changes in the social structure and lifestyles have led to more varied eating habits, with many people now seeking out gourmet foods and frequenting restaurants and further more convenience foods.

The food service industry is a 25.4 trillion yen market (as of 2016), and the cafeteria and restaurant business is a 13.9 trillion yen market. Within these industries, food and food products that can be prepared quickly and eaten quickly are labeled "fast food," and fast food franchises are popping up on busy streets and along roads with heavy traffic.

The "fast food" moniker conjures up images of American food chains (such as hamburger chains) and their cheap, easy-to-eat food, but Japanese beef-bowl restaurants and *udon* and *soba* noodle stand-bars fall into this category as well and are loved by the general public.

"Instant food" is the general term for preserved food that can be easily prepared in a short time with little effort. Powdered, dried, and concentrated food products and frozen, canned, and pouch-packed food

どである。
　中でもインスタントラーメン（即席麺）は日本が世界に誇れる大発明といっても過言でないほど普及している。1958 年に「お湯をかけて 2 分間」という味付即席麺の量産化に成功して以来改良が進められ、現在は「カップ麺」が主流である。日本では年間 56.9 億食（2017 年）生産され、また世界では 1,001 億食（2017 年）が消費され親しまれている。

b）和食（日本料理）
　　和食の特徴は、〈1〉多様で新鮮な食材とその持ち味の尊重、〈2〉栄養バランスに優れた健康的な食生活、〈3〉自然の美しさや季節の移ろいの表現、〈4〉正月などの年中行事との密接な関わりなどで、日本列島で生まれ発達した日本独特の料理である。新鮮な魚介類や野菜の持味を生かした料理が多く、ほとんどが米食と日本酒に調和するようにつくられている。材料や調理法に季節感を重んじており、食器の色・形・材質がさまざまで、盛りつけにも繊細な配慮が加えられる。これは、日本料理が舌だけでなく目で楽しむことも大切にしているからである。

　飯・汁・香の物のほか、前菜・刺身・焼き物・揚げ物・煮物・あえ物・酢の物などが加えられる。

　味は醤油・味噌・酒・酢・砂糖・塩などで調味するが、材料そのものの持味を生かすようにし、あまりゴテゴテした濃厚な味つけをしない。汁・煮物・揚げ物のつけ汁などには、特にうま味を出すため鰹節・椎茸・昆布その他を用いる。「ダシがきいていない」という味覚は塩味や酸味が足りないのとは違う感覚であることを経験的に知っていたからである。また「隠し味」と称して、ある種の調味料（たとえば塩・酒）を少量加えることにより、材料の持ち味のある要素（たとえば甘味）を引き立たせる用法もある。砂糖を用いるようになったのは近代以後であり、現代においても高級な日本料理では砂糖を多く使用しない。

that fall into this category have existed for some time.

Instant *ramen* (noodles in broth with vegetables and meat) can, judging from its universal popularity, safely be declared as one of the great inventions that Japan can take pride in having offered the world. The first mass-produced instant ramen, which could be prepared in two minutes by just adding boiling water, appeared in 1958 and was an immediate success. It exists today primarily as "cup ramen." As of 2017, Japan was producing 5.69 billion units of instant ramen per year, against global consumption of 100.1 billion units (2017), which only serves to underscore its popularity.

b) Japanese Cuisine

Japanese cuisine is unique to the Japanese archipelago where it originated and developed over the centuries. It is characterized by: <1> diverse fresh ingredients prepared with reverence for their natural flavors, <2> accent on a healthy diet excellent in nutritional balance, <3> expression of natural beauty and the changing seasons, and <4> close relationship with New Year's festivities and other events throughout the year. The majority of Japanese dishes are contrived to accent the natural flavors of fresh fish, shellfish, and vegetables, and almost all are prepared so as to go well with rice and *sake*. The season of the year is the prime factor in the selection of food and the choice of the manner in which to prepare them. As Japanese cuisine is supposed to delight the eyes as much as the palate, utmost care is used in arranging the foods on dishes of various colors, shapes, and ingredients.

In addition to rice, soup, and pickles, there are hors d'œuvres, *sashimi* (slices of raw fish), grilled fish, deep fried and stewed foods, vegetables and fish in various dressings, and vinegared dishes.

In seasoning, special efforts are made to enhance the natural flavor of the food. Typical seasonings are soy sauce, *miso*, sake, vinegar, sugar and salt, but in no case is the seasoning so heavy as to make the dish strong or cloying. In making broths for soups and boiled foods and sauces for fried foods, stocks prepared from such ingredients as dried bonito, *shiitake* mushrooms, and tangle (an edible seaweed) are used to bring out flavor. This way of enhancing flavor developed as the Japanese learned from experience that "broth doesn't have enough taste" expresses a different taste from "too little salt" or "not tart enough." Also, there is another technique, called "hidden seasoning," of adding certain kinds of seasoning (such as salt and sake) to enhance a certain element (such as sweetness) of the natural flavor of the food. For instance, a small amount of salt is added as a "hidden seasoning"

日本の代表的な調味料である醤油は、大豆と麹を用いて製造する発酵食品である。その起源は、13世紀ころ南宋の金山寺で作られていた金山寺味噌とされている。江戸時代のはじめに、大消費人口の需要に応えるために江戸周辺で1年で作れる「濃いくち醤油」が開発された。

　醤油は日本を代表する味として国際的評価を得ている。日本食が健康食として世界各国でブームとなるにつれ、日本の醤油は世界100カ国以上に輸出され、アメリカをはじめとしていくつか海外生産拠点もある。醤油の原型とされる味噌も日本の発酵食品として、味噌汁など日本人の食生活に欠かせないものとなっている。

　和食は「日本人の伝統的な食文化」として、ユネスコ無形文化遺産に2013年12月登録された。
　外国人に好まれる日本料理として、鮨（すし）・天ぷら・すき焼などがある。
　すしは代表的な日本固有の食物となっている。現在では世界各国ですしの愛好者が急増している。世界におよそ2万店あると推定されている日本食レストランでも人気第一のメニューである。にぎりずし（江戸前）は、一握りの酢飯の塊の上に、香辛料であるワサビを利かせた鮮度のよい生の魚介類の切身をのせただけのものであり、少量の醤油をつけて食する。職人の腕を客の前で見せる「粋」な感覚が特徴で、全国に普及している。江戸前ずしのほか、巻きずし、押しずし、ちらしずし、などがある。生の魚介類すなわち刺身を食べる日本の習慣は、広く外国にも知られるようになり、多くの国々で「刺身愛好者」も増えている。握られたすしが客の間を機械仕掛けで回る「回転ずし」が値段の安いこともあり、急激に増加している。

　天ぷらは魚介類・野菜類に水でといた小麦粉の衣をつけて油で揚げた料理である。
　すき焼は日本の伝統的な料理ではないが、19世紀後半以後普及したもので、牛肉を薄く切ったものを野菜などと

to bring out the natural sweetness of a dish. Use of refined sugar goes back only about one hundred years, and even today, sugar is used but sparingly in the best Japanese cooking.

The seasoning most associated with Japan is soy sauce, which is a fermented product made from soy beans and malted rice. Soy sauce is said to have originated in about the thirteenth century from the *kinzanji-miso* made at the Jingshan Temple in China during the Southern Song Dynasty. To meet the demand from the growing number of consumers in the early Edo period, a "strong flavored soy sauce" that could be produced within a year was developed in the Edo area.

The taste of soy sauce is recognized internationally as one that typifies the taste of Japanese food. Because Japanese food has become renowned to the world for being good for health, Japanese soy sauce has been exported to over 100 countries, and overseas production has been undertaken in countries such as the U.S. Miso, the precursor for soy sauce, is also a fermented Japanese food product. It is a staple of the Japanese diet and features in foods such as miso soup.

Washoku (traditional Japanese cuisine) was added to UNESCO's intangible cultural heritage list in December 2013.

The types of Japanese cuisine that are most popular among non-Japanese include *sushi*, *tempura*, and *sukiyaki*.

Sushi has become the most recognized Japanese food, and the number of sushi-lovers around the world is growing quickly. At estimated 20,000 Japanese restaurants around the world, sushi is a popular menu item. Sushi, which is also known as *nigiri-zushi* or *edo-mae-zushi*, consists of a handful of sushi rice (rice with vinegar added) formed into a lump, with a dab of *wasabi* (Japanese horseradish) paste added for flavoring, and topped with a slice of very fresh raw fish. It is eaten with a dash of soy sauce. Sushi is typically made in front of the customer, so that the sushi chef can show off his style, and this has helped to popularize it internationally. Other types of sushi (as distinct from edo-mae-zushi) include *maki-zushi*, *oshi-zushi*, and *chirashi-zushi*. The Japanese custom of eating raw fish—known as sashimi—is renowned worldwide, and there are increasing numbers of sashimi-lovers in countries throughout the world. The popularity of *kaiten-zushi*—low-priced sushi that is presented to the customers on a circulating conveyor belt—has exploded.

Tempura is a fritter-like dish of fish, shellfish, and vegetables dipped in a flour-and-water batter and deep-fried in vegetable oil.

Although not a traditional Japanese dish, sukiyaki has been quite popular from about the late nineteenth century. Slices of beef are braised

一緒に煮て、主として醤油と砂糖で味をつける。

うなぎを日本人が食べ始めた歴史は古代からと言われている。蒲焼（かばやき）という言葉は14世紀頃から登場し、現在の蒲焼の誕生には、醤油、味醂（みりん）、酒、砂糖などの調味料の普及とともに完成された。食用のうなぎの多くは養殖であるが、養殖用の稚魚である天然のシラスウナギの減少が危惧されている。

近年、ラーメンの人気が世界中に広がっている。伝統的な和食とは異なり、1958年にインスタントラーメンが発明されて以来ラーメンは日々の食生活の一部となった。日本と同様に、世界の都市に「こだわりの専門店」が登場して人気を呼んでいる。時間をかけて煮込んだスープと弾力のある麺に野菜、肉、卵などの材料から成り、日本では各都市ごとにそれぞれ異なる特徴のあるラーメンがあり、テレビや雑誌の題材になるほど、庶民に受け入れられている。

また、ラーメンにつづいて「日本のカレー」も世界中に広がりを見せている。
そのほか訪日外国人に人気のある日本の何処にでもあるメニューとして、「焼き鳥」、「餃子」、「お好み焼き」、「とんかつ」、「うどん・そば」、「おでん」などがある。
日本人が祝い事のときに食べる料理に、赤飯と鯛の尾頭付がある。赤飯はもち米に小豆を入れて蒸したもので、小豆の色が米について赤くなる。赤は火の色、太陽の色を表し、昔から縁起の良い色とされている。

鯛は日本語で「めでたい」という言葉と語呂が合い、色も赤く縁起の良い魚とされている。祝の席には、頭から尻尾まで完全な形のまま焼かれた鯛が出される。これには、形の完全さによって人を祝福するという意味がある。

c）酒
　　日本では、日本酒（アルコール含有量15～16％）をはじめ、世界各地の酒も飲まれている。

together with vegetables in a small amount of liquid seasoned mainly with soy sauce and sugar.

The eating of eels by Japanese is believed to date back to ancient times. The most popular eel dish today is *kabayaki*. The word itself appeared around the 14th century, but the cooking method evolved over the years and kabayaki now refers to eel flavored with soy sauce, *mirin* (sweet cooking sake), sake, and other ingredients, that is grilled over charcoal. Most eels eaten in Japan are farmed from natural baby eels called glass eels. So a dramatic decline in glass eel populations in recent years is a major concern.

Ramen (noodles in broth) continues to become increasingly popular worldwide. Although not a traditional Japanese dish, Japanese have come to enjoy it regularly, particularly since the advent of instant ramen in 1958. Cities both in Japan and around the world have seen the appearance of ramen restaurants that are attracting ramen connoisseurs on the claim of being "specialists who never compromise." The best ramen is made with broth prepared by hours of slow simmering, chewy noodles, and other selected ingredients, such as vegetables, meat, and egg. Nearly every town in Japan has its own special style of ramen, and these are frequently introduced on TV and in magazines as topics with wide popular appeal.

Other than ramen, Japanese *kare* (rice with curry sauce) is also beginning to spread internationally.

Other menu items popular among foreign visitors to Japan are *yakitori*, *gyoza* (Chinese dumplings), *okonomiyaki*, *tonkatsu*, *udon*, *soba*, and *oden*.

The Japanese celebrate particularly happy occasions with red rice (*sekihan*) and sea bream (*tai*) prepared with head and tail intact. Sekihan is made by steaming glutinous rice (an especially sticky variety) together with red beans which turn the rice red. The Japanese have long considered red to be a lucky color because of its association with the color of fire and the sun.

Tai (sea bream) is believed to be a fish that brings good luck, because its name sounds like "*medetai*" (happy) and its color is lucky red. On festive occasions the tai is served broiled completely whole from head to tail. The wish for good luck is thought to be better conveyed through the full and perfect shape.

c) Sake and Other Alcoholic Drinks

Not only *sake* (which has an alcoholic content of 15 to 16%) but alcohols from all over the world are popular in Japan.

日本酒は米からつくられる醸造酒である。全国各地でつくられるが、良い水の出るところ、あるいは良い米のできるところに、有名な酒の産地がある。日本酒の飲み方は、常温、冷して、温めてとそれぞれの味わい方で楽しめる。最近では外国人の日本酒の愛好者が増え、レシピに合わせてお酒選びをして楽しむことも普通に見られるようになった。

　焼酎（しょうちゅう）も広く飲まれている。焼酎は日本伝統の蒸留酒である。米、いも、麦などから作った醸造酒をさらに蒸留して作るので、アルコール分は日本酒より多く（25〜40％）、それぞれの原料の味と香りが楽しめる。泡盛は沖縄特産の焼酎である。その独特の香りと高いアルコール濃度（40〜50％）の愛好者も多い。

　また、ビールもよく飲まれるが、ほとんど国産である。ウィスキーやワイン（ぶどう酒）もかなり飲まれており、これらは国産のほか輸入されるものも多い。ほかにブランデー・ウォッカ・ジンなども輸入されている。

　日本の酒類の消費量は、年間約841万キロリットルである。生産量は約877万キロリットルで、そのうちビール（発泡酒を含む）が39％、チューハイや新ジャンル飲料を含むリキュールが25％、日本酒は6％、焼酎は10％を占めている（2016年度）。

　日本では、勤務時間後、会社の上司や同僚あるいはビジネスの相手と酒をくみかわしながら、本音で話し合ったり、人間関係を深めたりする習慣がある。

d）飲み物

　日本人のもっともポピュラーな飲み物は緑茶である。使用する原料の葉の品質によって、大まかに玉露・煎茶・ほうじ茶に分けられる。

　玉露はあまり高温でない湯を用い、煎茶は高温の湯を少しさまして用い、ほうじ茶は高温の湯を用いる。このほかに、玉露級の良質の茶を粉状にして湯を注いで、攪拌して飲む抹茶がある。緑茶には砂糖やミルクを入れない。

　コーヒーも今日、日本人に広く愛好されている。コーヒー好きの人は、好きな豆を買って自宅で調製して飲む。喫茶店や人気カフェチェーン店やコンビニでもコーヒーは

Sake is a fermented beverage obtained from rice. Although it can be made anywhere in Japan, famous sakes are produced in regions that have a supply of good water, or good quality rice. Sake is often drunk chilled but is also enjoyed warm. Recently the number of foreign sake enthusiasts has been growing and it has become common to see sake being chosen to match the dishes.

Another alcoholic drink with a long tradition that is popular in Japan is *shochu*. Shochu is made of spirits distilled from fermented rice, potatoes, wheat or the like and retains some of the original flavor. Being distilled, it contains more alcohol than sake (25 to 40%). *Awamori*, a kind of shochu made in Okinawa, is enjoyed by many for its very distinctive flavor and high alcohol content (40 to 50%).

Beer, most of which is domestically produced, is very popular.

Whisky and wine, some of which is domestically produced and some of which is imported, are also quite popular in Japan. Other imported alcohols include brandy, vodka, and gin.

Japan consumes 8.41 million kiloliters and produces 8.77 million kiloliters of alcoholic beverages a year. Of the amount consumed, 39% is beer (including *happoshu*, a low-malt beverage resembling beer), 25% is Chuhai and liqueurs including new-genre drinks, 6% is sake, and 10% is shochu. (Fiscal 2016 figures)

Many Japanese workers enjoy going out after work for a few drinks with their colleagues, superiors, or subordinates from the same company or with business associates from other companies. These occasions are used for frank exchanges of opinion and make deeper personal relationships.

d) Beverages

The most popular beverage of the Japanese people is green tea. Green tea is roughly graded into three categories depending on the quality of the leaf: refined, medium, and coarse.

Highest-quality tea (*gyokuro*) is brewed with lukewarm water, whereas ordinary tea (*sencha*) is brewed with once-boiled water that has been allowed to cool slightly, and coarse tea (hojicha) with boiling water. In addition, there is a tea called *matcha* which is made by powdering quality gyokuro. Hot water is added to the tea powder and the tea is drunk after stirring. No milk or sugar is used with green tea.

Coffee is also very popular nowadays. Those who are especially fond of coffee buy their favorite variety of coffee beans and grind and brew their own coffee at home. Coffee is also widely drunk in coffee shops,

よく飲まれる。一般の家庭でコーヒーを飲む習慣は、インスタントコーヒーが出現して以来著しく普及した。日本のコーヒー飲料状況として、一人1週間あたり約11杯が飲まれており、うち約7杯が家庭で飲まれている（2016年）。紅茶も広く普及し、各種の銘柄が好まれている。

その他の飲料としては、1980年代前半まではコーラがよく飲まれた。最近では缶コーヒーの売上が急上昇し、また各種のスポーツドリンク・ジュース・ウーロン茶・緑茶など、非常に多様な飲みものが飲まれている。

ペットボトルと温度調整がついた自動販売機の登場により、消費量の減少が見られた緑茶ならびにミネラルウォーター・天然水の販売量も急増している。

e) タバコ

日本はタバコ消費量で、中国、アメリカ、ロシアに次ぐ世界第4位であり、成人男子の27.8％、女子の8.7％がタバコを吸っている（2018年）。健康志向の高まりから、喫煙者の比率は年々低下の傾向が続いている。

また、非喫煙者の嫌煙権の主張が強くなり、他の多くの国と同じように、職場、公共の施設や交通機関、レストランなどでは禁煙が浸透している。

現在、日本で販売されているタバコは、外国産を含め100種以上がある。銘柄別ではセブンスターやメビウスなどが人気を保っていたが、喫煙者の健康志向の高まりから、より低タール、低ニコチンのメビウスワンやケントワンなどのほうが人気がある。

しかし、最近では自分の意思とは関係なく他人のタバコの煙を吸い込んでしまう受動喫煙や嫌煙の意識が高まり、喫煙所を探す手間がかかることもあり、比較的に周りを気にせず吸える電子タバコや加熱式などの無煙タバコを使う人も多い。

日本では、国産タバコは1985年に公社から民営化された日本たばこ産業（JT）によって販売されている。現在タバコの売値のおよそ60％超が税金である。

popular café chain stores, and convenience stores. Since the appearance of instant coffee there has been a great increase in the number of people who drinks at home. The per capita consumption of coffee is approximately eleven cups per week, with around seven of these cups drunk at home (2016). Black tea is also quite popular, and there is a demand for all the famous types.

Among other beverages, cola rapidly increased popularity shortly after the Second World War to the early 1980s. Recently, canned coffee drink sales have risen sharply, and a very wide variety of other beverages sold in cans or plastic bottles—isotonic drinks, pop, oolong tea, etc.—are being drunk in large quantities.

While consumption of green tea was once on the decline, the advent of PET bottles and temperature-adjustable automatic vending machines have led to a rapid increase in sales of green tea as well as of mineral and spring water.

e) Tobacco

Japan is the world's fourth largest consumer of tobacco, behind China, America, and Russia. 27.8% of adult males and 8.7% of females smoke (2018 figures). Increasing concern about the health effects of smoking has led to a steady decline in the overall percentage of smokers over the years.

At the same time, non-smokers have become more assertive of their right to smoke-free air, and, as in many other countries, the banning of smoking in workplaces, public facilities, mass transit, and restaurants are becoming the norm.

There are more than 100 brands of cigarettes, including imported brands. Seven Stars and Mild Seven (rebranded Mevius in 2013) were long among the most popular, but health consciousness among smokers has made low-tar, low-nicotine brands like Mevius 1 and Kent 1 more popular.

Recently, however, the awareness of passive smoking, the inhaling of other person's cigarette smoke regardless of their own intention, has increased, causing people to search for smoking spots. More people are now using electronic cigarettes or heated tobacco products that are smokeless, making them relatively easier to use without worrying about smoke bothering nearby people.

All tobacco products are sold through Japan Tobacco Inc. (JT), which was formed by the privatization of a public corporation in 1985. Currently, more than 60% of the price of tobacco products is tax.

f）自動販売機の普及

2016年末の日本全国の自動販売機の設置台数は約494万台で、内飲料系が247万台、食品自販機が7万台、たばこ自販機が19万台などで、人口や国土面積を勘案した普及率では、世界一と言える。またこれらの自動販売機の年間自販金額で見ると飲料系が2兆300億円、食品自販機が541億円、たばこ自販機が2,094億円となっている。

日本で自動販売機が普及した要因に、海外だとすぐに破壊されてしまう恐れがあるのに対して治安の問題が少なく、これが最も大きな原因だといわれている。また60種類以上のいろいろな自動販売機があり、タバコやアルコール類も自動販売機で購入可能である。さまざまな工夫が施されたものが開発されており、たとえば、外国人観光客も使えるように、商品情報や使用方法を4カ国語で表示するものや、電力消費ピーク時の使用電力を抑える省エネ対応型も登場している。

(12) 日本人について

a）国民性

日本人の国民性の特徴として多くの人が指摘しているもののうち、共通性のあるものを、いくつか取り上げてみよう。

〈1〉 日本人の国民性の軸となる思想は「和」であり、日本人は何人か集まると、たとえば、年齢とか社会的地位など何らかの基準によりお互いの序列が意識され、それにより礼儀正しく行動様式も影響を受ける。また日本語は敬語が非常に発達しているが、これらは日本人が上下関係を重視することによるものである。

〈2〉 多くの外国人は自分の意思や意見を直接相手にぶつけて強く自己主張するのに対し、日本人は「他人に迷惑をかけてはいけない」という心が基本にあり、相手の気持ちや立場を察して、それも考慮に入れて発言したり行動したりする傾向が強い。さらに、日本人にはイエス・ノーをはっきり表明しない傾向がある。日本人がこのような行動をとり、また相手に

f) Proliferation of Automatic Vending Machines

The number of automatic vending machines installed throughout Japan as of the end of 2016 was 4.94 million. Of these, 2.47 million were drink related, 0.07 million were food vending machines, and 0.19 million were tobacco product vending machines. Japan has more automatic vending machines per capita and land area than any other country. Annual sales through these machines amounts to 2.030 trillion yen for the drink vending machines, 54.1 billion yen for the food machines, and 209.4 billion for the tobacco product machines.

The main reason cited for the proliferation of vending machines in Japan is the high level of public order, while there is a concern that vending machines may be swiftly vandalized in overseas. There are more than 60 kinds of automatic vending machines. Tobacco and alcohol products can also be purchased from vending machines. There are machines that have been modified in various ways, such as to display product information and instructions in four languages for foreign tourists, and energy-saving machines that use off-peak power.

(12) About the Japanese

a) The Japanese Character

Below are some common features of the Japanese that have been pointed out by many people.

<1> The concept that forms the axis of the national character is "wa" ("harmony"). When Japanese people gather together in any numbers, the politeness of their behavior is influenced by an awareness of the order and rank of each person within the group according to age, social status, and other such considerations. Both this and the fact that the honorific forms of speech in the Japanese language have reached such an advanced level of sophistication because Japanese is sensitive to vertical relationships and considers it very important.

<2> In contrast to many Western people who are more likely to express their opinions openly in a self-asserting way, Japanese have a strong inclination to speak and act with due consideration for the other person's feelings and positions, a basic feeling that they should not disturb others. Furthermore, Japanese have a tendency to avoid being too assertively explicit in making answers either in the negative or in the affirmative. Japanese propensity to behave

もそれを期待するのは、日本人の同質性、無用の摩擦を避けようとする古くからの伝統などに基づくもので、「義理」「人情」が日本人の心情に作用しているからであろう。

〈3〉 日本人は「世間体」をかなり気にする。従来から「誇り」を基準に生きてきたからだろう。人からどう思われているかを非常に気にする。また日本人が一番避けたいのは「恥」である。「恥」を怖がって自分を表に出せないことがある。その結果「見栄」を張る行動をとることも見られる。

b) 日本人の集団帰属意識

日本人が個人より集団を重視する傾向が強いことは、アメリカのE・O・ライシャワー教授（ケネディ大統領時代の駐日大使）はじめ多くの研究者によって指摘されている。そして、日本人の集団帰属意識が、稲作文化の歴史とかかわりがあるとする見方も広く認められている。

日本の水田稲作農業では、集団作業と共同秩序が必要とされた。一定時間に集中的に行われる田植や稲刈などの作業には、近隣同士、力をあわせて共同作業をする必要があったし、田にひく水の割当なども近隣同士の配分の秩序が必要であった。このことから農民は、農村という地域社会への帰属意識を持たざるを得なかった。

また、中国から伝わった儒教の道徳が広がるにつれ、家に対する帰属意識が強まり、支配階級である武士は、自分の属する藩に対する帰属意識ももつようになった。

サラリーマンの企業への帰属意識も、このような歴史的基盤の上に、さらに日本の企業経営の特徴であった終身雇用制や年功序列あるいは企業内福祉により強められてきた。

c) 武士道

武士道は、鎌倉時代から発達し、江戸時代（17世紀から19世紀半ばまで）に儒教的思想に裏付けられて大成した武士階層の道徳体系である。忠誠・犠牲・信義・廉恥・礼儀・潔白・質素・倹約・尚武・名誉・情愛・相手への思いやり（武士の情け）、弱者や女性への愛情などの徳目が

like this and to expect the other person to do likewise may have derived from the homogeneity of the Japanese and a long, deep-rooted tradition of avoiding unwanted friction. Behind this may be the tendency for Japanese feelings to be influenced by a sense of *giri* (moral obligation) and *ninjo* (compassion).

<3> Japanese are quite concerned about appearances. The reason is probably that they have always been guided by a desire to be proud of oneself and are therefore very concerned about how they are seen by others. Of all things a Japanese wants to avoid, "shame" comes first. People are therefore sometimes unable to express themselves out of fear of shame. The result is that they tend to do things just to keep up appearances.

b) Japanese Group Consciousness

Dr. Edwin O. Reischauer of the U.S. (ambassador to Japan during the Kennedy presidency) is one of many scholars who have pointed out that Japanese tend to put group interests before personal ones. It is also widely acknowledged that the Japanese group consciousness is related to the country's long history of rice cultivation.

In Japan's wet-paddy rice cultivation, group working, and communal order was essential. For the planting and harvesting of the rice, which must be done concentratedly at certain times of the year, people in the neighborhood had to cooperate and work together, also making it necessary to establish order in the distribution of the water for the paddies throughout the neighboring areas. Because of this, farmers needed to have a sense of belonging to their regional farming communities.

Also, with the spread of the Confucian ethic from China, there was a strengthening of the concept of belonging to a family group, and among the warrior class, of belonging to a clan.

Against this historical background, the modern employee's sense of belonging to his company was further strengthened by the system of lifetime employment, ranking according to the numbers of years of service, and internal welfare schemes, which were features of company management in Japan.

c) Bushido

Bushido is the moral code of the samurai class. Based on Confucian ideas, it originated in the Kamakura Period (1185 to 1333) and reached perfection in the Edo Period (1603 to 1868). It puts emphasis on such virtues as loyalty, self-sacrifice, trustworthiness, sense of shame, refined propriety, integrity, austerity, thriftiness, warrior spirit, honor, sentiment,

重んじられた。

　武士が支配階級となる前、もっぱら戦うことを職業としていた時代には、死を讃える考え方が大きな比重を占めた。これは平和な江戸時代にも残り、佐賀藩では「武士道とは死ぬことと見つけたり」という思想（葉隠精神）が強調されたが、これは日本の武士道の全体系の中の、一部の考え方である。

　武士道の特徴の一つは尚武・名誉である。すなわち相手に勝つことである。勝つということは、ただ単に力ずくで他者を圧倒することではない。自分自身に勝つことによってのみ他者に勝ちうるという、精神的な構造の錬磨をも含むのである。強さは自己に勝つとき形成されるものであり、それは他者を精神的に圧倒し、他者から一目おかれる精神的な高さの表現でもある。このような精神的な強さを表現することの一部として、礼儀が重んぜられた。
　剣道・柔道など武術の流れを汲む現代のスポーツにおいても、はじめに礼儀が厳しくしつけられる。

　ヨーロッパの騎士道はキリスト教の影響を受けて発達し、勇気・敬神・礼節・廉恥・名誉・鷹揚などの徳を理想としている。騎士道はこのように武士道と多くの点で共通性をもつが、主従関係が契約的性質をもっていたため、この点で武士道が絶対的忠誠を重視するのと異なる。

d）切腹

　切腹とは、武士が責任をとって自害する方式のことで、平安時代末期に始まったといわれている。もちろん、現代日本では、切腹は自殺の手段としても刑罰の手段としても行われていない。

　日本では、精神修養のできた立派な人を腹のできた人といって尊敬する気風が強い。封建時代の武士は、腹を精神のやどるところとして尊重したので、武士として責任をとるために死ぬときに腹を切ったのである。

　江戸時代、切腹は武士に対する死刑の方法となった。これは、武士の人格・名誉を重んずる意味で、自ら死なせる

compassion (among samurai), affection for the weak and females, and so forth.

The glorification of death which prevailed in samurai thinking goes back to the days when these warriors fought strictly as professionals, before they became the dominant class, but such thinking remained strong even into the Edo Period when peace prevailed, and in the Saga clan, the concept (*hagakure* spirit) that "The way of the Samurai is found in death" was emphasized. This, however, is only a fraction of the entire system of bushido.

Bushido's other aspects include the warrior spirit and honor. That is, to win over the opponent. To win does not mean simply to overwhelm the other by force but requires tough-minded self-denying, only through which one can win over the other. Strength is obtained by a victory over oneself and is a manifestation of the heights one's spirits attain in the process, which overpowers the other mentally and commands his respect. As an element of such mental fortitude, propriety was strictly observed.

Even today, in *kendo*, *jujutsu* and the other modern sports which descend from martial arts, initiates are rigorously taught and trained in proper manners.

In Europe, chivalry developed under the influence of Christianity, upholding such virtues as courage, reverence, a sense of shame, honor, and generosity. Although chivalry had much in common with bushido, it was different from bushido in that the relation between a knight and his lords was contractual while bushido stressed absolute loyalty.

d) Seppuku

Seppuku is a ritual form of suicide that used to be practiced by members of the *samurai* class to show that they accepted responsibility for their actions. It is said to have its beginnings toward the end of the Heian Period, about one thousand years ago. In present day Japan, of course, seppuku is not practiced either as a form of suicide or as a form of punishment.

In expressing respect for someone of high moral character, the Japanese may use the phrase "person of determined and strong stomach." In feudal times warriors used to respect the abdomen because it was considered to be the receptacle of the spirit, so when they assumed responsibility as warriors for some action or course of conduct and had to die, they would cut open their abdomen.

In the Edo Era seppuku became the mode of capital punishment for members of the samurai class. To allow the warrior to die by his own

という形をとったものである。

なお、切腹については、森鷗外の小説『阿部一族』中に詳しく描かれている。

e) 日本人の微笑

長く日本に滞在して帰化したイギリス出身の文学者であるラフカディオ・ハーン（日本名：小泉八雲）（1850〜1904年）は、『日本人の微笑』という随筆で次のようにのべている。

「日本人の微笑から受ける第一印象は……まず、たいていの場合、すばらしく愉快なのが通例である。日本人の微笑は、最初はひどく魅力的なのだ。それが見る人に、へんだなと首をかしがせるようになるのは、よほど後になってからのことで、同じ微笑を常とはちがう場合に―たとえば、苦しいときとか、恥かしいときとか、がっかりしたときとかに見せられると、はじめは何だか妙てけれんな心持になってくるのである。……笑顔は、目上にものを言うときでも、対等の相手と話をするときでも、愉快な場合はもちろんのこと、愉快でない場合にも用いられる。だれにとっても一番愛想のいい顔は笑顔なんだから、できるだけ愛想のいい笑顔を、両親・身うちのもの・先生・友達・そのほか好意をもってくれている人にむかっていつも見せる。―これが生活の掟になっているのだ。……心は千々に乱れているようなときでも、顔には凛とした笑顔をたたえているというのが、社交上の義務なのである。」（小泉八雲全集『知られざる日本の面影』平井呈一訳）

このように、ラフカディオ・ハーンは、日本人の文化として定着している自制としての微笑に言及している。親愛・同調・共感などを示す微笑は、外国人にも共通であり理解されるが、この自制としての微笑は時に外国人をまどわせるようだ。

f) 日本人の自己紹介のしかた

日本では、特殊な職種を除いて通常新卒の従業員は、職種により採用されるのでなく、一般的潜在能力により採用されている。そして、会社が本人の希望や適性を加味しながら、各職場からの配属要求に基づいて、配属先を決定する。その後も地位の上昇あるいは事業の展開によって、経験のない職場にかわることはごく普通である。とくにホワイトカラーの場合、職種という観念が乏しい。

hand showed respect for his character and honor.

Mori Ogai's novel *The Abe Clan* examines the subject of seppuku in great depth.

e) The Japanese Smile

Lafcadio Hearn (1850–1904), an English man of letters who came to Japan and adopted Japanese citizenship under the name of Koizumi Yakumo, wrote the following in his essay, *The Japanese Smile*.

"The first impression is, in most cases, wonderfully pleasant. The Japanese smile at first charms. It is only at a later day, when one has observed the same smile under extraordinary circumstances—in moments of pain, shame, disappointment—that one becomes suspicious of it. … But the smile is to be used upon all pleasant occasions, when speaking to a superior or to an equal, and even upon occasions which are not pleasant; it is part of deportment. The most agreeable face is the smiling face; and to present always the most agreeable face possible to parents, relatives, teachers, friends, well-wishers, is a rule of life... Even though the heart is breaking, it is a social duty to smile bravely." (From The Writings of Lafcadio Hearn, *Glimpses of Unfamiliar Japan*, published by Houghton Mifflin Co.)

Here, then, Lafcadio Hearn refers to the Japanese smile as a form of the self-control rooted in the culture of the Japanese. Smiles to indicate affection, agreement, sympathy, etc. are the same wherever one goes, but this smile of self-control is something that on occasion seems to puzzle people from other countries.

f) How Japanese Introduce Themselves in Business Situations

Except in certain special fields, the focus in employing fresh college graduates in Japan is on latent potential rather than on skills for a specific job type. And, while taking some account of a person's wishes and aptitude, the decision as to where he or she is to be assigned is based on the needs of various sections which comprise the organization. Even later, it is quite usual for personnel to be moved, because of promotion or commencement of a project, to a post for which they have no experience. Particularly with white-collar workers, there is little

このようなことから、仕事の内容を表わすのには、会社名と現在の所属部門をいうのが、一番的確であるということになる。

(13) 日本の文化力

a) 文化力の再認識

文化力とは人の心を引き付ける魅力であり、真の豊かさと活力ある社会を実現する基礎であるといえる。同時に文化芸術は国の経済活動においても新たな需要や高い付加価値を生み出す源泉となり、また経済とも密接に関連しあうと考えられるようになった。21世紀に入って国の力として従来からの政治力、経済力、軍事力などに並立する概念として「文化力」の重要性が世界的に認識されるようになった。

ジョゼフ・ナイ、ハーバード大学教授は、「人や国の力には3通りがある。ひとつは脅威を与えること、次は金銭的見返りを与えること、そして相手を魅了することである。この3つはそれぞれ軍事力、経済力、ソフトパワーに対応する。ソフトパワーの源泉になるものは、外交政策と人権・平和などの普遍的価値観、ならびに文化力の3つである。これからはソフトパワーの重要性を重視していかなければなければならない」と述べ、国家の力として文化力の重要性を提唱している。ソフトパワーは、ハードパワーと相乗するとその威力は倍加すると言われている。広い意味での文化、すなわち衣食住などの生活習慣と国民の生活実態、言語、自然、芸術、伝統文化、各地の風習などを含めた価値の重要性を、国内において広く共有するだけでなく、インターネットなどを通じて世界中に発信して、日本を好きな国になってもらうことが肝要である。

b) 文化芸術立国にむけた政府の方針

文化芸術の振興により心豊かな国民生活を実現するとともに、活力ある社会を構築して国の魅力を高め、経済力だけでなく文化力によっても世界から評価される国づくり、つまり「文化芸術立国」を目ざすというものである（「文化芸術振興基本法」）。

concept of job classification by skills.

Because of this, the most precise way of indicating the nature of a person's work is for the person to mention the name of his or her company and the section to which he or she is assigned at the time.

(13) Japanese Cultural Power

a) Renewed Awareness of Cultural Power

Cultural power is the power to win the hearts of people and the foundation for the creation of a truly affluent and dynamic society. Moreover, culture and art are today viewed as the wellspring of new demand and high added value in the economic activities of a nation. They are also believed to interact closely with the economy. As we move forward in the twenty-first century, the concept of cultural power is coming to be recognized worldwide as an important aspect of a nation's power—alongside political, economic, and military power, which have up until now informed the power of nations.

In his book *Soft Power: The Means to Success in World Politics*, Harvard Professor Joseph Nye expounds on the importance of the cultural power of a nation. He lists the three ways a nation can exert power: through threats and force, through payments and sanctions, and through charm. These three avenues correspond to military power, economic power, and soft power. Soft power has three components: diplomacy, universal values related to concepts such as human rights and peace, and cultural power. The importance of cultural power cannot be ignored. Soft power is amplified through synergistic interaction with hard power. In its broadest sense, the term "culture" refers to lifestyle (including clothes, food, and housing) and the importance of values as they relate to aspects of life such as living conditions, language, nature, art, traditional culture, and regional customs. It is not enough for the Japanese to share their culture only within Japan. They also need use the Internet—and every means available—to broadcast Japan's cultural charm throughout the world, so that people everywhere can fall in love with Japan.

b) Government Policies Directed at Creating a Culturally and Artistically Vibrant Nation

The government is committed to promoting culture and the arts so as to create an energetic society that offers people a spiritually rich life and enhances Japan's attractiveness, and thus build a country that is admired by the world for its cultural power as well as for its economic power. In other words, Japan is determined to be a nation grounded in culture and

文化芸術振興の対象となるのは、次のような幅広い分野である。
〈1〉芸術：文学、音楽、美術、写真、演劇、舞踊
〈2〉メディア芸術：漫画、映画、アニメーション、コンピュータによるゲーム
〈3〉伝統芸能：雅楽、能楽、文楽、歌舞伎
〈4〉大衆芸能：講談、落語、浪曲、漫談、漫才、唱歌
〈5〉生活文化・国民娯楽・出版物：華道、茶道、書道、囲碁、将棋、レコード（CD、DVD）、出版物

また全ての国民が芸術文化に親しみ、自らの手で新しい文化を創造するための環境の醸成とその基盤の強化を図る観点から、安定的・継続的に多様な芸術文化活動に援助を行うことを目的として芸術文化振興基金が設けられている。

文化の海外への発信との観点から、国が中心となり現在進められている方策としては、以下が挙げられる。

〈1〉文化財の保存・活用
世界文化遺産、世界自然遺産をはじめとする各地の文化財の保存・活用の推進
〈2〉外国人旅行者の誘致増
2018年に日本を訪れた外国人観光客数は3,120万人となり、過去最高を記録した（国土交通省）。東京オリンピック・パラリンピックが開かれる2020年までに訪日客を4,000万人に増やす目標を掲げ、具体的な誘致策の検討を開始している。
〈3〉現代日本文化の発信と国際交流
「クールジャパン」は、外国人がクールととらえる日本固有の魅力（アニメ、マンガ、ゲーム等のコンテンツ、ファッション、食、伝統文化、デザイン、ロボットや環境技術など）として注目を集めている現代日本文化を計画的・積極的に発信している。
またクールジャパン戦略は、クールジャパンの、〈ⅰ〉情報発信、〈ⅱ〉海外への商品・サービス展開、〈ⅲ〉インバウンドの国内消費の各段階をより効果的

the arts (Basic Law for Promotion of Culture and Arts).

Promotion of culture and the arts includes activities in the following fields:

<1> Art: literature, music, fine art, photography, theater, dance
<2> Media Arts: *manga*, movies, animation, computer games
<3> Traditional Arts: ancient court music, *noh*, *bunraku* puppet theater, *kabuki*
<4> Popular Art: *kodan* (traditional storytelling), *rakugo* (traditional comic storytelling), *naniwabushi* (stories of loyalty and human feeling accompanied by the *shamisen*), *mandan* (comic monologue), *manzai* (stand-up comedy dialogue), *shoka* (singing)
<5> Lifestyle and Culture, Traditional Pastimes, and Publications: flower arrangement, the tea ceremony, calligraphy, *go*, *shogi*, records (CDs and DVDs), published works

The Japan Arts Council was established to provide support for diverse artistic and cultural activities in a stable and continuous manner, creating an environment with a strong foundation for people to develop an affinity for the arts and culture and be culturally creative.

The following policies are currently being put forward (principally by the central government) with a view to promoting Japanese culture overseas.

<1> Preservation and use of cultural properties: promoting the preservation and use of World Cultural Heritage sites, World Natural Heritage sites, and cultural properties in all regions.
<2> Attracting more foreign visitors: The number of foreign tourists who visited Japan in 2018 amounted to a record 31.2 million (Ministry of Land, Infrastructure and Transport). Japan hopes to attract some 40 million foreign visitors by 2020 when the Tokyo 2020 Olympic and Paralympic Games are being held and has begun considering concrete measures for realizing this goal.
<3> Promoting modern Japanese culture and conducting international exchanges: Under the Cool Japan slogan, interesting modern Japanese culture is being strategically and actively promoted based on what foreigners associate as being part of Cool Japan, such as anime, comics, games, fashion, food, traditional culture, design, robots, and environmental technology.

In addition, the Cool Japan strategy is <i> related information dissemination, <ii> overseas expansion of related products and services, and <iii> effective development at each stage of inbound

〈4〉海外・国内の外国人に対する日本語教育の推進

日本語の普及は、日本の文化、政治、経済、社会への理解を促進し、日本との交流の担い手となる理解者を育てるうえでぜひ必要である。現在、世界の日本語教育機関は約 1.6 万機関あり、およそ 365 万人（2015 年）が海外で日本語を学習しており、国際交流基金が中心となり支援している。日本語学習人口はこの 5 年で約 150 万人増加した。近年では、留学・就職の目的のために日本語を勉強するという人だけではなく、日本という異文化を理解したい、アニメ・マンガなどのポップカルチャーを日本語で楽しみたいなどの動機から勉強を始める人も増えてきている。

(14) 観光

a) 日本の自然景観を楽しむ

日本には山岳・渓谷・河川・湖沼などが多く、海岸線も複雑で地形が変化に富んでいること、四季の移り変わりがはっきりしていることなどから、美しい自然や景観を楽しめる観光地が多い。また、火山が多いので温泉地に恵まれており、それぞれ、よい保養地となっている。これらの代表的なものは、国立公園（34 カ所）や国定公園（56 カ所）に指定されている。また、松島（宮城県）、天の橋立（京都府）、宮島（広島県）は日本三景といわれ、水戸の偕楽園、金沢の兼六園、岡山の後楽園は日本三名園として知られている。

b) 日本の歴史や文化財をたずねる

日本の古都や史跡をたずね、古い寺院・神社の建物や庭園などを見学し、また仏像や美術工芸品を鑑賞しながら、日本文化の歩みをたどることができる。

奈良、京都はそれぞれ平城京、平安京と呼ばれた古都であり、中国の長安（現在の西安）の都市を模範として造営

consumption to tap into international growth, making it a brand strategy that leads to Japanese economic growth.

<4> Increasing Japanese language learning opportunities for foreigners inside and outside Japan: The spread of the Japanese language promotes an understanding of Japanese culture, government, economy, and society, and is thus necessary for the cultivation of people familiar with Japan who will drive exchanges with Japan.

Currently, there are some 16,000 Japanese language education institutions throughout the world and 3.65 million people studying Japanese overseas, and this is principally supported by the Japan Foundation. The number of people studying Japanese has increased by about 1.5 million over the past five years. In the past, people began studying Japanese in order to go to school in Japan or to find a job, but recently, a growing number of people have been studying Japanese in order to understand the culture of Japan or to enjoy aspects of popular culture, such as anime and manga, in the original language.

(14) Sightseeing

a) Japan's Natural Scenery

The rich topographical variety produced by many mountains, gorges, rivers, lakes, marshes, and a complex coastline together with the clearly defined four seasons, provides Japan with many sightseeing spots where the beauties of nature can be enjoyed. Also, the presence of many volcanoes provides an abundance of hot spring areas, many of which have become health resorts. The most representative of these have been designated national parks (34 areas) or quasi-national parks (56 areas). Also, there are what are known as the "Three Views of Japan" (the three famous beauty spots of Japan): Matsushima (Miyagi Prefecture), Amanohashidate (Kyoto Prefecture), and Miyajima (Hiroshima Prefecture); and the three famous gardens of Japan: Kairakuen, in Mito, Kenrokuen, in Kanazawa, and Korakuen, in Okayama.

b) Historical and Cultural Treasures in Japan

Those who wish to learn something about the progress of Japanese culture may do so by visiting Japan's old cities and other spots, by looking at old temples, shrines and gardens, and by admiring images of Buddha and objects of fine art.

The ancient cities of Nara, which used to be called Heijo-kyo, and Kyoto, which used to be called Heian-kyo, were modeled after the city

されたものである。

奈良は、8世紀に約70年間続いた古都である。神社・仏閣・仏像・彫刻・絵画など、国宝や重要文化財の宝庫である。

高さ16.21mの大仏（752年開眼、その後度々修復）がある東大寺や、五重塔が猿沢池に美しい影を写す興福寺、さらに放し飼いの鹿がたくさんいる春日大社などが、とくに有名である。東大寺には正倉院という校倉造りの木造宝物殿がある。

奈良近郊には、現存する世界最古の木造建築である法隆寺がある。

隣接する飛鳥地方は、6～7世紀ごろ、日本文化の開花した地方で、日本仏教の発祥地でもあり、天皇の御陵や古墳・史跡などが点在している。1972年に、極彩色の壁画が発見されて有名になった明日香村の高松塚古墳もこの一角にある。

京都は、8世紀末から約1000年間続いた古都である。清水寺・三十三間堂・鹿苑寺金閣・慈照寺銀閣・平安神宮および東・西本願寺・大徳寺・仁和寺・天龍寺・知恩院・南禅寺・西芳寺・龍安寺・京都御所・二条城・桂離宮・伏見稲荷など多くの寺社や史跡があり、その建築美や庭園美は訪れる人達を魅了する。

また、東山・嵐山・嵯峨野・加茂川など景勝地も多く、西陣織・友禅染・京人形・清水焼・京扇子などの名産品もある。

東京近郊の鎌倉は、12世紀末から約150年間、武家政権の幕府が置かれたところである。鶴岡八幡宮・長谷の大仏（高徳院）・建長寺・円覚寺などの史跡が多い。

日本の各地には、石垣・建物・配置などに日本独特の様

of Chang'an (present-day Xi'an) in China.

Nara was the capital of Japan for about seventy years, starting in the early eighth century. With its many shrines, Buddhist temples, statues of Buddha, carvings and paintings, it is rich in National Treasures and Important Cultural Assets.

Particularly famous are Nara's Todaiji Temple with its 16.21-meter-high (53.18 feet) statue of Buddha (dedicated in the year 752 and renovated several times since), Kofukuji Temple with its five-storied pagoda facing the beautiful pond called Sarusawa-no-ike, and Kasuga Grand Shrine with its many tame deer which are allowed to roam free. Todaiji Temple also has the Shosoin Treasure Repository, a wooden treasure-house with a special construction (called *azekura*) which has a unique feature of moisture-resistance.

On the outskirts of Nara is Horyuji Temple, the world's oldest wooden structure still in existence.

Also, the nearby Asuka district was where the culture of Japan flowered around the sixth and seventh centuries, and as such, was the cradle of Japanese Buddhism; in this area can be found Imperial mausolea, burial mounds, and historical relics. One such place is Takamatsuzuka, in Asuka village, which became famous when a tumulus with brilliantly colored wall paintings was discovered in 1972.

The ancient city of Kyoto was the capital for about a thousand years, starting at the end of the eighth century. Among its many historical places of interest are such temples and shrines as Kiyomizudera Temple, Sanjusangendo Temple, Rokuonji Temple Kinkaku, Jishoji Temple Ginkaku, Heian Jingu Shrine, Nishi-Honganji Temple, Higashi-Honganji Temple, Daitokuji Temple, Ninnaji Temple, Tenryuji Temple, Chion-in Temple, Nanzenji Temple, Saihoji Temple, and Ryoanji Temple. Other important sights are Kyoto Gosho, Nijo Castle, Katsura Imperial Villa, and Fushimi Inaritaisha Shrine. Each of these places has architectural and landscape beauty that leaves the visitor entranced.

In addition, there are many places of scenic beauty, such as Higashiyama, Arashiyama, Sagano, and the River Kamo, and many famous local products, such as *nishijin* brocade, *yuzen* dyed fabrics, *kyo* dolls, *kiyomizu* ware, and kyo fans.

Kamakura, which is not far from Tokyo, became the seat of the *bakufu* military government for a period of one hundred and fifty years, starting from the end of the twelfth century. The many historical places that can be seen there include Tsurugaoka Hachimangu Shrine, the Great Buddha of Hase, Kenchoji Temple, and Engakuji Temple.

In various regions of the country are found castles which are uniquely

式をもつ城郭が残されている。三名城といわれる姫路城・名古屋城（金の鯱鉾で名高かった。戦災で焼けたあと修復された）・熊本城のほか、大阪城・松本城・犬山城（その天守閣は、現存するもののうち最古）などが有名である。

なかでも姫路城は、14世紀中ごろにつくられ、その後しだいに拡張され、その規模の雄大さ、純白の天守閣の美しさなどで、一頭地を抜いている。別名、白鷺城とも呼ばれる。城郭の石垣の積み石は、重さ1トン前後のものが多いが、大阪城にはとくに大きなものが使用されている。大阪城の石は、遠く110 kmもはなれた小豆島から運ばれたもので、とくに重い石の場合は、海中に石をつるし、浮力分だけ軽くして運ぶ石釣船が使われたという。

現在の皇居は、徳川時代の将軍の居城であった江戸城の跡で、毎年1月2日と天皇誕生日には、国民参賀が行われるので、その一部が参観できる。また2014年から春季と秋季の一定時期に、皇居内の乾通りが一般公開され、春季には様々な種類の桜の花を、また秋季には紅葉がそれぞれ楽しめる。

c）日本にある世界遺産
1）概要

世界の顕著かつ普遍的価値を有する文化遺産と自然遺産およびその複合遺産を認定、保護する条約が、1972年ユネスコ総会で採択された。2018年7月現在、世界193カ国の総計1,092件が世界遺産リストに登録されている。その内訳は文化遺産845、自然遺産209、複合遺産38である。日本の世界遺産は下記の文化遺産18件、自然遺産4件である。

2）文化遺産

〈1〉法隆寺地域の仏教建造物（1993年12月登録）

奈良県斑鳩町にある。大陸の仏教建造物を寺院建築に取り入れた世界最古の木造建築群であり、その後の建築様式に多大な影響をおよぼした。

Japanese in their stone walls, architectural style, and choice of location. The three most famous are Himeji Castle, Nagoya Castle (famous for the golden dolphins on the roof; destroyed by fire during the war, this castle was later rebuilt), and Kumamoto Castle. Other famous ones include Osaka Castle, Matsumoto Castle, and Inuyama Castle (the tower of which is the oldest in existence).

Himeji Castle was built in the middle of the fourteenth century and gradually enlarged until now it is unrivaled for its size as well as for the beauty of its pure white tower. Another name it is known by is Shirasagi (which means egret) Castle. Most of the stones of the terraced walls of the castles weigh about one ton each, but the stones of Osaka Castle are particularly large. These stones had to be brought 110 kilometers (68 miles) from Shodo Island, and it is said that particularly large stones were suspended in the sea so that the buoyancy lightened them slightly, making it easier for the boats to transport them.

The present Imperial Palace was built on the site of Edo Castle, headquarters of the feudal government in the Tokugawa Era. A part of it can be visited on the second day of each year and on the Emperor's birthday, at which times the people are allowed to enter to offer their congratulations to the Emperor. In addition, since 2014 Inui Street in the Imperial Palace is opened to the public at a fixed time in spring and fall, enabling cherry blossoms to be enjoyed in spring and the colors of autumn leaves in the fall.

c) **Japanese Properties on the World Heritage List**
1) Overview

At its general meeting in 1972, UNESCO adopted a convention concerning the identification and protection of world cultural, natural, and mixed cultural and natural heritage of outstanding and universal value. As of July 2018, the list of registered world legacies had reached 1,092 in 193 countries. Of the total, 845 were cultural sites, 209 natural sites, and 38 mixed sites. Japan had the following 18 cultural and 4 natural site listings.

2) Cultural

<1> Buddhist Monuments in the Horyuji Area (Registered December 1993)

Located in Ikaruga-cho, Nara Prefecture. These are the oldest surviving wooden structures in the world, and incorporate elements of Buddhist architecture from the continent into the temple's architecture. This greatly influenced future architectural styles.

〈2〉 姫路城 (1993 年 12 月登録)
　兵庫県姫路市にある。16 世紀の日本を代表する城郭建築であり、設計技術と装飾美の両面において木造建築の最高峰に位置付けられている。
〈3〉 古都京都の文化財 (1994 年 12 月登録)

　京都府京都市・宇治市、滋賀県大津市に点在している。平安時代から江戸時代までの各時代の神社・仏閣、庭園および文化的背景を伝えている。木造建築でありながら古いものは 1200 年もの時を越えてその姿を今日に止めている。
〈4〉 白川郷・五箇山の合掌造り集落 (1995 年 12 月登録)
　岐阜・富山県境の山間部に発達した合掌造りの集落である。合掌造り家屋は、豪雪に耐え、養蚕にも利用できるよう工夫が施されており、巨大な茅葺き屋根と三角形の結合をベースにした独特の構造をもつ。集落として優れた自然景観が保存されている。

〈5〉 厳島神社 (1996 年 12 月登録)
　広島県廿日市市にある。海上に建ち並ぶ建造物群と背後の弥山原始林とが一体となった独創的な神社建築である。建造物の多くが平安時代の寝殿造りの特徴をもつ。日本三景の一つ「安芸の宮島」で知られる。

〈6〉 原爆ドーム (1996 年 12 月登録)

　1945 年 8 月 6 日、広島市に投下された原子爆弾によって破壊された広島県産業奨励館の残骸で、人類にとっては負の遺産であるが、後世に引き継ぐべき「歴史の生き証人」としての価値が評価された。核兵器廃絶と恒久平和を求める誓いのシンボルとして、平和へのメッセージを発信していく。
〈7〉 古都奈良の文化財 (1998 年 12 月登録)
　奈良県奈良市に点在する。8 世紀の中国、朝鮮半島との文化的交流を示す建造物や芸術品が数多く遺されている。
　また、日本国家の基礎が整った奈良時代の都市の様子を伝える貴重な史料としての価値をもつ。

<2> Himeji-jo (Himeji Castle) (Registered December 1993)

Located in Himeji, Hyogo Prefecture. An example of sixteenth-century Japanese castle architecture and an outstanding wooden structure in terms of design technology and decoration.

<3> Historic Monuments of Ancient Kyoto (Kyoto, Uji, and Otsu Cities) (Registered December 1994)

Located in Kyoto and Uji in Kyoto Prefecture and Otsu in Shiga Prefecture. Shrines, temples, gardens, and the background to Japanese culture from the Heian period to the Edo period are all to be found here. Although these wooden structures are very old, they can still be seen today, having survived for more than 1200 years.

<4> Historic villages of Shirakawa-go and Gokayama (Registered December 1994)

Nearly all of the houses in these villages are of the *gasshozukuri* style that developed in the mountainous region along the border between Gifu and Toyama prefectures. Well designed to withstand heavy snows and adaptable for sericulture, the gasshozukuri farm house has a unique structure based on interconnected triangles and is immediately recognizable from its enormous thatched roof. The villages are preserved for the outstanding natural scenic views.

<5> Itsukushima Shinto Shrine (Registered December 1996)

Located in Hatsukaichi, Hiroshima Prefecture. A collection of structures built in the sea in a unique style of shrine architecture, against the backdrop of the primeval forest of Mount Misen. Many of the structures are typical of a nobleman's residence in the Heian period. From old times it has been also called "Aki no Miyajima" (the shrine island of Aki Province) and admired as one of the "Three Views of Japan."

<6> Hiroshima Peace Memorial (Genbaku Dome) (Registered December 1996)

The remains of the Prefectural Industrial Promotion Hall after the A-bomb (*genbaku*) was dropped on Hiroshima on August 6, 1945. Although a site of negative heritage for humanity, it is valued as a surviving witness of history for future generations. As a symbol of prayers for the eradication of nuclear weapons and lasting peace, it conveys a clear message for peace.

<7> Historic Monuments of Ancient Nara (Registered December 1998)

Located throughout Nara, Nara Prefecture. There are many structures and works of art originating from the cultural exchanges with China and the Korean Peninsula in the eighth century.

Nara's monuments are also valued as an important historical record of city conditions in the Nara period, during which the foundations of

東大寺・興福寺・薬師寺など日本で独自の発展を遂げた仏教建築群、春日大社とその原始林、そして平城宮跡が指定範囲である。

〈8〉日光の社寺（1999年12月登録）
　栃木県日光市にある。江戸時代初期から中期に建てられ、日本近世の建築様式を代表する東照宮などの建築物群が残されている。また、自然環境と建造物が一体となった宗教空間は、古来の神道思想を顕著に反映したものとされている。

〈9〉琉球王国の城・遺産群（2000年12月登録）

　日本、中国、朝鮮半島、その他東南アジア諸国と経済的政治的交流をもっていたことを示す建造物群がある。また、失われた琉球王国の遺跡と失われつつある文化的伝統、および自然崇拝、祖先崇拝という沖縄伝統の信仰形態を今日に伝えている。

〈10〉紀伊山地の霊場と参詣道（2004年7月登録）

　和歌山・奈良・三重の3県にまたがる多数の神道・仏教の歴史的建造物および史跡群。自然崇拝に根ざした日本古来の神道と大陸より伝来した仏教が結びついた神仏習合思想をよくあらわしている。また、神社や寺院などの建造物が自然環境と一体となって文化的景観を構成している。加えて、吉野・大峯、熊野三山、高野山などの霊場を結ぶお参りのための古道があり、この「道」も世界遺産として登録されている。

〈11〉石見銀山遺跡とその文化的景観（2007年7月登録）
　島根県のほぼ中央にある。中世から近代まで400年の歴史をもつ世界有数の銀鉱山遺跡で、当時の生産現場から町並みまでの文化的景観が保存されている。「全盛期には、世界の産出銀の3分の1を占めた日本銀の相当部分を産出し、アジア諸国に輸出し欧州との交流をもたらしたこと」、「環境に配慮し、人と自然が共生しながら銀生産を実現させたこと」などが評価され、その周辺の景観とともに文化遺産に登録された。

the Japanese nation were laid.

Included are a group of Buddhist buildings, most notably Todaiji Temple, Kofukuji Temple, and Yakushiji Temple of a style that evolved independently in Japan, Kasuga Grand Shrine and the surrounding virgin forest, and the Heijokyu ruins.

<8> Shrines and Temples of Nikko (Registered December 1999)

Located in Nikko, Tochigi Prefecture. Constructed between the early Edo period and the mid-Edo period, many architectural structures such as Nikko Tosho-gu (Shinto Shrine) remain as examples of the architectural style of the early Modern period of Japan. In addition, the integration of the architecture with the environment is a striking reflection of ancient Shinto philosophy.

<9> Gusuku Sites and Related Properties of the Kingdom of Ryukyu (Registered December 2000)

This group of structures reflects the economic and political exchanges that took place between Japan, China, the Korean Peninsula, and other Southeast Asian countries. The remains still tell of the lost Ryukyu Kingdom and its fading cultural traditions, and of the traditional Okinawan religion that encompasses nature worship and ancestor worship.

<10> Sacred Places and Pilgrimage Routes in the Kii Mountain Range (Registered July 2004)

A collection of historical Shinto and Buddhist buildings, and remains spread throughout Wakayama, Nara, and Mie Prefectures. It provides a clear example of the fusion of ancient Japanese Shinto practice with its roots in nature worship, and the Buddhism brought to Japan from the continent. The Shinto shrines, Buddhist temples, and other structures merge with the natural environment to create a cultural landscape. Ancient roads that were used for pilgrimages to such sacred places as Yoshino-Omine, Kumano-sanzan, and Koyasan were also named a World Heritage Site.

<11> Iwami Ginzan Silver Mine and its Cultural Landscape (Registered July 2007)

Located in the center of Shimane Prefecture. This is one of the world's few surviving old silver mines, and boasts a 400-year history that runs from the Middle Ages to the Modern period. The production area and the surrounding town form a cultural landscape. This site is unique because, at the height of its prosperity, the mine accounted for one-third of world silver production and was a catalyst for exports to Asian countries and exchanges with Europe. It also demonstrates how consideration was shown for the natural environment and how the symbiosis between people and nature was preserved during mining. The

〈12〉平泉―仏国土（浄土）を表す建築・庭園および考古学的遺跡群（2011 年 6 月登録）

　平泉（ひらいずみ）町地域一帯には、平安時代末期、奥州藤原氏が栄えた時代の寺院や遺跡群が多く残り、5 件は中尊寺、毛越寺（もうつうじ）、観自在王院跡（かんじざいおういんあと）、無量光院跡（むりょうこういんあと）、金鶏山（きんけいざん）である。これらの仏堂と庭園の複合体から成る遺跡群は、現世における仏国土（浄土）を象徴的に明示しており、その他の都市の庭園・仏堂にも影響を与えた。

〈13〉富士山―信仰の対象と芸術の源泉（2013 年 6 月登録）

　神聖で荘厳な姿の富士山は、山域から山頂への登拝および山麓への巡礼を通じて、富士山信仰を育み、また美意識と関連し、今日まで人々に畏敬され、感銘を与え続けた名山である。さらに、海外の芸術家にも影響を与えた浮世絵など、多くの芸術作品に取り上げられてきた。信仰や芸術に関わる文化財が広い範囲に点在し、これら三保の松原・三嶋大社などを含む富士山全体を一体のものとして登録された。

〈14〉富岡製糸場と絹産業遺産群（2014 年 6 月登録）

　群馬県にある富岡製糸場は、官営製糸工場として 1872 年に創業された。近代西洋技術を導入し、日本独自の工法が融合してできた本格的な機械製糸工場で当時世界最大規模である。大量生産された高品質な生糸や養蚕技術は海外に広まり絹産業の発展に繋るとともに、日本の近代化、経済・産業発展の歴史を物語る証拠である。また、19 世紀後半の工場の主要な施設（製糸所・繭倉庫など）が創業当時のままほぼ完全な形で残っていることも希少な価値がある。

surrounding landscape is also registered as a cultural heritage site.

<12> Hiraizumi—Temples, Gardens, and Archaeological Sites Representing the Buddhist Pure Land (Registered June 2011)

Located in Northeastern Honshu. The region in and around Hiraizumi Town is the home of many temples, gardens, and archaeological remains from the height of the Oshu Fujiwara realm late in the Heian Period. The inscribed legacy comprises five sites: Chusonji Temple, Motsuji Temple, Kanjizaioin Temple Remains, Muryokoin Temple Remains, and Mt. Kinkeisan. As a whole, this group of temples, gardens, and archaeological relics symbolically represents the cosmology of Pure Land Buddhism. Their influence on the gardens and temples of other regions is also evident.

<13> Fujisan—Sacred Place and Source of Artistic Inspiration (Registered June 2013)

Fujisan, famous worldwide as Mt. Fuji, immediately evokes a divine and majestic impression. The mountain has long been an object of pilgrimages to the summit and through the surrounding foothills, and its aura as a sacred place has grown in proportion. It is revered as a mountain that never fails to overwhelm the beholder with its awesome beauty. It has often been the subject of *ukiyoe* and other works of art that had a strong impact on artists in other countries. The inscribed property encompasses many sites of religious and artistic significance spread over a broad area. These have been inscribed along with more distant sites closely associated with Mt. Fuji, such as Miho-no-Matsubara pine grove and Mishima Taisha Shrine.

<14> The Tomioka Silk Mill and Related Industrial Heritage (Registered June 2014)

The Tomioka Silk Mill in Gunma Prefecture was founded in 1872 as a government-run factory. The largest such facility in the world at the time, the full-fledged factory infused unique Japanese production methods with modern Western technology. As a result, sericulture technology and high-quality mass-produced raw silk spread abroad. The site clearly speaks to Japan's modernization and the development of the country's industry and economy. In addition, it is rare for a factory dating from the latter half of the 19th Century to have had most of its major facilities (such as warehouses and the mill for the reeling of cocoons and spinning of raw silk) remain in such good shape.

〈15〉明治日本の産業革命遺産　製鉄・製鋼、造船、石炭産業（福岡県、佐賀県、長崎県、熊本県、鹿児島県、山口県、岩手県、静岡県）（2015年7月登録）

　西洋から非西洋への産業化の移転が成功したことを証言する産業遺産群により構成されている。19世紀後半から20世紀の初頭にかけ、日本は工業立国の土台を構築し、のちに日本の基幹産業となる造船、製鉄、製鋼、石炭と重工業において急速な産業化を成し遂げた。一連の産業群は1850年代から1910年の半世紀で西洋の技術が移転され、実践と応用を経て産業システムとして構築される産業国家形成への道程を時系列に沿って証言している。具体的な物件名は次の通り。

　萩反射炉、恵比須ヶ鼻造船所跡、大板山たたら製鉄遺跡、萩城下町、松下村塾、旧集成館、寺山炭窯跡、関吉の疎水群、韮山反射炉、橋野鉄鉱山、三重津海軍所跡、小菅修船場跡、三菱長崎造船所（第三船渠、ジャイアント・カンチレバークレーン、旧木型場、占勝閣）、高島炭鉱、旧グラバー邸、三池炭鉱・三池港、三角西港、官営八幡製鉄所、遠賀川水源地ポンプ室

〈16〉ル・コルビュジエの建築作品―近代建築への顕著な貢献―（国立西洋美術館＝東京都）（2016年7月登録）

　フランスを拠点に活躍した近代建築の巨匠、ル・コルビュジエが手掛けた建築作品群で、非常に珍しいのが、7カ国に残る17の建築群が構成資産になっており、大陸をまたぐ初の世界遺産になっている。日本では東京・上野の国立西洋美術館が構成資産のひとつとなっている。日本で、また東アジアで唯一のル・コルビュジエ建築である。

〈17〉「神宿る島」宗像・沖ノ島と関連遺産群（福岡県）（2017年7月登録）

　沖ノ島は、福岡県宗像市の沖合約60キロの玄界灘に浮かぶ孤島。4～9世紀に朝鮮半島や中国大陸との交流成就と航海の安全を祈る大規模な祭祀（さいし）が行われた。朝鮮半島からの金製指輪、ペルシャからもたらされたと考えられるカットグラス碗（わん）片

<15> Meiji Japan's Industrial Revolution Heritage Iron and Steelmaking, Shipbuilding, Coal Industry (Fukuoka, Saga, Nagasaki, Kumamoto, Kagoshima, Yamaguchi, Iwate, Shizuoka) (Registered July 2015)

This consists of industrial heritage groups that testify to the successful transfer of industrialization from the West to the non-West. From the latter half of the 19th century to the beginning of the 20th century, Japan built a foundation for industrialization, and later achieved rapid industrialization in shipbuilding, ironmaking, steelmaking, the coal industry, and heavy industries, which became the core industries of the nation. This series of industrial heritage groups bore witness to how western technologies were transferred from the 1850s to 1910 and, through practice and application, following an arduous timeline, were brought together as an industrial system to build an industrial nation as an industrial system. The following are some of the items involved.

Hagi Reflector, Ebisugahana Shipyard, Oitayama Tatara Iron Works, Hagi Castle Town, Soka Sonjuku Academy, Old Assembly Hall, Terayama Charcoal Kiln, Sekiyoshi Sluice Gate of Yoshino Leat, Nirayama Reflector, Hashino Iron Mine, Mietsu Navy Dock Site, Kosuge Ship Dock, Mitsubishi Nagasaki Shipbuilding (No.3 Dry Dock, Giant Cantilever Crane, Former Pattern Shop, Senshokaku Guest House), Takashima Coal Mine, Old Glover Residence, Miike Coal Mine, Miike Port, Misumi West Port, Government Yawata Steel Works, Onga River Source Pump Room

<16> Le Corbusier's Architectural Works - Outstanding Contribution to Modern Architecture - (The National Museum of Western Art, Tokyo) (Registered July 2016)

These are architectural drawings from Le Corbusier, a master of modern architecture who was based in France. What is very unusual about the listing is that it covered 17 of Le Corbusier's projects in seven countries, the first time a World Heritage Site listing has spanned more than one continent. The National Museum of Western Art in Ueno, Tokyo, is part of the list. It is the only Le Corbusier architecture in Japan or East Asia.

<17> "The Island where God Dwells" Munakata, Okinoshima and Associated Sites (Fukuoka Prefecture) (Registered July 2017)

Okinoshima is an isolated island in the Genkai Sea, about 60 kilometers off the coast of Munakata City, Fukuoka prefecture. Large-scale religious ceremonies were held on the island from the fourth to the ninth centuries to pray for exchanges with Korea and China, and for safe navigation. Some 80,000 consecrated items that include gold rings

など約8万点の奉献品が出土し、全て国宝に指定されている。島全体が宗像大社の境内として信仰の対象とされ、女人禁制などの禁忌が残る。上陸は厳しく制限されており、許された場合も着衣を全て脱いで海に入り、みそぎをしなければならない。

〈18〉長崎と天草地方の潜伏キリシタン関連遺産（長崎県、熊本県）（2018年7月登録）

　17～19世紀の250年の禁教期間中、弾圧があっても祈りを捨てなかったキリシタンの歴史は世界的に稀有である。弾圧を逃れて移り住んだ当時の景観をとどめる長崎県本土や平戸諸島、五島列島、天草諸島の集落や、開国後にキリシタンがフランス人神父に信仰を告白した「大浦天主堂」（長崎市）など12の資産で構成されている。宗教が弾圧下もひそかに継承され育まれた日本独自の信仰の姿が、人類共通の価値を持つと認められた。

3）自然遺産
〈1〉白神山地（1993年12月登録）
　青森・秋田の両県の日本海側に広がる世界最大級のブナ原生林で、稀少な動植物も多い。

〈2〉屋久島（1993年12月登録）
　九州南方65 kmに位置し、年間雨量が10,000 mmに達する。亜熱帯植物から亜寒帯植物までの植物が平地から山頂へと連続的に分布する植生が見られ、希少植物の宝庫として知られる。樹齢数千年の屋久杉が多く見られ、その中には樹齢7200年の縄文杉がある。

〈3〉知床（2005年7月登録）
　北海道東部に位置する知床半島および周辺海域。季節海氷により海洋生態系と陸上生態系が相互に関係し合い、特異な複合生態系を生み出ている。動植物とも北方系と南方系の両種が混在する多様な生物相が見られる。類まれな原始性を残し、オオワシ、オジロワシ、シマフクロウ、トド、ヒグマ、光ゴケ、シレトコスミレなどの絶滅危機に立つ動植物が生息している。

from the Korea and cut grass bowls thought to have been brought from Persia have been excavated, and all are designated National Treasures. The whole island is regarded as the precincts of the Munakata Taisha Shrine, and therefore as the object of faith. Women are not allowed on the island. Landings are severely restricted, and even when permitted, the person must take off all his clothes and enter the sea to make a ritual purification.

<18> "Heritage Listing of Hidden Christian Sites in Nagasaki and Amakusa Region" (Nagasaki and Kumamoto prefectures) (Registered July 2018)

During the ban on Christianity that lasted 250 years from the 17th to the 19th centuries, the history of the Christians who carried on their faith and continued to pray even in the midst of repression is an unusual story. To escape the repression, the Christians moved and formed settlements in Nagasaki prefecture and on the Hirado and Goto Islands and Amakusa. After the religious ban was lifted, the Christians confessed their faith to a French priest at Oura Cathedral, in Nagasaki City. These are among twelve component sites that have been listed. It was recognized that the distinctive form of this faith, which was inherited and nurtured secretly under repression, has values common to mankind.

3) Natural

<1> Shirakami Sanchi (Registered December 1993)

One of the world's largest virgin beech forests extending along the Japan Sea sides of Aomori and Akita prefectures. Home of many rare animals and plants.

<2> Yakushima (Registered December 1993)

An island located 65 km south of Kyushu, Yakushima receives up to 10,000 mm of rain annually. Its plant life, ranging from sub-tropical to the sub-arctic, is distributed from the plains up to the mountain peaks. It is known as a treasure house of rare botanical species. Some of the island's cedars, the *yakusugi*, are thousands of years old (the oldest, 7,200 years).

<3> Shiretoko (Registered July 2005)

Includes the Shiretoko Peninsula in eastern Hokkaido and the surrounding sea. The seasonal ice drift creates a unique ecosystem that brings the ecosystem of the sea into contact with that of the land. The rare biodiversity of the region includes both northern and southern fauna and flora. Rare primitive nature remains unspoiled and many endangered plants and animals inhabit the area, such as Steller's sea eagle, the white-tailed eagle, Blakiston's fish-owl, the *todo* (sea lion), the brown bear, luminous moss, and Shiretoko violets.

〈4〉 小笠原諸島（2011年6月登録）
　　海によって隔てられた小さな島において独自の進化を遂げた多くの固有の生き物や、それらが織りなす生態系を見ることができる。小笠原諸島を構成する島々は、これまで一度も大陸や大きな島と陸続きになったことがなく、人間から受けた影響が極めて少ない大洋島で、亜熱帯の気候の中で独自の生態系が育まれてきたため、生物の進化を示す典型的な見本として、世界的な価値を持つことが認められ、登録された。
4）複合遺産（現在登録されたものはない。）

d) 日本での宿泊

　　日本の宿には、日本式と西洋式がある。西洋式のものは、設備・サービス・食事・会計など欧米の場合と大体同様である。ユニークな宿泊施設の形態のひとつに、カプセルホテルがあり、2段に積まれたカプセル状（箱形）の簡易ベッドを提供する宿泊施設で、都市の繁華街に多く立地している。

　　日本式の宿の各部屋は、日本家屋と同様に畳敷である。トイレは部屋ごとについている場合もあるが、トイレ・浴室ともに共同の場所に設けられていることもある。とくに温泉地では、共同浴室が売物なので広く豪華である。料金は通常、夕食・宿泊と翌日の朝食代が含まれている。食事は日本料理であるが、ふつうは客が選択するのではなく、宿側が用意したものが出される。また、食事は各部屋に運ばれる場合もある。

　　全国各地の観光地を主体に、民宿・ペンションと呼ばれる経営者の自宅を兼ねた簡便な宿泊施設もある。宿泊、食事を廉価で提供し、経営者の家族ぐるみでの家庭的なもてなしにより好評である。さらに近年、一般住宅（戸建住宅、共同住宅等）の全部又は一部を活用して宿泊サービスを提供する民泊も急増しているが、民泊営業で生じたごみや騒音などが原因で、近隣住民に対するトラブルも生じている。

<4> Ogasawara Islands (Registered June 2011)

More than 30 isolated small islands display a unique ecological system that interweaves many independently-evolved indigenous life forms. As oceanic islands that have never been connected to a large land mass and have been very little affected by human activity, the Ogasawara Islands were able to develop their own distinctive ecological system in a subtropical climate. They were registered in recognition of their universal value as a classical example of biological evolution.

4) Mixed

So far Japan does not have a mixed cultural and natural heritage listing.

d) Lodgings in Japan

There are two types of (hotel) lodging in Japan, Japanese-style and Western-style. In the Western-style hotels, facilities, service, meals, and method of charges are roughly the same as in Europe and America. A unique accommodation format is that of the capsule hotel, which provides two levels of squarish capsules in which the guests sleep. These hotels are located in many downtown areas of cities.

In the Japanese-style places, the floor of each room is covered with *tatami* mats, as in Japanese homes. At some places each room has its own toilet while at others toilets and baths are provided for the common use of all the guests. Particularly in hot-spring resorts, where bathing is the attraction, the communal bathrooms are large and luxurious. Charges usually include dinner, the night's stay, and breakfast of the following morning. The meals are Japanese style, and guests ordinarily do not choose the dishes, but are served whatever the hotel has prepared. Meals are sometimes served in the rooms of the guests.

All around the country, conveniently located bed-and-breakfast accommodation is also available—primarily close to tourist spots. Room and board are provided at low prices, and this type of accommodation has a good reputation, due to the warm family hospitality provided. In recent years, there has been a rapid growth in the number of private houses providing accommodation services by utilizing all or part of an ordinary house (detached house or apartment). However, the trash, noise, and so on that are generated by this kind of private housing business can be troublesome for people living nearby.

(15) 日本のノーベル賞受賞者

2018年までにノーベル賞を受賞した日本人は、次の24人である。

〈1〉 湯川秀樹（1949年、物理学賞）：陽子と中性子との間に作用する核力を媒介するものとして、中間子の存在を予言した。

〈2〉 朝永振一郎（1965年、物理学賞）：「超多時間理論」と「くりこみ理論」で有名で、量子電磁力学分野の基礎的研究につくした。

〈3〉 川端康成（1968年、文学賞）：人生の哀歓の幻想と美をみごとに描いた『雪国』は、近代日本抒情文学の古典といわれる。『伊豆の踊子』『古都』『千羽鶴』『山の音』など多くの名作を残している。

〈4〉 江崎玲於奈（1973年、物理学賞）：半導体・超電導体トンネル効果について研究し、エサキダイオードを開発した。

〈5〉 佐藤栄作（1974年、平和賞）：日本の首相として国を代表して核兵器保有に終始反対し、太平洋地域の平和と安定に貢献した。

〈6〉 福井謙一（1981年、化学賞）：「フロンティア電子軌道理論」を開拓し、化学反応過程に関する理論の発展に貢献した。

〈7〉 利根川進（1987年、医学生理学賞）：「多様な抗体遺伝子が体内で再構成される理論」を実証し、遺伝学・免疫学に貢献した。

〈8〉 大江健三郎（1994年、文学賞）：自らの障害をもつ子との共生の経験を背景に、詩的な想像力と言葉で、現実と神話が融合した世界を創り出し、窮地にある人間の姿を絵のように描いた。『万延元年のフットボール』、『個人的な体験』などの多くの作品を発表した。

〈9〉 白川英樹（2000年、化学賞）：絶縁体と考えられていたプラスチックに導電性を持たせることに成功し、現代社会を支える電子機器の開発・普及に貢献した。

(15) Nobel Prize Winners

Listed below are the twenty-four Japanese Nobel prize winners up to 2018.

<1> Yukawa Hideki (1949, Physics)

Yukawa won his prize for work predicting the existence of the meson as providing the nuclear binding force between the proton and the neutron.

<2> Tomonaga Shin'ichiro (1965, Physics)

Tomonaga's famous super-many-time and renormalization theories have become fundamentals in the field of quantum electromagnetics.

<3> Kawabata Yasunari (1968, Literature)

Kawabata's *Snow Country*, with its masterly depiction of the beauty and fleeting joys and sorrows of life, has become a modern Japanese classic. Other masterpieces by Kawabata include *Dancing Girl of Izu*, *The Old Capital*, *Thousand Cranes*, and *The Sound of the Mountain*.

<4> Esaki Reona (Leo Esaki) (1973, Physics)

For research on the tunnel effect in semiconductors and superconductors, and development of the Esaki diode.

<5> Sato Eisaku (1974, Peace)

Sato received the prize for his efforts as Prime Minister to keep Japan directed away from possession of nuclear weapons and his contributions to stability and peace in the Pacific region.

<6> Fukui Ken'ichi (1981, Chemistry)

Fukui pioneered the frontier orbital theory which contributed to advancing theories related to chemical reaction processes.

<7> Tonegawa Susumu (1987, Physiology or Medicine)

Tonegawa contributed to genetics and immunology by showing how pieces of genes form millions of combinations which can produce a vast number of antibodies.

<8> Oe Kenzaburo (1994, Literature)

Drawing on his experience of life with a mentally impaired son, Oe paints a vivid picture of human desperation using poetic imagination and words to evoke a world that is a blend of reality and myth. His works include *The Silent Cry* and *A Personal Matter*.

<9> Shirakawa Hideki (2000, Chemistry)

Shirakawa succeeded in imparting electrical conductivity to a plastic that is ordinarily an insulator. His achievement contributed enormously to the development and utilization of electronic equipment that is now an essential part of the infrastructure of modern societies.

〈10〉野依良治（2001年、化学賞）：必要な型だけを合成する「不斉合成」とよばれる手法を開発し、医薬・食品を安全かつ大量に生産することに貢献した。

〈11〉小柴昌俊（2002年、物理学賞）：「カミオカンデ」を利用して宇宙空間中の希少素粒子ニュートリノの検出に成功し、物理学の大統一理論の前進に貢献した。

〈12〉田中耕一（2002年、化学賞）：タンパク質の質量を精密・簡単に測定する技術（ソフトレーザー脱離イオン化法）を開発し、生命科学、医療の進歩に貢献した。

〈13〉小林誠および〈14〉益川敏英（2008年、物理学賞）：クォークが自然界に少なくとも三世代（六種類）以上あることを予言する対称性の破れの起源の発見をして、新しい理論で説明することに成功し、素粒子物理学の基礎の構築に貢献した。小林誠、益川敏英の共同受賞。

〈15〉下村脩（2008年、化学賞）：緑色蛍光たんぱく質（GFP）の発見と開発をして、医学や生命科学の発展の基となる貢献をした。

〈16〉根岸英一および〈17〉鈴木章（2010年、化学賞）：2種の有機化合物を結びつけて新しい化合物をつくりだすカップリングの研究開発で「有機合成におけるパラジウム触媒を用いたクロスカップリング」の業績で、アメリカのリチャード・ヘックとともに受賞した。根岸英一、鈴木章の共同受賞。

〈18〉山中伸弥（2012年、医学生理学賞）：人体をかたちづくるための大もとの細胞は胚性肝細胞（ES細胞）である。マウスを使ってES細胞に4つの特殊な因子を導入し、ES細胞と同様なiPS細胞の樹立に成功した。さらに人間の皮膚に4種類の遺伝子を挿入しiPS細胞の生成に成功した。イギリスのジョン・ガードンと共同受賞。

<10> Noyori Ryoji (2001, Chemistry)
Noyori developed a method called asymmetric synthesis that can produce only the useful form of molecules that come in two forms. Thanks to Noyori's research, many medicines and foods can now be more safely produced in large volumes.

<11> Koshiba Masatoshi (2002, Physics)
Koshiba used the Kamioka Underground Observatory to detect neutrinos (subatomic particles) released from supernova explosions for the first time. His findings have helped to verify the Grand Unified Theory.

<12> Tanaka Koichi (2002, Chemistry)
Tanaka developed a simple and accurate method for determining the mass of proteins (a soft ionization method called soft laser desorption). His method is helping to advance the life sciences and medical therapy.

<13> Kobayashi Makoto and <14> Masukawa Toshihide (2008, Physics)
Shared prize for the discovery of the origin of the broken symmetry that predicts the existence of at least three families (six types) of quarks in nature, which contributed to the foundations of particle physics.

<15> Shimomura Osamu (2008, Chemistry)
Awarded for the discovery and development of green fluorescent protein (GFP), which contributed to the fundamental development of medicine and bioscience.

<16> Negishi Ei-ichi and <17> Suzuki Akira (2010, Chemistry)
Shared prize with Richard Heck of the U.S. for achieving "palladium-catalyzed cross couplings in organic synthesis" through their research into the synthesis of new compounds by coupling two different organic compounds.

<18> Yamanaka Shinya (2012, Medicine)
Yamanaka discovered that adult somatic cells can be reprogrammed into pluripotent cells. The cells that make up the human body originally came from embryonic stem cells (ES cells). Working first with adult mice, Yamanaka found that introducing the genes for four factors into mouse skin cells made it possible to reprogram the cells into ones just like mouse ES cells. He named the reprogrammed cells "induced pluripotent stem cells (iPS cells)." He also succeeded in reprogramming human skin cells into iPS cells by the same method. Yamanaka received the prize jointly with John Gurdon of the UK.

⟨19⟩赤崎勇および ⟨20⟩天野浩（2014年、物理学賞）：高輝度で省電力の白色光源を可能にした青色発光ダイオード（LED）を発明した。赤崎勇、天野浩、中村修二の共同受賞。

⟨21⟩大村智（2015年、医学生理学賞）：寄生虫によって起こる感染症の治療法であるイベルメクチンの元となる抗生物質などを発見した。

⟨22⟩梶田隆章（2015年、物理学賞）：素粒子の一つニュートリノに質量があることを観測によって証明した。観測による証明は世界初。

⟨23⟩大隅良典（2016年、医学生理学賞）：生物の生命活動にはアミノ酸が必須であるが、このアミノ酸は、たんぱく質を消化液で分解することによって生成される。大隅の研究は、長らく研究が進まなかったこのメカニズム、すなわち細胞が細胞自身のたんぱく質を分解・再生する「オートファジー（自食作用）」という、細胞に備えられた分解機構の中心の一つを分子レベルで解明した。

⟨24⟩本庶佑（2018年、医学生理学賞）：もともと人間が持つ免疫力に着目し、がん細胞が人の免疫細胞の一種「T細胞」にブレーキをかける分子「PD-1」を発見。その働きを粘り強く研究し、そのブレーキを遮断する革新的ながん治療薬「オプジーボ」の開発につなげた。「オプジーボ」はがん免疫治療としては、過去に例がないほど様々ながん患者を劇的に回復させている。アメリカのジェームズ・アリソンと共同受賞。

なお、この他にアメリカ国籍を取得した2名とイギリス国籍を取得した1名がいる。

南部陽一郎（2008年、物理学賞）：素粒子物理学と核物理学における自発的対称性の破れを発見し、基本理論を数式化し、現在の素粒子論の基礎の構築に貢献した。シカゴ大学で研究を行い1970年にアメリカ国籍を取得した。

中村修二（2014年、物理学賞）：高輝度で省電力の白色光源を可能にした青色発光イオードを発明した。中村修二は日亜化学工業の研究者であったが、後にカリフォルニア大学サンタバーバラ校の教授となりアメリカ国籍を取得している。天野浩および赤崎勇と共同受賞。

<19> Akasaki Isamu and <20> Amano Hiroshi (2014, Physics)

Akasaki and Amano invented a blue light emitting diode that enabled high brightness and energy-saving white light sources. Akasaki, Amano, and Nakamura Shuji were joint winners.

<21> Omura Satoshi (2015, Physiology or Medicine)

Omura discovered antibiotics that are the basis of ivermectin, which is used to treat for infections caused by parasites.

<22> Kajita Takaaki (2015, Physics)

Kajita proved through observations that neutrinos have mass. The observation-based proof was a world first.

<23> Osumi Yoshinori (2016, Physiology or Medicine)

Amino acids are essential for the life activity of an organism, but these amino acids are produced by decomposing a protein with a digestive juice. Osumi's research elucidated at the molecular level the mechanism of autophagy, one of the central decomposition mechanisms that cells have for protein decomposition and regeneration.

<24> Honjo Tasuku (2018, Physiology or Medicine):

Focusing on human's original immunity, Honjo discovered a molecule, PD-1, that acts as a brake on the immune activity of human immune T cells. Tenacious research by Honjo led to the development of "Opdivo," a breakthrough cancer drug that blocks the braking action. The application of Opdivo immunotherapy has brought about dramatic and unprecedent recoveries of patients suffering from a variety of cancers. Received the prize jointly with James Allison of the U.S.

Besides these, there are two people who acquired American nationality and one who acquired British nationality.

Nambu Yoichiro (2008, Physics), a Japanese-born naturalized U.S. citizen, was awarded the Nobel Prize for the discovery of the mechanism of spontaneous broken symmetry in subatomic physics and nuclear physics. He also mathematized basic theories and contributed to the foundation of today's theory of elemental particles. He studied at the University of Chicago and acquired American nationality in 1970.

Nakamura Shuji (2014, Physics) invented a blue light emitting diode that enabled high brightness and energy-saving white light sources. He was a researcher at Nichia Corporation and later became a professor at the University of California, Santa Barbara, and acquired American nationality. Received prize jointly with Amano Hiroshi and Akasaki Isamu.

石黒一雄（イシグロカズオ）(2017 年、文学賞)：受賞理由は「偉大な感情の力をもつ小説で、我々の世界とのつながりの感覚が不確かなものでしかないという、底知れない淵を明らかにした」とされる。長崎県出身であるが、幼少のころ日本人の両親とともにイギリスに移住しイギリス国籍を取得した。

Ishiguro Kazuo (2017, Literature) was recognized as an author "who, in novels of great emotional force, has uncovered the abyss beneath our illusory sense of connection with the world." Originally from Nagasaki prefecture, moved to the UK with his Japanese parents at a young age and acquired British nationality.

［付録］

〔統計資料〕

（1）主要各国の面積と人口
(Area of Selected Countries)

国　　　　名	面積（2015 年）		人口（2018 年）
	(1,000 km²)	(1,000 sq.mile)	（千人）
ロシア（Russia）	17,098	6,602	143,965
フランス共和国（France）	552	213	65,233
スペイン（Spain）	506	195	46,397
ドイツ連邦共和国（Germany）	357	138	82,293
イタリア共和国（Italy）	302	117	59,291
イギリス（U.K.）	242	93	66,574
中華人民共和国（China）	9,600	3,707	1,415,046
インド（India）	3,287	1,269	1,354,052
サウジアラビア王国（Saudi Arabia）	2,207	852	33,554
インドネシア共和国（Indonesia）	1,911	738	266,795
イラン・イスラム共和国（Iran）	1,629	629	82,012
トルコ共和国（Turkey）	784	303	81,917
タイ王国（Thailand）	513	198	69,183
日本（Japan）	378	146	126,590
ベトナム社会主義共和国（Vietnam）	331	128	96,491
マレーシア（Malaysia）	330	127	32,042
フィリピン共和国（Philippines）	300	116	106,512
アラブ首長国連邦（U.A.E.）	84	32	9,542
カナダ（Canada）	9,985	3,855	36,954
アメリカ合衆国（U.S.A.）	9,834	3,797	326,767
メキシコ合衆国（Mexico）	1,964	758	130,759
ブラジル連邦共和国（Brazil）	8,516	3,288	210,868
アルゼンチン共和国（Argentine）	2,780	1,073	44,689
オーストラリア連邦（Australia）	7,692	2,970	24,772
コンゴ民主共和国（Congo）	2,345	905	84,005
南アフリカ共和国（South Africa）	1,221	471	57,398
エジプト・アラブ共和国（Egypt）	1,002	387	99,376

「世界国勢図会」（2018／2019）
国連人口部「World Population Prospects; The 2017 Revision」(2018 年 5 月 15 日閲覧) による。
但し、「日本の人口数」は、総務省 人口推計 2018 年 4 月確定値。

(2) 日本の主要都市人口 (2017年1月1日現在)
(Population of Selected Cities in Japan)

都　市　名	人口 (In thousands)
東京23区　（Tokyo）	9,303 千人
横　　浜　（Yokohama）	3,736 〃
大　　阪　（Osaka）	2,691 〃
名　古　屋　（Nagoya）	2,279 〃
札　　幌　（Sapporo）	1,947 〃
神　　戸　（Kobe）	1,546 〃
福　　岡　（Fukuoka）	1,515 〃
川　　崎　（Kawasaki）	1,474 〃
京　　都　（Kyoto）	1,418 〃
さ い た ま　（Saitama）	1,281 〃
広　　島　（Hiroshima）	1,194 〃
仙　　台　（Sendai）	1,059 〃
北　九　州　（Kitakyusyuu）	967 〃
千　　葉　（Chiba）	966 〃
堺　　　（Sakai）	844 〃
浜　　松　（Hamamatsu）	808 〃
新　　潟　（Niigata）	800 〃
熊　　本　（Kumamoto）	734 〃
相　模　原　（Sagamihara）	716 〃
静　　岡　（Shizuoka）	709 〃
岡　　山　（Okayama）	709 〃
船　　橋　（Funabashi）	631 〃
鹿　児　島　（Kagoshima）	607 〃
川　　口　（Kawaguchi）	595 〃
八　王　子　（Hachioji）	563 〃
姫　　路　（Himeji）	540 〃

「住民基本台帳人口」(2017年1月1日現在) による。

(3) 日本の統治機構 (2019年4月)
(Government of Japan)

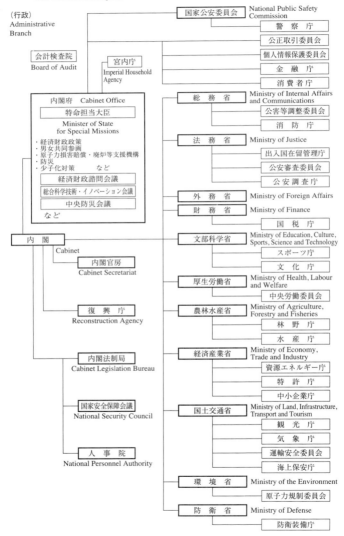

National Police Agency

Fair Trade Commission

Personal Information Protection Commission

Financial Services Agency

Consumer Affairs Agency

Environmental Dispute Coordination Commission

Fire and Disaster Management Agency

Immigration Services Agency

Public Securitry Examination Commission

Public Securitry Intelligence Agency

National Tax Agency

Japan Sports Agency

Agency for Cultural Affairs

Central Labour Relations Commission

Forestry Agency

Fisheries Agency

Agency for Natural Resources and Energy

Japan Patent Office

Small and Medium Enterprise Agency

Japan Tourism Agency

Japan Meteorological Agency

Japan Transport Safety Board

Japan Coast Guard

Nuclear Regulation Authority

Acquisition, Technology and Logistics Agency

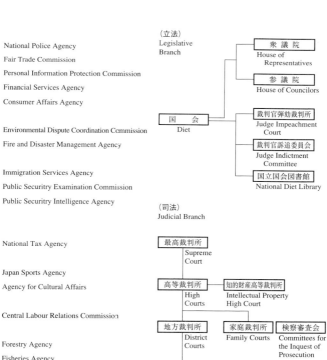

（立法）Legislative Branch
衆議院 House of Representatives
参議院 House of Councilors
国会 Diet
裁判官弾劾裁判所 Judge Impeachment Court
裁判官訴追委員会 Judge Indictment Committee
国立国会図書館 National Diet Library

（司法）Judicial Branch
最高裁判所 Supreme Court
高等裁判所 High Courts
知的財産高等裁判所 Intellectual Property High Court
地方裁判所 District Courts
家庭裁判所 Family Courts
検察審査会 Committees for the Inquest of Prosecution
簡易裁判所 Summary Courts

*
在外公館 Overseas Establishments
大使館 Embassies
総領事館 Consulates-General
領事館 Consulates
政府代表部 Permanent Missions and Delegations

(4) 各国の国内総生産 (GDP) と 1 人あたり GDP

(GDP and Per Capita Income)

	国内総生産 (億ドル)			1人あたり国内総生産 (千ドル)	
	2012年	2015年	2016年	2015年	2016年
アメリカ合衆国	162,446	181,207	186,245	58.1	57.8
中国	83,584	112,262	112,183	8.0	8.0
日本	59,602	43,799	49,362	35.5	38.6
ドイツ	34,260	33,756	34,778	42.1	42.5
イギリス	24,716	28,856	26,479	43.1	40.2
フランス	26,112	24,336	24,655	37.1	36.8
インド	18,752	21,328	22,596	1.6	1.7
イタリア	20,134	18,323	18,589	30.6	31.3
ブラジル	22,541	18,037	17,959	8.6	8.6
カナダ	18,214	15,528	15,298	42.5	42.2
韓国	11,296	13,828	14,112	27.4	27.8
オーストラリア	15,644	12,432	13,045	51.3	54.1
ロシア	20,298	13,263	12,460	9.0	8.7
スペイン	13,221	11,978	12,373	25.8	26.7
メキシコ	11,837	11,696	10,769	9.2	8.4
インドネシア	8,780	8,613	9,323	3.4	3.6
トルコ	7,883	8,598	8,637	10.9	10.9
オランダ	7,701	7,580	7,772	44.5	45.8
スイス	6,312	6,793	6,689	83.7	79.6
サウジアラビア	7,110	6,518	6,396	21.1	19.8
アルゼンチン	4,770	6,340	5,459	14.3	12.4
(台湾)		5,256	5,305	23.1	22.6
スウェーデン	5,238	4,979	5,145	51.5	52.3
ポーランド	4,809	4,774	4,714	12.0	12.3
ベルギー	4,834	4,552	4,680	40.3	41.2
イラン	5,516	3,934	4,254	5.0	5.3
タイ	3,857	3,992	4,070	5.5	5.9
ナイジェリア		4,946	4,046	2.6	2.2
オーストリア	3,945	3,821	3,908	43.7	44.9
ノルウェー	4,997	3,867	3,711	78.1	70.6
アラブ首長国連邦	3,838	3,581	3,487	39.3	37.6
(香港)		3,094	3,209	43.5	73.9
イスラエル		2,991	3,177	36.8	38.8
デンマーク	3,149	3,013	3,069	54.7	53.7
フィリピン		2,928	3,049	3.5	3.0
アイルランド		2,906	3,048	48.9	64.5
シンガポール	2,765	2,968	2,969	51.2	52.8
マレーシア	3,047	2,963	2,965	9.4	9.5

国連のデータベース (2018年5月16日閲覧) による。
中国には香港、マカオを含まない。名目値。米ドル。暦年。

（5）日本の産業別国内総生産（暦年）（単位 十億円）
（GDP by Industry in Japan）

	2000年	2010年	2015年	2016年	2016(%)
農林水産業	8,090	5,515	5,907	6,194	1.2
農業	6,837	4,628	4,899	5,240	1.0
林業	172	190	205	206	0.0
水産業	1,081	697	803	748	0.1
鉱業	611	304	315	291	0.1
製造業	118,815	104,239	110,223	113,337	21.0
うち食料品	14,093	12,538	13,260	13,656	2.5
化学	10,613	10,292	11,497	11,568	2.1
石油・石炭製品	5,490	5,234	3,852	4,880	0.9
一次金属	7,479	9,797	9,518	9,551	1.8
金属製品	6,037	4,197	4,764	4,924	0.9
はん・生産・業務用機械	14,370	13,206	16,213	16,875	3.1
電子部品・デバイス	7,920	5,684	5,173	4,983	0.9
電気機械	8,460	6,492	7,242	7,413	1.4
情報・通信機器	8,002	5,271	4,001	3,881	0.7
輸送用機械	12,652	14,800	17,709	18,011	3.3
電気・ガス・水道業	16,898	13,797	13,893	14,414	2.7
電気	9,312	6,092	6,167	6,737	1.3
ガス・水道・廃棄物処理	7,586	7,705	7,726	7,577	1.4
建設業	36,215	23,984	29,301	29,725	5.5
卸売・小売業	68,830	69,088	74,201	73,998	13.7
卸売	43,473	41,644	44,496	44,302	8.2
小売	25,358	28,044	29,706	29,696	5.5
運輸・郵便業	25,643	25,231	27,122	26,963	5.0
宿泊・飲食サービス業	16,580	12,847	12,372	12,865	2.4
情報通信業	24,236	25,514	26,681	26,830	5.0
通信・放送	11,267	11,636	12,218	12,312	2.3
情報サービス・映像音声文字情報制作	12,969	13,879	14,464	14,518	2.7
金融・保険業	25,637	24,115	23,187	22,462	4.2
不動産業	54,138	59,531	60,590	61,168	11.4
うち住宅賃貸業	47,018	51,732	52,539	52,699	9.8
専門・科学技術、業務支援サービス業	30,291	34,940	38,354	39,256	7.3
公務	27,314	26,306	26,572	26,679	5.0
教育	19,003	18,247	19,205	19,430	3.6
保健衛生・社会事業	27,874	32,025	36,229	37,744	7.0
その他のサービス	27,353	23,454	23,351	22,937	4.3
小計	527,527	499,136	527,502	534,292	99.2
輸入関税	3,869	4,847	8,755	7,676	1.4
(控除) 総資本形成に関わる消費税	3,525	2,898	5,747	5,776	1.1
国内総生産	526,706	500,354	531,986	538,446	100.0

内閣府「2016年度国民経済計算確報」（2018年2月1日閲覧）による。
構成比（％）は原資料掲載のものをそのまま引用し、各項目の内訳の調整を行っていない。

（6） 主要国のエネルギー自給率（2015年）（％）
(Self-Sufficiency in Energy)

	日本	アメリカ合衆国	ドイツ	イギリス	フランス
一次エネルギー	7.0	92.2	38.8	65.8	55.9
石炭	–	115.3	54.1	21.4	–
原油　1)	0.3	62.4	3.3	72.8	1.7
天然ガス	2.4	98.5	9.7	58.2	0.1

	カナダ	ロシア	中国	オーストラリア	サウジアラビア
一次エネルギー	174.4	188.0	83.9	304.3	292.6
石炭	166.2	172.1	94.2	695.8	–
原油　1)	214.3	184.9	39.7	71.0	281.4
天然ガス	159.8	143.9	71.0	174.9	100.0

「日本国勢図会」（2018／2019）
IEA（国際エネルギー機関）"Energy Balances of CECD Countries/Non OECD Countries"（2017年版）による。自給率は、エネルギー・バランスで石油換算された数値を用いて、生産量÷消費量×100で算出した。1) 天然ガス液など随伴物を含む。

（7） 主な国の農産物自給率（2013年）（％）
(Self-Sufficiency in Food Crops)

品目 (Items)	日本(Japan)	アメリカ(U.S.A.)	イギリス(U.K.)	ドイツ(Germany)	フランス(France)	中国(China)
穀類 (Grains)	24	126	87	113	190	100
小麦 (Wheat)	11	170	82	152	190	97
米 (Rice)	87	184	0	0	13	102
とうもろこし(Corn)	0	121	0	55	183	103
いも類 (Potatoes)	72	96	75	117	116	86
大豆 (Legumes)	7	174	0	0	18	16
肉類 (Meat)	51	116	69	114	98	99

「世界の統計」（2018／19）
FAOSTAT/Food Balance（2018年6月15日閲覧）による。

(8) 産業別就業人口割合（2016年）（単位 千人）
(Breakdown of Industrial Sector of Employed Persons 15 Years Old and Over)

	日本	アメリカ合衆国	イギリス	ドイツ	中国	韓国
農林漁業	2,281	2,561	361	540	140,244	1,297
鉱業・採石	30	738	92	85	3,483	19
製造業	10,962	16,039	3,058	7,908	131,145	4,519
電気・ガス・水道	637	1,459	441	553	2,317	187
建設	5,055	10,751	2,346	2,761	67,733	1,860
卸売・小売	11,178	18,279	4,205	5,826	130,077	3,760
宿泊・飲食	3,997	9,596	1,819	1,580	21,621	2,297
運輸・情報通信	5,938	10,823	2,475	3,279	29,697	2,216
金融・保険	1,952	6,373	900	1,301	24,860	803
不動産・専門サービス	6,339	15,819	5,059	4,627	16,959	2,990
公務・社会保障	2,378	10,566	1,584	2,888	34,985	1,004
教育	3,106	15,759	3,162	2,694	91,847	1,866
医療・福祉	8,175	23,412	4,578	5,294	35,324	1,871
計	65,136	154,263	32,167	41,292	763,980	26,455

「世界国勢図会」(2018／2019)
ILO "LOSTAT"（URL：http//www.ilo.org/ilostat）による。2018年5月時点の推定値。
15歳以上の統計。国の法律や慣習によって若干異なる場合がある。

（9）日本の学校体系図
(Japanese School System)

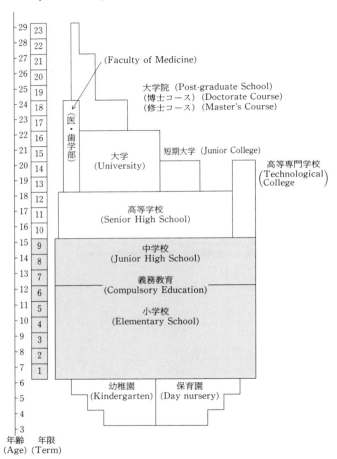

566 統計資料

〔参考文献〕

〈全般〉
「大日本百科全書」小学館
「世界大百科事典書」平凡社
「日本国語大辞典」小学館
「日本国勢図絵」（財）矢野恒太記念会
「世界国勢図絵」（財）矢野恒太記念会
「広辞苑」第7版　新村出編　岩波書店
「現代用語の基礎知識」自由国民社
「ウィキペディア」　ウィキメディア財団

〈政府刊行物〉
「日本の統計」総務省
「世界の統計」総務省
「外交青書」外務省　時事画報社
「防衛白書」防衛省
「警察白書」警察庁
「情報通信白書」総務省
「厚生労働白書」厚生労働省
「経済財政白書」内閣府
「通商白書」経済産業省
「ものづくり白書」経済産業省
「中小企業白書」経済産業省
「エネルギー白書」経済産業省
「日本の将来統計人口」国立社会保障・人口問題研究所
「環境白書」環境省
「文部科学白書」文部科学省
「科学技術白書」文部科学省
「宗教年鑑」文化庁
「少子化社会対策白書」内閣府

〈地理〉
「理科年表」国立天文台編　丸善
「日本列島の誕生」平朝彦　岩波書店

〈歴史〉
「詳説日本史」五味文彦他編　山川出版社
「詳説世界史」木下康彦他編　山川出版社
「世界史総合図録」成瀬治他編　山川出版社
「日本を決定した百年」吉田茂　日本健在新聞社
「後醍醐天皇」兵藤裕己著　岩波新書
「日本史のツボ」本郷和人著　文春新書
「上皇の日本史」本郷和人著　中公新書ラクレ

〈政治〉
「憲法」芦部信喜　岩波書店
「政治の精神」佐々木毅　岩波新書
「世界の憲法集」阿部照哉・畑博行編　有信堂
「アメリカとパレスチナ問題」高橋和夫　角川テーマ21
「新中国人」N・クリストフ、S・ウーダン　新潮社
「戦後日本首相の外交思想」増田弘編著　ミネルヴァ書房
「続・100年予測」ジョージ・フリードマン著　櫻井祐子訳　早川書房

〈経済〉
シュムペーター著「資本主義・社会主義・民主主義」中山伊知郎、東畑精一訳　東洋経済新報社
ケインズ著「雇用・利子および貨幣の一般理論」間宮陽介訳　岩波書店
マイケル・ポーター著「競争戦略論Ⅰ、Ⅱ」竹内弘高訳　ダイヤモンド社
クルーグマン著「マクロ経済学」大山道弘他訳　東洋経済新報社
クルーグマン著「ミクロ経済学」大山道弘他訳　東洋経済新報社
マンキュー著「経済学」マクロ編　ミクロ編　足立英之他訳　東洋経済新報社
藤本隆宏著「日本のものづくり哲学」「生産管理論Ⅰ、Ⅱ」日本経済新聞社
アルビン・トフラー著「第三の波」徳山二郎監修　日本放送協会出版
ピーター・F・ドラッカー著「マネジメント」エッセンシャル版　上田淳生訳　ダイヤモンド社
神野直彦著「財政学」改定版　有斐閣
宇波弘貴（財務省）編著　図説「日本の財政」平成29年度版　東洋経済新報社
野地秩嘉著「トヨタ物語」日経BP社
湯之上隆著「日本半導体敗戦」光文社
竹中平蔵著「第4次産業革命！日本経済をこう変える」PHPビジネス新書
野口悠紀雄著「平成はなぜ失敗したのか」幻冬舎
飯田泰之著「経済学講義」ちくま新書
ケヴィン・ケリー著「インターネットの次にくるもの」服部桂訳　NHK出版
田中道明著「（アマゾン社）ベゾスの大

参考文献　567

戦略」PHPビジネス新書

〈科学技術〉

「鉄の未来が見える本」新日鉄住金　日本実業出版
「鉄と鉄鋼がわかる本」新日鉄住金　日本実業出版
「1秒でわかる！先端素材業界ハンドブック」泉谷渉著　東洋経済新報社
「ホントにすごい！日本の科学技術図鑑」川口友万　双葉社
「はっきりわかる　現代サイエンスの常識事典」成美堂出版
「理化学研究所　100年目の巨大研究機関」山根一眞　講談社
「スマホ・ケータイ利用トレンド　ケータイ社会白書」NTTドコモモバイル社会研究所　中央経済社

〈文化・社会・教育・環境〉

「文化人類学の歴史」マーウィン・ガーバリーノ　新泉社
「文化人類学事典」祖父江孝男　ぎょうせい
「文明の衝突」サミュエル・ハンチントン　集英社
「比較文明」伊藤俊太郎　東北出版会
「日本文化論の変容」梅原猛　日本放送出版協会
「日本とは何か」堺屋太一　講談社
「日本人とは何か」宮城音弥　朝日新聞社
「日本文化史」家永三郎　岩波書店
「日本文化の歴史」尾藤正英　岩波新書
「日本文化史概説」中公新書
「日本人丸わかり辞典」PHP研究所編
「日本入門（全3巻）」早稲田大学編　早稲田大学出版部
「照葉樹林文化」上山春平　中公新書
「稲作文化－照葉樹林帯文化の展開－」上山春平　中公新書
「木と緑と土と」富山和子　中公新書
「福翁自伝」福澤諭吉　慶応通信
「西行」高橋英夫　岩波新書
「やさしい茶の湯入門」成井宗歌　金園社
「ソフトパワー」ジョゼフ・ナイ　日経新聞
「ホモ・ルーデンス」ホイジンガー　中公文庫
「菊と刀」ルース・ベネディクト平凡社世界教養全集
「日本人の微笑」ラフカディオ・ハーン下田衛註釈　学生社
「日本その日その日（1，2，3）」エドワード・モース　平凡社世界教養全集
「風土・人間的考察」和辻哲郎　岩波書店
「タテ社会人間関係」中根千枝　講談社
「日本のこころ・文化・伝統・現代」新日鉄住金　丸善
「本当の豊かさとは」岩波書店編　岩波書店
「世界宗教地図」石川純一　新潮文庫
「日本人の信仰心」磯部忠正　講談社
「ことばと文化」鈴木孝夫　岩波新書
「漢字なりたち辞典」藤堂明保監修　教育社
「日本語の特質」金田一春彦　NHK出版
「日本語（上・下）」金田一春彦　岩波新書
「コンサイス外来語辞典」三省堂編　三省堂
「日本の外来語」矢崎源九郎　岩波新書（赤）
「翻訳語成立事情」柳文章　岩波新書（青）
「ベルリッツの世界言語百科」チャールス・ベルリッツ　新潮選書
「日本美術の研究」吉田光邦　日本放送出版協会
「日本の美術百選」文化庁協力・朝日新聞社編
「日本美術史の歴史」辻惟男　東京大学出版会
「カラー版日本美術史」辻惟男　美術出版社
「講座日本美術史全六巻」佐藤康宏・板倉聖哲・長岡竜作・玉蟲敏子・木下直之　東京大学出版会
「日本文学の歴史」全集　ドナルド・キーン　中央公論社
「地球の歴史としくみ」山賀進　ベレ出版
「地球環境と資源問題」森俊介　岩波書店
「文明の崩壊（上下）」ジャレド・ダイアモンド　草思社
「少子社会日本」山田昌弘　岩波書店
「仕事と家族」筒井淳也　中央公論新社
「知識ゼロからのビッグデータ入門」稲田修一　幻冬舎
「コンテンツ業界の動向とカラクリがよくわかる本」第3版　中野明　秀和システム

〔年表〕

世紀	史実			
	時代	日本	東洋	西洋
紀元前	新石器	10000頃 縄文文化期に入る	2800～2300頃 中国、黒陶文化盛ん 2300頃 インダス文明	3500頃 メソポタミア文明 3000頃 エーゲ文明 3000頃 エジプトの統一
紀元前	縄文・弥生	300頃 弥生時代に入る (水稲稲作、金属器) (前1世紀頃、倭、小国分立)	1400頃 中国、殷王朝繁栄 1050 中国、周が殷を滅ぼす 770～403 中国、春秋時代 500頃 中国、呉越の抗争 500頃 仏教おこる 仏典結集 453 中国、晋分裂、戦国時代・諸子百家 268～232頃 アショーカ王、インド統一、仏教の布教 221 秦の始皇帝中国統一、万里の長城修築始まる匈奴活動活発化 202 前漢建国、匈奴との戦い 194 衛氏朝鮮誕生 104 前漢、朝鮮進出 37頃 高句麗誕生	1700頃 ハンムラビア法典 1600～1200 クレタ・ミケーネ文明 1200 トロイ戦争 753 ローマ建国 671 アッシリアの統一 525 ペルシャの大統一 500～449 ギリシャとペルシャの戦争 (マラトン・サラミス海戦) 334～324 アレクサンダー大王の大東征、ペルシャ滅亡 264～146 ローマ対カルタゴ戦争 (ポエニ戦争) 73～71 スパルタクスの乱 27 アウグストゥスの支配
1世紀		57 後漢に使者を送る	25 後漢建国、光武帝 37 後漢が全国統一 67 仏教中国に伝わる 74 後漢、西域平定、全盛	イエス・キリスト誕生 ローマ帝国地中海世界統一、以後200年間全盛 64～67 暴君ネロ、キリスト教徒迫害。ペテロ、パウロ殉教 79 ポンペイ市の埋没

1世紀				80 コロッセウム完成
2世紀	縄文・弥生	107 後漢に使者を送る（登呂遺跡）	104 後漢、衛氏朝鮮を滅ぼす 130～170頃 インド、カニシカ王ガンダーラ美術、大乗仏教普及 184 中国、黄巾の乱おこる	116 ローマ帝国、五賢帝時代、メソポタミア遠征領土最大期、キリスト教迫害 150頃 新約聖書成る
3世紀		239 邪馬台国卑弥呼、魏に使者を送る（前方後円墳出現） 266 邪馬台国台与、後晋に使者を送る	208 赤壁の戦い（天下三分の計） 220 後漢滅亡、三国時代となる（魏・呉・蜀） 250頃 朝鮮、三韓時代 265 中国、後晋建国	220以降 ゴート族、ゲルマン人がローマ帝国内侵入 224 サザン朝ペルシャ建国 260 ペルシャがローマ帝国と戦いローマ皇帝を捕える
4世紀	古墳	300年代前半、大和王権が全国統一 367 百済の使者来日 369 朝鮮出兵 391 日本、百済・新羅を破る	304～439 中国、五胡十六国時代 313 高句麗、後晋勢力を朝鮮から駆逐 316 後晋滅亡、東晋建国 346 百済建国 356 新羅建国 369 日本、新羅を破り、半島南部の加羅に進出 391 日本、百済・新羅と戦う（広開土王碑）	330 ローマ帝国、コンスタンティノープル遷都 370頃 フン族西進し、西アジア・東欧・ロシアを制圧 375 ゲルマン民族大移動開始、ローマ帝国内に侵入 380 ローマ帝国、キリスト教を国教化 395 ローマ帝国東西に分裂
5世紀		404 高句麗と戦う 413 倭王讃（仁徳天皇?）東晋に使者を送る この頃仁徳天皇陵（大山古墳）築造、大陸文化（漢字、儒教、暦、技術等）伝来 478 倭王武が宋に遣使	404 高句麗、日本と戦う 420 東晋滅亡、宋建国 439～577 中国、南北朝時代 450 高句麗、新羅を攻撃	5世紀から6世紀にかけて、東ローマ（ビザンツ）帝国とサザン朝ペルシャの争い継続 449 アングロサクソンがブリタニアに移住 476 西ローマ帝国滅亡 486 フランク王国建国

6世紀		513 百済、五経博士を日本に送る 538頃 仏教伝来 593〜621 聖徳太子の摂政政治	562 新羅、加羅を滅ぼす 589 隋の文帝、中国を統一、府兵制、均田制、租庸調制を整備	531〜579 ササン朝ペルシャ隆盛（ホスロー1世） 570〜632 ムハンマド（マホメット）
7世紀	飛鳥	600 遣隋使開始 604 十七条憲法制定 607 小野妹子を隋に派遣 607 法隆寺建立 630 遣唐使開始 645 大化改新 672 壬申の乱 680 東大寺建立	608 隋の煬帝大運河を開く、高句麗遠征失敗等で618滅亡 618 唐建国、隋の基礎に中央管制、科挙採用で律令国家を確立 高宗、太宗（貞観の治）唐全盛 663 朝鮮、白村江の戦い 676 新羅、朝鮮を統一 698 渤海おこる	610 イスラム教成立 622 イスラム暦元年 636 ササン朝ペルシャ、イスラム軍に敗北、651滅亡 673 イスラム軍、ビザンツ帝国と激突 697 イスラム軍、北アフリカ・カルタゴ占領
8世紀	奈良	701 大宝律令制定 710 平城京（奈良）遷都 712 「古事記」編纂 720 「日本書紀」 752 東大寺の大仏完成 754 鑑真上人来る 「万葉集」 794 平安京（京都）遷都	690〜705 則天武后の乱 712 玄宗皇帝即位、開元の治 唐文化全盛期 楊貴妃（745〜756） 唐文化、仏教、道教の全盛 755〜763 節度使（地方軍団長官） 安史の乱（安禄山・史思明） 760頃 チベット仏教成立 780 唐、両税法を施行	717〜718 イスラム軍、欧州西進 732 フランク王国、西フランスでウマイア朝イスラム軍を撃退、フランク王国内で封建制が進む アッバース朝ペルシャ(750〜1258)建国、唐を西域で破る 768〜814 フランク王国カール大帝、領土拡大（西ローマ帝国の復興）
9世紀	平安	804 最澄、空海唐に渡る 839 最後の遣唐使帰朝 858 藤原良房摂政となる 887 藤原基経関白となる 894 遣唐使の停止 かな文字の発生	唐、増税により均田農民が没落、宦官の横暴・異民族の侵入で唐の律令体制が崩れ始める。 唐の政治・軍事力は衰退 875 王仙芝の乱（農民の反乱） 875〜884 黄巣の乱（同上）	829 イングランド統一 この頃より約200年間ヴァイキングが欧州を荒らす 843 ヴェルダン条約、フランク王国がフランス、ドイツ、イタリアに分裂

世紀		日本	中国	西洋・その他
9世紀				871～899 イングランド、アルフレッド大王の統治
10世紀	平安	902 延喜式荘園整理令 905 「古今和歌集」 935～941 承平・天慶の乱 935頃 紀貫之「土佐日記」 藤原氏による摂関政治 1000頃 清少納言「枕草子」	907 唐滅亡 中国、五代十国時代 936 高麗が朝鮮半島を統一 960 宋建国 963 高麗、宋に服属 979 宋、中国統一	911 ノルマンディー公国成立 919～1024 東フランク・ザクセン朝マジャール人を撃退 962 神聖ローマ帝国成立 オットー1世戴冠
11世紀		1007 紫式部「源氏物語」 1016 藤原道長摂政 1051～62 前九年の役 1083～87 後三年の役 1086 白河上皇の院政始まる 武士の台頭	宋時代、火薬・羅針盤・木版印刷の発明。文治主義の為、武力が弱く、異民族の侵入に苦しむ 1069 王安石の改革（富国強兵） 1084 司馬光「資治通鑑」	1037 セルジューク・トルコ建国（首都バクダット） 1066 ノルマン人のイングランド征服ウィリアム1世（1066～1087） 1096 十字軍遠征始まる
12世紀		1167 平清盛太政大臣となる 1185 平家滅亡 1192 源頼朝征夷大将軍となり鎌倉幕府を開く。（武家政治の始まり）	1127 宋、満州人の金に滅ばされる 1127 南宋の建国 1142 南宋、金（女真族）と講和	1147～49 第2回十字軍 1143 ポルトガル建国 1150 オックスフォード大学建学 1180 パリ大学建学 1189～92 第3回十字軍
13世紀	鎌倉	1221 承久の変。北条氏が執権として鎌倉幕府を引き継ぐ 1232 貞永式目制定 元寇、鎌倉幕府、元軍（モンゴル）を撃退 　1274 文永の役（元、高麗襲来） 　1281 弘安の役（元、高麗、旧南宋襲来） 1297 永仁の徳政令	1206 チンギス・ハン、モンゴル統一（首都、カラコルム） モンゴル軍、アジア全域を侵略 1259 高麗、服属 1271 モンゴル、国号を元と称す、首都大都（北京） 1279 元、南宋を滅ぼす 1292 元、ジャワ遠征失敗、ジャワ、マジャパヒト王国建国	1202～04 第4回十字軍、コンスタンティノーブルを占領 1215 イギリス、マグナカルタ（大憲章）制定 モンゴル軍、中央アジア・中東・欧州を侵略 1237 モスクワ占領 1240 キエフ占領 1241 ワールシュタットの戦い 1258 バグダット占領

世紀	時代	日本	東洋	西洋
13世紀	鎌倉		1297 元、ミャンマー滅ぼす	1265 イギリス議会創設
14世紀		鎌倉幕府、元寇の影響で衰退 1333 後醍醐天皇、建武の新政（鎌倉幕府滅亡） 1336 南北朝の対立 1338 足利尊氏、征夷大将軍となり、室町幕府を開く 1392 三代足利義満、南北朝を統一 1397 足利義満、金閣寺を造営	1313 元、科挙実施 1328 元、内紛で分裂 1351～66 中国群雄割拠、紅巾の乱 1368 太祖洪武帝、明建国、元は華北へ後退 1373 明律、明令、兵制改革 1388 明、元を滅ぼす 1392 李氏朝鮮王国おこり、朝鮮半島を統一、明に服属	1302 フランス、三部会 1309 教皇アビニョン捕囚 1339 英仏百年戦争 1353～ヨーロッパにペスト（黒死病）大流行 1370～1507 ティムール王国、ペルシャ、トルコ、インド、ロシアを制圧 1378～1417 キリスト教会大分裂 英仏で農民の反乱
15世紀	室町・安土桃山	1404 明と通商（勘合貿易） 1428 正長の徳政一揆 1441 六代将軍足利義教、守護大名の赤松満祐に殺害される 1467～77 応仁の乱 戦国時代に突入 1483 足利義政、銀閣寺を造営 この頃、各地に土一揆おこる 1493 北条早雲、伊豆の堀越公方を滅ぼす	1402～24 明の永楽帝、積極的対外政策（北京遷都、南北遠征） 1405～30 鄭和南海遠征 1415 四書大全、永楽大全 1433 朝鮮ハングル文字 明、宦官の専横、国力衰退 1449 オイラト、華北侵入、明皇帝、捕虜になる。北虜南倭（沿岸部、倭寇の被害）	1414～18 コンスタンツ公会議 ローマ教皇権動揺、教会改革 1429 英仏軍、激突（ジャンヌダルクの活躍） 1453 オスマン帝国、ビザンツ帝国を滅ぼす 1453 英仏百年戦争終了 1492 コロンブスのアメリカ発見 1498 バスコ・ダ・ガマ、インド航路発見
16世紀		室町幕府弱体化、各地は群雄割拠、下克上相次ぐ 1543 ポルトガル人、種子島に鉄砲を伝える 1549 ザビエル、キリスト教を伝える 1553～64 川中島の戦べ5回 1560 桶狭間の戦い	1506 このころ「西遊記」、「金瓶梅」などできる 1511 ポルトガル、マラッカ占領 1521 マゼラン、フィリピン到着、セブ島で殺される	1500 ポルトガル人カブラル、ブラジル発見 1503～06頃 レオナルド・ダ・ビンチのモナリザ、ミケランジェロのダビデ像成る 1517 ルター宗教改革をとなえる 1519 マゼラン世界周航に出発

世紀	時代	日本	アジア	世界
16世紀	室町・安土桃山	1573 織田信長室町幕府を滅ぼす 1582 本能寺の変、織田信長死す 1590 豊臣秀吉、全国統一 1592〜1598 豊臣秀吉、朝鮮出兵	1592〜1598 日本軍、朝鮮侵攻、朝鮮、明軍と戦う（文禄の役、慶長の役） 1595 オランダ、インドネシアへ進出 明、日本との戦いに疲弊し、国力弱体化	1526 ムガール帝国おこる 1562〜1598 フランス、ユグノー（新旧キリスト教宗教）戦争 1581 オランダ、スペインから独立、ロシア、シベリア進出 1588 英国、スペイン無敵艦隊を破る
17世紀	江戸	1600 関ヶ原の戦い 1603 徳川家康、江戸幕府を開く 1612 幕府、キリスト教禁止令 1615 大阪夏の陣、豊臣氏滅亡 1637〜1638 島原の乱 1639 幕府、ポルトガル船の来航禁止（鎖国令） 歌舞伎おこる 1657 明暦の大火、江戸城本丸等、江戸の半分以上消失 1694 「おくのほそ道」松尾芭蕉	1602 オランダ東インド会社がインドネシア統治 1616 後金・清建国（満州人の女真族） 1621 後金、華北占領 1627 後金軍、朝鮮侵入 1636 後金、清と国号を改める 1636 清軍、朝鮮に再侵入、服属させる 1644 清、明を滅ぼす 1681〜1683 清、漢族の内乱を治め中国、台湾統一 1689 ネルチンスク領土条約（清・ロシア）	1603 オランダ、オーストラリア発見 1609 ガリレオが望遠鏡を発明 1613 ロシアロマノフ王朝はじまる 1620 メイフラワー号によるピューリタンのアメリカ東海岸への移住 1642 イギリスの清教徒革命 1687 ニュートン万有引力の法則発見 1688 イギリスに名誉革命おこる
18世紀		1702 赤穂浪士事件 1716 八代徳川吉宗将軍となる 1716〜1745 享保の改革 1720 洋書輸入禁緩和、蘭学おこる 1778 ロシア船、蝦夷地に来航 1782 天明の大飢饉、翌年浅間山大噴火、天候不順・凶作続く	インド、ムガール帝国、衰退に向かう。地方政権乱立 イギリス、フランス、オランダがインドに進出 1757 イギリス、プラッシーの戦いで、インドからフランス勢力を駆逐、以後、1世紀かけてインド支配を確立	1701 プロシア王国成立 1752 フランクリン電気発見 1769 アークライト、水力紡績機発明 イギリスに産業革命おこる 1775〜1786 アメリカ独立戦争 1776 アメリカ独立宣言 1788 アメリカ憲法制定

18世紀	江戸	1787〜1793 老中松平定信、寛政の改革 浮世絵全盛期	1796〜1804 清、白蓮教徒の乱 清、衰退に向かう	1789 フランス革命おこる 1792 フランス第一共和政 1795 ナポレオン、イタリア征服 1798 ナポレオン、エジプト遠征
19世紀	江戸・明治	1804 レザノフ、長崎来航 1808 間宮林蔵、樺太探検、フェートン号事件 1825 異国船打ち払い命令 1853 ペリー来航 1854 日米和親条約 1855 日露和親条約、エトロフ島は、日本に帰属 1858 日米修好通商条約 1868 明治維新、戊辰戦争 1877 西南戦争、東京大学開学 1889 大日本帝国憲法制定 1894〜1895 日清戦争、下関条約、三国干渉	1839 林則徐、広州でアヘン取締り 1840〜1842 アヘン戦争 1851〜1864 太平天国の乱 1856 アロー号戦争 清国、弱体化し、列強の中国進出相次ぐ 1858 ムガール帝国滅亡、イギリスがインドを直接統治開始 1877 イギリス領インド帝国成立 1887 フランス領インドシナ成立 1898 フィリピン、アメリカ領となる 1898 列強の中国分割激化	1804 ナポレオン皇帝即位 1805 トラファルガー海戦 1812 ナポレオン、モスクワ遠征 1815 ウィーン条約、ワーテルローの戦い（ナポレオン失脚） 1853〜1856 クリミア戦争 1861 ロシア、農奴解放令 1861 リンカーン、アメリカ大統領に就任、南北戦争（〜1865）奴隷解放宣言 1866 プロシア・オーストリア戦争 1870 プロシア・フランス戦争 1871 ドイツ帝国成立 1877 ロシア・トルコ戦争 1898 アメリカ・スペイン戦争
20世紀	大正・昭和	1904〜1905 日露戦争、ポーツマス条約 1910 韓国併合条約 1914 第一次世界大戦参戦 1915 中国に21ヶ条の要求 1918 シベリア出兵、米騒動、原内閣成立	1900 義和団事件 1901 北京議定書 1905 帝政ロシア、日本に敗れる、シベリア鉄道完成 1910 日本、韓国併合 1911 孫文、辛亥革命 1912 中華民国建国、清滅亡	1904〜1905 日露戦争、ポーツマス条約 1905 ロシア、血の日曜日事件 1912〜13 バルカン戦争 1914〜18 第一次世界大戦 1917 ロシア革命（指導者レーニン）

20世紀	大正・昭和	1922 海軍軍縮条約 1923 関東大震災 1925 治安維持法、普通選挙法 1927 金融恐慌 1928 普通選挙実施 1931 満州事変 1932 上海事変、五・一五事件 1933 国際連盟脱退 1936 二・二六事件 1937 日独防共協定 1940 日独伊三国同盟成立 1945 米軍、広島・長崎に原爆投下 1945 ソ連、対日参戦 1941～1945 太平洋戦争	1919 中国五・四運動、国民党成立 1921 中国共産党成立 1922 エジプト、イギリスから独立 1923 トルコ共和国成立 1926 中国国民政府軍、北伐開始 1931 満州事変、日中戦争開始 1932 上海事変 1932 サウジアラビア、イラク独立 1934～36 中国共産党軍、長征 1937 中国、第2次国共合作 1940 日本、インドシナ進駐 1942 日本、東南アジア各地を占領 1943～1945 連合国の反撃強まる 1945 日本降伏	1919 パリ講和会議、ベルサイユ条約 1922 ソビエト社会主義共和国連邦成立 1924 レーニン死去、スターリン後継 1928 不戦条約 1929 ニューヨーク市場の株価暴落、世界経済恐慌へ波及 1933 ドイツ、ナチス党政権成立 1935 ドイツ、再軍備宣言 1937 日独防共協定 1939 ドイツ、ポーランド侵攻、第二次世界大戦 1945 ベルリン陥落、ドイツ降伏
	昭和	1946 公職追放令 1947 日本国憲法成立 1948 極東国際軍事裁判判決 1951 サンフランシスコ平和条約、日米安全保障条約調印 1955 自由民主党、日本社会党による二大政党政治始まる 1956 日ソ共同宣言、国連加盟 1950年代後半から1970年代初めにかけて、日本経済の高度成長が続く 1960 日米安保条約成立 1964 東海道新幹線開通、東京オリンピック開催	1945 インドネシア独立 1946 フィリピン独立、インドシナ戦争（～54） 1947 インド、パキスタン独立 1948 韓国、北朝鮮成立、ミャンマー、スリランカ独立、イスラエル成立 1949 中華人民共和国建国 1950 中ソ友好同盟相互援助条約（～80）、朝鮮戦争勃発（～53） 1955 第1回アジア・アフリカ会議（バンドン） 1960 アフリカ諸国の独立続く	1945 国際連合成立 1947 アメリカ、トルーマンドクトリン、マーシャルプランで欧州復興援助 1949 北大西洋条約、ドイツ分裂 1951 ヨーロッパ石炭鉄鋼共同体条約 1955 ワルシャワ条約機構成立 1956 ハンガリー動乱 1957 ヨーロッパ経済共同体（EEC） 1962 キューバ危機 1967 EC発足 1968 ソ連、チェコスロバキアに侵入 1969 アメリカ、人類初の月面到着

20世紀	昭和	1965 日韓基本条約調印（賠償補償問題解決） 1968 GNP、世界第2位になる	1965 ベトナム戦争激化 1966 中国文化大革命 1969 中ソ国境紛争	
20世紀	昭和・平成	1970 日米安保条約改訂 1972 沖縄祖国復帰実現、日中共同声明 1973～76 石油危機で日本経済が大打撃を受ける 1978 日中平和友好条約 1980～ 行政改革、民営化推進。日米経済摩擦激化 1989 消費税初導入（3％） 1991 バブル経済崩壊 1993 自民党分裂、非自民、細川連立内閣成立 1994 社会・さきがけ・自民3党村山連立内閣成立 1995 阪神・淡路大震災、地下鉄サリン事件 1997 消費税3％から5％に増税	1971 国連、中華人民共和国の中国代表権承認（常任理事国） 1972 ニクソン大統領訪中 1973 第4次中東戦争、石油危機 1975 南北ベトナム統一 1976 周恩来・毛沢東死去、四人組失脚 1979 米中、国交正常化 1989 中国、天安門事件、以降鄧小平総書記、改革・開放経済路線を推進し、経済成長を達成 1991 韓国と北朝鮮、国連に同時加盟 1992 天皇、中国訪問 1998 北朝鮮、太平洋に弾道ミサイル発射 1999 中台関係緊張	1970 核拡散防止条約発効 1975 第1回主要先進国首脳会議（サミット）開催 1978 イラン革命 1979～89 ソ連、アフガニスタンに軍事介入 1985 ソ連、ゴルバチョフ書記長、改革開始 1989 東欧諸国で社会主義体制崩壊、東独ベルリンの壁撤去、米ソ首脳、マルタ会談で冷戦終結声明 1990 ドイツ統一、初代首相コール 1991 ワルシャワ条約機構解散、ソ連解体、湾岸戦争（米軍主体の多国籍軍対イラク） 1991 南ア、人種差別撤廃宣言 1993 EU発足
21世紀	平成	2001 中央省庁再編。テロ対策特別措置法 2002 小泉総理、北朝鮮訪問、日本人拉致被害者5人が帰国 2003 有事関連三法成立 2004 自衛隊、イラクへ派遣 2009 衆議院選挙で民主党勝利、政権交代実現	2001 中国、WTOに加盟 2003 中国、新型肺炎が猛威振るう 2004 スマトラ沖、大地震・大津波で死者不明30万人以上 2006 北朝鮮、第1回核実験を強行 2009 北朝鮮が6カ国協議離脱、第2回目の地下核実験実施	2001 アメリカで同時多発テロ 2002 EU、通貨ユーロ導入 2003 米英、イラク攻撃 2008 米証券リーマンブラザーズの破綻、世界同時不況が始まる 2009 米オバマ大統領就任、初の黒人大統領、米、経済・財政悪化

21世紀	平成	2011 東日本大震災（世界最大級の地震と巨大津波発生、犠牲者約2万人） 2011 東日本大震災、東京電力福島第1原発が壊滅、放射能拡散 2011 東京スカイツリー完成 2012 衆議院選挙で自民党勝利、民主党と政権交代 2013 日銀金融大幅緩和政策 2013 2020年東京オリンピック・パラリンピック開催決定 2014 消費税5％から8％に増税 2015 安全保障関連法が成立 2016 オバマ米国大統領、広島訪問 2017 衆議院選挙で自民党圧勝 2018 日本が主導するTPP11（環太平洋パートナーシップ協定）発効 2018 日欧EPA協定発効 2019 外国人材拡大法施行	2010 日本の尖閣諸島領海内で、中国漁船が日本の巡視船に故意に衝突 2011 中国の国内総生産、日本を追い抜き世界第2位に進出 2012 日本政府が尖閣諸島を国有地として買収し、日中関係緊張 2012 中国、習近平・李克強体制 2014 中国、「一帯一路」構想推進 2015 中国、アジアインフラ投資銀行（AIIB）設立主導 2017 韓国、朴槿恵大統領罷免、文在寅が大統領就任 2017 北朝鮮、核・弾道ミサイル実験強行 2018 南北朝鮮首脳会議（板門店） 2018 米国、北朝鮮首脳会議（シンガポール）	2009 米自動車大手GM、クライスラーが経営破たん 2011 「アラブの春」拡大 2011 ギリシャの財政危機からユーロ圏の金融不安拡大（ポルトガル、スペイン、アイルランド、イタリアなど） 2012 シリア内戦激化、死者急増 2012 米国がシェールガスの本格生産により天然ガス輸出国に転換 2013 米国経済、復活基調 2014 ウクライナ情勢緊迫化、ロシア、クリミア半島を併合 2015 欧州でイスラム過激派によるテロ続発 2015 欧州難民危機（100万人超） 2016 英国、「EU離脱国民投票」過半数 2017 米国、トランプ大統領就任 2018 米中貿易摩擦激化

〔索引〕

ACTA	124	SNS	280
ADB	108	TPP	72, 122
AI	148	WTO	106, 122

あ
葵祭	470
青色発光ダイオード(LED)	554
赤崎勇	554
亜寒帯	34
秋田犬	478
浅間山	42
アジアインフラ投資銀行	108
アジア開発銀行	108
アジア太平洋経済協力	108
アジア太平洋自由貿易圏	110
足利尊氏	52
阿蘇山	42
安土桃山時代	54, 398
アニメ	502
亜熱帯	34
アパレル	182
アフリカ開発会議	112
安部公房	388
安倍晋三首相	74
安倍政権(総理大臣)	112, 140, 228
アベノミクス	74, 140
甘酒	464
天の橋立	532
天野浩	554
アマミノクロウサギ	44
アラブの春	110
アルミ	170
阿波踊り	474
安定成長期	136

AIIB	108	
APEC	106, 108	
ASEAN	106, 108	
ATM	194	
BMD	120	
Brexit	114	
CATV	204	
COP	296	
DNA	318	
EEZ	32, 98	
EPA	112, 114, 122	
ESG	312	
EU	112	
e コマース	148	
Finance	194	
FTA	110, 122	
FTAAP	106, 110	
GDP	130	
H-IIB ロケット	326	
ICT	194, 206, 274	
IoT	148	
iPS 細胞	314, 552	
JBIC	124	
JICA	124	
JR	68, 196	
JT	68	
KOBAN	98	
KOMTRAX	348	
LCC	200	
LED	322	
MRJ	178	
NHK	204	
NTT	68	
ODA	124	
POS	350	
RCEP	106, 108	
Recycle	306	
Reduce	306	
Reuse	306	
RNA	318	
SDGs	292	

い
イージス艦	100
委員会等設置会社	216
イエズス会宣教師	54
いけばな	418, 458
違憲状態	94
違憲立法審査権	90
囲碁	488
石黒一雄	556
意思決定システム	212
伊勢神宮	454
一億総活躍社会	228
厳島神社	538

索引 579

	一帯一路	108, 116	
	一般機械	152, 170	
	1票の格差是正	96	
	稲作	36, 366	
	イノベーションのジレンマ	174	
	井原西鶴	386	
	イプシロンロケット	324	
	医薬品	154, 180	
	イラン革命	64	
	イリオモテヤマネコ	44	
	医療・福祉産業	208	
	医療保険	258	
	イロハカルタ	488	
	石見銀山遺跡	540	
	印鑑	482	
	インスタント食品	508	
	インスタントラーメン	186, 510	
	インターネット	148, 206, 282	
う	浮世絵	400, 422, 542	
	失われた10年	74, 138	
	失われた20年	74, 140	
	歌川広重	400, 422	
	打掛け	460	
	宇宙開発	324	
	うどん・そば	514	
	海の日	468	
	漆	424	
	雲仙岳	42	
	運輸業	194	
え	栄西	456, 458	
	駅伝	446	
	江崎玲於奈	550	
	江戸	54, 56	
	江戸時代	400, 460, 522, 524, 540	
	江戸幕府	54	
	エネルギー	332	
	エネルギー確保	142	
	エネルギー資源	136	
	エネルギーの安全保障	116, 124	
	エレクトロニクス	136, 174	
	演歌	492	
	円覚寺	534	
	縁日	462	
	遠洋漁業	164	
お	大阪万国博覧会	166	
	王貞治	444	
	欧州連合	112	
	応仁の乱	52	
	大浦天主堂	546	
	大江健三郎	388, 550	
	大阪城	398, 536	
	大隅良典	554	
	大村智	554	
	岡倉天心	402, 420	
	小笠原諸島	548	
	沖縄	62, 64	
	沖縄の基地問題	74	
	沖縄返還	64	
	沖ノ島	544	
	『おくのほそ道』	386	
	小倉百人一首	486	
	お好み焼き	514	
	おせち料理	462	
	織田信長	52	
	おでん	514	
	オバマ（前大統領）	104, 577, 578	
	お彼岸	466	
	お盆	452, 466	
	オリンピック	448	
	卸売	188	
	温帯	34	
	温帯モンスーン	368	
か	外貨準備高	156	
	外交	102, 118	
	外交三原則	102	
	外交文書の認証	78	
	開国	56	
	外国人材の受入れ	230	
	介護保険	208, 260	
	会社法	216	
	海上保安庁	96, 98	
	海上輸送	198	
	外食産業	508	
	懐石料理	420	
	回転ずし	512	
	海難救助	98	
	戒名	458	
	外来語	380	
	偕楽園	532	
	家屋	434	
	雅楽	412	
	科学技術	314	
	化学工業	180	
	書き初め	420	

580 索 引

隠し味	510	
学生野球	444	
核兵器禁止条約	104	
隠れキリシタン	458	
賭け事	484	
『蜻蛉日記』	378	
梶田隆章	554	
春日大社	540	
霞ヶ浦	42	
仮想通貨	148	
家族構成	234	
カタカナ(片仮名)	376	
活火山	42	
学校教育制度	262	
学校制度	58	
葛飾北斎	400, 422	
合掌造り	538	
桂離宮	534	
家庭用電気機器	172	
家電	308	
過度経済集中の排除	62	
門松	462	
カトリック	458	
嘉納治五郎	440	
歌舞伎	386, 406, 408	
株式持ち合い	210	
貨幣経済	54	
貨幣制度	58	
鎌倉	398, 534	
鎌倉時代	396, 456, 460, 522	
鎌倉幕府	50	
鎌倉仏教	456	
カミオカンデ	552	
上賀茂神社	472	
貨物	194	
カラオケ	492	
空手道	442	
カルタ	486	
川	40	
川端康成	388, 550	
観阿弥	408	
冠位十二階	48, 50	
官営八幡製鉄所	544	
環境保全	290	
環境問題	290	
観光	200, 532	
観光客	156	
観光業	194	
監査等委員会設置会社	218	
漢字	372, 376	
元日	462, 468	
間接金融	214, 220	
環太平洋地震帯	38	
環太平洋パートナーシップ協定	122	
神田祭	472	
竿灯	474	
関東大震災	38	
カンムリワシ	44	
き	紀伊山地の霊場と参詣道	540
	祇園囃子	472
	祇園祭	472
	企業間電子取引	190
	企業経営	210
	企業経営者	220
	企業倒産	138
	企業統治	216
	企業内労働組合	224
	企業別労働組合	222, 224
	菊	128
	季語	390
	気候	34
	気候変動	294
	気候変動枠組み条約	294
	岸信介首相	62
	技術貿易	356
	希少金属(レアメタル)	34
	規制緩和	72
	季節風	34
	貴族	50
	喜多川歌麿	400, 422
	北岳	42
	基本的人権	88
	『君が代』	126
	義務教育	86, 264
	着物	182, 460
	キャッシュカード	194
	キャッシュレス決済	148
	休暇	226
	九州	32
	旧石器時代	46
	弓道	442
	教育	262
	教育への経済的支援	270
	狂言	406

索　引　581

	餃子	514		経常収支	132
	共済組合健康保険	260		競馬	484
	行政	80, 86, 88		敬老の日	468
	京都	398, 532		劇画	500
	京都議定書	294		結婚	236
	京都御所	472, 534		ゲノム	318
	京都大学	270, 314, 316		元号	80, 128
	漁業	164		建国記念の日	48, 468
	清水寺	534		原子爆弾	62
	キリシタン	546		『源氏物語』	378, 384
	キリスト教	54, 458		原子力	142
	金閣	398, 534		原子力発電所	132
	銀閣	398, 534		遣隋使	48
	『金閣寺』	388		建設業	166
	緊急事態条項	86		現代	62, 66, 402
	金魚(きんぎょ)	478		建築物	402, 436
	銀行	192		建長寺	534
	近世	50		剣道	442
	金属工業	168		遣唐使	48, 396, 456
	金属工作機械	170		原爆ドーム	538
	近代	56, 402		憲法	58
	近代国家	58		憲法改正	78, 84, 88
	金融緩和	138, 192		憲法記念日	468
	金融再編	72		憲法第9条	66
	金融資産	192		建武の新政	52
	金融・保険業	190		兼六園	532
	勤労感謝の日	470	こ	碁	488
く	クールジャパン	504, 530		コーヒー	516
	空海	456		碁石	488
	熊本城	536		小泉純一郎首相	72
	組合管掌健康保険	258		小泉八雲	526
	組踊	410		五・一五事件	60
	クラウド	284		鯉のぼり	464
	クラシック音楽	494		公害	290
	グリーン経済	292		光学機器	154
	クリスマス	452, 466		後期高齢者医療保険	260
	クレジットカード	192		高機能素材	180, 182
	クローン文化財	404		皇居	536
け	ゲーム	504		工業用地	36, 132
	京	334		合区	94
	敬語	378, 520		航空機	154
	経済規模	130		航空輸送	200
	経済の安全保障	122		合区の解消	86
	経済白書	134		皇后	80
	経済連携協定	110, 112, 114, 122		高効率大型火力発電所	342
	警察庁	96		皇室典範	80, 82
	警視庁	96		皇室の歴史	78

582 索 引

『好色一代男』	386	国民所得	66
公職選挙法	90	国民性	520
合成ゴム	180	国民年金	256
厚生年金	258	国民の祝日	466
構造改革	70, 72	国立劇場おきなわ	410
高速道路	196	国立社会保障・人口問題研究所	232
小唄	406, 414	国立能楽堂	408
皇太子	82	国立博物館	404
講談	416	国立文楽劇場	412
紅茶	518	こけし	430
公的資金	138	『古事記』	48, 376, 384
公的年金	256	小柴昌俊	552
公的扶助	262	『個人的な体験』	388, 550
高等学校	264	古代	48
高等学校野球大会	444	後醍醐天皇	52
高等専門学校	266	国歌	126
高度経済成長	64	国花	126
高度成長期	134	国家安全保障	118
こうのとり(HTV)	326	国会	88, 90
紅白歌合戦	492	国会の召集	78
交番	98	国家制度	48
興福寺	540	国旗	126
鉱物資源	132	こどもの日	468
高分子化合物	330	小林誠	552
国宝	404	碁盤	488
弘法大師	456	古墳時代	48, 394
高野山	540	ゴム製品	182, 184
後楽園	532	雇用関係	222
小売業	188	雇用の流動化	222, 228
コーポレートガバナンス	214	雇用保険	260
コーポレートガバナンス・コード	218	コンビニエンスストア	188
高齢化	240	コンピュータ	136, 174
高齢化社会	246	コンプライアンス	216
高齢社会	240	さ 最高裁判所	90, 94
『古今和歌集』	126, 388	最高裁判所長官の任命	78
国債	138, 146	再生医療	316
国際協力機構	124	再生エネルギー	142
国際協力銀行	124	再生可能エネルギー	142
国際収支	132, 154	財政再建	146
国際平和協力法(PKO法)	68	最澄	456
国際連合	62, 66	財閥解体	134
国際連盟	60	財閥の解体	62
国事に関する行為	78	裁判員制度	90
国土面積	32	裁判所	90
国宝	534, 546	西芳寺	534
国民皆保険制度	232	裁量労働制	228
国民健康保険	258	サクラ	44

桜	126		失業率	66
桜島	42		自動運転	178
桜前線	44		自動車	308
酒	510, 514		自動車工業	176
鎖国	54, 56		自動車輸送	196
坐禅	458		自動販売機	190, 520
サッカー	446		信濃川	42
茶道	418, 458		士農工商	54
佐藤栄作	550		柴犬	478
佐藤栄作首相	64, 102		司法	80, 86, 88
ザビエル	458		死亡原因	232
参議院	88		資本主義	60
参議院議員通常選挙	86, 92		指名委員会等設置会社	218
産業革命	60		注連縄(しめなわ)	462
産業基盤	132		下鴨神社	472
産業構造	130, 148		下村脩	552
産業政策	134		社会党	70
産業の空洞化	136		社会保障	250
産業別労働組合	224		社会保障制度	150
産業用ロボット	170		社会保障費	250
三権分立	80, 86, 88		ジャポニズム	392, 402
三国干渉	58		三味線	408
三国同盟	60		車輪	344
三十三間堂	534		就学率	264
3種の神器	66		衆議院	88
三内丸山遺跡	46		衆議院議員総選挙	92
山王祭	472		衆議院の解散	78
サンフランシスコ平和条約	62		宗教	452
し	シームレスパイプ	346	十七条の憲法	48
	シェアリングエコノミー	148	集団帰属意識	522
	自衛隊	86, 100	集団的自衛権	120
	ジェネリック薬品	180	自由で開かれたインド太平洋戦略	120
	四季	34	重電機器	172
	磁器	422	柔道	440
	識字率	54	十二単	460
	四国	32	秋分の日	466, 470
	自己紹介	526	自由貿易協定	110, 112, 122
	慈照寺	398	自由民主党	62
	地震	38	重要文化財	404, 534
	氏姓制度	50	重要無形文化財	410
	自然遺産	530, 546	重量レール	344
	自然科学系論文	354	儒教	48, 522
	自然景観	532	宿泊	548
	持続可能な開発	292	主権在民	84
	時代祭	476	出生数	232, 238
	七五三	466	出生率	232
	漆器	424	出版	202

	主要先進国首脳会議(サミット)	64		『新古今和歌集』	388
	循環型社会	304		新国立劇場	496
	春闘	226		神社	454, 462
	春分の日	466, 468		人的資源	132
	生涯現役社会	246		神道	454, 540
	正月	462, 470		新聞	202
	小学校	264		神武天皇	48
	将棋	488		親鸞	456
	将棋盤	488		森林	36
	障子	434	す	水産業	164
	少子化	238, 242		水墨画	422
	少子・高齢化	132		水力	142
	少子高齢社会	238, 242		水力発電	42
	小選挙区比例代表並立制	92		スーパーコンピュータ	334
	正倉院	394		すき焼	512
	焼酎	516		鮨(すし)	512
	象徴天皇	84		鈴木章	552
	聖徳太子	48, 394		スチュワードシップ・コード	218
	消費税	68, 72		ストックオプション	214
	情報・通信業	206		『砂の女』	388
	情報通信社会	274		スポーツ	438
	縄文時代	46, 392		スポーツドリンク	518
	縄文土器	46		スマートフォン	154, 278
	醤油	510		相撲	438
	昭和時代	402		世阿弥	408
	昭和の日	468	せ	征夷大将軍	52
	職種別労働組合	224		生活保護	262
	食生活	506		青函トンネル	198
	食品ロス	310		政権交代	92
	植物	42		政権公約	92
	食料品工業	186		製紙	182, 184
	女系天皇	82		正社員	222
	初婚年齢	236		成人の日	468
	女性天皇	82		製造業	138, 166
	女性の社会進出	246		政党	92
	書道	420		西南雄藩	54, 56
	白神山地	546		政府開発援助	124
	白川英樹	550		生物多様性	302
	白鷺城	536		精密機械工業	172
	シリア難民	112		世界遺産	536
	知床	546		世界大恐慌	60
	真打ち	416		世界貿易機関	122
	進学率	268		関ヶ原の戦い	54
	新幹線	198		石炭	134, 142
	人権尊重	84		赤飯	514
	人口	40, 232		石油	142
	人口減少	150		石油危機	136

	世間体	522		大化の改新	48
	世帯数	234		待機児童	208
	摂政・関白制度	50		大正時代	402
	切腹	524		退職年齢	226
	節分	464		大政奉還	56, 80
	瀬戸大橋	198		大山古墳	394
	瀬戸物	424		大東亜戦争	60
	ゼネコン	166		大徳寺	534
	禅	458		第二次世界大戦	60
	繊維工業	182		第2次石油危機	64
	尖閣諸島	98		第2次湾岸戦争	68
	選挙	88, 90		大日本帝国憲法	58, 84
	全国健康保険協会健康保険	258		台風	34
	戦国時代	52		大仏	394, 534
	戦国大名	52		大名	52
	戦後経済の歩み	134		第4次産業革命	148
	洗浄便座	184		平将門	472
	扇子(せんす)	430		大陸棚	36
	戦争の放棄	84		高松塚古墳	394, 534
	先端医療	336		宝くじ	484
	線虫	338		瀧廉太郎	494
	銭湯	480		宅地	36
	千利休	400, 418		宅配便	188
	前方後円墳	394		太宰治	388
	占領政策	62		田沢湖	42
そ	早期退職	222		畳	434, 440
	箏曲	412		田中角栄首相	64
	総合商社	188		田中耕一	552
	造船	178		七夕	464, 474
	総選挙	78		谷崎潤一郎	388
	曹洞宗	456		タバコ	186, 518
	相馬野馬追	472		玉虫厨子	426
	創薬	316		短歌	384, 388, 390
	粗鋼	168		弾劾裁判	88
	『曾根崎心中』	386		団塊の世代	238
	ソフトウェア	206		談合	64
	ソフトパワー	528		端午の節句	464
	租庸調	48		男女雇用機会均等法	248
	そろばん	482		単身赴任	250
た	鯛	514		炭素繊維	182, 330
	体育の日	470	ち	治安	96
	第一次世界大戦	60		地域別の外交	104
	第1次石油危機	64		知恩院	534
	対外経済	132, 150, 156		近松門左衛門	386
	大学	264, 270		地球温暖化	294, 300
	大学院	274		地球環境保護	164
	大学入学共通テスト	272		地球シミュレータ	336

	畜産	160	同一労働・同一賃金	228
	地形	34, 36	東海道新幹線	66
	治験	316	陶器	422
	地上デジタルテレビ放送	114, 204	東京	32
	秩父の夜祭り	476	東京オリンピック	66
	知的財産権	156	東京大学	80, 270
	地熱	142	道元	456, 458
	地方自治体	90	陶磁器	182, 422
	地方制度	58	東洲斎写楽	400, 422
	茶室	420	東照宮	540
	『茶の本』	420	東大寺	394, 436, 534, 540
	中学校	264	銅鐸	392
	中世	50	統治機構	88
	中選挙区制	92	東南アジア諸国連合	106, 108
	中尊寺	542	動物	44
	長期景気低迷	138	土偶	392, 428
	朝鮮戦争	100	徳川家康	54
	超電導リニア	320	徳川幕府	54
	直接金融	214, 220	独占禁止	134
	賃金水準	226	独占禁止法	214
つ	月見	466	特別養護老人ホーム	208
	津波	38	『土佐日記』	378
	梅雨	34	土地制度	58
	鶴岡八幡宮	534	特許	356
て	庭園	432	利根川	42
	低炭素社会	300	利根川進	550
	鉄鋼業	168	土俵	438
	鉄道輸送	196	富岡製糸場	542
	鉄砲(火縄銃)	54	朝永振一郎	550
	デフレ不況	72	豊臣秀吉	52
	寺	462	トランプ(政権)	104, 158, 298, 578
	寺子屋	54	とんかつ	514
	テロ	86, 96, 110, 120	どんたく	470
	電気自動車(EV)	170, 176	な	内閣制度	58
	電子商取引	190	内閣総理大臣	88, 100
	電子書籍	202	内閣総理大臣の任命	78
	天神祭	472	内閣府	88
	伝統的行事	470	長唄	412
	伝統的な演劇	406	長崎	62
	天然ガス	142	中曽根康弘首相	68
	天然記念物	478	中村修二	554
	天皇	78, 80, 82, 90, 128	薙刀(なぎなた)	442
	天皇誕生日	468	名古屋城	536
	天皇の退位	80	夏目漱石	386
	天ぷら	512	浪花節	406, 416
	天龍寺	534	ナノテクノロジー	328
と	銅	170	なまはげ	476

	奈良	394, 532
	奈良時代	50, 394, 456, 460, 538
	南禅寺	534
	南蛮貿易	54
	南部陽一郎	554
	南北朝時代	52, 396
に	新潟県中越地震	40
	にぎりずし	512
	ニクソンショック	64
	錦鯉(にしきごい)	478
	二条城	534
	日英同盟	58
	日米安全保障条約	62, 104
	日米安全保障体制	118
	日蓮	456
	日蓮宗	456
	日露戦争	58
	日光の社寺	540
	日章旗	126
	日清戦争	58
	日ソ共同宣言	62
	日中戦争	60
	日中平和友好条約	64
	二・二六事件	60
	日本アルプス	40
	日本犬(にほんいぬ)	476
	日本映画	496
	日本画	402, 420
	日本海溝	36
	日本経済	130
	日本語	372, 378, 532
	日本語教育	532
	日本国憲法	62, 84, 90, 102
	日本国の起源	46
	ニホンザル	44
	日本三景	532, 538
	日本式ビッグバン	138
	『日本書紀』	48, 384
	日本人の祖先	46
	日本人の微笑	526
	日本刀	426
	日本猫(にほんねこ)	476
	日本のカレー	514
	日本の文学	382
	日本の歴史	532
	日本美術	392
	日本舞踊	414
	日本文化の特質	366
	世界貿易機構	106
	日本放送協会	204
	日本民族	46
	日本民謡	416
	日本料理	510
	日本列島	32, 34, 36, 38
	日本労働組合総連合会	224
	入浴	480
	韮山反射炉	544
	人形	428
	人形浄瑠璃	386, 410
	『人間失格』	388
	仁徳天皇陵	394
	仁和寺	534
ね	根岸英一	552
	ネット通信販売	190
	ねぶた	472
	年金制度	150, 256
	年中行事	462
の	ノーベル賞受賞者	550
	能	406
	農業	160
	農業の6次産業化	162
	農業用地	36, 132
	農耕社会	366
	農地改革	134
	農地解放	62
	農林水産業	132
	ノーベル平和賞	102
	飲み物	516
	野茂英雄	444
	野依良治	552
	『ノルウェイの森』	388
は	パートタイマー	222
	廃棄物再資源化	306
	俳句	386, 388, 390
	排他的経済水域	32, 98
	廃藩置県	56
	廃仏毀釈	402
	ハイブリッド車	176
	羽織袴(はおりはかま)	462
	破壊的イノベーション	174
	葉隠精神	524
	博多人形	428
	幕藩体制	54
	幕府	52, 56

	羽子板	430		琵琶湖	42
	恥	522	ふ	ファイナンス	220
	橋本龍太郎首相	72		ファインセラミックス	184
	長谷の大仏(高徳院)	534		フィンテック(Fintech)	194
	働き方改革	228		プーチン大統領	116
	パチスロ	484		フェノロサ	402
	パチンコ	484		付加価値税	68
	発光ダイオード	322		福井謙一	550
	鳩山一郎首相	62		福島第一原子力発電所	140
	花見	464		福田赳夫首相	64
	花道	408		武士	50
	埴輪	394, 428		富士山	42, 542
	ハブ	44		武士道	458, 522
	バブル経済	70, 136		武士の棟梁	50
	バブルの生成	136		伏見稲荷	534
	バブルの崩壊	138		婦人参政権	62
	はやぶさ	324		襖	434
	パラサイト・シングル	240		仏教	48, 394, 456, 540
	パラリンピック	448		扶養係数	242
	パリ協定	298		プライマリー・バランス	146
	版画	400, 422		プラザ合意	66
	判子	482		プラスチック	152, 180
	藩校	266		プラスチックごみ	312
	犯罪件数	96		ブラックアウト	40, 144
	阪神・淡路大震災	38		フリーター	222
	版籍奉還	56		不良債権	138
	半導体	152		風呂敷	482
	半導体等製造装置	152		プロテスタント	460
ひ	ビール	516		プロ野球	444
	美意識	460		文化遺産	404, 530, 536
	日枝神社	472		文化芸術立国	528
	非核三原則	102		文化財	530, 532
	東アジア地区包括経済連携	108		文化の日	470
	東・西本願寺	534		文化力	528
	東日本大震災	38, 74, 130		文楽	406, 410
	非正規雇用	222, 238	へ	平安京	50
	ビッグデータ	148, 284		平安時代	50, 396, 456, 460
	非鉄金属工業	170		平安神宮	534
	人づくり革命	270		平安朝	50
	ひな人形	464		平均寿命	232
	ひなまつり	464		米軍再編	118
	日の丸	126		『平家物語』	384
	卑弥呼	46		平城京	50
	姫路城	400, 536, 538		米食	508, 510
	百貨店	188		平成時代	402
	ひらがな(平仮名)	376		平和憲法	102
	広島	62		平和主義	84

	平和条約の締結	116
	ベビーブーム	238
	ペリー	56
ほ	貿易	132, 150
	貿易赤字	158
	貿易慣行	158
	貿易黒字	66, 136
	貿易収支	132
	貿易摩擦問題	106
	邦楽	412
	放送	204
	ポーツマス条約	60
	法然	456
	法隆寺	394, 426, 436, 534, 536
	捕鯨	164
	北海道	32, 34
	北海道胆振地方	40
	ポツダム宣言	62
	北方領土問題	116
	盆踊り	466
	盆栽	432
	本州	32, 34
	本庶佑	554
ま	麻雀	490
	『舞姫』	386
	蒔絵(まきえ)	426
	マグニチュード	38
	正岡子規	390
	益川敏英	552
	マスコミ	202
	松尾芭蕉	386
	松飾り	462
	松島	532
	松の内	464
	松本城	536
	祭り	470
	マニフェスト	92
	麻薬	120
	マラソン	446
	マルタ会談	70
	まわし	438
	マンガ	500
	漫才	416
	満州国	60
	満州事変	60
	『万葉集』	378, 384
み	ミサイル防衛システム	120
	三島由紀夫	388
	ミシン	346
	湖	40, 42
	「瑞穂の国」	368
	味噌	510
	三菱長崎造船所	544
	みどりの日	468
	源頼朝	50
	三原山	42
	宮沢喜一首相	68
	宮島	532
	味醂(みりん)	514
	民営化	68
	民主党	72
	民族的特性	368
む	無常	370, 384, 456
	無店舗販売	190
	村上春樹	388
	紫式部	384
	村山談話	70
	室町時代	398
	室町幕府	52
め	名刺	480
	明治維新	56
	明治時代	402
	明治政府	56
	明治天皇	56
	メタンハイドレート	332
	メディアコンテンツ	502
も	毛越寺(もうつうじ)	542
	文字	48, 372, 374
	ものづくり	342
	もののあわれ	370
	森鴎外	386, 526
や	八百万(やおよろず)の神	454
	焼き鳥	514
	野球	444
	薬師寺	540
	屋久島	546
	八坂神社	472
	野生生物	302
	山	40
	邪馬台国	46
	ヤマト王権	46, 48
	大和朝廷	46
	山中伸弥	314, 552
	山の日	468

	山鉾	472		領海	32, 86, 98
	弥生時代	46, 392		領土	86, 98
ゆ	有機EL	330		旅客輸送	198
	郵便事業	192		緑茶	516
	湯川秀樹	550		臨海工業地帯	132
	『雪国』	388, 550		林業	162
	雪祭	470		稟議(りんぎ)	210
	輸出	152		臨済宗	456
	輸入	152	る	ル・コルビュジエ	544
	ユネスコ無形文化遺産		れ	レアメタル	34, 170
		408, 410, 412, 512		冷戦	62, 70
よ	容器	306		連合	224
	窯業	182		連合軍	134
	謡曲	408		連立政権	92
	横綱	438	ろ	ロイヤリティ	356
	吉田茂首相	62		浪曲	416
	吉野ヶ里遺跡	46		労災保険	262
ら	ラーメン	514		労使関係	224
	ライシャワー	522		労働組合	224
	ライフサイエンス	314		労働権の確立	134
	落語	406, 416		労働時間	226
	ラフカディオ・ハーン	526		労働者の権利	62
り	リーマンショック	72, 130, 140		労働条件	226
	理化学研究所	316, 318, 334		労働力の流動化	138
	離婚	236		鹿苑寺	398
	立憲君主国家	56		轆轤	424
	立憲君主制	80		ロシア正教	460
	立憲君主制度	58		ロシアの南下政策	58
	立法	80, 86, 88		ロボット	330
	律令制度	48	わ	和歌	384, 388, 486
	リニア中央新幹線	166, 198, 320		『吾輩は猫である』	386
	リニアモーターカー	320		和食	510
	琉球王国	410, 540		和服	460
	流行歌	490		湾岸戦争	66
	龍安寺	534			

Printed in Japan

日本 —その姿と心—
NIPPON
THE LAND AND ITS PEOPLE

1982年 7月20日	第 1 版初刷発行
1984年 5月 1日	第 2 版初刷発行
1988年 5月25日	第 3 版初刷発行
1993年11月25日	第 4 版初刷発行
1997年 4月 1日	第 5 版初刷発行
1999年 9月30日	第 6 版初刷発行
2002年 9月30日	第 7 版初刷発行
2006年 5月25日	第 8 版初刷発行
2010年 4月25日	第 9 版初刷発行
2014年 9月15日	第10版初刷発行
2016年12月 5日	第10版新訂版初刷発行
2019年 9月 5日	第11版初刷発行

ⓒ著者　**日鉄総研**

編集者　中島　裕史

発行者　実原　幾雄
発行所　日鉄総研株式会社
　　　　東京都千代田区丸の内 3 丁目 1 − 1 国際ビル 9 階
　　　　電　話　03 − 3213 − 8560
　　　　F A X　03 − 3213 − 8790
　　　　U R L　https://nsri.nipponsteel.com

発　売　東洋出版株式会社
　　　　東京都文京区関口 1 丁目 23 − 6
　　　　電　話　03 − 5261 − 1004（代）
　　　　U R L　http://www.toyo-shuppan.com/
　　　　振　替　00110 − 2 − 175030
印　刷　日本ハイコム株式会社

ISBN978-4-930825-31-5

■お問い合わせについて
本書の内容に関するご質問等は、書面または FAX にてご連絡いただくか、
下記のお問い合わせフォームをご利用ください。
https://nsri.nipponsteel.com/inquiry/send/shoseki
https://nsri.nipponsteel.com/en/inquiry/send/shoseki　（English）